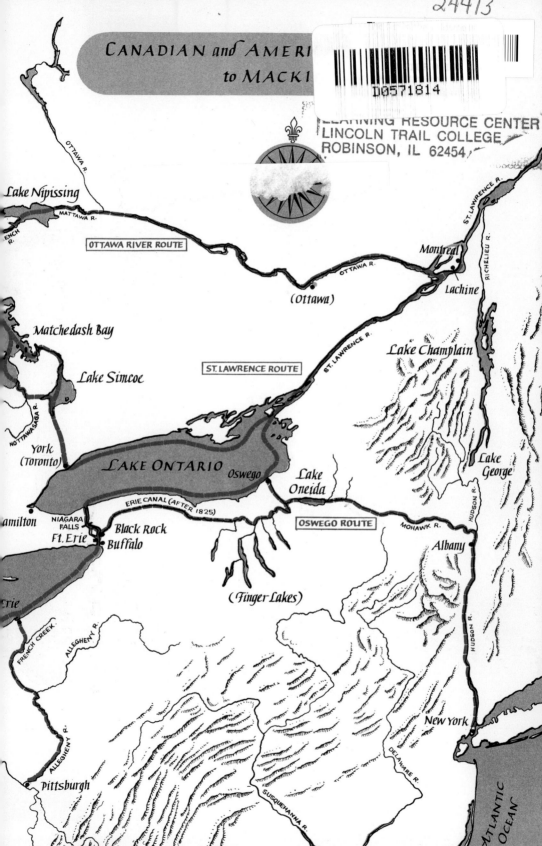

CANADIAN and AMERI
to MACKI

OTTAWA RIVER ROUTE

ST. LAWRENCE ROUTE

OSWEGO ROUTE

ERIE CANAL (AFTER 1825)

Lake Nipissing

MATTAWA R.

FRENCH R.

OTTAWA R.

(Ottawa)

OTTAWA R.

ST. LAWRENCE R.

Montreal

Lachine

ST. LAWRENCE R.

RICHELIEU R.

Lake Champlain

Matchedash Bay

Lake Simcoe

NOTTAWASAGA R.

York
(Toronto)

LAKE ONTARIO

Oswego

Lake
Oneida

Lake
George

Hamilton

NIAGARA
FALLS

Ft. Erie

Black Rock

Buffalo

MOHAWK R.

HUDSON R.

Albany

(Finger Lakes)

Erie

FRENCH CREEK

ALLEGHENY R.

ALLEGHENY R.

Pittsburgh

SUSQUEHANNA R.

DELAWARE R.

HUDSON R.

New York

ATLANTIC
OCEAN

The Fist in the Wilderness

BY DAVID LAVENDER

Non-Fiction

THE FIST IN THE WILDERNESS

WESTWARD VISION

THE STORY OF CYPRUS MINES CORPORATION

LAND OF GIANTS

BENT'S FORT

THE BIG DIVIDE

ONE MAN'S WEST

Fiction

RED MOUNTAIN

ANDY CLAYBOURNE

Juveniles

THE TRAIL TO SANTA FE

GOLDEN TREK

MIKE MARONEY, RAIDER

TROUBLE AT TAMARACK

The Fist in the Wilderness

DAVID LAVENDER

Doubleday & Company, Inc.,
Garden City, New York.

Library of Congress Catalog Card Number 64–16203
Copyright © 1964 by David Lavender
All Rights Reserved
Printed in the United States of America

For those who have made all this groping worth while:
MILDRED, DAVID, VAL, JIM, JUDY, CHRIS, *and* LEITH.

Contents

MAPS (*in center of book*)
1. *Mackinac and Environs*
2. *Hunt's Westbound Trip and Route
    followed by Stuart and Crooks*
3. *Missouri River Fur Country*
4. *Mackinac Island*

A Side View for Clarity

Decadence and the dissolution of nations begin, the spartans say, when life grows soft. Nevertheless every human race grasps with innate fierceness at any political panacea or mechanical gadget that promises to ease the ordeals of daily living. The Indians of North America were no exception.

They greeted the early Europeans as if they were demigods—not because of the whiteness of their skins or the loveliness of their morals or the superiority of their brains, but because they provided an almost naked people with guns for hunting and warfare, with knives and cloth for convenience, silver earbobs and blue beads for prestige (which is a form of soothing), and whisky for euphoria. In exchange the Indians offered the best they had—fur—and the whites seized it just as avidly. This theme of pioneer barter is, of course, an old story, but like all supposedly easy tales it is susceptible to distortion. And that is what has happened to parts of the history of the fur trade.

Most schoolboys know that the glamour fur to both the traders and the historians was beaver—to the traders because of its peculiar adaptability for the making of fine hats. To obtain beaver, the storied pioneers of the fur trade pressed deeper and deeper into the western wilderness, unraveling the geography of the new world and preparing the way for future generations of more permanent settlers. During nearly two centuries of ever broadening exploration, they brought back across incredible distances—in fragile canoes or on top of cantankerous pack animals—tens of thousands of beaver pelts whose value ranged from about two to six dollars a pound.

This was glamour. This made good stories—so many good stories that the glitter of beaver mythology has obscured the everyday staples of the Indian commerce: muskrat and raccoon skins, deer hides, and, later, buffalo robes. These were the pelts the Indians could take with relative ease and in relatively great numbers. During the two centuries of the wilderness commerce, they produced these humbler products not by the thousands but by the millions. (In one triumphant *single day* in New York, Astor sold upward of half a million muskrat hides.) Their value ran in cents, not dollars, but it did not take a John Jacob Astor to multiply the totals and see where the everyday bread and butter of the business lay.

This was the backbone of the trade, the casually mentioned, unglamorous routine that supported the beaver hunters at their work of frosting the cake. It was for this that the white men kept open the supply routes, did their day-by-day chores, and sent their ships around the world. This was the true foundation of the huge mercantile empires that influenced the destiny of nations. This great power of ordinary things is the first point that must be understood about John Jacob Astor. Save for one upheaval, his disastrous transcontinental leap to the mouth of the Columbia River just before the War of 1812, he was not an innovator. He preferred a volume turnover, where he could exercise his superior abilities at squeezing pennies, to the risks inherent in stampeding for virgin ground. His great field manager, Ramsay Crooks, was bolder. But Astor never gave Crooks his head, never let him expand until after the paths had been securely marked by someone else's feet. Then they moved in with their vast concentrations of capital and sought to control the fields which others had opened. No, it was not glamorous. But it was effective, and a recognition of it is essential to an understanding of the American Fur Company.

The enormous power of ordinary things: behind the great mercantile houses in Paris, London, and Montreal, behind those in New York, Albany, and St. Louis stood national governments (France and England first, then England and the United States) whose colonial aspirations led them to back with big sticks the threatening gestures that rival traders made at each other in the distant wilderness. Despite their very limited numbers, these wilderness entrepreneurs sometimes seemed worth the risk of international war. As providers of a better way of life, they exerted a paramount influence over the savages with whom they dealt and whose women they generally married. Because their canoes, barges, and packhorses roamed far in advance of any other national force, the possibility always existed that a handful of scheming traders backed by a small army of Indians might upset the political destinies of empires of empty land.

Actually history never quite worked out that way, save in the rarest of instances. But the possibility always troubled national strategists, to whom it was a basic law that one must never allow the other fellow to get in the first jump. Accordingly Presidents, premiers, governors and generals found themselves listening to the men who, through intricate chains of debt and supply, controlled the traders who in turn controlled the Indians. These considerations, and not the mysterious emanations of corruption, explain why Astor was able to gain the ears of Jefferson, Madison, and Monroe. The channels were so routine that after 1819 or so Astor went off to Europe on extended visits and left government interfering largely to Ramsay Crooks, who visited the wilderness every year, clashed personally with the Indian agents and military men, and came back knowing at first hand which particular screw in Washington ought to be given a particular twist.

In the other lane of this two-way political street flowed the day-by-day influences which international jockeyings for power exerted on the fur trade. For instance, David Thompson's strange "race" (or failure to race) to the Columbia with the banners of the North West Company as opposed to the Pacific Fur Company appears not so strange after all when viewed against the background of Astor's maneuvers with the Nor'Westers to split the trade of the borderlands. Those maneuvers were influenced in turn by each new whirl of policy in the Congress of the United States concerning the Embargo and Non-Intercourse Acts against England and France, an essential point historians have strangely overlooked.

Similarly, politics born from the strident nationalism that followed the War of 1812 account for the courses which Astor and, more importantly, Ramsay Crooks pursued around the Great Lakes while shifting an essentially British trade into American hands. Talk of low influence in high places and of secret bribes as evidenced by pages supposedly missing from old ledgers makes dramatic and even soothing reading for those who wonder how someone else was able to wax so rich. The truth, however, is more prosaic—from which it should not be inferred that this account is a whitewash of the American Fur Company. Astor, Robert Stuart, and, to an extent, Ramsay Crooks knew very well how to use their metaphorical thumbs for gouging when the occasion demanded. But in the main the slick cunning generally associated with a criminal mind was not their style. They were intelligent enough and the American Fur Company was strong enough for them to adapt to their own ends the frontier moods and political tensions that surrounded them. The competitors they crushed in the process generally were not so smart. Hurt without quite understanding how, the injured cried "Foul!" and the complaint has been echoing in some quarters ever since. It is time for another look.

Today we have largely forgotten how tightly the Indian problem was woven into the fabric of the young nation's existence. Because of the life-and-death mastery which the fur trade held over the Indians, the Indian commerce inevitably became a matter of public concern. Yet the traders furiously resisted the government's contention and insisted that their work, as private as any grocer's, should not be subjected to public meddling.

This clash of interests spread to related fields. The government, for example, wished to obtain Indian lands for its citizens by moving the savages onto constricted reservations, there to prepare them for civilization by teaching simple crafts and farming methods, meanwhile protecting the red students from the whisky and the unethical business practices of the traders. The wilderness merchants wished, on the other hand, to preserve the patterns which held the Indians to be hunters, not farmers. They defied in courts of law and the halls of Congress the efforts of the Indian Bureau, of military men, and of Indian agents to interfere with established routines. They insisted with some justice that they filled the needs of the Indians better than the government did. They defended their exorbitant profits on some transactions by pointing out how much they lost at other times to defaulting creditors and natural disasters. One cannot understand either the American Fur Company or its peers in Detroit and St. Louis without also understanding the contradictory complexities of the Indian problem.

As settlement pushed west and the new states began to chafe over the semi-independent Indian "nations" within their borders, the tempo of change increased. In the beginning the Indian trade was a leisurely business. Years passed between the buying of goods in London (young America did not produce satisfactory blankets or guns) and the paying for the merchandise with furs caught somewhere in the wilds beyond Lake Superior. The traders, who were often part Indian themselves, did not hurry their customers. Furthermore they accepted the savages' contention that each band owned the game that roamed within certain time-hallowed boundaries. Indeed, the early white traders seldom hunted even for table use, but acquired what they needed through barter. They were not being considerate so much as canny. They had stumbled into something which many businesses lack—a two-way profit, first through marking up the goods they sold the savages and then in selling the furs they obtained.

Pressure from settlement brought two changes to the pattern. During the prosperous years of the American Fur Company, the United States Government purchased millions of acres of land from the Indians. Payment was made by installments called annuities. Some annuities were in the form of services—blacksmith shops, schools, cows, plows, and the like. Some—and this tendency increased—were in the form of cash. Quite naturally the Indians hunted less and less and used this money to purchase what they needed from their usual traders—and to pay off old debts to the traders, who quickly made an art of horning in on treaties between the government and its wards.

This was called the money trade in contradistinction to the fur trade. At first the fur companies did not like it, for it deprived them of the furs that once had been their reason for being. Gradually, however, they swung with the times and at various strategic spots were running what amounted to little stores when the first white settlers began drifting in. These settlers traded amiably with men who once had hated settlers; they also brought in for pin money (it was one of the few sources of cash in the barter-oriented frontier) the furs from small animals they caught around their farms. Thus, insensibly and without planning it, the local fur dealers survived the transition from a wilderness to a pioneering economy. Through their established connections in the East and through their established transportation facilities they and the army sutlers provided a dependable source of merchandise for many young towns that eventually grew into cities—Chicago, Fort Wayne, Minneapolis–St. Paul, Rock Island, to name only a few. Inevitably they were training arenas for young men who developed into leading bankers and merchants, mayors, governors, congressmen. This process was well begun when Astor surrendered control of the American Fur Company to Ramsay Crooks in 1834.

Meanwhile, in the mountain West, other changes were developing at headlong pace. There the Indians had not learned to trap beaver, and the increasing numbers of adventurous young whites invading the field were unwilling to waste time trading for deer skins and muskrat hides (it took many muskrats to equal one beaver in value) and then transport the pelts long distances in huge pack trains through the lands of Indians noted for their ability to steal horses. They decided, contrary to the express laws of their nation, to short-circuit the Indians and do the trapping themselves, confining themselves mostly to beaver hides, which were relatively compact in respect to value. The result was the storied stampede to the beaver streams of the Rockies, the frenzied rendezvous, and ceaseless clashes with resentful Indians—the short-lived era of the mountain men.

This was radical, illegal, dangerous. Most entrenched concerns are conservative. Under Astor the American Fur Company was no exception. Furthermore, the Western burst came when, old and sick, he no longer tingled to the sort of dreams that led him to the one great fling—and the one great debacle—of his life, the Pacific Fur Company. He entered the Missouri trade reluctantly and only at the prodding of Ramsay Crooks.

Both of them soon decided that the lawlessness and bloodshed that accompanied the effort were not worth the gains. Astor retired (not entirely because of this, but because of age), and Crooks withdrew to his familiar grounds around the Lakes and the headwaters of the Mississippi, where muskrat and deer and raccoon were the staples, as they had always been. In some sections in that area farmers were producing more of the humble furs than the Indians ever had. There too the money trade was adding a fillip to the commerce. These things all entered Crooks's calculations, but accounts which focus on Astor's retirement miss them entirely.

Ramsay Crooks participated in—helped guide—the entire transition of the fur trade from an instrument of history to a plain business. His was the true fist in the wilderness. He learned his business at the custom-bound stronghold of Michilimackinac and along the Missouri River in the vibrant days immediately following the Louisiana Purchase. A Scot by birth, he threaded an adroit path through the hatreds that preceded the second war with Great Britain. He went to the Pacific with the Astorians, disliked what he saw, and returned to the Lakes. There he watched the lonely, desperate little battles by which the British fur men hoped to regain the wilderness they had lost during the Revolution. After the war he, more than any other man, Astor included, implemented the devices and worked out the compromises by which Americans seized a trade that they never before had been able to touch. He led the battle against every form of government interference with what he fiercely contended was private enterprise—and he won. He went West in spite of Astor, reassessed what he was doing, returned home again and presided over the changing ways of the industry that had opened the continent.

Once during a bull session at the Thacher School in Ojai, Wilmarth Lewis remarked to me that one way of gaining fresh insight into Shakespeare's plays was to read them from the viewpoint of a minor character, and he used Albany in *King Lear* as an example. A similar flanking approach may also shed new light on our frontier history by telling the story of the American Fur Company not through the familiar Astor-eye view, but through Ramsay Crooks, who really isn't so minor a character. And, like Albany, he saw what was happening when the others lost their grip.

Anyway, here it is.

DAVID LAVENDER

Ojai, California
February 10, 1964

CHAPTER *1*

Michilimackinac: The Key and the Door

This is a difficult story to launch. In spite of the eminence which its subject achieved—by the time Ramsay Crooks was forty-five years old his shadow touched nearly every person, red and white, in the wilderness half of the United States[1]—we can resurrect very few documents connected with his formative years. Most of this scanty information hinges around five dates. After that, imagination must take over.

Fortunately, the first date is his birth—January 2, 1787, in the vigorous Scottish seaport town of Greenock, beside the Firth of Clyde. His father, a shoemaker, died before Ramsay was well into his teens. His widowed mother decided to migrate with the boy and perhaps with his sister to Niagara, Canada, where one or two of his older brothers had settled. They sailed from Greenock on April 25, 1803. Significantly enough to Ramsay's future career, 1803 was also the year of the Louisiana Purchase.

Mother and daughter may have located at Niagara, but the teen-age boy soon dropped back down the St. Lawrence to Montreal. There he found a job with the supply firm of Maitland, Garden and Auldjo, whose business was importing coarse dry goods and cheap hardware for the Indian trade of the far West. A year and three quarters there were more than enough for a restless, ambitious youngster. In the spring of 1805, Crooks left the gray countinghouse beside the river and became a trader himself, traveling with a supply flotilla 900 watery miles to the uproarious rendezvous on Michilimackinac Island, in the narrow strait between Lake Huron and Lake Michigan.

From Michilimackinac he ranged far. On July 9, 1806, for instance, he bought two bushels of corn from a trader in infant Chicago. And in early May 1807, when he was barely twenty, he appeared in St. Louis with a boatload of furs. These pelts he and his French-Canadian voyageurs had collected during the preceding winter from Maha Indians who dwelt eight hundred miles up the Missouri River, across from where Sioux City, Iowa, now stands.

That is the extent of the information which can be documented.

Few as they are, however, the facts permit conjectures. Young Crooks must have received a sound common-school education in Scotland, or he could not have handled the letter writing and commercial arithmetic which his early work in Montreal demanded. He must have been adventurous, aggressive, and competent, or he would not have advanced so swiftly to full charge of a trading post (crude though it undoubtedly was) at the dimly known edges of the Midwestern plains. More importantly, once we have recognized the patterns of the trade, we can surmise that if he was in one place on such-and-such a date and at another place a year later, he probably followed certain characteristic routines in between. Perhaps it is possible to venture farther. Perhaps by grasping the forces that shaped him, we can gain some understanding of the man himself. But this imaginative reconstruction of character out of the rough materials of milieu cannot be done quickly. There are many threads, none simple.

By the time Ramsay Crooks entered the fur trade of the Great Lakes, it had been evolving for fifteen decades. Out of this long communication with the Indians a highly peculiar and potentially explosive social pattern had taken shape. Its basis was the ownership of game. Indians had no concept, in Anglo-Saxon terms, of land as private property. If anyone owned the magnificent sweep of North America, so the great leader Tecumseh was to argue in the fiery days before 1812, then it belonged by gift of the Great Spirit to all Indians communally—neither one council of chiefs nor one tribe, however powerful, could alienate a foot of it.

In spite of this mystic brotherhood of ownership, however, each tribe and each band within that tribe recognized what amounted to property rights in the deer and raccoon, the muskrat, beaver, and other game which ranged definable hunting grounds. Splits within tribal families and wars immemorially long against outsiders developed from efforts to seize or to protect these ownership rights.

The first whites to reach the northern wilderness accepted this condition. They did not invade the hunting grounds in order to kill the game themselves, as later Americans did in Kentucky, say, or more particularly, in the lands toward and beyond the Rocky Mountains. Rather, they enticed the Indians to bring the pelts to them. The lures they used were the manufactured goods that seemed to promise to each savage an easier way of surmounting his crushing environment.

Habit soon turned the luxuries which the Indian received into necessities: he could not hunt successfully without a gun, make fire readily without a flint, cook happily without a metal bowl, or dress himself comfortably in anything other than the woolens he himself was unable to manufacture. Furthermore, he was swayed in his barter not only by the quality of the goods offered him but also by his friendship for the men who brought the goods. The inevitable result was a fierce competition to command his loyalties. Generally speaking, he yielded more readily to vice than to virtue. Ruthlessly, therefore, an entire race was debased by a commerce which in its beginnings had promised a more tolerable plane of existence.

During the long degradation, the Indian's prowess as a fighter intensified his value as a consumer. In normal years, white merchants preferred peace among their customers; a war party did not produce beaver pelts. But whenever the purveyors themselves fell to blows, each side tried to enlist the support of the Indians.

Their merciless involvement started during the long series of wars which France and England waged for the control of North America. Most of the tribes around the Great Lakes preferred the French, but the English won and the native inhabitants were swung willy-nilly under the suzerainty of King George. Before they were well adjusted to this new situation, the American Revolution upset their status once again. Thousands of them in the Ohio-Illinois country were told by strange white paper bearers from America that whether they liked it or not they were now wards of the United States, an apparently trivial power confined for the most part to the Atlantic seaboard.

Unfortunately the telling lacked conviction. Even the geographic boundaries of the Old Northwest beyond Lake Superior had been left unsettled by the Peace of Paris, which in 1783 formally closed the American Revolution. The social and political future of the Far Western frontier was even less resolved. What eventually happened would depend in large part on asserting economic control over the savages. And so the traders of Canada and the United States began a semiofficial, early-day cold war for the minds of the red men. Meanwhile far-off international upsets reached out to trouble this chaos in the *pays sauvage*, the savage country. Whenever Napoleon blockaded a fur-receiving port in Europe, adjustments had to be made in the Sioux villages of Minnesota. But the emperor's critical gesture was his sale of Louisiana to the thrusting young United States. At that moment the tensions on the fur-trading frontier became unbearable.

As 1812 drew near, every fur man between the Great Lakes and the Columbia had to make his choice according to convictions that had solidified during this swirl of trouble. Ramsay Crooks's answer differed from that of most Canadian traders. He became and stayed an American. It would be interesting to find a diary entry that told just why. The best we can do, however, is establish the background against which the decision was made, and then guess. But the long antagonisms of the frontier are not quickly outlined. To start we have to turn far back of Crooks's own time, to the strange folkways and lovely geography of the trade, to ancient conflicts born from the way rivers flow, and above all to the tragic choices which the Indians repeatedly had to make in struggles they could not possibly win.

For many years a sharp rivalry over the Indian commerce of the Great Lakes area had existed between the supply houses of Montreal and those of Albany. Every spring huge wooden rowboats, each thirty or more feet long and up to eight feet wide amidships, their oars supplemented by sails when the wind was right, toiled up the St. Lawrence into Lake Ontario. (Canoes equally large struggled up the Ottawa River and over the Nipissing portage to Lake Huron; it was the romantic route of the storied voyageurs, but in the years bracketing the revolution a greater tonnage probably used the St. Lawrence.) Arrived at Lake Ontario, the barges avoided the dangerous rocks of the north shore and skirted the safer beaches to the south. Soon they reached the port of Oswego, New York, and there encountered the hardheaded Yankees from Albany, whose goods had arrived in the same kind of rowboats via the Mohawk Valley and Lake Oneida. The rest of the journey to Detroit or even Michilimackinac was a race of straining backs and oar-blistered hands.

The war froze the rivalry. After the revolution was over, the Canadian government obliged its Montreal merchants by slamming shut the Oswego gateway—and all other direct routes into the United States. The embargo was absolute. Trade goods could not enter Canada legally from the south. Furs could not go out. Strange wanderings resulted. A beaver trapped near present Milwaukee, say, or a muskrat caught in the swamps of northern Indiana traveled first to Michilimackinac or Detroit (both on American soil) and thence to Montreal. From Montreal the pelts crossed the Atlantic and then came home, enriching several British commission men along the way before finally the fur could be turned into felt by a hatter in New York City.

This devious commerce soon became familiar to John Jacob Astor, an emigrant whose immense resources eventually gave focus to Ramsay Crooks's career. Born July 17, 1763, in Waldorf, Germany, Astor reached New York almost penniless in 1784. Various legends attend his initial ventures. One of them has him tramping through the backwoods of New York State trading for furs out of a pack of trinkets he carried on his own back. Perhaps so. But he did not gather skins that way for long; there was more profit in letting others handle the grubby work in the field while he concerned himself with the furs only after they had left the wilderness.

By 1788 Astor was making annual trips to Montreal to buy from the merchants there. The pelts he acquired he shipped home legally through London—or possibly he smuggled some of them, as many traders did, south through the Richelieu Valley and Lake Champlain to the Hudson. From the beginning he resented the roundabout procedure. Surely furs caught within the United States should be able to move directly to United States customers.

His long brooding over the problem—it extended across two decades— was intensified by the huge volume of the commerce which the Canadians each year siphoned out of American lands. As early as 1790, for instance, Upper Canada sent to Quebec, for export, furs worth £140,000 —about $700,000 early-day dollars. Translating the amount into modern currency is next to impossible, but the figure reaches well into the millions. And well over half of the total, approximately £100,000, came from lands which the Peace of Paris in 1783 specifically said belonged to the new United States of America.

Areas tributary to Detroit—northern Ohio, northern Indiana, and the eastern streams of the Michigan Peninsula—sent out to Quebec in 1790 furs worth £40,000. But the richest amount, £60,000, came through Michilimackinac from the sprawl of forest and stream and prairie that constitute most of what Americans call the Old Northwest—western Michigan, northwestern Indiana contiguous to Lake Michigan, much of Illinois, all of Wisconsin, and the watery parts of Minnesota between Lake Superior and the upper Mississippi. It also included bits of the forbidden land claimed by Spain beyond the great river. Even in 1790 British and French-Canadian traders were illegally coursing the rivers of Iowa, southwestern Minnesota, and the eastern fringes of the Dakotas. Moreover, 1790 was not a peak year. During the next several years, throughout most of the Michilimackinac area, the trade kept growing.[2]

Ramsay Crooks reached the island in the flush of its great days. He saw American arms fail to hold it in the War of 1812, but American diplomats succeed in 1815. After that, for the rest of his life, he visited it continually on Astor's or his own behalf, laid critical plans that swung on its unique geographical hinge, and insensibly molded its ways while being in turn molded by them. Trying to understand either him or the American Fur Company without also understanding something of little Mackinac's long history and odd quirks is inconceivable.

Michilimackinac is an Ojibway (Chippewa) Indian word. In formal correspondence during French and British administrations, white men generally used the full term. Colloquially, however, they shortened it to Mackinac, pronounced Mackinaw, which still prevails. Some etymologists suggested that the name, almost as long as the island, meant "green turtle," because its humped oval form and heavy forests reminded aborigine imaginations of a turtle sleepily afloat on the limpid waters.

It is about two miles wide and three long. Its major axis runs from northwest to southeast. A projection of that axis leads immediately to dot-sized Round Island and then to larger Bois Blanc, named for its deciduous trees and pronounced, in a hard Anglo-Saxon abuse of the French, "Bob Low." These three islands sit like teeth across the throat of water leading from Lake Huron into Lake Michigan. Michilimackinac, although somewhat northeast of the throat's opening, is the closest island to it. Accordingly the strait also became known as Michilimackinac, a glitter of crystal water so compressed between forested points that today a bridge leaps the span in a single mighty suspension.

Long before any British colonist had crossed the Alleghenies, a French Jesuit priest, Claude Dablon, recognized the significance of this narrow passage between the lakes. "The key and the door for all the people of the south," he called it; and in 1670 he erected a crude mission on Michilimackinac Island. The location did not please the man who would have to run the mission, however—Father Jacques Marquette. In 1671 Marquette moved the station to the northern shore of the strait and renamed it St. Ignace.

Two years later, on May 17, 1673, Marquette and a younger companion, fur trader Louis Jolliet, left St. Ignace with two small canoes and five voyageurs to find a huge river of which the Indians spoke and which the whites hoped would lead to the Southern Sea, as the Pacific was then called. What they actually did was pioneer a vaguely kite-shaped route that ever afterward functioned as the standard highway of the fur trade.

The first section, the deeply scalloped northern shore of Lake Michigan, was familiar to the Frenchmen. Bright water sparkled against tree-shaggy headlands; shoals were dangerous in spots but compensation came from occasional small islands that afforded shelter from sudden squalls. About a hundred miles due west of Michilimackinac, a long snout of land bent the travelers to the southwest. After leaving its tip they held to the same direction, hurrying from island to island in the open lake until at last they gained the reassurance of another long peninsula. This welcome, cliff-lined tongue of land (today it is called Door Peninsula) formed the eastern side of a long, narrow bay, the explorers' first goal.

The bay teemed with trout, sturgeon, and whitefish. Attracted by the food, great numbers of Indians gathered in the area. Many of them were Winnebagos, the most sullen and unlovable of the Northwestern tribes. Their diet gave the Winnebagos so overwhelming a stench that the French called the tribe *Puants*, or Stinkers, and their fishing ground *La Baye de Puants*. Later the emerald foliage on the shores produced a more euphonious name—*La Baye Verte* or, today, Green Bay.

A river named *Reynard*, or Fox, for still another Indian tribe, flowed from interior Wisconsin into the southwestern tip of Green Bay. Six miles up the Fox, at the foot of the first rapids, French Jesuits had in 1670 built still another of their western missions, naming it St. Francis Xavier. Jolliet and Marquette rested here briefly and then tackled their first real obstacle—a twenty-mile stretch of river broken by four saults of white water where goods had to be portaged and the canoes dragged up by ropes. Beyond the last rapids stretched Lake Winnebago, thirty-five miles long by ten or so wide. The upper part of the Fox poured into the lake halfway along the western shore, where Oshkosh now stands.

Beyond Lake Winnebago the river twined like a dropped cord. Indian mythology said that once a huge snake decided to leave its home in the Mississippi for a visit to the Great Lakes. The trail the monster left collected rain and became the Fox River. Occasionally the meanders widen into shallow lakes. The mucky bottoms of some of these lakes sprouted acres of tall rushes which the Indians wove into mats; other lakes produced such tight stands of wild rice that in the fall boats could scarcely push through the heavy-headed stalks. Indians harvested canoefuls of the kernels (wild rice became an important item of trade as well as a food) and ducks, which congregated in unbelievable flocks on the small lakes, grew so fat they could scarcely fly. On either hand stretched rolling prairies broken by groves of trees. It was the heart of what eventually would be called the dairyland of America.

The coils of the upper river grew so tight that the long canoes and bateaux of the later fur trade would have difficulty negotiating the bends. Finally, near present Portage, the Fox bent almost completely back on itself. Less than two miles beyond the tip of this hairpin curve lay another river, the Ouisconsing, later refined to Wisconsin. The intervening land was low and swampy. During some spring floods, canoes could actually float across the stretch. Still, it was properly called in the idiom of the times "a height of land," a divide between major watersheds. After toiling through its mud, Marquette and Jolliet thought that they had reached Pacific drainage.

The Wisconsin's current was swift but punctuated with interfering islets and sandbars. After 110 miles of this, the explorers reached ("with a joy I cannot express," wrote Marquette) the immense sweep of the Mississippi, island-strewn, bluff-lined. Twice on their swift journey downward they were dismayed by its difficult rapids—eighteen miles of transverse stone ledges just above present Rock Island and another long boil north of the mouth of the Des Moines. The return?—but that was a problem that would have to wait. On they drove, past the surging entry of the Missouri and, with growing dismay, along what is now the eastern border of Arkansas. This persistent southern course would not take them to the Pacific. And then they encountered Indians with European artifacts and tales of winged ships that visited the river's mouth—Spaniards obviously. And so this must be the *Espíritu Santo,* the lower Mississippi, its course already known. Furthermore, the Indians they met were growing hostile.

Disheartened, the Frenchmen turned back. As they struggled against the current, they remembered the long rapids at the mouth of the Des Moines and at Rock Island. Fortunately, the questions about geography which they asked of every Indian they could reach revealed that there was an easier way to Lake Michigan. Just above the boisterous mouth of the Missouri, where the Mississippi makes a surprising sideways curl, the Illinois River comes lazily down from the north. Neither its sluggish current nor that of the tributary Des Plaines offered any particular difficulty. From the Des Plaines the explorers crossed a portage as swampy and as low as that between the Fox and Wisconsin.[3] This carrying place opened onto a short stream called Chicagou, which in turn led to the lake.

In spite of gales which often whipped the water, paddling along Lake Michigan's shores was far easier than fighting the currents of the Mississippi and Wisconsin, both rivers relatively swift. But the Fox, despite its lower rapids, wasn't bad. And so the slowly developing trade tended to follow exactly in Marquette's and Jolliet's path. Merchandise bound for the central Mississippi Valley and, later, for the Missouri River generally left the lakes by way of the Fox-Wisconsin route. After St. Louis was founded in 1763, a few boats did go south to the new town via the Illinois. But variations in the return path were rare. Almost without exception furs procured in the central valleys went north to Michilimackinac by the Illinois, not by the Mississippi, an economic pattern that eventually led the United States to establish a fort and trading factory at Chicago[4]—and, as will appear, one which allows certain deductions about Ramsay Crooks's first hurryings to and fro between Michilimackinac and the Missouri River.

Marquette and Jolliet traveled farther that summer of 1673 than the strength of young Canada could follow. For a time the western thrust of the trade paused at Detroit. But the beckoning passage out of Lake Huron to unexploited fields in the south and west was too alluring to be ignored for long. About 1714, Fort Michilimackinac was hewn out of the forest on the strait's southern shore, directly across the way from abandoned St. Ignace. An annual summer trading fair sprang up under the protection of its guns. By 1750 canoes were gathering there that had been laden in northern Indiana and brought down the St. Joseph River into southern Lake Michigan. The western wilds of Michigan Peninsula poured out more—Grand River, Muskegon, and the Ottawa Indian town of *L'Arbre Croche* (today's Harbor Springs, Michigan). All Wisconsin fed in its precious, evil-smelling bales, either through Green Bay or along the savage south shore of Lake Superior.

So much colonial wealth inevitably became entangled with the quarrels of the mother countries in Europe. During what was called in America the French and Indian Wars of 1754–60, English colonists challenged the French for the continent and won. Alarmed by the tremendous implications of the victory, diplomats in Europe tried to put brakes on Britain's vaulting ambition by giving the land west of the Mississippi to Spain.

At first the transfer to Spain was an abstraction only. The English merchants who elbowed aside the old Gallic traders of Detroit and Michilimackinac were too busy east of the river to worry about the west. One did not just walk into the *pays sauvage* on the say-so of a treaty. The Indians of the border country were profoundly conservative. They wanted to cling to the trade forms they knew; furthermore they were deeply suspicious of the English land-grabbing tendencies which had shattered other red tribes along the Atlantic coast. And so, under the leadership of a farseeing Ottawa chief named Pontiac, they tried to weld themselves into a confederation strong enough to fight for the old ways.

In an effort to awe the savages, the English had established thirteen tiny garrisons from Fort Pitt in western Pennsylvania and around the fringes of the Great Lakes to Michilimackinac and Green Bay. In 1763 the Indians stormed them. Nine fell, including Michilimackinac. Green Bay was abandoned. Pittsburgh and Detroit were placed under heavy siege.

Michilimackinac was overturned by cunning one sultry June morning. Pretending a game of bagataway (Canadian voyageurs called it *le jeu de la crosse*), the Indians lured the new British commanding officer and most of his garrison outside the stockade to watch. As the noisy game progressed, squaws waddled through the untended gateway with guns and tomahawks under their blankets. Suddenly the ball sailed over the pickets as if by accident. Whooping and laughing, the players ran after it. Once inside, they seized the weapons from the squaws and leaped for the garrison buildings and the trading houses. Meanwhile, warriors on the outside took care of the startled soldiers there.

Michilimackinac's French-Canadian traders, who neither joined the Indians nor tried to restrain the slaughter, were not harmed. But nearly every Briton died. One who escaped was Alexander Henry of New Jersey. At the onset of the battle Henry hid himself in the garret of a Canadian's house without the owner's knowledge. Through a chink he looked out on carnage:

> The dead were scalped and mangled; the dying were writhing and shrieking under the unsatiated knife and tomahawk; and from the bodies of some, ripped open, their butchers were drinking the blood, scooped up in the hollow of joined hands and quaffed amid shouts of rage and victory.

The wild triumph did not long endure. Strong British forces hurried to help besieged Pittsburgh and Detroit. Winter chilled the ardor of the braves, and French officials added to the dismay by advising peace. Moreover, the Indians had become totally dependent on the white man's marvelous blankets, kettles, guns and powder. Convinced at last that only the English could now supply them, they let their loose alliance fall apart. Band by band they turned to colonials pushing west from the Atlantic seaboard—to Alexander Henry and to Peter Pond of Connecticut as two notable examples, and to a growing influx of young Scots, many of them displaced from their families' stony crofts by the spread of large-scale sheep raising through their native land.

For their labor force these newcomers retained, pragmatically enough, the sturdy French-Canadian voyageurs who long ago had adapted themselves like energetic beavers to the arduous life of the waterways. In addition the British often employed educated Montreal French youths as clerks in their trading houses. A few French merchants at such outlying spots as Green Bay even managed to hang on to the tatters of their independence—but the goods on which they depended and for which they paid in otter and muskrat came from Montreal and Detroit suppliers bearing such alien names as McGill, Todd, Richardson, Askin, and so on.

Along with absorbing men, the new bourgeois, or employers, also absorbed the culture and language of the trade. They endeavored, further, to follow methods which experience had shown to be most efficient in drawing furs away from the Indian hunters. And right there they ran into trouble with the government, just as their Gallic predecessors had done with their administrators, and as the American fur men in time would do with theirs.

For a hundred years the French, English, and American governments in sequence fought three linked trading abuses—the granting of credits, the following of Indians to their hunting camps, and the use of alcohol as an article of barter. Critics of the American Fur Company during the 1820s and 1830s (and some historians since then) often sounded as though they believed Astor and Crooks had invented these three villainies out of their own deep-seated wickedness. But the least glance backward shows that when the British took over Canada in 1761 and set up supervisory posts at Detroit and Michilimackinac, they also took over the same persistent set of problems.

Indians were improvident. When the time came for them to move themselves and their families to their hunting camps, they had wasted the previous year's intake and had nothing with which to buy equipment for the coming winter—ammunition, cooking utensils, knives, axes, warm clothing. The traders had to furnish the items on credit, taking their chances of being repaid in due time with furs. Obviously a man needed to judge his debtor's character accurately (hence the frequent employment of knowledgeable halfbreeds related to the consumers' tribe) and, as is equally obvious, he had a strong interest in keeping the Indians at work throughout the winter.

One way to spur industry was to go to the Indians' camp. And of course one took a few goods along, just in case the Indians needed anything during the winter. When the new British government tried to stop the practice, fifty-seven merchants signed a protest, dated Montreal, September 20, 1766. The Indians, they argued, would not come long distances, often through the land of unfriendly tribes, simply to trade at some post the government had designated as official. The savages would rather deal with foreign traders coming up the Mississippi, "to the great Detriment of our Manufactures in Great Britain, and the utter ruin of this our Province of Quebec." Furthermore, the memorial went on,

> It is well known that the Support of an Indian and his Family is his Fusee; now if any Indian Family who perhaps Winters at the Distance of five or six hundred Miles from one of these Established Forts, should by any Misfortune either break his Fusee, or the least screw of his Lock be out of Order, or want Ammunition, where would that Indian Family be supported from, or how get their Sustenance? they must either perish with Hunger, or at least loose their Hunting that year, which will be so much Peltries diminished from the Publick Quantity. . . . Without the Indians have Credit given them, 'tis impossible to carry on a Trade to Advantage. And when we are on the spot to winter with them, we have always an Opportunity of knowing their Dispositions, pressing them to exert their Diligence . . .

Not only that, said another statement, of February 20, 1765, but also by living among the Indians the traders can "Excite a desire in them to have the commodities of Europe"—all of which of course sounded very reasonable in the manufacturing towns of Great Britain.[5]

The memorials were not wholly candid, however. They did not mention still another reason why traders liked to winter among their debtors. Indians were easily seduced, particularly by alcohol, into selling to a competitor furs which they had promised to a supplier. One protection against this loss, and against simple defaulting—a trader anticipated writing off half his credits each year—was to mark the goods up high enough to cover the risk. But a better way was to station either himself or an engagé at the camps in order to snatch up the furs as fast as they were produced. If one snatched up his rival's furs in the process, so much the better. The rival of course retaliated in kind, and a cutthroat war, with liquor as its chief weapon, was soon underway.[6]

Liquor, indeed, was always the paramount problem of the trade. One famous Canadian merchant, Duncan McGillivray of the North West Company, summed up the reason cynically enough: "When a nation becomes addicted to drinking, it affords a strong presumption that they will become excellent hunters"—in order to satisfy their craving. It was not a matter of physiology. The average Indian probably could tolerate alcohol as well as the average white. What the savages lacked was that built-in remonstrance called conscience. Their lives most of the time were barely endurable. They labored dreadfully, squaws in the homes and men at hunting, for negligible rewards. Hundreds of them starved to death or perished of disease every winter. So why worry about the future? Now was the time to forget.

One story will suffice as illustration. It is a little outside our present chronology, for its events occurred during the winter of 1784–85, two decades after the British had first moved into the Old Northwest. But time does not matter very much in a yarn typifying the labors, dangers, and debasements of an entire era.

The narrator is Jean Baptiste Perrault, who entered the trade in 1783, when he was twenty-one. He spent his first winter taking goods to Cahokia, Illinois, from whence they were smuggled across the ice of the Mississippi into Spanish Missouri. Returning to Michilimackinac in 1784, Perrault signed on as clerk with a tough party led by a bourgeois named Alexander Kay. Kay was bound through Lake Superior to the wilderness around the headwaters of the Mississippi. It was a hard trip. Near Fond du Lac, at the western tip of Superior, where Duluth now stands, a November gale drove the flotilla onto the beach. In Perrault's words, "Our canoes were broken up, our goods thrown here and there. . . . We were all soaked and chilled with cold. It was at that time that I deplored my fate." But accidents were normal. Swallowing their dejection, the men dried the soggy merchandise, patched the canoes, and trudged up the forbidding portages beside the St. Louis River.

Counting Kay's Indian mistress, there were sixteen persons in the group. Since they expected to meet another party shortly, they carried with them only a single bag of flour, one keg of butter, and a little sugar. The other party did not appear on schedule, however, and murmurs grew against the thin rations. Kay leveled a pistol and threatened to shoot the complainers. Sullenly they went on. When finally the expected friends appeared, they had no food either. Splitting into small groups, the men lived through bitter Christmas weather on wild-rose hips sweetened by sap drained from trees. Fortunately they were later able to fortify the diet with roots and a few fish.

In April 1785 they reassembled at Sandy Lake, a favorite Indian hunting ground where the Mississippi makes a big eastward curve through upper Minnesota. Wise traders stayed sober while dickering with savages. But Kay was not wise. At one trading session early in May he let the entire gathering, red and white, drift into what was referred to in the jargon of the commerce as "a drunken frolic."

An Indian named Cul-blanc held a grudge against Kay. But Cul-blanc was afraid of the white man. He turned to a friend called Le Cousin, worked on his vanity as a warrior, and persuaded Le Cousin to attack Kay in the trader's own tent. Le Cousin was clumsy with drink. He succeeded only in slashing the side of the white man's neck. Blood streaming, Kay seized a knife and took after Le Cousin, who fled among the round bark wigwams of the Indian camp.

The pursuit precipitated an uproar among the white voyageurs and the Indians, most of whom were sitting around a big fire drinking. "In a moment," Perrault remembered, "every man Seized his arms, knives, guns, hatchets, and War Clubs, lances, etc. and I found myself quite confounded; me! who never before witnessed such a scene . . . I judged we were to have a critical time." Indeed they were. Le Cousin's mother pushed up beside Kay as he was surrounded by the surging, gesticulating crowd. Coolly she stabbed him in the side. "He fell under the blow; we lifted him, and carried him to his tent; he weltered in his blood."

The confusion of putting the wounded man into bed aroused a comrade who had passed out in a corner. He donned Kay's blood-soaked smock and reeled out to avenge him. Somehow he learned who the instigator was—Cul-blanc. Spotting Cul-blanc lolling contentedly by the fire, he seized him by his scalp lock, cried "Dog, you are dead!" threw the Indian down and knifed him. (Cul-blanc later recovered.)

By this time most of the other Indians had caught panic and were packing up to flee. In the midst of the turmoil, Kay's avenger ordered his wife to fetch him a certain root. He chewed this into a paste, tottered into the tent, sucked the clotted blood from Kay's wound, and slapped on a poultice. Kay fainted but after a while regained consciousness. An Indian medicine man then undertook to complete the cure if the trader promised "to eat nothing salted or peppered, to guard against Drink, and not to touch a woman." Perrault was not around to learn whether his bourgeois heeded. He went off to Leech Lake, trading, while Kay was packed on a litter to Fond du Lac and shipped by canoe to Mackinac. Later that summer Perrault met him there, in dreadful pain from his supurating wound. Shortly thereafter Kay was lugged on toward Montreal in another canoe, to no avail. En route he died.[7]

Abuses such as Kay unleashed could not be controlled by handfuls of troops stationed at a few wilderness forts—and of course that was one reason for the government's trying to concentrate the trade at central points where it could be supervised. But the trade was too volatile to be squeezed. The government's next resort, accordingly, was a system of licensing.[8]

A trader wishing to enter the Indian country applied for permission to the commander of the appropriate fort, who in theory knew the applicant's reputation and reacted accordingly. As an additional guarantee of good behavior, the licensee had to post a bond which became forfeit if he was convicted of breaking the law. Predictable vexations immediately followed. Traders who were refused licenses complained that the commander was playing favorites, often collecting bribes in the process. Conversely, those who won licenses felt the document carried with it exclusive privileges, and they complained that the officials were ruining the trade by turning loose in the interior hordes of irresponsible adventurers. The system nevertheless stayed in effect for a century, passing with slight modifications to the government of the United States—and eliciting the same threnody of grievances from the American Fur Company and its rivals.

Best-known of the Michilimackinac commanders to be impaled on the quarrels of the trading fraternity was Robert Rogers. During the French-Indian wars Rogers had become the military hero of the Atlantic colonies for his exploits as leader of a troop of commando-style rangers. Later he had come to the relief of Detroit during Pontiac's siege; and in 1766 he applied for the command of Fort Michilimackinac, still located on the south shore of the strait. Most of the motives which prompted him to turn west (he was heaped with debt and struggling for an escape) lie outside the scope of this work. But one of his desires is very pertinent—to discover the New World's ancient hope, an interior Northwest Passage to the Pacific and the trade of China.

Immediately after his arrival at Michilimackinac, Rogers sent two exploring parties, one led by James Tute and one by Jonathan Carver, off through Green Bay and the upper Mississippi to locate the mythical river Ourigan, which supposedly would lead to the rainbow. The men scarcely got untracked. Carver did winter an unknown distance up the St. Peter's River (today's Minnesota) but in the spring came back to the Mississippi, met Tute, and returned with him via Lake Superior.

Workaday traders were more resolute, however, and in succeeding years kept pushing their birchbark canoes farther and farther west. By the time of the American Revolution they had paddled so far up the rivers of the Canadian plains that to continue they had to end their rivalries and form a series of cooperative associations. These in 1787 became the famed North West Company. Very soon some of the company's boldest partners—Peter Pond, Alexander Henry, Alexander Mackenzie—began wondering about bringing goods into and taking furs out from their most distant posts via the Pacific. Navigable west-flowing rivers were the first requirement. Searching for one, Mackenzie in 1793 made the first transcontinental crossing, but the route he traveled was impracticable even for canoes.

The hunt dropped to the south. Alexander Henry proposed that the British government help subsidize the effort; and without question John Jacob Astor, during his visits to Montreal, heard Henry expatiate on the subject. The British government did not act, however, even though Mackenzie, who was knighted for his discoveries, wrote a book of travels which concluded with a prophetic chapter about the future of the fur trade. In the United States, Thomas Jefferson read the account. It was one of the many reasons why he hurried the Lewis and Clark expedition overland to the Columbia ahead of the North West Company. And that triumph led in turn to Astor's attempt, implemented in part by young Ramsay Crooks, to establish at the mouth of the great River of the West the post which Robert Rogers of the Rangers had dreamed of nearly fifty years earlier at Michilimackinac. But this is getting far ahead of the story.

Rogers' schemes had been doomed from the start. During the French and Indian wars his semiautonomous rangers had aroused bitter enmities among regular army officers. When he was at Michilimackinac, two of those unfriendly officers turned out to be his direct superiors. Their headquarters were in Albany, and they listened with grim delight to charges that Rogers was favoring the merchants from Montreal. (Again, the old struggle between North and South for control of the border commerce: Astor and Crooks would become its heirs.) Accusations of treason were trumped up against Rogers: he was planning, it was said, to establish an independent government in the West with himself at its head. Arrested, he was put into irons for the winter. The next summer he was loaded like a stone onto the other ballast in the hold of a sailing ship and taken east for trial. Eventually he was acquitted, but he never returned west; nor did Jonathan Carver, who left Michilimackinac on the same sailing ship, comfortably as a passenger.

One of Rogers' guards on the miserable, pitching trip—and one who relished maltreating his prisoner—was Ensign Robert Johnson. Most people found life at Michilimackinac dull, with some reason. Traders complaining against government rules that they stay in the vicinity of the post said in 1765 that since "nothing is produced but Indian corn, the Traders cannot Winter there for want of provisions but have always been obliged to quit that Place to winter with the Indians in their villages . . ." Ensign Johnson, however, found ways to spice his living if not his diet. According to gossip, he seduced Rogers' wife while Rogers was in jail at the fort during the winter of 1767–68; and when he returned to Michilimackinac after delivering the prisoner, he sought the same sort of solace. He dallied with the wives of a sergeant or two and endeavored to rape the ten-year-old daughter of one his paramours. He drank heavily and was embroiled in frequent rough-and-tumble brutalities.

All frontier posts probably suffered from men like Ensign Johnson, but we know about Michilimackinac because one of Johnson's favorite victims was the post's fussy little surgeon's mate and diary keeper, Daniel Morison. As example: Johnson and Forrest Oakes, a trader who later achieved prominence in Montreal, broke into Morison's room one night after a drinking party, picked a quarrel, "pelted me pell-mell with incessant blows repeatedly . . . my shirt, sheets & pillowcase [were] all bespattered with gore and blood." In the end, however, Morison had revenge of sorts. For nearly three years he kept in his journal a running account of Johnson's misdeeds. As a by-product of his secret retaliation he also left a sharp contradiction of the common romantic concept of the forest outposts. They were not exciting. They were dull, and boredom is stultifying anywhere, especially in the wilderness.

For the next decade boredom was Mackinac's story, until the shock of the American Revolution rolled across the lakes and caused a flurry of change.

CHAPTER 2

Robert Dickson and the Ways of the Trade

Early in 1779 George Rogers Clark topped a series of spectacular frontier victories in Illinois by leading his Virginia rangers on an "impossible" winter march over the flooded plains of the Wabash to seize Vincennes. Tremors of the upheaval reached to Michilimackinac and persuaded the commander there that he had better tighten security regulations.

Recalling that the post had been captured in 1763 with arms smuggled inside the stockade by squaws, he decreed that Indian women were no longer to be admitted. The order disturbed trader John Long. Life at Michilimackinac was still dull, war or no, and Long knew a comely pair of copper-cheeked girls who were willing to brighten the days for him and his friends at his store inside the gate. Security indeed! He persuaded the two young women to curl up inside a huge hogshead. Then he closed the end and hired some soldiers to roll the barrel through the gate. Just possibly the men were tipsy. Anyway, the barrel escaped, careened down a slope, smashed into a boulder, and burst asunder. The post commander, it is said, was not amused.

The next year Clark's prowess touched off still greater alarms. Hoping to dislodge the American from the Mississippi Valley, officers at Michilimackinac called on the traders to help enlist an Indian army of 700 men. In May 1780 this ill-disciplined force moved by canoe and barge down the Mississippi to attack the enemy garrison at Cahokia, Illinois, and their Spanish allies in St. Louis across the river.

Clark resoundingly defeated them. The raiders fled north in confusion, some by way of the Chicago portage, some through Prairie du

Chien, a hamlet on the east bank of the Mississippi just above the mouth of the Wisconsin River. The traders in the vicinity (including John Long of squaw fame) were so terrified by the thought of Clark's pursuit that they gathered up at Prairie du Chien as many furs as they could carry in their boats—300 packs—burned sixty-five more bales, and stampeded for the protection of Michilimackinac on the south shore of the strait.

The place looked strong. Sharp-ended pickets twenty-two feet tall surrounded the establishment's thirty-odd buildings. Wooden bastions equipped with six-pounder cannons jutted out from the stockade's corners. A defensive walkway of two-inch planks gave instant access to the rifle ports. But everything was of timber. Either fire or a bombardment by even tiny artillery could be disastrous. Accordingly, the newly arrived commander, Patrick Sinclair, wrote for and received permission to move his garrison to turtle-shaped Michilimackinac Island and relocate the soldiers behind ramparts built of stone.

Sinclair paid the Indians five thousand dollars for the island. As a landing place he selected a small cove on the southeast shore, where ships at anchor would be somewhat protected from the weather by dot-sized Round Island a few hundred yards away. Steep limestone cliffs guarded both flanks of the cove. Between them was a smooth beach and a strip of open meadow where Indians often camped. Behind the flats, its top somewhat to the east as one approached the cove by water, rose a steep hill 150 or more feet tall. Where the slope leveled off just short of the summit, Patrick Sinclair determined to erect a bastion so strong that neither George Rogers Clark nor anyone else could ever seize it.

He began construction in 1780. In 1781 the buildings were far enough advanced to receive the garrison. When the troops moved, so did the handful of traders and voyageurs who earlier had clustered around the stockade on the mainland. Quickly a new village of small homes and cavernous warehouses took shape along the bend of the cove, under the guns of the fort. The hamlet by no means filled the area, and there was still room at either side of the village for visiting Indians to set up their bark wigwams.

By 1782 Sinclair's expenses had reached a reputed $300,000 and he was haled to Quebec to explain. He exonerated himself and work went on. An imposing complex resulted. Timber was stripped from the steep face of the hill behind and somewhat to the right of the village. The fort's long stone-front rampart was approached by a diagonal ramp that slanted across the bared hillside to a sally port well right of the wall's center. Behind this barrier of whitewashed stone rose the steep roofs of the garrison buildings.

The other two walls of the fort formed, with the front base, a rough triangle. They also were of stone but topped by pickets. Each rampart contained a half-timber blockhouse and gun platforms, and the whole looked imposing indeed when viewed from the strait. But any British resident on the island could at once have pointed out the weakness in the defense. Inland behind the fort was the actual top of the hill. From that high point the guns of an invader could command the post's interior.

Builder Patrick Sinclair must have recognized the danger. But he evidently felt he had to stay forward on the slope so that his guns could cover the harbor. Hoping perhaps that troops from the fort could repel any attempt by an enemy to invest the high point at his rear, he faced resolutely toward the water. During the next war, thirty years later, when Americans held the fort, the British seized it from behind. And so, ironically enough, Sinclair served his country better by making a mistake than he would have by creating the impregnable stronghold he had first envisioned.

The last major shooting in the Revolution occurred at Yorktown in 1781, while Sinclair was still at work on the fort. The Treaty of Paris, confirming American independence, was signed in 1783. By its terms every British fort south of the new international boundary—Niagara, Detroit, Michilimackinac and the rest—was to be surrendered to the United States with all convenient speed.

The surrender of the posts and of all the fur country south of the lakes stunned the Canadian merchants. Their diplomats might as well have given up Montreal and Quebec, too. A mourner in Parliament cried, "All Canada is in fact lost . . . All the country from the Allegheny Mountains lost, all the forts, settlements, carrying places, town, inhabitants upon the lakes, lost. The peltry and fur trade, lost." In Montreal, men conversant with the trade tried to console themselves with the thought that they could keep the commerce even if the posts were surrendered. The Canadians possessed over the Americans "every advantage that we could wish . . . such as experienced Guides, expert Canoe men and able interpreters, to those may be added the facility of procuring Birch Canoes and above all the Knowledge which our Traders have of the various articles necessary for the many Indian Nations."[1]

Various responses to the loss were suggested—a chain of new forts inside the line from which the trade could be conducted as of old; a luring of Indians out of the United States into Canada, and so on. But the easiest thing was simply to ignore the peace treaty, keep the forts, and let the Americans lump it.

This was the strategy that was adopted. There was nothing whatsoever that either the first loose confederation of American states or the more perfect union which succeeded it in 1789 could do about the defiance.

The discontented little army of the new nation could not possibly have marched across the wilderness to force the issue. The entire intervening frontier was aflame. The Indians beyond the Allegheny Mountains who had fought on the side of the British during the war refused to acknowledge the peace, which had been signed without anyone's consulting their wishes. To them the struggle was one for existence. If the land-greedy American settlers already pouring into Kentucky were allowed north of the Ohio River, entire tribes would vanish, just as those east of the mountains had disappeared before the Revolution. No, they were not putting down their arms.

So far as the American frontier was concerned, the next decade was bloodier than the war years had been. In hit-and-run attacks that bred monstrous retaliations, fighters of both sides burned each other's villages; scalped, skinned and roasted each other's men; tomahawked each other's women; made slaves of each other's children. People died not by the dozens, as they did in the later, better-publicized wars west of the Mississippi, but by hundreds, even thousands.

The knives and guns with which Indians did the killing, the clothes that warmed them, the pots that cooked their food, the paint that made their faces hideous—nearly all came from British traders operating out of border posts held illegally on American soil. The Americans believed the British added provocation as well. Probably the government of Great Britain did not do so as a phase of official policy. But a few rash army officers and several private traders certainly did so unofficially, and urged the Indians to press home attacks the red men might have made anyway.

The British of course claimed justification for keeping the forts. They said that various of the American states were wrongfully obstructing the collection of certain debts due British citizens, especially loyalists whose property had been confiscated during the conflict. As late as 1791 Minister Hammond told Thomas Jefferson that England intended to retain the posts as long as necessary as security for the debts. In addition, so the British argued more unofficially, they were bound to help their former Indian allies secure an inviolate nation between the Great Lakes and the Ohio River, where the savages could maintain their ancient culture safe from encroachment from the east. And finally, the traders said, the posts could be used to keep the Indians under control while negotiations on these points continued.

Whatever the justice of the arguments, the British-supplied Indians did maintain for a dozen years an impassable barrier in the Ohio country. Behind its protection, Michilimackinac's trade, most of it on American land, grew vigorously. Other factors helped. During the war several Albany fur merchants, electing to remain loyal to Britain, had emigrated to Montreal. There they looked about for new fields in which to invest their capital. Because their former adventures through Oswego had made them familiar with the lakes, they pushed the use of the roundabout Ontario-Erie-Huron route to Michilimackinac, as against the classic canoe path from Montreal up the Ottawa River. The war over, the Canadian government gradually relaxed its restrictions against private shipping, and little sailing ships of twenty to forty tons burden began bringing such staples as flour, pickled meat in barrels, whisky, and the like to the distant and always hungry island. The displaced Albany men also began urging goods on credit on ambitious traders. They were involved in the formation of the potent North West Company, and they were particularly active in stimulating the commerce through Green Bay into the upper Mississippi and beyond the river to the Spanish lands of upper Louisiana.

Buoyed by this new energy, the village under Sinclair's fort grew until there were two streets winding parallel to the cove's shore. The first, Water Street, lay quite literally at the lake's margin, with not a building between it and the water. Short log docks furnished means for unloading the big canoes and little schooners. On the inland side of Water Street, looking across it to the lake, were a few storehouses and commercial buildings. Directly behind them ran Market Street. Its houses too all stood on the inland side, looking toward the source of their existence, the crystal lake.

By the turn of the century a few prosperous merchants had erected attractive dwellings of white clapboard, with dormer windows and tasteful fanlights. Most of the homes, however, were unimaginative, cedar-roofed cubes, often built of logs set upright in the ground and covered with plaster. Many were rented during the summer by traders from the interior and stood empty the rest of the year. Always, winter or summer, there were Indian camps of varying size at either end of the village—an odorous confusion of round-topped huts, the intervening spaces littered with beached canoes, cooking tripods, sleds, fur-drying racks, and miscellaneous junk. Dogs swarmed everywhere; but since drayage was almost entirely by human back, very few horse-drawn carts or even riding animals moved through the streets. Only a handful of the permanent residents boasted anything so exotic as a cow.

Foodstuffs imported by schooner were luxuries. Everyday staples included lyed corn imported from Indian villages along the Michigan Peninsula; maple sugar made in quantities each spring in community sugaring camps on Bois Blanc Island, reached by dog sled over the ice; bits of game and waterfowl traded from the Indians; and fish—especially and everlastingly fish.

Seines scooped up bulging loads of delicious whitefish. Weighing five to ten pounds each, these fish could be salted and kept for long periods, and even shipped to such places as Detroit. In addition, huge Mackinaw trout, as heavy as sixty-five pounds apiece, were dragged out of deep water by hook and line. Trader Robert Dickson, soon to be a major figure in this account, once declared that a rattlesnake with fifteen rattles on its tail was found inside one of these monsters.

Because the island produced little hay, the inhabitants during winter even fed whitefish to their few horses, cows, and pigs. The animals seemed to thrive on the flesh—but entrails, especially trout entrails, were harmful. In spite of borough ordinances against offal, these collected in foul heaps, particularly behind the Indian village. Now and then hunger drove hogs or an occasional colt to sample the putrefying intestines. Invariably the creature lost its hair, became stunted, and sometimes partially paralyzed. Another Dickson story said that once a starving man ate some trout entrails he found near an Indian camp, then paddled on to Mackinac. Every hair he had, together with much of his skin, sloughed off. Although in time he partly regained his health and the use of his limbs, he never again grew hair or beard.[2]

Winters were long and severe. The wives of army officers and of traders who were off in the interior traveled from house to fort by dog sled, entertaining each other with tea carefully measured. As the vernal equinox passed, soft winds occasionally blew the harbor free of ice, then betrayed the promise by reversing and piling the shattered floes onto the shore in dazzling, tooth-edged piles twenty feet high. In some laggard years the French-Canadians erected their Maypole on the still frozen cove and held their spring rites amid snow and ice.

The sighting of the season's first sail from the top of the hill behind the fort touched off a day of rejoicing. From then on the tempo of life increased. Soon the merchandise canoes from Montreal began to appear. The arrival was dramatic and the voyageurs knew it. Pausing just out of sight, they shaved and put on their guarded finery—fresh pink-and-white shirts, gay sashes, beaded pouches. Then on they came, songs rising, paddles flashing. The beach was thronged with people out to stare and shout greetings—soldiers from the whitewashed fort on the hill, sailors from ships lying spike-masted at the docks, villagers, engagés, and hundreds of Indians.

That excitement was scarcely over when the winterers began arriving from the other direction. The year's justification: canoes and big Mackinaw boats heavy with glossy, stinking pelts. The frost-blackened voyageurs at the paddles were even cockier than the Montreal men had been. They were the *hivernants,* the winterers, and the feathers in their caps were the boast of their prowess. For them this was the time of the regale, the explosive summer reward for a winter of denial. They prayed first in the little parish church and then rushed outside to strut. The strong man of one outfit would do bloody battle with the champion of a rival group, for exuberance and for another feather. They all fought the Montreal greenhorns. They drank and sang. Then off they reeled, arm in arm, to the Indian camp for the attentions they generally could buy for a handful of beads.

Their employers were just as eager to relax. As one of them, John Johnston, a veteran of Lake Superior, recalled the scene:

> . . . they think themselves entitled to make up for what they call lost time, by making the most of the short interval elapsed between the sale of their furs, and their repurchase of goods for a new adventure. The chief traders and Montreal merchants keep open table for their friends and dependants and vie with each other in hospitality to strangers. But the excess to which this indulgence is carried, seldom ends without a quarrel, when old grudges are opened, and language made use of that would disgrace a Wapping tavern, and the finale a boxing match as brutal and ferocious as any exhibited in ancient times by the Centaurs and Lapythe.[3]

The young clerks had little time for such carryings-on. It was their job to supervise the opening of the bales of furs that arrived bound in buffalo hides or bear skins, to count the pelts inside, to have each skin beaten free of moths and dust, sorted, graded, valued. Furious arguments erupted as the traders rejected the prices set by the Montreal merchants. While the bosses vociferated, the clerks winked at each other, yawned and waited. At last agreement was reached. Notes were taken so that the paper work—a balancing of payments in furs against debts for goods—could be completed in the loft at night by candlelight.

The furs that had been purchased from many different traders were then lumped in a noisome mass in the warehouses and sorted according to kind, size, and quality. Uniform lots were pressed into compact bundles and lashed tight. Shipping invoices were prepared for each bundle; and when each package had been branded with the merchant's distinctive mark, the weary clerks rounded up the voyageurs, most of them sullen from hangovers, and watched sharply while the bales were loaded aboard various craft for shipment east.

Meanwhile the sobering traders were making up their outfits for the next season. Engagés lifted down the bundles of goods that had been brought from Montreal and opened them on the long counters in the stores. Purchasers dillied and dallied, trying to gauge how much credit they could command and what particular types of merchandise they could sell most readily to the Indians within their area. As part of their dickering they complained routinely about quality and about prices, both the basic cost and the astronomical markups.

The standard unit of a trader's outfit was a "piece." The name derived from a piece, or bolt, of strouding twenty to twenty-five yards in length. Stroud was a kind of heavy, coarse woolen cloth, generally colored red or blue, which Indians made into garments. Buckskin no longer suited the savages. In the words of David Thompson, far-ranging map maker for the North West Company, leather "when wet sticks to the skin and is very uncomfortable, requires time to dry, with caution to keep its shape. . . . Every [Indian] is glad by means of trade to change his leather dress, for one of woollen manufacture of England."

Other dry goods joined the piece of strouding in what was called an "assortment." The most common items were calico, melton, cotton, and heavy blankets. "A blanket," wrote Lewis Cass, early governor of Michigan Territory, ". . . is frequently [an Indian's] house and it is always the most essential part of his dress. The heavy Mackinac blankets are almost impervious to rain, and are . . . large enough to cover an Indian completely." More specifically, a doubled three-point British blanket measured 6'6" by 5'6" and weighed 8½ pounds. Two-and-a-half-point and two-point blankets were smaller. The name derived from black markings woven into the textile to designate size at a glance.

Along with dry goods in the assortment went household equipment—axes, kettles, needles, thread, awls, looking glasses. Hunting items: traps and skinning knives; flints, powder, lead and bullet molds; and the famous short-barreled North West trade musket, invariably decorated by a small bronze, fork-tongued, curling sea serpent screwed to the wood beneath the lock. Adjuncts to vanity were essential—vermilion, combs, gay ribbons, black-silk handkerchiefs, hawk bells (falconry bells the Indians sewed to their clothing for adornment), silverwork, and fathom-long strings of polished bits of white, red, gray, purple and black seashell, called wampum. Besides being used in personal adornment, wampum was also employed as a medium of exchange and, when made into belts, for accompanying such ceremonial affairs as treaty-signing or inviting another tribe to participate in a war party.

Silver was the great prestige item. Its tremendous attraction dated from the time when early officials had handed out to influential chiefs imposing breastplates like those worn by European army officers. For a time its use in ordinary trade was forbidden. But gradually the winterers added, as normal articles of barter, gorgets, half-moons, wristlets, arm bands, and a dazzling variety of ear pendants. During post-Revolutionary days on Michilimackinac, flamboyant male dandies were still slitting the bottom rim of each ear and attaching weights to the lower part of the separation to make it dangle. (The cartilege was often wrapped with brass wire to keep it from breaking.) To the bowlike deformity that resulted, the Indians attached enormous earrings that hung to their chests. Even after actual mutilation passed out of style, red males still demanded earrings as large as our silver dollars, but thinner and decorated with patterns of perforations. Their wives, equally fond of silver, were daintier about size but more varied about shape—tiny wheels that could be set entirely around the rim of the ear, or pendants of balls, triangles and disks. When white men's tall stovepipe hats came into vogue, the savages flossed them up with silver hatbands an inch and a half broad.

In addition to all this, an assortment might contain such miscellany as jew's-harps, occasional pairs of women's shoes; and, for the voyageurs themselves, red caps, striped shirts, warm capotes, playing cards, and incredible numbers of short-stemmed clay pipes. And always there were strands of tobacco twisted into "carrots" weighing one or two pounds each. Plus, of course, small eight-gallon kegs of West Indies rum (later Pennsylvania whisky) or high wine, a concentrated distillation whose bulk, after transport, could be tripled by adding water.[4]

Practice long since had showed that although a voyageur could carry about two hundred pounds as a routine load over the portages (some legend-breeding cocks-of-the-walk went up to five hundred pounds for extra pay), he could maneuver the weight better if he could swing the burden onto his back in two pieces, one on top of the other. Custom decreed, therefore, that everything be packed in compact bundles weighing from ninety to a hundred pounds each. Hence the eight-gallon kegs for liquor: full, they tipped the scales at about ninety pounds.

Assorting was as important as weight. Sometimes single bales were dropped off en route at subsidiary sites, and the contents of these had to be varied enough to suit a maximum number of customers. Furthermore, whatever remained unsold in the spring had to be returned to the outfitting point, because obviously there was risk in leaving merchandise unattended at a log cabin throughout the summer. Besides, the supplier who sold the goods on credit preferred to start each season with a fresh slate. But there is not much charm in an unsold piece of calico or an unwanted pot. When packing-up time arrived, these dull items had a way of disappearing to the Indian wives of the engagés or to their relatives. The more open packages there were lying around, the greater the chance of loss. The ideal, therefore, was to put into each bale a varied enough assortment that only one package would have to be opened at a time to find what the buyer wanted. Exactitude was of course impossible. Still, Indians were swayed in their purchases by habit; and a trader familiar with each customer in his area was able to make surprisingly accurate judgments.

Learning this mass of picayune details was arduous. Not many young men possessed the necessary talent or temperament. One who did show aptitude was quickly spotted by the veterans and hired as a clerk. In the fur trade the title had strong connotations. A clerk was the trader's alter ego; often he was given full charge of a boat, its crew, and its lading. He might even assume command of a secondary post for a season. If he did well there and if his habits, far from supervision, were reasonably sober, he could rise fast. Indeed, given the proper mixture of luck, imagination, endurance, and courage in moments of extreme danger, a young man could achieve independence faster during those post-Revolutionary days on Michilimackinac Island than anywhere else in the West. The extreme distances then being opened beyond Lake Superior made monopoly in that section of Canada almost inevitable, and monopoly is always jealous. The partners in the new North West Company held their shares closely. But south and west of Michilimackinac, where the initial demands were not so rigorous, an individual operator had a chance. Ironically, the area's greatest drawback—furious competition among the individuals—arose from this very fact.

Allured by these hard opportunities around the island, still another young Scot—the one who in his turn would introduce young Ramsay Crooks to the trade—drifted across the lakes in 1785 or so.

His name was Robert Dickson. His boyhood is even more obscure today than is Crooks's. He was born in Dumfries, in the southern Highlands, but the date is uncertain. It was probably 1765. We do not know when he came to Canada. Tradition says that for a time he lived at Niagara, as some of Crooks's family later did. Moving on soon to Michilimackinac, he found a job clerking in the government store there.

In a wilderness where most of the French-Canadian voyageurs were small, Robert Dickson was a striking figure. He stood more than six feet tall. His craggy, florid face was topped by a heavy thatch of red hair. Later associates grumbled that he was vain. In part the braggadocio may have started as a pose. The savages admired monumental dignity, and Dickson perhaps cultivated such an air when he began dealing with them on the island. He was only twenty or twenty-one at the time, totally on his own in what soon became a responsible position, and he may have needed whatever assurance he could muster. Later, though, he did not have to muster vanity. It had become as permanent and as inescapable as his physical bulk.

Dickson had a knack for Indian languages. Either at Niagara or in the store at Michilimackinac, he became fluent in Chippewa. This accomplishment proved of moment to him in the winter of 1785–86. The Sioux and Chippewa of the upper Mississippi had resumed their intermittent fighting.[5] Their hunters stalked each other instead of stalking furs; they roughed up a few white traders in their excitement; and the uneasiness threatened to spread to other tribes in the vicinity, the Menominees and perhaps the Winnebagos.

All these so-called nations occupied United States land and were theoretically under United States jurisdiction. But the United States was involved with the Indians of the Ohio Valley, a thousand miles away, and could not possibly attend to the matter—did not even know of it.

With no sense of incongruity, the British undertook to impose peace on another country's legal wards.

The king's interpreter was put in charge of the mission. His name was Joseph Louise Ainse. He was a native of Michilimackinac, forty-two years old, and had been a witness against Robert Rogers in 1767, when the latter had been charged with plotting to set up his own private country in the West.

One way to persuade Indians to listen to peace overtures was to shower them with gifts of merchandise. The government furnished some of this material. A loose association of interested traders, called the Michilimackinac Company, chipped in thirteen more bales[6]—an unlucky number for Ainse, as matters turned out. To be one of his helpers with the Chippewa during the negotiations, Ainse hired young Robert Dickson. The dim path that developed out of this adventure led, over the years, straight to Ramsay Crooks and the American Fur Company.

Twice thirteen bales would not have necessitated more than a single canoe. Since Ainse seems to have had six interpreters along with him in addition to his crew, this craft may have been one of the remarkable *canots du maître*, the great Montreal canoes of legend. Developed primarily for bringing goods up the Ottawa River from Montreal, the vessels were thirty-five to forty feet long and six feet wide. They could carry up to four tons of merchandise plus a crew of eight, ten, or even fourteen, and their equipment, yet themselves weighed no more than five hundred pounds. Or perhaps Ainse preferred the smaller, more manageable *canots du nord*, only twenty-five feet long, such as the Nor'Westers were beginning to use on their herculean trips to the Athabaska country, eighteen hundred miles beyond Grand Portage on the northwestern shore of Lake Superior.

Either canoe was indigenous to the country. Strips of birch bark were laid over thin slats of red cedar and laced together by thread twisted from the fibers of spruce roots. Melted pine resin served for waterproofing. High prows and sterns curved like scimitars. To the functional, dancing grace of the canoes, the voyageurs added color, painting the paddles and the rims red and green and white. The faces of the bow boasted bright geometric designs or perhaps an Indian's challenging profile.

In August the peacemakers started west, probably in company with traders returning to Prairie du Chien. The bales were stowed carefully on long poles laid lengthwise in the canoe's thin bottom to distribute the weight. Private equipment and food enough for the journey to Green Bay followed; there would be no time for hunting or fishing along the way.

As the canoes (and perhaps a wooden barge or two) slipped away from the docks, the steersman in the rear of each craft struck up one of the repertoire of songs that belonged to every voyageur. The words of some were obscene; others were naïve jingles about shepherdesses, fountains, and bouncing balls. All were rollicking, designed to keep the red paddles moving in unison. Sometimes the crew sang together; sometimes in dialogue with the steersman. Nearly always the songs ended in a wild Indian whoop.

Digging their paddles into the water forty or more times a minute, the crew built the canoe's speed, during favorable weather, to six miles an hour. The occasional rest stops, determined by the guide according to the distance or time or difficulty of the water, were called "pipes." On this first trip of Dickson's there was probably one pipe at Point Seul Choix, some sixty-five miles west of Michilimackinac. Here voyageurs making their first trip carved their names into the rock of the headland and gave small presents to the old hands; Dickson may have been so initiated. Then on they went again, for fourteen hours or more, utilizing to the full each minute of visibility in the long summer days.

Circumstances at times forced additional pauses. If baggage was wet through by rain, spray or upsetting, the bales had to be opened and the cloth spread on trees and shrubbery to dry. High winds also made the voyageurs seek land, for the bark canoes were fragile and could be broken in half by a big wave. In 1787, one year after the peace trip, a canoe belonging to Charles Patterson, a partner of the Michilimackinac Company, was swamped along the northern shore of Lake Michigan. Ten people drowned. When the bodies were picked off the pebbly beach, Patterson's dead Indian "slave girl" was clinging to his corpse. The only survivor was the trader's big white dog. Ever since then the scene of the accident has been known as Patterson Point.

A bark canoe could be easily punctured, too, by scraping on a rough bottom. Accordingly a vessel was seldom driven ashore at a camping place. Instead, just before the bark grated on the shingle, the voyageurs jumped overboard into the cold water and checked the momentum. They carried their bourgeois or clerk pickaback ashore (Dickson, as a government interpreter, would have been so carried), then lifted out the bales, and finally eased the canoe itself onto land. The craft had to be unloaded every evening. The waterproofing gum did not keep its virtues long; each day the canoe had to be overturned and touched up again.

As the men worked, the cook prepared supper. Twice every day each man devoured a quart of lyed corn boiled into a thick soup and flavored with bear oil or, farther west, with buffalo grease. (Finicky engagés making their first journey from Montreal to Michilimackinac had to be pampered with dried peas instead of hominy, boiled with strips of fat pork and fortified with broken pieces of biscuit. The veterans scorned such gourmets with the contemptuous epithet, *mangeurs de lard*.) At night there were a few swallows of rum. The gentlemen clerks and the bourgeois might have tea and a taste of wine.

In spite of each day's long labor, the men retained enough energy to want to dance together in the evening, to the tune of their singing. But not for long. Morning began about three o'clock. Soon they were asleep, the crew under blankets stretched between twigs or under the overturned canoe; the bosses more luxuriously in tents. The caste system, incidentally, was rigid. Bourgeois and clerk did no manual work, often wearing in the wilderness white-duck trousers or even frock coats and tall beaver hats as symbols of their status.

The poles of tents, however, were used in the canoe bottoms to support the baggage. If a sleepy clerk or interpreter was not ready in the morning, no matter. The canvas tumbled impudently about his ears to the ribald jokes of the men. Then in went the bales, the songs swelled under the pallid sky, and the miles flowed back again until sunrise, when a pause was make for breakfast—corn soup again, invariably.

At Green Bay, Ainse's peace mission probably rested briefly and bought fresh supplies of corn. The little town of La Baye had sprouted on the east side of the Fox River, a mile or two above the marshy, insect-infested head of the bay. Farther on, near the first rapids, was the older French community of De Pere. Occasional houses were scattered in between. All stood close to the river; a man could pull his canoe almost to his front door. Though the owners liked to think of the holdings as farms, agriculture was desultory. Most of the male population was away with the Indians during winter and at the Michilimackinac rendezvous during the heart of the summer.

At some point in Green Bay's languid history, an enterprising citizen began earning small fees, during the season when traders passed by, hauling goods in a cart around the rapids on the way to Lake Winnebago. But the custom may have developed after 1786. In that case Ainse's voyageurs lugged the bales on their own backs while the empty canoes were "lined up" the turbulent water—that is, pulled up by a line or rope; during the journey a man or two inside the craft fended it with poles away from dangerous rocks. About every third of a mile along the portage there was a *pose*, or pause. All bundles were brought to this point before any were taken on to the next pause. The Fox River, with only four carrying places in twenty miles, was gentle. One portage on the Montreal River between Lake Superior and Lac du Flambeau in northern Wisconsin was forty-five miles long and divided into 120 pauses.

Beyond Lake Winnebago the main difficulty for Ainse's party was working the long canoe through the tight curves of the upper Fox; the bowsman had to spend most of his time pushing the prow away from the curving, muddy bank. Years later, in 1832, Juliette Kinzie, daughter-in-law of a Chicago trader, described the scenery along this stretch as monotonous. Robert Dickson had a sharper prescience: "Any quantity of hay may be made," he told an American explorer, Zebulon Pike, in 1805, "and it is as fine a country for raising stock as any in the same latitude through all America." He correctly predicted, also, that one day a canal would link the Fox and Wisconsin rivers.[7] On this mission, however, and on every other trip Dickson took across the divide, the way was a mush of mud and a torment of mosquitoes.

In August the Wisconsin River was probably low and the voyageurs frequently needed to jump overboard and boost their fragile craft across the sandbars. At the mouth of the Wisconsin they turned north to Prairie du Chien—the Plain of the Dog, so named perhaps for the Fox Indians.

The Prairie was a strip of flood plain running for about ten miles north from the mouth of the Wisconsin, between the islanded Mississippi and a steep, timbered limestone bluff on the east. Three miles above the Wisconsin a backwater or slough, called Marais St. Friole by the French, curved through the Prairie. Between the Marais and the river was a large, low mound, believed by some observers to have been heaped up in ancient times by human hands. This area was a favorite gathering place for Indians, and each spring and fall a brisk commerce flourished there.

For years there was no white settlement—just Indians. In 1767 Jonathan Carver found three hundred bark wigwams on the Prairie. The erratically spelled reminiscences of Peter Pond report that the camp of 1773 "Exeaded a Mile & a half in Length." Lured by the prospects, "One hundred and thirty Canoes . . . Came from Mackena Caring from Sixty to Eighty Hundred Wate Apease." Up from Spanish New Orleans came ponderous barges "navagated By thirty six men who row as maney oarse. Thay Bring in a Boate Sixty Hogseates of Wine . . . Besides Ham, Chese &c-all to trad with the french & Indians." But the English traders had the know-how and went back to Michilimackinac with 1500 packs of fur of "a Hundred wt Each"—some 75 tons of pelts—in exchange for 450 tons of merchandise, every pound of it transported on a thin rind of birch bark.

In 1781 Patrick Sinclair, builder of new Fort Michilimackinac, prevailed on the Fox Indians to cede nine square miles of the Prairie to a trio of French Canadians. Other French gathered around them. Like the town founders of Detroit, Green Bay and every other Gallic settlement in the Old Northwest, each settler wanted his property to face the water. As a result, the land was divided into long strips rather than squares. As at Green Bay, these plots were loosely called farms. A few cattle and a little seed wheat were brought in from Illinois, the Michilimackinac Company erected a small store, and civilization

made its first tentative incursion onto the upper Mississippi. Among
the traders whom Dickson met there in 1786–87 were two fellow Scots,
Murdock Cameron and James Aird, the latter of whom would first take
Ramsay Crooks to the Missouri. Eventually both Cameron and Aird
became Dickson's partners; and for all three of them little Prairie du
Chien would come as near being a place of residence, in the legal
sense of the word, as they would ever know.

From Prairie du Chien the peacemakers continued northward up the
Mississippi—shaggy islands, rocky bluffs, an occasional meadow, and low
side valleys matted with cedar trees. At the mouths of the larger tributaries there was generally an Indian camp and a trader's hut. This
was Red-Leaf country; frost-bright foliage, clinging stubbornly to scrub
oak trees throughout the winter, gave its name to a hereditary line of
Sioux chiefs who ruled from Black River (present La Crosse, Wisconsin)
north to Lake Pepin—*wapa* or *waba,* red, and *sha,* leaf: Wabasha.

Unquestionably Ainse stopped to see the current Wabasha—or perhaps
was stopped by the chief's men. Trading boats were eagerly awaited.
The Sioux charged down to the riverbank and fired welcoming shots
across the bow, much too close for comfort. The leading whites were
pressed to attend a dog feast in the chief's lodge. Then the oratory.
During it the savages wept copious tears—literally. The Sioux could
turn grief on and off like a faucet. How poor the Indians were—and
how rich their father. Be generous! Ainse presumably made the routine
reply: a little whisky and tobacco, a few more durable presents, and
a long speech urging the Indians to abandon unproductive warfare, take
up the hunt, and become prosperous.

The Sioux temporarily beguiled, on the emissaries went, into what
was called Lake Pepin. The "lake" was really a widening of the river,
forty miles long and one or more broad, the current scarcely percepti-
ble. Save for a meadow or two, bold hills crowded hard against the
water. One stony overlook was called Maiden Rock because of a young
girl's death. As in most tribes, a Sioux brave could buy a wife from
her parents or brother with horses and merchandise. Normally the prospective bride was allowed a voice in the decision, but not if the bid
was high. Rather than add an objectionable husband to a squaw's
standard drudgery, reluctant Sioux brides now and then hanged themselves. One creator of legends varied the pattern by throwing herself
off Maiden Rock onto the jagged boulders beneath. Murdock Cameron
of Prairie du Chien told the yarn to Zebulon Pike in 1805; Pike put
it into the story of his expedition, and a long line of travelers repeated
it after him to the delectation of romantic readers in the East. True love
and all that—but behind the mists was the grimmer truth of unbearable
misery. No wonder Indians got drunk. Like suicide, it was a way to
escape.

Above Lake Pepin the current quickened and islands became numerous again. The bordering hills grew less rugged, the stretches of prairie more frequent. Some 270 river miles above Prairie du Chien (about 210 land miles) the Mississippi bent sideways in a reclining S. Into the southern point of the upper hairpin curve came another river, the St. Peter's, its name later changed to Minnesota. (The suburbs of Minneapolis and St. Paul straddle the confluence today.) Between the two streams reared a striking escarpment. Out in the channel was a big island, later Pikes Island. Sioux Indians were accustomed to camp on the island or the bottom lands round about, and that meant that traders had built their cabins in the vicinity.

In March, 1787, nine or ten weeks after Ramsay Crooks's birth in far-off Scotland, Ainse's party found at the mouth of the St. Peter's a conclave of Sioux beating war drums and boasting of another attack on the Chippewa as soon as the weather should allow. Ainse lectured them on the error of their ways. As part of the usual formula he also asked for a delegation of leading men to go back with him to Michilimackinac, where they could scratch their X's to a formal treaty and, more importantly, be impressed by the generosity and the might of their government. (The British government—not the United States. No Sioux on the St. Peter's had ever heard of the United States.)

Farther up the Mississippi the peacemakers apparently found some Chippewa—none of this is clear in the records that survive—and prevailed on a few of them also to attend the council at Michilimackinac. Dickson, the Chippewa interpreter, would have been the logical person to have shepherded this delegation southward, traveling, one assumes, at a circumspect distance from the glowering Sioux.

At Prairie du Chien these Indian animosities were paled by an acrimonious dispute among the whites. In livid fury James Aird charged that he had been undercut on the St. Croix River during the winter by a rival trader using goods obtained at cheap rates from Ainse— goods, mind you, which had been given to Ainse in part by the Michilimackinac Company, in which Aird was an associate. In short, he had financed his own ruin, thanks to that man Ainse. Other traders brought up other accusations, there were attempts to halt the delegation entirely, and a great turmoil of words developed. In the midst of it Dickson started for Michilimackinac ahead of Ainse, perhaps to keep his Chippewa apart from the Sioux or perhaps to disassociate himself from his beleaguered boss.[8]

Soon Ainse followed with his savages. On his appearance he was fired; later he and the government storekeeper, John Dease, would be tried for misappropriation of goods, be convicted, and eventually lose again on appeal. Meanwhile 196 Indians were waiting and the council had to be held. Experienced interpreters were hard to find.

The annual importations had arrived from Montreal, traders were feverishly making up the next season's outfits, and no one who knew the language of these distant Indians was willing to help. So twenty-two-year-old Robert Dickson became the chief interpreter, which suggests an intelligence nimble enough to have mastered at least some of the Sioux dialects during the preceding winter.

During the council, everyone promised to love everyone else. The fort commander distributed a few British flags and medals, and the Indians went happily home to start fighting each other again. The ancient routine would continue until the last Sioux-Chippewa battle at Shakopee, near Minneapolis, on May 27, 1858. But there would be those during the 1820s who seemed to think that traders of the American Fur Company invented it all.

When the council of 1787 ended, Dickson had nearly a year's pay coming—$300 or so, less whatever he had spent for personal necessities. And the things he had seen during the previous winter and spring had stirred his imagination. He wanted to go back—not to the Chippewa, but to the Sioux, to the big woods that stretched across the confluence of the Mississippi and the St. Peter's, to the prairies that began just beyond them and reached—no man knew how far.

He could not have financed the venture for $300. But a three-hundred-dollar down payment, added to his winter's experience and the regard he had won from the traders at Prairie du Chien, enabled him to find credit, probably from the Michilimackinac Company. With this backing he bought a *canot du nord*. He assembled an appealing assortment of trade goods, he hired voyageurs, and in August 1787 he started back toward the prairies and the beginning of one of the most extraordinary careers of the turbulent Canadian-American frontier.

CHAPTER *3*

The Americans Stir

Each year Dickson prospered a little more. Each year he pushed his canoes farther up the St. Peter's, the *Wattapaw Menesotor* of the Sioux, today's Minnesota. It was a pleasant stream. From its junction with the Mississippi—*Mendota,* the Sioux said, "the meeting of the waters,"—it led the traders seventy-five miles to the southwest. Then abruptly the valley bent like an elbow and pointed northwest. The course remained gentle. In its full 475 miles the river dropped 270 feet; only two portages were necessary because of rapids. There were other navigational problems, however. As the traders advanced, the way narrowed until in places the huge old oaks and alders, the elms and cottonwoods along the riverbank met overhead to form a sun-flecked tunnel of greenery. In the low water of fall the down logs, the mud-banks, and the sandbars created dreadful labor for the voyageurs who had to climb out into the stream and tug the easily damaged canoes ahead foot by foot.

The rolling sides of the upper valley were punctuated by granite outcrops left bare by ancient glaciers. Although early map makers called the long lake at the head of the river Teton Lake after the Teton band of Sioux, the French voyageurs responded more directly to its surrounding outcrops and named it *Lac des Grosse Roches.* Dickson and other English traders translated this into the name it still bears, Big Stone Lake.

North of Big Stone Lake a continental divide separates the waters of the Minnesota, which flow to the Gulf of Mexico, from those of the Red River, which flow via Lake Winnipeg into Hudson Bay.[1] Some people believe that in 1362 a Viking ship sailed out of Hudson Bay through Lake Winnipeg, up the Red River, and, during a season of high water, across a low divide at the head of one of its tributaries into the heart of today's Minnesota. Be that as it may, the portage from Big Stone Lake to Lake Traverse at the source of the Red River was no problem to Dickson's French Canadians. Over they went some-time in the early 1790s, and on Lake Traverse's eastern shore, opposite a village of Teton Sioux, he built a fort. For the next decade it was his trading headquarters, even his home, for in 1797 he married the sister of a Sioux chief who lived near there.

Using packhorses, Dickson and men associated with him followed the Indians from Lake Traverse westward into a totally new environment, the illimitable plains of the Midwest. Crossing still another, almost imperceptible watershed, they reached streams draining due south into the Missouri River. First came the Big Sioux River, which reaches the Missouri at present Sioux City, Iowa. West of the Big Sioux and flowing parallel to it was the Rivière au Jacques, today's James. This was the transitional area from lands of ample rain to the arid West, from canoe to horse culture, from forest animals to almost inestimable herds of buffalo.

On one of his maps, William Clark of the Lewis and Clark expedition noted, concerning the expanse between the Big Sioux and the James, "Between these Rivers the different Bands of SIOUX meet every spring to trade with each other and the white traders who visit them." What the Sioux obtained from the whites at these meetings they did not use entirely themselves. Certain select items they carried on west to other Indian trading fairs on the Missouri River. One was held each summer at the villages of the Aricara Indians near present Pierre, South Dakota. (About the turn of the century Sioux pressures forced the Aricaras upstream to the vicinity of the present South Dakota-North Dakota boundary.) Another trading center was among the Mandans and Minnetarees, who lived in central North Dakota.

The Aricaras, Mandans, and Minnetarees were sedentary Indians. They dwelt in earthen lodges shaped like big inverted bowls. Their women raised squash, melons, pumpkins, and maize, cut the vegetables into pieces and dried them. The men raised and cured a wretched species of tobacco—women were considered too unclean to handle anything as intimately connected with ritual as was tobacco. This garden produce, a few handsomely painted buffalo robes, and occasional furs the Missouri River Indians swapped to red men from the southwest for horses, and to Sioux from the east for manufactured articles which the Sioux had obtained from British traders like Robert Dickson.

This aborigine commerce was not particularly rich, for the savages of the Missouri remained unsophisticated. Except for iron, guns, and

ammunition their wants were few. As Lewis and Clark discovered a
little later, they even rejected alcohol. The myriad buffalo of the
plains made living easier than it was in the forests to the east. Hides
for clothing, for tepees (of interest to the sedentary bands only during
journeys) and even for bullboats in which to navigate the rivers; bones
for hoes; sinew for thread; skulls for ceremony; and inexhaustible larders
of meat readily preserved with pounded berries as pemmican—all came
easily from a single animal. Hunting it was an exhilarating race on
horseback. By contrast, digging beaver or muskrat or otter out of their
riverbank burrows was hard work. Why bother? Said one Mandan to
Charles Mackenzie of the North West Company in 1804, the Indians
might be interested if the hunting could be done on horseback, but
they did not wish to degrade themselves by digging in the bowels of
the earth just to satisfy the avarice of the traders.

> White people [this uncivilized red man went on] do not know how to
> live, they leave their houses in small parties, they risk their lives on the
> great waters, among strange nations, who will take them for enemies.
> What is the use of beaver? Do they make gun-powder for them? Do
> they preserve them from sickness? Do they serve them beyond the grave?[2]

The traders who first encountered the upper Missouri savages were
baffled by this indifference to manufactured goods. Still, so mused one
St. Louis merchant named Pierre-Antoine Tableau, the British eastward
on the Mississippi knew how to create desire. And, given an opportunity,
they would have been delighted to try their temptations on the virgin
Missouri as well. Like all untried fields, this one glowed with promise—
if only it could be reached and developed.

The Sioux did not want the whites to reach it. Though the profits
from the area might not be great until stimulated, still the red middlemen wanted to keep what they had. They tried. Although geography
prevented them from interfering seriously with Canadians coming out of
the north to the Mandan towns, they were able to block the western
thrust of Dickson and other traders from the St. Peter's. Meeting the
wall, the English turned south down the Big Sioux to find the Indians
along the eastern fringes of Nebraska. The Sioux allowed this. That
section of the Missouri was already being exploited from St. Louis. But
the Indians had no intention of letting the higher parts of the river be
used as a way to outflank them. If they could prevent it, nothing from
any direction was to reach the Aricaras—and if a trader did happen to
penetrate that far, then the Aricaras would try to stop him from going on
to the Mandans. At least the blockade was impartial. The Sioux and the
Aricaras applied it not only against the English using land routes from
the east, but also against the Spanish and later the Americans pressing
out of St. Louis.

Another obstacle in the way of Dickson's men was Spanish law. Government edict said, on paper, that Louisiana Territory was closed to aliens. Trading licenses, which were sold by competitive bidding, went only to Spanish citizens, either native-born or naturalized. (As a matter of record, most of the St. Louis traders were of French origin.) The administration in St. Louis had no teeth to put into the order, however. They kept foreign traders out of the lower Missouri, but they had no power to close either the Des Moines or the St. Peter's, and the traders from Michilimackinac went into those areas as blithely as they went into the lands of the United States.

In 1792 the Spanish roused themselves somewhat. The occasion was the appearance in St. Louis of a naturalized trader named Jacques D'Eglise—the Spanish called him Santiago Yglesia. He had managed to reach the Mandan towns and on his return he brought alarming information that the North West Company was sending representatives to the villages overland from the Assiniboine River in Canada. His information reached the administration very shortly after troubles about the sea-otter trade at Nootka Sound, off Vancouver Island in the Northern Pacific, had come within a hair of plunging Spain and Britain into a general war. These difficulties, added to a persistent misconception about the size of the American West, bred fears that the British might at any time launch an attack through Hudson Bay against the silver mines of northern Mexico.[3]

One defense would be to turn the Missouri River into a barrier, not by stringing forts along its unknown length (though that was considered) but by the old device of wooing the loyalties of the Indians through trade. Considering the superiority of English goods and traders over anything Spanish St. Louis could produce, the scheme, in hindsight, looks feverishly optimistic. Nevertheless, the government in 1794 chartered The Commercial Company for the Discovery of the Nations of the Upper Missouri and sent it off to forestall the Canadians, to find if possible a way to the Pacific and to repay itself for its efforts by collecting, under exclusive franchise, whatever furs the Indians offered.

A series of expeditions foundered far short of their goals. Leader of the most ambitious thrust, that of 1795–96, was James Mackay, a Scot turned Spaniard. Associated with Mackay was a Welshman named John Evans, who thought that the light-skinned Mandan Indians might be descendants of a lost colony from Wales and who had turned fur trader in order to learn.

During the unusually cold fall of 1795, the Mackay-Evans party reached as far as the extreme northeastern corner of Nebraska. There, approximately across the Missouri from where Sioux City now stands, they were stopped by the Maha Indians and their villainous chief, Parajo Negro, or Blackbird.

The entire area quailed before the old devil. On one occasion when beleaguered Poncas were begging the Maha chief for an armistice, they sent out their peace pipe not with elders as was customary, but in charge of an alluring maiden, whom Blackbird kept. Somehow he obtained arsenic from St. Louis. Whenever one of his own tribesmen murmured against him, Blackbird invited the complainer to a dog feast. He predicted death and then complacently watched the victim's agonies as he perished by some mysterious agency which the chief apparently had summoned from the nether regions. On the arrival of white traders in the village, Blackbird helped himself free of charge to whatever goods he wished. Satisfied, he ordered a crier to the top of his earthen lodge and summoned his terrified tribesmen to bring in their furs. Trading then went on under whatever terms Blackbird permitted, and no one dared protest.

Unable to get past him, Mackay built a crude post called Fort Charles and settled unhappily down for the winter. Blackbird, the trader wrote, "is so arbitrary, despotic, cruel and implacable a tyrant toward the whites, that one cannot hope that the hunt from this tribe . . . can compensate for the excessive expense." However, Blackbird did let John Evans, the Welshman, start north on foot toward the Mandans with a small party. Sioux chased them back, but the next summer they got by in canoes. It was a fruitless trip. The Mandans proved to be ordinary Indians, not strayed Welshmen; and the North West Company, in the person of notorious René Jessaume, was there ahead of the Spaniards. Jessaume, Evans said, even tried to kill him, and in the spring the disillusioned searcher decided he might as well go back to St. Louis.

Meanwhile Mackay was gaining still more evidence of English penetration into the forbidden lands of Louisiana Territory. Blackbird mocked him for the Spanish gifts he passed out and said blandly that the English who visited him were more generous. In December 1795 reports arrived that English traders working west from the Des Moines River of Iowa had crossed the ice of the Missouri with twelve laden packhorses, bound for the Pawnee villages on the Platte. Other English traders escorting thirty canoeloads of goods from the "San Pedro [St. Peter's] River" were said to be within four days of the Maha village—and one may assume that either Dickson or his clerks were with them, somewhere up the Big Sioux River. In the journal that he was keeping for the Spanish lieutenant-governor in St. Louis, Mackay boasted that his arrival had frustrated the Britons' scheme to build a fort in the area, as they had among the Mandans. But he also warned that English intrigue among the Missouri tribes was increasing to such an extent that the Spanish must adopt strong countermeasures, "unless we desire to see ourselves exposed to abandon this magnificent country."

Mackay's alarms were exaggerated in 1795. Nevertheless a threat was there; the English were chipping patiently away at obstacles they had overcome before—naïve customers, greedy red middlemen, foreign interdicts. If Dickson thought much about his long-range prospects, he must have been confident that sooner or later he and his associates would gain the middle Missouri in force. And then, contrary to every anticipation, the United States in 1803 suddenly acquired Louisiana Territory, a name that then embraced a vast million square miles of largely unknown wilderness between the Mississippi River and the Rocky Mountains. When that word reached Michilimackinac, every trader had to adjust his planning.

While the Spanish were making faint efforts to defend their lands beyond the Mississippi, the Americans were also stirring east of the river. First, they won breathing time against the Indians. In August of 1794, Mad Anthony Wayne at last defeated the savages of the Ohio Valley at the battle of Fallen Timbers, near modern Toledo. During the campaign the Indians failed to receive from their British allies the support which, rightly or wrongly, they had anticipated. Dejected by the seeming perfidy, the vanquished bands assented to the Treaty of Greenville. In exchange for various annuities, they ceded to the United States the southern two thirds of present Ohio. The northern third—in Indian minds it extended to the Mississippi, despite reservations within the area for American forts (at Chicago, for instance) and American roads—was the shrunken remnant of the Indian nation which the British had hoped to interpose between Canada and the United States. Until after the War of 1812 many disappointed traders kept hoping for another chance to push those boundaries back to the Ohio—and so did the brooding savages.

Meanwhile diplomacy was at work. Using the victory at Fallen Timbers to bolster his country's bargaining power, John Jay, American envoy to Great Britain, signed a treaty calling for the surrender, in 1796, of the British-held forts along the Canadian border. In theory, Jay also brought commercial order to the economic wastes around the Great Lakes. Embargoes disappeared. John Jacob Astor, for instance, could now buy pelts anywhere he wished in Canada and ship them directly to New York. Similar freedom extended, on paper, to all intercourse with the Indians. Traders from either nation could venture with merchandise into the wilderness areas of the other country with no more than routine political restrictions. That is, they paid standard duties on their imports and abided by whatever laws the host country asserted over its own citizens.

On the face of things this was reasonable. Before the signing of Jay's Treaty, British traders working out of Michilimackinac had paid no more duties on their goods than if the United States had not existed. After 1796 they would have to stop at the new American customs house in

Michilimackinac, declare their imports, and add appreciable sums of excise money to the revenues of the country they had ignored so long. Reciprocally, on paper at least, Americans going into Canada would heed the same requirements.

In actuality, the privileges for American traders were meaningless. The infant industries of the United States had not learned by 1800 to turn out blankets, coarse woolens, calicoes, and sturdy hunting guns of high enough quality to attract the increasingly sophisticated Indians around the lakes. To win the red men's trade, an American for many years would have to import goods from Great Britain. He had to pay duties on these goods when he brought them into an American port. But the Canadian importer paid no duty when he brought identical goods into Canada. Thus if the American tried to go from Michilimackinac into Canada, as Jay's Treaty said he could, he found himself saddled with more costly goods than his competitors were using. Yet when a Canadian came into the United States, he paid exactly the same duty that an American did. What sort of privilege, so far as Mr. Jay's countrymen were concerned, was that?

Even if the price differential had not existed, the individual American traders could not have bucked on their home ground either the powerful North West Company or its vigorous young rival, the XY Company. Those warring concerns, backed by ample funds, were cutting prices to the starvation point in their struggle with each other; a would-be invader would be ground mercilessly between them. Moreover, as against Americans, those traders possessed years of experience and the ancient loyalties of the Indians. They knew as intimately as they knew the shape of their own canoes each crooked stream in their forbidding lands. They were versed in devilment; their own bloody in-fighting had taught them every dirty trick in the trade. Was it a privilege to venture into a buzz saw like that? Helplessly the Americans stayed on their own side of the border.

Not so the British. Once they had paid duties and secured licenses, they were as free as ever to continue their invasion of the American fur lands. They had trained men, superior goods and better canoes. Above all, they themselves had molded the habits of the conservative Indians, which of itself was an almost insurmountable advantage. Impressive profits flowed from these circumstances. According to an estimate made for the Canadian government by Robert Dickson in 1797 (the year after the border forts had been turned over to the Americans) Detroit and Michilimackinac sent to Montreal a total of 5826 packs of furs. Their value, which accounted for almost half of Montreal's pelt trade that year, amounted to at least £87,390.[4] Records of the furs that went from the same area directly to New York, without enriching Canadians along the way, do not exist; but the total was negligible. Yet these were American furs, save for those that came from Spanish lands beyond the Mississippi. Moreover, matters were likely to grow worse. Uncertain of how long their welcome under Jay's Treaty might continue, the British would have no interest in conservation. Instead, they would strip the land bare. Meanwhile, if one were to judge from past performances, at least some of these Canadian fur men would continue to keep the Indians stirred up against any American citizen who dared try to enter into his country's own wilderness.

What the frontiersmen of the Ohio Valley wanted was not some empty trading right in Canada, but protection within their own land as they built up their own trade—just as a new manufacturing enterprise might be protected by a tariff wall. One form of protection would be to exclude all foreigners. Instead of that, Jay had legalized their ravages. The very name of the treaty came to be spoken, on the frontier, like an oath.

But in the middle 1790s the frontier's voice, though shrill, was not strong. After acrimonious debate in Washington, Congress ratified the document. Late in the fall of 1796, an American garrison moved into the stone fort above Michilimackinac's French and British village. American administrators assumed charge of the customs house and judiciary.

It was a pinprick. Scarcely half a dozen United States civilians followed them into the area. In 1800, when Indiana Territory was established (it included Indiana, Illinois, Wisconsin, Minnesota east of the Mississippi and, until 1805, Michigan), there were not enough Americans along the fringes of the area to fill even the simplest administrative posts. As a result, Governor William Henry Harrison had to rely on British citizens to keep the territory functioning.

John Johnston, an English trader on Lake Superior, became for a time a deputy United States collector of customs at Sault Ste Marie. At least Johnston, a highly educated and well-read man for the area, was not eccentric. Harrison's appointee as justice of the peace for Green Bay certainly was. He was Charles Réaume, of French extraction but a British citizen. Legal formalities never interfered with Réaume's decisions. One voyageur, charged with the attempted rape of an Indian girl, was ordered to replace her torn frock with a new one—and to labor for a week in the judge's garden. Another time, deciding that both disputants in a quarrel were wrong, Réaume fined both: the plaintiff had to bring His Honor a load of hay, the defendant a load of wood. He kept a particular eye on the contracts of convenience which the French-Canadians of his jurisdiction regularly entered into with the half-breed parents of young girls who caught their fancy. The hirer agreed on paper to give the old folks so much a month for the girl's services and to pay an additional amount for her board and room if she stayed with her parents while he was away. The contracts might cover six months' time, a year, or longer. The girls, it is said, were faithful to their part of the bargain and resented infidelity by their employers. Réaume benignly settled squabbles and made sure that time limits were strictly observed. Though none of it accorded with the laws of Indiana Territory, the people of Green Bay seemed to be satisfied and Réaume held the post for several years.

A greater anomaly was Robert Dickson. Not only was he a leading British trader, of the sort the American frontiersmen resented, but he was also, in the eyes of the Spanish officials at St. Louis, an outlaw for his continuing violations of their territory. Yet Dickson was the man whom Harrison selected to be justice of the peace for Prairie du Chien.

Cynically enough, while some American officials were utilizing the services of a few British traders, other American officials were at the same time inventing ways to sidestep Jay's Treaty and harass them. For example, the treaty said that Canadian goods crossing a segment of American territory en route to another point in Canada were not to be charged duty. Thus, merchandise moving west out of Lake Superior over the Grand Portage route, which lay just inside the United States, should not have been taxed. But Americans charged that some of the goods traveling those waterways ended up on United States soil on the upper Mississippi and Red rivers without paying duty—as, indeed, some did. Accordingly they threatened to levy a portage tax on the whole. To avoid this and other possible bedevilments, the North West Company in 1803 began preparing another expensive rendezvous, Fort William, north of the border, and another portage route up the Kaministiquia River. It was far more difficult than the Grand Portage way, but at least it was out of reach of the Americans.

The normal United States duty on goods imported from England was ten per cent of a sum obtained by adding transportation charges to the original purchase price. Thus if an American trader introduced a hundred dollars' worth of English strouding that cost him ten dollars to ship to New York, his duty amounted to ten per cent of $110, or $11. But the American customs collector at Michilimackinac devised a way to circumvent this formula. He arbitrarily said that transportation costs on a hundred dollars' worth of strouding from England to Michilimackinac amounted to $33.33. The duty then rose to $13.33. As a result, a Canadian going into the Indiana or Illinois country, where he was challenged by the spreading American traders, started with a cost handicap of twenty per cent.

The indignant suppliers in Montreal cited other annoyances. They pointed out that for decades they had packed rum in eight-gallon kegs so that voyageurs could carry it over the portages. But the Americans found an obscure government ruling which they interpreted to mean that rum had to be imported in casks. Casks averaged thirty-two gallons each, an impossible weight to load on human back. Mere harassment, so protested the Montreal men, was the only reason for the regulation. Furthermore, Jay's Treaty said commerce between the countries was to be free, yet the Americans charged six dollars for each trading license. In the opinion of the Canadians, malice, not revenue, was behind the exaction.[5]

These annoyances, petty enough, were not official products of the federal government. But in 1802 the United States Congress also showed a disposition to contravene Jay's Treaty by adding to its laws concerning Indian commerce certain provisions which to the Canadians smelled like the beginnings of overt anti-British attacks.

The Act in question, passed on March 30, 1802, repeated a few routine prohibitions: traders in America were once again forbidden (as they had been from time to time in Canada since 1763) to follow the Indians to their hunting camps or to take liquor into the Indian country. Fresh appropriations were authorized for maintaining the government's trading posts, called factories. The first of these factories had been established in 1796 in the southern United States. Their purpose was twofold: first to woo the friendship of the savages, as other governments tried to do, through the blandishments of commercial intercourse, and second to set up standards of fair dealing with which private traders would have to compete.

The initial factories had been too far from the border to concern the Canadians. But the Act of 1802 authorized two more which obviously the United States hoped would be political weapons as well as centers of aborigine trade. One was put at Detroit, another at Fort Wayne, Indiana. The locations were not particularly judicious. The interlude in the Indian wars that followed Wayne's victory at Fallen Timbers had induced settlers to hurry westward. As settlement spread, Detroit and Fort Wayne lost some of their importance as Indian trading centers. Posts there, manned by inexperienced political appointees and stocked with second-rate goods of American manufacture, did not pose a serious threat. But the motives behind them might be indicative of more vigorous measures in the richer regions of the West.

Of more immediate concern was the clause in the Act of 1802 which dealt with licenses and which seemed to say that trading permits would not be issued in the future to any except United States citizens. At once the Canadians protested. Such an exclusion would be a flat violation of Jay's Treaty, which granted citizens of each country unrestricted trading rights within the borders of the adjoining nation.

The remonstrance succeeded, in fact if not by government edict. Caught between the paws of the contradictory rules, the United States officers commanding at Detroit and Mackinac continued issuing licenses to British traders just as they had been doing since 1796. But, as the

Canadians realized, some officious American might at any time or any place decide to force the issue.

The test came in Louisiana Territory. Napoleon had acquired the enormous wilderness from Spain by the treaty of San Ildefonso in October, 1800. Since the treaty was secret, Spanish officers in New Orleans and St. Louis continued in their administrative posts. Although President Jefferson of the United States knew of the transfer, he continued to treat with the Spanish as he prepared to send an army expedition, headed by Meriwether Lewis and, as Lewis' associate, William Clark, overland through alien territory to the Pacific.

This expedition was pointedly anti-British. True, Jefferson hoped that the explorers would find a water highway that would allow direct American commerce with the Orient. But he also wanted to strengthen the claims of the United States to the Columbia River drainage system. The American President further hoped to discover northern tributaries of the Missouri, which might lead toward easy portages to the Saskatchewan. Being more southerly than the frigid Saskatchewan route to Winnipeg, these tributaries might furnish relatively ice-free routes whereby furs could be siphoned out of the Canadian west to the United States, much as American furs were siphoned through the Great Lakes into Montreal.

In the summer of 1803, while the American captains were moving men and equipment toward St. Louis in preparation for the western strike in 1804, the astounding information reached them that the United States had purchased Louisiana. At once their mission took on still stronger anti-British overtones. They were to inform any British traders they met that the fur commerce was now under United States jurisdiction and that the men must be licensed accordingly. They were to inform the Indians that they now owed allegiance to a new overlord. To impress the savages with American strength, and thus wean them from the British, the captains were to send East delegations representing different tribes from the entire length of the Missouri River, so that they could see the white men's might and also meet their new father, the President of the United States.

In Montreal and Michilimackinac, the fur merchants were stunned by the news. What might this portend? Men like Robert Dickson had developed a valuable, if illegal, trade in that portion of the Purchase lying between the Mississippi and the James River. The furs they brought out of the area were worth between £40,000 and £50,000 a year —an amount equal to half the treasure which by Dickson's estimate had come from the entire United States in 1797.[6] And furs were only part of the story. To obtain the pelts another fortune in trade goods—West Indies rum; English blankets and strouds and guns; Montreal silverwork and beaver traps, to say nothing of wages and provisions for scores of voyageurs—each year moved back up the forbidden St. Peter's and Des Moines rivers into the *pays sauvage*.

And now the Americans owned the land.

Would they throw the country open under the terms of Jay's Treaty? Or would they try to exclude foreigners according to the act of 1802?

The bulk of the traders at Mackinac believed that Jay's Treaty would prevail.[7] Strong desires to reach the Missouri may have prompted the conclusion. The lower Missouri and its many tributaries, once locked tight in the grip of a few monopolistic, Hispanicized French in St. Louis, could now be seized by anyone strong enough. Farther upstream were the rumored riches of the Kansas and the Platte. Beyond those rivers (and the allure increased, the farther one's dreaming strayed) were the Aricaras, the mysterious Cheyennes and Crows, the Mandans. No longer need one fear the Sioux of eastern South Dakota or the arduous way through Prairie du Chien and up the St. Peter's. Now it was possible to float easily down the Mississippi to the mouth of the Missouri and row in the time-proven way in big Mackinaw boats up the western river. Or so most of them reasoned.

The theory could not be tested in 1803, for the word of the Purchase arrived too late for outfits to be made ready that fall. The stampede, relatively speaking, began in 1804. Supplies to meet the demand were scratched together out of every warehouse in Montreal and Quebec, and hurried west as soon as the ice went out of the lakes. Any winterer who was not otherwise committed and who could manage the necessary credit hurried to Michilimackinac to buy. Then, in unprecedented numbers, they tramped from the village up the long diagonal ramp to the white-washed fort and demanded of its commanding officer licenses which would permit them to trade within the boundaries of the United States. Bound by Jay's Treaty to comply, he signed them as he always had. If any question about their applicability to the newly purchased territory entered his mind, he shrugged it aside. Let the officials in St. Louis worry about that.

Worry they did. The United States Indian agent for Upper Louisiana (soon to be called Missouri Territory) was Pierre Chouteau of St. Louis, a scion of the city's founding family. As a long-established trader in his own right, Chouteau quite possibly viewed this inrush of Englishmen with not disinterested eyes. On November 19, 1804, he wrote to his superior, Secretary of War Henry Dearborn, that so much freedom of trade was harmful to the interests of the United States. His, Chouteau's, situation was not happy. "An immense number of merchants coming from Michellimakena with licenses from the commandant of that post presented themselves to obtain permits. I could not refuse, since they furnished security [i.e., bonds for good behavior]." It was dangerous, Chouteau continued, to let potentially unfriendly persons enter territory where they might poison the minds of the Indians, "who are easy to seduce." And what of the liquor which the foreign traders brought with them? The United States Government in his opinion should "take vigorous measures to avoid the incalculable miseries which a longer tolerance of this article could occasion." If he tried to seize the kegs and met resistance, what response was he legally entitled to make? He was tired of hearing from the invaders about their rights under Jay's Treaty. How could that outdated document, signed before Louisiana was a part of the United States, be offered as authorization for everything the alien traders wanted beyond the Mississippi? Please send instructions! But the government evidently did not know its own mind, and no official pronouncement was forthcoming that winter or the next spring.

Oddly enough, Robert Dickson seems not to have joined the first rush to the Missouri. Perhaps he could not free himself soon enough from his other responsibilities. More probably, he did not want to go until he could invade the area in strength. The Missouri would soon be swarming with small operators—not just established traders from Michilimackinac and Prairie du Chien, but also with St. Louis merchants who previously had been denied ingress under Spain's system of granting monopoly rights to high bidders. Americans, too, would cross the river from Illinois to take advantage of the sudden opening of what had been a closed door. As Dickson saw matters, this chaos of independents would founder under the stresses of its own frantic competition. He was not averse to helping the collapse along its way, but he wanted to be sure he had power enough to survive the initial shocks. And that could come only through an association of chosen individuals.

A combination for survival seems already to have been on his mind. In spite of the local stimulus given to the trade by this rush to Louisiana Territory, the fur business as a whole was in poor shape. The old Michilimackinac Company, under whose auspices peculating Joseph Ainse had tried to make peace between Sioux and Chippewa, had long since collapsed. Increasing numbers of traders, a few of them Americans, were edging into the Great Lakes area. Unbridled competition led to a wanton stealing of each other's credits. Indian debts mounted on each man's books. Troubles abroad matched those at home. Prices were dropping because of tremors which the Napoleonic wars sent through the fur-buying centers of Europe, while at the same time sea raids on commerce increased the cost of importing goods from England.

Caught in these iron jaws, Dickson began preaching unity to the traders gathered at the Michilimackinac rendezvous of 1804. In association they could stop the price cutting that flowed from competition. By avoiding duplication they could effect economies in ordering and in operating. He proposed a sweeping plan. He wanted to include at least the western part of the Michigan peninsula, the Indiana-Illinois country around the tip of Lake Michigan, and of course his old stamping grounds between Prairie du Chien and the head of the St. Peter's. He needed to come to terms with an existing, more limited combination of Green Bay traders headed by Jacques Porlier, Noel Rocheblave, the Grignon brothers, and that exceedingly rare phenomenon of the wilderness trade, a Jew, Jacob Franks. He hoped to extend operations as far up the Mississippi as possible, even at the risk of colliding with the North West Company. And when the Missouri River was so unexpectedly opened, he obviously needed to include it as well.

Mackinac representatives of the Montreal wholesale firm of J. and A. McGill & Company agreed to discuss with their principals the possibility of backing the venture. They too were being pinched by the same factors that pinched the traders in the field. Any scheme to increase stability among their own numerous small debtors, so that the wholesale firms could collect enough furs to pay what they in turn owed their suppliers in England, was certain to find a sympathetic hearing.

Some progress evidently occurred in Montreal during the winter, for in the spring of 1805 a quantity of goods consigned to Robert Dickson & Company moved through the lakes to the rendezvous at Michilimackinac. In the field, however, a few of the traders were dragging their feet. Jealousies were deep-rooted, suspicions a habit. Dickson's aloof, red-headed arrogance raised hackles. Look at the name the fellow was proposing for the area-wide combination: Robert Dickson & Company, though his own trade was limited to the Sioux of southwestern Minnesota and eastern South Dakota. Who did he think he was, reducing everyone else between the Wabash of Indiana and the Missouri of Louisiana Territory to "& Company"?

The strongest knot of traders, the ones Dickson needed most, were those who worked out of Prairie du Chien—Jacob Franks of Green Bay; Allen Wilmot of the Prairie itself; and James Aird, who knew the Sioux west of the Mississippi almost as well as Dickson did. Early in the spring of 1805 they and the other Wisconsin winterers met as usual at Prairie du Chien to go over the returns from the area between the Rock River of northern Illinois and the Falls of St. Anthony, where Minneapolis now stands. Indians gathered on the plain also, to buy with their choicest remaining furs those luxuries which were rarely sold on credit—silver, fancy guns, and, inevitably, rum. This was the frosting on everyone's winter cake. The traders submerged the bitterness of the field while they settled accounts between themselves and made ready the flotilla of barges that would take their pelts to Michilimackinac and return with the next season's outfits.

Dickson was there, talking earnestly. The need for association had grown. The world-wide economic squeeze had forced the XY and North West Companies to end their long feud and amalgamate. The closure of many erstwhile competing posts threw several clerks and traders out of work. Blocked by the powerful monopoly from entering the Canadian west, many of these unemployed would be forced to turn southward into the United States. Unless the traders already there pulled themselves together, strife would grow more vicious, profits more scanty.

While Dickson was absorbed in these discussions, and in the maze of details connected with his own business as well, a crowd of Sioux appeared, escorting one of their own tribesmen who had committed a murder. To whom should they surrender him?

The timing of the approach was highly inconvenient. But Dickson, as American justice of peace for Prairie du Chien, was the only authority within hundreds of miles. Somewhat impatiently, one guesses, he snapped that he would hold a preliminary hearing.

This is what he learned. A little earlier, somewhere up on the St. Peter's River, in country which had belonged to the United States for less than a year, two Canadian voyageurs had visited an Indian hunting camp to collect credits belonging to their bourgeois. As was customary in such cases, they had carried spirits with them. (Both the visit and the liquor were violations of the Congressional Act of March 30, 1802.) During the frolic that developed, the Indian prisoner now in front of Dickson had killed both white men.

The murder sobered the camp. During more than a century of dealing with the French and English, the Indians had been taught that white blood could not be spilled with impunity, any more than one Indian could slay another (save in war) without making restitution—often, in the custom of the tribes, by giving rich presents to the bereaved family.[8] When whites were dissatisfied, they retaliated in a way that hurt the Indians most—by withholding their trade goods. So after this particular murder the worried tribesmen decided to turn the killer over to white officials.

The nearest one was John Campbell. Like Dickson, Campbell was a justice of the peace for St. Clair County, Indiana Territory. That winter, however, he was far outside his jurisdiction, carrying on his trade somewhere along the upper Des Moines River, near the present Minnesota-Iowa border. The Sioux went overland from the St. Peter's to see him. For undisclosed reasons their sudden appearance outside his cabin doorway startled Campbell. Seizing a pistol, he fired. The shot broke the jawbone of the accused Indian, hummed on, and removed the nose tip of a second savage.

Incredibly, the Indians still wanted to abide by the law. By unrecorded stages they went on to Prairie du Chien and presented themselves to Robert Dickson. Campbell may or may not have been with them; records are unclear. He certainly had as much authority over the affair as Dickson had (the murder occurred in Louisiana Territory, where neither of them held jurisdiction), but perhaps he was embarrassed by his ill-judged shooting. In any event, Dickson took the matter into his own hands.

The preliminary hearing finished, he could have ended the vexation by refusing further responsibility and telling the Sioux to report to Pierre Chouteau in St. Louis, since Chouteau was the legally appointed Indian agent for Louisiana Territory. Less adroit men, especially if they were as busy as Dickson then was, probably would have done just that. But the big redheaded Scot saw in the situation an opportunity to win the good will of the American authorities with whom his proposed company might soon be dealing. Dropping everything, he said he would travel to St. Louis himself, not just with the accused, but with the entire Sioux delegation—thirty-six warriors and four principal chiefs.

Persuading them was a remarkable feat and indicative of Dickson's influence over the tribe. Indians everywhere were profoundly suspicious of the Americans. William Henry Harrison was even then pushing a series of treaties that would take millions of acres of land through from the tribes east of the Mississippi and kindle resentments that would flare up into Tecumseh's confederation. Furthermore, thanks to the British, the Indians had little reason to respect the United States. A trader continually sought to hold the Indians' good will by establishing his own importance in their eyes. A favorite whipping boy was the United States: how poor and weak its people were as compared to the British king and his delegates, the traders. And finally, most Indians were reluctant to venture very far into strange lands. Who could tell what dangers might be lurking in wait, there where the wanderers were helpless?

In spite of these objections Dickson was able to load his forty Indians into canoes and take them to St. Louis. The accused was jailed (but later freed on grounds of insufficient evidence), and the chiefs were so bemused by the white man's busy town that they handed over to Pierre Chouteau their British medals, symbols of allegiance to King George. Chouteau replied by giving the chiefs in exchange four shiny new American medals. That too was notable. Lewis and Clark were sending down the Missouri as many Indians as they could persuade to go, and in all St. Louis there were only seven medals to be divided among them. (The rest of the government's stock had been destroyed several weeks earlier when Chouteau's house was burned to the ground by a disgruntled slave.) Yet the Indian agent considered this visit by Dickson's Sioux important enough to merit more than half his remaining tokens.

In reporting the episode to Secretary of War Henry Dearborn, Chouteau described Dickson as "a respectable inhabitant of Prairie du Chien, whose zeal for the government is well known." And of course that had been Dickson's purpose—a recommendation to the American government.

He needed a favorable opinion. The United States was determined to strengthen its hold over its Indians. As the entire West knew, President Jefferson believed the savages could be saved from extinction if they were lifted from a hunting economy to one of agriculture. The traders of course wanted to maintain them as hunters, and since the traders had always been the purveyors of desirable goods, the Indians listened to them. Jefferson wished to counteract this influence by extending the government trading factories throughout the wilderness as rapidly as congressional appropriations allowed.

With his own lips the President promised a delegation of Osages who visited Washington in 1804 that soon their new father would build trading establishments near enough their lands for them to visit and buy whatever they needed at fair prices. Adjoining these stores, Jefferson said, would be agency buildings where friendly Indian agents would help the savages learn the mysteries of farming. During that same summer of 1804, Lewis and Clark repeated the promises to other tribes higher up the muddy Missouri. Indeed, the explorers had even picked out sites, as instructed by Jefferson, where forts and trading factories might be located—one at Fire Prairie in western Missouri, not far east of today's Kansas City, and another above the mouth of the Platte at Council Bluffs, near present Omaha. For the moment, however, those sites were too far west. The government's newest factories (Detroit was closed in 1805) were scheduled for Chicago and Bellefontaine, the latter near the junction of the Missouri and the Mississippi. Quite possibly Dickson heard discussions about Bellefontaine; the post was built within months after his St. Louis visit. And he knew that British traders would be its prime target.

Other evidences of Lewis' and Clark's diligence were apparent right in Chouteau's own office. A notable old squaw man named Pierre Dorion came down the river the same May that Dickson was in St. Louis with a delegation of Yankton Sioux from the mouth of the James; the Indians had promised Lewis and Clark the previous fall that they would go to Washington with Dorion in 1805. (The Teton Sioux farther up the river had proved less amenable. They tried to stop the explorers. The move failed, but the Tetons were in ugly humor, which boded ill for traders hoping to work past them to the Aricara and Mandans.) Delegates from other tribes were also wandering around town, ready to journey east to see the President—Otos, Missouris, Iowas, and some Sacs and Foxes from the Mississippi.

Most curious of all was an Aricara chief who had just arrived with a party of voyageurs whom Lewis and Clark had no longer needed. This unusually bold chief (his name has not survived) was probably the first of his tribe to see St. Louis. Winning his allegiance might be a key to Indians residing unknown distances west of the Aricara villages, and the government was accordingly eager to impress him.

Agent Chouteau, however, disliked the wholesale junketing. Since some of Dickson's Sioux were selected to go with the other Indians to Washington, he may have growled out his objections to the trader—objections that he put on paper in the middle of May for William Henry Harrison. It was very foolish, he said, to send Indians East during warm weather; the change in climate was likely to prove disastrous to them. He therefore was holding the Indians in St. Louis until the cooler weather of fall. The complications that resulted from his decision will appear in the next chapters.

Dickson saw none of this. By summer he was back in Michilimackinac, receiving his goods and completing the formation of his hopeful new company. As a mere incident in the hurly-burly he greeted a young, eager, dark-haired clerk who had come from Montreal with the crews transporting the merchandise—an eighteen-year-old Scottish immigrant named Ramsay Crooks.

CHAPTER 4

Citizenship by Necessity

At least we know that Robert Dickson stood more than six feet tall and had a florid face. But no one bothered to write down what Ramsay Crooks looked like, talked like, or believed in. He simply appears, an eighteen-year-old immigrant working in the Montreal offices and warehouses of the wholesale firm of Maitland, Garden and Auldjo. Yet something about his looks or his way of doing things must have suggested substance. He attracted the attention of a man named George Gillespie, who was not a member of the firm that employed Crooks. And somehow Gillespie also knew that if Robert Dickson succeeded in putting his new company together in the summer of 1805, he would want a capable clerk.

Gillespie, a shadowy figure in surviving records, was an old hand around the Great Lakes, and a respected one. He belonged to the famous Beaver Club of Montreal, membership in which was restricted to men who had wintered beyond the frontier with more than ordinary skill. Of his actual experiences, however, only this remains: in 1798 he ran the North West Company post on St. Joseph Island, in the mazy, rapid-flecked St. Marys River, which tumbles out of Lake Superior into Lake Huron.[1] He was a believer in Sir Alexander Mackenzie's policy of expansion by establishing posts on the Pacific. When Mackenzie quarreled with the other directors of the North West Company over implementing that policy and left the firm to join the rival XY Company, Gillespie followed him and became Mackenzie's representative on Michilimackinac Island. He also became a partner in Parker, Gerrard, Ogilvie & Co., one of the Montreal houses that backed the XY group. When the

XY and North West companies ended their ferocious rivalry and amalgamated in 1804, Gillespie continued his annual trips to Michilimackinac for the new combination.

He was particularly valued as a negotiator, representing not only his own company but various other wholesale houses in setting up combinations of traders or in closing out short-lived concerns. As we shall see, he carried to Washington the protest of the entire body of Montreal merchants against the United States Government's embargo of 1807–08; and he was one of those who dealt with Astor when the American began making gestures toward the Great Lakes trade. It is a fair assumption that such a man would recognize talent, and when Dickson's firm needed a new clerk, Ramsay Crooks was the young man Gillespie picked.[2]

What talents? Hindsight suggests several: physical stamina, unusual perseverance, adaptability, charm, leadership, loyalty, aggressiveness. It is impossible to say which, if any, of these traits struck Gillespie most forcefully. Perhaps he was won primarily by the lad's good nature and faithfulness in doing small tasks totally devoid of that Homeric glitter now associated with the words "fur trade" and "mountain man."

Crooks's time in Montreal had probably gone something like this. He had arrived in 1803 well after the year's shipment of goods to the interior had started up the rivers. The spring's wild bustle was over; a boy had time to adjust not only to a new job but to an entirely new way of living. In the soft light of evening he could wander through the narrow streets of the gray-stone city, listening to the patois of the French-Canadians or leaning against a post at the wharves and wondering about the sources of the great bright river in front of him. On free days he might climb for a wider view to the top of the shaggy peak that gave the island city its name. But mostly he was inside an office, bent over a slope-topped desk, copying his employers' business correspondence into big gray letter books. In preparation for the annual fall rush of ordering he climbed short ladders beside long wooden shelves and took inventory of hawk bells, awls, black-silk handkerchiefs, and bolts of gaudily printed calico.

In late summer expresses (canoe-borne messengers) began racing in with estimates of the year's take in beaver, muskrat, and deer skins. Information had already arrived from London about the results of the March and April fur auctions. The merchants gathered in the coffee-houses to gossip about developments and to gauge the coming year's orders against the past season's experience. In view of current returns, how many tin kettles should a man in the field pay for a hundred raccoon skins? Or should the Indians be asked to concentrate on muskrat instead? Would the disappointing profits on deer skins hurt the sale of stroud in Iowa? Parchment beaver (the highest quality) was up slightly, but was it up enough to justify increasing the order for blue beads from

Venice? And what of the complaint from Fond du Lac about the weak springs in the last order of traps? Late in the summer of 1803 there was additional speculation: what effect would the Louisiana Purchase have on the fur trade in general? Could a sharply increased demand for goods be met if Napoleon continued to interfere with shipping?

In short, part of the trade's health depended on swift contact around nearly half the world—"swift" in terms of sailing ships, birchbark canoes, and packhorses. In years to come, part of the success of the American Fur Company (and of J. J. Astor & Son, which bought the supplies and marketed the furs) would spring from its mastery of communications from Leipzig and London to St. Louis and Michilimackinac, and from those points on to Big Stone Lake and the Mandan villages. The critical importance of the problem first dawned on Ramsay Crooks during his initial year in the warehouses at Montreal.

Soon the furs themselves and the final order lists from the traders began to come in from the frontier. Skins that had been assembled at Detroit and a few of the bulkier, less valuable packs from farther west arrived by schooner through the lakes. The best furs, particularly those destined for Europe, came in canoe over the faster Ottawa River route, so that they could reach Montreal before the St. Lawrence froze to ocean shipping.

The clerks rushed about in a frenzy of effort. The bales had to be opened, inspected, graded. Representatives from the various London fur houses were on hand to watch and make deals for whatever pelts they needed that were not already committed to them. John Jacob Astor was up from New York to fill his requirements. Once destinations had been determined, the right quantities of furs had to be pulled together and loaded onto the waiting ships. Meanwhile the merchandise orders were checked against inventories and lists prepared for the London suppliers.

The bulk of the fabricated merchandise was delivered from England in the spring, as soon as the lower river was open to shipping. Unfinished material arrived as convenient during the summer. During the winter local craftsmen transformed the raw goods into salable products. Tailors turned bolts of wool into capotes and trousers; seamstresses prepared shirts and occasional dresses for the Indian wives of prosperous bourgeois. Blacksmiths shaped bar iron into axes and traps. Silver workers tapped out bracelets and earrings. Local products also found a market. Leather workers made oxhide shoes for the portages (moccasins could not stand the punishment of rocky paths) and the tumplines called portage collars, which held the bales to the porters' backs. Oilcloth had to be provided for covering the goods, tents for sheltering the bourgeois and his clerks. Boat and canoe builders throve.

Overseeing the articles and collecting the finished products was in general the responsibility of the clerks. As spring neared, they supervised

the packing of goods going by canoe into the standard ninety-pound bales
and the transferring of spirits from barrels into eight-gallon kegs. They
then marked each bale, filed an invoice of its contents, and entered the
charges into the proper ledger.[3]

While the packing went on, other company agents visited the outlying
hamlets to hire voyageurs, invariably French Canadians. Two classes
were sought. One group replaced laborers coming out of the interior
after serving stints of three to five years. These were the *hivernants*,
the winterers. The others were common workhorses—*mangeurs de lard*,
pork eaters—who took the canoes to Michilimackinac or Sault Ste Marie
or as far as the North West Company's huge new Fort William on the
northwestern shore of Lake Superior. The goods delivered, the voyageurs
reloaded the canoes with furs and returned to Montreal at the close of
the same season. Many of the shuttling *mangeurs de lard* never saw the
pays sauvage and were correspondingly scorned by the *hivernants*.

Each individual of both groups signed his name, or more probably an
X, at the bottom of an indenture, printed in French, that bound him
rigorously to his employer. A pork eater might be paid as little as four
hundred livres for his season's work. (A livre varied between sixteen
and twenty cents.) An experienced steersman might earn three times
that much. In addition each hand received equipment—a blanket, shirt,
trousers, handkerchiefs, tobacco, and so on in amounts varying according
to the bargaining power of the worker. A portion of both goods and
money was paid in advance. The money part was often spent during a
last wild roister. On sobering up, many a simple-minded, impulsive voyageur had second thoughts about his agreement and tried to hide. An
annual spring exasperation for company agents and clerks was the rounding up of these would-be deserters.

As ice began leaving the upper rivers, the agents posted on the doors
of the little parish churches "warnings" of the date when the brigade
would leave Lachine. Lachine was a hamlet eight miles up the St.
Lawrence from Montreal, at the head of the St. Louis rapids. Goods
went there in oxcarts over an abominable road. The voyageurs, many
accompanied by their sad-faced families, assembled at the chapel of
St. Anne for a blessing by the priest. The ceremony over, the plumes,
bright sashes, beaded pouches and other bits of finery were stored away
until arrival at the rendezvous. Clad now in workaday cap of red wool,
long shirt, Indian breechclout, trousers or perhaps deerskin leggings
bound below the knee with gay gartering, the men loaded the goods
into the river craft and took their own places on the thwarts.

As a rule the flotillas journeyed only far enough on the first day to
remove the men from temptation. The crews then camped on an island
to wait for the bourgeois to come up with the laggards and the apprehended deserters. Here greenhorn clerks like Ramsay Crooks obeyed

tradition and treated the men to a round of drinks, receiving their cheers in return.

Goods carried in Schenectady or Mackinaw boats, sometimes called barges or bateaux, went directly up the St. Lawrence into Lake Ontario. The current was swift; much of the way the men had to drop their oars and thrust the boat ahead with iron-shod setting poles. The barges weighed far too much to be portaged. Flat-bottomed, pointed at bow and stern, and built of oak strips fitted to a stout frame, they were thirty or more feet long and eight or more feet wide. If the wind served, a mast could be stepped in a footing ready in each boat and the lucky crew could then sail at ease for as much as seventy miles a day. The advantage of barges over canoes was not capacity (a big Montreal canoe could carry as much), but durability. They lasted several seasons; a canoe seldom outlived one. They did not have to be unloaded every night for gumming and they could continue moving against waves that forced the more fragile canoes ashore.

Sometimes the barges went only to Kingston, at the lower end of Lake Ontario. There the cargoes were transferred to little sailing vessels that took them to Niagara. Wagons hauled the goods around the falls, and another vessel continued the journey southwest through Lake Erie, around the long wedge of land formed by the extremity of Ontario, and so reached Detroit. Barges, too, occasionally made this roundabout trip.

Boats traveling on to Michilimackinac found the way by Detroit too long, however. They shortened it by skirting the north shore of Lake Ontario as far as York, now Toronto. There they were lifted with their cargoes onto wagons. Ox teams pulled them due north twenty miles or so to Lake Simcoe. Riverways opened out of Lake Simcoe into bleak Penetanguishene Bay on the southeastern flank of Huron's vast Georgian Bay. The rest of the route to Michilimackinac was smooth sailing, with the long barrier of the Manitoulin Islands to protect the tiny fleets from the area's quick, lashing squalls.

Even counting the cost of the Niagara portage, the cheapest way to reach Mackinac was in a sailing vessel or barge by Detroit. It was risky, however, because of the long expanses of open water, and because of delays caused by uncertain winds, especially on the St. Clair River between Lake Ontario and Lake Huron. The next cheapest way was the York-Lake Simcoe route. The most expensive, but fastest, route was by canoe up the Ottawa River.

Speed was often critical. Merchandise bound for the Athabaska country had to reach the transfer point at Fort William in time for the winterers to carry it on to their distant posts before ice closed the streams. Goods destined for the newly opened Missouri had to reach the Michilimackinac rendezvous almost as promptly. Furthermore, furs from both points had to start back early enough to reach the St. Lawrence while the river was still open to ocean-going vessels. Thus the Ottawa route persisted almost as long as the fur trade did, a rare instance when human muscle was able to hold its own against sail, wind, and even steam.

The speed was obtained at fearful cost. The Ottawa River, which entered the St. Lawrence just above Montreal, was a harrowing sequence of saults, or rapids. At the milder obstacles the canoes were partly unloaded and dragged upstream by towropes. At more severe interruptions everything came out and was backpacked bale by ninety-pound bale to the next navigable water, a fantastic labor whose plague of mosquitoes one trader, John Johnston, described as "beyond all endurance."

I who had nothing else to do but defend myself . . . was left a perfect spectacle of deformity, my eyes closed up, and my mouth distorted in a most frightful manner; judge then the condition of the poor men, engaged in carrying baggage . . . with their faces, necks and breasts exposed, and the blood and sweat in commingled streams running from them. But they seemed to mind it very little, making game of some young men whose first trip it was, whom they . . . treated with great contempt if they expressed pain or fatigue.[4]

Where the Ottawa River's northwesterly trend shifted north, the brigades turned into a tributary, the Mattawa. This and one last portage brought them to Lake Nipissing. Now the worst was over. Joyfully they threw away their setting poles and sped down the French River into Lake Huron due east of Manitoulin Island. There they might pick up favoring winds and reach Michilimackinac within three weeks of leaving Montreal, though the average time for laden canoes on the nine-hundred-mile trip was closer to a month.

Light express canoes could make it in half that time. Generally the agents of the Montreal supply houses sent the goods ahead by barge through York or the big *canots du maître* up the Ottawa, and then overtook the laden craft by record-breaking feats of speed.[5] As one who would have important work to do as soon as the traders assembled on Michilimackinac, Gillespie may well have traveled by express in 1805, taking young Crooks with him. Or perhaps Crooks went in more ordinary fashion, working his way with the merchandise canoes.

Very few changes had come to Michilimackinac since the transfer of the fort to the Americans. The burr in the voice of the traders was still primarily Scotch, the talk of the workers French, and the loyalty of the Indians totally toward England. The advance of the United States frontier was a benefit in one way, however: foodstuffs were a little easier to obtain. The end of the Indian wars and the Treaty of Greenville had quickened a stream of migration through western New York State to Buffalo, Erie, Pennsylvania, and Cleveland, Ohio. These hamlets became supply ports. Tiny schooners loaded aboard flour, Monongahela whisky, tobacco, kegged butter, lyed corn, and pickled meat that had been brought up the Allegheny River from as far away as Kentucky and northern West Virginia. On July 5, 1805, for instance, the sloop *Sagnah* landed 95 kegs of liquor on Michilimackinac for Robert Dickson & Company.

By Crooks's time these ships were beginning to return a few furs to other markets than Montreal. Detroit and Erie absorbed deerhides for leather, buffalo robes for bedding and lap robes in sleighs, bearskins for rugs. Hatters in Pittsburgh and the growing towns of the upper Ohio River called for muskrat fur that could be transported to them down the Allegheny and made into felt. A trickle of choice pelts was even beginning to go again toward Albany, in a resumption of the competitive pattern that had prevailed before the Revolution. In the main, however, the Montreal merchants held the winterers so firmly in their debt that no one on Michilimackinac in 1805 would have forecast any serious American threat to the established order.

The officials of the United States, to be sure, continued what the Britons called a policy of deliberate harassment. In June 1805 two North West Company canoes bound for the Canadian side of Lake Superior and hence not subject to duty were detained at Michilimackinac by wind. The bourgeois in charge had no intent of trading during the delay —he said. Captain David Duncan, in charge of the United States customs house, thought otherwise. He seized and impounded the cargo of the canoes; the company sued; the case was shifted to Detroit, and commerce worth nearly $5000 was lost for the year.[6] The event fired resentments and Crooks certainly heard mutterings about it as he disembarked at the short log docks of the cove and began learning his way through the turmoil of the rendezvous.

Dickson formally launched his company that summer. It walked on shaky legs. To win the support of the suppliers the organization as a whole had to assume the debts of each individual member, a staggering total of about £40,000, most of it due to J. and A. McGill & Co. Only energetic trading could bear such a load. Although the company sent a few individuals into Indiana and Michigan, its main reliance was to be the familiar St. Peter's, the more dangerous upper Mississippi, where the North West Company was certain to cause trouble, and the newly opened Missouri.

Confident of his own prowess as a trader, Dickson turned the St. Peter's over to a subordinate and assigned the Mississippi to himself. For handling the equally critical Missouri, particularly that section where the Sioux could be reached near the mouths of the Big Sioux and James rivers, he called on James Aird.

Little is known of Aird save that he was a Scot and had been at

Michilimackinac as early as 1779, before the fort had been shifted to the island. He was in Prairie du Chien in 1785 during the troubles with Joseph Ainse and had met Dickson there. He had a dignity and a roughhewn charm that impressed explorers who met him, yet some unexplained lack of thrust kept him from reaching quite to the top. Dickson, a younger man, quickly assumed ascendancy over him. Still, he was a good trader and knew the Sioux well. After the Louisiana Purchase he quite probably was one of the British adventurers who hurried south to look over the prospects of the Missouri River. When he returned to the Mackinac rendezvous in the summer of 1805, Dickson persuaded him to add his new knowledge, contacts, and hopes to the shaky young firm of Robert Dickson & Company. Ramsay Crooks, eighteen years old and newly arrived from Montreal with one of Gillespie's boats, was assigned to him as clerk.[7] Only a dozen years later Aird would be working for Crooks.

Something of the young man's drive must have been apparent as Aird started his four laden boats, manned by thirty or so voyageurs, away from the rendezvous toward the almost untouched West. To him the way was familiar—the long arms of Green Bay, the twisting Fox, the portage—but to Crooks it was as fresh as a sunrise. No doubt Aird told him condescendingly that times were easier now than in the good old days. For example, two white men, enduring continual bullying by Winnebago Indians, now helped travelers across the Fox-Wisconsin portage with a wagon. They charged $1 for 300 pounds of merchandise and $8 for a barge, paid in goods charged off at double their original cost. Thus, for an outlay of less than $75 in cash, Aird got his four thirty-foot boats and twelve or so tons of merchandise carted with relative ease across the two-mile stretch. But he could remember when traders made the portage with their own muscle.

They soon found work enough. The Mississippi was low. The eighteen miles of transverse rock ledges that gave their name to Rock River Rapids, just above present-day Davenport, Iowa, loomed like teeth. It was impossible to run the stretch with laden boats. Aird cached half his goods on shore and risked the ledges with the lightened craft. Three boats made it; one was badly smashed. He emptied the three survivors and sent them back for the cached merchandise. He himself camped on a sandbar with a few voyageurs to repair the damaged boat.

Work began as usual at dawn. A little after sunrise there was a pause for breakfast. During it a keelboat appeared, making toward them across the water. The craft, much larger than the trading barges, was seventy feet long, equipped with a small cabin amidships and, near the front, a mast from which a cordelle, or towrope, could be run to human draft animals on the shore. In this keelboat were eighteen disgruntled American soldiers (the weather had been humid and wet) and a ruddy, blue-eyed, twenty-six-year-old lieutenant, rather short (five-feet-eight) and stocky. The officer's manners were unusually punctilious and he had an odd way of tipping his head to the right, so that at times the brim of his hat almost touched his shoulder. Jumping ashore as his rowers nosed the keelboat against the bank, he introduced himself as Zebulon Montgomery Pike.

Aird invited him to breakfast. As they ate, the trader learned that the new governor of Louisiana Territory, James Wilkinson, had ordered Pike to the upper Mississippi to explore, to win the amity of the Indians, to select sites for military forts, and (this no doubt was put delicately) to order out of United States territory any illegal British fur men he encountered. Aird must have known that Nor'Westers went regularly without paying duty on their goods to posts at Sandy Lake, Leech Lake, and other spots in north-central Minnesota. Embarrassment for these rival Nor'Westers might help Robert Dickson & Company; but the anti-British motives behind Pike's expedition might also forebode trouble on the Missouri.

To preclude the difficulties, Aird set about being gracious. He supplied Pike with considerable geographic information and the two men parted amicably. As the lieutenant's oarsmen struggled with the rapids, he learned why traders preferred ascending the Illinois River when traveling to Mackinac. He smashed the rudder on the keelboat, repaired it, and then nearly split the vessel itself on a boulder while using his sail to bull ahead into quiet water. At the top of the rapids he passed Aird's other three boats tied to rocks in midstream, a cryptic maneuver Pike does not explain. Presumably Crooks was with the moored barges.

After the Americans had gone by, the three merchandise barges worked their way down the rapids to their bourgeois's camp. Shortly thereafter a trader named Maurice Blondeau appeared with two soldiers. Aird may have heard of the pair earlier from Pike. The two men had vanished from the Americans' camp several days earlier while trying to whistle out of the underbrush some strayed dogs which the party had started out with for help in hunting or, in case of emergency, for eating. When the searchers had not returned in due time, Pike had concluded that they were dead and had gone on.

Now Aird learned that the pair had been wandering forlornly in the wilderness for five days, eating nothing but a few mussels. At last they had stumbled onto a village of Fox Indians. The savages fed them, gave them new moccasins, and turned them over to their trader, Maurice Blondeau. Blondeau in turn delivered them to Aird. No doubt the Americans would have gone happily downstream with him to St. Louis. That would have been the easiest solution for Aird too. But it was not a useful gesture, and he was worrying about the new governor in St.

Louis. So he did the obliging thing: he hired Blondeau and two Indians to hurry the soldiers after Pike in a canoe.

They caught Pike at the lead mines of Julien Dubuque. Some years earlier, Sac and Fox Indians had discovered (perhaps with the help of the Frenchman) extensive bodies of lead ore in the vicinity of present Galena, Illinois, and Dubuque, Iowa. Only a thin overburden covered the deposits. The Indians scraped the soil off with bone hoes, chipped the crumbly ore into baskets and dragged it on sledges to their villages. There they threw the chunks onto roaring fires. When the ashes cooled they picked out the solidified gobs of lead that had melted free and swapped them to traders who hovered about. Except for Julien Dubuque, to whom they granted extensive concessions, they would not let the whites mine.

Governor Wilkinson of Louisiana wanted a report on the deposits.[8] Pike arrived too ill from dysentery to make a personal inspection, but Dubuque obligingly supplied him with oral data. While the American lieutenant was working over the notes, he was delighted to see his missing privates appear.

Good for Aird! A little later Pike wrote Wilkinson from Prairie du Chien (where the American selected a site for a fort and exchanged his clumsy keelboat for nimbler Mackinaw barges) a letter which was intended to be helpful.

> Dickson is at Michilimackinac. I cannot say I have experienced much spirit of accommodation from his clerks when in their power to oblige me; but I beg leave to recommend to your attention Mr. James Aird, who is now in your country, as a gentleman to whose humanity and politeness I am much indebted.

The gesture came too late. On August 24, less than two weeks before Aird reached St. Louis, Wilkinson had written to James Madison, then the United States Secretary of State, that St. Louis was overrun with British traders, clerks, and engagés bound for "a river, where they have no right." These foreigners were whispering to the Indians, "Beware of the Americans, they mean to take your country from you, as they have done that of your Red brethren East of the Mississippi." He said that if the other officials of Louisiana Territory agreed with his stand, he would close the Missouri to British citizens.

The officials supported him, as Wilkinson had known they would. On August 26, 1805, he issued in English and Spanish a sweeping proclamation: "Notice is hereby given that no person the Citizen or Subject of a foreign Power, will be permitted to enter the Missouri River for the purpose of Indian Trade." No goods could be imported save by citizens or residents of the United States. "All agents, patrons, & interpreters, are to take & subscribe an oath of fidelity to the United

States and of abjurgation to all other Powers." By Wilkinson's own admission to Secretary of War Dearborn, this arrogation of authority was "somewhat extrajudicial," but he justified himself on the ground that the British commercial invasion of Louisiana Territory called for special measures.

For several of the British citizens caught by the edict with their goods in St. Louis the loss was severe. Their merchandise had been ordered a year before, in 1804. Before leaving Michilimackinac, they had ordered more for 1806, confident that Jay's Treaty would protect the move. This sudden interdict, coming too late in the season for them to shift plans, threatened to leave them with two years' stock on hand. Distraught, they rushed expresses to Michilimackinac and Montreal; the alerted merchants in the latter city fired off hot protests to their own government and to Washington.

Aird found his own way around the impasse. The second clause of Jay's Treaty stated that residents of the border areas at the time of the surrender of the forts in 1796 should be considered American citizens unless they elected otherwise. Aird had been in the area in 1796 and had not declared himself. Therefore he was automatically a citizen of the United States. As soon as he landed in St. Louis, he went to Wilkinson and on that basis demanded his license.

Wilkinson had to comply. But he did not want to be circumvented again. Angrily he wrote Secretary Dearborn, asking for more discretion when it came to refusing licenses to men like James Aird. "Extraordinary provision should be made," he said, "to detect or repel the impositions daily practised by persons calling themselves American, but who are in fact Zealous British Partizans—Michilimackinac is the Den from which this description of Persons annually issue forth."

Meanwhile he could harry the Scot. The crews of Aird's four boats were foreign. Brushing aside Pike's letter of recommendation, which had arrived by then, Wilkinson refused to grant permits to the boatmen. Aird had to pay them off in a strange city, after making what arrangements he could to return them to Mackinac, and scour the countryside for new crews who, though probably of French origin, could qualify as American citizens. The search, complicated by a spell of illness, consumed a month and set him far behind schedule.

With official attention thus focused on the party, Aird's clerks would not be likely to risk the law by entering the river without licenses. Sometime in September 1805 they probably took and subscribed "an oath of fidelity to the United States and of abjurgation to all other Powers." Since the oath was in a sense forced on them, the young men could hardly have felt truly bound by it. Yet this is quite likely the occasion on which Ramsay Crooks became a lifelong American citizen— technically if not yet emotionally.

While Aird was recruiting both his strength and his boatmen, the new "American" clerks wandered curiously around the town, center of so much western ferment. There were fewer than two hundred buildings, none of brick and only thirty-five or so of stone. Hotels were poor. Travelers lodged generally in the homes of residents with whom they had business. Since George Gillespie represented the Chouteaus at times in Michilimackinac and at Montreal, it is possible that Crooks may have been welcomed even then by the famous family who in time would be related to him by marriage and who would take over, under his direction, the running of the Western Department of the American Fur Company.[9]

Although a few pretentious residences boasted sawn lumber, most were framed of squared logs eight feet tall standing vertically against each other, French fashion, rather than laid horizontally as American log cabins were. Neatly whitewashed, the buildings were shaded on two or more sides by wide galleries. In back of nearly each home was ample space for a kitchen garden and fruit trees.

The houses sprawled for nearly a mile along a low limestone flat that resisted the gnawings of the river. At the foot of the flat's low sides was a long sandbar to which keelboats, barges, pirogues and canoes tied up—no steamers yet. Years earlier, residents wielding picks and crowbars had chipped out two steep troughs between the water's edge and the town proper. Merchants in tall hats and frock coats, dipping now and then into golden snuffboxes, sauntered down these rough streets to watch Negro slaves unload the boats. French peasants walking beside their squeaking, high-wheeled oxcarts, hauled the merchandise up into the town.

One of the streets leading from the water and on across the three roads which paralleled the river became today's Market Street. The other was named Rue la Tour because it ended at the base of a forty-foot, tree-green bluff on the upper lip of which stood a round stone tower capped with a funnel-like roof. The Spanish had built that strange, squat, loopholed structure, together with three other unfinished towers, as defenses against the British and Indians in 1780. In 1805 the building still housed a few American soldiers. The next year it became the town jail.

The permanent population numbered no more than a thousand. Most were French, plus a sprinkling of Spaniards, half-breeds, and Negroes. By 1805 numbers of Americans were arriving also—military men, civil officials, merchants. The largest store in town, Hunt and Hankinson's, was owned in part by a young man from New Jersey, Wilson Price Hunt, whom Ramsay Crooks soon would know well. The bulk of the emigrants who crossed the Mississippi did not linger in St. Louis, however; they were leather-clad backwoodsmen from Kentucky, eternally restless, and they were searching for farmlands on the prairies west of town or along the creeks that opened into the rivers.

When Aird reached St. Louis in the fall of 1805, the town was still housing, in addition to traders bound west, the delegation of Indians which had been assembled in May to go to Washington to see the President. Records are incomplete, but apparently the Sioux whom Dickson had brought from Prairie du Chien in May and those whom Lewis and Clark had sent down the Missouri with old Pierre Dorion were not among the group. During the summer those wild Indians had grown bored with city living and had gone home. (Later a single Sioux was recruited from the Des Moines River to represent the twenty-odd bands of his nation.) But there were others waiting around, willing to make the trip—Sacs and Foxes from the Mississippi; Iowas, Missouris, and Otos from the middle Missouri. Still in town, also, was the famous, important Aricara chief from the upper river, in charge of his own special interpreter, Joseph Gravelines. But he did not want to stay. During the summer, he and one of the Oto chiefs had fallen ill, and by September they were clamoring to be taken home.

In Wilkinson's eyes the Aricara was an exceptional Indian. "I understand Him to be a great traveller," the governor wrote Washington, "a warrior & Geographer, and He is certainly a learned Savage, because he not only speaks eleven different languages, but is Master of the *Language* of Arms, Hands, & Fingers [sign language]." The governor hoped that even if the Aricara did not go to Washington, still it might be possible to "convert Him to an important Instrument of Humanity & of Policy." Furthermore, unless the Aricaras were impressed by the Americans, the tribe might cause trouble for Lewis and Clark on the explorers' homeward journey. Therefore the governor proposed to send this noble savage and the ailing Oto chief back to their homes with a "Military Escort loaded with presents." The duty completed, the escort would then settle down at the mouth of the Platte and build a fort against mysterious threats Wilkinson thought he detected emanating from the Spanish in New Mexico.

Without waiting for official endorsement of the plan, he started thirty soldiers up the river with the two chiefs. At St. Charles, just above the mouth of the Missouri, the Oto died. Other troubles piled up. The suspicious Kansa Indians objected to any such force marching through their lands as escorts for members of a hostile tribe; the equally suspicious American War Department wondered at Wilkinson's real reason for wanting a fort at the Platte. The expedition was ordered back to St. Louis and Wilkinson was censured for his arrogation of authority. The Aricara chief meanwhile recovered and decided to go to Washington after all.

Twenty-seven Indians made the trip. Each was given a capote, two shirts, a hat, blanket, moccasins, and other equipment. They refused to walk. Wilkinson accordingly had to rent horses for them. They would ride these as far as Louisville and then catch a boat on up the Ohio to either Wheeling or Pittsburgh, depending on the state of the water. After disembarking, they would travel by squads in stagecoaches with their interpreters and military supervisors to Washington. Later they would visit New York and Boston. The idea, of course, was that they would return home so awed by the might of the United States that they would cease listening to subversive talk by the British traders.

Aird and his clerks almost certainly were aware of the bustle accompanying the preparations, and probably speculated among themselves about the outcome. Naturally they had no way of foreseeing how severe the repercussions would prove to be—or how contrary to the hopes of the United States. Besides, they had worries enough of their own to engross them.

Finally, sometime in October, the hiring of the new crews was completed, Aird's health improved and the delayed boats started west. It was an ominous beginning. It wasn't just that he had to race winter in his effort to reach the Yankton Sioux up toward the mouth of the James. Even if he succeeded in traveling that far, every other trader would have been there ahead of him. The Indians would have made their purchases and be starting for their hunting grounds. Unless he broke the laws of the United States and followed the savages to their camps, he could not hope for anything more than random furs picked up from stragglers. But now that he was in this deep he had to keep on wading.

First the rowers struggled back up the Mississippi past the new American fort and trading factory at Bellefontaine, then turned in a horseshoe loop into the gray-brown Missouri. Twenty-one miles up this (and no more than that overland from St. Louis) they reached St. Charles, a village of perhaps a hundred small wooden houses on the north bank of the river. Always there were delays at St. Charles. Discipline was not yet established. The voyageurs indulged in another last fling and had to be bailed out of hock from the tavern keepers. Or some of them deserted and tried to slip overland back to St. Louis.

St. Charles was the last considerable village. Above it were a few clearings where American woodsmen had thrown together rough log cabins backed by gardens of pumpkins, potatoes and Indian corn. Near the houses roamed droves of hogs and half-wild horned cattle. During winter the shaggy beasts would have no other fodder than the tall rushes that grew thick along the riverbank. Overlooking these rushy bottom lands were huge cottonwood trees, their leaves beginning to show golden from early frosts. Out on the islands, where cedar trees grew, axmen were splitting timbers to float downstream to St. Louis.

Fifty miles above St. Charles they came to the dozen rude huts that made up the French settlement of La Charette. Beyond it lay only wilderness. In places limestone bluffs rose two hundred or more feet above the toiling boats. The bordering forests were choked by brambles and nettles. Channel-twisting islands were frequent. All this cut off wind, and sails gave only rare relief to the oarsmen.

There were other interruptions. The low water of fall bared yellow sandbars and upside-down forests of dangerous snags. Now and then an arm of matted driftwood, called an *embarras* by the voyageurs, reached out from the bank. Sometimes the water dammed behind the obstruction whirled around its point too rapidly for the boats to be able to thrust upward against the current. Then the men had to land and chop a passage through the mat. In other places they had to rely on towropes and setting poles. But at least their Mackinaw barges were easier to maneuver than were the big keelboats favored by the St. Louis merchants. Also, in the fall the current was not the raging thing it became by spring, and the cooling nights had ended the plagues of mosquitoes. So on they went: the beat of the songs, the endless lean-pull, lean-pull; twenty miles from dawn to dusk was a good day's work. And the Sioux were nine hundred river miles away.[10]

By winter Aird had pushed his boats at least 600 miles up the Missouri to the broad mouth of the shallow, sandy Platte River of central Nebraska. How much farther he may have penetrated or where his clerks wintered is unknown. It is unlikely he reached the Sioux. But one party may have ventured to the Maha village, 200 miles beyond the Platte. Once this had been the domain of the ferocious old chief Blackbird, but in 1802 he had died indescribably of smallpox with four hundred of his people in their festering lodges.[11] During the winter of 1805–06, a Briton named Joseph La Croix reach the Mahas and during his trade with them cut prices so drastically that his American rival in the area, Robert McClellan, lost $2000 trying to compete with him. Possibly Aird was La Croix's principal. If so, the price war availed the Britons very little. When spring came, Aird had quantities of unsold goods still on hand.

Morosely he assembled his scattered clerks at a rendezvous near the mouth of the Platte. There they took inventory of what remained and dug a jug-shaped hole in the earth for hiding it.[12] After wrapping the merchandise carefully in buffalo hides and lowering it into the cache, they replaced the sod in the opening. They then made camp on the site, burned fires and scattered ashes to conceal all traces of the storage place from wandering Indians. That done, Aird had his men toss the few bales of fur they had obtained into the boats and start for St. Louis. It was a glum trip. Robert Dickson & Company had banked heavily on the new lands bordering the Missouri; but unless the other partners had done far better than Aird, the firm was not likely to survive even its first year. And of course that was exactly the sort of thing the frontiersmen of the western United States were eager to see happen. As long as foreign traders could work undisturbed, no American could hope to profit substantially from his own country's tempting resources.

CHAPTER 5

The Meeting at La Charette

Dickson joined the Missouri traders in St. Louis in the middle of May, 1806. Going there was an unusual detour for him. His normal spring program would have been to take his furs from his winter camp near present-day St. Cloud, Minnesota (some seventy-five miles north of Minneapolis) to a rendezvous with his partners at Prairie du Chien and thence to Mackinac. But at Prairie du Chien he learned of Wilkinson's anti-British proclamation and was alarmed. He could not plan for the ensuing year unless he first obtained exact information about what had transpired and was likely to transpire on the Missouri. Turning affairs over to the company's second-in-command, Allen Wilmot, the big redhead hurried in a light canoe for St. Louis.

He was following Zebulon Pike downstream, much as he had followed the American explorer up the river the previous fall, and so he knew at first hand something of Governor Wilkinson's attitudes concerning the trade and the British. For example, Pike, operating under Wilkinson's orders, had called the Sioux into council at the mouth of the St. Peter's River late in September 1805. There he had prevailed on the Indians to cede to the United States Government a nine-mile strip of land on either side of the Mississippi above the confluence of the rivers for use as a military reservation. The American's speech on that occasion furnished sharp indication of what British traders might expect.

Pike had promised the Sioux that the United States would soon establish trading factories in the vicinity, "in which the Indians may procure all their things at a cheaper and a better rate than they do now, or than your traders can afford to sell them to you, as they are single men, who come far in small boats. But your fathers [the American government] are many and strong, and will come with a strong arm, in large boats." In other words, the government of the United States was going to attack private trade. Furthermore, while Murdock Cameron and other Scots sat there listening, Pike blamed the British for fomenting hostility among the Indian tribes. "I think the traders who come from Canada are bad birds among the Chippeways, and instigate them to make war on their red brothers, the Sioux, in order to prevent our traders from going high up the Mississippi." He also told the council that traders absolutely could not sell them rum and recommended that the Indians not pay their debts if their creditors dealt in liquor. He added a private warning to Murdock Cameron, ordering the Scot to keep spirits out of the St. Peter's Valley. He then concluded with a promise to the Sioux that "before my departure I will give you some liquor to clear your throats."[1]

From this council at the mouth of the St. Peter's, Pike had continued north up the Mississippi to the vicinity of Little Falls, Minnesota. The portages, the icy rains of autumn, and the everlasting wading in the numbing river to push the boats ahead made the trip an ordeal. On October 16, Sergeant Henry Kennerman, "one of the stoutest men I ever knew, broke a blood-vessel and vomited nearly two quarts of blood. One of my corporals, Bradley, also evacuated nearly a pint of blood when he attempted to void his urine." These unhappy circumstances, as Pike called them, convinced him to halt and spend two weeks building a stockade thirty-six feet square for winter quarters.

A month after he had settled in and while he was "powerfully attacked with the fantastics of the brain called ennui," an Indian appeared with word that Robert Dickson was spreading sly tales designed to undermine Pike's work. On December 3 Dickson himself arrived. Taxed by Pike, the Scot denied everything. "He assured me that no liquor was sold by him, nor by any houses under his direction." This would suggest either that Dickson was not truthful, or that his French-Canadians consumed the entire 95 kegs which the sloop *Sagnah* had delivered to Robert Dickson & Company at Michilimackinac only five months earlier, or that he and his associates perhaps "gave" (not sold) liquor to the Indians to help oil commerce. Be that as it may, he allayed Pike's suspicions, supplied him with useful geographic information, and impressed the American lieutenant with his "general commercial knowledge and . . . open, frank, manners. He gave me many assurances of his good wishes for the prosperity of my undertaking."

Fortified by Dickson's maps, Pike led half his men northward to find the sources of the river and to prevail on the Chippewas to make peace with the Sioux. They worked hard, walking over the frozen prairie and dragging their equipment on sleds. Occasionally they broke through the river ice; often they went hungry. But they were hardly exploring and they did not reach the true source of the Mississippi. Every significant point they visited—Cedar Lake, Sandy Lake, Leech Lake, and so on—was already occupied by a trading house belonging either to Dickson's firm or to the rival North West Company.

Although located on American soil, the North West Company posts flew the Union Jack. Just an innocent old custom the Indians expected, one trader told him. Pike did not like it. He did not like the British medals he saw the Chippewas wearing. He certainly did not like hearing that each year the North West Company brought through Fond du Lac, at the end of Lake Superior, forty canoeloads of goods on which they paid no duty. More untaxed goods, so he was informed, went annually to Red River. By his estimate, the United States annually lost $26,000 in revenue.

During Pike's stop at the North West Company post at Leech Lake he was royally entertained by the bourgeois in charge, Hugh McGillis. He ate lavishly, talked for hours with the traders, harangued the Chippewas, and read avidly in McGillis's library. For the sake of the record he wrote McGillis a long letter on February 6, 1806, telling him that henceforth the Canadians must not fly the British flag or distribute British tokens to the savages. McGillis must henceforth pay his legal duties at Michilimackinac and obtain proper trading licenses from the commander at that fort. (Pike added parenthetically that he doubted whether the licenses would be good in Louisiana Territory, west of the river.) He rumbled about liquor, but added to the unhappy Indians that since McGillis had brought great quantities of expensive rum into the country, he would be allowed to sell it bit by bit "that you may forget it by degrees." Next year there would be no more.

On February 10 the English flag was still flying. Furious, Pike "ordered the Indians and my riflemen to shoot at it, who soon broke the iron pin to which it was fastened, and brought it to the ground." Five days later McGillis got around to answering Pike's letter of the sixth. In effect he agreed to everything the American said and then helped Pike gather the Chippewas for a council.

The whole business was futile. Only two Indians were willing to start with the Americans for St. Louis. They soon deserted. And the soldiers were scarcely out of sight on February 18 when McGillis went back to conducting his affairs as he always had.

In April enough ice went out of the river in front of the stockade near Little Falls for the Americans to load their boats and start home. At the mouth of the St. Peter's, Pike held another council with the Sioux. Dickson interpreted for him as the American tried to explain what he had been up to with the Chippewas. The Sioux were unimpressed. They also declined to send a delegation with him to St. Louis. To his further mortification, the lieutenant learned that Murdock Cameron and a fellow trader had taken liquor to the St. Peter's in flat defiance of his orders. Hotly he vowed to prosecute them, though if any suit was instituted the record seems to have vanished.[2]

Dickson of course was aware of the implications behind these American gestures toward establishing control over the upper river. He nevertheless offered the angry young man supplies and did what else he could to be obliging. Pike went on ahead of him to Prairie du Chien and was entertained there at dinner by other members of the company. Yet the amiability could not soften the fact that Pike was carrying information southward which might very well stiffen Wilkinson's determination to keep British traders out of as much American territory as possible. Before Dickson could face his creditors at Michilimackinac, particularly J. and A. McGill & Co. as represented by Thomas Blackwood, he must learn at first hand what to expect west of the river. Accordingly he followed Pike to St. Louis.

Records go blank again. It is not possible to say whether or not Dickson himself saw Wilkinson. Aird, however, succeeded in having his license renewed for another year. In his hurry to recoup he decided against accompanying his dab of winter furs to Michilimackinac. Dickson and some of the clerks could do that. Meanwhile Aird would go straight back up the Missouri to the Platte, retrieve his cached merchandise and trade it for summer deerskins—or red skins, as the out-of-season pelts were called, not so valuable as winter hides but salable. He would also set up a winter camp between the mouth of the Big Sioux and James rivers in southeastern South Dakota. In the fall he would come back down the Missouri to meet the fresh supply of goods which Dickson would send him from Michilimackinac. For overseeing this critical job of transportation, the partners selected James Reed and Ramsay Crooks. Of Reed we know only that William Clark described him later that summer as a "young Scotch gentleman." Crooks too was young to have merited such responsibility; he was nineteen that year.

The plan assumed, optimistically enough, that Dickson would be able to win leniency from the company's creditors. Yet the outlook was discouraging. To be sure, the Green Bay partners had done well among the Menominee Indians (sometimes called the *Folles Avoines*) in northwestern Wisconsin; and by cutting prices almost to the break-even point, Dickson had held his own against the Nor'Westers on the upper Mississippi. Elsewhere results had been below expectation. Total production would not reach a thousand packs, a gross income of perhaps $75,000. Even this figure might prove optimistic.[3] Mercantile gossip floating through St. Louis indicated that the Napoleonic wars were still depressing the fur market. Well, there was nothing to do but make the best of a bad situation and hope that the next year might be better.

On June 7, 1806, just before the boats carrying the Missouri pelts started for Mackinac, Aird put his own feelings into a letter to partner Jacob Franks of Green Bay. Whatever money the company realized, he said, should be divided equally among the firm's many creditors, without favor toward anyone. "God knows all wont be near Enough, but it is our duty to act honorably and honestly Toward all men and not get discouraged or dispirited for one bad Year . . . Keep up your spirits and I think we have a fair Chance of overcoming all our difficulties."

He and Crooks and Reed waved the fur boats on their way to Mackinac and then set about preparing Aird for his summer venture. As they hustled about the humid town they picked up other unsettling bits of information. The navy of Great Britain was seizing neutral American ships which they thought might be helping Napoleon and was impressing English citizens employed as seamen on American merchant vessels. In April 1806 one of two English warships blockading New York Harbor fired a shot that struck an American fishing smack and killed the brother of the captain. The incident touched off public demonstrations in New York City and reverberated across the nation. Such episodes were not likely to make Wilkinson any easier for British traders to get along with.

Still more potential trouble for the Missouri River was inherent in the death, that same April, of the lone Aricara chief who had finally gone to Washington the previous fall. Others of the Indian delegation had also perished on the trip (as agent Chouteau had gloomily predicted), but the Aricara's demise was the fatality that worried the government the most. At once plans were launched for placating his tribesmen.

Either Thomas Jefferson or some ghost writer in the President's employ devised a speech which illiterate Joseph Gravelines, the dead chief's special interpreter, was to memorize and deliver to the Aricara tribe for the Great Father. Gravelines was then to hand around lead and powder, give the chief's medal and personal possessions to his favorite son, and distribute two or three hundred dollars' worth of presents to his wives and other offspring. Dignity was to be lent the mission by an escort composed of (so Secretary of War Dearborn instructed Governor Wilkinson by a letter of April 9, 1806) "A sober, discreet Sergeant & four faithful sober soldiers." Old Pierre Dorion, long-time trader among the Sioux, was delegated to help Gravelines pass the unruly band of Tetons, who had come within a heartbeat of stopping Lewis and Clark in the summer of 1804. Dorion was also instructed to recruit new chiefs to visit Washington in place of those who had dropped out during the

summer of 1805. Finally, there were a few Mahas around St. Louis who
had to be given a ride home.

All this was of more than passing interest to traders in St. Louis.
Very few adventurers had succeeded in reaching the Aricaras by way
of the lower Missouri, and fewer still had gone beyond. If the river
tribes stayed well disposed in spite of the fatalities in Washington, then
an almost incalculable commerce might yet be opened across the plains
and on to the mountains. Surely Aird and Ramsay Crooks, like everyone
else in town, took note of and speculated about the preparations Wilkinson made to further Gravelines' mission.

The man the governor selected to transport soldiers, interpreters, and
Indians was a wild and colorful former Indian scout named Robert
McClellan, whom Wilkinson may have met first during Mad Anthony
Wayne's campaigns in the Ohio country. McClellan was about thirty-
six years old in 1806. He had been born near Mercersburg, Pennsylvania,
on a date now unknown (probably 1770). In his teens he helped his
older brother take pack trains of supplies through the Indian-infested
mountains between his home town and Pittsburgh. He absorbed the
wilderness so completely that he even talked and looked like an Indian.
He was a fabulous athlete. Once while walking through Lexington, Kentucky, he accepted a companion's bet and, to the amazement of nearby
pedestrians, leaped entirely over two draft oxen who happened to be
trudging across his path. Another time, aided by a down-slope run, he
reputedly cleared a canvas-covered army wagon that measured eight
feet tall from the ground to the top of its bows. Trained high jumpers
today cannot spring so high, but legend insists that Robert McClellan
could.

Tales equally extraordinary are told of his adventures as an Indian
scout—savage escapades that impressed the entire army and won him
the friendship of William Clark. Once, it is said, two Miami squaws
detected McClellan and a companion as they were lurking outside a
village in quest of information. To stifle any alarm, they started to drown
the women in a handy creek. Indeed, McClellan's companion did kill
his prisoner and shoved the corpse off downstream, out of sight. But
McClellan's prize turned out to be a white captive and he lifted her
from the water in the nick of time. Grateful and adroit with a rifle, she
helped stand off an attack that developed soon after, then at dark
guided the scouts through a crashing thunderstorm to safety. By all
romantic conventions McClellan should have married her; but he didn't.

During Wayne's campaign, the scout served in a select group of
rangers led by famed William Wells, who, though raised by Potawatomi
Indians, had rejoined the whites on attaining manhood. Two days before
the battle of Fallen Timbers, Wells, McClellan and three others, dressed
like Indians, rode into a camp as if they were warriors coming to join

the fight. They gleaned useful information, seized an Indian and his wife as they left, and started back to Wayne. On the way they saw another Indian encampment. Cocky from their earlier success, they decided on the spur of the moment to tie up their captives out of the way, ride into the camp, kill an Indian apiece, and run for safety during the confusion. But the Indians suspected them and struck first. One scout, William May, was captured, bound to a tree, and later used for target practice. Wells was shot through an arm, McClellan through a shoulder. They broke loose, however, retrieved their prisoners, and hid in a copse. The one man not wounded brought help and all ended well, save that McClellan's wound kept him from participating in the subsequent battle of Fallen Timbers, which ended the Indian wars of Ohio.

For three or four years after the war McClellan made his living as a hunter. In 1799 he took a flatboat to New Orleans, caught yellow fever and nearly perished. For a period after that he did errands among the frontier forts for the quartermaster's department of the army. About the time of the Louisiana Purchase he entered the fur trade of the Missouri. In the spring of 1805 he purchased his goods from the firm of Lisa and Benoît, but ran afoul of Joseph La Croix (perhaps a clerk of Aird's) at the Maha village and took such a commercial drubbing that he could not pay his bill. Lisa and Benoît sued him. McClellan insisted he had lost out in the trade because they had given him goods of poorer quality than his contract with them called for, and he entered a countersuit for damages. The court believed the suppliers, dismissed McClellan's suit and awarded Lisa and Benoît $1185.[4] The ill will springing from the encounter bred passions that soon would engulf Ramsay Crooks as well and would even add a small footnote to the continent-wide planning of John Jacob Astor.

Harried by the law, McClellan needed a fresh source of money. Accordingly he accepted with alacrity the proposal that he conduct Gravelines, Dorion, the soldiers and the Mahas up the river to their destinations. The errand completed, he planned to drop downstream to his trading post at the Maha village. As still another quasi-official function he was authorized by Wilkinson to seize the persons and property of any unlicensed traders he encountered during his travels. Lastly, he was to try to find some trace of the Lewis and Clark expedition, about which not a word had been heard for more than a year.

Before McClellan was ready to leave St. Louis, Aird had completed his own arrangements. Leaving his clerks James Reed and Ramsay Crooks in town to order food, equipment and perhaps American crews for the fall importations, he started upstream on June 10 or thereabouts. He either departed with three barges or later picked up one he had hidden somewhere near the Platte. Anyway, when a hailstorm hissed down the river on July 25, he had three craft with him.

Two years earlier, on July 14, 1804, William Clark had described the ferocity of the squalls which swept the vicinity of the Platte.

> The atmispr. became Sudenly darkened by a black and dismal looking Cloud . . . the storm which passd. over an open Plain from the N.E. Struck the our boat on Starbd quarter, and would have thrown her up on the Sand island dashed to pices in an Instant, had not the party leeped out on the Leward side and kept her off with the assistance of the ancker & Cable.

Aird was not so lucky. One of his craft, caught broadside, heeled over and sank with its cargo.

No good would come from quitting. And in the fall Crooks and Reed would be along with fresh supplies. To make ready for them and for whatever recouping the winter might bring, Aird kept his remaining two bateaux laboring up the meandering channel, past Blackbird's hilltop grave and on toward the mouth of the James, where he hoped to meet the Yankton Sioux.

On July 25, 1806, the day Aird's boat sank, Meriwether Lewis and a small party were far to the northwest on Marias River, almost to the Canadian boundary in what is now Montana. Though eager to reach home after their epochal trip to the Pacific, they had visited this northern tributary of the Missouri to find, if possible, a portage that might lead to the Saskatchewan and thus furnish a route for enticing furs away from the British into the United States. Convinced finally that no such portage existed and "biding a lasting adieu to this place which I now call camp *disappointment*," Lewis on the morning of the twenty-sixth started his group back toward the Missouri. During the gray, stormy day they ran into a party of eight Piegan Indians.

The Piegans were one of the confederated tribe of Blackfeet. Repeatedly the Nez Percé and Flathead Indians west of the mountains had warned the explorers to beware of Blackfeet. This small group seemed friendly, however, and so the whites camped with them that night. Toward dawn, the sentries growing careless, the Indians tried to jump the explorers. In the fight that erupted, Reuben Fields stabbed one Piegan to death; Lewis shot and killed another. The survivors fled. Fearing reprisals, the whites saddled up and rode with only short rest stops more than a hundred miles to the Missouri to join the rest of their party. Although the Blackfeet did not pursue them, the Indians did not forget. The enmity bred by the killings very soon would be intensified by other clashes with white trappers. An implacable resistance developed against the United States that would alter the trade of the northern Rockies and affect, directly or indirectly, the lives of many men, including Ramsay Crooks.

Lewis of course foresaw none of this. He soon had more immediate hurts to worry about. As he was crashing through a stand of willow brush on August 11, a one-eyed hunter of the party mistook him for an elk and shot him through the buttocks. The next day, as he was lying stomach-down in great pain in one of the boats, his section of the exploring party overtook the group led by William Clark, who had been examining the lower Yellowstone River. Two days later the reunited party reached the contiguous villages of the Minnetaree and Mandan Indians, near which they had camped during the winter of 1804–05 on their outward trip.

The Mandans in particular were a key tribe in the trade and for the past twenty-five years had been visited regularly by merchants coming south out of Canada. As part of the American policy of winning the good will of the western Indians, Lewis and Clark were eager to take a few Mandan and Minnetaree chiefs with them to visit President Jefferson. The year before, several leading men of both tribes had promised to make the trip when the explorers returned from the Pacific. Now that the moment was at hand, however, they refused. They dared not try, they said. They would never be able to pass alive through the lands of their enemies, the Aricaras and the terrible Sioux.

The impasse was broken on the sixteenth by René Jessaume, though in a fashion not entirely to the liking of the American captains. Jessaume was a Canadian trader who lived in the villages and was interpreting for the explorers. Evidently he decided he would like a free trip himself, and so made a deal with a chubby Mandan of such light complexion that he was called Shahaka, or Big White. Coached by Jessaume, Big White said that he, his wife and son would go see the wonders of America if Jessaume, Jessaume's wife and their children could accompany the delegation. "We wer obliged to agree," Clark grumbled in his journal.

With sail and oar the home-eager party pushed down the river as fast as they could. On August 21 they met three French trappers a little above the Aricara villages in northern South Dakota. From these men they heard a garbled account of the death of the Aricara chief whom they had persuaded to go to Washington. Curiously, news of the chief's death seems not to have reached the tribe itself—nor did the captains risk enlightening the Indians when they hove to at one of the earthen towns a few hours after talking to the trappers.

Using Shahaka, or Big White, as an ambassador, the Americans urged peace between Mandans and Minnetarees on one hand, Aricaras and Sioux on the other. Everyone at the council puffed smoke and nodded agreement, but when the captains proposed that more Aricaras travel downstream with them, the Indians demurred. They said they were worried about their chief, who had not come home, and they wanted to talk to him first. Some headmen of the little-known Cheyennes, several lodges of whom were camped outside the village trading for vegetables, proved equally reluctant. They wanted white men to visit them and teach them to trap beaver, of which they had a plentiful supply in their country, but they were a wild, shy people, afraid of strange places; and they certainly would not venture out until they knew what had befallen the missing chief. All this while, so the journals seem to suggest, the captains stayed silent about what they had heard. After all, the gossip of the Frenchmen may have been rumor and spreading it would be obviously injudicious at the moment.

On they went, with Big White their only Indian. They passed the place where Teton Sioux had bullied them two years earlier, scolded some of the tribe whom they met for their evil ways, and said that traders would not be permitted to visit them. At the mouth of the James they had a more pleasant meeting with some Yankton Sioux. Then, on September 3, just beyond the Redstone (today's Vermilion) they were saluted by rifle fire from two bateaux tied to the bank. Pulling over, they met James Aird of Robert Dickson & Company, duly licensed by Governor Wilkinson and bound for the land of the Yanktons.

Aird was the first informed, intelligent white man Lewis and Clark had seen in two years. They drained him of everything he knew—Aaron Burr had killed Alexander Hamilton in a duel two years earlier, American troops were quartered at Bellefontaine, Pierre Chouteau's house had burned down, British ships blockading New York had fired on an American vessel, killing the captain's brother. They spent the night with Aird, still talking. He gave them tobacco and flour; they presented him with six bushels of Indian corn, "well calculated for his purpose as he was about to make his establishment and would have it in his power to hull the corn &c."

Nearly every day thereafter they met other traders struggling upward against the imperious river. From one party they obtained "the first spiritious licquor which had been tasted by any of them since the 4 of July 1805." Several of the tattered soldiers "exchanged leather for linen Shirts and beaver for corse hats." On past the Platte they rowed, past the Nemaha, out of the barrens into timber, on among sandbars, snags, and sawyers; past the Nodaway and so to St. Michael's Prairie, about where the city of St. Joseph, Missouri, now stands. There they met Robert McClellan with two or three boats carrying Gravelines, old Dorion, and some Mahas.

The rumor was true. The Aricara chief had died. The Sioux whom the captains had sent downstream in 1805 with Dorion had not continued to Washington. The interpreters were now traveling upstream to make amends and, if possible, to persuade other Sioux to undertake the eastern trip. And so that policy-making part of the Lewis and Clark expedition had failed—an insignificant fault in view of the rest they had accomplished.

On again. More traders, more drams of liquor—more policy. One young trader named Robidoux did not seem to have a proper license. (Wilkinson had been removed as governor; Joseph Browne was acting pro tem and his signature on Robidoux's unstamped paper meant nothing to the captains.) "We . . . cautioned him against . . . attempting to degrade the American Charector in the eyes of the Indians." On, on. No food now but papaws. Never mind, home was close: "the party appear perfectly contented and tell us they can live very well on the pappaws."

Endless sun on the water inflamed their eyes. On September 20 three of the crew "was unabled to row from the State of their eyes." Never mind! The rest of the party "being extreemly anxious to get down ply their ores very well." Near La Charette "we saw cows on the bank [plain, ordinary, wonderful cows] which . . . caused a shout to be raised for joy." Shortly afterward they sighted the village itself, the first white habitations they had seen since leaving this same spot twenty-eight months earlier. "The men raised a Shout and Sprung upon their oares . . . & they discharged 3 rounds with a hearty cheer." The villagers poured to the riverbank, dumfounded. From the Pacific!

Five trading barges were tied nearby. Lewis and Clark landed beside them "and were very politely received by two young Scotch men from Canada one in the employ of Mr Aird a Mr [blank space in ms] and the other Mr. Reed." In the confusion and excitement of the greetings, Clark evidently missed the name of Mr. Aird's clerk, although in time he would learn it well enough. For almost certainly Reed's companion was Ramsay Crooks.

For a nineteen-year-old youth Crooks had passed a responsible summer. After seeing Aird start back for the Missouri, Reed and he had made what arrangements they could for their own return trip in September. Toward the middle of June they started up the Illinois River, perhaps traveling in a canoe or perhaps in one or more barges—they may even have been transporting furs to the island rendezvous for St. Louis merchants. On July 9, 1806, they sighted Lake Michigan. The approach was dreary. A traveler from the south left the Des Plaines River and struck into twelve miles of muck, broken by stagnant Mud Lake. The soupy paths led to the sluggish south fork of the Chicago River. About a mile from Lake Michigan, the south fork joined the north. Thwarted by sandbars along the shore, the combined streams slanted into the lake at a sharp angle.

On the desolate ground between lake and stream, shaded by scrubby pines, stood a log stockade which had been built in 1803 by the United States Army and named Fort Dearborn for the Secretary of War. Four log barracks housed the soldiers; a brick magazine held powder. Southwest of the stockade were the garrison stables, a garden, and the log buildings of the Indian agent and the government trading factory, erected in 1805. Nearby was the establishment of John Kinzie, a silversmith and trader whose outfits visited Indians as far north as Milwaukee, as far south as Peoria. Kinzie bartered supplies to the families of the troops and to travelers using the portage. He sold young Crooks two bushels of corn for $5, an outrageous price in those days.

On arriving at Michilimackinac some two weeks later, the young clerk must have learned that company affairs were in bad shape. Although Dickson and Wilmot had renegotiated the firm's debts, no one was happy about it. Meanwhile a new name had entered the involved picture—John Jacob Astor. In order to raise $4800 in American money for paying duty on Dickson's imports, Thomas Blackwood, the agent of J. and A. McGill & Company, had given the collector of revenue at Mackinac a draft on Astor, due October 1. In return Dickson & Company consigned some of their best muskrat and martin to Astor, via Montreal. "I wished to avoid it," Blackwood wrote gloomily, "but . . . I could not refuse."

Crooks had probably heard Astor's name before. The German-born American had been buying heavily in Montreal for several years. Just the previous October, 1805, he had purchased in the Canadian city beaver, martin, and otter valued at $75,000, much of it from Parker, Gerrard, Ogilvie & Company, of which George Gillespie was a partner.[5] Gillespie had brought Crooks west in 1805. He was on Michilimackinac again in 1806, and it is reasonable to suppose the two men saw each other. Gillespie may even have dropped word to Crooks that Parker, Gerrard, Ogilvie & Company, together with the other suppliers of the powerful North West Company, were dissatisfied with developments south of the border. Dickson apparently could not resist either the economic slump or the Americans. More strength was needed. The Montreal supply houses were contemplating a southern monopoly to be known as the new Michilimackinac Company. If the firm materialized as planned, and talks were already underway with possible wintering partners, its capitalization would amount to a resounding $800,000. (The capitalization of the giant North West Company was $1,000,000.) To avoid competition along the border, the new concern and the North West Company would set up zones of influence, which was something the Nor'Westers would not do with Robert Dickson & Company. So far, Dickson had held off from the proposals, but once the Michilimackinac Company was functioning, his smaller concern was likely to find the pace too grueling. Most probably he and his partners would have to give in and ride along.

How many of these preliminary maneuvers Crooks grasped is problematical. He had his hands full preparing goods worth between $12,000 and $15,000 for the Missouri.[6] Yet surely he sensed that he must go back to the West and tell Aird that their company was about to founder. What next? Would he, Ramsay Crooks, backed by only a little more than a year's experience in the wilderness, be offered a job with the huge monopoly? Did he want to be a minor member of such a concern? How successful was the company likely to be if the Americans stepped up their counterthrusts against all things British?

Surely Reed and he talked these questions over on the long trip through Wisconsin and down the Mississippi. Surely echoes of the speculations were very much alive in the backs of their minds on September 20 as the crews moored the five laden boats opposite La Charette. Then the sudden gunfire interrupted and everything else was forgotten as they rushed with the rest of the townspeople to the riverbank, to greet the explorers just returned like sun-blackened ghosts from the Pacific.

Words poured out. "Every person," Clark wrote in his journal, ". . . express great pleasure at our return, and acknowledged themselves much astonished they informed us that we were supposed to have been lost long since."

The occasion demanded celebration. The captains paid a villager eight dollars for two gallons of whisky, "an imposition," Clark growled. Crooks and Reed were more generous. "those two young Scotch gentlemen furnished us with Beef flower and some pork for our men, and gave us a very agreeable supper. as it was like to rain we accepted of a bed in one of their tents."

Nineteen years old, thunderheads piling over the trees. A meal and a night's talk with men who had stood where no other white men had ever been before. A comparable situation is no longer possible, unless one were somehow to seize upon an unexpected astronaut and monopolize him for twelve hours. Anyone's guess will do concerning Lewis' and Clark's subject matter that night. Black herds of buffalo on plains rolling endlessly away from the yellow river. The eroded fantasies of the badlands. Collapsing riverbanks, roar of grizzlies, the stab of cactus thorns on the eighteen-mile portage around the Great Falls; the incredible emptiness waiting for—what? Afterward, the white peaks of the Rockies, mountains such as Americans had scarcely dreamed about. And finally the glitter of the Columbia, carving a resonant gorge through the Cascades to coastal forests whose trees were so mighty that it was an affront for a man just to swing out his hands in an effort to suggest their size. And underneath the matter-of-factness of the telling there must have run a timbre of voice that a boy would catch: a wonder of discovery so overwhelming that every now and then the talker must have had to pause, look inward with his sun-assaulted eyes and re-evaluate once again the implications of what he had seen, of what he was saying.

Young fur traders would surely ask about beaver. The American captains had no reason to hold back information. All the way down the river they had been checking trading licenses. Presumably they also examined the permits of Crooks and Reed and found the papers in order. That meant the young men had been accepted in St. Louis as American citizens, whatever reservations they may have held in their own hearts. And so the explorers probably told them at least part of what Meriwether Lewis would write to Thomas Jefferson three days later from St. Louis, in a letter announcing the party's safe return:

> That portion of the Continent watered by the Missouri and it's branches from the Cheyenne [of central South Dakota] upwards is richer in beaver and otter than any country on earth particularly that proportion of its subsidiary streams lying within the Rocky Mountains.[7]

A remark like that would be one more thing to contemplate the next morning as the voyageurs edged the Mackinaw boats again into the current and rowed slowly upstream to resume business for a company which probably could not last out the year.

CHAPTER 6

Bold Hopes

Aird built his winter post somewhere between today's towns of Vermillion and Yankton, South Dakota. Then he rowed back down the river to meet the arriving goods. Once again we have no definite way of knowing the different points at which he dropped off clerks and merchandise. It seems probable, however, that Crooks spent the winter near the earthen town of the Maha Indians, where Robert McClellan also had a trading house. By May 1 the two men were partners, and their acquaintanceship could hardly have ripened to such a point unless they had spent time in the same vicinity.[1]

Like the other semisedentary tribes of the Missouri River, the Mahas lived in permanent lodges built of logs and earth. The habitations looked like inverted bowls. They varied from thirty feet to as much as ninety feet in diameter. In constructing them, the builders first laid out a square of six or more feet to the side. At each corner of the square they dug a hole three feet deep with their hands and with sharp sticks. Into each hole they fixed a heavy, flat-topped post that rose twelve feet or so above the ground. Heavy stringers were placed across these posts and lashed tight by wet rawhide. This structure was the center of the house's frame.

The center of the square itself was found by intersecting its diagonals. From this intersection an exact circle was determined by the use of cords. Twelve or more heavy posts that rose six feet above the ground were set at equal distances around the circumference. Stringers, beveled to fit the tops of the posts, were run from upright to upright. The builders then laid rafters from these outer stringers to the higher ones in the center; these rafters did not quite meet in the middle, so that smoke could escape through the opening. Willows tied with rawhide were laid across the rafters. Dried grass and earth, the latter carried onto the house in hide bags, were spread over the willows and tamped hard. These gently sloping rooftops made fine places on which to sit in the cool of the evening, and also for storing the owners' skin boats and other bulky paraphernalia.

The sides of the lodges sloped. Slabs of wood were leaned from the ground against the outer stringers; these slabs too were covered with grass and with chunks of sod cut like bricks out of the prairies. The entry was a sod-roofed tunnel protruding six or ten feet from the inner circumference of posts out to and beyond the circle formed by the feet of the leaning slabs.

The fireplace was a sunken circle under the smoke hole; the edge of this shallow, stone-lined pit doubled as a fireside seat. As many as eight or ten elevated willow bedsteads, covered with buffalo hides and bearskins, occupied little apartments under the slanting outer slabs. Goods were stored in grass-lined caches to the left of the door. Prized horses sometimes were penned in a cramped stall to the right of the entry. Weapons, headdresses, and clothing hung from the center stringers. Willow mats were scattered about as lounging places. During the hot growing season of the gardens, when the village was occupied, the lodges were cool. They sound cozy, but very little air and light entered except through the smoke hole. Pierre-Antoine Tabeau, who lived one season in an earthen Aricara lodge 108 feet in circumference, found the place noisome almost beyond toleration, a den fit "only for Ricaras, dogs, and bears."[2]

The arrival of Aird and his clerks was an exciting event. The Mahas had been waiting along the riverbank for days. When the boats appeared the Indians fired off volleys of gunfire and probably lugged the bourgeois and his clerks on buffalo robes into the chief's lodge for a gorge of dog meat. Afterwards they wept unabashedly, begging for gifts. They were so poor! Aird or Crooks moaned in reply that he too was crushed by poverty; that he had obtained these wonderful goods on credit; that the Indians must hunt industriously during the winter and make many furs so that the white man could buy his way out of bondage and return the following season with a truly magnificent assortment.

The gambit completed, the trader doled out as little free material as he thought he could get away with—paltry measures of beads and vermilion, a few twists of tobacco, a swallow or two of whisky for his likeliest customers. Then Aird went on up the river, leaving Crooks to make ready for winter. Crooks's first step was to find a spot for a cabin within range of purchasers, yet far enough from the village to free him from the continual importunities of mere visitors, from the sound of family uproars, and the night-long racketing of innumerable dogs.

Farther up the Missouri, timber was limited mostly to cottonwoods on the islands or on points of land around which the river curved. Along the Mahas' stretch of the broad valley, however, there were still many sycamores close to the water and, farther back, scattered stands of walnut, hickory and oak. The groves were parklike; the rushes and brambles that choked the forests farther downstream had largely disappeared. So Crooks and his voyageurs would have little trouble picking an attractive site beyond probable reach of the spring floods, and then felling enough trees for a cabin.

The simplest kind of structure sufficed—hardly as complicated as an Indian lodge. The logs for the side walls were piled horizontally, one on top of the other between upright pickets lashed together at their tops with strands of twisted bark. The end walls were made of logs set perpendicularly and rising gradually toward the centerpiece, which was a tall forked stick that held the ridgepole. The roof consisted of split logs sloping from this ridgepole down to the tops of the side walls and held in place by a few wooden pins. On top of the roof the builders spread a daubing of clay and ashes covered by a thick layer of grass held down by still more logs.

Puncheons (logs split and roughly smoothed into thick boards by a tomahawk) served for floor, door and table top. The window, if any, was a rectangle eighteen inches by two feet or so cut out of the wall opposite the door. In the winter this was covered by a heavy piece of paper impregnated with bear grease, through which a dim light suffused. Sometimes a single room served as both store and dwelling for the clerk and his voyageurs. More often two rooms were built, shelves and counters in one, living quarters in the other.[3]

Double bunks softened with buckskin, grass, or reed mats lined the walls of the living space. The fireplace was made of crisscross sticks covered with a mortar of mixed clay and ashes bound with grass. Food consisted of the inevitable corn soup (quantities of maize were traded regularly from the Indians), wild turkey, venison, bear steaks and bear oil, fresh or jerked buffalo, and pemmican, a highly nutritious mixture of dried meat and berries pounded into a powder and solidified with melted fat. Catfish, wild pigeons, and migrating ducks and geese lent variety. Flour for pancakes was reserved for Sundays. All cooking was done in the fireplace, in kettles or frying pans, or by dangling roasts on cords in front of the blaze.

The clerks made some effort to maintain dignity by wearing civilized clothing. The voyageurs generally dressed like Indians (and so might a clerk on a trip to a hunting camp)—first a calico shirt and breechclout, buckskin hunting shirt over these, or perhaps a cloth capote belted with a gay sash. Attached by another belt to a man's waist were a sheathed knife and a quill-decorated pouch for holding tobacco, flint, steel, and punk for tinder. In cold weather, folded pieces of blanket served as socks beneath moccasins. All squaws made moccasins readily—but moccasins wore out, could not turn cactus, and were hard for a novice to walk in. Like other magical white products, shoes soon replaced the native product for those who could afford the luxury and became regular if unglamorous items of trade, as invoices for later American Fur Company outfits amply demonstrate.

Crooks himself left no account that reveals how he passed his days in the wilderness. Other traders reminisced, however. One who was particularly articulate was Gurdon Hubbard, who went to work for the American Fur Company twelve years later in Illinois, close enough to Crooks in time and area that with a few adaptations for geography the account can be taken as representative of the life on the Missouri also. First, an Indian customer and his squaw came to the cabin and looked over the wares to see what they might need for their winter hunt. Dickering was protracted and sometimes acrimonious. Spendthrift customers had to be turned away from luxuries (those were sold only in the spring when a purchaser actually had his furs in hand) and poor credit risks had to be held to minimum purchases. The Indians did not always take kindly to denials. Hubbard (who was eighteen at the time of this episode) says that once a disappointed savage tried to creep up behind him with a tomahawk as the young clerk sat reading in his cabin on a three-legged stool. Warned by a flickering shadow, the lad flung up his arm and partially deflected the blow as it fell. Nevertheless it sliced open his forehead. Blood filled his eyes. Desperately he clung to the tomahawk until he could blink his vision clear. Then he got hold of his stool and with it beat the Indian unconscious. This "firmness," as Hubbard called it, pleased the chief of the band, and he kept the revengeful savage away from the youth during the rest of the winter. Indeed, says Hubbard, "firmness" about credits was a trader's chief requisite. Presumably Crooks had it.

The credits advanced and duly recorded in the clerk's ledger, the Missouri Indians loaded their skin tepees onto horse-drawn travois and left the earthen village for hunting camps beside small streams where beaver and muskrat might be found, or on the plains where the buffalo fed, or in bottomlands beside the river itself, where deer abounded. After that, there was little for the trader to do but stay alive under the immense sky, beside the endless plains, and wait for his furs.

For company a man had two or three voyageurs, perhaps a squaw— sometimes a casual liaison, sometimes a permanent union—and generally an interpreter. The engagés chopped mountains of firewood, fished through the ice and (if they had received permission from the jealous

Indians) trapped on their own account. Clerks read and reread the few books they had been able to bring with them. They hunted wild turkey and deer. There at the edge of buffalo country Ramsay Crooks probably obtained a good running horse from the Mahas and learned the exhilaration of the most exciting chase the continent could afford. But nights were long and cold, boredom was colossal, and unstable fur men often turned to drink.

Breaks in the monotony came from rare "expresses" from the other post—messengers who traveled sometimes on horseback but often afoot or with dog sleds. And always one could fill time by spying on one's rivals, lest they slip off to a hunting camp first and steal the credits. Then every so often a man packed up a few trinkets and some alcohol and went off on his own, partly to make sure he got what was due him, partly to exhort the Indians to greater effort—and partly just to have something to do.

Gurdon Hubbard tells of snowshoeing as much as seventy-five miles a trip in the Illinois country, his feet so chafed by the straps that they bled; of scratching a sleeping space out of the snow beside a fallen tree that could serve as a windbreak; of dining on a porcupine he clubbed to death as he traveled. On one trip, during which he and his men had to wade several icy streams, a voyageur ruptured himself so severely that later in the summer, bound in a canoe for Mackinac, he grew seasick, vomited blood from the old hurt, and died. On another occasion Hubbard distributed only part of his alcohol in a hunting camp and hid the rest, hoping to keep the frolic in hand. But his Indian interpreter and two other drunks found the keg and resumed the celebration. A squaw came to Hubbard's tent with a warning. Instantly the eighteen-year-old boy rushed barefooted into the snow, hurled himself onto the interpreter, "threw him on his back, and placing my knees on his stomach choken him so he could neither move nor speak. . . . He was considerably injured." But he surrendered the keg. Firmness again. Presumably Crooks could have related comparable experiences, had he chosen.

Such firmness by the French and English during more than a century of trading around the Great Lakes had taught the Indians of the Old Northwest to respect white men. Spain's weaker policies on the Missouri, however, had bred contempt. Until 1803 the lieutenant-governor in St. Louis had customarily sold trading monopolies to the highest bidder. The trader naturally added the exorbitant cost of his license to the price he charged for his goods. The not so naïve savages soon compared these Spanish prices with those being charged by British traders on the Des Moines and St. Peter's rivers, and came to the conclusion that they were being cheated. Angry and rapacious, a few of them seized what they wanted. More frequently, however, they balanced accounts by a form of extortion. They would not allow the trader to go down the river in the spring unless he advanced them credits for a summer hunt. The Indians did hunt: thousands of red (summer) deer skins were shipped out of the Missouri country every year. But the pelts were not valuable and rarely paid for the items the tribes demanded in exchange for the trader's safe passage home.

Retaliation seldom visited the extortionists. The one sure way of forcing the savages into line was deprivation of the trade on which they had come to depend. The merchants seldom were able to invoke the embargo, however. They had indebted themselves to secure their monopoly; the cost of their license went up each year whether they traded or not. To avoid bankruptcy they had to keep going back and demeaning themselves before the Indians on whom their commercial existence depended.

Sometimes a man went broke and had to turn his license back to the Spanish lieutenant-governor. Again the monopoly was open to bidding. Because of the failure, the price generally dropped. To gain the good will of the Indians, the new licensee generally passed on the saving by reducing the cost of his goods. The Indians naturally assumed that their arrogance was what had brought about the improvement and they treated the new man with even greater contempt. Convinced that they could get away with almost anything, some bandits even stopped furs bound for St. Louis, forced the whites to load the packs on their own backs, and hike overland to the tributaries of the Mississippi. There the Indians sold the hijacked furs to British traders. Indeed, some of the Americans who were beginning to trickle into St. Louis blamed the British for instigating the robberies. Meriwether Lewis specifically charged Murdock Cameron of Prairie du Chien and the St. Peter's with being deeply involved in the nefarious business.

After the Louisiana Purchase, the contempt that had attached to the Spanish was transferred to the Americans. When Meriwether Lewis was appointed Governor of Missouri Territory in the spring of 1807, he reported to his superiors, in italics, that the Osage, Kansa, Sioux and other Indians of the western river went around grinning at each other and saying, "*the white men are like dogs,* the more you beat them and plunder them, the more goods they will bring you and the cheaper they will sell them."[4] By 1808 the conduct of the Osage and Kansa tribes had become so reprehensible that they were declared outside the protection of the United States, and other tribes were actually invited to make war on them. Trading on the Missouri River was, in short, a hazardous occupation.

It may not have been quite so risky for the British. Many years earlier they had come into contact with the tribes higher up the river

and out of the weight of their experience had been able to turn aside
much of the opprobrium. No doubt many of them, including those who
had sworn allegiance to the United States, continued trying to inflate
their own importance with the Mahas, Otos, and Pawnees by denigrating
all Americans. But it is not likely that Ramsay Crooks indulged in similar tactics. If he had, he would have run into trouble with hot-tempered
Robert McClellan, who bore Wilkinson's authority to arrest irregular
traders.

McClellan was not above turning the authority to his own advantage.
He spent much of the winter roaring at teen-age François Hortiz of
St. Louis because Hortiz, who was also trading with the Mahas, did
not have a proper license with him. The young man claimed his father
had the document and until spring this kept McClellan at bay. On
May 11, 1807, however, the old scout exploded. When Aird paused at
the Maha village on his way downstream, McClellan had him translate
Wilkinson's sanction into French for Hortiz. He then seized the younger
man's goods and, so Hortiz charged in a suit instituted that summer,
abused him physically and for three months prevented him from going
home.

If Crooks had been overtly hostile, McClellan would have clashed
with him too. Instead, although the American was seventeen years older
than the Scot, they became good friends. As they visited back and
forth, whiling away the long winter evenings in each other's cabins,
McClellan perhaps grumbled about how crowded this section of the
river was becoming and how good it would be to find unexploited fields
somewhere off toward the mountains. Crooks and he no doubt repeated
to each other what both of them had heard from Lewis and Clark. The
old dream of young America—something better out beyond. And suddenly they must have looked at each other and said in effect, "Let's
do it! Let's get backing from our friends, and go ahead before every
other trader in St. Louis has the same idea!"

On April 5, 1807, McClellan announced something of their plans in a
strangely incomplete letter to Meriwether Lewis. He did not name
Crooks. He did not reveal whether Gravelines, whom he had taken
upstream in 1806, had reached the Aricaras on his mission of placation.
He did not indicate what mood the Aricara tribe might be in. He
reported only that he had brought his Mahas safely home, save for
one who had died of a chronic ailment en route. He added ominous
information that the Teton Sioux had refused Pierre Dorion's overtures
on behalf of the government and had said they "would lay in the banks
of the Misouri this Summer for the purpose of Stopping boates Should
any atempt to pas." Then he tried to line up a little business for the
new company.

I have aranged my business for to visit the upper parts of the Missouri as soon as I posably can after my arival at St. Louis . . . . Should Govermint think proper to send the Mandaine Chiefe to his respective hoame I will with Pleasure take him under my charge as there will be but little danger to feare. I shall have two boates well Mand. and armed.

By "boates well Mand. and armed" McClellan meant keelboats.[5] Keelboats were expensive. They averaged between sixty and eighty feet in length, sixteen to eighteen of beam. They were fully decked, carefully framed, and steadied by a heavy keel that ran from bow to stern. Shallow of draft, they offered holds only three to four feet deep, but storage space was increased by a cargo box rising four or five feet above the deck and occupying all but a small part of the front and rear ends of the craft. Each boat boasted a mast so that a square sail could be used when the wind served, which was seldom. Mostly the keelboat was moved by oars, by setting poles thrust against the bottom of the stream, or by a long towrope or cordelle that was attached to the mast and manipulated by men struggling up the riverbank. Cordelling required upward of twenty hands per boat, and these in turn involved a relatively heavy outlay for wages and Indian corn to supplement the game of the countryside. Nor was there any point in having so much cargo space unless it was filled. That too suggests a heavy expense. In other words, the new partners felt sanguine about their ability to secure financing. Yet all they could offer in return was their reputation and a willingness to risk the unknown for the riches which Lewis and Clark had said were there.

Keelboats and the number of men involved in moving them suggest further that Crooks and McClellan planned not only to trade but also to send white trappers into the Indian country. Having eighty men hanging around the posts throughout the winter with little to do would be wasteful. (The operators in the Great Lakes area used no such numbers for ordinary trading.) The best way to keep at least some of the hands occupied was to have them hunt. This of course was a flat violation both of custom and of the laws of the United States.

It was not a new violation. While toiling up the river in 1804, the Lewis and Clark expedition had encountered a few French-Canadian trappers and had helped them on their way. They had let John Colter drop out of their party in 1806 and go with two American trappers back to the mountains. Lewis' own report of the beaver riches of the Rockies was calculated to stimulate the trend. Once the Indians recognized the value of the furs they were losing to these aliens, they were sure to react in fury. Meriwether Lewis had recognized the dangers, but he also said that "the use of the trap . . . is an act which must be learned before it can be practised to advantage." He felt therefore that white trappers should be allowed on the upper reaches of the Missouri until the Indians could be induced to undertake the hard work of trapping for themselves. He supposed that white hunters would then withdraw and that normal trade patterns could be resumed.

It was a singularly unrealistic hope. Although Indians and French and British fur men had some interest in conserving game for the future, the American approach was to strip an area bare and move on. American hunters were far more efficient than Indians. They had never relinquished a good fur area so long as profitable numbers of animals remained in it, and they were not likely to do so in the Rockies. It was quite a different philosophy of fur production from the one to which Ramsay Crooks had been first introduced, yet he seems to have had no trouble absorbing it during his short association with Robert McClellan. By and large the other naturalized Americans on the river did not make the radical switch. Most of those former Britons stuck to the more familiar patterns of the business.

No matter who financed the trading-trapping company, its goods could be best secured at Michilimackinac. Crooks knew the practices of the island, and had had experience bringing merchandise from there to the Missouri; McClellan had not. McClellan therefore stayed behind at the Maha village to finish his spring trade while Crooks, undoubtedly with Aird's permission, went on down the river in April, presumably taking McClellan's letter to Lewis with him. He went early because he would need time to line up prospective backers, then hurry to Michilimackinac, purchase the goods and return with them to the Missouri in time for the new company to reach the upper river ahead of the ice. It was an arduous program, demanding luck and ability for its completion.[6]

Just short of the city, perhaps at St. Charles, the young man realized that his and McClellan's idea of how best to exploit the upper river was not as original as they may have supposed during the enthusiasm of planning. He met a large keelboat commanded by McClellan's old enemy, Manuel Lisa. Lisa, too, was headed for the sources of the Missouri. He had on his boat forty-two men, trappers and traders both, and goods worth $16,000.

Nor was Lisa's party the only one. About the time Crooks reached the area, Frederick Bates, who was acting as governor of Missouri Territory until Meriwether Lewis returned from the East, rode overland from St. Louis to St. Charles to tell the Spaniard that other parties were forming behind him. Auguste Pierre Chouteau, the twenty-one-year-old elder son of Indian agent Pierre Chouteau, Sr., freshly graduated from West Point, was bound for the Mandan villages with thirty-two traders and trappers. William Dorion, son of interpreter Pierre Dorion, with ten men and two interpreters, was intending to risk the Yankton Sioux. Both

parties were fortified by escorts of American soldiers returning junketing
Indians to their homes. Accompanying Dorion were Lieutenant Joseph
Kimball and seven soldiers protecting eighteen Sioux men, women and
children. Accompanying young A. P. Chouteau were three non-commis-
sioned officers, eighteen privates, and four civilian helpers under Nathaniel Pryor, who had been a sergeant with Lewis and Clark but who
had since been promoted to ensign.[7] Pryor's command was delegated
to return to the Mandan villages the chief Big White, René Jessaume,
and their families.

The combined Dorion-Kimball-Chouteau-Pryor parties numbered
close to eighty men, a formidable force for the Indian country in those
days. Frederick Bates did not think it was enough, however. He asked
Lisa to wait and add his forty-two men to the others. Lisa reportedly
agreed, then had second thoughts. He had much farther to go than
any of the others. Why should he delay to help potential rivals? Off
he went ahead of them, in violation of his word.

Young Crooks must have felt a twinge of disappointment that his new
company, unaided now by a contract for escorting Big White, would be
dragging up to the beaver grounds behind so many other parties.[8] But
Big White had never been more than a hopeful notion at best, and the
upper Missouri was vast enough to hold many groups. He obtained a
trading license from Acting Governor Bates and began hunting for what
later mineral prospectors would call a grubstake.

He soon found two backers—Sylvestre Labaddie and the dean of St.
Louis fur merchants, Auguste Chouteau, uncle of the A. P. Chouteau
who was bound with Big White for the Mandan villages. Winning the
approval of such men was a remarkable feat for a twenty-year-old.
Circumstances were in his favor. Excited by the reports Lewis and
Clark had brought from the mountains, every fur dealer in St. Louis
was eager to find steady men with enough know-how and bravery to
risk the huge, untried field. McClellan possessed both courage and experience in abundance. But he had also defaulted on a debt to Lisa,
and this must have created some doubt among St. Louis financiers. Yet
Crooks was able to brush the reluctance aside. He suggested a long
list of articles McClellan and he wished. Labaddie and Chouteau no
doubt examined the order minutely, made challenges and revisions, then
furnished him with letters of credit to the traders at Michilimackinac
and told him to take the jump.[9]

He probably left St. Louis for the north early in June. About two
weeks later Aird and McClellan arrived in the city, perhaps traveling
together from the Maha village where Aird had paused to trade during
May. Immediately McClellan was named defendant in a lawsuit for
having seized the goods and furs of young François Hortiz on May 11,
under his supposed authority from James Wilkinson. In his suit Hortiz

charged that the furs McClellan had unlawfully impounded—902½ pounds of deerskin, 167½ pounds of beaver, 230 raccoon skins—and his strouds, blankets, knives and so on were worth $4900. He wanted these returned and demanded $8000 in damages to pay for the trade he had lost through having no merchandise. A more modest figure came from William Clark, who had been made a brigadier-general by Congress as a reward for the Pacific expedition and who had hurried back to Missouri to organize the militia. Clark in a letter to Secretary of War Dearborn estimated the value of the goods at $800 to $900. But he added that things looked dark for McClellan. Hortiz's father produced a license that he said he had taken out a year before (Clark doubted the date), and the grand jury thereupon refused McClellan's request that it indict the son for illegal trading. With that as an indicator, Clark predicted that McClellan "will pay . . . seveerly for his solisitude to do a service to his Country."[10] (McClellan did lose the suit, won a retrial on technical grounds, lost in 1810, and was directed to pay damages amounting to $121.)

Unaware of his stormy partner's fresh troubles, Crooks reached Mackinac. He must have been plied with questions. Where was Aird? How well had Aird done with the five boatloads of merchandise, worth 76,500 livres, which Crooks and Reed had taken to him the previous summer? Every last skin counted now. Robert Dickson & Company had failed even more disastrously than anticipated, and the painful process of liquidation was underway. It could not be completed until Aird's returns were in, and his partners were growing impatient over his delays.[11] (He finally arrived July 29 after a month's trip from St. Louis. By that time Crooks was already bound back through Green Bay and down the Mississippi with his new stock of trade goods.)

During the involved settlements John Jacob Astor's name again bobbed up. Needing immediate cash, Dickson sold 17,500 choice muskrat skins to George Gillespie, acting as agent for Astor. This was the second time Astor had bought directly on the island rather than in Montreal, and the notion may have occurred to some of the dejected traders that if times grew harder for British subjects, the American might decide to move his own outfits into the field. Well, that was one of the reasons why the new Michilimackinac Company had been formed the previous December 31, 1806—to keep American furs flowing to Montreal. The Canadians could not slack off now. They needed to press every advantage. The Michilimackinac Company even absorbed the reluctant Dickson and his partners. That swallowing completed, the company could boast that it controlled the best talent in the American wilderness, save possibly for the Missouri River.

Nevertheless there were signs of trouble ahead; and Crooks may even then have thanked his hunches and his luck that he had pulled away from the Canadians when he did. The officials of Missouri Territory were certain to continue harrying British citizens who tried to go west of the Mississippi. Indeed, so Aird told Thomas Blackwood of J. and A. McGill & Company, the trend was likely to grow worse rather than better. East of the Mississippi, meanwhile, the Indians were causing increasing worry. They were restive and not hunting as vigorously as before. Dickson blamed their lack of production as contributing in a large measure to his poor showing during the winter. And that trend, too, was likely to grow worse.

The agitation had been kindled by twin Shawnee Indians of Ohio, Tecumseh and Tenskwatawa. Nothing quite like the pair had ever been seen before, even in the times of Pontiac. After their father and two older brothers had been killed in wars with the Americans, the twins had traveled by different routes to two passionate visions of how the Indians might yet be saved. Though totally different in appeal, their messages to the desperate red men combined into an energizing force of tremendous potential.

Tecumseh, who has been called the most extraordinary Indian in United States history, correctly saw that lack of unity among the tribes was their greatest handicap in the struggle for survival. He began preaching a vast brotherhood. As a practical manifestation of his philosophy, he challenged the numerous treaties which William Henry Harrison was concluding with separate tribes and even with minority groups inside a tribe. (Between 1795 and 1809 these treaties would take from the savages forty-eight million acres in Ohio, Indiana, and Illinois.) As each document was signed, Tecumseh declared that it was illegal and void. The land belonged to the Indians in common and no single group could alienate a foot of it. When American officials brushed his arguments aside, he and his representatives began carrying wampum belts and pipes to every tribe from Florida to Wisconsin and even west beyond the Mississippi. With the eloquence of despair they preached a confederation of Indians mighty enough to hold back the American flood. As a concrete goal to fight for, Tecumseh seized upon a political entity which British fur men had advocated many years earlier—a strong, independent Indian nation between the Ohio River and the Great Lakes.

His brother Tenskwatawa meanwhile took a mystical rather than a political bent. Twins could scarcely have been more different in appearance or in character. Tecumseh was handsome, ascetic, practical, and highly disciplined. Tenskwatawa wore a brass ring in his nose; his seamed, homely face was disfigured by an empty eye socket. In his youth he had been wildly dissipated and had struck those who knew him as unusually stupid.

One day a trance that may have been epileptic in nature dropped him into apparent lifelessness. When he was about to be buried, he mysteriously recovered and announced that he had been in the spirit world receiving a new revelation of life. His claim to divine authority for these revelations was enormously increased in the summer of 1806 when, acting on data supplied by a trader, he correctly predicted an eclipse of the sun. Ever afterward he was called the Prophet.

His appeal was emotional, conservative, and unoriginal. Other red prophets had used and would continue to use the same arguments throughout the long disintegration of the Indians within the United States. But the orthodoxy of the idea in no way diminished its strength. The hope of the red men, so Tenskwatawa proclaimed, lay in a return to their old beliefs and customs. They must remove all white taint, rejecting alcohol and even the manufactured items that seemed to make life softer.

Amazingly, the Indians heeded. John Askin, Jr., wrote his father from St. Joseph Island that "all the Ottawas from L'arbe au Croche adhere strictly to the Shawney Prophet's advice they do not wear Hats, Drink or Conjure. Whiskey & Rum is a Drug, the Indians do not purchase One Gallon per month." Even worse, great numbers of Indians of all tribes were leaving their villages and hunting grounds to visit the Prophet and hear his revelations. Such savages, as Robert Dickson & Company had painfully learned, raised little corn and took few furs.

At first the western frontier underrated the Prophet. Acting Governor Bates wrote William Clark, July 25, 1807, saying that a red preacher was predicting an imminent appearance of God to help the Indians retaliate for their wrongs, though "what these wrongs are, it is impossible for me to conjecture . . . His Divinityship has indeed created some little stir and bustle, as these imposters always do," but, Bates said, he had sent out Nicholas Boilvin, the canny old agent of the Sac and Fox Indians, to investigate, and "seriously General, I beg you to give yourself no uneasiness on the subject."

Within less than a month he was writing in a different vein. Word reached the West (probably while Crooks was on the last leg of his trip down the Mississippi) that the British warship *Leopard,* while searching for deserters, had on June 22 poured three broadsides into the American frigate *Chesapeake,* killing three men and wounding eighteen. Fury swept the nation; war talk boomed in Congress. Frontiersmen, remembering the Indian wars that had ravaged Ohio only fifteen years before, reached for their guns. What would the British incite the savages to in this newest crisis?

The threat of war did indeed offer the new Michilimackinac Company certain dubious advantages. Although the Prophet decried white trade in general, he reserved his particular venom for the Americans, quoting words which he said the Great Spirit had spoken to him:

I am the father of the English, of the French, of the Spaniards, and of the Indians . . . . The Americans I did not make . . . . They grew from the scum of the great water, where it was troubled by the evil spirit, and the froth was driven into the woods by a strong east wind.

A man who talked like that was a potential ally in case of war. True, a war would completely demolish trade for a time—but a war might also win back a portion of the Old Northwest which had been surrendered to the Americans after the Revolution. Creating on that recovered land an Indian state such as Tecumseh dreamed of would preserve the fur trade to the Canadians for an indefinite time. Conspirators have been known to go to work on slimmer hopes.

It is impossible to say how actively the partners of the Michilimackinac Company really did conspire with the Indians in 1807, apart from the normal trade routine of inflating one's own importance in front of the savages by belittling rivals. Certainly the Americans suspected the worst.

St. Louis, which had been attacked by British-led Indians during the Revolution, fell into a panic. To calm the fright, Acting Governor Bates and William Clark called up units of the newly formed militia. In one breath Bates said he was sure there was nothing to fear. In the next he wrote the Secretary of War (on August 12), "The British merchants of Canada are plotting mischiefs—and will dispose as many northern Indians to hostility as possible." Eight days later Josiah Dunning, the commander of the American garrison at Fort Mackinac, warned William Clark, "There is not a man in the Michilimackinac Company, who does not feel a Spirit of Opposition to the American Interest; and who would not wish to Annihilate the Arm of American power, so far as it extends over the Indian Country. . . . They assume a high tone— No goods can go into the country but through them— Every inch of the Indian country is partitioned among them."[12] He gave examples of how the Canadians poisoned the minds of the savages against the United States and urged the Americans to stir themselves in opposition.

Crooks and McClellan caught only ripples of this. McClellan had won a stay in his lawsuit so that depositions could be taken from Aird on his arrival in September, and the partners were anxious to start their long journey up the river. While St. Louis speculated in agitation about the accursed British, they loaded their two keelboats with goods and dragged their eighty men out of the grogshops. As the clumsy craft nosed into the yellow Missouri, they may even have congratulated themselves that at last they were bound for an unspoiled region where a man's prospects did not hinge on quarrels over which he had no control.

Exactly where they planned to go is uncertain. So far as they knew, young A. P. Chouteau was already established in the Mandan villages, a spot which British traders were also accustomed to visit. Lisa was somewhere on toward the headwaters. But plenty of attractive ground lay in between—the mouth of the Yellowstone, perhaps. It was close to 1900 twisting river miles away, roughly a four-month trip, yet with luck and continual pressing they might make it in early December. If ice closed the river before then, they would have to adapt. But at least they were on their way in one season, thanks to herculean efforts at preparation.

They pressed hard. But their luck failed. A little above the mouth of the Platte, hardly a third of the way to the Yellowstone, their expedition was brought to a dead halt by a quarrel over which they had no control.

7

Frustrations

Nathaniel Pryor, young A. P. Chouteau, and their bedraggled men were coming back down the river, Big White and Jessaume still in tow. The party had been soundly whipped at the earth town of the Aricaras by an alliance of villagers and Teton Sioux. As the whites told Crooks and McClellan about the disaster, they indulged in furious recriminations whose truth cannot now be determined.

Their story went like this. The handful of Yankton Sioux and the small escort under Lieutenant Kimball had been dropped off near the James without incident. Kimball's interpreter, William Dorion, had continued with the main party to help in case they met Tetons. They did. As Pryor's soldiers and Chouteau's traders neared the lower of the two towns, 650 armed men, Aricaras and Teton Sioux together, swarmed to the riverbank and fired shots for the boats to stop.

A brief conference revealed that the Mandans had declared war on the Aricaras and Tetons. The latter Indians naturally considered Big White, a Mandan, fair game. Pryor barricaded the chief in the cabin of his keelboat. Through his interpreters he then prevailed on a few Sioux and some of the Aricaras of the lower village to sit down and talk things over. He felt he made progress with them, but was told that the chiefs of the upper town were still recalcitrant. He decided to move his forces up there for further talks. Dorion and Jessaume recklessly walked along the bank while the boats rowed. A hooting gang tagged along, and a great concourse was waiting when they arrived.

While the Indians yammered on the beach, one of their chiefs came aboard the keelboat and demanded the surrender of Big White. Peremptorily Pryor ordered the fellow ashore. Words flew, then bullets. After a fifteen-minute battle, Pryor signaled a retreat. As the party started downstream, young Chouteau's boat stuck fast in a narrow channel between sandbars. Bullets frothed the water as his men leaped overboard to free it. The running fight continued until at last a soldier killed a Sioux chief and his followers dropped back. All told, casualties amounted to three white men killed and ten wounded, one of whom died later. René Jessaume, who had persuaded Big White to go with Lewis and Clark on this lark to Washington, was shot through the thigh and shoulder.

What on earth had set the Indians off like that? Two explanations were voiced. Pryor blamed Manuel Lisa, who in the ensign's mind had started the debacle by breaking his word to Bates and going off ahead of the other parties. The Aricaras had stopped Lisa too (though Pryor felt they would not have dared tackle the combined parties) and had told the Spaniard that he must do his trading with them, not with their enemies upstream. Lisa later insisted that he bluffed his way through by aiming the two swivel cannon on his keelboat at the mob on the beach. But a female Mandan captive whispered a different version to Pryor during his pause at the lower village. She said Lisa had bought his passage by selling the Aricaras several guns and then telling them that the bulk of his goods were in boats that would be coming along later. Those people would trade. And by the way, a Mandan chief was in one of the boats. That was tempting prey. According to the captive, the excited Aricaras decided to demand presents from Lisa, then let him go on. They would use the guns he had sold them to pounce on the boats following him, seize the Mandans and the goods, and kill Lisa when he returned downstream.

After talking to his son, Indian agent Pierre Chouteau (in a letter he wrote the President of the United States on November 14, 1807) assigned a different cause to the trouble. He blamed the traders of Canada, saying they came overland to the Missouri from the St. Peter's and the Red rivers and stirred up the tribes in order to keep Americans away from the rich grounds of the upper country.[1] No one publicly mentioned a third possibility, that the Indians, who liked to fight, were finding motive in protecting their position as middlemen from the growing tendency of the whites to bypass them. Whatever the cause of the violence, the mere recounting of it was enough to freeze the voyageurs with Crooks and McClellan. Although the humble, French-speaking rivermen of the fur trade would cheerfully perform labors and endure privations an American worker would reject, they were notoriously reluctant to fight. Yet if they continued upstream they would have to fight; Pryor's defeat would have turned every Indian on the middle river completely cocky. Giving battle would produce no trade. So why push the dismayed voyageurs into a pointless struggle? Glumly the partners decided to stop where they were.

Since they had eighty men with them, they probably staffed as many posts as seemed justifiable along the lower Platte and as far up the Missouri as the Maha village.[2] It was a strategic area for trade. From it one could reach not only up and down the Missouri but also eastward into Iowa and westward onto the unknown plains as far as a man had nerve enough to go with packhorses. But it was not an area suited to the partners' plans. The Indians of the vicinity were used to normal trade customs, and it is not likely that Crooks and McClellan risked offending them by using to any great extent the traps they had brought along. Thus, since only a limited number of trading posts were economical for a given area, no matter how strategic, the partners found themselves paying wages to and providing food for several unnecessary hands. They could not possibly have collected enough peltries to offset the burden, for when they returned to St. Louis in the spring they found that world politics had caused prices to drop disastrously.

President Jefferson had resisted the country's war talk following the gunning of the *Chesapeake*. Believing his country's produce to be more important to France and England than it really was, he hoped to humble those countries and win respect for American shipping by depriving them of United States commerce. (Various white administrators, especially Spanish, at times tried to humble Indians in the same way, by depriving them of trade.) He pushed through Congress an Embargo Act, effective December 27, 1807, which forbade American ships to clear for foreign ports. The act also reinvoked the non-importation decrees of 1806 and forbade the landing in this country of many articles of British manufacture. Most of the excluded items were necessary for the Indian trade.

St. Louis languished under the embargo almost as much as did the ports of New England. In the spring of 1808, for example, Auguste Chouteau was unable to trade for furs certain deer skins belonging to a Montreal client, though in normal times deer skins were a standard item of barter. But the embargo had glutted the market with both skins and furs; prices were so bad dealers would not trade anything and were sitting tight, waiting to see what developed. Unable to dispose of the skins in St. Louis, Chouteau finally sent them off to Montreal in charge of two boats bound through Chicago to Michilimackinac.

Quite possibly Ramsay Crooks was the bourgeois who transported the skins; for he traveled to Mackinac that summer, hoping that as an American citizen he could somehow evade the non-importation act and secure the goods his firm needed. In other words someone, Chouteau probably, was still willing to back him in spite of the winter's failure. Or perhaps it wasn't willingness so much as a desperate hope of salvaging part of what had already been invested.

He found the traders on the island in a lather of indignation over recent developments. On learning of the embargo, the Montreal partners of the Michilimackinac Company had rushed George Gillespie, barely back from St. Louis, on to Washington with a protest. From Washington, Gillespie had continued to London with an appeal for support to Lord Castlereagh, Great Britain's Secretary of War. Meanwhile Canadian negotiators named Michaels and Nicholl stayed in Washington, trying to win from the government special dispensation for the introduction into Michilimackinac of those goods which the company had ordered in England before the embargo and which were already being shipped. The Montrealers contended that so far as the Indian trade was concerned, the non-importation acts were illegal, since they tried to supersede by unilateral action of the United States an international agreement, Jay's Treaty, which gave Canadian traders every right to cross the border with their merchandise. To this the negotiators added a more pragmatic argument. The Indians for whom the United States Government was morally responsible would suffer severely if deprived of their normal flow of goods. It was therefore to the advantage of the Americans, both legally and practically, to except at least this 1806 importation of goods from the strictures of the embargo. That done, diplomatic representatives of the two countries could discuss matters of ultimate right. But at the moment there was no time.

Underlings in Washington apparently listened with some sympathy. That was enough for the Michilimackinac Company. It loaded twenty Mackinaw boats with merchandise and started them West. They did take one precaution against an adverse ruling by the Americans; they directed the barges to land at St. Joseph Island, a British post in the St. Marys River between Lake Huron and Lake Superior. The flotilla was to travel in sections up the St. Lawrence, through Lakes Ontario and Erie to York, and then by way of Lake Simcoe to the eastern shore of Huron. Their bourgeois would wait in Montreal for last-minute information from Washington, then would hurry up the Ottawa River route in light express canoes and overtake the barges somewhere around the Manitoulin Islands.

On May 21 the first two boats of the caravan entered the Niagara River, where British and American forts stood almost opposite each other. If Washington had granted any special dispensation to the Michilimackinac Company, the collector at Niagara had not heard of it. Though the trading barges had not yet touched United States soil, he decided that they could not reach their destination without doing so. On the strength of this wholly hypothetical violation of the non-importation laws, he ordered the commander at the fort to seize the Canadian vessels.

The boatload of troops sent to apprehend the unsuspecting barges pushed so near to the Canadian side of the river that the warning shots they fired struck Canadian soil close to startled witnesses. Learning that more boats were coming behind, the Americans dispatched another force to apprehend them. Six were seized. Three landed safely in Canada and sent a warning to the nine boats in the second contingent. Although the Americans pursued the second group for thirty miles, it escaped to Kingston. The shootings and frantic rowings so terrified the voyageurs of all the boats that they immediately deserted and new crews had to be brought up from Montreal to take the twelve unattached vessels on to St. Joseph. Because of the delays, they arrived too late to fill the needs of the more distant winterers. Furthermore, the loss of eight boatloads meant that many assortments could not be properly filled. All told, the company said, damages came to $100,000.

Company representatives hurried to Niagara to investigate. Their outrage frightened the collector into trying to compromise. He offered to release the impounded boats and merchandise if the company would post a bond, to be forfeit if decision in the controversy went against the Canadians. The Montrealers refused. A bond would by implication acknowledge American jurisdiction over the commerce of the lakes. This the Canadians denied. The Americans cried in pain when their vessels were stopped on the Atlantic, yet look what they were doing here! This shipping too should be free.[3]

The Americans meanwhile were repeating their old grievances about British meddling with the Indians. In the spring of 1808 Tecumseh and the Prophet had built a new village in western Indiana, near the junction of Tippecanoe Creek with the Wabash River. Tribal delegates from the entire Midwest and even from the Gulf states were flocking to Tippecanoe to listen to the Prophet's fiery sermons and to discuss confederation with Tecumseh. As relations between the United States and Great Britain grew more and more strained, Tecumseh inevitably began looking north of the border for help.

The British had recently appointed as head of Canadian Indian affairs an ex-trader named Matthew Elliott, and Tecumseh promptly visited him at his headquarters post in Amherstburg, near Detroit. The American frontier was furious. Elliott, who was married to a Shawnee (Tecumseh's tribe), had been a notoriously effective British agent during the Ohio Indian wars, and the pioneer settlers of the Midwest hated him passionately. When it became known in the United States that Elliott and Tecumseh had decided at their meeting to assemble a great council of 5000 Indians at Amherstburg in the fall of 1808, alarmists south of the border were convinced that an uprising was in the immediate offing.

Still other crossruffs were agitating the main tensions. One complicated series of events engulfed Robert Dickson in a killing. The sequence began in the fall of 1807, when Acting Governor Bates of Missouri decided that the rigid exclusion of British traders from every foot of land west of the Mississippi was turning into a boomerang. Although American and French merchants had moved into the void along the Missouri, no United States citizen seemed interested in wooing the British-oriented savages of eastern Iowa and southern Minnesota. As a result, Bates wrote Secretary of War Dearborn on October 22, 1807, "the Indians of the upper country [are] destitute of those comforts to which they have been accustomed and which are indispensable during the winter season." To calm the Indians he promised that next year the United States Government would build a trading factory for them near the mouth of the Des Moines River. (The site chosen became Fort Madison.) So that the savages would not suffer in the interim, he proposed to have agent Nicholas Boilvin of the Sac and Fox tribes stock one temporary post on the Des Moines with trade goods worth $1037 and another at Prairie du Chien with merchandise valued at $1200. It didn't work. The army commander at Bellefontaine declined to detach soldiers to escort the boats, Boilvin was unable to undertake the assignment, and the plan collapsed.[4]

As a final effort at conciliation, Bates in November 1807 granted a special license to Robert Dickson to trade for the Michilimackinac Company in Iowa. In defending the action to Meriwether Lewis, Bates admitted that the licensing was an extraordinary move—his first and probably his last departure from an unswerving anti-British stand—but in this case something exceptional had been necessary. Hopefully he predicted, "Dickson's deportment and profession proclaim that we may grant him every indulgence. He will cooperate in all our Indian measures"—meaning those designed to woo the Indians from Great Britain to the United States.

To most Americans on the frontier the trust was frighteningly naïve. Every British trader who passed through St. Louis that fall, including James Aird, was asked about the attitude of the Indians. Every one of whom there is any record said that in case war did break out between the United States and Britain, the Indians would fight solidly on the side of the British. This was a deliberate exaggeration, of course. Nevertheless there was enough truth in it that alarmed citizens asked what wisdom there could possibly be, with tensions as they were, in turning so influential a British citizen as Robert Dickson loose with government blessing among the susceptible savages.

One who asked was John Campbell of Prairie du Chien. Campbell, like Dickson, was of Scottish blood though he had been born in Ireland. He bobs into the records in 1792 during a brawl on Michilimackinac. A Chippewa was fighting with a trader. Another merchant, trying to stop the quarrel, was stabbed by the Indian, who was thereupon seized and started toward the fort. This was too mild for John Campbell and six other friends of the wounded merchant. They took the Indian from the soldiers and beat him to death. All seven were arrested but available records do not indicate that any of them was punished.

Ten years later Campbell was considered a respectable enough citizen of Prairie du Chien that William Henry Harrison appointed him, like Dickson, a justice of the peace for St. Clair County, Indiana Territory. He was the man to whom the Sioux of the St. Peter's had taken a tribesman charged with slaying two voyageurs. Campbell, it will be recalled, had shot in alarm at his visitors; thereupon they had repaired to Dickson, who led them to St. Louis to visit Pierre Chouteau. At some point after that Campbell, like Crooks, had sworn allegiance to the United States. He declined an invitation to become a member of the Michilimackinac Company, and on December 7, 1807, shortly before the passage of the Embargo Act, he had been appointed U. S. Indian Agent at Prairie du Chien.

Evidently he took his new duties seriously. The next summer he visited the usual rendezvous at Michilimackinac. When Dickson appeared with the special license he had acquired from Bates, scurrilous remarks were bandied concerning loyalties, character, bribery, favoritism, and so on. A Mississippi trader named Redford Crawford picked up Dickson's side of the quarrel. Heated by liquor, he and Campbell agreed to a duel with pistols. Crawford chose Robert Dickson as his second.

Mackinac authorities stopped the first exchange. Still breathing fire, the contestants paddled in dancing bark canoes to a deserted stretch of mainland northeast of the island. There Campbell was mortally wounded and died shortly after being carried to St. Joseph. He had been well liked. Feeling ran high. Traders on Michilimackinac openly declared—and Crooks must have heard it all—that if either Crawford or Dickson dared return to Prairie du Chien, where Campbell's family lived, they would pay for the killing.[5]

The episode climaxed Dickson's growing discouragement. Prices were down, the seizure of the barges at Niagara had hopelessly delayed the goods he needed for his trade, and ardent Britons looked on him as a traitor for accepting favors from Bates in return for keeping the Indians peacefully disposed toward the United States. Now came this death of a long-time acquaintance, a death for which he was at least partly responsible. Motivated more by remorse than by the threats of Campbell's friends, he decided not to trade that winter.

He used the "vacation" to make his first visit in years to Montreal. There the greatest merchants and adventurers on the continent showed their opinion of him by electing him a member of the sacrosanct Beaver Club. Quite possibly he sat down with them in uncomfortable broad-

cloth and high stock collar at the lavish dinner with which they honored
John Jacob Astor, when the New York fur merchant visited Montreal
in September, partly to buy furs as usual, but also to launch, with the
help of these international tensions, his long, roundabout attempt to gain
control of the entire fur trade of the United States. But, again, that is
getting ahead of the story.

In spite of the seizure of the eight Michilimackinac Company barges
at Niagara, young Ramsay Crooks was able to buy the goods he needed.
Uncertain when the embargo might let their furs reach market and
dismayed by the high cost of merchandise imposed by the shortages,
many traders were deciding, as Dickson had, to sit out the winter in
hopes of better times next year. Crooks thus was able to obtain at
least part of what he wanted, but before he could move the goods, he
had to secure clearance from the U.S. collector on the island, George
Hoffman.

Hoffman hesitated. To him the young man sounded like one more
Scot, out to stir up the Indians perhaps, and he tried to cover himself
by having Crooks swear an oath of allegiance. Crooks declined. He
was already an American citizen, he said, and expected to be treated
as such. Hoffman let him go. Almost at once a hue and cry arose from
British citizens unable to obtain clearance. That fellow was as much
a Briton as they were (it was a charge that would follow Ramsay
Crooks for years) and if he could get through with goods, why couldn't
they? Shortly thereafter Aird came along, insisting that he too was a
citizen under terms of Jay's Treaty, and he also talked his way into a
clearance. It kept Hoffman squirming and he wrote unhappy letters to
St. Louis, trying to explain his actions. When the letter of the law said
one thing but when his suspicions suggested something else, just what
was a man supposed to do?[6]

Clearance did not mean an end to the troubles besetting private
traders within the United States. The United States Government's poorly
located factory at Bellefontaine had been closed and its goods distributed between two more strategic houses. One was Fort Madison near
the mouth of the Des Moines, the post which Bates had promised in
1807 to the Sacs and Foxes and to the Sioux of Iowa. The other was
Fort Osage (sometimes called Fort Clark) at Fire Prairie on the south
bank of the Missouri River near the present western boundary of the
state. Fire Prairie was an idyllic stretch of rolling country but grue-
somely named: several Indians had been burned to death there not
many years before by a grass fire.

Like other early factories, those at Fort Madison and Fort Osage
were designed to counteract British influence and at the same time
hold American traders in line on their prices. Furthermore, both were

associated with military garrisons designed to frighten the savages into whatever cooperation the blandishment of trade goods failed to produce. In 1808, muscles rather than cajolery seemed necessary. For uncertain causes (some people blamed the British), the Osage and Kansa Indians of western Missouri were in a particularly truculent mood.

On August 8, 1808, six boats carrying eighty-one soldiers started up the curling Missouri to begin work at Fire Prairie. With them as sub-agent for Indian Affairs went Reuben Lewis, younger brother of Meri-wether Lewis, the latter of whom had belatedly reached St. Louis in the spring of 1808 to begin his term as territorial governor. Somewhere a little short of Fire Prairie, this river party met Robert McClellan, bound downstream to meet his partner. He told them what to expect at the Prairie, but it is not clear that he returned there with them. One of his hunters did, however, a tremendously muscled, six-foot Kentuckian named John Day, once as famous an athlete as McClellan but by 1808 beginning to turn flabby because of his gigantic, if intermittent dissipations.

General William Clark was simultaneously riding overland with eighty mounted militia, enlisted to protect the fort builders during their work. His force and the river party met on schedule, and on September 5 began raising a triangular fort on top a spectacular bluff. The river curved around its feet in so wide and glittering a sweep that anything moving on the water could be seen for miles. The site, Clark remembered in his diary, had delighted him in 1804 on his way to the Pacific, and it still did.

As soon as work was underway, he sent out scouts to bring in the Osage and Kansa Indians so that he could make a treaty with them for this land he was already appropriating. He told them further that any who did not appear would be considered enemies of the United States and no traders would be allowed to visit them. Thus threatened, representatives assembled grudgingly. Although Clark was miserable with dysentery, he warmed them up with a little liquor, held a council, and then lay awake the rest of the night, agonized by cramps while the savages outside "danced and hollered and sung."[7]

On September 16 Clark, who was very sick, felt that both the construction and the Indians were well enough under control that he could go home. John Day, McClellan's athletic hunter, went along in another canoe, to meet his employers and have a taste of the fleshpots before cold weather set in. They arrived on September 22. Crooks was already there with his load of merchandise from Michilimackinac.

On September 24, 1808, the firm of Robert McClellan & Company applied for a trading license. It was given to them on September 30 with a very curious restriction. No place was specified, as was normally the case. Instead they were told that they could trade at Fire Prairie (where they would be in direct competition with the new government factory) but that the agent at Fort Osage could extend the area to as much of the upper river as he saw fit.

The agent they saw was either Reuben Lewis or Pierre Chouteau, Sr. Whoever it was told them that they could spend the winter at the Black Snake Hills on the east side of the Missouri River in the northwestern part of the territory. This was 175 river miles short of the nearest point where they had traded before. Furthermore, it was in an area that for years had been dominated by the fabled Robidoux clan, whose patriarch, old Joe Robidoux, was closely allied by many economic ties to Auguste Chouteau.

Traders of course had no hesitation about thrusting into any area where they thought they could do well. Possibly Crooks and McClellan supposed that prospects around the Black Snake Hills were alluring enough for them to try challenging the old regime. But it does not seem likely. Their ambitions had been centered on the upper river, a fact well known in St. Louis; and it is within plausibility that in being exiled to the Black Snake Hills the partners were feeling the claws of a new monopoly that hoped to absorb every bit of the trade from the mouth of the Platte to the head of the Missouri.

Lisa was the reluctant initiator of the monopoly. His 1807 expedition had turned up the Yellowstone River to the mouth of the Bighorn in south central Montana. There he had built a post. He sent messengers, notably George Drouillard and John Colter, both veterans of the Lewis and Clark expedition, south and west to invite the Indians to visit the fort for trade. Trappers examined the streams for beaver; and although the winter's proceeds had not been particularly rich, the prospects revealed by these pilot operations were dazzling. In the summer of 1808, therefore, Lisa had hurried down the river to finance and set up another expedition big enough to exploit the area to the fullest. He arrived in St. Louis six weeks or more before Ramsay Crooks came in from Michilimackinac.

Lisa's reports touched off a fierce jockeying for power. Everyone wanted in. Soon he found that to get what he wanted he had to link himself to people he might rather have done without. Among them were the Chouteaus and, in a mingling of interests which today would be intolerable, Reuben Lewis, brother of Governor Meriwether Lewis and subagent of Indian affairs, and William Clark, general of the territorial militia. The company these men and a few others formed was known as the St. Louis Missouri Fur Company. They meant their control to be exclusive. Not another partner was to be admitted to the firm without the unanimous consent of all the charter members.

In February 1809 Governor Lewis signed with the St. Louis Missouri Fur Company, of which Reuben Lewis was a director, a most advantageous contract. The government would pay the company $7000 if it agreed to hire 125 effective men, 40 of them expert American riflemen, for returning Big White, Jessaume, and their families to the Mandan villages. The United States was of course morally bound to atone for Pryor's 1807 defeat and make sure that the Mandan chief and his interpreter did reach their homes. If the expedition also made the river safe for the St. Louis Missouri Fur Company, that was just an interesting by-product. As a further inducement, Governor Lewis promised that he would grant no licenses to any other trading company above the Platte River, and would let no other party move up the river ahead of the company.

These specifics were put into writing on February 24, 1809. Robert McClellan & Company, which always before had traded between the Platte and the Maha village, applied for its license five months earlier, on September 24, 1808. This was the license which told them to check in at Fire Prairie, where the agent would extend their range as he saw fit. The agents there were Reuben Lewis and Pierre Chouteau, both of whom would soon be associated with the St. Louis Missouri Fur Company.

Since the company had not come into formal existence when the partners asked for their license, it is perhaps straining the evidence to suggest that Crooks and McClellan were sent to the Black Snake Hills, well below the Platte, in anticipation of the monopoly. On the other hand, there was time enough in the six weeks or more between Lisa's arrival and Crooks's appearance for the Chouteaus, Reuben Lewis and Clark to have started pressuring the Spaniard to let them into his proposed company. Shackling potential competitors may have been an object lesson to Lisa about the ways in which the game could be played. Guesswork—but it does explain what otherwise seems a curious place for an aggressive pair like Crooks and McClellan to have spent the winter of 1808–09.

They soon grew discouraged at their new locale. The Indians were restive and not hunting. In November unknown savages killed one of their men. Prices stayed down and there was no telling how much longer the embargo would continue crippling the fur business. They may have found the Robidoux family too deeply entrenched to buck; and if they were not to be allowed above the Platte for an indeterminate time, the struggle hardly seemed worth while.

In mid-February they prepared an advertisement for insertion in the St. Louis *Missouri Gazette*.

TAKE NOTICE

The partnership formerly subsisting between us under the firm of Mc-Clellan and Crooks, is this day disolved by mutual consent.

All persons indebted to said firm are requested to make immediate payment—and those who have claims, on the same, will present them to Ramsay Crooks, who is fully authorized, to settle all the affairs of said partnership.

Robert McClellan
Ramsay Crooks
Black Snake Hills, River Missouri, 17th Feb. 1809

As soon as the ice went out of the river, Crooks took the notice to St. Louis. It appeared on April 12, 1809. Almost immediately thereafter news arrived that changed the entire outlook of the fur trade.

As one of his last official acts President Jefferson in early March signed a bill that repealed the general embargo which for months had kept American ships shackled beside their docks. Although the non-intercourse decrees against England and France remained in effect, ways were provided for ending the restrictions. In anticipation of freer international commerce, fur prices jumped. At once Crooks began regretting that notice he had published. Perhaps the firm of McClellan and Crooks should reconsider . . . if financing could be found . . . if suitable goods could be obtained at reasonable prices on Michilimackinac.

While the possibilities were dancing like sparks through his mind, he was approached by a man with whom he probably had had commercial dealings before, young Wilson Price Hunt, junior partner of the mercantile firm of Hunt and Hankinson, which owned the largest store building in St. Louis. Hunt had electrifying news of his own. How would Crooks and McClellan like to join an expedition being formed by John Jacob Astor to follow Lewis' and Clark's route to the Pacific?

He explained as much of the background as he knew. For some time Astor had been planning to stretch a chain of posts from the upper Missouri over the Rockies to a headquarters station at the mouth of the Columbia River. He hoped to assemble at this station both beaver from the Rocky Mountains and sea-otter pelts from the North Pacific, send the furs to Canton in exchange for choice tea, silk, and chinaware, and bring the Oriental goods to New York in ships which he already had plying the trade. Although details of the plans were not yet firm, he proposed sending one party around the Horn to build the principal post on the Columbia. Another party was to travel overland by the Missouri and Columbia. As leaders for the land party Astor wanted a few young, dependable Americans to help balance the large numbers of Canadian Scots he was going to have to employ for the sake of their experience. He had just sounded out Hunt by letter, and Hunt in turn was considering possible American associates for the great adventure.

The beginnings of this dream of Astor's are obscure. No doubt many impulses contributed. He was familiar with the Canadians' search for a navigable river beyond the Rockies by which their westernmost posts could be supplied through the Pacific. He knew the Chinese market. For several years he had been sending to it aboard his own ships the best furs he bought each year in Montreal and Albany. On reading the reports of Lewis and Clark he instantly grasped the full significance of their remarks on the richness of the upper Missouri, the practicability of pack-train crossings of the mountains, and the use of ships on the Columbia.

The trouble was that the North West Company, which had posts close to the eastern slope of the Rockies, might reach the Pacific watersheds long before he could prepare his expeditions—especially since Jefferson's anti-British embargo of December 1807 froze the ships he needed right in their harbors. And if the Canadians once took root in the Columbia, their know-how would make them hard to dislodge. The only safe way for him to move West—and Astor always liked to be safe—would be to work out some sort of joint agreement with the North West Company for exploiting the new land.

The first problem was to persuade the Montreal partners to listen to him. Astor knew the Nor'Westers. He was sure that if he went to them with a request that he be allowed to share in *their* western enterprise, they would either refuse or impose harsher terms than he could endure. By being indirect, however, he might exert such pressures on them that they would come to him, asking for a share in *his* enterprise. It was an extraordinary plan and would succeed only if he could safely work a gigantic bluff. And that too was characteristic of the cautious, devious ways in which John Jacob Astor liked to operate.

He knew of course that the Montreal partners of both the North West Company, which was reaching toward the Pacific, and of the Michilimackinac Company, which operated entirely south of the border in the Great Lakes area, were, by and large, the same men. His idea was to offer them an escape from the embargo-created troubles inside the United States if they would cooperate with him on the Columbia.

His first step was to create an image of strength solid enough to make the Montreal fur men heed him. In January 1808 he approached De Witt Clinton, mayor of New York City and a member of the New York State Senate. He asked Clinton to introduce a bill into the New York Legislature granting a charter to a concern to be known as the American Fur Company. He wanted a full monopoly in "the Lusianas & Missouri," arguing that a monopoly's "best & True Policy" would be to treat the Indians well. ". . . with Independent Traders it is not so, they go one year to trade with the Indians perhaps never to see them again, why then they care little how much they cheat them."

To these pious generalities he added specifics for Clinton to use in supporting the measure. He pointed out that each year American citizens imported from Canada $400,000 worth of furs that had been caught within the United States but taken by alien traders to Montreal. He said that he hoped to combat the intrusion (if the charter was granted) by stringing posts along the route followed by Lewis and Clark to the Pacific. He would be solicitous about attaching the western Indians to the United States. In the process he would relieve the government of the expenses involved in maintaining its trading factories—a completely disingenuous argument, since any extension of the factories by the government would result in competition for the American Fur Company.

All this Clinton dutifully repeated to the New York Legislature. The bill was passed without debate on March 29, 1808, and the charter formally assigned ten days later. Like most careful bluffs, this one had substance to it. Astor wanted to seize control of the United States fur trade if he could, and would develop the American Fur Company to that end as events warranted. Accordingly the document was carefully drafted. It was good for twenty-five years. It established the company's maximum capitalization during the first two years at one million dollars and at two million thereafter. Detailed provisions were laid down about the election and power of directors, the value and sale of stock (only citizens of the United States could be shareholders) and so on and so on—most of it window dressing, since Astor had no intention of a public stock issue or of anything other than a nominal board of directors. When and if the American Fur Company came into existence, John Jacob Astor was to be its sole power.

Even before the legislature acted, he was in touch with the Secretary of Treasury of the United States, Albert Gallatin, and through Gallatin with President Jefferson.[8] He very carefully did not tell Jefferson that he intended a monopoly. The President made a few inquiries about Astor, received commendatory replies, and on April 13, 1808, wrote the New Yorker wishing him well and saying that he hoped the proposed American Fur Company could induce the Canadian Michilimackinac Company to retire from the fur trade of the United States.

When Astor visited Montreal in September 1808, he surely took copies of the charter and the letter with him. There he used them as topics of conversation at the parties which the Montreal partners of the North West and Michilimackinac gave in his honor. He no doubt asked a few rhetorical questions about the supply troubles which the Michilimackinac Company was having because of the non-importation decrees. How very unfortunate! Under the circumstances, he said, it almost seemed as if the Canadians would be wise to abandon the fur business inside the United States. Apparently changing topics, he then mentioned in an offhand way the visits of his ships to the Chinese markets, from which the Canadian fur traders were excluded by the franchise of the monopolistic East India Company. Switching back, he suddenly offered to free the Canadians of the troublesome Michilimackinac Company by purchasing it from them for $550,000. In fact, he said generously, he would even throw in another $50,000 if the Canadians would guarantee him a clear field everywhere south of the border, including the disputed Columbia River watershed.

If the Michilimackinac Company was truly capitalized for $800,000, Astor's bid of slightly more than half a million was low, but he was counting on the embargo, which was still in effect, to do his squeezing for him. He did not believe, surely, that the Montreal fur traders would surrender the Columbia Basin to him, undeveloped though it still was, for a mere $50,000. What he wanted, rather, was for the Canadians to counter his suggestion with an offer that he share in their western trade in return for his lifting the Michilimackinac Company off their backs.

The Montreal men held a few trumps of their own, however, Their winterers were working farther west than Astor perhaps realized at that time. David Thompson had pushed into Montana and northern Idaho and was beginning to unravel the complex geography of the upper Columbia. Simon Fraser was examining the river in British Columbia that now bears his name, hoping that it might provide a suitable way for supplying the interior posts from the western ocean. The doughtiest of the North West Company directors, Sir Alexander Mackenzie, first man to cross Canada by land, had already applied to the English Board of Trade for an exclusive charter to string North West Company posts across the Canadian Rockies and to establish a commercial colony at the mouth of the Columbia.[9] Very soon this government franchise, backed by their own explorations, might establish them unassailably on the Pacific watershed. Under those circumstances they were not about to be stampeded by a paper company. Politely, since Astor was being entertained in their homes, they declined to discuss the Columbia at all and told the American that if he wanted the Michilimackinac Company he would have to pay $700,000 for it.

Thus Astor's opening gambit failed. In March 1809 Jefferson dealt the devious scheme a second blow. He signed the bill repealing the general embargo. The non-importation decrees against England seemed destined to follow, and with a little luck the Michilimackinac Company could soon go to work again south of the border. (Actually, they had never been entirely out of business. The Indians around the Lakes had to be supplied. Bowing to expediency, customs officers had let American citizens, not Britons, move some merchandise off the island every year, as Crooks had done in 1808 and again in 1809. The ruling about citizenship was ineffective, of course. Various Britons, posing as Americans under the cloak afforded by Jay's Treaty, managed to take many boatloads of goods over the border into the Indian country.)

Astor either had to move with events or be left behind. Rather reluctantly, one feels, he decided to challenge the Nor'Westers and began
actual preparations for the sea and land expeditions to the Columbia
which until then had been only talk. The decision brought several practical problems immediately to the fore. One was the impossibility of
finding enough trained winterers in the United States to manage the
large, complex, and dangerous enterprise he envisioned. He would
have to lure experienced Canadians away from the North West Company. Yet the American government was likely to raise a great hue
and cry if he sent a party to the Pacific entirely under control of British
citizens. Moreover, he himself was reluctant to risk using only former
Nor'Westers, in case out-and-out competition developed with the Canadian company. Therefore he began wondering how to find at least a
few qualified Americans with whom to dilute the alien cast of the
enterprise.

St. Louis was the place to look. The land expedition would leave
from there, and it was the only trade center that contained American
fur men of stature. But he did not turn to the town's leading merchants,
the Chouteaus, for help. In 1800 they had stung his pride with their
lofty rejection of his offer to import goods and sell pelts for them. Besides,
the Chouteaus had joined Lisa to invade the Rocky Mountains and it
would cost him too much to buy them out.

He did have a western representative in St. Louis, old Charles
Gratiot. Gratiot would have been willing to participate. Months earlier
he had somehow learned that Astor had talked to Jefferson about possible expeditions to the Columbia, and on December 9, 1808, he had
written eagerly to New York, offering his services. Astor put him off.
Gratiot was too fulsome.[10] He was heavily in debt to the New Yorker
and seemed unable to do anything more about it than make excuses.
He was growing old and Astor wanted a man vigorous enough to lead
the continental crossing in person. So he turned instead to the only
young, unattached merchant of consequence in St. Louis, Wilson Price
Hunt. Presumably he sounded Hunt out during the winter of 1808–09,
and became urgent when the repeal of the embargo warned him there
was no time to lose.

Hunt, a native of New Jersey, was twenty-six, four years older than
Ramsay Crooks. He had come to St. Louis in 1804, and for a time had
done well. But the embargo had hurt him and his partner Hankinson,
and he was in a mood to listen to new proposals. When Astor's messages arrived shortly after Crooks (an American now) came down from
the Black Snake Hills with glum intentions of quitting the Missouri,
the two young men got together and began to talk.

No matter how anxious Astor might be to beat the Nor'Westers to the
mouth of the Columbia, April was too late in the year for preparing

the expedition. The New Yorker would have to wait until the spring of 1810. But should the whole year of 1809 go to waste? Would it not be logical for an advance party to press up the Missouri ahead of the main overland group and prepare a winter base for the overlanders to use the following winter, 1810–11? (The experiences of Lewis and Clark suggested that a big group might not be able to make the full jump to the Pacific in a single season.) While waiting for the overlanders to come up the Missouri in the summer of 1810, the advance party could explore, make friends with the distant Indians, and perhaps set up on the far side of the Continental Divide some of the outposts that could start funneling furs to the headquarters fort at the mouth of the Columbia as soon as it was established.

Conceivably Astor suggested this idea to Hunt. More probably Crooks and Hunt dreamed it up themselves as a way whereby Crooks could support himself during the next year. Hunt could promise nothing definite. Astor had been merely asking questions. No firm contracts for the Pacific trip would emerge until after Hunt had gone to New York for personal discussions. But once the contract was signed, events would have to move fast. Sending Crooks and McClellan up the Missouri in the interim as Astor's agents would secure their services and, in case anything did upset the Pacific plans, would provide Astor at least with an opening on the Missouri, should he wish to exploit it.

Furthermore, thanks to President Jefferson, it was a way to keep up with the St. Louis Missouri Fur Company and forestall any trouble they might want to make for Astor in the mountains. The year before, while Astor's proposal to send parties to the Columbia was still just talk, the President had written Meriwether Lewis (July 17, 1808) of the formation of the American Fur Company "under the direction of a most excellent man, a mr Astor merch^t. of N. York, long engaged in the business & perfectly master of it," and had recommended Astor to Lewis' attention. The letter had arrived after Lisa's return from his post on the Yellowstone, and was a warning to the embryo St. Louis Missouri Fur Company that a powerful competitor might at any time try to thrust into the area. The threat alarmed Lisa's partners, but there was not much they could do about it, in spite of Lewis' promises to grant no licenses on the upper river. It was one thing to brush Crooks and McClellan off into the Black Snake Hills, but quite another to deal in so cavalier a fashion with Crooks and Hunt as agents of John Jacob Astor. Galling though it might be to his brother and to William Clark, Governor Lewis would have to give Crooks a permit.

To make the license mean anything, Crooks had to obtain goods. Lisa's expedition had drained the embargo-impoverished stores in St. Louis. Crooks lined up what little he could from Hunt and then prepared to rush to Michilimackinac and, using Hunt's letter of credit, secure a share of whatever was available on the island. As soon as he returned he would have to hurry up the river to acquaint McClellan with these unexpected developments. Meanwhile someone in St. Louis would have to arrange for a keelboat, hire a crew of voyageurs and trappers, wait for the goods, and bring them up the river. Crooks could not do it all himself; and this may be the time when he took Joseph Miller, a retired army officer and experienced trader, into the firm to help.[11]

By pressing his paddlers hard he reached Michilimackinac late in May. He found the island stirring with fresh excitement as expresses came with still more good news from the East. Commerce was completely free again!

The bill of March 1809 removing the general embargo had added that as soon as either Great Britain or France repealed certain obnoxious orders in council concerning American shipping, then the United States would lift its non-intercourse edicts against that particular country. The bait had apparently worked. The British minister to the United States, David Montague Erskine, all but gave his diplomatic oath that Britain's orders would end as soon as the American government offered an earnest of its own intentions. President Madison thereupon issued, on April 19, a proclamation stating that free trade with Great Britain would be resumed on June 10.

The country rejoiced. The *National Intelligencer* rushed extra editions onto the streets of Washington; bells pealed throughout New England. Merchants ordered foreign goods; ship owners hurried repairs. Within three weeks 670 vessels of every description made ready to sail for Great Britain and her colonies. Messages bearing the glad tidings followed the receding ice into the north country.

What Crooks did not realize during the excitement was the additional hurt which this relaxation might cause Astor's schemes. The Michilimackinac Company could breathe again. By the mere payment of ordinary import duties, the Canadians once more could take goods anywhere in the United States east of the Mississippi. (The exclusion of foreigners from the Missouri still held, however.) As a result the partners in Montreal were less eager than ever to give Astor concessions on the Columbia in order to have him buy the Michilimackinac Company, which he must have if he were to control the American fur trade.

Meanwhile title to the Columbia country remained in dispute. True, Britain's Board of Trade had denied Alexander Mackenzie's 1808 appeal that the North West Company be granted an exclusive franchise to the Columbia watershed lest such a monopoly infringe on United States territory, but this did not mean that England had given up her own claims. The area was as open to the North West Company as it was to Astor. Some of its winterers had already built posts on the western slope of the northern Rockies and would soon be pushing down the river to-

ward its mouth. Let Astor start his belated expeditions. They were off
ahead of him. And they were used to fighting experts.

Unaware of these distant problems, Crooks bought and packed his
merchandise. When an unexpected chance presented itself for a quick
trip back through Lake Michigan aboard the sailing ship *Selina,* he seized
the opportunity. He loaded on his merchandise and prevailed on the
Selina's captain to tow behind his vessel a barge or two for carrying the
material on down the Illinois River to St. Louis. On June 18 he was in
Chicago. According to the account books kept by the trader there, both
Ramsay Crooks and a Mr. Bodain, "Mr. Creich's conductor"—surely a
phonetic rendering of Crooks—went across the portage that day.[12]
Bodain's job was to shepherd the merchandise on down the Illinois.
Crooks, carrying perhaps a few bales of choice merchandise with him,
hurried ahead in a canoe or light bateau to St. Louis. There he gave the
bills of lading for the barges to Joseph Miller, so that Miller could transfer
the material to a keelboat and start it up the Missouri.

Presumably he consulted also with Hunt about last-minute plans. They
must have discussed the stimulation which the ending of the non-
intercourse decrees would almost certainly bring to the entire fur trade.
Other adventurers could be expected to risk the long river. All the more
reason for Crooks, McClellan, and Miller to thrust as far up the Missouri
as possible before winter, build a stout post, and be ready for major
activity beyond the Rockies the following year.

What they had no possible way of anticipating was the new gyration
which the dizzy politics of the Napoleonic War was about to give to
American diplomacy—and hence to the fur trade. With a worried eye on
Napoleon, the British government repudiated the semiofficial promises
of its minister, Erskine. The hateful orders in council against American
shipping were not revoked. On August 9, 1809, therefore, Madison
reinstated the non-intercourse decrees against England. If the American
government next chose to enforce the restrictions tightly along the
northern border (and the temper in Washington indicated that it would),
then the fur trade, politically speaking, was back where it had been
under the general embargo, its freedom of movement almost fatally
crippled.

Half a month before this unexpected reversion occurred, Crooks was
on his way up the river. The brigades of the St. Louis Missouri Fur
Company were scattered out for miles ahead of him. The section escorting Big White and Jessaume—ten barges loaded with about 160 soldiers,
voyageurs, trappers and Delaware Indian hunters led by agent Pierre
Chouteau—had started in the middle of May and was creeping along at
a snail's pace. More hunters (190 altogether) had followed in sections.
Lisa and the last eighty of them had pulled out of St. Louis on June 17,
the day before Crooks crossed the Chicago portage, and were straining

furiously in a keelboat and two or three barges to catch up. A little short
of Fort Osage they did. On July 8, the combined flotilla labored to a
landing under the triangular post on the bluff.

Crooks arrived at Fort Osage at almost the same time. It had been a
phenomenal trip. In a day less than Lisa had spent coming from St.
Louis—twenty-one days all told—Crooks had coursed 400 winding miles
down the Illinois, had paused probably at St. Louis, and then had overtaken the rival company before it was out of Missouri Territory.

He could not possibly have made the trip if handicapped by a keelboat or by any appreciable amount of goods. Nevertheless his arrival
disconcerted Lisa. Perhaps the Spaniard feared there were more goods
upstream with McClellan, who had moved back toward the Platte for
the summer hunt. Now that Crooks had secured a license, the partners
perhaps would try to rush off ahead of Lisa and cause trouble—though
how the Spaniard expected them to pass the Indians he was so afraid
of does not appear. Anyway he badgered Crooks into promising to wait
at McClellan's, perhaps on the strength of Meriwether Lewis' assertion
that no other trader would be permitted to travel up the stream ahead
of the monopoly. Since Crooks's goods were far behind, he agreed amiably and went on to catch McClellan. Still Lisa distrusted him. On July
10 the Spaniard wrote Clark from Fort Osage, "If we do not find him
there [with McClellan] I will be obliged to take an assortment and go
after him with my boat which is the fastest going boat we have."

Crooks and McClellan, who had to wait for Miller to bring up their
keelboat, did not go ahead. At the end of July, Lisa's ungainly trading
party found them just short of the Platte, where McClellan had been
staying obediently on the permitted side of the river, trading with the
Otos who lived a little above its mouth.[13] By this time Lisa's American
trappers were ready to quit. The size of the flotilla, the need to exercise
the soldiers, and Lisa's insistence that all groups camp together each
night had created confusion and built resentment. To keep up with the
light barges, the heavier vessels and the keelboat had to labor each day
until after dark. The boiled corn on which the French-Canadians throve
did not satisfy the Americans, especially after they discovered several
barrels of salted meat in one of the holds. Lisa's autocratic airs annoyed
them still more. Numbers of them deserted. A few more were discharged
for incompetence. By the time the bickering party reached the Platte,
morale was in a deplorable state. McClellan, who despised the Spaniard,
no doubt watched with a broad grin as Lisa resorted to frantic cajolery
to keep the men from leaving. He managed somehow, and the party
toiled slowly on.

Impatiently Crooks and McClellan waited for their own keelboat. It
appeared in late August or early September, with the new partner,
Joseph Miller, in charge of the forty singing voyageurs and trappers.

Eagerly they loaded onto the vessel everything at their post that might be of service. Then off they went, around the extraordinary twists of the muddy river, beside the rolling hills that Lewis and Clark had named Council Bluffs, past the striking yellow mound where Blackbird, fierce chief of the Mahas, was buried. In high spirits they dragged the boat 350 miles or so. And then, somewhere in southern South Dakota, perhaps near the mouth of the James River, hundreds of painted Teton Sioux, black raven feathers in their hair, swarmed to the riverbank and sent a volley of arrows and bullets across their bow.

The whites landed. Arrogantly the Indians said that they could go no farther. The savages were tired of being promised traders and then seeing every boat row by. The American government had even kept British traders from bringing in as many goods as usual from the Des Moines and St. Peter's. Enough was enough. Crooks, McClellan, and Miller would have to stop, build a post right there, and trade with the Sioux on the Indians' own terms.

Crooks and McClellan were instantly suspicious. Two years earlier they had talked to Nathaniel Pryor when he came limping down the river from his defeat by Aricaras. Pryor had told them that he blamed Lisa for setting the Indians on him (what justice the charge had no one today can say) and when the Sioux turned ugly in 1809, Lisa got the blame for that too. He had been nervously anxious back at Fort Osage to keep Crooks and McClellan well behind him. Perhaps he was using the Tetons to make sure that they stayed behind.

Surmises helped nothing now. Helplessly outnumbered, its voyageurs in a blue funk of terror, Astor's would-be advance party pulled over to the bank far short of its goal and went through the pretense of heeding the orders of the triumphant savages.

CHAPTER 8

Ripostes

Lisa's party may or may not have had difficulty passing the same Teton Sioux. Thomas James remembered nothing untoward. Pierre Chouteau, Sr., however, reported to Secretary of War William Eustis that although trouble had not progressed beyond angry words, things had been touch and go for a time. Finally peace was achieved and on the party went. Another peace was made with Aricaras. Those two achievements opened the Missouri River—to the St. Louis Missouri Fur Company, that is. Big White's escort delivered him safely to his home among the Mandans, and some of Lisa's traders began building a trading post nearby. The trappers, except for a few who had deserted, pushed on up the river toward the Yellowstone and the Rocky Mountains. Some of them would cross the Continental Divide shortly; probably others of the same company already had. So affairs were in good enough shape up there.

Circumstances were different farther down the river. Glumly Crooks and his group felled trees and built a cabin. They had no intention of staying in it—not among Indians in so dangerous a mood. Their best hope now was to hoodwink the savages, spirit a few trappers up the stream if possible, and at the same time slip their trade goods downstream beyond reach of the Sioux and try to establish friendlier relations among tribes they could count on, the Omahas and Otos near Council Bluffs.

Outsmarting the Sioux proved easy enough. The cabin finished, the whites told the Indians that if they wanted to trade, they had better bring in their furs. In great excitement over their apparent success, most of the savages rushed off to their village, twenty miles away, to gather up their pelts. Confident they had thoroughly cowed the whites, they left only six or eight of their number behind as guards.

Even to French-Canadian voyageurs the odds were now acceptable. Led by the fiery McClellan, they pounced on the guards and tied them up where the captives could see only part of what was going on. One thing they did not see was that Crooks sent the trappers of the party on up the river, probably in hastily constructed dugout canoes, to take whatever beaver they could. He promised that later in the winter he would try to slip past the Sioux and join them.

To keep the Tetons from detecting the ruse and following the trappers, the remaining voyageurs and the partners staged an elaborate show of preparing to flee downstream in the keelboat. To concentrate still more fury on themselves, and hence away from the trappers, they entrusted the writhing captives with several scurrilous remarks for delivery to the tribe. Waving derisively, they then disappeared toward the lower river.

In the neighborhood of Council Bluffs, safely beyond the normal range of the Tetons, they halted and opened a substitute trade. Hunt and Astor might not like this poor beginning to his thrust toward the Pacific, but what else could they do? A few days later, while their resentment was still hot, along came Chouteau and Lisa, fatly content with the success of their own mission. Presumably the partners upbraided Lisa violently for their misfortunes and the Spaniard retorted as earnestly as he could that their suspicions were baseless. He failed to convince McClellan. With sulphurous oaths the old scout swore that if he ever caught Lisa away from the protection of his private militia, he would kill him on the spot.

Records go blank again. Did either Crooks or McClellan risk the Tetons to join their men farther up the river, as promised? How far? Or did the trappers go only a short distance, lose their nerve, and retreat to Council Bluffs? Unhappily no record survives to tell. But wherever the partners were that winter, trapping and trading were poor. On June 10, 1810, Charles Gratiot of St. Louis wrote to Astor, "Mr. Crooks. . . . returned yesterday from his Winter ground, which has been very indifferent on account of the Indians being at War with each other during the Season."

Although Gratiot's letter did not mention either McClellan or Miller (by this time the merchants in St. Louis recognized that young Crooks was the real force behind the partnership), the pair may nevertheless have paddled down the river with him. Their first plan had collapsed and what they did next would depend on what they heard from Hunt, who had gone to New York the previous November for detailed discussions with Astor. There was no recent news. All Gratiot could tell them, on the basis of a letter Astor had written him in February, was that preparations for the project were still underway. If so, Hunt probably was already on his way West via Montreal and Michilimackinac, where he planned to go to hire voyageurs.

It sounded hopeful. Still, mere expectations were thin timber on which to support livelihood. Arranging for a winter's trade took time, and many things could have happened in New York since February. If the partners were to sit around St. Louis (or at their post on the river) waiting for Hunt to appear and then were to learn late in the summer that some hitch had occurred, they would be left to face the winter with empty hands. Probably they had long since decided that Crooks should go as usual to Michilimackinac and try to make arrangements for another outfit they could use for their own trade if Hunt did not appear. McClellan and Miller meanwhile would do such summer bartering as they could and also prepare for the winter, building a post as high up the river as circumstances and the Sioux allowed. If, on the other hand, Crooks did encounter Hunt at Michilimackinac, the independent trading plans would be dropped and the partners would join the overland expedition without loss, as originally planned.

Sometime in mid-June, then, Crooks told the other two farewell in St. Louis (if they were there), loaded the company's skimpy harvest of pelts into a barge, and once again started the long pull back up the now familiar Illinois. At Chicago he had one bit of luck. The sailing ship *Selina* had just brought another shipment of supplies to the fort and the Indian trading factory there, and was on the point of returning to Mackinac. Grateful to miss rowing the barge through the lake, Crooks boarded her. In Mackinac he found Hunt already on hand and from him learned what had happened during the winter just past.[1]

President Madison's April 1809 repeal of the Non-Intercourse Act against Great Britain scarcely rippled Astor's plans. He simply ordered a large stock of first-class Indian-trade merchandise from England and went stubbornly ahead with his preparations to send both sea and land expeditions to the Columbia. And then, as if in compensation for his earlier bad luck with the embargo, he ran into a Russian who, as a mere incident in solving his country's own colonial problems, was quite willing to help him strangle the Canadians in the Pacific.

Under charter from the Czar, the Russian-American Fur Company, with field headquarters at Sitka, held a paper monopoly to the otter trade of Alaska. Actually the company was not able to enforce its exclusive rights. Its supply caravans across Siberia to Kamchatka and from there over the ocean to Alaska were undependable. Often the hungry colonies had to buy what they needed from American vessels coasting the wild shores in search of whatever pelts they could entice from the natives. Once allowed in the area, these irresponsible traders plied the savages with liquor and sold them guns that might be used against their masters.

It occurred to the Russian consul-general in America, Andrew Daschkoff, that these unwelcome, irregular traders might no longer visit Alaska if they knew they could not sell their surplus goods to the Russians. Perhaps someone like Astor could set up a dependable supply system to take their place. His captains could carry merchandise around the Horn from New York on ships destined for China, unload the goods at Sitka, and fill the space with Russian sea-otter pelts. These would be sold in Canton on consignment or speculation. Astor's ships would then pick up their normal cargoes of tea and silk and return to New York.

Or perhaps Astor proposed the plan to Daschkoff; origins are uncertain. In any event, Astor saw in it not just a profitable commerce for his ships, but also a device for hurting the North West Company. He told Daschoff he would agree not to trade with the Indians in Alaska if the Russians, who were already looking for posts in the south, agreed to stay away from the Columbia River. For if Russian trade agreements helped Astor establish himself on the Columbia and if his subsidiary posts linked with the Russian posts to the north, the chain quite conceivably could strangle the North West Company's ancient desire for an outlet to the Pacific.

Daschkoff nodded tentative agreement.[2] Almost immediately thereafter international politics gave the Montreal men another shock. The British government, as we have seen, repudiated Erskine and the Americans reinstated the non-intercourse decrees. Once again the Michilimackinac Company was a liability. Sensing this, Astor immediately reverted to his old, cautious plan of protecting himself on the Columbia by setting up a trade agreement with the Nor'Westers. After all, a man was foolish to fight a powerful enemy if he didn't have to.

He used his as yet unsigned contract with the Russians to apply still more pressure to them. On September 1, 1809, he bought the ship *Enterprise,* 291 tons. As her captain he hired John Ebbets, a veteran sea-otter trader with several years' experience on the Northwest coast. He loaded the *Enterprise* with tempting goods for the Russians and instructed Ebbets to use them in winning the assent of the Russian governor at Sitka, Alexander Baranoff, to the agreement with Daschkoff. He also told Ebbets to visit the Columbia and prepare the Indians for a party of white men who would soon be coming to live among them. He then went to Montreal. Casually he mentioned Ebbets and Daschkoff to the Nor'Westers, and said he had been corresponding with an Indian trader in St. Louis, Wilson Hunt, about leading a party overland to the West Coast. He then remarked that he might consider buying half of the Michilimackinac Company (no longer all of it) so that as an American citizen he might be able to bring goods across the border for the firm's traders—*if* the North West Company would take up a third of this Pacific enterprise, not counting the Russian agreement. That third, of course, would be enough to keep them from competing with him, yet he would have two thirds of the business.

The price seemed too much to pay for solving some of their troubles in the Great Lakes area. The Montrealers shook their heads. No, thanks. But behind their bland smiles they were beginning to worry. They had just learned that Simon Fraser had found the fearful canyons of the Fraser River to be unnavigable. Therefore the North West Company must depend on the Columbia for its transmontane operations. Yet incredibly—a year ago they had not been sure Astor meant business— incredibly his ship was all but on its way there. An overland party also. A Russian tie-in . . . Perhaps they could not reach the mouth of the Columbia, where an essential depot must be built, in time to forestall the American.

Nor was Astor the only Yankee bound West. The St. Louis Missouri Fur Company, with prominent officials of Missouri Territory on its board of directors, was pressing hard for the upper Missouri and would certainly spill over onto the Columbia if its traders found they could do so unchallenged. Finally, the Winship brothers of Boston, experienced sea-otter traders, were rumored to be working on a plan exactly like Astor's —simultaneous sea and land expeditions to a post at the mouth of the Columbia River.[3]

Why the Nor'Westers did not immediately send a ship of their own to the Columbia is impossible to say. The Napoleonic Wars had of course hurt the entire trade, and the partners in London, highly sensitive to shocks from France, may have felt times were too uncertain to justify expansion. Perhaps the Montrealers themselves were relying too much on the activities of Simon Fraser and David Thompson beyond the Rockies and on their own hard-won experience in driving other competitors from the field. Perhaps they feared rousing the United States Government to diplomatic action on Astor's behalf. In any event, the Montreal partners contented themselves with directing on September 30, 1809, a surprisingly lackadaisical appeal for help to the British minister in Washington, advising him that various Americans contemplated establishments on the Columbia, "to which they have no pretensions by Discovery . . . the right clearly belonging to Great Britain. . . . No establishments of the States . . . should therefore be sanctioned."[4]

This was hollow talk. Only protracted negotiations between the two nations could settle the issue of sovereignty over the Pacific Northwest. Meantime any citizen of either nation could build posts in the area. Rather than simply write his government, Astor acted. In mid-November he started the *Enterprise* toward the Pacific. Almost simultaneously Hunt left St. Louis for New York to consult with him about the overland expedition. And finally, through channels now unknown, Astor offered partnerships in his Columbia enterprise to several dissatisfied clerks of the North West Company.

Troubles were mounting south of the Lakes also. The American government, angered by what seemed Erskine's faithlessness, was determined this time to make the non-intercourse restrictions work. Manuel Lisa, for instance, was so desperate to obtain merchandise for his new concern that he and a friend left St. Louis on January 23, 1810, for a winter trip to Montreal to see what they could achieve in person. In Detroit—after his horse had fallen with him twice in icy water along the way—Lisa had a chance to see the effectiveness of the blockade with his own eyes. Dejected, he wrote home to Pierre Chouteau,

> . . . it is impossible for me to get a needle across due to the embargo.
> . . . Guards are all along the river, who watch if one takes anything across, and the fines are very harsh, confiscation of the goods, five hundred dollars fine & twenty-five days in prison.[5]

Astor, however, had a large stock of merchandise on hand, ordered during the brief summer of commercial freedom. With his help the Michilimackinac Company might stay afloat until government action somehow solved this international quarrel. Some of the Canadian partners wanted to turn to him immediately. Others repeated that the cost was excessive and that it was better to fight.

Their confusion shows in the contradictory lines of action they adopted. With one hand they continued trying to block Astor through government action. On January 23, 1810, they wrote urgently to their London partners, saying that in spite of the war with Napoleon, the government of Great Britain must be prevailed on to devote some attention to holding the Columbia against the claims of the United States. American trading posts must not be allowed "on what has been considered British Territory. . . . We request you to make such application to government on part of the North West Company, as . . . may be most likely to succeed."

With the other hand the company extended to Astor the overtures he had been maneuvering to get. In the middle of February 1810, before the letter to London could have reached its destination, two of the principal Montreal partners, John Richardson and William McGillivray, went to New York to talk terms.

They did it reluctantly. On February 17, three days after reaching New York, John Richardson wrote to partner Thomas Forsyth in Montreal,

> To this measure nothing but dire necessity would reduce me to consent, but it seems to be evident under present circumstances, that unless something of the kind can be effected, utter ruin to the property invested

in the concern [the Michilimackinac Company] must be the consequence—So many impediments are thrown in the way of the Trade, that
it is impossible to be carried on profitably.[6]

Knowing their helplessness, Astor refused to budge from his original
stand. He would buy half of the Michilimackinac Company (and send
some of his goods to it) if the Canadians would take a one-third interest
in the Columbia enterprise. His only lapse was that he did not try to
define the boundaries of the Columbia country, probably because he
had no idea of how to describe them.

These terms were no easier to choke down in February and March
than they had been in September. Richardson and McGillivray temporized. To keep them off balance, Astor on March 10, 1810, negotiated
a provisional contract with three former clerks of the North West Company who, hardly by chance, had arrived in New York shortly after the
Montrealers. On the face of things they were an excellent trio for taking
charge of his proposed sea-land expeditions to the Pacific. One was
Duncan McDougall (later on the Columbia he disappointed Astor's expectations). Another was Donald McKenzie, big as a bear, a famous
shot with a rifle, and veteran of ten rugged years in the wilderness. The
third was Alexander McKay, who had gone with Alexander Mackenzie
on his historic trips to the Arctic and Pacific oceans nearly twenty years
earlier—trips that had been intended to implement just such a continent-
wide fur trade as Astor was now proposing. Furthermore, Wilson Hunt
was also in New York, awaiting instructions.

Thus beset, Richardson and McGillivray tentatively agreed. Either
honestly or in an effort to stall for time, they then said that before the
contract could become binding it would have to be approved both by
their associates in Montreal and by the wintering partners—the men, that
is, who were out in the wilderness but who would assemble late in June
or early in July for their annual rendezvous at Fort William on the
northwest shore of Lake Superior.

Astor demurred. A reply from Fort William would not reach him until
fall. That would delay his expeditions a full year. If the Montreal partners really meant to do business, they should make the agreement
promptly and then inform the winterers. He would expect George
Gillespie to come back to him with a definite answer in May, by which
time Hunt and the Canadian partners would be in Montreal hiring men.
If Gillespie did not appear, Astor would assume that the proposal had
been rejected and would press ahead accordingly.

This ultimatum Richardson and McGillivray took back to Montreal. It
caused consternation and bickering, but a majority at last agreed to go
along. Yet they could not dismiss the wintering partners quite so cav-
alierly as Astor suggested. Under guise of consulting them, McGillivray

sent a special express through the thawing rivers and lakes to Fort William with a letter explaining the circumstances.

The winterers were even more upset than the Montreal supply houses had been. The same Montreal supply houses, it will be remembered, were involved in both the North West and Michilimackinac concerns. But the trade of the wintering Nor'Westers was confined entirely to Canada. They had no interest in baling the Michilimackinac Company out of its troubles. They consequently debated the proposed tie-in with Astor on the basis of its own worth. Their primary objection to the arrangement was the length of time that might pass before they could realize a return on the investment. On the other hand, McGillivray's letter led them to believe that Astor's sea and land expeditions would be well on the way before the North West Company could make any concrete moves in opposition. Unhappily deciding there was nothing to do but fall in line, they wrote McGillivray of their consent.

We perfectly coincide with you in the opinion that Mr Astor's expedition to the North West Coast of America, if successful . . . may prove injurious to our concern & we are willing . . . that you accept the third proposed, provided our share of Capital does not at any future period, without the sanction of the N.W. Co. exceed £5000 to £10,000 Currency.[7]

Astor had won completely. He had guaranteed himself freedom from the North West Company's competition on the Columbia. But where should the American's territory end and that of the Canadians begin? To keep Astor from spreading too far too fast, the winterers decided they would need a representative on the spot, one who would reserve as much of the country as possible wholly to them and not just the undivided third of it which was all that Astor's company would concede.

David Thompson, who had already established posts for the company on the upper Columbia, was the logical man. And Thompson was already on his way to the rendezvous at Fort William. Enclosing a copy of their letter to McGillivray to clarify their stand, the winterers sent out an express to turn him back. The messenger caught Thompson at Rainy Lake on July 22. The great geographer—Koo-Koo-Sint, the Star Man, the Indians called him from his custom of observing the heavens every night—obediently retraced his steps.[8]

It was a dreadful journey. Revengeful Indians drove him far north to a January crossing of spectacular Athabaska Pass. The herculean feat availed him little. Desertions by his men and mammoth snows pinned him for weeks to the western slope of the Rockies. And so far as his immediate purpose was concerned, it was all needless. Even before the winterers at Fort William had written to McGillivray in Montreal that they were accepting Astor's proposal, the deal had crumbled.

Documents revealing the reasons for the collapse have not survived. Probably they were connected with the antics of the United States Congress as it tried to devise some satisfactory response to Great Britain's repudiation of the so-called Erskine agreement. Madison, it will be recalled, had reimposed the Non-Intercourse Acts on August 9, 1809; and this in turn had helped drive Richardson and McGillivray to New York the following winter. But to many congressmen embargoes and non-intercourse decrees were inadequate. Such laws had hurt Americans more sorely than they had hurt either the British or the French—so sorely that New England had been at the point of secession.

Throughout the winter of 1809-10, in debates filled with recriminations and digressions, Congress had sought for more effective alternatives. None was found. What emerged instead was a strange stopgap known as Macon's Bill No. 2. This in effect told the belligerents that the United States was giving them one more chance to realize the error of their ways. Unless they revoked their obnoxious orders in council by March 3, 1811, trade would be stopped. Meanwhile commerce was to be again resumed, presumably so that France and England could learn how much they really liked trading with the United States after all. Then came a dangerous lure. As soon as one of the powers recognized the neutral rights of the United States, this country would trade with it but refuse commerce with the other—becoming, in effect, a non-shooting ally of the agreeable country. Obviously this provision courted ripostes from the belligerents that might turn out to be risky indeed.

Macon's Bill No. 2 became law on May 1, 1810. To the Michilimackinac Company it guaranteed importation of enough goods for one more year of life independent of John Jacob Astor. But after that—what?

There was the rub. No one could guess how either France or Great Britain might respond to Macon's Bill. In discussing probabilities, the four Montreal supply houses behind the North West and Michilimackinac companies fell into bitter arguments. Two of them—Forsyth, Richardson & Co. and McTavish, McGillivrays & Co.—were willing to chance Great Britain's favorable reaction. In that case Astor's help would not be needed for sending goods to the rendezvous at Mackinac Island and from there throughout the central United States. With this freedom assured, they could repudiate their agreement with him and also compete freely on the Pacific coast.

The other two supply houses—J. and A. McGill & Co. and Parker, Gerrard, Ogilvie & Co.—were tired of the uncertainties. They wanted to continue with Astor as agreed. After all, his agents were already in Montreal, hiring men at their very elbows, and the Americans would be on the Pacific Coast before the Nor'Westers could arrive. Was it not better to work for what was assured rather than grasp at what might happen? But they were not aroused enough to fight for their contentions. In

the end they threw up their hands and sold their interest in the Michilimackinac concern to Forsyth, Richardson and McTavish, McGillivrays.
The purchasers promptly reorganized the firm, whose trade would still
be confined almost exclusively to areas south of the border, and renamed
it the Montreal-Michilimackinac Company.

Presumably purchasers hurried another express to Fort William to inform the winterers that the arrangements with Astor had been canceled.
The word arrived too late for the winterers to stop Thompson, however,
and he kept slogging westward as instructed. George Gillespie, meanwhile, was sent not to New York, as Astor had requested, but to Michilimackinac with Toussaint Pothier, to settle affairs with the wintering
partners of the old Michilimackinac Company and transfer their credits
and, if possible, their loyalties to the new Montreal-Michilimackinac concern.[9]

Before the month of May was ended, Astor realized that he was the
victim of what must have looked to him like a double cross. He still
could have dropped the Pacific plan, even though his partners were
already in Montreal hiring men. But his German stubbornness was fired.
The *Enterprise* was on its way to the West Coast, and the Russian
agreement might be formally consummated at any time. Should he stop
all that now? As for the Montreal-Michilimackinac Company, it might
yet fall into his lap. Political friends, of whom he had many, quite possibly predicted that England would not be bluffed by Macon's Bill
No. 2. If these prophets were right, and anyone not blinded by desire
must have believed so, commercial restrictions would soon be imposed
again and by spring the Canadians might find themselves in as sore
straits as before. He could then treat with them as he chose.[10]

As already indicated, Hunt, McKenzie, and McKay had opened, at
some point during these abrupt changes, an office in Montreal for recruiting voyageurs and clerks. At first, according to Alexander Ross, who
signed on as a clerk to travel to the Columbia by sea, "The flattering
hopes and golden prospects held out to adventurers, so influenced the
public mind that the wonder-struck believers flocked in from all quarters
to share in the wonderful riches of the Far West." Then trouble developed. The North West Company "tried to throw all the cold water
of the St. Lawrence on the project," presumably because that firm had
suddenly disassociated itself from Astor and now wanted to do him every
sort of damage possible. Their minds poisoned by rumors of danger and
suffering, good men held back and it was with great difficulty that
qualified workers could be obtained—or so says Washington Irving.

A far more serious difficulty lay in a clash of policy between Hunt and
McKenzie. Was it best to hire their full complement of men in Montreal?
For the crews leaving New York by sea the answer was evident. The
eastern United States did not contain experienced fur men. Save for a

leavening of clerks hired in New York City and some common laborers picked up at the Sandwich (Hawaiian) Islands, the bulk of the group would have to come from Montreal. The land party was a different matter. It would be passing through St. Louis, where a growing labor pool of experienced Kentucky backwoodsmen and of French-speaking Missourians was available. Hunt, who knew St. Louis, wanted to draw most of his party from among these men.

His preference was based on sounder reasons than local patriotism. The anti-British mood of the frontier being what it was, it would not be politic to overload the group with Canadians. Furthermore, the average Canadian voyageur did not understand the new kind of fur gathering that would prevail when the party reached the Rocky Mountains. As Hunt had learned from Lewis and Clark, from Lisa, and from the aborted plans of Crooks and McClellan, the distant Indians were not accustomed to normal trade patterns. Furs would have to be produced largely by the party's own trappers, or hunters as they were generally called. The Canadian voyageur had neither the experience nor the temperament for that risky craft, but there were men in St. Louis who had.

McKenzie, who knew by experience the prodigious feats the voyageurs could accomplish on the Canadian rivers, thought that this soft-handed St. Louis storekeeper was prejudiced. Or as Ross put it, Hunt "detested the volatile gaiety and ever-changing character of the Canadian voyageurs." McKenzie on his part distrusted the surly independence of the American frontiersmen, who could not and would not endure the toil and privations which the Canadians accepted as routine. He was suspicious of trapping, for it might agitate the Indians. Anyway, the Canadians could learn as much of the new procedures as they had to.

Hunt, who had never been in the wilderness, overruled him, and the barrel-bodied Canadian never quite got over it.[11] They hired fourteen men only, enough to move a single big *canot du maître* at maximum speed up the Ottawa. To be clerk of the group, partner Alexander McKay signed on the veteran Jean Baptiste Perrault, who in the winter of 1784–5 had gone to the headwaters of the Mississippi with an incompetent bourgeois who, as we saw, ended up being mortally stabbed during a drunken frolic.

On June 14 Perrault received a letter ordering him to report at once in Montreal. He went with heavy heart. He had been away from the trade for two years, earning a meager living as a schoolteacher in the village of St. Francis, northeast of Montreal. McKay lured him out of the rustication by promising him £80 a year for five years. His pregnant wife was disconsolate. It did not help her frame of mind, or his, that the baby, another son, was born a few hours after his orders arrived. But Perrault had promised. He gave her £25 and strode away, leaving her still in bed.

When he reached Montreal he waited. Delays had occurred in the signing of the final agreements with Astor. Time was precious, yet the document that established the Pacific Fur Company was not executed until June 23, 1810. One assumes the lag had to do with straightening out the uncertainties caused by the withdrawal of the North West Company. Evidently the trouble entailed considerable traveling between New York and Montreal. Neither McKay nor McKenzie, both of whom had come to New York to sign the first provisional contract on March 10, was on hand for the final formality. Duncan McDougall signed for them and for David Stuart, another Scot and former Nor'Wester who recently had been added to the roster of partners. Hunt signed for the American partners—himself, Ramsay Crooks, Robert McClellan and Joseph Miller.

Stock in the Pacific Fur Company was limited to one hundred shares. Astor, who was to conduct all business save that in the field and who assumed financial responsibility up to $400,000, held fifty of those shares. McDougall, McKenzie, McKay, David Stuart, Hunt, and Crooks held five shares each, a distribution which put the twenty-three-year-old Crooks on the same footing as the other, older field partners. McClellan and Miller each received two and a half shares. The remaining fifteen were reserved for such future partners as Astor might appoint, but none was to have more than three shares. No partner was to trade independently. Each was to receive every year free of shipping charges clothing and merchandise that together were worth two hundred dollars. Lest they grow discouraged by early setbacks, Astor agreed to absorb all losses during the first five years. In return, Hunt committed Crooks, McClellan and Miller to a minimum of seven years of service each.

Hunt was named resident manager of the post on the Columbia. A meeting was to be held there once a year and every partner was obligated to attend either in person or by proxy. Obviously the principal shareholder, Astor, would always be represented by proxy. A partner could vote all of Astor's shares, but no non-partner could vote more than a third of them. Thus Astor could not upset the desires of the field men without sending three representatives to the Pacific. Three fourths of the total votes possible were necessary to carry any major point.

The terms completed, Hunt and McDougall hurried to Montreal to join the Canadian partners and the gathering crews. No time was wasted now in starting the overlanders on their long trek. On July 4 the big canoe was hauled by wagon to Lachine. The next morning the sobering voyageurs paid their devotions in the chapel of St. Anne and then, singing to the beat of their red paddles, started up the Ottawa River toward Mackinac.

What really happened on the 900-mile trip cannot be determined. Writing a quarter of a century after the event, Irving says the trip was so "slow and tedious" that the party did not reach the island until July 22. The voyageurs "were fit to vie with the ragged regiment of Falstaff. Some were able-bodied but expert; others were expert, but lazy; a third class were expert and willing, but . . . broken down veterans, incapable of toil." The inexperienced Hunt could not manage them. They played the soldier and balked their work, ever disposed "to come to a halt, land, make a fire, put on the great pot, and smoke and gossip, and sing by the hour."

Alexander Ross, writing after having read Irving's *Astoria,* in effect contradicts the impression by saying that the canoe reached the island on July 17. This would be excellent time for the laborious journey. One inclines toward Ross's estimate. Hunt may have been inexperienced, but neither McKenzie nor Perrault was.

Shortly after their arrival at Michilimackinac, Crooks appeared. At once he gave over his and his associates' alternate plan for an independent trading venture on the Missouri. Then, with the others, he sat motionless for three weeks, although more than half the continent stretched ahead. The strange inertia was caused by the century-old custom of the trade.

Crooks wanted more men. On the basis of painful experience he said he would not risk the Sioux and Aricaras of the Missouri with the meager thirty men Astor had authorized—Astor was always tightfisted in small matters.[12] Especially they could not depend on French Canadians alone. To be safe the overlanders would need at least twenty or thirty riflemen—American backwoodsmen who, after the fighting was over, could be used to set traps. Moving them and their paraphernalia would require another boat. The additional boat in turn would require another crew of willing French-Canadian voyageurs. These could be best obtained at Michilimackinac.

Voyageurs could not be gathered at will, however. The only ones who were free were those who had just completed a long tour of duty in the wilderness. They had no intention of going back to the *pays sauvage* without the regale they considered an almost inalienable right. As Ross put it, "Every nook and corner of the whole island swarmed, at all hours of the day and night, with motley groups of uproarious tipplers and whiskey hunters . . . a great bedlam, the frantic inmates running to and fro in wild forgetfulness." Or, in Irving's words, "They feast, they fiddle, they drink, they sing, they dance, they frolic and fight until they are all as mad as so many drunken Indians."

Irving adds that the voyageurs were reluctant to face the unknown dangers of the distant land, a timidity characteristic enough of the French Canadians. But then he says that Hunt overcame the reluctance by giving out colored feathers which anyone who signed on could wear in his hat as a childish symbol of his hardihood. Perhaps. But dates are also suggestive. The party left the island on August 12. This was the normal time for Missouri River boats to start out.[13] Knowing their men, Crooks and McKenzie probably persuaded Hunt to let the frolic run its course.

They employed the time to sell their canoe, which would not be useful on the snag-filled Missouri, where no birch bark grew for repairs, and buy in its place two barges. They assembled goods to use as presents for the Indians they would meet. They were inconvenienced by Perrault. He took to brooding about the five-year stretch he would be away from his wife and asked for a release. A dissatisfied clerk was no asset. Hunt not only freed him but helped him secure winter work from a Lake Superior trader, so that when the old-timer returned home he would have something to show for his aborted adventure. In his place they hired a man who proved highly capable, John Reed. This may be the same man as the "James" Reed who had been with Crooks on the Missouri a few years earlier, but Reeds, both James and John, were too common in the area for positive identification.[14] They also picked up a hunter or two among the soldiers whose enlistments were expiring. Then, when the regale was over and the voyageurs were flat broke, Hunt showed his cash. No doubt the Canadians liked the feathers—feathers had always been a sign of superiority in the craft—but money was what they needed. In return for a picayune advance he got their names down on the printed indentures all traders used, and away they went.

They made fine time up the Fox River, down the Wisconsin and the Mississippi. They reached St. Louis on September 3. Here again they ran into trouble obtaining men, this time experienced hunters. At best the supply of qualified hands was limited, and by September most trappers were either on the river or spoken for. Manuel Lisa planned to send a boat to his fort above the Mandan villages the next spring and did not wish good men snatched away from him before then. He was also deeply suspicious of Astor's true intent. Although Hunt protested that the party had no intention of pausing in the rich beaver grounds of the upper Missouri where the local company was struggling to get established, Lisa did not believe him. To him this party smelled like dangerous competitors. Furthermore he did not want them on the Columbia, where he himself hoped to expand if all went well.

William Clark, Lisa's associate in the St. Louis Missouri Fur Company, endeavored to find out exact details. On September 12 he wrote Secretary of War William Eustis, saying, "Mr Hunt & McKinzey are at this place, prepareing to proceed up the Missouri, and prosue my trail to the Columbia. I am not fully in possession of the Objects of their expedition but prosume you are, and would be very glad to be informed." Lisa meanwhile spread rumors (so Irving says) about the horrid dangers ahead. Hunt's frightened riflemen demanded bonuses for signing. The voyageurs then grew jealous and in their turn pressed for wages that would match those received by the Americans. Legend has it that only the arrival of Joseph Miller at this critical juncture saved the day. By dint of his popularity on the waterfront he overcame the petty bickering and filled the quota of sixty men Crooks wanted, roughly twenty riflemen and forty voyageurs—double what Astor had authorized.

By this time it was October 21. Fall's warning was on the trees. Hunt was eager to push as far up the river as possible before ice blocked the way. Several motives impelled him. Wintering sixty men in St. Louis would be expensive and risky; many might desert. But starkest of all were the demands of distance. Ascending the Missouri to its head and crossing to the mouth of the Columbia had taken Lewis and Clark two full spring-summer-fall seasons. Granted, the explorers had had to treat with Indians and grope for the right way across the Continental Divide. Hunt could avoid those delays. Even so, he dared not assume he could reach the Pacific during the ensuing summer, as the sea party expected him to do, unless he utilized every minute of open water the weather allowed.

In two barges and a keelboat the group toiled upward at the limit of endurance for 450 crooked river miles. Then fingers of ice began to reach. Reluctantly, on November 16, Hunt halted at the mouth of the Nodaway in the northwestern corner of what is now Missouri.[15] They had scarcely unloaded their boats when Robert McClellan and a few men appeared, floating with the current. They were in wretched frames of mind.

It developed that McClellan had built a post during the summer no higher than Council Bluffs. A group of Sioux appeared while he was off hunting table meat. They cowed his men and rode off with plunder worth $3000, quite possibly in revenge for the trick McClellan and Crooks had played on them the year before. In one of his fits of wild passion McClellan prevailed on his athletic hunter John Day and a few others to help him run the thieves down. The reckless move netted little. Though they overtook some of the Indians, they managed to recover only five hundred dollars' worth of the stolen merchandise. That dab was not worth a winter in the wilderness. In black disgust, McClellan divided the remnant among his men to do with as they liked and started down the river. If he met Crooks and the Pacific party on the way and if the contract Hunt had negotiated for him was suitable, he'd go west. Otherwise—well, he would have to adjust as best he could. In any event, this sort of life was getting him nowhere.

At the Nodaway, Hunt showed him the contract. McClellan, touchy at best, was offended by its terms. Two and a half shares? And Ramsay Crooks, his erstwhile junior, had five?

Hunt assured him that no animus attached to the figure; Joseph Miller also had been limited to two and a half shares, yet had joined. In turns,

Crooks, Hunt, and Miller argued for six days. At last McClellan swallowed his pride—there was not much else his destitution would let him do—and agreed to go along.

The decision made, he wrote what was almost a last testament to his brother at Fort Hamilton, Ohio.

Six days ago I arrived at this place from my settlement, which is two hundred miles above on the Missouri. My mare is with you at Hamilton, having two colts. I wish you to give one to brother John, the other to your son James, and the mare to your wife. If I possessed anything more except my gun at present, I would throw it into the river or give it away, as I intend to begin the world anew tomorrow.[16]

Both Crooks and he must have felt some wryness at starting out once again there at the Nodaway. This was the vicinity of the Black Snake Hills, where they had been isolated two winters earlier by the machinations of the St. Louis Missouri Fur Company. Once again, thanks partly to delays caused by the same group, the company they were with had been brought up short of its desirings at almost the same spot. But this time, so they may have promised themselves as they built their rough log huts and settled down for the winter, they were going to show their heels to Manuel Lisa.

CHAPTER 9

By Sea

Shortly after Hunt's party left Lachine for the west, the sea group began drifting toward New York. Some traveled by public conveyance, but partner Alexander McKay, clerk Gabriel Franchère, and nine voyageurs were more original. They paddled in a birchbark canoe up the Richelieu River, across Lake Champlain, and down the Hudson. They neared New York City on a Sunday. Pausing as they might have if approaching Michilimackinac, they donned sashes, ribbons and feathers, and enthralled the strollers along the waterfront by singing their French songs as they crossed to temporary lodgings in the village of Brooklyn. The rest of the sea party, Franchère says, were already assembled there.

The group consisted of thirteen voyageurs, five mechanics, twelve clerks, and partners Duncan McDougall, Alexander McKay, and David Stuart. A few American clerks softened the foreign cast—Russell Farnham, William Wallace, and William W. Matthews. But the great majority were Canadians of Scottish ancestry. To this account the one of primary concern was Robert Stuart, nephew of partner David Stuart.

Robert Stuart was born February 18, 1785, two years earlier than Ramsay Crooks, on a croft in the hamlet of Ruskachan, parish of Balquhidder, Perthshire, in the southern highlands of Scotland. His father John Stewart (as he spelled the name) was called *Ian Mohr na Coille*, Big John of the Woods. It was a proud clan. David Stuart, whom Robert called "Old Uncle," insisted that the family was not descended from the royal Stuarts of Scotland, but that the royal branch sprang from *their* line. They cherished a coat of arms befitting the boast: a demi-lion rampant and above it the motto *Nobilis ira est leonis*, "Noble is the anger of lions." Noble or not, young Robert often flashed in full the clan's leonine temper.

Nicknamed fondly Little Robert of the Hills, he was one of nine children and the third son. As a younger son, he had few prospects in Scotland. While still in his teens he was apprenticed to work in the Orient for the East India Company, but his mother lost heart and held him at home. In 1807, when he was twenty-two, he could no longer be restrained. His father died sitting in a chair, the croft passed to the eldest son, and Robert left for Montreal, where Old Uncle had promised him a job as clerk with the North West Company. The bond between uncle and nephew was strong. Years later Robert wrote one of his daughters about David, "To him, under God, I owe everything." It was through Old Uncle's recommendation that he was signed on with Astor's sea party.

While the 300-ton ship *Tonquin* was making ready to sail for the Columbia, Robert either boarded with or lived near the family of John Sullivan, an Irish revolutionist who had fled from his homeland to sanctuary in Brooklyn. In America, John Sullivan, a Catholic, married Mary Palmer, a Protestant, agreeing that if the boys of their union were raised Catholics, the girls could be Protestant. In spite of the arrangement, daughter Elizabeth Emma, born June 27, 1792, was baptized in the Roman Catholic Church in New York City, one of her sponsors being Cornelius Heeney, at that time a partner of John Jacob Astor in the fur business. Later the arrangement about religion took effect perhaps by default, for her father died in 1807. Anyway, Elizabeth Sullivan received her education at a Moravian seminary in Bethlehem, Pennsylvania.

A warm attachment quickly formed between Robert Stuart, a Presbyterian by birth though not yet by conviction, and eighteen-year-old Betsy, as he called her. He may even have proposed as the last trade goods were being hoisted aboard the *Tonquin*. If so, the prospects of a clerk about to sail for the savage mouth of the Columbia, where he would earn four or five hundred dollars a year, did not appeal to Betsy's widowed mother. Perhaps that was why Old Uncle, David Stuart, deeded to Robert, for considerations unknown, two of his five shares of stock in the Pacific Fur Company. The young man thus became a partner, in name at least, of fabulous John J. Astor, but the mother remained unconvinced. Betsy was young enough to wait. She would talk further with Robert when—and if—he returned.

Mrs. Sullivan had reason to hold back. Even Astor was nervous about the *Tonquin*. Despite the free trade allowed under Macon's Bill No. 2, British warships continued to stop American vessels and impress British citizens. Astor heard that the North West Company might inspire some eager British naval officer to halt the *Tonquin* and whisk off its alien passengers. He asked the Canadians in his employ to become citizens of the United States (this was probably the occasion of Robert Stuart's becoming an American). He filled the *Tonquin's* twenty gun ports with ten live cannon and ten wooden dummies, expecting of course that these might also prove useful in awing the belligerent Indians of the Northwest coast. As the *Tonquin's* captain he hired a naval lieutenant on furlough, Jonathan Thorn, whose bravery in battle against the Tripolitan pirates had drawn an official commendation from Stephen Decatur. And finally Astor obtained from the government an escort ship, the *Constitution,* to protect the *Tonquin* until she gained the open sea.

On September 8, the *Constitution* convoyed the *Tonquin* as far as Sandy Hook and then signaled the private vessel good speed. It was the beginning of a miserable trip. Though the clerks were used to bobbing canoes, the roll of the ship made them ill. They grew dirty and unkempt and odorous, to the disgust of Captain Jonathan Thorn. After they found their sea legs they quarreled with Thorn over rations and goods, which the captain felt he was duty-bound to conserve, and over the navy-type discipline which he exacted in waters where unfriendly ships might appear at any moment. Thorn was a choleric man and so was Duncan McDougall, the partner in charge of the civilians. At one point the captain threatened to blow out the brains of anyone who disobeyed him; at another McDougall drew a pistol and defied Thorn's threat to put him in irons. Meanwhile water grew short, gales battered the ship, and two fires caused frantic commotions before being quelled.

Climax of the unfriendliness came at the Falkland Islands. The *Tonquin* paused there several days while the crew repaired her rigging and took on water. During the layover, the clerks and partners pitched a tent on the island and amused themselves exploring and hunting wildfowl. A mix-up occurred concerning the date the ship would weigh anchor. Thorn set one day and said he would fire a signal shot for those on shore to come aboard. The traders thought he meant another day. McDougall and David Stuart wandered off hunting. McKay, with clerks Franchère, Farnham, and Ross, employed themselves carving fresh wooden markers for the graves of two seamen who had perished on the island years before. No one heard a shot, but suddenly a man who had been at the tent near the harbor came shouting over a hill, "The ship's off!"

They piled eight strong (Ross says nine) into a boat twenty feet long and set out to overtake the *Tonquin* by rowing. Heavy seas almost swamped them. They plied the oars until dark—six hours, Ross says. Franchère's more modest three and a half hours is probably nearer the truth. Just as they were abandoning hope, the ship put about, partly because of contrary winds and partly because lion-tempered Robert Stuart aimed a pistol at Thorn's head. Just why the young man waited so long has not been explained. Conceivably he had been in his cabin at the time of departure and had not been aware of the marooning.

From that point on the clerks deliberately annoyed Thorn by disregarding his officious little orders and whispering among themselves in Gaelic, so that the captain grew convinced they were hatching a conspiracy. He clashed with McDougall over perquisites. The animosity spread to others. McDougall and McKay fell out; Thorn clapped his own mates into irons for petty breaches of discipline.

A break came at the Hawaiian Islands, where the party reprovisioned and hired Kanaka laborers. Even this respite ended unhappily. Thorn ordered sailors who overstayed their leave to be flogged; one was beaten insensible and thrown overboard, to be rescued by natives. As the ship pressed northward during March, 1811, the captain refused the traders' request for warm clothing. Out came pistols again, and only the intervention of David Stuart prevented an explosion.

A gale swept away or killed all the livestock on board. Seas were still high on March 22 when the *Tonquin* neared the Columbia's estuary. In the best of weather the bar across the river's broad mouth was dangerous. By unlucky coincidence the uncle of the *Tonquin's* first mate had drowned a few years earlier in the maelstrom. When Thorn ordered the nephew out in a small boat to find the channel, the man protested in horror. Let him wait for calmer water. Thorn refused. Off the mate went with four men. None of them was seen again.

For another day the ship beat back and forth outside the bar. Some of the experienced Canadian rivermen then embarked in the longboat to find the channel but were so battered by the mountainous breakers that they had to retreat. On March 25, the third mate and a crew of four in the pinnace at last located the passage. The ship followed, but did not pause to pick up the pilots. The pinnace vanished. The *Tonquin* grounded, but was saved by a shift in the tide. When at last a rescue party sought for the pinnace, it found only two survivors. The boat had swamped; two men had drowned at once and of the three who reached land one had soon died of his injuries. All told, the crossing of the bar had cost eight lives.

As Lewis and Clark had done half a dozen years before them, the whites searched the north shore of the broad inner bay for a site on which to erect a post. Finding no adequate break in the dense, swampy forest, they crossed to the south and picked a spot within easy walking distance of Lewis' and Clark's already decayed Fort Clatsop. Reminiscences written long after the event contend that the site was dreadful but that Thorn, eager to start trading along the coast of Vancouver Island, would not allow a longer search to be made. A more contemporary account by Robert Stuart, who had no reason to love the captain, gives a different picture of Astoria's location. The post, Stuart wrote, "is delightfully situated on the Southwest extremity of point George,

which is a commanding as well as in every other respect a commodious
station."

Slowly the Canadians and the Sandwich Islanders cleared away the
underbrush and planted a vegetable garden. They then attacked the
enormous trees, some so big that four men could chop together at
different parts of the same monster. The impact with which the giants
fell killed two men. The gunpowder used to blast the stumps apart
blew off another worker's hand. The curious, thievish Indians who lurked
about dispatched three more. The perpetual fog and the diet of roots
and fish sickened everyone. Men now and then deserted in the insane
hope of reaching Spanish settlements to the south, but were apprehended
by Indians and brought back for the sake of a small reward.

The nervousness that sprang from the disasters and discomforts intensified the quarrels between Thorn and the partners. The captain
charged that the builders were wasting time in their long surveys to
determine which way a tree might fall, in "smoking parties" with the
Indians, and in their reconnoitering trips along the river.[1] Toward the
end of May, when a warehouse was finally roofed, he rushed into it a
few trade goods and food staples (another supply ship was scheduled
to arrive shortly), took aboard partner Alexander McKay, and early in
June started north on his delayed trading trip. Just outside the bay he
picked up an Indian interpreter to help with the venture.

Dispiritedly the post builders went on with their work. Original plans
had called for a stockade 360 feet to the side. Difficulties soon shrank
the dimensions. Rumors that the Indians were planning an attack turned
some of the workers into guards; sickness reduced the remaining force.
To obtain logs small enough for the stockade and the houses, the able-
bodied had to push inland, harness themselves like horses, and drag
the timbers back to the building site. In the end the stockade, built of
logs seventeen feet tall and a foot and a half in diameter, became 75 by
80 feet, enclosing only a sixth as much area as Astor had envisioned.
Inside this cramped space four buildings gradually took shape.

In mid-June the Astorians were startled by the arrival of two strange
Indians, ostensibly man and wife. The pair, dressed in buckskin quite
different from the slovenly wood-rat cloaks and skimpy cedar-bark skirts
of the coastal Indians, bore a letter written by one Finan McDonald at
Spokan House to John Stuart (not a relation of the Astorians of the
same name) at Estekatadene House, New Caledonia.

The former Nor'Westers knew that New Caledonia was the name for
the section of Canada west of the Rockies that is now called British
Columbia. They knew that Finan McDonald, a great red-bearded bear
of a man six feet four inches tall, was David Thompson's clerk. But
the names of the posts meant nothing to them—yet. They tried to find
out, though communication with the two messengers, who could speak

a skimpy bit of English, was unsatisfactory. From what the pair said, however, it appeared that Thompson had not yet returned to the upper Columbia when the messengers had departed. Spokan House was a post built a few months earlier near the site of today's Spokane by Finan McDonald and Jacco Finlay. John Stuart, also a Nor'Wester, was supposedly building another post off north beyond the headwaters of the Okanogan River, a tributary of the Columbia.[2] The messengers had been told to ascend the Okanogan in their search for him, but had missed the river's mouth (in north-central Washington) and instead had followed the Columbia to the sea. They said.

Various things about the account seemed odd. The letter's contents did not appear urgent enough to merit so extraordinary a journey. It seemed even more strange that the two Indians would have grown so mixed about routes that they would land on the coast a thousand miles from where they were bound. Yet without question a white man had written the letter. More significantly, the episode revealed that the North West Company was working westward from the posts which David Thompson had established earlier in northern Idaho and western Montana.

The move was potentially dangerous. If, as the partners at Astoria supposed, the proposed purchase by the Nor'Westers of a third of the Pacific Fur Company had come to nothing, then competition would be the order of the future. It behooved them, therefore, to establish posts of their own on the upper river as soon as possible, even though this meant weakening half-formed Astoria still more.

The most they dared risk was a party of eight under David Stuart. To transport the group and its packs of trade merchandise, Stuart and his men began hollowing out of tree trunks three clumsy pirogues.[3] As they were finishing the work toward noon on July 15, 1811, a shout went up from workers on the upriver side of the stockade. A large canoe, different from those used by the local Chinook Indians, was bobbing through the waves from Tongue Point, a tree-covered promontory two miles to the north. A British flag rippled on the prow. The man standing in the bow, obviously the bourgeois, was black-haired and stocky. He was clad in neat European clothes, apparently donned on Tongue Point for the impression they would make. Five of the nine engagés flaunted the bright caps and sashes of French-Canadian voyageurs. Two were Iroquois Indians; their tribesmen were moving west in numbers to trap for the North West Company because the mountain Indians were not doing the job well. The other two men in the canoe were natives from higher up the Columbia, evidently interpreters.

The bourgeois leaped ashore as the canoe nosed onto the bank. Duncan McDougall exclaimed in recognition and reached out his hand. Later Alexander Ross and Washington Irving would complain of the warmth, seeing the beginnings of treachery in it. Yet one wonders how else McDougall could have acted. True, Thompson represented a rival firm. But he was an old friend, a fellow trader, and the first white man outside his own party that the Canadian had seen for months. Naturally he drew Thompson inside the stockade, fed him well, and listened in amazement to the story the Nor'Wester told.

Thompson had had a harrowing trip. By means of an unbelievable January crossing of Athabaska Pass, he had reached the Columbia where it makes a sharp hairpin curve around the Selkirk Mountains in south-eastern British Columbia. Hoping to gain Saleesh House (Flathead Post) in extreme western Montana (near today's Thompson Falls), he turned south *up* the Columbia. Five grueling days in deep, wet snow took him only twelve miles and exhausted his sled dogs. Retreating to the point where the trail from Athabaska Pass met the river, he built a hut. Some of his engagés deserted. Others, more loyal, fought a way back over the pass and returned with sleds loaded with merchandise and dried provisions.

While waiting for spring he built a canoe. Unable to find satisfactory birch bark, he split out thin slats of pliable cedar and joined them tightly over a light frame, sewing them in place with thread made from pine roots and hide. The canoe that resulted was twenty-five feet long and four wide. Into it he loaded 270 pounds of goods, 180 pounds of dried meat, and a little grease, salt and flour. With his three remaining Canadians he pushed south again, upstream toward Saleesh House.

They waded in snow and ice water, humped against the cold rains, ached with snow blindness and mosquito bites. They met a few Iroquois trappers whom Thompson hired to help them. They portaged from the headwaters of the Columbia to the Kootenai and followed that river into northern Idaho. There they took to horses, floundered through swamps and chopped down trees to bridge the flooded streams. On May 27, 1811, after forty-seven agonizing days, they reached Saleesh House. It was deserted. Indians had frightened away Finan McDonald and his men.

The next morning, before setting out in search of the missing clerk, Thompson "wrote a few lines in Charcoal on a Board in case the Americans [Hunt's overland party] should pass." Then he moved with his men west down Clark's Fork. Through Indians he made contact with McDonald, who met the wayfarers with horses and took them to newly-finished Spokan House. After three days' rest Thompson and nine men started for the coast. He followed a strange route. Instead of going forty miles directly west to the Columbia, he went twice that distance northwest to a favorite Indian fishing village called Kettle Falls. Perhaps he traveled that far out of his way in order to find suitable wood for a canoe. Or, more probably, he wanted to meet the Indians who con-

gregated at the falls and through them launch the job he had been
sent across the mountains to accomplish—hold the Americans on the
lower Columbia. As other Britons farther east had long ago learned,
the best weapon in a trade rivalry was the loyalty of the Indians.

He kept wooing them throughout his journey down the river. The
effort required diplomacy. The savages of the Columbia had never seen
a white man and might easily react by flight or battle. On sighting a
camp, therefore, seven of the voyageurs landed behind Thompson with
their rifles cocked. They spaced themselves a few feet apart and stayed
unostentatiously in the rear as Thompson advanced unarmed toward
the suspicious natives. The two men remaining in the canoe followed
along the shore, ready to disembark the party in a hurry if need arose.
The interpreters called out reassurances. Communication established,
Thompson passed around tobacco, sat patiently in the fish-stinking
lodges, showed samples of merchandise, and talked of the wonderful
English trade goods that he would bring in later if the Indians were
industrious hunters. English: he kept emphasizing that: and finally
at a savage village in the vast brown valley where the Snake River
(Sawpatin, he called it) pours into the Columbia he put the essence
of what he had been doing into writing, attaching a continent-wide
notice to a small wooden stake.

> Know hereby that this country is claimed by Great Britain as part of
> its territories, and that the N.W. Company of Merchants from Canada,
> . . . do hereby intend to erect a factory in this place for the commerce
> of the country around.

Alexander Ross, who came up the river from Astoria a month later,
adds in his reminiscences, "This edict interdicted the subjects of other
states from trading north of that station." Thompson's mission was as
complete as one man could make it. The Pacific Fur Company—and
he supposed that his own firm owned one third of it—could have the
lower river and the coastal trade. But the full three thirds of the upper
company was to be the property of the Nor'Westers. The single remaining chore was to paddle on to the coast and see how the river and the
harbors at its mouth could best be adapted to supplying the inland
posts—a water highway which their lower-river partner, J. J. Astor, would
have to let them use.

Since his entire journey had been conditioned by the thought that
Astor was a partner, he must have been surprised to hear from Mc-
Dougall and the others that the arrangement had collapsed. When? In
late May? Ah, but that was before the wintering partners, meeting at
Fort William on Lake Superior, had written to William McGillivray,

approving the plan. Would not that letter have led to a resumption of discussions?

McDougall thought not. The *Tonquin* had not sailed until September. If changes had occurred during the summer he probably would have heard of them.

Thompson was not convinced. It was a long way from Fort William to New York City. There may have been delays. And since it was impossible at the mouth of the Columbia to be certain of what was happening on the other side of the wilderness, the representatives of the two firms protected themselves by a curious exchange of letters. On July 15, the day of his arrival at Astoria, Thompson wrote a formal note to "Messrs McDougall, Stuart & Stuart," congratulating them on their buildings and commerce and adding,

> With pleasure I acquaint you that the Wintering Partners have acceded to the offer of Mr. Astor, accepting one third of the business you are engaged in . . . I have only to hope that the respective parties at Montreal may finally settle the arrangement between the two Companies which in my opinion will be to our mutual benefit.

To this information Messrs McDougall, Stuart and Stuart replied the next day in a letter almost duplicating Thompson's in form and wording. They congratulated him on his safe arrival by "so unusual a route" and acknowledged receipt of his note

> communicating the pleasant intelligence of the Wintering Partners of the North West Company having accepted of Mr. Astor's offer of one third share of the Business we are engaged in, and with you sincerely wish that final arrangements may take place to the mutual satisfaction of both parties, which would inevitably secure to us every advantage that can possibly be drawn from the Business.[4]

The Astorians closed this letter by saying that when Thompson arrived they had been on the point of setting out to meet their friends who were coming across the continent by land. The remark was untrue. They did not expect Hunt before October at the earliest, and their casual allusion to David Stuart's three new pirogues, which Thompson certainly had seen, was probably designed to deceive the Nor'Wester about the purpose of the upriver trip.

Thompson was not taken in. And although he was unusually religious for the time and place, he was not above duplicity of his own. Only a week before he had posted a claim stake for his company and a flag for his country at the junction of the Snake and Columbia, yet he now blandly stated (according to the recollections of clerk Gabriel Franchère) that if the Astorians wanted the country they could have it;

"the wintering partners [of the North West Company] had resolved to abandon all their trading posts west of the mountains, not to enter into competition with us, provided our company could engage not to encroach upon their commerce to the east side."[5] Furthermore, Thompson continued, he had just been through the bleak country and could not say much in its favor. Furs were scarce, dangers great.

The Astorians were not naïve. The two Indians who had arrived a month earlier with Finan McDonald's letter had told an entirely different tale about the furs along the upper river. McDougall and the Stuarts quite probably gauged Thompson's contradictory report for what it was: an attempt to discourage them from invading the upper country. In other words, they realized that although Thompson might turn out to be a partner west of the Cascades, he and his company were going to fight to control the entire trade farther inland. To show that they accepted the challenge, the Astorians went right ahead loading David Stuart's canoes with trade goods. When Thompson started back upstream, Stuart's party went along with him.

Either at the beginning of the trip or shortly thereafter the two letter-bearing Indians, who had posed at Astoria as man and wife, appealed to Thompson for help in getting back to the head of the river. He was dumfounded. Man and wife nothing! The "husband" was a Kootenai squaw. Three years earlier she had been living with one of his voyageurs and he had thrown her out of camp for her loose morals. Her tribe refused to have her back, so she wandered off to other bands. Somehow she had set herself up as a prophetess. Declaring her sex changed, she adopted male clothing and took a "wife." Early in 1811 she had turned up at Spokan House. To get rid of her, Finan McDonald had given her a bogus letter to John Stuart. Instead of searching for Stuart, the pair had journeyed to the mouth of the river, perhaps hoping to encounter trading ships. Since arriving they had been trying to frighten the Chinooks around Astoria by predicting dire diseases which they said they could control. The Chinooks decided to meet the threat not by buying them off but by slaying them. Now the pair wanted Thompson's protection as they traveled back to their own people. He proved uncordial and so they attached themselves to David Stuart's small party of eight, but ranged far and wide between camps, especially after they had secured horses east of the Cascade Mountains.

Thompson traveled with Stuart's group until they reached the Cascade rapids. There Stuart's canoes proved too heavy for his men to carry and he had to hire Indians who, halfway through the portage, drew daggers and exacted extra tribute in the form of tobacco. Thompson's canoe was light enough for his men to handle. Not needing to depend on the savages, he pushed on to the junction of the Snake and Columbia, obtained horses, and cut overland to Spokan House. When Stuart reached the confluence a few days later, he found the famous claim stake. Indians camped nearby added force to its pretensions by trying to divert him eastward up the Snake—at Thompson's behest, he was sure. Well, the Nor'Westers could not have the whole upper Columbia *that* easily. Stubbornly he pushed on up the main river to the mouth of the Okanogan.

Liking the brown, treeless, sun-smitten spot, he built out of driftwood the Pacific Fur Company's first inland trading fort. Resorting to the eastern custom of maintaining only small parties in the interior, he sent four of the men back to Astoria. With three others he set out to explore the headwaters of the Okanogan. He expected to be back in a month, to relieve Alexander Ross, who was left alone at the cabin. Snow trapped the explorers. They could not return until March, and Ross wolfed out the winter alone. By his own account he bartered trade goods worth $170 for furs that in Canton would bring $12,000. And in the north, where Kamloops, British Columbia, now stands, David Stuart found another fine location for a post. No wonder Thompson had been eager to keep them away!

Affairs at Astoria developed less prosperously. The throngs of light-fingered Indians, who at first had been an almost unbearable nuisance, drifted away. The emptiness worried the whites. Something was afoot. A few savages who remained friendly confirmed the suspicion. The local tribes were planning to attack the fort before it could be completed and were delaying only long enough to enlist allies from among other tribes visiting the estuary to fish for sturgeon. Alarmed to energy by the report, the whites finished the stockade, built bastions at opposite corners and hauled in four-pound cannon. They made a show of practicing rifle shooting and posted sentinels at night. One-eyed Chief Concomly, who posed as a friend, asked that Robert Stuart and Gabriel Franchère visit him and help cure his sore throat; but an Indian friend of Stuart's said it was a sham, and the two whites stayed at home.

Disaster struck not at Astoria, however, but at the *Tonquin*. Vague rumors that the ship had been lost trickled in along the Indian grapevine and then were confirmed by the interpreter whom Captain Thorn had picked up just outside the Columbia's mouth. He said that Thorn's arrogance had enfuriated the savages of Clayoquot Sound on Vancouver Island. By a stratagem they overwhelmed the ship, killed the captain, partner Alexander McKay, and the entire crew save for five sailors who managed to barricade themselves in the hold. When the triumphant Indians withdrew during the night, four of the survivors tried to escape in the longboat but were captured and tortured to death. The fifth, who had been wounded too seriously to join the flight, prepared in the *Tonquin's* hold a monstrous booby trap from 9000 pounds of gunpowder. When the ship was swarming again with Indians the next day, he blew the lot, himself included, into fragments.

The men at Astoria were stunned. Twelve whites and seventeen Hawaiians had died in the debacle. The company had lost a veteran partner, necessary goods and provisions, its chief contact with the outside world, and any hope of profit for a long time to come. The Indians' victory was certain to rouse savages everywhere along the coast to increased truculence. Until Hunt's overland party arrived and a new supply ship appeared from New York, there was little the marooned traders at Astoria could do other than sit tight and hope.

Food ran short. The Indians who once had supplied the post with fish and elk meat withdrew to their villages for winter. To find a new source of provisions Robert Stuart embarked with a small party in the newly completed thirty-ton schooner *Dolly,* whose frame had been brought to the river aboard the *Tonquin.* The foragers fell to quarreling and in another fit of leonine temper young Stuart ordered the insubordinate part of the crew back to Astoria. Short-handed though this left him, he nevertheless collected enough foodstuffs to avert hunger for a time. He also heard of the beaver-rich valley of the Willamette, and on December 5 left with a few men to explore it.

Perhaps he was back in time to join the dismal celebration with which the post welcomed the New Year of 1812. At sunrise, drums and cannon fire launched a day of games. Puddings and extra rum enlivened the main meal, and the night was spent in dancing—without female partners, or so says Washington Irving after research among men who might not have been willing to admit for print what kind of female solace they did have. Until New Year's there had been no lack of venereal-tainted Chinook squaws.

Underneath the forced gaiety a fresh alarm was growing. Hunt's land party was overdue. Had some disaster struck it down too?

CHAPTER *10*

And by Land

Hunt's winter camp at the mouth of the Nodaway in north-western Missouri was unpleasant. Although Crooks, McClellan, and Miller carried on some trade with Indians as far away as the Platte, most of the men were idle. Several hunters whose rifles might be necessary to force a way past the Sioux grew disgruntled and vanished.[1] The need to replace them gave Hunt one more urgent reason for going to St. Louis. He had planned the trip anyhow, to pick up last-minute dispatches from Astor, to find if possible a good Sioux interpreter, and to meet John Bradbury and Thomas Nuttall, English naturalists whom he had agreed to take up the river with the party in the spring.

He began the 450-mile trip with eight men on January 1, 1811, exactly one year before the gloomy New Year's Day celebration at Astoria. He had to start afoot, perhaps on snowshoes, for the river was frozen and no Indians had visited the Nodaway camp with horses for sale. At Fort Osage he was able to obtain three riding animals. He sent six of his engagés back to the Nodaway, and with the other two continued to St. Louis, arriving January 20—excellent time. He stayed until the middle of March. Recruiting men could hardly have absorbed that many days, even though Lisa again threw obstacles in his way, and the presumption is that he was waiting for letters from Astor.

Letterbook copies of those that at length did arrive have not survived, but it is reasonable to suppose they brought word of fur-trade developments in the East which might affect operations on the Pacific. In October 1810, for example, Astor had ordered exceptional amounts of merchandise in England. Some of the goods he planned to send to

the Columbia aboard his favorite ship the *Beaver,* as soon as she returned in the summer of 1811 from a routine trip to China. But the
bulk of the articles were intended for the trade south of the Great
Lakes. He knew the Montrealers would hear from their London associates of his English orders; he knew too they would learn that he
had been making offers to experienced traders on Michilimackinac
Island; and he intended that they should worry about these maneuvers
as they prepared the Montreal-Michilimackinac Company for its own
first year of business within the United States.

Napoleon unwittingly applied more pressure. The French emperor
suggested to American ministers in Europe that he was on the point
of removing his restrictions against neutral shipping. If these restrictions
were revoked, then the United States was bound by the terms of Macon's
Bill No. 2 to end commerce with Britain while maintaining it with
France. President Madison was warned that Napoleon's good faith in
dangling this bait was not above question. In November 1810, nevertheless, at about the time Hunt had been nearing the Nodaway, the
President issued a proclamation stating that if the British government
had not, by February 2, 1811, matched the French in removing its
restrictions on shipping, then all commerce between Great Britain and
the United States would cease.

The proclamation placed the Montreal-Michilimackinac Company in
jeopardy. Their own goods, like Astor's, were already on order and
would leave England before the suppliers there could learn definitely
whether or not the embargo was to be invoked. If it was imposed,
they could not take these goods to Michilimackinac Island and their
trade for the ensuing season would be sorely hurt. On the other hand,
if England complied with the American demands—but that seemed too
thin a chance on which to risk a year's business.

Once again an alliance with Astor seemed the only escape. Always
before, no matter what the embargo, United States citizens had been
able to move at least some trade goods into the wilderness. It seemed
reasonable to suppose that Astor could do so again. Swallowing their
pride, they sent William McGillivray once more to New York City to
talk terms.

Circumstances had changed since the abortive discussions of the preceding year. At that time Astor had been interested in joining the
Montreal firms on the Lakes in order to secure their cooperation on the
Pacific. When the Non-Intercourse Acts had been relaxed, they had
grown toplofty and had backed off, needing him no longer. He had
sent out a ship and land party anyway, which perhaps had surprised
them. In an effort to check him, the Nor'Westers had then stepped up
their appeals to their government. On November 10, 1810, Simon
McGillivray, the London representative of McTavish, McGillivrays (note

plural) and Company, November 10, 1810, waited on the Earl of Liverpool to urge that the navy send a warship to the Columbia immediately. If the government furnished that protection, then the company would send traders overland to establish forts and stop Astor. Haste, Simon McGillivray argued, was essential, for the ultimate possession of the entire Northwest might hang in balance. Once again, however, the English government refused to make a public cause out of a private commercial rivalry.

Through his agents Astor was aware of the North West Company's actions. Undisturbed, he continued his own countermeasures. Even while William McGillivray was in New York to discuss some sort of agreement for the Lakes trade, Astor was writing out detailed instructions for his son-in-law, Adrian Bentzon, to take to St. Petersburg in an effort to conclude terms with the Russian American Fur Company for dividing the trade of the Northern Pacific. Bentzon was to try to persuade the Russian government to remove its duties on certain furs in favor of the American Fur Company. Such a concession, Astor wrote, would "encourage [the company] greatly in opposing with vigour the dangerous rival of both Russian and american enterprise in this quarter, the Canada Company— We would thereby be enabled to prevent them completely from extending themselves to the Northwest coast."

Believing the proposal stood a good chance of acceptance, Astor coolly informed William McGillivray that any agreement between him and the Montreal supply houses would not include either the Columbia watershed or the Missouri. The last exclusion must have been a bitter pill. Although the laws of Missouri Territory barred aliens from the river, the Canadians had maintained a hold of sorts through traders who could assert American citizenship. Aird, for instance, was again wintering on the Missouri for the Montreal-Michilimackinac Company; and the Montrealers must have hoped that through Astor they could extend the operations. He refused, and for the sake of the rest of the trade McGillivray had to submit.

As a final rub Astor refused to pay one cent for a share in the company, although less than three years before he had offered $550,000 for the firm's predecessor. Now he simply offered his citizenship and connections as the equivalent of the experience and good will which the Canadians around the Lakes had built up during decades of effort.

McGillivray accepted that, too, and they settled down to implementing a joint organization to be known as the South West Company. The new firm was to last for five years, beginning April 1, 1811. The Montreal men paid six sixteenths of the price of the goods, canoes, warehouses and other Great Lakes properties belonging to the old Montreal-Michilimackinac Company. Astor paid the remaining ten sixteenths. Goods and property were then turned over to the new South West

Company. Thereafter half of each year's merchandise was to be imported through New York and half through Canada, "unless from political or other events it shall hereafter be found for mutual benefit to vary the proportion"—the hedge for which McGillivray was paying so high a price.

Other clauses discussed accounting procedures, the sale of furs—some through London and some through New York—and the sending of agents to Mackinac Island to represent both Astor and the Montreal houses concerned (Forsyth, Richardson & Co. and McTavish, McGillivrays & Co.). As soon as practical the North West Company was to surrender to the South West Company its posts within the United States, principally along the south shore of Lake Superior and around the headwaters of the Mississippi. The South West Company agreed in turn to send no traders into Canada, except for two or three posts held by the old Montreal-Michilimackinac Company on the eastern shore of Lake Huron.

A curious proviso was then worked into the agreement. Astor and the Montreal firms were each to supply one half of the merchandise needed by the South West Company traders—unless the trading factories maintained by the United States Government were abolished. There were seven factories which in one way or another might hurt the business of the new firm—at Sandusky, Ohio; Fort Wayne, Indiana; Chicago, Michilimackinac Island, Green Bay, Fort Madison on the Mississippi and Fort Osage on the Missouri. Astor evidently thought that he could do something about eliminating them. If he succeeded, then his returns through the South West Company would rise appreciably: he would supply two thirds of the merchandise and would market two thirds of the furs. It was the beginning of a long struggle against government competition which, though delayed by the War of 1812, would outlive the South West Company and reach its climax under Ramsay Crooks a dozen years later.

The agreement establishing the South West Company was signed January 28, 1811. The goods that had been ordered by Astor and by the Canadians the preceding fall were thereupon consigned through Montreal to British-held St. Joseph Island in the strait between Lakes Huron and Superior. From St. Joseph the merchandise could be taken directly to Michilimackinac if no embargo followed. If restrictions followed, then Astor was to apply, as an American citizen, for an exemption. That much of the business was patently a subterfuge. The traders in the field were to be, almost without exception, the same British citizens who had worked earlier for Robert Dickson, for the Michilimackinac Company, and, during a single season, for the Montreal-Michilimackinac firm. Many American frontiersmen, on learning of the Mackinac traders' new disguise, were enraged by it and would stay enraged for years, to the discomfiture of Crooks and Robert Stuart when, after the war, they tried to Americanize the fur commerce of the United States.

Six months later, on July 15, 1811, the wintering partners of the North West Company agreed, at their Fort William rendezvous, to purchase one third of the interest which the two Montreal supply houses held in the South West Company. By the terms of the agreement establishing the South West Company, the Nor'Westers were now officially Astor's allies in the East—and his competitors in the West.

News of the actual signing at Fort William could not have reached Wilson Hunt in St. Louis. Yet the possibility must have been recognized during Astor's discussions with William McGillivray, and the results of those discussions were almost certainly dispatched to Hunt, for it was important for him to know that on the Pacific no holds would be barred.

Under such circumstances, Astor naturally wanted an American, not a former Nor'Wester, in charge. He therefore reaffirmed Hunt's command of the overland party. According to Alexander Ross, the letter announcing the decision gave great umbrage to Donald McKenzie, the veteran Canadian trapper who was traveling overland with the American. Bitterly Ross adds that delivering the party to an inexperienced St. Louis storekeeper was the cause of its later difficulties in the wilderness. Perhaps so. But, granting Astor's inordinate caution, what other choice could he have made?

Hunt's troubles began even before he reached the *pays sauvage*. The additional hunters he managed to hire in St. Louis were frightened off by the appearance of still more deserters from the Nodaway camp. He clashed with Lisa over the interpreter he needed to help with the Sioux—Pierre Dorion, Jr., another half-breed son of the Pierre Dorion whom we noticed earlier taking Sioux to Washington for Lewis and Clark. Although young Dorion had violated his contract with the St. Louis Missouri Fur Company in a quarrel over a liquor bill, Hunt hired him to go all the way to the Pacific and even agreed to take Dorion's Iowa Indian wife Marie and their two children with the party. Either the young interpreter was a mighty good man or Hunt was growing desperate.

At the last minute he lined up a few hunters and on March 12 started his boat toward the mouth of the Missouri. The two English-born naturalists whom he had promised to take up the river with the company, middle-aged John Bradbury and young Thomas Nuttall, somehow learned that Lisa intended to recover Dorion's services by suing out a writ for debt. They left St. Louis at 2 A.M. with the alarm and reached St. Charles about noon. Dorion and his squaw fled into the woods, escaped attachment and, after a stormy family quarrel of their own, rejoined the boat farther upstream.

A little above La Charette, where Ramsay Crooks had first met Lewis and Clark, they paused for a long talk with one of Lewis' and Clark's most famous hunters, John Colter, recently returned from his trapping adventures at the head of the Missouri. With ominous headshakings Colter told them of the furies of the Blackfeet, who the preceding summer had driven Lisa's partner, Andrew Henry, from the Three Forks country in Montana to refuge somewhere west of the Continental Divide. In Colter's opinion, Hunt would be well advised to avoid that area and try to find a safer way across the Rockies.

Shortly thereafter Dorion picked up alarms nearer at hand. Osage war parties were roaming the neighborhood, searching for Iowas and Sacs. A small party of whites might look like a tempting substitute. The frightened voyageurs checked their arms and Hunt posted sentinels around the camp at night. The fears did not keep the two naturalists from wandering along the banks with the hunters. One evening they lost themselves, and Hunt had to stuff dry weeds into a hollow tree and light a dazzling beacon to guide them back.

On the morning of April 8 the travelers sighted triangular little Fort Osage on its river-girt bluff. A flag went up, and as they neared the short loading dock, rifle fire added its chatter to the welcome. A swarm of Indians, soldiers, and traders crowded around to hear what probably was their first news from the outside that spring. Among the greeters was Ramsay Crooks. He had boated down from the Nodaway with nine men, either to break the boredom or to apprehend deserters or possibly to deliver furs for shipment to St. Louis by the fort's supply barges.

During the two-day layover he and the post's doctor introduced the naturalists to the corrupted edges of the American frontier. Just outside the fort's stockade stood an odorous village of Osage Indians—small round or oblong frames covered by rush mats. Waving from sticks on the chief's house were seven fresh Iowa scalps. These caused periodic whoops of exultation, late dances, drum beatings, and arrogant struttings among the bucks. Even more disturbing to sleep were the unearthly predawn lamentations that were customary among the tribe. Someone waking in the darkness would remember a dead spouse or child, a vanished horse or dog, and would begin to wail. As others were wakened, they joined the ululation. Hundreds of dogs chimed in and rest was shattered for miles around.

Although the Osages were taller and more muscular than some of the other native tribes, visitors did not find them prepossessing. Another naturalist, Henry Brackenridge, who reached the village with Lisa two weeks behind Hunt and Bradbury, wrote that the savages had "a filthy, greasy appearance," wore nothing but a loincloth and dirty buffalo robe, and spotted themselves unattractively with vermilion. The women were dirtier than the men, morally as well as physically. Bradbury sniffed that they joked among themselves with appalling obscenity. All the young ones seemed willing to prostitute themselves among the voyageurs, the standard rate being a handful of blue beads worth $1.50 for themselves and scalping knives worth fifty cents each for their husbands or fathers. Hunt's men paid the price eagerly, drawing the articles from the boat's stores in spite of Hunt's remonstrances and charging the cost against their wages of $80 to $100 a year.

On April 10 the party resumed its voyage, twenty-six strong with the addition of Crooks's men. For four straight days the wind favored them. The only disturbance came when Dorion began abruptly to beat his squaw; he had refused to let her stay at Fort Osage and her pouting got on his nerves. Then the weather began to storm as well—contrary winds and drenching rains. To avoid the full thrust of the spring current, the boats crept behind islands and sandbars, sometimes grounding so that the men had to leap overboard and drag them free. At each promontory the force of the water was such that they had to cross to the far side of the channel and search for gentler eddies. They struggled around mats of driftwood and watched apprehensively for sawyers—monstrous snags caught to the river bottom and seesawing on the current with violence enough to impale the stoutest craft. Clay banks were continually crumbling; trees collapsed; even a man's campground might threaten to disappear from under his feet. Putrefying corpses of dead buffalo lodged in stinking heaps against the driftwood or floated soggily in the backwaters, attended by hordes of vultures. Mosquitoes and agonizing sunburn were routine. And yet when the steersman started a song, the indefatigable French Canadians always managed to answer with a ringing shout, take a fresh grip on the oars, and keep the boats moving ahead.

On April 17 they reached the Nodaway camp, a few rough cabins set back against the bluffs. On the twenty-first they moved on, through rains, under enormous flocks of passenger pigeons, sixty persons now, traveling in three barges and a large keelboat that mounted a swivel gun and two small cannon. Toward the end of the month they passed the Platte. At night they saw the glow of prairie fires set by war parties covering a retreat. In spite of this warning, Crooks decided to risk the spring-bright land. He was bored by the slow progress of the boats through the coils of the river and suggested to Bradbury that they walk ahead to his and McClellan's trading house near Council Bluffs.

The foot journey went so well that next they decided to strike inland to the bend of the Platte, collect credits due Crooks from the Otos after the winter's trade, and then overtake the boats several score miles to the north at the Maha village. They impressed two voyageurs as auxiliaries. Each man loaded himself with eighty bullets, a full powder-horn, a knife and tomahawk, and blanket. Bradbury carried a portfolio for bringing back plant specimens; the Canadians lugged a few pounds of dried meat and a single kettle for cooking it in.

Crooks led west at a fast walk. They spent the first night on the banks of the Elkhorn River, crossed it the next dawn on a raft they had built, and came unerringly onto the Platte opposite the earthen huts of the Oto village. By Bradbury's calculation they had walked forty-five miles, apparently for nothing. Although the shallow river was half a mile wide at that point and details in the village were hard to discern, no Indians were evident. To make sure, they fired their rifles in unison. An answering shot came from a brushy island a little downstream. They waded out to it, up to their armpits at times, and found two traders hiding with their goods from a rumored war party of Pawnees. The Otos, the traders said, were at a hunting camp about twenty miles away.

One of the wilderness merchants, a man named Rogers, had some sort of connection with Crooks. He volunteered to visit the Oto camp and collect what credits he could. The next day he returned with a single horse which already belonged to Crooks. This hardly made the hike worth while, but Crooks decided they would have to go on empty-handed in order to catch the boats at the Maha village.

Rogers' wife was a Maha. He asked if she and her small child could travel with the whites. Crooks agreed, put the two on the horse, and started north. The squaw soon fell into panics. She quit the horse at the Elkhorn and swam across the river on her own power, the child clinging to her long hair. As soon as she reached the other shore she wanted to go back and rejoin her husband. One of the disgusted voyageurs escorted her and did not rejoin the group until two o'clock the following morning.

Not long afterward the excitable Canadians opened fire on a herd of elk. The animals stampeded unscathed—and so did the single horse. They tossed its useless saddle into a creek, shouldered their gear and walked on. That night a fantastic electrical storm bombarded them. They covered their powder with the kettle, rolled themselves in their blankets, and all night lay flat on the bald plains while lightning crashed around them. At dawn they wrung out their soaked buckskin clothing and hobbled on to restore circulation. They passed the hilltop grave of Chief Blackbird, and ten days after leaving the main party limped into the Maha village. The boats were four miles upstream at Aird's post, swapping beads and vermilion for foodstuffs.

The trade completed, they labored on against the spring flood. Near the mouth of the Niobrara River, in northeastern Nebraska, a chattering gang of Ponca Indians appeared with two messengers from Manuel Lisa. One was a half-breed. The other was Toussaint Charbonneau, husband of Sacajawea, the famous Shoshone "Bird Woman" who had gone with him and with Lewis and Clark to the Pacific. Charbonneau and Sacajawea had then tried farming near St. Louis. There the young Indian woman had grown homesick and now they were returning to the Minnetaree villages, Charbonneau as an employee of the St. Louis Missouri Fur Company.

Lisa had left St. Louis nineteen days after Hunt in a specially built keelboat manned by twenty chosen voyageurs and carrying as a passenger still another journal-keeping naturalist, Henry Brackenridge. From his own experience Lisa knew how dangerous the Sioux could be. He also knew that Crooks and McClellan blamed him for having set those Indians on them two years before. Fearing they might try to repay him in kind, he hoped to overtake the Astorians before they reached the Sioux, quell suspicion, and travel in force with them through the territory of the unfriendly savages. By driving his men frantically, he cut Hunt's lead from nineteen days to four. But when he reached the Maha village, he learned that the advance party had left it under sail—in other words, traveling fast.

Fast meant river time, not land time. The Missouri twisted prodigiously. By short-cutting its bends (as Crooks and Bradbury had done after their side jaunt to the Oto village), good walkers could overtake Hunt before he reached the Sioux and ask him to wait. Charbonneau and the half-breed were delegated to carry the message; they reached the Ponca settlement near the Niobrara without incident.

Crooks and McClellan objected violently to Lisa's proposal. In their minds Lisa was not to be trusted. If he got ahead of them he might cook up some devilment among the Sioux or Aricaras. Besides, his opposition in St. Louis had not entitled him to consideration. The thing to do was to give him a taste of his own medicine: lull him into slowing down by promising to wait at the Ponca village, then use the respite to race ahead and shake the Spaniard for good. Back Charbonneau went with the pledge, not knowing that it was false.

If knowledge of the plot leaked to Hunt's voyageurs, and it is difficult to believe it did not, they must have been distressed. They wanted reinforcements. Both the Mahas and the Poncas had warned that the Sioux were in a dangerous frame of mind. Now along came the very man who a year before had helped stir their anger—Alexander Carson, traveling downstream in a log canoe with Benjamin Jones, another ex-employee of the St. Louis Missouri Fur Company. Yes, Carson admitted, he'd killed himself a Sioux the summer before. He had been standing with some Aricaras on one bank of the Missouri when a group of Sioux had appeared on the other bank. They had waved insults back and forth; Carson had snapped a rifle shot just for the hell of it. He had not expected to hit anyone—the river was half a mile wide—but by luck, good or bad depending on a man's viewpoint, one of the Indians had dropped. The enraged tribe had slain three whites in revenge and were said to be lying in wait for whatever group came along next.

The threat worried Hunt. Whatever advantage he might gain through Dorion's interpreting was likely to be offset by the presence of Crooks, McClellan, and Miller; for the Indians had not forgotten how those three had hoodwinked them two years before, tying up their guards and vanishing with the desirable trade goods the whites had promised to barter. Force, not cajolery, might well be the only way to pass the savages. Yet desertions had continued to plague the Astorians as they fought the river. If Lisa's rifles were to be rejected, then Hunt needed to pick up any other help he could find. In desperation he hired the very pair the Sioux would most resent, Alexander Carson and Benjamin Jones.

To shake Lisa he crowded on sail whenever the wind served. The voyageurs grew more and more terrified. When the boats heeled under the strain, they cried, "O mon Dieu, abbattez le gale." When they thought of Sioux, they crossed themselves fervently. The leaders sought the safety of islands for each night's camp, and even the stolid American hunters scoured game off the brushy bars rather than risk the exposed, almost treeless riverbank.

On May 26 they hired three more white trappers—John Hoback, Jacob Reznor and Edward Robinson. Like Carson and Jones, the new trio had worked the upper river for Lisa's company. They had been at Three Forks when Blackfeet had struck and had fled with Andrew Henry across the Continental Divide to the headwaters of the Snake. They confirmed everything that John Colter had already said at La Charette: white men trying to cross to the Columbia through the lands of those implacable savages were certain to suffer.

The result was an ironic inversion of fears. As the boats drew near the terrible Sioux, the leaders laid plans for avoiding the distant Blackfeet. At a camp on Cedar Island (near today's Chamberlain, South Dakota), Hunt decided to press no farther up the Missouri than the Aricara villages. The Aricaras were horse traders. If he could buy enough pack animals from them, he would transfer the expedition to horseback and strike due west, aiming for a pass in the Rockies which Hoback, Reznor and Robinson said they could guide him to.

The Sioux could not be so easily dodged. Soon several hundred warriors appeared on the high banks, near which the current soon would force the boats. A spyglass revealed that only a few of the savages carried firearms, and the Astorians decided to try a bluff. They loaded the swivel gun and small cannons on the keelboats with as much powder as they could stuff in and fired them with the loudest bang the savages had ever heard. While the Sioux were still disconcerted by the unexpected crash, the voyageurs headed the boats straight toward the bank. The hunters ostentatiously aimed their rifles, and in a sudden fading of truculence some of the Indians began waving their buffalo robes in a signal for peace.

Under cover of the hunters' rifles, the leaders of the party—Hunt, McKenzie, Crooks, McClellan and Miller, accompanied by Bradbury and Dorion—landed for a council with fourteen of the principal Sioux. A peace pipe of red stone, its six-foot stem decorated with dyed horsehair, made the rounds. Hunt calmed the economic nerves of the Indians by saying he was going far to the west and would not trade with their enemies upriver. He passed out some presents and although some of the savages continued to follow along, yelling threats, the general tension melted enough that Crooks and McClellan even embraced the chiefs of the party they had hoodwinked two years before.

A little later they fell in with a wandering war party of Aricaras and Mandans. That summer, for a change, the Aricaras were at peace with the whites. While the white men and red were holding the usual ceremonials of brotherhood, they were astounded to see Lisa's keelboat laboring around a bend below them. The indefatigable Spaniard had guessed that something was amiss when he reached the Ponca villages and learned that Hunt had broken his pledge to wait. In a passion of effort he set out to catch him. One night he risked grounding to travel by moonlight. In an exhausting twenty-four-hour period he drove his men a phenomenal seventy-five miles. The ordeal brought unexpected dividends. The Sioux did not see him. Either they were not expecting him so soon and had left the river to search for game, or he had passed their camp unnoticed during the night.

In spite of McClellan's noisy threat to shoot the Spaniard on sight, no breach occurred until a few days later, when adverse winds pinned the five boats to the riverbank. During the enforced pause, the old quarrel between Dorion and Lisa erupted. Before it was over they were facing each other with pistols, Hunt was holding back Crooks and McClellan, and the voyageurs were ranged behind the principals, waiting to see which way to jump. Lisa sneered at Hunt's peacemaking. Hunt lost his temper and shouted back an offer to duel. At that point the naturalists of the two parties returned from a joint ramble and managed to pull the adversaries apart.

From that point on the parties rowed sullenly up opposite sides of the river, communicating only through the naturalists. Late in the morning of June 10, after a night of lightning and heavy rain, they neared the Aricara villages, 150 oval dirt lodges clustered on the south side of the river in two towns eighty yards apart. Each cluster was surrounded by a dry moat and a ramshackle barricade of pickets nine feet tall. High, barren hills rose to the rear. Few trees were visible anywhere. Squaws kneeling in round little boats made of hide paddled toward home with driftwood tied behind their fragile craft.

The whites landed on the north bank, opposite the lower village. Each group suspected that if the other reached the Indians first, it would stir up animosity against its rival. Accordingly the naturalists arranged for the leaders of each party to visit the chiefs together. With stiff politeness they filed one after another through the low, tunnel-like door-way of the principal lodge and took seats on the rush mats and buffalo robes scattered around the sunken fireplace. Their host bawled directions up through the smoke hole to a crier, who shouted invitations across the village. About twenty chiefs assembled. While the Astorians watched suspiciously, Lisa made the first speech. At once tension relaxed. The Spaniard furthered Hunt's aims (and also helped get the Astorians away from the river) by urging the Indians to trade horses to him so that his party could continue west by land.

Peace restored, the whites settled down below the lower village for a long session of bargaining. They soon grew hungry. In normal seasons there might have been a surplus of dried vegetables. Like the women of all the sedentary tribes along the Missouri, the Aricara squaws raised a surplus of beans, pumpkins, and maize in gardens a little distance outside the stockades. This surplus the men traded in part to the nomads of the plains for furs and horses. The rest they cached in cellars to use later in the summer when buffalo withdrew and the new crops were not yet ripe. But that year unusually heavy rains had flooded some of the storehouses and spoiled the contents. Fear of the Sioux kept hunting parties from ranging far, and food for the whites was limited to substitutes they did not particularly relish. One was bloated buffalo corpses which the Indians dragged out of the river and ate with gusto. The other was dogmeat from the packs that roamed snarling throughout the town, some destined for the cooking pot and some for pulling sleds the next winter.

The towns were filthy. There were no streets, the lodges being placed at random. Rains mixed the ground and the offal that lay wherever it was tossed into a noisome bog. The Indians were no more cleanly. The men greased, painted, and gummed their long hair into tufts—it hung almost to their heels and many of them increased its length by at-taching horsehair. A later trader, Edwin Denig, who disliked the Aricaras, described with gloomy relish the vermin that "pastured" in these profuse locks.

On almost any fine day, a stranger promenading in their village will see hundreds of lazy men lying down [on the earthen rooftops] with their heads in the laps of their wives, who . . . pick off and smash with their teeth enormous crawlers, retaining the same in their mouth until enough is collected to spit it out in the shape of a ball as large as a good-sized walnut.

Traders were convinced that the Aricara had the loosest sexual mores on the continent. They were indiscriminately incestuous. Denig declined to do more than allude to the rites that accompanied their corn-planting ceremonies. A full description "would serve only to show men in the lowest state of animal degredation." And then he went on:

There are neither handsome men or women among them. The former have sharp, sneaking, thieving looks . . . The latter coarse features, thick lips, short and thick set persons. Both young and old of either sex are more or less tainted with venereal disease. This also makes its appearance in their children in the form of scrofula and other cutaneous eruptions, and these know no end.

Hunt's voyageurs were a match for them, nevertheless. They assured each other that since the Aricaras did not use either alcohol or salt, the diseases were mild. So why worry? Every evening, according to Bradbury, the Aricara men led wives, sisters, and daughters to the white camps for barter. Hunt protested, but many of the voyageurs drew in advance their entire salaries; one fellow divested himself of his clothing to buy what he desired. The lustiness aroused the wonder of even the Aricaras. One chief asked Brackenridge a question that became well exploited among later novelists. Did the white people have no women of their own? Was that the reason they acted as they did among the Indians?

Barter for horses went more slowly. Unlike the nomads of the plains, among whom horse stealing was an honorable profession, the Aricaras did not have a surplus of animals. They refused to part with good buffalo horses at a price Hunt could afford, and haggled endlessly over the second-rate mounts they did offer. Then Lisa came to the rescue by agreeing to trade several horses he owned at his fort near the Minnetarees for Hunt's boats and a quantity of merchandise.

Crooks was sent for the animals. He went on horseback with five men, including Bradbury, although Sioux war parties roamed the neighborhood and Manuel Lisa was starting up the river by boat that same day. Perhaps Crooks thought his party could go faster overland; perhaps the keelboat was too crowded for additional passengers. Or perhaps he preferred risking Sioux to traveling in close company with his old enemy.

It was an exhausting ride. Unable to secure food to take with them, the party had to depend on whatever game they encountered en route. They went at a jolting trot in crude wooden Indian saddles, concealing themselves from war parties by winding in and out of rough ravines.

They did not eat until noon of the second day, when they killed a
deer. Thereafter buffalo abounded. In spite of protests by Crooks and
Bradbury, the engagés shot the animals wantonly, letting them lie untouched where they fell.

On the fourth day they reached the Mandan villages. There they
paused to smoke and eat and shake hands with Shahaka, or Big White,
the chief whose return from Washington had caused the government
so much trouble. At sunset Crooks pressed them on. Just before dark
they reached the Knife River opposite one of the Minnetaree villages
and shouted for ferry service. Several Indian males swam across; six
squaws came in round skin boats. Each boat transported one white man
and his saddle. The Indians swam the horses over. And still the whites
had seven miles to ride to reach the fort. They arrived a little before
midnight, dead-tired from eighteen hours in the saddle. Mosquitoes
were so ferocious they could not sleep. Even the fort's horses fought
each other for choice positions in the dense smudge which the workers
built for them.

If Crooks had thought to gain time by riding, he learned better.
His party's riding horses were so jaded he had to let them recuperate.
Lisa arrived by keelboat before he could start back, traveling again by
forced marches. A little after his safe arrival at the Aricara camp, a
traveling village of Cheyennes appeared from somewhere off toward
the Black Hills of western South Dakota. Hunt bought a few more
horses from them. Now he had eighty-two head, enough for baggage
and provisions and for each partner to ride, but not enough for the
voyageurs. In obtaining them he had spent a month of valuable time
and dared wait no longer. On the assurance of the Cheyennes that he
could buy more horses at one of their villages in the west, he began
preparations to push on.

The men were ordered to discard all non-essentials and repack their
equipment for transport on horses. (Bradbury, who with the other naturalists left the party there, was able to buy seventeen trunks from
the Canadians for transporting his plant specimens.) They mended saddles, parched corn, pounded it and stowed it into bags. During the
hurried work a war party came marching triumphantly home in full
panoply, waving aloft several Sioux scalps. The villagers roared with
excitement, but the whites were so busy they scarcely noticed.

Each night a guard detail that included one of the partners paced
about the camp. In spite of it a cask of powder and a gun belonging to
Bradbury disappeared. Since Indians could not well have stolen the
material, some of the workers must have. This suggested a plot by an
unknown number to desert. Hunt sent the boats to Lisa's camp, where
they might be harder to steal. Under pretense of cheering the depart-
ing naturalists, he ordered the men into a line, then harangued them

earnestly about the powder, the future, and their *esprit de corps*. Afterwards one abashed Canadian came privately to his tent and confessed where the powder was buried.

Morale somewhat restored, Hunt gathered the party on the far side of the river. It made an impressive column—eighty-two horses, forty-five engagés, eleven hunters and guides, one clerk (John Reed), an Indian woman (Marie Dorion) and two children. On July 18, 1811, slowly and with the confusion of inexperience, the ungainly group crawled ahead to blaze a new trail across the West.

CHAPTER *11*

The Harrowing

Although water and game were plentiful and grass was knee-deep, the caravan spent a week advancing a meager seventy miles. Many men were sick, including Ramsay Crooks. Unable to sit his horse, he had to be dragged on a litter—the first recorded instance of a long sequence of unidentified illnesses that throughout the rest of his life would fell him at inconvenient times. By July 24 so many invalids were groaning on Hunt's hands that he halted for twelve days while they recuperated. During the pause hunters found a camp of Cheyenne Indians and from them he bought thirty-six more horses. When the party moved again on August 6, every two engagés had a riding horse to share. Crooks, though, was still too feeble to sit a saddle and for several more days was bounced along on a litter.

Speed picked up. On good days the caravan traveled as much as forty miles between camps. In general, they followed the Grand River due west just below the present border of North and South Dakota. Heading the stream, they traversed a corner of Montana, veered southwest into Wyoming, crossed the Powder River, and probably camped one night where the town of Buffalo now stands.

The country was arid. For weeks they had seen no trees save a few cottonwoods beside the streams. They learned to cook—they long since had divided for convenience into small messes—in classic Western fashion over dried buffalo manure. Grass on the long ridges was sparse. The coarse soil showed volcanic origins; the sun's heat was often intense (McKenzie's dog died of it); and the marchers often suffered from thirst. But when they did encounter water—they could see the white-topped peaks of the Big Horn Mountains ahead of them—it was bright and cold. And though the hunters were lost for one period in the bewildering immensities, the men in general ate well on limitless deer, buffalo, elk, and antelope.

It was not an unknown country even then. Frenchmen living with the Mandans and Minnetarees had visited northeastern Wyoming a quarter of a century earlier. At least one American knew its stream courses and its people, the Crow Indians. He was Edward Rose, a scarred mixture of white, Negro and Cherokee Indian blood. In 1807 Rose had traveled with Manuel Lisa's first expedition to the Yellowstone River. During the winter he was sent south into Wyoming with a load of trade goods to barter and to use for attracting Crow Indians with their furs to Lisa's new trading post at the confluence of the Bighorn River with the Yellowstone. He gave the goods away to achieve prestige among the savages and returned to the post empty-handed. Lisa, who was on the point of starting in a keelboat to St. Louis, flew at him in a fury. Rose methodically beat his employer until a trapper named Potts pulled them apart. As Lisa was boarding the keelboat, Rose tried to blow it apart with one of the fort's small cannon, failed, and decided he might as well rejoin the Crows. In spite of the altercation, he afterward worked a time for Lisa's partner, Andrew Henry, then drifted off to the Aricara villages, where Hunt hired him as a guide.

In some ways the Crows were the most amiable Indians of the plains. The men were tall and strapping, given to the usual barbaric decoration of long hair, feathers, and vermilion. (But the women, says Denig, were foul witches, as abandoned as the Aricara squaws.) The Crows boasted that they had never slain a white man. But they could not resist horseflesh and were known even among enemy tribes as the most adroit thieves on the prairies.

Hunt bought several animals from the first Crows the party met and then began to fret about keeping them. When an informer told him that Edward Rose planned to desert to the tribe with as many voyageurs as he could seduce and steal all the group's horses, the leader believed the tale. He bought Rose off by giving him half a year's salary for six weeks' work, a horse, three beaver traps and some merchandise. With nothing but verbal directions to guide them, the overlanders then worked on south of the Big Horn Mountains toward Wind River. Along the way the travelers were joined by eight Flathead and Snake Indians from west of the Rockies. Six of these nomads soon wandered off, but two more hung along near the whites and probably furnished more guidance than records reveal.[1]

By mid-September, nights in the Wind River region were nippy with frost and the leaders of the party began to worry about breaking clear of the mountains before snow caught them. To compound the problem, game vanished. Although the three trappers whom Hunt had hired on the Missouri (Hoback, Reznor and Robinson) wanted to continue up the Wind River and cross Togwotee Pass to Jackson Hole, Hunt was turned aside near present Dubois when someone (the two Snakes?) assured him that buffalo abounded across the divide on the Spanish River, today's Green. After a hard climb through the evergreens, the caravan emerged onto rolling, high-altitude meadows dotted with groves of spruce, the apex of what is now called Union Pass. In the distance, hazy with autumn, they glimpsed the snow-topped peaks of the Tetons, called Pilot Knobs by the trappers, who said that one of the sources of the Columbia surged past the eastern flanks of the peaks and then cut west through a howling canyon.

Today the river is called the Snake. (Hunt called it first Mad River, then Canoe River; other mountain men called it Lewis River.) The overlanders could easily have gone directly to it from Union Pass, but first they needed meat. Accordingly they continued south to the Green and followed it out of the mountains onto a vast sagebrush plain. Grass waved high in tributary valleys. They found a pleasant campsite, turned the weary horses loose to rest, and settled down to killing and butchering buffalo, slicing the meat thin and laying it on racks to dry under a cloudless sky.

Hunters reported a nearby Indian camp of conical skin tepees. Here was an opportunity to launch the trade they had come so far to establish. Hunt, Crooks, McClellan "and two other persons"—the two Snakes?—saddled up to pay a visit. The appearance of white men stampeded the savages. After a wild eight-mile pursuit the traders overtook one terrified pair, calmed them, and through them gained welcome to the village. Its inhabitants turned out to be Shoshone or Snakes.

Somehow (the two Snakes?) Hunt arranged to swap merchandise for a quantity of dried meat later estimated at two thousand pounds. The mobile village must have hummed with excitement when packhorses arrived bearing wealth more overwhelming than these distant savages had dreamed of before. In addition, Hunt and Crooks paid out more incredible treasure in cloth, knives, and bright beads for a few buffalo hides and beaver pelts. Then, as other whites had been doing since the day when Jacques Cartier had first nosed his ships into the St. Lawrence River, they promised that if the Indians would hunt diligently and procure more furs, other whites would return with even better goods.

The party's voyageurs meanwhile had dried another two tons of meat. Adding the provender to the group's normal equipment loaded every horse but six. Dragging the troublesome pack stock along with lead ropes, the displaced rivermen clambered over a high ridge to a turbulent stream named for John Hoback, who had trapped it the year before. "Abominable," Robert Stuart described the Hoback's rough gorge several months later. Each time Hunt's men splashed from one bank to the other to avoid the crowding cliffs, the current nearly battered them from their feet.

Sore-limbed and disgruntled, they reached the Snake on September 27. To their river-trained eyes, the broad rush of its green current looked like heaven and they were eager to hollow out log canoes and abandon their accursed pack animals. So was partner Joseph Miller, who was suffering from some unnamed ailment that made riding irksome. But scouts reported that the canyon ahead was unnavigable and that they would have to walk across at least one more mountain range. After waiting out an alarming sleet storm, they hiked disconsolately on, following the two Snake Indians (reference to them is at last specific) over what is now called Teton Pass, near today's Wyoming-Idaho border. Along the way they detached four trappers to work Jackson Hole to the north. After procuring as many pelts as they could handle, the quartet were to follow along to the mouth of the Columbia in the spring.

West of Teton Pass the overlanders came onto the lovely meadows that later trappers would call Pierre's Hole. But this group found no relish in the scenery. It was October 8. Gusts of snow blew against their bent heads as they trudged up to the deserted cabins which Andrew Henry had built the year before, after fleeing from the Blackfeet on the headwaters of the Missouri. The ramshackle buildings stood on the west bank of Henry's Fork of the Snake, a mile or two below the present-day town of St. Anthony, Idaho.

Surely—so the overlanders thought with the conviction of desire—surely the mountains were behind them at last. Eagerly they chopped down fifteen big cottonwoods and with fire and ax began shaping them into dugouts. During the work four more hunters departed to trap and learn the country—Hoback, Reznor, Robinson and Martin Cass. As they were saddling up, partner Joseph Miller decided to join them. The decision against canoes a week earlier had started him sulking. Now the canoes he had wanted were taking shape, but in the meantime the men who had gone against his wishes had become intolerable. In a fit of pique he gave up his shares in the company and rode off with the hunters as a common trapper. Their guides were the two Snake Indians. The savages promised that as soon as they had taken the trappers to good beaver ground they would return and guard the horses until a party came from Astoria for the animals the next spring.

On October 19, in a snowstorm, the travelers launched their fleet. They soon ran into the Snake and rejoiced. It was rushing south and southwest, not the direction they wanted, but the Indians said that it soon bent west and northwest. And it was a lovely stretch of water, a quarter of a mile wide, swift and generally smooth. Here and there a few rapids bounced them about, but nothing to alarm a trained voyageur. So for two blissful days. Then, on the twenty-first, near present-day Idaho Falls, perpendicular lava cliffs compressed the stream into a plunging cataract only sixty feet wide.

They were able to avoid the stretch by portaging the goods for a mile and a half. The heavy log canoes they let down through the white water at the ends of ropes, losing only one on the way. Then the cliffs dwindled; the current resumed its steady thrust, westward now in the direction they wanted to go. Hearts lightened, only to be betrayed by more deep lava troughs, more bawling rapids. One tumult that seemed no worse than the others troubled an otherwise placid stretch of stream west of Burley, in south-central Idaho. The lead canoe shot through without trouble. The second dugout, holding Crooks and four others, was not so lucky. In spite of the bourgeois' warning shout, the steersman, Antoine Clappine, let the pirogue ram into a boulder. The soft cottonwood split apart. Crooks and three voyageurs managed to flounder to the bank, but Clappine was drowned and many goods were lost.

Horrified by the accident, the party swung into shore and camped. What next? Ahead of them loomed the slit of another chasm. Could they get through that without more drownings? Two small groups of explorers trudged down both banks to see, Hunt himself leading the party that followed the north rim. The sight was appalling. The compressed river, once eight hundred yards broad in places, slammed over a narrow cascade into a monstrous whirlpool, and shot out of that through a roaring slot not forty feet wide. This terrifying stretch the explorers named Caldron Linn, after the Scottish word for a whirlpool at the base of a cataract. And that was just the beginning. The rent in the earth through which the river howled grew deeper and wilder.[2] If the voyageurs did succeed in portaging canoes around Caldron Linn, where could they reach the river again? In thirty-five miles (by his calculation) Hunt was able to crawl down to the river's edge at only two places. Even this was no gain. The water along the north bank was so furious that not even an empty canoe on a towline could live in it.

The explorers on the south bank returned a more hopeful report. The dugouts, they said, could be portaged six miles around the Linn and the river regained through a side gully. For a way at least the canoes could then be lined along the edge of the torrent.

Hunt was not convinced. From what he had seen of the canyon, he thought they had better quit the river entirely. If so, horses would help.[3] He sent John Reed and four men down the north bank to find Indians who might be able to supply the party with livestock and food. Reed might not succeed, of course. In that case it would be well to know exactly what the river did offer. Accordingly Hunt ordered sixteen voy-

ageurs to shoulder the four best canoes, lug them around the south
bank of Caldron Linn, and test the water below.

Whether the main group went ahead by canoe or by horse, it would
have to travel light. While awaiting reports, the men started to dig
caches in which to store all but the barest minimum of traps, powder,
and trade merchandise. Icy rain—it was October 31—fell in such torrents
that they had to give up the effort and huddle under blankets and
behind rocks. While they were in this dismal situation the sixteen voyageurs returned to report that river navigation was hopeless. They had
reached the stream, but on attempting to line the dugouts through the
canyon they had lost one with its cargo. The other three were stuck fast
among the boulders.

Soddenly they finished the caches, arguing the while about the next
move. They had to have horses, and suddenly Reed's party, which had
not yet returned, seemed far too small to be their sole dependence in
the unknown immensities. Other searchers must go out to supplement
the effort.

The scattering began November 2. Each partner led a group. McClellan and three men went down the side of the canyon opposite to the
one Reed was already exploring. McKenzie and four men started north
across the lava plains. Each party understood that if it found no Indians
it was not to return and burden the others, but was to keep traveling
toward the Columbia as best it could. Finally, as a desperate coppering
of bets, Crooks turned back upstream with five men, intending, if he
met no Indians, to retrieve the horse herd at Henry's Fort. During the
search Hunt and the bulk of the party—thirty-one men, Dorion's Indian
wife, and the two children—were to sit beside the river and wait for
whatever developed.[4]

Leadenly Crooks and his companions slogged eastward. Walking was
difficult—sand, rocks, rough side gullies, and miles of high, dense, knotted
sagebrush. Two days of toil thoroughly disheartened the men. At this
rate they could never reach the horses. Nor did it seem likely they
would find Indians capable of helping the party; at least the few savages
they had seen on their way down the river had been poverty-stricken
and too terrified even to give them directions, let alone concrete as-
sistance. Would it not be wise to use their strength going toward the
Columbia rather than back into the desolate Rockies, already whitened
by the nearness of winter?

Turning around, they found that the main group had moved upstream
to a better campsite, dragging their canoes by towropes and losing one
more in the process. To increase their scanty food stocks while waiting
for word from the other searchers, the reunited group—forty-one persons
now—trapped a few beaver but had scant luck netting fish. On November 6 two of the scouts who had left Caldron Linn with Reed

returned. They had seen no Indians—nothing but the interminable, impossible canyons, which Reed was still stubbornly exploring.

What now? Records say only that Crooks and Hunt consulted. But one can almost hear Crooks's voice, hammering out arguments similar to the ones that had turned him back from the forlorn march toward Henry's Fort. They had lost nine precious days and were not a foot nearer the Columbia than when Clappine had drowned. If Indians were close enough to be of help, the whites would have heard by now. Was it not better to starve while moving forward rather than while sitting motionless?

Since two small groups might be easier to feed than a single large one, the leaders decided to split. Each took nineteen men. To his group Hunt added the squaw, now in advanced pregnancy, and her children. They divided the food—about five pounds of meat per person, a little corn, grease, and bouillon tablets. On November 9, in another rain, they straggled away from each other, Hunt along the north bank, Crooks along the south.

For twenty-eight days Crooks's group walked an average of eleven or twelve miles a day. Each day for the first eighteen days they ate the equivalent of half of one normal meal. During the next ten days, twenty men subsisted on a single beaver, one dog, some chokecherries, and the boiled soles of a few worn moccasins. On this diet they completed the great arc which the Snake River makes through southern Idaho and found themselves headed north. They passed Burnt River, along which later wagon trains would travel going toward Oregon, and plunged into terror. The canyon of the Snake deepened; in places the shaggy hills dropped a mile from peaktop to river. In their weakened condition the travelers could not flounder across the snowy Wallowa Mountains of northeastern Oregon. They struggled down to the river, determined in their despair to build rafts, but when they saw the wild tumult of the rapids they lost heart.

White men appeared on the opposite slope—Reed's party and McKenzie's. McKenzie had found the dry, fractured lava beds north of Caldron Linn too formidable to cross and had veered west. By chance his party had fallen in with Reed's and McClellan's. Since none of them had located food, horses, or information they decided to push on rather than rejoin Hunt. Bristle-tempered McClellan soon left the others to find his own way across the mountains.[5] These items Crooks learned by shouting across the narrow canyon. But he could not get himself over the torrent. His friends, who had found more to eat than he had, waved and went on. For three days Crooks and his men tried to follow on their side of the canyon, then gave up in waist-deep snow. Crooks was so ill he could scarcely walk. His party's only hope, he decided, was to return to an impoverished Indian camp they had passed several days before.

They started slogging back upstream. On the morning of December 6 they were astounded to see Hunt's party marching along the opposite (east) side of the river. Wildly they signaled for help. During his own desolate wanderings Hunt had been able to buy several horses from the Indians and the night before had butchered one of them to eat. He had his men build a canoe by stretching the slain animal's hide over willow sticks. In this flimsy craft one bold voyageur crossed the river with a load of horsemeat, then returned with Crooks and a man named François LeClaire.

Until this meeting Hunt had hoped to push north through the mountains to the main branch of the Columbia. On Crooks's insistence that recent snows would defeat the attempt he decided that both parties should return to an Indian camp he had visited earlier in the vicinity of present-day Weiser, Idaho. As soon as the decision was known, his men began straggling in that direction. Unable to keep up with them, Crooks wanted to rejoin his own group. He failed. The horsehide canoe had floated away during the night, and two efforts to cross the river on an Indian-style raft made of willow branches ended in collapse. Presumably Crooks was dumped into the icy river at each upset. On the night of December 8 he became so violently ill that Hunt did not expect him to live. The crisis passed before morning, but he could not possibly travel for awhile. In the meantime most of Hunt's hungry men had gone ahead along their side of the river; Crooks's had followed on theirs. Chilled by the freezing night, the five loyal ones who had remained with the leaders now said that they too were leaving.

Hunt felt that he must pull the fragmenting groups back together. Prevailing on two men to stay with Crooks and LeClaire, he gave them two of his three remaining beaver skins to eat, promised to send help as soon as he could, and hurried after the others. On the tenth, well before he expected it, he found Indians from whom he inveigled five horses. He immediately sent meat and a riding animal to the invalids. Thus fortified, Crooks and LeClaire reached Hunt's camp.

Crooks's party was still on the opposite bank. They had seen the purchase of the horses and were crying piteously for food, but the enervation of despair was on Hunt's men, some of whom had just finished their first meal in four days. They refused to risk the river. In outrage Crooks ordered a canoe built, but when he tried to launch it his trembling legs crumpled beneath him. His dismay shamed one of the hunters, Benjamin Jones, into taking over one load of meat. Joseph Delaunay took a second. As Delaunay was about to return to Hunt, one of Crooks's voyageurs, demented by his sufferings, leaped into the tipsy craft, gyrated wildly, upset it, and drowned. Delaunay barely escaped.

John Day, one of Crooks's party, thought he was dying and asked to spend his last hours with his bourgeois. They got Day across the river to him and now Crooks was in a dilemma. The scanty resources of the area had been exhausted and the desperate voyageurs on both banks were determined to continue to the Indian camp at the Weiser River. There was no possibility of Day's keeping up. Abandon him? Crooks refused. He urged Hunt to go with the party, hold them together, and get them to the Columbia. He would wait until Day either recovered or died, and then follow if he could.

An ailing voyageur named Dubreuil asked to stay with the invalids. The Shoshone Indians nearby promised to do what they could for the trio. Hunt left them some meat and two horses and went unhappily on. For a time the Shoshone treated their charges well, but ran out of food and drifted away, taking horses and tepees with them. In an effort to combat the cold the whites built a hut of branches and dry grass and collected a little firewood. Day grew too sick to stand. With the last of his own energy, Crooks hacked some roots from the frozen ground but returned to find the fire out. He was unable to rekindle it with his chilled, trembling hands. For a day and a night the trio lay in a torpor. Then two Indians chanced by, lighted a fire and prepared a meal. They threw away the roots Crooks had dug, saying that they were poisonous. Having done what they could, they wandered on.

Revived by the food, Day managed to kill a wolf that was prowling about the camp. They banqueted on it; some of their strength returned and they were able to hunt better provender. Soon three voyageurs appeared. They said that Hunt had found an Indian guide who had been willing to lead the overlanders across the Blue Mountains of eastern Oregon to the Columbia. This trio, however, had stayed behind, preferring the miseries they knew to the unknown ones ahead.

They remained on the Snake when Crooks, Day and Dubreuil finally felt able to strike along Hunt's trail. In the Blue Mountains Crooks's trio got lost in the snow and wandered forlornly for weeks, rescued from time to time by small bands of Indians who were scarcely better off than the whites were. One such band agreed to care for Dubreuil when he collapsed completely. (Recovering, Dubreuil returned to the Snake, lived with the Shoshones for awhile, and eventually fell in with the trappers who had been detached from the main party at the mouth of the Hoback River nearly a year before.) Crooks and Day meanwhile staggered on toward the Columbia. In mid-April they reached the river near the mouth of the Umatilla. An old Indian named Yeckatapam fed them, let them rest, and set them off along the south bank toward Astoria with renewed hope.

They traveled seventy miles or so and passed what is now the John Day River. Then other Indians—the first unfriendly ones they had met—fell on them and stripped them of everything: guns, knives, fire-making equipment, even their clothes. Stark naked, subsisting on few rotten fishes, bones and a scanty meal one solitary old couple gave them, they hobbled on bleeding feet back to Yeckatapam. He clothed them, killed a horse, dried the meat and gave it to them. Fearful of the Indians farther downstream, they decided in their desolation to walk all the way back to St. Louis. They were tying as much jerky as they could carry into packs when an Indian called that four canoes were coming down the other side of the broad, bright-blue river.

They rushed to the bank. White men, far off across the sun-dazzled water! They shouted in unison. An agonizing moment passed. The four canoes floated into a cluster and slowed. Obviously the paddlers were listening. Again Crooks and Day whooped full-lunged. The canoes turned toward them. To their amazement they saw among the bearded, staring men two of their former trail companions, John Reed and Robert McClellan.

From the river party Crooks and Day learned that Reed, McKenzie, McClellan and their men had crossed the mountains after a dreadful ordeal. Near present-day Lewiston, where the north-flowing Snake bends sharply west to join the Columbia, they had obtained two Indian canoes. On New Year's Day, McClellan's canoe upset, but he and his men clung to its sides until fished from the frigid water. In mid-January, 1812, they reached Astoria, the first of the overlanders to appear. Hunt's emaciated party arrived a month later. During the arduous crossing of the Blue Mountains, Marie Dorion had given birth to a child that soon perished; and one sick voyageur had wandered off with Indians to be seen no more. They were the final casualties of the journey.

Except for Robert McClellan. He too in a way was a casualty. Like Joseph Miller, who had dropped out in Idaho, he had grown to despise the work and the country and felt that enduring them merited more than the two and a half shares allotted him—a meagerness over which he had brooded since the beginning of the expedition. He told the others he wanted more. They refused. In a fiery huff he tossed away his partnership and vowed to return home at the first opportunity.

It presented itself on March 22. Three expeditions started together up the Columbia from Astoria. One, led by Robert Stuart, was to supply the post his uncle David had built the previous summer at Okanogan. Another, led by twenty-eight-year-old, Massachusetts-born Russell Farnham, a clerk who had arrived with Stuart on the *Tonquin*, planned to retrace Hunt's route as far as Idaho and retrieve the goods which had been cached near Caldron Linn. En route they were to try to

succor John Day and Ramsay Crooks. Their guide as far as the caches
was to be John Reed, who had completed the grueling crossing only
a month earlier. After locating the caches for Farnham, Reed and four
men were to continue east with dispatches for Astor. McClellan decided
to return as far as St. Louis with them.

In spite of their herculean assignments, the total muster of the three
groups came to only sixteen men. At the upper end of the long series of
rapids that fret the gorge by which the Columbia breaks through the
Cascade Mountains, they ran into more trouble than they could handle.
Cruelest stretch of the "rioting, rock-strewn water" was The Dalles,
fourteen narrow, bellowing miles, terminating at their upper end in
Celilo Falls, where throngs of Indians gathered with long-handled nets
to scoop up migrating salmon. Two days of portaging were necessary
to surmount the stretch. Stuart hired several savages to help with the
carrying. They were so truculent, however, and so many armed loiterers
gathered to watch the work that he decided to finish without them.
That night he settled into camp as usual and the Indians returned to
their temporary village. At 1 A.M. he roused his men and they began
secretly moving the bales to the quiet water above the falls.

They had not quite finished at dawn. The savages discovered the
ruse and rushed to the lower camp, where McClellan and Reed were
on guard. The two whites were not able to face in all directions at once.
A soft-footed Indian got behind McClellan and threw a buffalo robe
over his head. He jerked free, killed his assailant with his rifle, and
turned back just as Reed was felled by a tomahawk. McClellan dropped
the attacker with his pocket pistol. Both his guns were empty now. He
started to reload. Enraged Indians began hammering on Reed's unconscious body. There was no time for fresh bullets. McClellan gave
one of the wild Indian war yells he had learned with Wayne's army
in Ohio, brandished his rifle as if it were loaded, and charged so
ferociously that the savages retreated, taking Reed's dispatch box with
them.

Stuart heard the shots and came running back with eight armed
men. Instead of fighting the revengeful Indians, however, he followed
McClellan's advice and bought them off with three blankets and some
tobacco. But irreparable damage had been done. Reed was in no shape
to cross the continent, and without his guidance Farnham could not
find the caches. Accordingly the entire group continued with the supply
canoes to Okanogan. There they picked up David Stuart, who had
wintered in British Columbia. At least the fur harvest had been good.
They loaded 2500 pelts into four canoes and started downstream. At no
great distance above the scene of their fight they heard English words
shouted from the bank, swung over, and picked up Day and Crooks.

Rescued and rescuers reached Astoria on either May 11 or 12. The fort bustled. Astor's supply ship *Beaver* stood in the harbor. It had come to anchor shortly before, after several days spent groping cautiously for a way across the tumultuous bar. Aboard were one new partner, six clerks (most of them Americans), fifteen American mechanics, six Canadian voyageurs, and several Kanaka laborers recruited at the Sandwich Islands. Equally important, half the *Beaver's* hold was filled with goods for Astoria, the other half with merchandise for the Russians in Alaska. When the party from the river arrived, some of the *Beaver's* passengers were still being rowed ashore, and the little schooner *Dolly* was preparing to help lighter the freight to the warehouses. The appearance of 2500 pelts from Okanogan and encouraging reports about other sections of the country fired enthusiasm still higher.

But not for Ramsay Crooks. At a meeting of the partners on May 14, he relinquished his five shares in the company, even though the action meant that he must return with McClellan through the very country where both had suffered so dreadfully.

Strangely, no contemporary account suggests more about motives than that his travail had discouraged him. But why should the discouragement have afflicted only the three former associates—Miller, McClellan, and Crooks—and no one else? Were unrecorded personality clashes still at work? Or did Crooks look beneath the surface excitement caused by the *Beaver's* arrival and decide, as McClellan already had, that Astoria's future was far less bright than it had appeared in St. Louis?

At least two of the men aboard the ship may well have possessed detailed information about Astor's serious difficulties in the East. One was the new partner, John Clarke, a native of Montreal and a former Nor'Wester whose German mother was said to be distantly related to Astor. Another, George Ehninger, was Astor's nephew. From them, the partners at Astoria could have heard several disquieting facts.

The new South West Company was in trouble. President Madison, it will be recalled, had fallen into Napoleon's trap and in November 1810 had issued a proclamation stating that unless England revoked restraints on American shipping within three months, trade with Great Britain must end. The prescribed date passed without response. By that time Napoleon's duplicity in pretending to relax the French orders was recognized, and France was included in the rigid Non-Intercourse Acts that went into effect March 2, 1811.

The South West Company goods had already started for Montreal and from there would go to St. Joseph Island. Astor made routine application for exceptions that would allow him to take the merchandise to Michilimackinac for distribution to the company's traders, most of them British citizens. Always before the government had granted variances on the ground that Indian tribes were independent "nations."

Congress, so reasoned fur traders and Thomas Jefferson, could forbid importation of foreign goods to its own citizens but not to the citizens of another "nation," that is, the Indians. It could, however, refuse transit rights to British citizens and thus put the Indian trade into American hands.[6] The Montreal supply houses and Astor had supposed that as an American citizen he could keep the South West Company in business in spite of embargoes. This time, however, government officials said that no exceptions would be allowed.

The fur traders did not really believe the statement. Astor's field representative, another nephew named Henry Brevoort, went to Montreal in May to start the goods off to St. Joseph Island on schedule. In a special express canoe he hurried on ahead to consult with George Gillespie and Toussaint Pothier. The importation permit, daily expected, failed to follow. On Michilimackinac bewilderment heated into resentment. The traders, Brevoort wrote his friend Washington Irving, were "as desperate as so many famished wolves," and, in a later note, "the Savages are beginning to raise the war hoop [sic] against their brethren the big knives." The Indians, Brevoort said, considered the Non-Intercourse Acts criminal. "Hundreds of children of these unprovided savages must starve, and their furious parents will assuredly avenge their deaths upon the unoffending whites who inhabit the frontier." To his uncle John Whetten he confided somberly, "The aspect of the Fur Company's affairs at present looks as unfavourable as is possible."

When the Beaver cleared New York Harbor on October 13, 1811, there had been no change. Nor had any official agreement yet been concluded with the St. Petersburg headquarters of the Russian American Fur Company. Astor, however, was so confident that a contract would materialize that he filled half the ship's hold with goods for Baranoff at prices that would be ruinous if any hitch occurred. None did—but Crooks could not foresee that in May 1812 on the Columbia.

Finally, there was the threat of North West Company competition. Clarke dispelled any lingering notion that the Canadians might own a third of the Pacific Fur Company. The Nor'Westers were commercial enemies and would fight for the Pacific trade. They were still bombarding their government with requests for help. Rumors reaching Astor and his associates in New York said that at last the Canadians were going to send a ship of their own, the Prince, to the Northwest coast. Land parties were also on the way.[7] Actually the Prince never appeared (though the land party did in time) but Crooks had no way of foreseeing that either. As he and McClellan discussed the situation, they must have surmised prompt opposition by forces as strong, well equipped, and experienced as the Astorians were.

What had they seen that was worth fighting for? The coastal Indians had been debased by trading ships and produced relatively few good pelts. Those at The Dalles promised to be as troublesome to supply flotillas as were the restless tribes of the Missouri, whose power to upset plans they knew well. Although David Stuart had gathered 2500 pelts along the Okanogan, the Indians farther south, whom Crooks and McClellan had measured with experienced eyes, seemed less promising. Completely unsophisticated, those would need to be tutored carefully in trapping before they produced a trade worth the effort involved in reaching them.[8] So slow a business could not offset for years the losses arising from the *Tonquin* disaster.

Did such prospects merit more suffering while they waited for dividends? Like McClellan, Crooks answered the question by resigning. Almost surely McClellan's urgings played a part in the decision.

Outsiders now, they loafed around the fort while the Astorians planned for the future. It was decided that Hunt, now in command of the entire operation, should sail to Alaska on the *Beaver*, conclude the trade with Baranoff, return with whatever pelts he obtained there, pick up the Astorians' harvest, and go to Canton to sell the whole cargo.

Several new posts were designed for the interior. John Clarke was to build one at Spokan and another among the Flatheads in direct competition to the Nor'Westers. Donald McKenzie was to erect one on the Snake near the mouth of the Clearwater and from there work southern Idaho. Clerk John Reed, his wounds healed, was to help him with the construction and then retrieve the caches Hunt had left near Caldron Linn. David Stuart was to reinforce Okanogan and build another post at Kamloops, British Columbia. And finally, Robert Stuart was delegated to finish Reed's earlier errand by carrying dispatches to Astor in New York City.

As companions for the journey young Stuart selected four veterans of Hunt's overland crossing—hunters John Day and Benjamin Jones, engagés François LeClairc and Andrew Vallé. Crooks and McClellan attached themselves to the group for safety in returning home.

The different expeditions—John Clarke's, David Stuart's, Donald McKenzie's, John Reed's and Robert Stuart's—left Astoria together on June 29, 1812. Their first trouble was with John Day. Deranged by his earlier sufferings, he began muttering, as Stuart related it in his journal, "the most incoherent absurd and unconnected sentences," reviled every Indian he saw "by the appellations of Rascal, Robber &c &c &c," put two loaded pistols to his own head and pulled the triggers. Incredibly he missed. His friends bound him under guard in one of the canoes and at the mouth of the Willamette found Indians to take him to Astoria, where he recovered and until his death in 1820 trapped usefully for the North West Company.

Nearly sixty strong, the Astorians passed the thievish Indians of the rapids without trouble. In one gang were two of the men who had robbed Crooks and Day earlier that spring. The whites pounced on the pair, bound them hand and foot, and threw them into a canoe, but released them when alarmed friends of the captives returned the rifles that had been stolen from Crooks and Day.

At the mouth of the Walla Walla River, Stuart's small party traded merchandise for horses and on July 28 struck southeast through intense heat toward the Snake. Until they reached the Blue Mountains they suffered from thirst; their single dog collapsed and "Le Clairc to preserve respiration drank his own Urine." On August 12 they reached Farewell Bend, where the Oregon Trail in later years left the river. As Crooks and his nineteen starving men had done during the preceding November, they followed the south side of the stream as nearly as the rugged tributaries and sterile hills allowed.

A series of extraordinary meetings began. First they encountered one of the far-ranging Snake Indians who had followed Hunt's party from the land of the Crows, had guided the overlanders across the Tetons, and had promised (faithlessly, it developed) to guard the horses at Henry's Fort. This Indian told Stuart there was no use going back east by way of Teton Pass. There was a shorter route south of the Wind River Mountains in Wyoming, the South Pass of later migrations. He promised to guide the returning Astorians to it in exchange for a pistol, a blanket, some tools and ornaments, but soon changed his mind and vanished with Stuart's fine riding horse.

Shortly thereafter the travelers stumbled across Hoback, Reznor, Robinson and Joseph Miller—but not Martin Cass. These were the trappers who had left Henry's Fort the preceding October. Since then they had rambled far and wide and had caught many beaver, but had been robbed by Arapaho Indians of everything. During the wanderings Cass had deserted (or, ugly rumors said, had been eaten by his companions during hungry times). For weeks they had barely managed to stay alive. Yet when they reached the caches beside Caldron Linn—six of the nine store cellars had been opened and robbed—Hoback, Reznor, and Robinson accepted Stuart's offer of supplies and went cheerfully back to their trapping.[9]

Not Joseph Miller, however. According to Stuart, Miller had had enough of the Indian country and wanted to return to civilization. He may also have been influenced by learning that his former partners, Crooks and McClellan, had, like himself, surrendered their shares in the company and were going back to the Missouri. To do what? We have no way of knowing. But surely something was on their minds beyond disgust with the Far West, and they may have invited Miller to join them in their plans.

From Caldron Linn the party continued eastward along the south bank of the Snake. On reaching the Portneuf River, they turned south, aiming for the pass of which the Snake Indian had told them. A war party of Crow Indians frightened them north. As they fled along the present Idaho-Wyoming boundary, the Crows followed, stole every horse and left them afoot in the wilderness. During their subsequent wanderings, McClellan grew disgusted with Stuart's cautious maneuverings to avoid being seen and stalked off by himself.

Crooks fell so ill he could not travel. The others wanted to abandon him. Stuart refused. He purged Crooks with castor oil, built a small oval frame of willows, covered it with hide, made the naked invalid crawl inside, and steamed him red by throwing water onto hot stones. After four days of recuperation Crooks was able to travel again.

They crossed Teton Pass on the route Hunt had taken and plodded with the numbness of despair up the arduous canyon of the Hoback River. From its upper reaches they crossed to the sagebrush plains, immense beyond seeing, which surround the Green. There they left Hunt's trail, as McClellan had done ahead of them, and once more aimed for the pass south of the Wind River Mountains. Their desperate detour, they realized all too painfully, had taken them four hundred miles out of their way.

As they trudged southeast, parallel to the spectacular peaks of the Wind River Mountains, game disappeared. Ahead of them McClellan collapsed and lay down to die. Overtaking him, they shouldered his few possessions and persuaded him to struggle back onto his feet. That night one of the French Canadians suggested cannibalism by lot. The others were about to agree when Stuart cocked his rifle and silenced the proposal. The next noon they managed to kill "an old run down Buffalo Bull . . . and so ravenous were our appetites that we ate part of the animal raw."

They rested a day, stuffing themselves with meat, and walked on. On October 18 they met Snake Indians from whom they obtained more meat, leather for moccasins, and the single horse the natives had retained after a battle with the Crows. Shifting their loads to the animal made walking easier, but they suffered from thirst and cold as they moved into the broad gray defile of South Pass, so gentle in its ascent that later travelers would have trouble determining exactly where its apex lay.[10]

In early November, near present Caspar, in central Wyoming, they decided to halt for winter. They built a hut "8 feet by 18 with the fire in the middle Indian fashion, the sides are 3 feet high and the whole covered with Buffaloe skins." Time passed pleasantly until mid-December, when Arapaho Indians frightened them 150 miles farther down the Platte to the vicinity of modern Torrington. There, in intense cold, they began another hut. They celebrated New Year's Day, 1813, by banqueting on buffalo tongues and cutting up and smoking Joseph Miller's tobacco pouch.

They hollowed two cottonwood trunks into canoes, and after the ice went out of the river in early March spent several days trying to float down the Platte's shallow, island-sprinkled current. The effort failed. On March 20 they loaded their bony horse once more and resumed their footsore march. From traders among the Oto Indians in eastern Nebraska they learned "the disagreeable intelligence of a war between America and Great Britain . . . but in such a confused manner was it related that we could comprehend but little."[11]

They traded their horse for enough skins to build a hide canoe. In that and in a wooden canoe which they found on the banks of the Missouri they floated to Fort Osage. There Lieutenant Brownson confirmed the disagreeable intelligence. War had been raging for ten months, having been declared in June, 1812, before their departure from Astoria.

At sunset on April 30, 1813, they reached St. Louis. By then they knew that the upper Great Lakes area was entirely in British hands and that Indians from as far away as the Missouri River were flocking toward Prairie du Chien and Green Bay to join Crooks's old bourgeois, Robert Dickson, and join the fight against the Americans. As they docked their canoe, they must have felt as displaced as men from Tibet. For almost three years their world had been limited to the unmapped horizons which they could see around them; to an extraordinary degree their concerns had been the elemental ones involved in staying alive from one day to the next. Now, abruptly, they had to ask themselves, Staying alive for what?

Dazed, they wandered from store to house to tavern, trying to absorb not only the facts but the implications of this disastrous conflict. The unfolding news was not heartening. Not just their future or even Astor's, but that of the entire Indian trade as they had known it was inscrutable indeed.

CHAPTER *12*

The Pawns of War

In the eyes of American frontiersmen the Indian settlement
called Prophetstown, built in May 1808 at the junction of Tippecanoe
Creek and the Wabash River, had grown to formidable proportions.
Journeying north as far as Green Bay, west beyond the Mississippi, and
south into Florida, Tecumseh had won promises of support for his confederation from many tribes. Hundreds of savages migrated to his settlement to be near the center of the promised renaissance and to listen
to the frenzied orations of Tenskwatawa, the Prophet.

Seeking still more power, Tecumseh traveled late in the summer of
1809 to the Mohawk Valley to try to enlist the aid of the Iroquois.
Taking advantage of his absence, William Henry Harrison, Governor of
Indiana Territory, assembled at Fort Wayne several chiefs who had little
claim to the area save through Tecumseh's contention that all land belonged to the Indians communally. He plied the gathering with speeches,
passed out a little whisky, and for $10,500 in cash and annuities obtained
for the United States a tract one hundred miles wide on either side of
the Wabash River—nearly 3,000,000 acres. For another $3000 the chiefs
of two other tribes who had not been at the first signing agreed to
recognize the Treaty of Fort Wayne. Their signatures completed a series
of diplomatic victories by which Harrison in a five-year period of unprecedented avarice wrested from the Indians many thousands of square
miles in what is now Ohio, Indiana, and Illinois.

On his return from the Iroquois, who had resisted his overtures,
Tecumseh declared he would not accept the Treaty of Fort Wayne. The
next August, 1810, he met Harrison at a council on the governor's lawn

at Vincennes. Most of the territory's officials and their ladies were on hand to witness the encounter. They almost got more excitement than they wanted. Tempers flared, weapons flashed. Harrison checked the display, and after a cooling-off period the discussions resumed—fruit-lessly. Neither man gave ground. Tecumseh blurted out a prediction of war and stalked away.

Tecumseh was echoing the opinion—even the desire—of most of the Indians throughout the Old Northwest. They were convinced that war was unavoidable. British traders fostered the belief. Agencies of the British government added to the restiveness by passing out, free of charge, blankets, food, guns and powder to the red warriors who each summer flocked across the Detroit River to the headquarters of Indian Superintendent Matthew Elliott at Amherstburg. Tecumseh himself con-ferred with Elliott in November 1810, shortly after his clash with Harrison at Vincennes, and went away convinced of British aid in case of open conflict between the Indians and the United States.[1]

In spite of Elliott's offer, Tecumseh himself was not quite ready for war—yet. But many of the tribes were. Raids and bloodletting began with good weather in the spring of 1811. They increased when the Indians learned that because of the new, severe Non-Intercourse Acts of early 1811 they were not likely to receive goods in the fall. Soldiers were killed on the Missouri; surveyors were driven off the ceded lands along the Wabash. Tecumseh, parading brazenly through Vincennes with 175 armed warriors, told Harrison he was going south to ask the powerful Creek and Cherokee Indians to join his confederation. Another ominous, if less spectacular threat of trouble lay in an unprecedented drought that was shriveling Indian cornfields around Lake Michigan and on to-ward the Mississippi. If the crops failed, the hungry Indians would be more ready than ever to strike at the government which, as they sup-posed, was depriving them of the manufactured items they needed in order to keep on living.

The traders who assembled at the Mackinac rendezvous in August 1811 were equally desperate. Under the prodding of their Montreal suppliers they had obediently swung aboard one more corporate merry-go-round. First it had been Robert Dickson & Company, then the Michili-mackinac Company, and finally the Montreal-Michilimackinac Company, each with its quickly dimming promise of survival. Now it was the South West Company, created by their Montreal agents on the hope that Astor would find legal gateways across the border for their merchandise. But Astor had turned out to be as helpless as the Canadians. The American government refused to grant him or his new company any importation rights whatsoever.

The result was wholesale smuggling. Crossing from Michilimackinac to St. Joseph Island, Robert Dickson, James and George Aird, Allen

Wilmot, Joseph Rolette, Thomas Anderson and various other South West Company traders loaded goods worth $50,000 into their canoes. By dark they skirted Michilimackinac and passed through the strait to Lake Michigan and Green Bay.[2] As usual hundreds of Menominee, Winnebago, and Sioux Indians were waiting at Prairie du Chien for the year's importations. This fall they had little hope. When, to their shouted delight, the flotilla unexpectedly appeared, they were profoundly impressed. This action showed who their friends were. It showed, too, in their minds, which nation was the more powerful: the Americans had not been able to halt the Canadian traders.

The only American on hand in Prairie du Chien to counter the impression was the United States Indian agent, Nicholas Boilvin. He merits a digression. Born in Quebec, probably in 1761, Boilvin had first come to St. Louis, presumably with his parents, in 1774. Thereafter he was in Canada and Detroit until the mid-eighties, when he returned permanently to St. Louis, venturing with his trading canoes as far up the Mississippi as the St. Peter's River. He became an American citizen after the Louisiana Purchase and was appointed agent to the Sac and Fox Indians on the Des Moines River. He inherited the Prairie du Chien agency on the death of John Campbell following Campbell's duel with Redford Crawford. Symbolically enough, the buildings of Boilvin's new agency were squeezed between Robert Dickson's home on one side and the warehouse of the Michilimackinac Company on the other. Although his loyalty to the United States remained unswerving and his influence over the Indians was almost as great as Dickson's, he was in continual hot water with the bureaucrats in Washington. He could not keep accounts the way the War Department ordered him to, could not write English, and reduced French to a weird phonetic system all his own.[3]

The summer of 1811 taxed his abilities. He stopped a few of the Indians who were swarming to Amherstburg to receive presents and listen to Matthew Elliott. He managed to keep the Sacs from going on the warpath when an American mining company, having obtained a lease from the administrators of Julien Dubuque's estate, tried to settle sixty men among the lead mines which the Indians had granted to Dubuque—and to Dubuque only, they said. There was little Boilvin could do about Dickson, however, other than report him and his fellow smugglers to William Clark.

No reaction followed. Clark simply did not have force enough to police the distant wilderness. In triumph, Dickson moved up the St. Peter's, arriving just in time to succor with gunpowder 100 lodges of starving Sioux. Behind him, Rolette, Anderson, and Wilmot paused at a fort on Pike's Island in the Mississippi, opposite the mouth of the St. Peter's. High wine flowed for the first time in months. Hoping to prevent violence, the squaws hid the men's weapons. Even so one

Indian was stabbed, another's skull was fractured by a stick. When the grog ran out toward midnight, the reeling savages scaled the stockade to find more. The traders cocked their guns—according to Anderson, Rolette trembled so with fright that he broke his own ramrod—and drove the Indians off. At dawn quiet returned.

But not peace. Uneasiness was rippling everywhere throughout the Old Northwest. Isaac Van Voorhis, the surgeon at Fort Dearborn, Chicago, wrote in October 1811:

> I cannot but notice the villainy practiced in the Indian country by British agents and traders . . . They labor by every unprincipled means to instigate the Savage against the American . . . Never until a prohibition of the entrance of all foreigners, and especially British subjects, into the Indian Country takes place, will we enjoy a lasting peace with the credulous, deluded, and cannibal savages.

In their eagerness to further their commerce by exploiting the grievances of the Indians, the Canadian traders did the red men a profound disservice. They gave American resentment a focus. In its outrage, the entire United States West—indeed, most of the nation—closed its ears (which were not very open anyway) to whatever justice the Indians might have asked for. Grimly the frontier determined to strike back before the alliance between Tecumseh's federation and the British army in Canada could take shape.

Acting on the strength of very ambiguous authorization from Washington, William Henry Harrison in early November marched a thousand men against Prophetstown. Tecumseh was in the South seeking allies; otherwise he might have forestalled open conflict for a more auspicious time. His brother was less judicious. Just before dawn on the seventh, after mumbling charms designed to turn enemy bullets soft, the Prophet launched a fanatical attack. The white lines held, then in roaring confusion under the brightening skies drove the Indians back across a marsh. After plundering Prophetstown for supplies, Harrison turned the village into ashes. The price was high—sixty-one dead, 127 wounded—but the reward proved to be great: thirty years later Tippecanoe helped elevate William Henry Harrison to the presidency of the United States.

The battle also furnished an immediate sounding board for the new Congress which assembled in November. Recent elections had put control within grasp of the War Hawks, most of them ambitious young men from the frontier regions. They made the most of Harrison's report of finding British rifles and tomahawks in Tecumseh's settlement; in oration after oration they cried to the country that the time had arrived for action against the real enemy and not just against his pawns, the red men. To say that the fur trade and the Indian problem were primary causes of the War of 1812 is to overlook other complex issues.

But certainly the two intertwined difficulties ranked high. Jingoists throughout the land declared that the best medicine for both sores would be an invasion of Canada. As further balm, the United States would acquire from the victory the rich farm lands of the Ontario peninsula; the West's long economic depression would end; the frontier could spread unchecked.

On November 29 a Select Committee on Foreign Relations of the House of Representatives brought in a special report that amounted to a recommendation for war. It touched off long debates about strengthening the army and navy, about finances, about extending the embargo. During the arguments the Indians added more fuel. Tecumseh's return from the South with pledges of support from the Creeks and Cherokees sent shivers of alarm through Indiana. Farther west, Winnebagos attacked American miners near Galena, Illinois, burned a smelter, killed two men, stripped off their flesh and scattered the bones. Frontier newspapers wrote fiery editorials and the War Hawks grew steadily more truculent in their speeches.

Quite naturally the British army officers in Canada used this long period of debate to consolidate their strength. Key garrisons were fortified. In January 1812 letters were sent to the wintering partners of both the North West and South West companies, asking how many voyageurs and Indian auxiliaries, how many boats, and how much ammunition they could furnish in the event of war. On February 27, François Réaume and two Chippewa Indians were sent on foot from York (now Toronto) through bitter weather to find Dickson and obtain from him an exact accounting of the support the British could expect from the Indians along the Mississippi.

Scouts from Fort Dearborn seized the three emissaries as they were passing around Chicago and turned them over to their commander, Captain Nathan Heald. Heald examined them suspiciously but missed finding the written questions Dickson was to answer. One of the Chippewas had hidden the paper in the toe of his moccasin. Released, the messengers went on to Green Bay and up the Fox River to the Wisconsin portage. There, in mid-June, they met Dickson and approximately 170 Indians.

The big redhead had been busy. Later, when submitting a bill to the government in Quebec for expenses, he said that on reaching his trading grounds he had learned that American agents were diligently wooing the neighboring Indians to the American cause. As a countermeasure he distributed free of charge, principally to the Sioux, merchandise worth £1875.5.9. In thus lightly skirting the edges of the truth, Dickson was buttering his claim. The United States was as unprepared for 1812 as it has been for all its other wars. The only agents in the area were half-blood runners whom Boilvin sent out from Prairie du Chien to see what Dickson and his fellow traders were up to. Far away on the Missouri, Manuel Lisa's winterers may also have played down British war talk in order to keep the Indians at their hunting. By and large, however, there was very little American pressure for Dickson to counter. "Agents" simply read more dramatically than did the real enemy he found stalking the Indian camps—hunger.

Dry days had withered the corn. Storage cellars gaped. Game animals moved north to find pasture. Faced with a desolate winter, the savages needed their usual credits from the traders more urgently than ever, yet could offer little security. Dickson responded with a free hand. Why not? American officials throughout the West knew of his smuggling and he might never again be able to bring in goods. These savages, not white men, were the people among whom he had spent most of his life. His wife was one of them. Should they have cause to remember his last trip as niggardly?

As he extended credits he did not expect to recover, he also sowed bitterness against the country that had brought him to the edge of ruin. He did it effectively. When he started in the spring with his scanty harvest of furs for Michilimackinac, to pay off such of his debts as he could and to learn what the future might hold, scores of Indians followed him.

He could hardly have intended them as soldiers. War had not been declared and no messengers had yet reached him. But he knew that Indians from the St. Peter's seldom made the long trip to Amherstburg or even to St. Joseph to receive presents and to listen to the appeal of British army officers for their loyalty. This might be a good time to start propagandizing them.

His Sioux wife helped him overcome the reluctance of some of the chiefs and off they went in a barbaric fleet of canoes. At Prairie du Chien, Boilvin prevailed on a few important pawns—five Sioux chiefs, three Iowas, and two Winnebagos—to forsake the British and join him on a trip to Washington. Undisturbed, Dickson continued with 170 Indians up the Wisconsin. War still had not been declared, and the St. Louis *Gazette* did not know quite what to make of the movement. It finally decided (June 6, 1812) that the "celebrated British trader" intended to seize a year's supply of goods at St. Joseph and use the Indians for fighting his way back past Michilimackinac. And that just possibly could have been in his mind.

The messengers who met him at the portage put a new light on affairs. Judging from their talk that a crisis was approaching, Dickson sent thirty or forty of his Indians directly to Fort Malden, the British army post just outside Amherstburg. With the remaining savages, he continued to St. Joseph. He had not been there long when word arrived, by avenues which cannot now be determined, that the inevitable conflict had begun. Strangely enough, the information was common property on St. Joseph long before the American garrison at Michilimackinac, scarcely seventy miles away, knew anything about it.

For years Astor and his friend, Secretary of the Treasury Albert Gallatin, were blamed as the sources of the British information. To show why, it is necessary to backtrack to the Non-Intercourse Act of March 1811.

As already noted, that stringent embargo had frozen the South West Company's goods in the warehouses at St. Joseph. When Astor at last was convinced that he could not obtain a variance through his usual channels, he wrote in August 1811 directly to President Madison. Madison politely rebuffed him. Undeterred, Astor in March 1812 petitioned Congress for a special act allowing the American Fur Company to take goods into the Indian country for the benefit of the Indians. He appealed to Thomas Jefferson for aid in having the act passed. Although Jefferson agreed in May that Astor and the Indians were victims of a hardship not intended by Congress when passing the Non-Intercourse Acts, he declined to interfere.

As the probabilities of war increased, Astor changed tactics. Instead of arguing the needs of the Indians, he warned Madison that the goods at St. Joseph included rifles, powder, lead, and many other items that would be useful to the British in case of conflict. Would it not be better to move the merchandise for safekeeping to Michilimackinac?

The argument prevailed. As Gallatin recalled matters in a letter to Astor on August 5, 1835,

> I was directed to instruct the collectors on the lakes, in case you or your agents should voluntarily bring in and deliver any parts of the goods above mentioned, to receive and keep them in their guard, and not to commence prosecution until further instructions, the intention being then to apply to congress for an act remitting the forfeiture of penalties.

It was too late. War was next to inescapable. Realizing this long before Astor would admit it, Governor William Hull of Michigan Territory went to Washington to urge the building of a fleet on the Lakes as the only sound defense for his territory. Washington preferred offense. Hull was offered not a defensive fleet but command of an army of 1500 men for invading Canada. He accepted reluctantly. Though as a young man he had fought in the Revolution, he was by nature peaceful. He was also sixty years old and fond of his small comforts. He probably would not have characterized himself with the adjectives his detractors used—timid and indecisive—but at least he knew he was not fitted for army command. Unfortunately, he let himself be flattered out of his reservations.

Late in May 1812 he met his troops at Urbana, in Western Ohio. From there he began hacking a supply road north toward the site of modern Toledo. The job went slowly in wretched weather. During the labors war was formally declared (June 18), but for many days Hull knew nothing about it. Reaching Maumee Bay on Lake Erie he decided to save transport by loading various stores, including his papers and military instructions, onto a schooner and shipping them ahead to Detroit while he and the army marched on around the lake by land. Canadians, who had been more promptly informed of the existence of hostilities, captured the vessel and its store of valuable papers.

Hull reached Detroit July 5. He was understandably out of sorts to learn that the Canadians were somehow better posted than he was. At that point two letters fell into his hands, one written by Astor and one by Gallatin, both intended for Mackinac and both containing news of the declaration. They had reached Detroit ahead of Hull; and in compliance with a request from Astor, the Detroit postmaster, James Abbott, had arranged for an express to carry them north. Indians frightened the messenger back. On his return he surrendered the letters to Hull. There was no evidence that any Canadian had seen those letters, but the mere fact that they were traveling ahead of Hull's own communications from Washington gave him a concrete object on which to vent his spleen and he jumped to a conclusion of treason in high places. James Abbott became a scapegoat, was later tried for disloyalty to his country, and was acquitted.[4]

Hull (who on his part took no immediate steps to alert the American troops on Mackinac) was barking up the wrong tree. But he had caught a whiff of the right scent. Word from somewhere did reach St. Joseph far ahead of any American dispatches. Today there is little likelihood of discovering the exact channels. But evidently the agent of the South West Company, Toussaint Pothier, picked up the startling news in Montreal from one of the numerous associates to whom Astor had written from Washington immediately after the declaration. Pothier then carried it with him when he traveled by express canoe up the Ottawa. He may have been quite surprised on reaching St. Joseph to discover that until his arrival the commander there, Captain Charles Roberts, had known nothing about the matter.

Since the information was unofficial, Roberts was cautious about using it, to the exasperation of Pothier, Robert Dickson, and John Askin, Jr., who ran the North West Company store on St. Joseph. As was usual each summer, many canoes filled with traders and Indians moved freely back and forth between Mackinac and St. Joseph. From observant travelers the men on St. Joseph learned that the soldiers in the American fort were probably unaware of hostilities. (The preponderant British sympathies of the neighborhood kept comparable information from floating back to the Americans.) Heatedly the traders—Dickson, Pothier, and Askin—urged Roberts to attack while the possibility of surprise favored him.

Roberts declined to move without official sanction. He did make preparations, however. From the nearby islands and from Sault Ste Marie he assembled, as reinforcements for his forty-odd regular soldiers, a force of one hundred and eighty armed voyageurs and an even greater number of Chippewa Indians to add to the ones Dickson had brought from the West. He armed and equipped these auxiliaries in part with merchandise Astor had been trying to get off the island. He assembled canoes, barges, and the North West Company's brig *Caledonia*. And either he or Pothier rushed William McKay in an express canoe on west to ask help from the great rendezvous at Fort William, nearly five hundred miles away.

Before the voyageurs and Indians from Fort William could arrive, Roberts received orders from Major General Sir Isaac Brock to move against Michilimackinac. Thanks to his preparations he lost no time. Pothier's French Canadians dragged two unwieldy cannon into a barge. Another South West Company trader, Lewis Crawford, assumed command of the armed half of the voyageurs. The other half, unarmed, were to man the boats under Pothier's direction. Dickson and young Askin, dressed like Indians, led the savages in their birchbark canoes. Soldiers boarded the *Caledonia*. Rendezvous was set for three in the morning at a point on the northwest shore of the enemy island where the cliffs flattened out. From that ancient Indian landing a narrow trail led through thick forests and dense underbrush to the hilltop overlooking the American fort from the rear.

On the afternoon of July 16 the heterogeneous fleet started along the regular canoe route around Point Detour. As the slow twilight fell, the songs faded, lest the sound, traveling far across the water, serve as a warning. No premonition alerted a big canoe coming toward the invaders, its bourgeois sound asleep. The fleet closed around it and found they had captured a prize—Michael Dousman, acting as special scout for the American garrison.

Roberts and the other leaders frightened Dousman into telling what was going on at the island. He said that Lieutenant Porter Hanks, in command of the fort, had recently grown disturbed. Traders were not coming to the island in their usual numbers. Indians were withdrawing from their camps on the beach. The disappearance had been caused by Roberts' appeal for reinforcements, but Hanks of course did not know that. He asked Dousman, a trader who owned a farm on St. Joseph, to go there as if on business and learn whether anything was afoot that the military should know about. The spy had been on his way when captured.

Learning from this that they must be very careful not to arouse the garrison, the invaders assembled at the rendezvous point on schedule. Dousman, watched by a British trader, was sent around the west bluffs (an hour and a half walk) to waken the villagers, but not the soldiers, and draw them to a point where they could be guarded and at the same time be out of danger. Meanwhile the Canadians dragged one of the six-pound cannons up the trail to the hill above the fort (a forty-five minute stroll if one is unencumbered). The gun was in place by dawn. Soldiers, voyageurs, and Indians led by the area's most responsible traders—John Johnston and Charles Ermatinger of St. Marys, Jacob Franks of Green Bay, Joseph Rolette of Prairie du Chien—took up strategic positions. Under cover of a flag of truce, Pothier carried a letter from Captain Roberts to Lieutenant Hanks, demanding his surrender. Dousman earnestly recommended compliance to prevent a massacre by Indians aroused by blood, and at eleven in the morning Hanks complied. Not a shot had been fired.

The word was flashed back along the trail to the landing place. Indians and Canadians ran to their barges and canoes and rowed into the cove, whooping and banging their muskets. Other Canadians swarmed into the fort and touched off its cannons in welcome. The Indians danced wildly through the streets. "Their minds," Roberts reported in a dispatch sent that afternoon to General Brock, "were much heated . . . [but] not one drop of either Man's or Animal's Blood was Spilt." Credit for the restraint belonged to the whites who led them—Dickson, Askin, Johnston, and a courageous handful of others.

As a reward for their participation, the savages were clothed with goods worth $9600 plundered from the United States trading factory on the island.[5] Scores more flocked in to share the excitement. Soon 1460 of them were howling improvidently through the town, devouring food at such a rate that Roberts had to send most of them away, as he did the reinforcements from Fort William who came, disappointed, into the cove after the fun was over. A few American soldiers of French-Canadian origin were persuaded to enlist in the British army. Roberts accepted the parole of the others and loaded them with a few American civilians onto two sailing ships and sent them to Detroit. There they found themselves in the middle of another siege.

Obedient to orders from Washington, General Hull had crossed into Canada on July 12. For the rest of the month he fiddled nervously in front of Fort Malden, fighting pointless little skirmishes while he tried to steel himself to a frontal assault. What little nerve he did muster evaporated when Chippewa runners brought him word of Mackinac's fall. His flanks were exposed. Fearing that hordes of inspired savages and Canadian voyageurs might fall on him at any moment, he dropped back into Detroit.

With Lake Michigan blockaded, Fort Dearborn could no longer be supplied. By Indian messenger Hull ordered its garrison to retreat to Fort Wayne. At approximately the same time he tried to clear his own threatened supply lines to the south. Tecumseh's Indians drove the party back and then strung a garrote around Detroit. Isaac Brock advanced with reinforcements from Niagara and demanded Hull's surrender, warning coldly, "It is far from my intention to join in a war of extermination, but you must be aware, that the numerous body of Indians who have attached themselves to my troops, will be beyond controul the moment the contest commences."

When the cannonade began, Lieutenant Porter Hanks, who had survived the fall of Fort Mackinac, was sitting under guard in an improvised prison room, awaiting a military investigation into his conduct at the capitulation. A chance ball crashed through the building and killed him. Out in a tent in the field Hull was chewing and drooling tobacco in a misery of irresolution. As the bombardment increased, he groaned, "My God! What shall I do with the women and children?" and surrendered.

Just twenty-four hours earlier the garrison at Fort Dearborn had begun their withdrawal, accompanied by wives and children and escorted by thirty friendly Miami Indians under famed scout William Wells, with whom Robert McClellan had served in Ohio. In the sandhills two miles from the fort, Potawatomi Indians fell on the column. An indeterminate number of the Miamis and upward of forty whites died, including two women and twelve children. The survivors, many of them wounded, were taken captive to various Indian camps and, in some cases, sadly abused. At the same hour that Hull was running up his white flag at Detroit, a frenzied clutch of savages burned Fort Dearborn and the government trading factory to the ground. Once more the entire country around the upper Great Lakes and off to the Mississippi belonged to the British.

The Canadian traders were determined to keep it that way. Small in numbers themselves, they planned, as all whites had in each of North America's earlier wars, to augment their strength by enlisting armies of Indians. Without waiting for approval from Quebec, Dickson appropriated twelve boatloads of merchandise from the United States trading factory at Mackinac and took it to Green Bay. From there he sent runners throughout Wisconsin and up and down the Mississippi, inviting Indians to meet him for presents and to hear what further rewards lay in store for those who fought the Americans.

Not all responded. The Foxes, who were used to looking toward the United States for protection against the truculent Winnebagos, held back. Their reluctance was shared by some of the Illinois Indians, including that part of the Sac tribe that was under the sway of Thomas

Forsyth and of Boilvin's interpreter, Maurice Blondeau. The more distant Sioux of the St. Peter's and on toward the Missouri also had second thoughts. The wars they were being asked to fight were far away. During their absence enemy Indians and Missouri militia might strike at their undefended villages. These were exceptions, however. The bulk of the Mississippi tribes—the forest Sioux, the Menominees, Winnebagos, and some Chippewas listened to Dickson's runners. So, thanks in large part to American bumbling, did the warlike majority of the Sacs, led by Black Hawk.

Shortly before the declaration of war, a delegation of Sacs had visited Washington. There they had shaken hands with President Madison and had understood him to say that the government trading factory at Fort Madison, Iowa, supposedly built for their especial benefit, would abandon its insistence on cash and would grant credit to the Indians, as private traders did. The factor, however, received no such instructions and refused. Convinced they had been deceived again by the Americans, the Sacs at Rock River gave a rousing welcome to Dickson's agent, Edward Lagoterie, when he visited the village with a British flag and a keg of rum. Black Hawk led two hundred chanting warriors to join the throng gathering at Green Bay. His "army" swelled to five hundred by Black Hawk's addition, Dickson started east to join the attack on Detroit. He arrived after the city had fallen, but the stories of the triumph which the savages heard in no way lessened their ardor to help King George's men drive the Americans out of the Midwest.

The fear that swept across the frontier bred frantic reactions. The settlers along the Ohio River cried for the blood of the friendly chiefs whom Nicholas Boilvin was bringing back from a visit to Washington. An abortive attack on Fort Madison so unnerved its commander that he convinced himself the government trading factory outside the stockade was a danger: the Indians might fire it as soon as the wind was right and let blowing sparks set off the post. To forestall this, the commander had volunteers slip out one calm evening and burn the place themselves. The loss in goods and furs, apart from the buildings, came to $5500.

Missouri militia destroyed a peaceful Indian settlement at Peoria, a wantonness that almost cost the government the services of trader Thomas Forsyth (not to be confused with the Montreal merchant of the same name), who lived there. Governor Benjamin Howard of Missouri wrote nervously to Washington that enemy cannon could be easily floated down either the Illinois or Mississippi rivers. Supported by artillery and given cohesion by a few skillful British traders like Dickson, Indians could overrun all Missouri. Had not Detroit fallen? St. Louis was even more vulnerable, he said, and urged a fleet of gunboats to patrol the rivers. William Clark supported the recommendation, but the harried War Department in Washington authorized only four of the awkward craft.

The provokers of these fears were private traders who until this point had acted on their own responsibility. Everything Dickson had done so far—distributing supplies during the winter of 1811–12, taking Indians to St. Joseph and leading them in the battle of Mackinac, even his recruiting activities at Green Bay and his freehanded signing of notes for supplies—had lacked official sanction. His personal expenditures amounted to close to $10,000. He had assumed, of course, that formal authorization would come in due time. But one cannot keep fighting a private war forever. To collect the reimbursements owed him and to win station as a government officer—without it he was a mere freebooter, subject to instant hanging if he was caught by the enemy—he went from Detroit to Montreal in the fall of 1812.

He was lionized by merchants and military men alike. The court of inquiry that reviewed his claims used their report to eulogize his activities. His monumental self-assurance purring under these warm strokes, he asked that he be appointed superintendent of all Western Indians, responsible only to Matthew Elliott; that he be given blanket authority to requisition whatever he needed from any of His Majesty's Indians storekeepers in the West; and that he be made captain of a ranger force which he himself would raise among the western fur men.

The proposal for a ranger force was shelved. Otherwise he was given everything he asked for. But the job entailed its responsibilities. Since an American counterattack on Detroit was anticipated early in the spring, he was ordered to go west immediately, through the dead of the winter, and start recruiting red auxiliaries for the defense. As stage properties he took with him several impressive wampum belts colored red, the symbol of war, many medals and several large silk flags for distribution to important chiefs. He was authorized to proclaim an official war aim for the Indians: a boundary between them and the Americans along the old Greenville Treaty line of 1794. (At the trader's behest, Great Britain was reviving the old dream of an independent Indian nation between the United States and the upper Great Lakes.) He was told that as soon as weather allowed, supply depots would be established at Chicago and at "the portage of the Ouisconsing." Orders to prepare boats went by special winter express to Mackinac, and Dickson was given to understand that until the goods arrived he could keep his savages happy by drawing from whatever sources were available such goods, tobacco, and liquor as he felt were necessary. In time, when there were not enough supplies to go around, that blanket authorization would breed deep resentments.

He made a fantastic trip west. After rumors of it had trickled back to Montreal, the governor of Canada asked for an account, but Dickson never got around to complying and so the exact details of the journey have been lost. Clearly he did not spare himself, though he was no longer young—forty-eight or so—and the weather was ferocious even for the Lakes. He reached Detroit about February 15. Blizzards pinned him there for two weeks. The weather calming, he hired a half-blood named Jean Baptiste Chandonnai as interpreter and with a small party plowed through the snow-heaped woods of southern Michigan to Burnett's trading post, near the point where the St. Joseph River empties into Lake Michigan. There, while proselytizing the Indians, he learned of the whereabouts of various survivors of the Chicago massacre and made arrangements for their release.

Leaving Chandonnai to carry on the propagandizing of the Chicago area, he went to Rock River, spread his inflammatory arguments among the Sacs and Foxes, and continued to Prairie du Chien, arriving April 17. His shadow went with long strides ahead of him. In January, before he had even left Montreal, rumor reported that he and Aird were on the Mississippi with eight or ten cannon and a contingent of British troops. (Almost simultaneously he was also reported to be icebound on a sloop at the mouth of the Milwaukee River.) Nearly everyone in St. Louis believed that as soon as the rivers opened he would descend on them with a large force of Indians—a move the Sacs and Foxes at least would have much preferred to marching against Detroit. Many white families had no intention of waiting for him. On February 7, 1813, Joseph Charless, the editor of the St. Louis newspaper, wrote the new Secretary of War, James Monroe, that several citizens were planning to move to Kentucky and Tennessee as soon as the weather allowed.

Reports of real trouble came in to intensify the imaginary dreads. Even before Dickson reached Prairie du Chien, a trader who lived there, a friend of Nicholas Boilvin, wrote to the agent in St. Louis that things looked grim. Indians had killed Boilvin's cattle; Jacob Franks was carrying on Dickson's recruiting at Green Bay; other runners were visiting the Sioux on the St. Peter's. "In short, Sir, I must tell you every thing is against you Americans, all nations in general have given their word to the English." The contagion was even reaching to the distant Missouri. There, early in March, Minnetaree Indians, incited by British traders, fell on Manuel Lisa's fort in central North Dakota, inflicted an indeterminate amount of damage, and drove the St. Louis Missouri Fur Company off the upper river.

The Americans were able to launch a few effective countermeasures. Boilvin sent his two best half-bloods, Maurice Blondeau and Augustin Ange, to Chicago and to Prairie du Chien to keep track of Dickson's movements. They sowed one very effective seed of doubt in the In-

dians' minds. The British, the interpreters whispered, were far away
and very busy; they might not be able to send in as many supplies
as Dickson promised; and if that happened, who would take care of
the warriors' families while the men were away fighting the white man's
battles? Meanwhile Boilvin himself journeyed on Dickson's heels to
the great village of the Sacs and Foxes at the mouth of Rock River. He
found a large segment of the tribe reluctant to risk themselves fighting
far to the east and began arrangements to split these doubters from
their hostile fellows and settle them for the duration among the Osages
of western Missouri, beyond reach of British seduction. No more modest
than Dickson about his abilities, Boilvin thought that a few soldiers at
his back would have enabled him to triumph entirely: "If I had the
authority to levey 200 men, I should have chased this rabble to Mackinac." In Illinois, Thomas Forsyth subverted Jean Baptiste Chandonnai
and others of Dickson's agents; though pretending to work for the
British, they began reporting on Dickson's movements to the Americans.[6]
Lisa and his men worried the Sioux of South Dakota by threatening to
cut off their supplies. They even hinted broadly that scalping parties
of their enemies might attack the Sioux villages if the men were foolish
enough to leave for a distant war which did not really concern them.

In spite of these maneuvers, Dickson succeeded in recruiting 1400
Indians to join the British army at Detroit. He sent 800 by land around
the southern tip of Lake Michigan; the rest he led east himself in
canoes through Green Bay and Michilimackinac. But in April, when
definite news of his imposing force reached St. Louis, no one there
supposed he was going east. The inhabitants were convinced he was
coming straight after their city. William Clark and Benjamin Howard
recruited fresh companies of militia. A committee of safety soberly discussed the advisability of repairing the Spanish forts on the bluff above
the city—forts which during the Revolution had helped turn back an
attack launched down the Mississippi by other British traders and their
red allies.

The arrival of Stuart, Crooks, McClellan, Jones and their two voyageurs from the Pacific on April 30 gave the frightened city something
fresh to talk about for a change. Not at once, however. A full apprecia-
tion of what the overlanders had done seemed to dawn with strange
slowness. The first issue of the weekly newspaper which could have
carried a notice of their arrival, that of Saturday May 8, 1813, relegated
the news to a small paragraph on page 3 of the four-page edition.
The bulk of the same column was filled with the usual worries about
Robert Dickson. After speculating at length on the redhead's intentions,
the editor threw out his chest and breathed defiance of an inverse
sort back at him:

But who are we in God's name? When we are proud, we call ourselves *Americans:* and in peaceable times we have always entertained the notion that previously to the surrender of any one of our rights, we should choose to have a little fighting—a few interchanges of blows at least.

The next issue was different. After interviewing the Astorians, editor Joseph Charless on May 15 devoted his entire front page and half the second to an account of Hunt's overland trip, the activities on the Columbia, and Stuart's return. No other single item, war stories included, ever received comparable emphasis in the *Gazette.* Today we can only guess at the excited talk which the account released like a heady elixir in St. Louis, the speculations about the Far West that made even talk about Dickson seem momentarily irrelevant. Lewis and Clark over again—renewed visions of an untouched continent waiting to be exploited, of St. Louis as the jumping-off place to an unguessable future . . . and then, inevitably, the present intruded: War. If men like Dickson had their way, and so far nothing appeared able to halt them, that vast region, like the Great Lakes area, would be British land.

The Astorians did not long relish the sensation their stories caused. The day after the *Missouri Gazette* printed its long account, Robert Stuart left for New York to deliver his year-old news of the Columbia to Astor. Two days later the creditors of Robert McClellan, untouched by the heroics of his transcontinental journey, had him imprisoned for debt. He shortly obtained his release by taking bankruptcy, but obviously he was no longer in a position to go ahead with whatever plans he may have been discussing with Ramsay Crooks during their long walk.

If McClellan's debts arose from his and Crooks's hard-luck ventures on the Missouri, the naturalized Scot must also have been threatened with jail. Apparently nothing happened. Either he was not concerned in the matter, or he was able to clear himself. But for what? The man who had first brought him to this western land, Robert Dickson, was now turning it upside down in a determined effort to destroy at least some of the things which had caused Crooks to forsake the Canadians and become a citizen of the United States. Now he was twenty-six years old. He had been in the wilderness for eight years, trying to establish himself. In return for the ordeal of those years he had only experience, much of it the experience of failure.

Perhaps even that would be worth something to Astor. Anyway, there was no place else to turn. Early in July, Crooks too started toward New York City. By the time he reached Pittsburgh he was so broke that he had to borrow $310 from a friend, giving a delayed draft on Astor as security, in order to complete the trip.

CHAPTER *13*

Small Fights for Large Stakes

Stuart's ride East took nearly six weeks. The inhabitants of much of the Illinois country he crossed had fled from their homes for fear of Indians. Rain mired long stretches of the road, and for days fever added to his discomfort. It was a relief to shift finally from saddle to stagecoach, rough though the latter was, and finish the trancontinental epic with someone else doing the driving. He reached New York on June 23, 1813.

His year-old news of affairs on the Columbia—the safe arrival of the *Beaver* and the establishment of posts in the interior—inspirited Astor. The merchant needed a lift. His last prior advice, brought more than a year earlier by the *Enterprise* on her return from Alaska and Canton, had told of the destruction of the *Tonquin*. Recent warnings from his agents in London said that the North West Company had gained from the government of Great Britain letters of marque authorizing the firm to arm a raider, the *Isaac Todd*, and send her to the Columbia in company with British warships, the thirty-six-gun *Phoebe* and the smaller *Raccoon*.

By employing various ingenious subterfuges, Astor had done what he could to bolster his colony. He cleared one supply ship, the *Lark*, through the British blockade of New York on the pretense that she was carrying goods to a British ally, the Russians in Alaska. His London agents spent nearly $60,000 outfitting another, the *Forester*, and dispatched her under British colors with a British convoy bound for the Pacific.[1]

Neither the *Lark* nor the *Forester* carried armament. Throughout the

fall and winter of 1812–13 Astor importuned Washington for more powerful help. At one point the frigate *John Adams* was assigned to him,
but the orders were canceled when her crew was transferred to the
Great Lakes. At that discouraging moment, Robert Stuart arrived.
Aroused by his reports, Astor redoubled his assault on William Jones,
the incompetent Secretary of Navy. Between times he fired a few salvos
at President Madison.

In his letters he emphasized over and over the importance of the
fur trade to the nation. The area between the Lakes and Columbia was
capable of grossing $2,000,000 a year, by his estimate, and it was within
the power of the United States to secure it all. His overland party had
proved that posts could be stretched entirely across the continent. The
western anchor of this chain, his fort of Astoria, could also serve as the
advance base of a lucrative trade with China, California, and Alaska,
excise duties on which would fatten the coffers of the nation. The presence of United States traders throughout this vast stretch of North
America would guarantee the friendship of the Indians—or so he wrote
without mentioning their attack on the *Tonquin*. But all this had been
endangered by the British capture of Michilimackinac. Now the Columbia remained the only point from which the Canadian traders could
be opposed. With so much at stake, surely it was the duty of the United
States Government to help guard that vital outpost.

He denied that his primary concern in seeking government aid was
the welfare of John Jacob Astor. To be sure, he had invested half a
million dollars and could not risk more without the assurance of support,
but others were also interested, "many of whom have Spend 3 years of
there Lifs enduring the Severest hardships while others will Loose the
fortunes acquird by Industory."[2]

In other letters he added that although the *Isaac Todd* and her escort,
Phoebe, had left England several weeks earlier, both were slow sailers
and would be delayed by heavy weather off Cape Horn. A fast frigate
could overtake them. Furthermore, he would equip the *Enterprise* at
his own expense for supplying whatever vessel was dispatched; indeed,
he was already loading the ship. Only a few soldiers would be necessary.
Robert Stuart said that twenty-five or thirty men could defend Astoria
against three or four hundred. (If Stuart said any such thing, he must
have been thinking about defense against Indians, not against warships
armed with heavy cannon.) Communication, Astor went on, would be
easy. Stuart had just discovered a new route across the continent and—
shades of the Oregon Trail!—"is of the opinion that the jurney may be
performed from the mouth of the Columbia to St. Lewis in 4 months
that is after having Some few establishments on this Side of the Rocky
mountains."

Nothing resulted. In October Astor lost heart. Unwilling to risk the

Enterprise without an escort, he unloaded her and laid her up for the duration. The men at Astoria would have to improvise as best they could to meet whatever arose.

Meanwhile he tried to keep the rest of his fur business alive. At the outbreak of the conflict he anticipated that pelt prices would skyrocket in New York while remaining depressed in Europe because of the long-continuing Napoleonic turmoils. Accordingly he wished to divert every skin possible into the United States.

He expected a considerable quantity. By the summer of 1813 he knew that appreciable amounts of South West Company merchandise had reached the Indian country in spite of the Non-Intercourse Acts and that furs would return as usual to Michilimackinac or St. Joseph in payment. Arrival of expresses with news that the Canadians had captured Mackinac in no way altered his prospects. By terms of the capitulation private property was to be respected. Indeed, the Canadians might prove more lenient about moving the furs to Montreal than the Americans would have been, and the company agent, Toussaint Pothier, almost certainly would start forwarding the bales as soon as transport became available.

These were not the only furs Astor counted on. Before the declaration of war he had, as usual, contracted with the North West Company and with independent traders for large numbers of pelts. The agreements having been concluded before the outbreak of hostilities, he and his Montreal partners were able to persuade both warring governments that it was legal for him to bring the furs out of Canada into the United States. The route he planned to use was the familiar one through Lake Champlain. He would clear the furs at Plattsburg, where the collector of customs, Peter Sailly, was, conveniently enough, an old friend of his.

The procedure he set up in conjunction with Albert Gallatin, Secretary of the Treasury, was this: Astor would inform Peter Sailly when a shipment of furs was on its way. Sailly would seize them on their appearance, as required by law, but would release them when either Astor or his agents posted bond to their full value—a guarantee, in effect, that the goods were not contraband. The furs would then go on down the Hudson to New York. Astor would meanwhile submit proof that the transaction was legal and would recover the bond.

Immediately after the declaration of hostilities he secured special passports and went to Montreal to arrange the details of the plan in person. Thereafter he entrusted the movement of the furs to various agents, coppering his bets in his usual cautious fashion by sending out several men on the same errand. If one failed to cut through the enormous snarls of red tape and wartime confusion to a particular batch of muskrat hides in a forgotten corner of some warehouse, another might succeed.

Time proved the precaution wise; in general the duplicating agents supplemented each other's activities very well.

Each movement—and the furs traveled in small consignments—was always subject to the danger that some privateer greedy for bounty or some zealous army officer resentful of this commercial fraternizing would pounce upon a cargo as it traveled through the border wilderness and create more trouble than restitution of the pelts would be worth. Transport and storage therefore had to be entrusted to dependable men. Fortunately Astor had operated in the Lake Champlain area for two dozen years. He had many useful acquaintances. Writing to one of them from Montreal on July 9, 1812, he remarked that he would send "segars" to the men in the area who helped his cause and books and earrings to their wives. He also said that the first shipment—2693 wolf skins, 143 beaver, the whole "Bulkey and not much value"—was already on its way, though he had been in Montreal scarcely twenty-four hours.[3]

The shipments dribbled along throughout the winter of 1812–13. Disappointingly few pelts arrived from Mackinac, however. One batch, surprisingly enough, turned up in St. Louis through the efforts of traders Jean P. Cabanné and Antoine Chenié. The two men were United States citizens, respected and influential in the Missouri River trade. But in their desperation they were not above violating the law. Caught in Mackinac in 1811, unable to obtain goods because of the Non-Intercourse Act, they had apparently copied the Canadian traders and successfully smuggled in what they needed. In 1812 they decided to repeat. Taking along a boatload or two of furs for settling their accounts, they toiled up the Illinois River and through Lake Michigan. While they were on St. Joseph Island, making up their assortments, word arrived that war had been declared.

The excitement of the attack on Mackinac engulfed them and they were not able to leave until quiet returned in mid-August, which was normal departure time for Missouri boats anyway. As they were readying their crews, they were approached by Toussaint Pothier. Pothier was looking for a way to ship out enough furs that the new South West Company could raise American dollars for meeting at least some of its current obligation. Detroit seemed too risky a way: Hull and Brock were maneuvering their armies for position and no one knew what was likely to happen. Besides, transport was tight. Voyageurs and Indians hurrying to Brock's help had requisitioned most of the large barges on the lake and all of the canoes suitable for carrying shipments down the Ottawa River to Montreal. Cabanné and Chenié, however, had barges of their own and perhaps could obtain more of the small kind needed for navigating the Fox-Wisconsin route. Would they take as many South West Company furs as they had room for? From St. Louis they could then ship the pelts to Astor without undue risk. Roundabout, to be sure, but what other way was there?

Cabanné and Chenié agreed, no doubt for a price. All told, they managed to crowd aboard 602 packs of skins. Some of these were the same furs they had brought out of St. Louis; there was no other way of getting them to market. When they reached St. Louis, they tried to land their smuggled merchandise undetected at midnight on September 12, 1812. In 1811 they had had no trouble. But the war put a different light on matters and this time an angry posse of citizens, apprised by some informer, pounced on them. Goods and furs were confiscated, and the two traders had to post bonds of $30,000 as surety for their appearance at a trial held in May 1813.

Astor had already settled the legality of importing furs which he owned in full or in part. He came to the aid of the beset traders and the jury cleared them.[4] The furs were declared released, but during the period while they had been impounded, close to 200 packs were lost to theft and destruction by vermin. This ended any hope of profit, but at least some furs had come out of Mackinac. Very few others had. In brooding about the matter, Astor convinced himself that there must be two thousand more packs on the island.

Canny though he was in most respects, Astor sometimes fell victim to such moments of self-delusion. In 1812 he had not wanted war and so had refused to accept its possibility almost until the cannons were being loaded. In 1813 the first thin showings of American aggression led him to persuade himself that victory and peace were in the offing.

In hindsight one wonders how even unbridled optimism leaped to such a conclusion. The projected American marches to Montreal in late 1812 had died at the border, and in the early summer of 1813 the New York frontier was bogged in a stalemate. In the West, William Henry Harrison had replaced Hull after the fall of Detroit, but his campaign to retake the city had been halted by a near disaster: British-led Indians surprised a thousand of his men at River Raisin, south of Detroit, and massacred or captured most of them. Withdrawing into northern Ohio, Harrison built three defensive forts and in the spring staved off heavy enemy assaults. These defensive victories were not very strong foundations on which to build hope, but the frontier managed. When Harrison began strengthening his army with fresh troops, the West ecstatically concluded that a victory march was all but underway.

Astor caught the contagion. With anticipations of peace pushing his pen, he wrote Ramsay Crooks at St. Louis, care of Charles Gratiot, on July 19. He began by regretting Crooks's resignation from the Pacific Fur Company and remarked in an offhand way that as soon as the war ended, an event he expected shortly, he planned to resume his Great Lakes Indian trade. Was Crooks interested?

The letter passed Crooks as he was on his way to hit Astor for a job. On reaching New York, he told Astor that his preference was to return to the Missouri, where he had served so hard an apprenticeship.[5] That area did not intrigue Astor, however. Late in 1812 the merchant turned down an offer to buy shares in one of the many reorganizations of the St. Louis Missouri Fur Company; and although he had commissioned Charles Gratiot to buy deer skins for him in St. Louis, that was as far as he wanted to commit himself. Indians had closed the upper river and Lisa was firmly entrenched at Council Bluffs, where Crooks once had made his headquarters with McClellan. No, the Missouri was out for the time being.

The talks lagged. During the stagnant time Crooks sought out Robert Stuart. In his own way, that young man had had a busy time. After reporting to Astor on his arrival, June 23, 1813, he had hurried to Brooklyn and resumed his impetuous courtship of Betsy Sullivan. On July 21 they were married. For a year thereafter Stuart vanishes from the records. It seems certain, however, that at the end of the honeymoon Stuart continued working for Astor in his New York warehouses and on buying trips north into Canada.[6]

While Crooks was dawdling in New York, American military prospects in the Detroit area suddenly brightened. Using the Indians which Dickson brought to Amherstburg during the summer of 1813, the British late in July renewed their attacks on the three forts which Harrison had built in northeastern Ohio. The Americans again beat them back with heavy losses. The disheartened Indians, who did not relish siege warfare anyhow, began fading away toward the Mississippi. Shortly thereafter (on September 10) Oliver Perry gained control of Lake Erie and cut the British supply lines to the west by his brilliant naval victory at Put-in-Bay. Scenting victory, Harrison marched north to invade the Ontario Peninsula.

These developments gave a sharp new direction to Astor's talks with Ramsay Crooks. The merchant was still trying to bring as many furs as possible into the United States. In September 1813 he again sent agents to Montreal to meet the fall collections and divert whatever was due him through Lake Champlain to New York. He had received no communications from Mackinac or St. Joseph, however, and had no way of knowing how many furs from that area might be coming down the Ottawa. Because of continued transportation difficulties he was inclined to doubt that very many would. This worried him. Goods had gone to St. Joseph and Mackinac in 1812, before the declaration of war. During the subsequent winter some Indians must have received those goods and had hunted to pay for them, particularly the distant Chippewas west of Fond du Lac at the far tip of Lake Superior. Some traders would be bringing in the returns. These pelts, added to the ones Astor envisioned as already accumulated in the warehouses on the two islands, might represent rich profits—if he could get them.

On hearing of Perry's victory, Astor jumped characteristically to the conclusion he desired. Detroit would soon fall and a man with proper connections should be able to work his way on to Mackinac without trouble. Why not Crooks? He knew the area. Though an American now, he was a Scot by birth and was friendly with many of the Canadian traders.

He blurted out his proposal, but Crooks held back. He was reluctant to undertake the difficult trip to Mackinac in the dead of winter, especially if the island was still in enemy control. But he agreed to travel as far as American troops went, so that he could be on hand for whatever developed. On that basis they came to an understanding—too quickly, perhaps. When Crooks actually began working under it, he found that it was full of uncertainties.

Astor did not want him wasting time while the army made its preparations. He directed Crooks to busy himself in whatever fur areas he could reach and buy as many pelts as he safely could—with emphasis on the ill-defined term "safely." He could spend $36,000 for skins delivered to Buffalo, New York, at Astor's risk (but Astor wanted the risk to be minimum), and up to $100,000 if the sellers undertook the risk of delivery. For this work Crooks was to receive one third of the profits. Astor was also eager to secure Indian goods for filling the merchandise vacuums that existed around Fort Wayne and on west as far as St. Louis. He had ordered his agents in Montreal to bring out as much of his property as the British government would allow (he was not optimistic on this score) and he hoped Crooks could pick up more from Detroit traders who had been bankrupt by the war. If Crooks found enough goods and could hire the necessary men, he might even launch a few trading outfits for the winter season, if it seemed safe as the British and Indians withdrew. He would be paid for handling the mass of detail involved, but it wasn't quite clear on what basis, since no one could venture a sound guess as to what might evolve.

In so fluid a situation, Crooks would obviously need to improvise on the spot—yet Astor disliked improvisation by his underlings. The result was instructions whose full ambiguities Crooks did not appreciate until he was out in the field. Much of his correspondence during the winter would be devoted to sharp requests for clearer authorizations. It proved to be good training for the highly responsible position he would assume under Astor a few years later: a man had to keep hammering hard at the merchant to nail him down to firm commitments on major policy. Crooks never forgot that early lesson.

Astor sent him off from New York City on October 8 with $150 for expenses. The young man—Crooks was approaching his twenty-seventh birthday—lived more than four months on that pittance. He traveled to Albany by steamboat and on west by stagecoach over bone-racking roads to Buffalo, arriving October 19. Along the way he learned that on October 5, beside the River Thames in Ontario, Harrison had crushed a retreating British army commanded by General Henry Proctor. (In 1807 Crooks's sister had married Proctor's younger brother William.) Tecumseh died in the battle. Kentucky cavalrymen skinned a body they thought was his for souvenirs. Indians insisted, however, that they had recovered his corpse. The matter was largely academic. His death and Proctor's defeat ended any hope (it was never very great) of unified action by the American Indians against the United States.

Confusion was racketing through Buffalo when Crooks arrived. Harrison was about to move in some of his troops and the village was in a frenzy preparing accommodations. Crooks found a miserable room in a house that carpenters noisily transformed about his ears into a barracks. From Harrison, whom he met through letters provided by Astor, he learned that no attack on Mackinac was contemplated for so late in the year. The general added that he saw little gain in Crooks's struggling against transportation jams in an effort to reach Detroit. The only furs he might find there would be whatever paltry amounts the citizens had been able to conceal during the British occupation. No Indian goods were available either; traders had not been able to import during the summer of 1813.

Other rumors Crooks picked up (presumably not from Harrison) were more exciting. People in Buffalo were sure that an American attack on Montreal was imminent. If the city fell, Mackinac would automatically have to surrender and the entire Lake area would lie open to the traders who moved in first. "You must be well aware," Crooks wrote Astor on October 21, "how propitious and inviting the present crisis is." He then coolly challenged his principal. If Astor expected Crooks to manage any sweeping bid for trade supremacy, then Crooks wanted a better agreement than the one under which he was working. He suggested that he return to New York and discuss the situation. To occupy himself while awaiting Astor's decision, he began drawing up long lists of goods which the new concern might need for trading outfits as far away as the Missouri.

Astor shied away from the bait and concentrated on those troublesome furs at Michilimackinac. He professed amazement that the army of the United States would not make the move he desired. "Surely our people know not the importance of Michilimackinac & St. Joseph," he wrote Crooks on November 15. "I was sure they had gone & taken it." Nevertheless Crooks should not come to New York. He should be ready to hurry to Mackinac for the furs the instant the island fell, and Detroit was the best place to wait. Astor then admitted that "it is of course my object to take hold of the whole [fur trade] . . . and I cannot believe you entertain fears of our agreeing as to the terms, but at this moment it would be premature to fix anything."

Thus put off, Crooks went as far as Erie, Pennsylvania, on his way to Detroit. There, using another letter of introduction provided by Astor, he met General Lewis Cass, who through the succeeding years would be as useful a business friend as Ramsay Crooks would ever know. Though only thirty-one at the time of their first interview, Cass already had had a notable career. He had been admitted to the Ohio bar at the age of twenty, had served four years in the Ohio Legislature and had been United States Marshal for the territory. At the outbreak of the war he had joined the Ohio volunteers as a colonel. He was soon appointed a brigadier-general in the regular army and then Governor of Michigan Territory.

Cass told Crooks in Erie not to push his luck. Word had just arrived that British raiders had crossed the Niagara River late in December, shortly after Crooks's departure from Buffalo, and had burned most of the town to the ground. A British counterattack on Detroit appeared imminent. Indians were gathering, and boatwrights were busy building three brigs at Matchedash Bay, where the Nottawasaga River emptied into the southern tip of Huron's broad Georgian Bay. Eventually Crooks would learn that this report of the brigs was not quite accurate, but even so it was obvious from Cass's information that the British were going to make a concerted effort to forestall any American moves toward the upper lakes.

The disruption of his plans initiated a winter of almost aimless wandering. Hearing of a man who had ninety packs of furs for sale, he pursued him to Pittsburgh, but the price was too high. After a siege of illness he drifted back to Erie to learn the prospects for spring. Astor kept writing cheery letters—when peace came, "we shall make as mush money as you please by the Indian trade." In the raw weather of March that happy day looked a long way off.

Astor, however, was more resourceful than Crooks yet realized. Early in April 1814, he conceived the idea of sending his own private vessel to Mackinac to remove the furs. He began the attack with his usual bombardment of letters to influential men in Washington. He knew they would be read. After all, he had subscribed and was subscribing millions in war loans. On May 16 the United States capitulated and gave him permission to send the vessel through the lines provided that the Canadian government also agreed. Straightway the merchant rushed George Astor, another of his multitudinous nephews, to Montreal to approach the Canadians through the good offices of his partners in the South West Company. The commanding general of Canada, Sir George Prevost, agreed on June 8 with the stipulation that the ship follow a certain course during the loading. George Astor thereupon departed for Erie to buy the necessary vessel.

Crooks meanwhile remained sick, discouraged, vacillating. He was working for a share of the profits, yet so far had not obtained a skin, let alone a profitable one. As spring neared, he wavered between going to Detroit for whatever might be there or to St. Louis where he might find deer skins. When he heard that Astor contemplated sending another agent to Mackinac, his hurt pride took umbrage. Was Astor withdrawing his confidence? Did he think that Crooks's incompetence had caused the luckless winter?

Astor soothed him. Anyone else who represented Astor on Mackinac would be subordinate to Crooks. "You *must* be satesfaid that I have full confidence in your Integrity and as to your ablielitys untill they fail I shall have no cause to Doubt tham." Somewhat mollified, Crooks went to Detroit, but found traders demanding exorbitant prices for their few pelts. Unable to bring "these lunatics to their senses by dint of argument," he told them what he would pay "and left them to their reflections for a few days." Then a fresh difficulty arose. The Detroit traders heard that Astor sometimes rejected drafts if he disapproved of his agent's actions, and they demanded either specie or bank notes, neither of which Crooks had. Unable to procure more than a handful of furs, he busied himself trying to set up trading parties for the Michigan Peninsula and for northern Indiana. He needed, he wrote Astor urgently, at least thirty pieces of stroud, gunpowder, lead, shoes, hats, chocolate, coffee, tobacco, high wine, wampum, silverworks, playing cards. He also made investigations as to how many boatmen he might be able to hire. The effort came to nothing. But it too was good practice.

The army meantime was preparing to storm Michilimackinac. Commander of the troops was Major George Croghan, twenty-two years old, who the preceding summer had performed spectacularly in turning back a British-Indian attack on one of the Ohio forts. The fleet for transporting the troops was commanded by Captain Arthur Sinclair.

Crooks, who knew the island, watched the proceedings with a jaundiced eye. Mackinac's fort was too high on the hill to be injured by ships outside the cove. In his opinion the attackers would have to land on the back side of the island, where the British had, and fight their way into the citadel. It might be difficult. The trails from the beach, he wrote Astor in a letter outlining his doubts, were mere "winding paths where not more than two men can walk abreast." The heavy undergrowth was suited to ambush. Furthermore, Indian report said that the defenders had built a new fortification on the highest part of the island, to prevent a repetition of their own surprise attack from the rear.

In spite of his reservations, he nonetheless arranged to go along with the fleet, his knowledge of the island making him a welcome addition to Sinclair's staff. If the attack succeeded, he would be on hand to make sure the furs were not confiscated as Canadian contraband. If it failed, perhaps he could arrange to be landed under a flag of truce, gather the pelts together, and wait with them for George Astor's ship. So far he had not heard a word directly from George about his plans.

Sinclair's little fleet sailed July 3. It consisted of six vessels, each towing a gunboat—evidently nothing more than a large barge mounting small cannon. Crowded aboard the sailing ships were six hundred soldiers.

The British had been expecting the move ever since the fall of Detroit. The common sense of strategy demanded that the Americans protect their flanks by neutralizing Michilimackinac and its satellite, Prairie du Chien. Success would then leave Canada exposed. On learning of the American preparations in Detroit, General Prevost summed up the stakes of the campaign in a letter of July 10, 1814, to Earl Bathurst:

> . . . the Island and Fort of Michilimackinac is the first importance, as tending to promote our Indian connexion and secure them in our interest: its geographical position is admirable; its influence extends . . . among the Indian tribes to New Orleans and the Pacific Ocean; . . . it gives security to the great trading establishments of the North-West and Hudson's Bay Companies.

Prairie du Chien shared the importance, and for the same reasons. If the settlement on the Mississippi should fall to the Americans, so wrote the commander at Mackinac,

> tribe after tribe would be gained over or subdued . . . Nothing could then prevent the enemy from gaining the source of the Mississippi, gradually extending themselves by the Red River to Lake Winnipic, from whence the descent of Nelson's River to York Fort [the key bastion on Hudson Bay] would be easy.

The defense of the southern flank of these strategic posts had been assigned several months earlier to Robert Dickson and his savages. Before following the attack on Michilimackinac, it is necessary to revert to his activities and American counterthrusts along the Mississippi in the winter and spring of 1813–14.

Most of Wisconsin's Indians, it will be recalled, had drifted home in discouragement after the failure of their attacks on Harrison's Ohio forts. Dickson feared that their dejection might lead them to listen to American agents. In order to hold their wavering favor, he hurried from Detroit to Montreal, started more supplies west, and gained from officials there fresh authority to requisition whatever he needed from the store-houses on Mackinac and St. Joseph.

When he arrived back on the Lakes in mid-October, 1813, he exercised his authority with so heavy a hand that he enraged John Askin, the government storekeeper on St. Joseph, and sowed the seeds of other enmities that would hurt him later on. No one had goods to spare. Food, too, was critically short. To remedy matters Dickson took twenty-seven Michigan Fencibles to Green Bay—the Fencibles were the French-Canadian militia on the island—and with two local traders, Louis Grignon and John Lawe, scoured the surrounding farms for provisions that he sent to distant points.

In so doing he injured his own work. Later in the year he ran short of supplies himself. He wintered on Garlic Island in Lake Winnebago, a little north of modern Oshkosh. The weather was bitter. The ice was so thick the Indians could not cut through it to spear fish. He kept begging the men at Green Bay to send wheat. "I hear nothing," he wrote on Christmas Day "but the cry of Hunger from all Quarters." And again on February 4, 1814, "I am sorry to distress you by sending you so many men but necessity has no law."

There was never enough food. Many Indians died; the survivors grew restless. The tug of war for their support intensified. Boilvin, Forsyth, and their agents worked busily throughout Illinois, eastern Iowa, and as near to Prairie du Chien as they dared. Dickson charged that Forsyth offered the Indians bounty money for his redheaded scalp, and Forsyth retorted with a similar accusation. Both insisted that they escaped hired assassins only by the narrowest of margins.

The Indians did achieve one signal success on behalf of the British. Early in September 1813 they laid such heavy siege to Fort Madison on the Mississippi that the commander decided to evacuate. By night the garrison dug an escape trench to the river. They then set fire to their own fort (they had burned down their own trading factory a year earlier), crawled out through the ditch, and fled in boats to St. Louis. The Mississippi lay completely open.

The frightened citizens of Missouri poured demands on their own officials and on Washington for some sort of counteraction. Resentment centered on Prairie du Chien. Armchair strategists in St. Louis urged that their militia capture the settlement, build a fort and erect a government trading factory whose supplies would make the Indians less vulnerable to Dickson's presents. William Clark, who not long before had been appointed Governor of Missouri Territory, was at first re-luctant. He felt that maintaining a fort deep in hostile territory would prove difficult, particularly if it had to be garrisoned by militia. The militia in those days signed on for short terms only (often for as little as two months) and declined to linger on duty a moment longer than specified. Trying to keep such troops moving back and forth along the Mississippi obviously would create problems.

In April 1814, however, Clark was able to obtain sixty-one regular troops, commanded by Lieutenant Joseph Perkins. This nucleus might be able to maintain a fort at Prairie du Chien, once it was built. Enlisting 140 short-term militiamen as a supporting force for the "invasion," he started up the river on five big keelboats. Boilvin went along with his family to reoccupy his agency headquarters at the Prairie.

They had no trouble. Exaggerated reports of the American "army" flashed through the Indian country ahead of the expedition and so frightened the Sacs and Foxes at Saukenuk, their village near the mouth of Rock River, that they were cowed to peace by the bark of a few rifles. The same rumors slowed Dickson's recruiting. He had been ordered to bring at least three hundred Indians to Michilimackinac, to await the expected attack from Detroit. But the American movements on the Mississippi seemed more urgent to the Indians. Many said they would not leave their homes, and it was only after extreme effort that Dickson managed to produce the number he had been asked for. He left Prairie du Chien with them shortly after Clark's five boats started up the Mississippi. He hoped that Black Hawk's Sacs would forestall the enemy advance; but when that did not happen, Indians everywhere along the river lost heart and the Americans entered the Prairie without firing a shot.

Commandeering the South West Company warehouses as temporary barracks, Clark's soldiers went quickly to work. Part of their activities, according to inflamed rumors reaching the British, were atrocities. In outrage the commander at Mackinac wrote General Drummond about Clark:

> This Ruffian on taking Prairie des Chiens, captured eight Indians of the Winnebago Nation; they cajoled them at first with affected kindness, set provisions before them; & in the act of eating treacherously fell upon them & murdered seven in cold blood—the eighth escaped to be the sad historian of their horrible fate . . . . He shut [four others] up in a log house, & afterwards shot them thro' between the logs.[7]

On June 5 Clark selected as a site for the fort a small mound, believed to have been built by prehistoric Indians between the slough Marais St. Friole and the rears of the two dozen clay-daubed, bark-covered houses that straggled along the river front. There he stepped off the outlines of a triangular post. On June 7 he left with three of the gunboats and most of the militia. The remaining two gunboats stayed behind to protect the fort builders for so long as the volunteers aboard them would stay.

It was not long. Toward the end of June, the smaller of the two boats started for St. Louis with those among the militia whose enlistments were due to expire. Only thirty-five or so remained aboard the *General Clark,* commanded by an ex-tanner named Fred Yeiser. Their terms of service were also running out. Growing alarmed, Lieutenant Perkins pushed his workers hard. He surmised that Indian messengers had sped to Michilimackinac with word of the Prairie's fall and he expected a counterattack. If he hoped to have his barricades up and occupied before his outside support left him, he would have to hurry.

Michilimackinac was ready for battle, thanks in large part to a noteworthy exploit by Lieutenant Colonel Robert McDouall. Early in February, in the same severe weather that had distressed Dickson on his island in Lake Winnebago, McDouall led two hundred picked infantry, twenty-two artillerymen with four cannon, and a dozen officers from Kingston, at the eastern end of Lake Ontario, to York, near its western end. From York they turned north along the voyageur route to Lake Simcoe, then west to the upper reaches of the pine-girt, frozen Nottawasaga River. There they found a small group of boat builders already at work. Word of these activities reaching Crooks in Erie, Pennsylvania, said that the shipwrights were building three brigs with which to control Lake Huron. The reports were wrong. The men were constructing thirty barges for carrying McDouall's troops and their equipment to Michilimackinac.

The soldiers put together several huts beside those of the boat builders, chopped out a road through the dense forest—called Yonge Street, it would henceforth be the highway for heavy matèriel moving out of York—and helped whipsaw tree trunks into planks. By April 19 the barges were finished and loaded.

The ice in the river was beginning to rot. In a hurry to be moving, McDouall's soldiers started chopping out a channel. Six strenuous days of this brought them to Georgian Bay. The sight was terrifying. Agitated by violent gales, the lake was heaving its ice up into crunching floes. Grimly McDouall ordered his deeply laden bateaux into the narrow seams of black water. Fending off jagged chunks of ice with their oars, soaked by spray, ill rested in their rocky camps at night, the reinforcements crept forward an average of sixteen miles a day. They lost one boat, but saved its crew and lading. After nineteen days they reached Michilimackinac. There, on May 18, McDouall took over command of the defenses.

Dickson arrived a little later with his Indians—Chippewas, Winnebagos, Menominees, Sioux, a few Sacs. McDouall sat them in a square eight deep in the open air, listened to their headmen promise allegiance, and replied in a speech exhorting unflagging vigor against the common enemy. "May the Great Spirit give you strength and courage in so good a cause and crown you with victory in the day of battle."

That day obviously was not far distant. Canoe messengers followed one after another with the newest word of the American preparations in Detroit. Hard on the heels of those reports came word that Prairie du Chien had fallen. Faced with the prospect of being caught by a pincer movement, McDouall did not wish to split his force by moving toward the enemy. The report of Clark's supposed atrocities against the Winnebago captives put the Indian auxiliaries in such a frenzy, however, that Dickson said they could not be controlled unless some of them were sent back to avenge the wrong. McDouall reluctantly acceded. To spare his own force, he authorized two traders of Prairie du Chien, Joseph Rolette and Thomas Anderson, to enlist volunteers among the voyageurs who were assembling in the village for the annual summer rendezvous, a semblance of which resounded ever year, war or no.

In two days Rolette and Anderson recruited sixty-three men. One hundred and thirty-six Indians were detached to go with them. Additional voyageurs and Indians were to be gathered at Green Bay. To this untrained, undisciplined force McDouall added "twelve smart fellows of the Michigan Fencibles" and a small three-pound cannon under charge of Sergeant James Keating, of whom more hereafter. As commander in chief of the expedition he selected a tall, grim wintering partner of the North West Company, William McKay, brother of the Alexander McKay who had died aboard the *Tonquin* when it was blown apart off Vancouver Island. William McKay was famous for his physical strength and for his severe treatment of his subordinates. The nature of his command considered, he probably seemed like a good choice, though Thomas Anderson later grumbled that during most of the campaign he was half drunk.

Dickson and the bulk of the Indians were held at Michilimackinac. Hoping to strengthen the island still more, McDouall urged trader John Johnston to recruit as many voyageurs as he could find at Sault Ste Marie and St. Joseph, even though this left those two spots quite defenseless. Provisions for the anticipated siege proved harder to come by than men. To General Drummond, McDouall wrote urgently, "I have therefore to beg, to suplicate, to entreat, my dear General, that every possible effort be made—every step be immediately taken, which can facilitate our being supplied . . . which if not acted up to, with the utmost promptitude & vigor, there is no prospect for us but famine and starvation."[8]

These steps taken, his guard details doubled, and Indian sentries posted at the far beaches, he settled down to await the assault.

CHAPTER *14*

Sweet Fruits of Defeat

At Green Bay, William McKay increased the force advancing against Prairie du Chien to 120 whites and 530 Indians. The canoes and barges carrying these men and their equipment jammed the winding Fox River and clogged the portages. In spite of the confusion the army reached the mouth of the Wisconsin on July 17, nineteen days after leaving Michilimackinac. The first man to see them as they crept behind small islands in the Mississippi toward Prairie du Chien was a drover taking cattle toward Boilvin's agency. He cried out an alarm, and panic was instantaneous. Boilvin hustled his family onto the gunboat, *General Clark*. A few American sympathizers rushed into the fort, but most of the citizens scampered out onto the prairie, to be away from the fighting.

Thomas Anderson entered the fort under a flag of truce and demanded its surrender. Lieutenant Perkins refused. Sergeant James Keating thereupon aimed his little three-pound cannon at the *General Clark*. His skill was devastating. At least two thirds of the eighty-six rounds he fired hit their mark. The gunboat was less effective. Counting coehorns (small mortars mounted on wooden blocks) it carried fourteen pieces of artillery, the largest a six-pound cannon. It inflicted one casualty: flying splinters from a smashed fence post drew blood from an Indian's thigh.

On the gunboat, five men were dead, ten wounded. Damage was severe. Fearful that if the vessel suffered many more hits it would sink, its commander, Fred Yeiser, cut the cable and fled downstream. Keating thereupon switched his aim to the fort. Its guns had been even less effective than those of the *General Clark;* they had not scratched anyone at all.

McKay intended to let Keating soften up the defenses during the evening and attack at dawn. The Indians spoiled the plan. The excitement had turned them wild. They ran in and out of the houses, pilfering even bedclothes. (Agent Boilvin lost $4000 worth of property.) They swarmed out to the farms to butcher cattle, now and then interrupting themselves to fire their rifles at the fort from impossible distances. McKay had to post guards throughout the village that night to keep his own allies in hand. When he did assemble the savages for the morning assault, they were tired and refused to carry out a frontal charge.

Thus frustrated, the commander tried mining. The tunneling proved too hard and the sappers gave up after twelve feet. By the morning of the nineteenth the indiscriminate rifle shooting had about exhausted the Canadians' powder, and only six rounds remained for Keating's three-pounder. McKay decided his only hope was to set fire to the fort. Sappers crawled out and built protective breastworks; the cannon was pushed up behind them, close to the stockade. As the attackers were building a fire to heat the last balls red-hot, planning to crash them like brands into the timbers, they were astonished to see a white flag over the pickets.

Only five of Lieutenant Perkins' men had been wounded during the bombardment, but he had neither doctor nor medicines for them. He too was almost out of ammunition. His well had run dry and when he tried to deepen it, the sides caved in. He did not know that the tunneling, whose start he had detected, had been abandoned, and he expected a combined assault, inside and out, at any moment. Most discouraging was his realization that he had been abandoned. When the gunboat had floated away, he had supposed it was seeking safer mooring. Later he and his disheartened men had to face the truth that they could expect no help from outside.

The Indians were so intent on murdering the surrendered Americans that McKay kept the vanquished inside their own fort until the excitement simmered down. Accepting their parole, he then sent them downstream with a guard to help them pass the Sac village at Rock River.

They needed the guard. The Sacs and Foxes were even wilder over an unexpected triumph than the Indians at Prairie du Chien had been. When the *General Clark* had started downstream, McKay had given a party of Indians four kegs of powder with orders to get ahead of the gunboat, arm the Sacs and Foxes, and harass the vessel as it was passing through the Rock River Rapids.

While the raiders were lurking along the riverbanks, waiting for the *General Clark,* several American army keelboats and supply barges appeared unexpectedly from below. The craft held replacements for the militia at Prairie du Chien whose terms were about to expire. Since Clark had passed Rock River without trouble on his earlier trips, Major John Campbell, in charge of the reinforcements, was not as alert as he should have been. A perfunctory parley lulled him still more. As he neared the rapids, a heavy wind occupied his attention and finally forced his vessel, the largest of the flotilla, ashore into the arms of the hidden savages. Black Hawk led the attack that killed sixteen whites, wounded fifteen, and captured a barge loaded with supplies. Other vessels swung to Campbell's aid, but if the *General Clark* had not come bumbling down through the rapids and unlimbered its guns at this opportune moment, the disaster might have been even more severe.

Apprised of the victory, the delighted McKay sent more powder and lead to the Sacs and told them to keep the rapids closed. In St. Louis, General Benjamin Howard vowed to open them. On August 22 he ordered 330 rangers and militia onto eight boats and started them up the Mississippi under Major Zachary Taylor. Learning of Taylor's advance almost immediately, the Indians rushed an appeal for help to Thomas Anderson, McKay's successor at Prairie du Chien. Anderson responded with thirty men, one of them Sergeant James Keating with his dwarf three-pound cannon. A thousand Indians joined the ambush. On a day of gusty rain they surprised the Americans completely. Sergeant Keating's fire slammed out as awesomely as it had at Prairie du Chien; Taylor, totally astounded, turned and ran.

During the opening phases of the Prairie du Chien campaigns, Arthur Sinclair's small fleet was moving north from Detroit. He wasted time looking for the Canadian supply base at Nottawasaga River. Balked by fog and uncharted shoals, he gave up and sailed to St. Joseph Island. Its small garrison had just been transferred to Michilimackinac and he won an easy victory. He captured the North West Company's schooner *Mink* as she lay against the shore, waiting for favorable winds to move her with her cargo of flour up the river to Sault Ste Marie. He burned the British fort and the buildings of the North West Company. He did not touch the warehouses and store of the South West Company, possibly because Ramsay Crooks pointed out that they belonged in part to an American, John Jacob Astor.[1]

Another prize, the North West Company schooner *Perseverance,* was waiting at the head of the St. Marys sault, or rapids. She expected the *Mink;* in the normal run of things that ship would have halted at the foot of the rapids and unloaded her 230 barrels of flour; these would have been carted around the sault and reloaded on the *Perseverance* for shipment across Lake Superior to Fort William. Instead of the *Mink,* several longboats appeared, rowed by sailors from the American schooner *Tigress,* Lieutenant Daniel Turner commanding, and filled with American soldiers under Major Arthur Holmes. The startled crew of the *Perseverance* made a futile effort to scuttle her and took to the woods. Securing the schooner, Lieutenant Turner tried to run her down "the swift leaping falls." It turned out to be a wilder ride than he had anticipated. Fearing he could not succeed, he ran the schooner into the bank and set her afire.

Holmes's soldiers destroyed the buildings of the North West Company on the Canadian side of the river and then crossed the strait to the mansion of John Johnston on the American side. Johnston was a wilderness oddity, slender, debonair, gentle. Born in Ireland in 1762, he had joined the North West Company at the age of nineteen. While trading on lovely Madeline Island off the southwest shore of Lake Superior, he had married the daughter of an Indian chief. Highly intelligent, she transformed herself into a gracious, cultured hostess for the home he later built at the Sault. In this wilderness mansion Johnston assembled fine furniture and a large library. Each long winter night he gathered his sons and daughters around the fire, read the classics to them, and led discussions on whatever subject the reading had suggested. But he was an enemy. He had abjured the oath he had taken when appointed deputy United States collector of customs at the Sault, and he had just led a hundred voyageurs to Michilimackinac to aid in the defense of the island. No doubt he would kill all the Americans he could. Grimly ignoring the appeals of Mrs. Johnston, who had managed to spirit away the family valuables, the American raiders seized her husband's supply of trade goods and then reduced the home to ashes.[2]

On July 28 the six American ships, gunboats in tow, appeared off Mackinac. Fearing a landing in the cove, the townspeople fled with what choice possessions they could carry into the forest or the fort. Arthur Sinclair did not land, however. As Crooks had predicted, he found that he could not elevate his guns high enough to duel on equal terms with the stone bastion which his namesake, Patrick Sinclair, had built during another British-American war thirty years earlier. In a quandary he beat back and forth just out of range for seven days. A siege might have been his wisest step. The defenders were down to two or three weeks' provisions, including the jerked meat of every horse on the island. Sinclair did not know this, of course, and anyway could not keep six hundred men inactive on his ships for an indeterminate time. In spite of Crooks's earnest doubts, he sailed on August 4 to the northwest side of the island, where the British had landed two years before.

There was no surprise this time. Anticipating Sinclair's move, McDouall had placed cannon on each of the four heights commanding the trail to the breastworks his defenders had erected on the hilltop overlooking Fort Mackinac. Regulars occupied predetermined positions. Dickson scattered his Indians through the ravines, behind trees and logs.

Sinclair covered the landing with a crashing bombardment. It hurt no one. The English had expected that, too, and were waiting out of range. They let Americans advance well into the underbrush before striking. It was short and bloody. At first the Americans maintained a semblance of order and tried to swing around the left flank. Indians faded with them and kept their attention occupied while McDouall shifted his regulars to meet the change. Later Sinclair wrote plaintively in his report:

> . . . the farther our troops advanced the stronger the enemy became and the weaker and more bewildered our force were; several of the commanding officers were picked out and killed or wounded by the savages. The men were getting lost and falling into confusion . . .

Completely routed, the survivors tumbled in a panic back to the beach. There at last the fleet's cannon did some good; they held off the Indians while the troops were embarked.

The next day under a flag of truce the Americans picked up their dead, including the second-in-command, Major Holmes.[8] During the arrangements for the truce one of the American officers asked McDouall, on Crooks's behalf, whether the trader might remove the South West Company furs from the island. McDouall agreed. Sinclair, however, refused. Crooks then asked to land by himself, in order to have things ready when George Astor arrived. Again Sinclair declined. "As the future movements of the fleet where not determined on," Crooks explained dryly to Astor, "it was thought improper to suffer any communication with the Island."

When Sinclair did decide upon a move, it was a strange one. Though he knew he could not shoot back at the fort, he sailed his ships boldly into the narrow channel between Round Island and the cove, his troops at parade on the decks. The defenders were convinced (so John Johnston recalled years later) that the foolhardy Americans intended to land without artillery protection and storm the fort head-on. If so, a blast of red-hot cannon balls from above quickly changed Sinclair's mind. Heeling the ships around, he fled out of range.

Persuaded at last that assault was impractical, Sinclair detached the schooners *Tigress* and *Scorpion* to blockade the island. They were also to seize if possible the flotilla of North West Company furs which were due to pass through the St. Marys River some time after the middle of August. His hundred wounded groaning aboard the other ships, Sinclair then bore off toward Detroit. On the way he detoured again toward the Nottawasaga River, hoping to aid his blockading ships by destroying the Canadian supply station located in the area.

This time circumstances favored him. He found the place and trapped the British ship *Nancy* inside the river, which near its mouth ran almost parallel to the lake shore. Exultant American artillerymen dragged a howitzer onto the intervening ridge of sand and scrub pine, and started lobbing shells. Suddenly there was a shattering explosion. Lieutenant Miller Worsley of the *Nancy* had mined his ship and the blockhouse at the station so that he could blow them up if necessary. Before he had a chance to fight back, a freak ricochet from the American howitzer ignited the powder train he had laid, and the *Nancy* sank in a ball of fire and smoke.

Confident they had crippled the British, the Americans chopped down several trees to choke the river and continued to Detroit, arriving August 17. Shortly thereafter George Astor appeared with a ninety-ton schooner he had managed to charter after great difficulty at Grand River, between Erie and Cleveland. Wearily Crooks prepared to sail back to Mackinac for Astor's elusive furs.

Behind him Lieutenant Worsley decided to abandon the Nottawasaga River. He had his twenty-five men patch up a canoe and two bateaux that had escaped the full violence of the explosion, dragged them around the tree-blocked channel, and started rowing toward Mackinac. They followed the normal, island-studded canoe route between the Manitoulin chain and Huron's shaggy north shore. As they neared St. Joseph, they spotted the *Tigress* and *Scorpion*. By unrecorded means Worsley reconnoitered the American ships. He grew excited. The enemy sailors, bored by their assignment of merely watching, had grown careless. Worsley was sure that a small, well-armed force could capture both vessels. Hiding his two clumsy barges, he paddled in the canoe with a few men by night to Mackinac and eagerly laid his plan before McDouall.

McDouall already knew from Indian report that the ships were there, and probably had surmised why. And since his communication system by water was remarkably effective, he quite likely had learned that the North West Company fur brigade had already eluded the watchers.

It may have been the biggest brigade in the history of the North West Company—335 men in 42 canoes bearing furs said to be worth a million dollars.[4] In addition to the normal collections from Fort William, the convoy also included the furs which the Astorians had been gathering on the Columbia. For that post, too, had been the victim of wretched luck. And here another reversion in time becomes necessary.

After separating from Robert Stuart's overland party at the mouth of the Walla Walla in the Oregon country in August 1812, the other Astorians had pushed on to their different posts in the interior. Though David Stuart at Okanogan, John Clarke at Spokan, and Russell Farnham in Montana had straightway fallen into competition with the Nor'Westers, they made out fairly well. Donald McKenzie, however, could not persuade the Nez Percé Indians along the lower Snake to trap. Discouraged by his poor returns, he rode to Spokan to talk things over with Clarke. He had scarcely arrived when trader John George McTavish appeared with a group of grinning Nor'Westers and said that war had been declared. The *Isaac Todd,* a raider armed by the North West Company, McTavish added, would shortly appear in the Columbia to batter Astoria to submission.

Stampeded by the threat, McKenzie picked up clerk John Reed on the Clearwater and hurried down the Columbia to warn Duncan McDougall at Astoria of the danger. Together McKenzie and McDougall decided that all personnel should leave Astoria for St. Louis in July. McKenzie and Reed then hurried back up the river to alert the other traders and urge them to start procuring the three or four hundred horses that would be needed to transport men and furs across the continent.

When the other partners gathered at Astoria in June 1813 for the annual rendezvous, they were not disposed to accept the decision. In spite of the competition inland, they were sure they could improve their trade as the Indians fell under the spell of their goods. The *Isaac Todd* had not appeared. (During the talks John George McTavish of the North West Company was camped outside Astoria's stockade, short of supplies and considerably embarrassed by the *Todd's* failure to arrive.) Perhaps the vessel had sunk; perhaps the talk of it was pure bluff. Meanwhile the Astorians were as strong inland as were the Nor'Westers. Why not take a chance?

McKenzie and McDougall shook their heads. *Their* trade had been very poor, and no doubt that colored their thinking. They pointed out that a supply ship had not arrived from Astor that spring and probably would not if the British were blockading New York Harbor. Meanwhile what had happened to Hunt? He had left aboard the *Beaver* the August before to deliver goods to Baranoff at Sitka and take on sea-otter pelts for shipment to Canton. Before going to China he was supposed to have returned to the Columbia for the Astoria pelts. Though he had been scheduled to appear in two months, eleven months had passed without sign of him. If a disaster like the *Tonquin's* had befallen the *Beaver,* the Astorians had no contact left with the outside world.

After protracted discussions the partners compromised. They would continue trading for one more year. If no help had arrived by then, they would leave the country as best they could. To keep the Nor'Westers off their backs during this period they sold supplies to McTavish and with him delineated areas within which each company would have exclusive rights for the ensuing season.

The decisions reached, the various parties returned inland. Shortly thereafter, on August 20, 1813, Hunt reappeared on a strange ship, the *Albatross*. He had a gloomy saga to tell. After concluding a profitable trade with Baranoff, he had gone late in October 1812 to one of the Bering Islands to load sealskins. Arctic gales so racked the *Beaver* that the captain refused to risk her to the Columbia's bar before he had made extensive repairs. Since any long delay would put the lading of furs in China too late for the best markets, Hunt agreed and sailed on the *Beaver* to the Hawaiian Islands. There he dropped off to wait for the annual supply ship from New York.

None appeared. On June 20, 1813, he learned from arriving ships that war had been declared a year earlier and that the Atlantic coast was tightly blockaded. Fearful that the next British move might be against Astoria, he chartered the *Albatross* for $2000, planning to take supplies to the Columbia from Hawaii and return with the furs that had been accumulating during the past two years. He did not intend to abandon Astoria—just remove its valuables in anticipation of trouble.

When McDougall told him that the *Todd* might appear at any moment, Hunt agreed reluctantly that the decision to abandon the post the following July had probably been wise. But he could not keep the *Albatross*, which had another charter scheduled. Therefore he would have to go back to the islands and buy a ship for the evacuation of men and furs. Strangely, he took no pelts with him when he left.

In the fall fresh parties of Nor'Westers arrived from Fort William on Lake Superior. No, they said triumphantly, the *Todd* was not a bluff. They showed letters from London announcing her sailing in company with two warships, the *Phoebe* and *Raccoon*. That was why the Nor'-Westers had made their overland journey to Astoria—to greet the vessels and take over the post.

At that point someone—McTavish of the North West Company perhaps or maybe McDougall of the Astorians—asked what gain there would be in fighting. They were traders, not soldiers. If the Astorians resisted, everything in the post might be destroyed by a bombardment. On the other hand, if they surrendered to naval vessels, the post, its supplies, and its furs might be considered prizes of war and be sold at auction for the benefit of the British government. Would it not be better to make a deal among themselves that would benefit everyone?

That was what they did. After long haggling, the Nor'Westers bought Astoria, its subordinate posts, all supplies and furs for $58,000. The figure included $14,000 in wages due the employees, an obligation the purchasers agreed to assume. When Astor learned of the figure he was enraged and insisted it should have been "nearer two hundred thousand dollars." Neither he nor his historian, Washington Irving, ever forgave McDougall or McKenzie. They imputed treachery to the Scots and ignored the possibility that by being resistant the men might have lost everything.

The arrangement was completed October 16, 1813. On November 30 the warship *Raccoon* at last appeared outside the bar, without the *Todd*. When a group of Astorians and Nor'Westers rowed out to meet her, they saw, walking painfully across the deck toward them, a great hulk of a man so fearfully scarred the Canadians did not recognize him until he spoke. John McDonald of Garth, a partner in the North West Company! He explained many things. The *Isaac Todd* had indeed left London with the *Phoebe* and *Raccoon*. McDonald of Garth had started on her with another company partner, Donald McTavish, who had brought along for solace on the journey a rosy Portsmouth barmaid named Jane Barnes. Disgusted with the wallowing ship and with the scandal, McDonald transferred at Rio de Janeiro to the *Phoebe*.[5]

Storms had separated the snail-slow convoy south of the Horn. The *Todd* did not appear at the rendezvous at the Juan Fernández Islands. Meanwhile the captain of the *Phoebe* had decided his ship was too big to cross the Columbia's bar. He transferred McDonald to the *Raccoon* and sent her ahead under Captain Black to seize the post unaided. During gunnery practice one day an accidental explosion killed or injured twenty-six men. McDonald lost his long red hair and bushy beard. The back of his head, he declared later, "could not have been known from my face had it not been for my conspicuous nose." The ship's surgeon told him that only a life of temperance had enabled him to pull through his painful convalescence.

Because of the sale there was no post for Captain Black to seize. Somewhat disgruntled by his long and fruitless errand, he held a ceremony of possession anyway, broke a bottle on the flagstaff, and hoisted the Union Jack. In January 1814 he departed. The next month Hunt returned in the brig *Pedler* to evacuate the post. He bore more bad news he had picked up in Hawaii. Astor had sent two relief ships, but the *Lark* had sunk off Maui and the crew of the *Forester*, rebelling against extending help under British colors to an enemy post, had diverted the ship to Alaska.

According to Washington Irving, Hunt was infuriated when he learned that Astoria had been sold. It seems, though, he must have realized that if McDougall and McKenzie had not struck a bargain with the enemy, the *Raccoon* would have seized the post outright. Accepting the *fait accompli* in what may have been better grace than Irving admits, Hunt helped wind up the last details and on April 3, 1814, left the Columbia in the *Pedler* for Alaska to start trading off such goods as the Pacific Fur

Company still retained. He may also have intended to pick up more merchandise from the *Forester*.

Three clerks went with him—J. C. Halsey, Alfred Seton, and Russell Farnham. Knowing that his projected trade might delay him for an indefinite time, Hunt dropped the trio off at different places with instructions that they find means of carrying dispatches to Astor about developments at Astoria. Halsey lingered in Sitka, hoping to catch a wandering trader. Farnham, described by Ross as a "bustling, active and enterprising man," switched to the *Forester*, which landed him on the Kamchatka Peninsula of eastern Siberia. He supposed that he could make his way with Russian travelers across Asia and northern Europe to some Atlantic port, but the Russian wilderness proved more primitive than he had anticipated. The trip took more than two years. Details are unknown, except that he walked most of the way and at one point ate the tops of his boots to escape starvation. In October 1816 he reached Copenhagen, caught an American-bound ship, and so came home.

Seton was still aboard the *Pedler* when Spaniards captured her at Santa Barbara, California, and impounded her for two months at San Blas, Mexico. Freed at last, Hunt sailed for the Hawaiian Islands. Seton made his way south to the Isthmus of Darien, fell ill, but struggled through the jungles of Panama to the city of Cartagena in Colombia. By then he was a skeleton, totally destitute. A revolution saved him. A British squadron appeared to evacuate the British citizens in the city and Seton threw himself on the captain's mercy. The man graciously took him to Jamaica. From there Seton was able to obtain passage to New York.

Neither of the ordeals was necessary. Astor had already learned the fate of the Pacific Fur Company from the men who came back overland with the Nor'Westers and their bargain furs—furs which the schooners *Tigress* and *Scorpion* were waiting to seize off St. Joseph Island.

The Pacific part of the brigade—ninety men in seven canoes and barges—had left the Columbia on April 4, the day after Hunt's departure on the *Pedler*. Among the overlanders were a few Astorians who declined to accept service with the North West Company. (Those who wished jobs were hired by the purchasers as part of the sale agreement.) The travelers crossed the Rockies at Athabaska Pass and worked down the roily rivers of the plains to the great rendezvous at Fort William. There they decided to increase their strength by waiting until the canoes from Fort William were ready to go.

A few unencumbered men decided to press ahead in a single canoe— John Clarke, Donald McKenzie, David Stuart, Gabriel Franchère, four voyageurs, and John McDonald of Garth, his singed beard beginning to grow out again. Avoiding the American side of the lake, they traveled along the bleakly beautiful, foggy north shore. One hundred and twenty-five miles from Sault Ste Marie they met Captain McCargo of the burned schooner *Perseverance,* heading west in a small canoe to apprise the men at Fort William of the American raid on the Sault and St. Joseph.

The flotilla at Fort William had to be warned. Most of the men turned back with McCargo. Franchère, David Stuart, and two voyageurs went ahead in McCargo's canoe—it was the small one—to reconnoiter. Although the ruins of Johnston's home were still smoldering when they reached the Sault, a few traders had already returned to start the slow work of rebuilding. Determined to resist more effectively if the Americans returned again, the whites recruited a few Indians, managed to scrape together a few rifles and some powder that had escaped the raid, and prepared breastworks. They could not find food, however. For nineteen days they lived on wild raspberries and trout. Then the flotilla appeared. Cautiously the boats wound among the many islands of the river, turned east along Huron's rugged north shore, and reached the French River undetected. This led to the Ottawa. By September Astor knew that a few of his erstwhile partners were in Montreal, and he sent Robert Stuart to the border to arrange passports for them.

For some reason Astor supposed Crooks might have encountered the displaced Astorians on their way past St. Joseph or Michilimackinac. On September 14, 1814, while Crooks was preparing to return to the island with George Astor, the merchant wrote sorrowfully to him,

I supose you have seen or heard of Some of your old Companyons who I am told have Returned. I hope to See some of tham here soon as Mr. R. Stuart is gone towards the line to procure a passport for tham to com here   was there ever an undertaking of more merit of more hazzard & enterpriz attended with a greater variaty of Misfortunes . . . I do not know what has been done at Columbia River only that it is taking [taken].

Meanwhile the *Tigress* and *Scorpion* beat in boredom back and forth off St. Joseph. Now and then one or both vessels sallied out into the lake to make sure no supply ship was bearing toward Mackinac. It was probably during one of these absences that the fur brigade slipped by.

Mackinac was hungry. McDouall agreed instantly with Lieutenant Miller Worsley's scheme to capture the blockading schooners. The very morning of Worsley's arrival, September 1, 1814, he ordered four bateaux outfitted, two with small fieldpieces in their bows. Worsley and his sailors manned one boat. Lieutenant Andrew Bulger and fifty volunteers, including Robert Dickson and William McKay, the latter just back from

Prairie du Chien, handled the others. Two hundred of Dickson's Indians followed in their canoes.

At sunset on September 2 they reached The Detour, where the shore
bends north toward St. Joseph. Scouts located the *Tigress*. They crept
close through the dusk, hailed her in the last twilight, and immediately
opened up with cannons and rifles. In the short, violent scuffle, each
of the three officers aboard the *Tigress* was killed; three sailors were
wounded. Three Canadians also died; seven were wounded. But they
gained the ship.

The next day they sent the prisoners to Mackinac. The boarding
force then sat tight on the prize, American flag still flying, in the hope
that the *Scorpion* would reappear. On the evening of September 5
she did, anchoring two miles away. At dawn of the sixth, reported
Lieutenant Andrew Bulger, "We slipt our Cable ran down under our
Jib and foresail, everything was so well managed by Lt. Worsley that
we were within 10 yards of the Enemy before they discovered us
it was too late."

Jubilantly the British used the captured schooners to bring in supplies for themselves and a few goods for the Indians. In October, during
the feverish preparations for winter, Ramsay Crooks and George Astor
reached the neighborhood on the ship young Astor had obtained. They
anchored at Bois Blanc Island, as General Prevost had instructed, and
repaired to the town to collect the furs—far fewer, it developed, than
Astor had anticipated. As they dragged the dusty bundles from the
warehouses and dumped them into rowboats, the young Scot no doubt
listened dourly as his former employers, Dickson and Aird, boasted
about what they had already done to the Americans and what they
planned to do when spring let them strike again.

The exultant Canadians were determined to hold the land their arms
had won. Almost surely Crooks heard that the merchants in Montreal had
sent to London the preceding May (1814) a memorial for British
negotiators to use in peace talks with the Americans. Those discussions
had begun at Ghent, Holland, in August, more than a month before
Crooks returned to Mackinac with George Astor.

Basis of the traders' memorandum was the old idea of a buffer Indian nation between the United States and Canada. The paper proposed three possible boundaries for it. The most ambitious one would
halt the United States east and south of a line that ran from Erie,
Pennsylvania, to Pittsburgh, down the Ohio to the Mississippi, then
by the Missouri and Platte rivers to the Rocky Mountains and the Columbia. The most modest line for which Britain should settle, the traders
urged, was one that followed the Wabash to the Ohio and the upper
Missouri to the Rockies.[6]

The British negotiations at Ghent adopted the proposal in principle, and the Indian traders of Canada were optimistic about eventual success. Not only was the fur country theirs; British raiders had also succeeded in burning Washington, D.C., and General Prevost was massing an army on Lake Champlain for a fall drive down the Hudson toward New York City.

When Crooks and George Astor started back to Erie with their furs (they also carried a few paroled prisoners to Detroit aboard their schooner), no word had reached the frontier about the progress of negotiations at Ghent. But Crooks could hardly have been optimistic about the outlook. Even his errand to Mackinac had been of dubious worth. The bulk of the disappointingly few furs they had secured were muskrat skins, and old Astor already had a plethora of those in New York. So Crooks was told to take 100 packs of the unwanted pelts from Erie down to Pittsburgh and try to dispose of them among the hatters in the growing little towns of the Ohio Valley.[7]

He passed a drab, dispiriting winter—small-time peddling in depression-ridden Pittsburgh, Cincinnati, Louisville, and Lexington. Recurrent illness forced him to bed from time to time in gray, unfamiliar boardinghouses. When he tried to vary his routine by buying ginseng root for Astor to export to China on the ending of the blockade, and by dickering for such beaver and raccoon as were drifting out of the Wabash country, he found he could not succeed at the niggardly prices Astor authorized him to pay. Yet for the time being he had to keep plugging along. In the face of the Canadian strength he had seen at Mackinac, what other choice did he have?

On Mackinac, meanwhile, a conviction gripped military men and traders alike that the eventual peace settlement would take into account the amount of territory controlled by each belligerent at the end of hostilities. The Canadians were aroused, accordingly, when they picked up rumors during the fall of 1814 that the Americans were planning a determined counteroffensive up the Mississippi in the spring, to regain lost ground.

After the defeats at Prairie du Chien and Michilimackinac, William Clark on August 24, 1814, had appointed Manuel Lisa special agent to the Indians on the Missouri River, salary $548 per year, and had strengthened Lisa's hand with presents worth $1335 for the express purpose of "engaging those tribes in offensive operations against the Enemies of the United States, particularly on the Mississippi who are too numerous for our thin population to oppose." The probable direction of Lisa's strategy was easy for the Canadians to guess. Using promises of scalps and booty to excite those Indians over whom he exerted the most influence—Mahas, Otos, and the Sioux of the middle Missouri— he would send them eastward across the Des Moines River, harrying the Iowas, the Sacs, the Foxes. The marauders need not secure victory in the white man's sense of the word. It would be enough to frighten the British Indians into staying quiet during the ensuing season. If this pacification-by-terror spread far enough (and many of the Indians were growing tired of war), the Americans might well follow it by launching fresh attacks on Prairie du Chien and even Chicago.

The obvious British answer was to hold their Indians in line. If peace had not come by spring, then it might be well to give the negotiators at Ghent something fresh to think about in the form of a hard drive down the Mississippi toward St. Louis.

Prairie du Chien was the nerve center of the operation. To be military commander there, Colonel McDouall selected Andrew Bulger, twenty-four years old and one of the leaders of the successful attacks on the *Tigress* and *Scorpion*. Bulger, who was raised in rank from lieutenant to captain for his exploit, was physically brave but pompous, self-congratulatory, and given to feeding back to his superiors the opinions they wanted to hear.

The last quality guaranteed friction at Prairie du Chien. McDouall did not like Robert Dickson's bland arrogance. The crisis came, in McDouall's mind, when Dickson assumed on his own responsibility that the Wisconsin theater overrode in importance everything else within McDouall's jurisdiction. He requisitioned so many of Mackinac's limited supplies that the neighboring Ottawas and Chippewas felt deprived of their fair share and complained to Quebec, blaming McDouall. Infuriated, McDouall sought to have himself appointed in Dickson's place as Superintendent of Western Indians.

Bulger was well aware of the animosity when he and Dickson left together on October 29 with five heavily laden boats for Prairie du Chien. Snow was falling. Spray damaged four hundred pounds of irreplaceable gunpowder. Starving Indians kept wheedling material that should have been saved for later use. The Wisconsin River was freezing and the boatmen had a dreadful battle with ice before reaching their destination on Bulger's twenty-fifth birthday, November 30.

At Ghent, on November 30, a proposed treaty of peace was nearing completion. From the outset the American negotiators had rejected the claim of the British diplomats to be representing the Indians as well as themselves. The war was with Great Britain, the Americans retorted; when peace came with Great Britain, it would automatically follow with the savages. Most certainly the English had no right to talk of creating a separate Indian nation inside the United States.

They made the point stick. Later, after Prevost's would-be invasion of New York turned into a fiasco and the English people, exhausted by twenty years of war, began clamoring for any kind of honorable peace, the Americans were able to carry an even more important proposition:

boundary lines should remain as they had been at the outset of the war. This provision was incorporated into the treaty signed December 14, 1814, and ratified by the United States Senate the following February.

As a whole the Treaty of Ghent was by no means a diplomatic victory for the United States. But to the Canadian traders it seemed so. From Michilimackinac westward to the Pacific they had won every major encounter with the enemy. They controlled, largely through the allegiance of the Indians, hundreds of thousands of square miles of unexploited fur country. Yet they were being compelled by a piece of paper to return everything they had won east of the Rockies. In the ambiguous area west of the mountains, where Astor had been completely eliminated, they would shortly have to concede to the Americans a right of joint occupation.

Were these the fruits of victory? In this kind of war it seemed better to be defeated.

For several months McDouall, Bulger, and Robert Dickson did not know they were defeated. Hating each other, often conniving against each other, they went on waging the war whose sudden, unexpected termination would throw ironic highlights on the pettiness they wrought: each little mess was totally useless.

The troubles began in December with objections among Bulger's soldiers which, in Dickson's own words, amounted almost to mutiny. He helped quell the outbreak and approved when Bulger had the worst offenders either flogged or placed in solitary confinement. He did not receive reciprocal help from Bulger, however, during his own simultaneous quarrel with Joseph Rolette, one of Dickson's erstwhile partners in the South West Company.

According to Dickson, Rolette sowed discord among the Indians. When Winnebagos killed one of his calves, Rolette urged some Sioux, over whom he had great influence, to kill the Winnebagos. An internecine Indian fight was the last thing Dickson wanted. He ordered Rolette arrested for "seditious words and discourse tending to excite insurrection against His Majesty's government, also illicit, illegal, and dangerous conduct toward the Indians, His Majesty's allies."

Since Bulger recently had declared Prairie du Chien under martial law, Rolette's trial was a court-martial over which Bulger presided. Dickson's testimony sprang more from passion than from facts, and Bulger declared for the accused. The verdict did not improve relations between the two men.

Immediately there was another tempest. Rolette received messages from a band of Sioux who said they must have powder or starve. Since these particular Sioux were suspected of listening to the blandishments of an agent of Manuel Lisa's, a one-eyed Indian named Temaha, there was some doubt as to what the band really intended to hunt with that powder. Nevertheless Rolette entrusted two of his voyageurs with a couple of kegs for delivery to the suspect Indians.

A savage who was friendly to the British followed the two Canadians, killed both while they lay asleep in their overnight camp, and returned with the booty. Dickson flew into a rage. If the Sioux really were wavering, that sort of irresponsible antic would simply turn them against the British. Furthermore, as Superintendent of Indian Affairs he could not tolerate any sort of murder, no matter what the reason.

He set up another court-martial. This one sentenced the Indian to death, and Bulger had no choice but to execute the sentence. He did not like it and poured out his grievances in a letter to McDouall. McDouall's reply on February 16, 1815, indicated which way the wind was blowing so far as Dickson was concerned:

> I have been totally disappointed in the assistance I expected from him . . . . Wherever he has been, all has been confusion & mismanagement . . . . *Where he is not*, I have seen method, order & regularity revive, and in some instances followed up by a degree of courage and judicious daring which saved the country which it was his peculiar duty to watch over.

McDouall could afford to talk that way. He had won his request to be named Indian Superintendent in Dickson's place. Henceforth Dickson would be his subordinate, with authority over only the Indians of the Mississippi.

Bulger did not respect even this authority. Complaining that Dickson did nothing but sit around and make promises, he decided to work among the Indians himself, knowing that McDouall would support him. He ordered out detachments of soldiers to drag in extra supplies of powder and lead on hand sleds from Green Bay. He took long trips, he wrote later, "into the Indian Country—a wild inhospitable region—in which, with the exception of a few adventurous fur-traders, a white man had not previously been seen. . . . I travelled fully seven hundred miles, partly in winter vehicle on the ice, occasionally on foot and upon snowshoes, and upon horseback over prairies after snow had begun to melt. . . . At night, we often slept before a fire in the open air, with arms prepared for defence—two hunters keeping watch—the country on our route being infested by evil disposed bands."

As spring neared, he announced a great council at Prairie du Chien to discuss the attack on St. Louis. Twelve hundred warriors assembled. "Upon no other occasion of the war had so choice a body of Indians been arrayed under the British flag, and a reserve of another thousand had engaged themselves to join the expedition . . ."

To fire them to frenzy Bulger, in mid-April 1815, read a speech prepared by McDouall. The commander at Mackinac had received word a little earlier that the American negotiators at Ghent had summarily rejected British proposals for an Indian nation between the Ohio and the Lakes. McDouall decided to turn this to propaganda. The British, he wrote, were fighting not for themselves but for justice to the Indians and would continue to fight until the Americans agreed to an inviolate nation for the red men.

When the council gathered and was quieted, Bulger placed on the ground before him an ornate wampum belt "with its blood red colour as the symbol of war" and over it read McDouall's extravagant declaration. The success was tremendous. In whooping excitement the savages declared that the rumors of peace emanating from St. Louis must be false. Drums beat, war dances racketed. After starting advance parties down the river, Bulger prepared his own garrison of voyageurs, militia, regulars, and gunners to follow to an appointed rendezvous.

Just as the Canadians and the main body of Indians were ready to march, a messenger brought devastating news from below. The American gunboat *General Clark* had just ascended the Mississippi to Rock River with word of peace. At Rock River the *Clark's* commander met trader Duncan Graham, whom the St. Louis paper called Dickson's "deputy-scalping-master-general." Graham agreed to carry the information through hostile Indian country to Prairie du Chien.

Bulger and Dickson were stunned. From what Graham said—he had brought no copy of the treaty—the land the Canadians had conquered was to revert to the Americans and the international boundary run as it had before the war.

The exact status of the Indians was not made clear by the message, but obviously the war parties had to be recalled. The dismayed Canadians sent runners after them. Not all were overtaken, but by May 10 eight hundred savages were milling around Prairie du Chien in a state of intense excitement. Great Britain had just promised, through McDouall and Bulger, that she would fight to the end for them. Now they were being told they must lay down their arms. Why? They had not been defeated. They had won their battles on the Mississippi. Were the Canadians suddenly turning into women?

During this uneasy period, no instructions reached Bulger from his own commanders. He marked time as best he could. While the garrison in Fort McKay stayed on full alert, he went each morning to the open-sided, bark-roofed, Indian-style council house a little beyond the stockade. There he and his interpreters talked to the chiefs of the different bands as they came boiling in to learn what was wrong.

Most of the savages reluctantly agreed to wait for definite word from their Great Father, the English king. Some, however, including the Sac chief Black Hawk, were too furious to heed. Black Hawk shook in Bulger's face the war belt he had received at the outbreak of hostilities and said his Indians would keep on fighting. With a handful of impassioned warriors he paddled back down the Mississippi. Near Fort Howard they killed eleven whites and wounded three. War parties Bulger had been unable to recall added to the havoc. In a froth of excitement after one raid, the St. Louis newspaper called for

> the extermination of these miserable beings excited to murder by the nation that has been impudently called the *'Bulwark of Religion'* . . . . It is probable that, as in 1794, many Englishmen are among the savages, exciting them to these horrid deeds. If any such are found, they ought to be capitally punished on the spot without mercy.

Instead of exciting the Indians, whatever some traders might have been doing, the unhappy Bulger was trying to calm them. About May 20 he at last received orders from McDouall. These directed him to read to the Indians the terms of the Treaty of Ghent, an official copy of which accompanied the instructions, and deliver another speech prepared by McDouall, this one much more abject than the inflammatory talk from the same hand which Bulger had read aloud less than two months before. And finally Bulger was to surrender Fort McKay and its cannon to a force of Americans who would ascend the Mississippi to accept capitulation.

The copy of the treaty confirmed earlier rumors. There was to be no Indian nation. Article IX said simply that the aborigines would be "restored" to the possessions they had enjoyed before the war. In other words, the hated prewar treaties that had taken so much land from them before the conflict were to remain in force.

To the Indians this looked like complete betrayal by the English, who had promised so much. Bulger feared violence as he announced the terms. Before he went to the council house for the final great meeting he prepared a stratagem. There was a smoke hole in the roof of the meeting place. A flagpole rose through the opening. Bulger ordered his chair placed beside the pole. If trouble developed, he would drop the flag. At this signal the guns of the fort were to open fire immediately on the thousand or more Indians who would be jammed around the house. In the confusion perhaps the whites could fight clear.

Other signals were carefully arranged to lend impressiveness to the ceremony. A cannon boomed to assemble the chiefs. Upward of seventy crowded inside with the handful of whites while their followers surrounded the open-sided chamber. An interpreter placed on the ground in front of the assembly a belt of blue wampum, the color of peace. Bulger started the prepared speech, addressed "To the brave and faith-

A NOTE ON THE MAPS

Two main points of entry funneled supplies into the fur country between the Great Lakes and the Pacific—little Mackinac Island, just inside Lake Huron, and the mouth of the Columbia River. As early as 1810 John Jacob Astor sought, by controlling both spots, to monopolize the best fur-producing territory in the United States.

The first of the following maps indicates the strategic canoe and barge routes which French voyageurs had anchored on Mackinac Strait by the middle of the eighteenth century and which their successors, the British fur giants, yielded slowly and with stubborn reluctance to American dominance.

The second sketch shows the river and land routes followed by Wilson Price Hunt's Astorians in going from Mackinac to the Columbia, hoping to locate inland trapping bases which could be coordinated with an ocean-supplied post (Fort Astoria) at the Columbia's mouth. Also shown is Robert Stuart's famous return journey through South Pass, eventual gateway of the emigration to California and the Pacific Northwest.

After the War of 1812, which cost Astor his Columbia hopes, Stuart and Ramsay Crooks, basing themselves on Mackinac, consolidated the American Fur Company's hold south and west of the upper Lakes. Only belatedly, in 1827, did the company thrust into the highly competitive trade of the Missouri River. The third map indicates the extent of that commerce and the sites of the Western Department's principal posts.

The final single-page map portrays the geography of critical Mackinac, which the British seized in 1812 but lost to the United States (and to the American Fur Company) at the Treaty of Ghent, 1815.

LAKE SUPERIOR
TO FOND DU LAC
MICHIGAN
POINT PATTERSON
TO GREEN BAY
Green Bay
LAKE MICHIGAN
L'Arbre

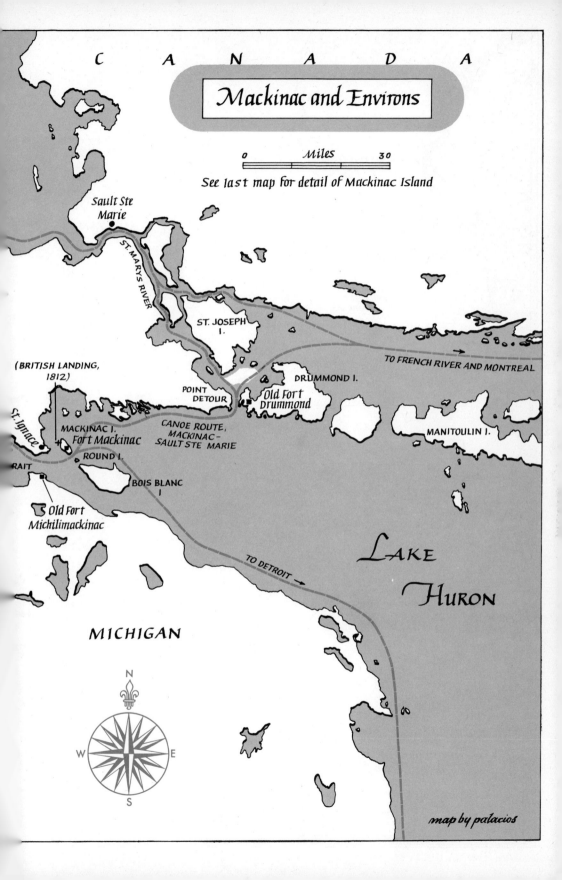

C A N A D A

Mackinac and Environs

0 Miles 30

See last map for detail of Mackinac Island

Sault Ste Marie

ST. MARYS RIVER

ST. JOSEPH I.

TO FRENCH RIVER AND MONTREAL

(BRITISH LANDING, 1812)

POINT DETOUR

DRUMMOND I.

Old Fort Drummond

St. Ignace

MACKINAC I.
Fort Mackinac

CANOE ROUTE, MACKINAC–SAULT STE MARIE

MANITOULIN I.

ROUND I.

RAIT

BOIS BLANC I

Old Fort Michilimackinac

TO DETROIT →

LAKE HURON

MICHIGAN

N
W E
S

map by palacios

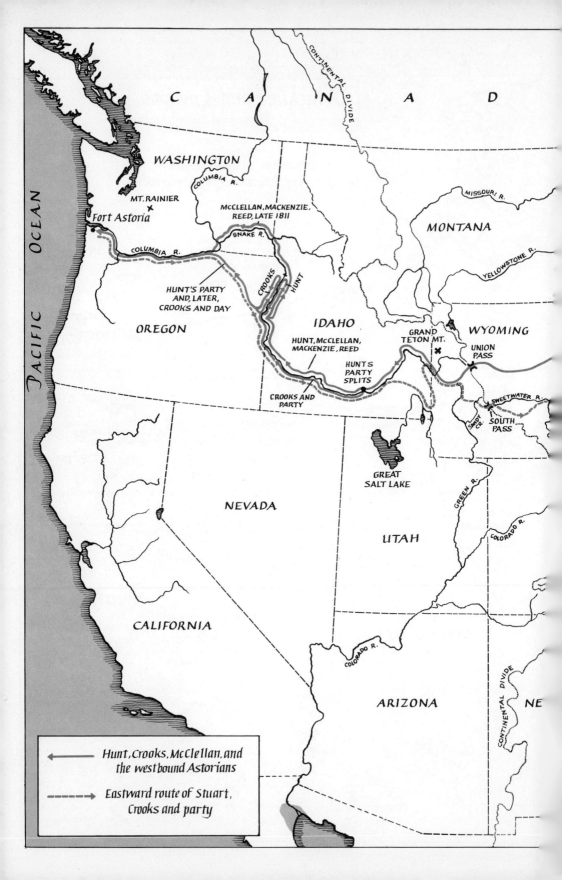

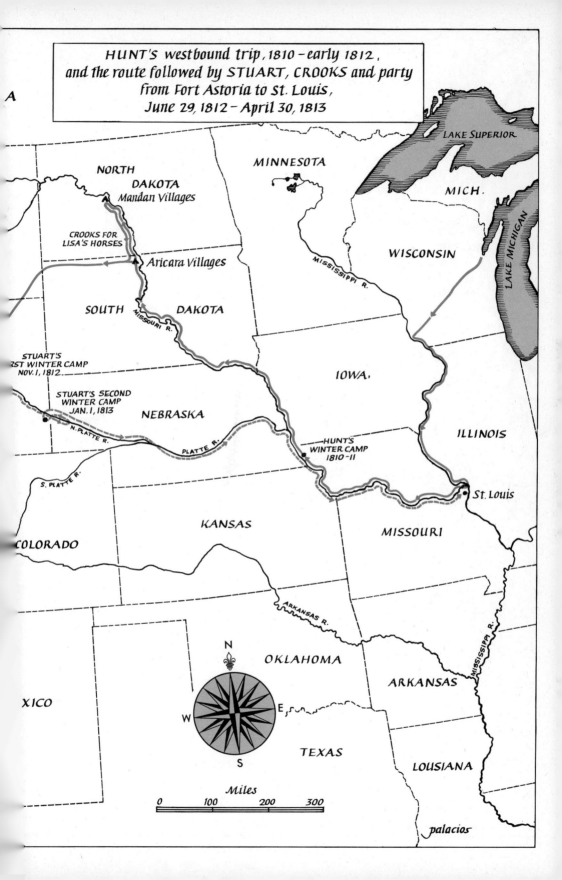

HUNT'S westbound trip, 1810 – early 1812,
and the route followed by STUART, CROOKS and party
from Fort Astoria to St. Louis,
June 29, 1812 – April 30, 1813

A

LAKE SUPERIOR

MINNESOTA

NORTH
DAKOTA
Mandan Villages

MICH.

WISCONSIN

CROOKS FOR
LISA'S HORSES

Aricara Villages

MISSISSIPPI R.

LAKE MICHIGAN

SOUTH   DAKOTA

MISSOURI R.

STUART'S
RST WINTER CAMP
NOV. 1, 1812.

IOWA.

STUART'S SECOND
WINTER CAMP
JAN. 1, 1813

NEBRASKA

N. PLATTE R.

PLATTE R.

HUNT'S
WINTER CAMP
1810 -11

ILLINOIS

S. PLATTE R.

St. Louis

COLORADO

KANSAS

MISSOURI

ARKANSAS R.

N

OKLAHOMA

ARKANSAS

XICO

W   E

MISSISSIPPI R.

S

TEXAS

LOUSIANA

Miles

0   100   200   300

palacios

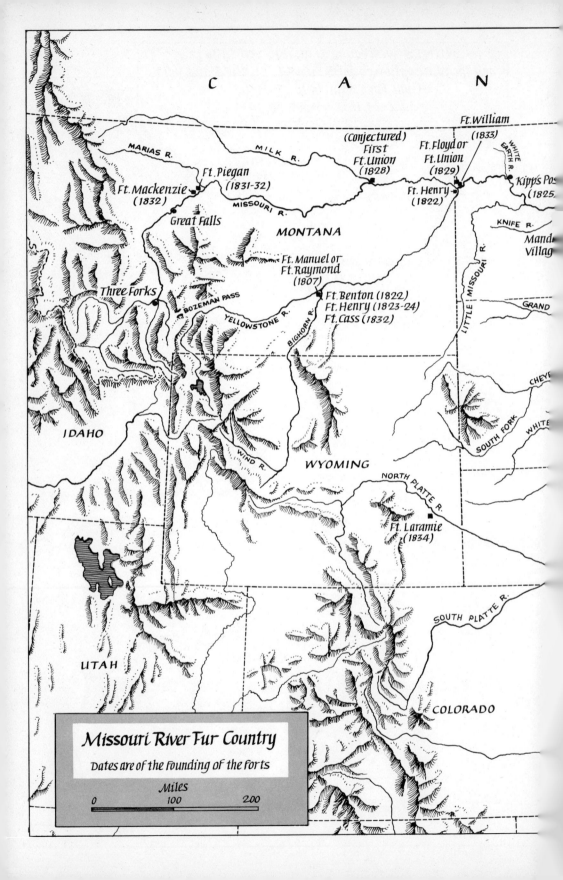

C A N

MARIAS R.

MILK R.

Ft. Piegan
(1831-32)

(Conjectured)
First
Ft. Union
(1828)

Ft. William
(1833)

Ft. Floyd or
Ft. Union
(1829)

WHITE
EARTH R.

Ft. Mackenzie
(1832)

MISSOURI R.

Ft. Henry
(1822)

Kipp's Pos
(1825

Great Falls

MONTANA

KNIFE R.

Mand
Villag

Ft. Manuel or
Ft. Raymond
(1807)

LITTLE MISSOURI R.

Three Forks

BOZEMAN PASS

YELLOWSTONE R.

BIGHORN R.

Ft. Benton (1822)
Ft. Henry (1823-24)
Ft. Cass (1832)

GRAND

SOUTH FORK

CHEYE

WHITE

IDAHO

WIND R.

WYOMING

NORTH PLATTE R.

Ft. Laramie
(1834)

UTAH

SOUTH PLATTE R.

COLORADO

Missouri River Fur Country

Dates are of the founding of the forts

Miles

0   100   200

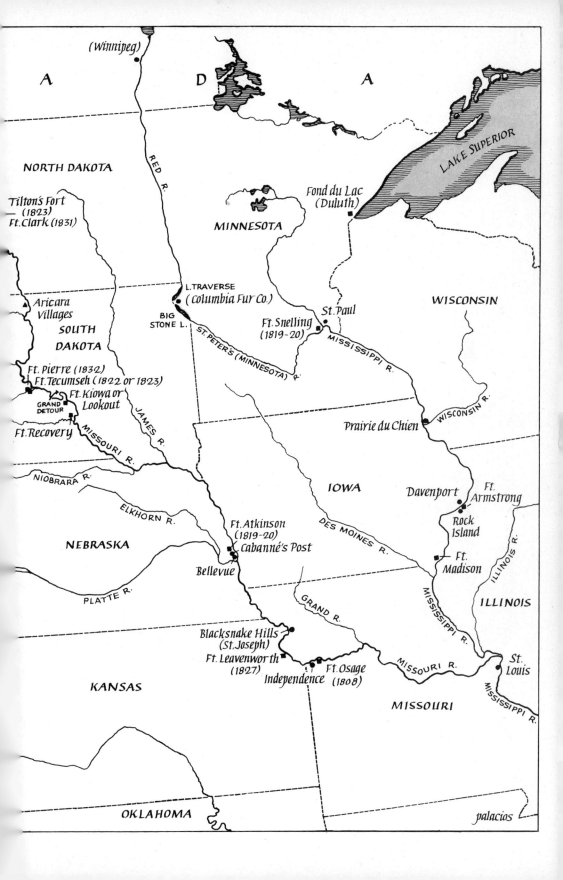

CANADA

(Winnipeg)

A   D   A

LAKE SUPERIOR

NORTH DAKOTA

RED R.

Tilton's Fort
(1823)
Ft. Clark (1831)

MINNESOTA

Fond du Lac
(Duluth)

Aricara
Villages

SOUTH
DAKOTA

L. TRAVERSE
(Columbia Fur Co.)

BIG
STONE L.

St. Paul

WISCONSIN

Ft. Snelling
(1819-20)

ST. PETER'S (MINNESOTA) R.

MISSISSIPPI R.

Ft. Pierre (1832)
Ft. Tecumseh (1822 or 1823)
Ft. Kiowa or
Lookout

GRAND
DETOUR

Ft. Recovery

JAMES R.

MISSOURI R.

Prairie du Chien

WISCONSIN R.

NIOBRARA R.

ELKHORN R.

IOWA

Davenport

Ft.
Armstrong

Rock
Island

NEBRASKA

Ft. Atkinson
(1819-20)
Cabanné's Post

Bellevue

DES MOINES R.

Ft.
Madison

ILLINOIS R.

PLATTE R.

GRAND R.

MISSISSIPPI R.

ILLINOIS

Blacksnake Hills
(St. Joseph)
Ft. Leavenworth
(1827)
Independence

Ft. Osage
(1808)

MISSOURI R.

St.
Louis

KANSAS

MISSOURI

MISSISSIPPI R.

OKLAHOMA

palacios

Mackinac Island

Point aux Pins

British Landing

BATTLEFIELD
X

Fort Mackinac

N
W E
S

ful, the Chiefs and Warriors, of the Nations of the Mississippi; from their Great Father, the King of England." At the word "king" prearranged signals flashed and the guns of the fort roared a salute. This and the groundwork which Bulger, Thomas Anderson, and Dickson had laid during the preceding days of suspense impressed the Indians. The chiefs agreed to cultivate peace with the Americans, but said they could not promise to keep it if new acts of aggression were practiced against them. After five hours of speeches the pipe circulated and a salute of nineteen guns confirmed the end of the war on the Mississippi.

One order Bulger could not bring himself to execute—the surrender of his fort and cannons to the Americans. That would look like total cowardice to the Indians. For the safety of his men (so he excused his act) he burned the structure to the ground, loaded the guns into barges, and started for Mackinac.

On the glum retreat he took Robert Dickson with him as prisoner. During the conciliation of the chiefs, the redheaded trader had made speeches which to the distraught Bulger sounded treasonable. He arrested Dickson and at Mackinac ordered him confined in the island's fort.

A day or two later Dickson was quietly released without trial or any mention of the charges against him. Seeking vindication, he went to Quebec and won a hearing. It exonerated him completely. He was given the title of Lieutenant Colonel and a military pension of £300 a year. But he sensed that the trade as he had known it—as he had helped to make it—was forever ended. Rather than return to the scenes of his defeat, he joined the colony which the Earl of Selkirk, governor of Hudson's Bay Company, had founded at Red River in defiance of the Nor'Westers.

All the traders of Michilimackinac faced a future as uncertain as Dickson's. The war had left a commercial vacuum in the Indian country. Could they reaffirm their prestige with the savages and fill the void in the old way? Or would the Americans rush in to exploit their unexpected and, to the Canadians, undeserved victory? More specifically, would Astor decide to end his agreement with the Montreal supply houses and seek to dominate the trade for his own exclusive benefit? If so, how? With what men?

CHAPTER *15*

Bright New Vistas, American Style

Even in the darkest days of the war, Astor had sensed that peace might bring with it an opportunity to break away from his Canadian associates and establish himself as the controlling force on the Indian border. In October 1813 he had instructed one of his agents in Montreal to sound out Forsyth, Richardson & Co. and McTavish, McGillivrays & Co., his partners in the South West Company, about selling their interests to him. Three weeks later, as we have seen, he had told Crooks that he intended to take over the entire American fur trade.

On March 21, 1815, little more than a month after peace came, he summoned thirty-year-old Robert Stuart to his office and reaffirmed his intention, in Stuart's words, to establish posts "in all the Indian Countries within the line of demarkation between G.B. & the U.S." He hinted of important places in the new organization for both Stuart and Crooks, but cautioned that time might elapse before the ambitious plans matured. To keep themselves busy in the meantime, why didn't Crooks and Stuart try a venture of their own, which Astor would back?

Stuart hurried home to Brooklyn and penned an excited letter to Crooks, who was still wandering about the Ohio Valley with Astor's unsold muskrat furs. "The old Cock," Stuart wrote, hoped

you and myself would come to some arrangement either to purchase the goods [which Astor expected soon to arrive from England] and try the S.W. on our own Acct, or take them to Mackinac and give him a certain share of the profits .... If something like this plan would meet your ideas, it will give me much pleasure for on your judgement I can entirely rely, knowing you are perfectly conversant in every branch of that business, and there is no mortal living, I would prefer being concerned with.

Crooks found Stuart's letter waiting for him in Pittsburgh when he drifted back on April 16, 1815. With it was a letter from Astor himself, dated April 5, suggesting an "arrangement for something more important."[1] Presumably the combined promises left him as excited as Stuart. After his first swift start in the wilderness trade, he had been felled continually by circumstances—on the Missouri River, during the terrible ordeal of his venture to the Pacific, by the ignominious failure of American arms on the upper Lakes. Now perhaps, under the new alignments which peace would make possible, he might find a way to begin again, either on the Missouri of his first adventurings (the "S.W." of Stuart's letter) or around the Lakes.

Before making up their minds about areas, the partners wanted to investigate both fields. They spent much of 1815 conducting the examination. The thorough study suggests that their ambitions had quickly reached out to embrace much more important arrangements than Astor had originally contemplated with his first stopgap proposal. Nevertheless the merchant let them drive ahead. Probably he was not sure himself what he thought their adventure might lead to. It was part of his character to let the ripples start and then to improvise. That was one form of his caution. John Jacob Astor preferred to adapt rather than to originate. Fortunately he had money enough to wait until the first shimmers began to settle into a picture. Then he jumped and jumped hard.

Although no record survives about Stuart's activities during the summer of 1815, it is probable that he traveled to St. Louis to check on opportunities there.[2] Crooks meanwhile journeyed to Mackinac. It was a miserable trip, according to the recollections of James Lockwood, another young man who was venturing west that same season to see what possibilities peace held out for an American to thrust into the British-dominated Indian trade. Lockwood and Crooks left Buffalo together on June 10, 1815, aboard an ancient vessel devoid of conveniences for passengers. On the captain's refusal to improve matters Crooks himself stormed ashore, bought dishes and tableware. Later, when the schooner was becalmed for ten days near the entrance to Lake Huron, he rowed out in a skiff for a sheep to enliven their fare.

Their vessel was bound for Drummond Island, westernmost of the Manitoulin chain that stretches along Huron's north shore. Drummond lay in the opening of the St. Marys River, just southeast of St. Joseph Island. Because its snout commanded the narrow channel around Point

Detour, which canoes followed in traveling between Sault Ste Marie and Mackinac, McDouall's British garrison chose Drummond as a new site after surrendering Mackinac on July 18. No one ever liked the place. In time desertions would become almost routine. One tale has it that Indians sent after five deserters fleeing across the ice caught them, killed them, and brought their heads back in a sack as proof of success.

Crooks wasted no time on the island. Hiring a canoe and voyageurs, he continued with young Lockwood to Mackinac. There Lockwood's record ends. Conceivably, after looking over the field, Crooks continued through Green Bay to St. Louis and met Stuart. In any event, by fall the two men had decided to risk their venture not on the Lakes but on the Missouri.

One can only guess at the reasons. Crooks may not have liked the hostile temper in the Lakes area toward all things American. British officials were making earnest attempts to hold the savages' good will. Immediately after the peace, for instance, McDouall had sent boatloads of presents and food to the Mississippi in charge of Thomas Anderson. Although Anderson urged good behavior on Indians, he also extended invitations for them to visit either Malden or Drummond Island every summer for more gifts, a clear indication that the British government would do all it could to support the Canadian traders in their efforts to maintain their business within the United States. In Montreal, Astor's partner, William McGillivray, who had first urged the post on Drummond Island, was insisting that if the government vigorously supported the new location, "the village of Michilimackinac would consequently dwindle away."[3]

The Canadian traders cooperated vigorously in this commercial offensive. Word of peace reached Montreal early enough for the South West Company to dispatch for the West at least eight canoeloads of merchandise under its new agent and partner, Pierre Rocheblave. Independents brought in more. They hurried the goods to the wintering camps before American officials could arrive and impose drastic new duties amounting to 31¼ per cent of Montreal prices. Every one of these men knew the country better than Crooks or Stuart, and would be dangerous to challenge. Furthermore, they were backed in part by the same man, Astor, who would be backing him and Stuart. If open competition developed, repercussions were certain to follow.

Lastly, there was the threat of competition by the American government itself. The trading factories at Mackinac and Chicago were being revived; new ones were to be established in conjunction with military forts at Green Bay, Prairie du Chien, and Rock Island on the Mississippi. Rumor added others at Sault Ste Marie, Fond du Lac, the mouth of the St. Peter's, and Red River. Of these last only the one at the St. Peter's would become a reality, but the shadows were worrisome. On the Missouri, however, the sole government factory was located at Fort Osage, well below the country Crooks knew.

Deterred by all these difficulties, Crooks and Stuart told Astor they wanted to try the Missouri. He agreed. Then in the spring of 1816 he abruptly changed his mind. He did not want them in the West after all, but up on the Lakes.

Various considerations operated. The St. Louis firm of Cabanné and Company (which included members of the Chouteau family) was seeking an American source of goods that would avoid the high duties imposed on importations through Canada. In the winter of 1815-16 they dropped hints to Astor—nothing definite yet—that they might increase their orders appreciably and use him as marketing agent for some of their furs if he promised to outfit no one else in their area. Should this Cabanné business materialize and should Astor be able to include other St. Louis merchants in the arrangement, profits might be higher than anything Crooks and Stuart could realize by routine trading along the river, where competition would be ferocious. So perhaps, even though they had ordered their goods, the idea really wasn't as sound as it had seemed when first the two young men proposed it.

Furthermore, Astor's interest in the Missouri as a route to the Pacific had been rudely jolted by the peace. The negotiators at Ghent, unable to agree about the boundary line between Canada and the United States west of the Rocky Mountains, had wearily agreed to let future commissions decide the question. They had not even reached a consensus about Astoria. If the post and its satellites had been transferred peacefully to the North West Company by McDougall's unauthorized sale, there could be no enforced restitution. But if Astoria had been seized militarily by Captain Black and the *Raccoon*, it should be restored to its original owner under terms of the treaty. Astor wrote his usual spate of letters, trying to press the United States Government toward that contention. By the spring of 1816, however, it was evident that matters were going to drag. Meanwhile the North West Company was digging into the area so strongly that the expenses of driving them out with no help from Washington was likely to be prohibitive. Slowly Astor reconciled himself to abandoning his great dream for the Pacific Northwest.[4] This failure made an advance up the Missouri by Crooks and Stuart seem less attractive than it otherwise might have.

These were minor considerations. Astor's main motive for calling off the Missouri adventure was a swiftly developing need to send someone he could trust up to the Lakes to represent his interests there. The old British fur-trade patterns under which he and his Canadian partners were accustomed to operate—patterns long resented by American frontiersmen—were at last being attacked directly by the United States Government itself, and not just by western newspapers and western politicians.

The war had released a surge of nationalistic feeling throughout the country. "America for Americans" was a popular slogan. "Yankee Doodle" was a favorite song, Uncle Sam a new national folk symbol. In the words of one British traveler, "The national vanity of the United States surpasses that of any country, not even excepting France. It blazes out everywhere, and on all occasions." In Washington this fiery patriotism became concrete in the authorization of new military forts at frontier points where British influence had been strong during the war—Chicago, Green Bay, Prairie du Chien. Indian agents, responsible to the governors of the territories in which they operated, were slated to occupy these spots and Mackinac. In conjunction with government trading factories, the agents were intended to regulate the wilderness commerce and see to it that the British winterers lost their baneful hold over the savages.

An official decision concerning the status of those winterers took shape more slowly. Under Jay's Treaty, British citizens possessed a legal right to carry on their commerce within the United States. Various technical steps abrogating that treaty had to be completed before Congress could pass, without violating international agreements, some sort of measure either excluding or controlling the hated foreign traders. Many officials were certain the measure would come, international agreements notwithstanding. On June 12, 1815, for instance, John Mason, Superintendent of Indian Trade, wrote Astor, "It is the intention of the government to prevent altogether the British Indian traders coming within the United States."

In jingoistic newspapers such declarations made fine reading. At Detroit, Mackinac, and Prairie du Chien, however, they created only uncertainty; for no law by Congress could alter the ancient fact that every tradition and practice of the Northwest Indian trade was oriented toward the British. If Americans upset those routines, then what new methods for supplying the Indians could be substituted in their place?

By the very nature of its operations, the Indian commerce could not endure uncertainties. Merchandise flowed very slowly over enormous distances—from England to receiving ports in the United States or Canada and then in primitive canoes and barges into the wilderness, to be replaced after an equal number of months by furs traded from the aborigines. The effects of this time lag cannot be overestimated. It made the trade deeply conservative. A man venturing capital across so many months needed assurance that the routines under which he launched his outfits would still prevail when his investment returned. But after the war, the temper of the United States was such that assurance simply did not exist. As a result neither John Jacob Astor nor his Montreal partners in the South West Company knew quite which way to jump.

The only answer the Montrealers could devise was to temporize. Their agreement with Astor establishing the South West Company was due to expire with the outfits of 1816—that is, when furs reached the rendezvous in 1817 to pay for the goods received the year before. The Canadians decided that the best way to defend their accustomed trade south of the border was to renew the agreement, in the hope that Astor, as he had in the days before the war, could help soften whatever anti-British blows befell them. Accordingly, in September 1815 (while Crooks and Stuart were perhaps in St. Louis, deciding to press with an Astor-supplied outfit up the Missouri), William McGillivray traveled to New York on behalf of his worried partners.

No laws had yet been passed against Canadians. It was conceivable that the American War Department, aware of the usefulness of the old-line British traders in supplying the Indians, would prevail on Congress to make haste slowly. In that event the South West Company might continue to function for an indefinite time. Thus if Astor broke too abruptly with the Montrealers he might find himself faced inside his own country with their practiced competition. Unwilling to take so dangerous a commercial risk, he agreed with McGillivray to extend the contract. But, as usual, he coppered his bets. If anti-British laws were passed, he might find South West Company merchandise (half supplied by him) excluded from the Lakes. He wished to avoid this too. Therefore he inserted into the contract a clause stating that if the government of the United States passed any laws against foreign traders, the agreement was to end.

Possibly Astor intended, at the moment he signed the contract, to murder it by pressing for the exclusion of foreigners. The accusation has been leveled at him with varying degrees of contempt. But it is also possible that he was simply being his usual prudent self, trying to bulwark his investments against whatever might develop. In any event, McGillivray, a notably canny man, could read the temper of the times as well as Astor could. Knowing the chances he took, the Canadian signed.

The Montrealers lost the gamble. Seven months later, on April 29, 1816, Congress passed almost without debate the long-anticipated bill barring foreigners from the Indian trade within the borders of the United States. One concession was made to the War Department: the President was authorized to grant exemptions to certain winterers if he found variances to be necessary. Before the fur trade died as an international force, infinite misunderstandings would reverberate around that seemingly mild precaution.

Young James Lockwood, among others of Astor's contemporaries, flatly states that the New Yorker instigated both the exclusion bill and its modifying clause. Perhaps. But the anti-British climate was such that the law almost surely would have passed regardless of John Jacob Astor's desires. And if he did meddle, he certainly created problems for himself.

By April 29, the day the law took effect, goods for the 1816 rendezvous at Mackinac (the last one under the original South West Company agreement) had been packed. Loaded schooners were yawing up the Hudson toward Albany and the ancient Mohawk route to Buffalo; heavy carts were rumbling from Montreal toward barges waiting at Lachine. Stopping them would result in heavy loss both to Astor and the Canadians. Yet if the merchandise continued to Mackinac and if zealous American officials there took the April act at face value and refused to let a Canadian boatman touch even a stroud, how was the material to reach the Indians? No American manpower was available; if the year's trade went ahead, it would have to be under presidential exemption, applied on the spot by someone who understood wilderness needs. And finally there was the problem of making sure that the furs which the British adventurers would bring back to Michilimackinac that same summer of 1816 were not confiscated on the grounds that the traders were now operating illegally.

Astor, in short, urgently needed a qualified American representative on the island. The man he turned to was Ramsay Crooks. But Crooks and Stuart, banking on Astor's support to smooth their way with the Missouri traders, were ready to embark on their Far Western trip.

As late as May 21 they still planned to travel west.[5] But by May 26 Astor had induced them to abandon the project. Inasmuch as they had spent a year in preparation, he must have held out a potent lure. It could hardly have been anything less than a promise of the top managerial posts, salaries to be fortified by profit sharing, in the revitalized American Fur Company, first chartered in 1808 but dormant ever since its prewar stirrings.

Whatever the understanding, it was too tentative to be put into writing. Perhaps there would be no American Fur Company. That was part of Crooks's errand—to determine whether or not an American firm could obtain the experienced manpower it needed for its operations and then launch the commerce in a region where hostility was almost certain to meet the change-over. Obviously the assignment dovetailed neatly with the work he would be doing at the same time as Astor's agent in helping the South West Company finish its existence with a decent profit. Indeed, if he worked well in closing the South West Company's affairs, he might even become, in the eyes of the disgruntled winterers, an acceptable heir of the Canadian firm to which they were used. In other words, Astor had reason to suppose that in that rough-

and-tumble trade Ramsay Crooks would prove an adroit hand at public relations.

So much for what Astor hoped to gain by diverting Crooks to Mackinac that summer. For Crooks himself, twenty-nine years old, the implications were tremendous. If he manipulated these touchy problems successfully—if he brought what had been half of Astor's trade fully into the merchant's hands—if under his management an American monopoly at last proved able to thrust aside the Canadians, then he, Ramsay Crooks, shoemaker's son from Scotland, potentially was on his way toward becoming one of the most powerful men on the American frontier. Surely he was aware of this when he agreed to surrender once again the Missouri River trade which had tantalized him so long.

Robert Stuart, who was Crooks's elder by two years, his superior on the transcontinental crossing, and the one whom Astor had approached first about a postwar adventure, seems to have dropped without protest into a relatively minor part. His assignment was St. Louis. There he was to dispose of the merchandise which he and Crooks had bought for the Missouri. Astor, ever the tightwad, had declined taking back the goods himself. But he did promise to help them dispose of the cloth and hardware to J. P. Cabanné. On May 26 he wrote Charles Gratiot:

> it is natural to Supose that Mr Crooks & Stuart must have some Compensation for time Lost & perhaps giving up the object of which they might make Some money and under this consideration I have Encouraged Mr. Stuart to believe that Mr C. will give him a Liberal Profit

Stuart was also delegated to try, with Gratiot's help, to win Cabanné and other principal traders of St. Louis to firm contracts appointing Astor as their agent for importing goods and marketing furs. In return Astor would promise not to outfit anyone else for opposing them on the Missouri.

Acting under the provisions of the exclusion act of April 29, 1816, Astor next sought to help Crooks's work in the Lakes area by appealing to the President of the United States for the exemptions authorized by law, so that the South West Company's usual complement of traders could return to their normal wintering grounds with their 1816 purchases. Before he made his plea, however, a development occurred which, oddly enough, escaped his notice.

The War Department, which was responsible for Indian affairs, had already realized that for the sake of supplying the savages, certain concessions had to be made in the granting of licenses. As soon as the problem was pointed out to President Madison, he agreed to delegate his powers to men who were already on the spot and familiar with the wilderness commerce, the Governor of Michigan Territory and the Indian agents of the far Northwest. Secretary of War William H. Crawford explained matters thus to Cass in a directive of May 10, 1816:

> The want of Capital in the hands of men accustomed to the trade, and who have enterprize to bear the fatigue, and brave the dangers incident to its prosecution, will, it is believed, render it necessary for the present to permit foreigners to carry on this trade. . . . [Accordingly] the President has judged it expedient to vest in the governor of Michigan territory, and in the agents for Indian affairs at Michilimackinac, Green Bay, and Chicago, the exclusive right of granting licenses to foreigners to carry on the trade.

Unaware of this delegation of the President's licensing power, Astor supposed he had to apply directly to the Chief Executive for exceptions, as provided by the law passed on April 29. He forwarded his request on May 27 through an influential acquaintance, James Monroe, then Secretary of State, a man who still owed Astor five thousand dollars borrowed from him a few years earlier. Since Astor had no way of knowing what winterers might be available at Mackinac (the war had upset routines), he asked Monroe "that the President would please to give six to Nine Licenses, they might be sent in blank & filled at Michilimackinac to such persons as the Collector [of customs] or Commanding officer shall judge best."[6] Crooks of course would be on hand to help the officials do their judging.

Having dispatched this letter to Monroe, Astor then wrote to Jacob Franks, a Canadian trader with whom he had long done business, and told him of the request. In this letter he expressed regret over the hardships which the exclusion act might create among his old acquaintances and held out the hope that there still might be a way for Franks to carry on his lifetime work. The communication was normal enough, but, as we shall see, it caused agitation on Mackinac.

Monroe presumably answered Astor's request for blank licenses by informing him of the War Department's directive of May 10, delegating the power to make exceptions to Governor Cass and the various Indian agents. Astor thereupon wrote the War Department asking that the three men he was sending to Mackinac—William W. Matthews, Joseph B. Varnum, and Ramsay Crooks[7]—be recommended to the Indian agent on the island, Major William H. Puthuff. The request was granted June 5 by George Graham, chief clerk of the department. It was not a special favor. The War Department also wanted the Indians supplied, and only Astor's men, of whatever nationality, seemed available.

Armed with this recommendation, Crooks and Wallace hurried off through Buffalo and the Lakes ahead of Varnum, who followed more slowly with a consignment of goods. On arriving at Michilimackinac, they found agent Puthuff embroiled in bitter quarrels with the entire trading fraternity and with the British army officers on nearby Drummond Island.

In some ways Puthuff's uproars were petty enough, even comic; but they were also symptomatic of the demoralizations that peace had brought to a commerce which cried for stability. In an effort to reestablish that stability for the sake of an American merchant—America for Americans, as the frontier was loudly demanding—Ramsay Crooks found himself allied with aliens against his own adopted government. The bitternesses that flowered from this strange and ironic hybridization drew gall from ancient roots. In order to understand more fully what he confronted as he plunged into the turbulent scene, it is necessary to digress for a look at Major Puthuff, the Indian agent on Mackinac, and what, in the eyes of the French Canadians, Puthuff typified.

CHAPTER 16

Taste of Power

At the outbreak of the war, William Henry Puthuff had been working as a clerk of the Ohio Supreme Court. By the end of the conflict he was a major in command of the Detroit area. He took his duties seriously. One wartime military law, for instance, forbade the selling of ardent spirits by unlicensed citizens to American troops; another prohibited the hoarding of breadstuffs. On learning that a man named Daniel Ames was violating the first edict, Puthuff decided on March 27, 1815, after the fact of peace was known in Detroit, to inflict the authorized penalties.

He went with half a dozen soldiers to Ames's house (Ames was absent but his wife and children were there), kicked down the door, and rolled out four kegs of whisky and one of cherry bounce. As military law said he could, he put the kegs two at a time in a cart, broke open their heads, and drove around letting the spirits spill into the street. As military law said he should, he then ordered all the Ameses to remove themselves three miles from the premises where the whisky had been sold.

Two days later Mrs. Ames was still defiantly occupying the house, and her husband was still away. Though a hard rain was falling, Puthuff directed his troops to place Mrs. Ames, her children and her furniture in the street. Finding a hundred bushels of corn and wheat in the residence during the eviction, he decided it was hoarded contrary to military law and ordered it destroyed. When Ames returned and rushed to headquarters with a protest, Puthuff had him locked in the guardhouse until he calmed down. Released, Ames sued. The often-delayed trial was held in September 1820. On the ground that the military laws which Puthuff offered in defense were not operative in time of peace, the jury awarded Ames damages of $570. The supreme court of Michigan upheld the verdict.[1]

Other persons found Puthuff's administration praiseworthy. When he was demobilized in the summer of 1815, fifty-one citizens chipped in to buy him a ceremonial sword; accompanying the presentation went a scroll extolling his activities. And when Governor Cass, who always liked Puthuff, recommended him for the new Indian agency at Michilimackinac, he declared to the acting Secretary of War, "A better soldier has not drawn a sword in the defense of his country."

As usual, bureaucratic wheels rolled slowly. Washington had not projected an agency for Michilimackinac, supposing the ones scheduled for Chicago, Green Bay, and Prairie du Chien to be enough. Cass wrote urgent letters to the War Department, pointing out the importance of the island in countering the activities of the British at their new post on Drummond Island and in supervising the traders who operated around Lake Superior and the head of the Mississippi, far beyond the control of either Green Bay or Prairie du Chien. Knowing that confirmation of his request for the agency could not be expected for months, Cass asked Puthuff whether he would accept temporary appointment in the hope that it would later become permanent.

Puthuff agreed on August 18. (His position was confirmed in December.) He reached Mackinac toward the end of the month. Knowing he was there on sufferance, so to speak, he presumably wanted to make a good showing. By this time, however, most of the traders had left for their wintering grounds. Furthermore, they had departed in suspicious haste ahead of the American forces and consequently had paid no duties on their goods. Sternly Puthuff vowed to look into that point when the traders returned with their furs. Meanwhile he called councils with the Indians, in order to counteract the ones already held by Lieutenant Colonel Robert McDouall on Drummond Island.

A principal bone of contention in this tug-of-war for the loyalty of the savages was the plan of the United States to establish new military forts at Green Bay and Prairie du Chien. The Indians long since had grown used to the post at Mackinac; they even accepted the rebuilding of the one they had destroyed at Chicago. Both those forts were legalized by earlier treaties. But the Indians contended that they had never granted permission for the Americans to enter either Green Bay or Prairie du Chien. Those villages were in the heart of the Indian country; and the savages insisted that, save for ancient grants to the French-Canadian settlers (with most of whom they had intermarried), they had alienated none of the ground. When the Americans said they were coming anyway, the tribes swore not to permit the invasion.

Robert McDouall abetted the Indians. He was a very unhappy man, his pride cruelly scarred. Though he had held Michilimackinac and Prairie du Chien under adverse odds, a mere piece of paper, the Treaty of Ghent, was making him crawl away in front of the Indians as abjectly as if he had been defeated. Wabasha of the Mississippi Sioux told him bitterly (in translation) when McDouall offered presents to mollify the Indians' hurt, "We never knew of this peace. We are told it was made by our Great Father . . . that it is your duty to obey his orders. What is that to us? Will these presents pay for the men we have lost in battle? . . . Will they make good your promises?" Little Crow, whose tribe lived near the mouth of the St. Peter's, was even more scornful. "You no longer need our services, and offer these goods as compensation for having deserted us. But no! we will not take them; we hold them and yourselves in equal contempt."

McDouall eased his humiliation by supporting the Indians' objections to the forts at Green Bay and Prairie du Chien. In letter after letter to his superiors he declared that the posts violated that clause of the Treaty of Ghent which confirmed the Indians' right to the lands they had occupied before the war. If the British government tolerated the usurpation now, its prestige would sink still lower and it could never hope to enlist the savages' help in case of future need. He became so importunate, indeed, that the British government finally told him sharply to confine himself to his military duties and let Indian policy alone.

American officials were convinced the forts were necessary to awe the most warlike of the tribes—the Winnebagos, the Sacs, and some of the Sioux. They further believed that the British government was deliberately using English traders, in Puthuff's words to Cass, "to restore and maintain their wonted influence over that people." In outrage the new agent continued:

When the Indians shall see those [Britons] who, during the late war, gave direction to their ruthless Tommahawks, who . . . received from their hands, with plaudits and rewards, the scalp fresh torn, alike from the hapless Father, the defenceless tender and affectionate Mother, or innocent unoffending Babe, I repeat, Sir, when the Indians shall see these people again sent and stationed among them, when they shall be told by them, that *they* are the only persons Enabled to supply the Indian wants, that were not for them the Indians would perish . . . what effect may it not have upon their unenlightened Minds.

So responsible a person as Ninian Edwards, Governor of Illinois, actually recommended that all residents of Green Bay and Prairie du Chien be expelled by military force from their homes. They were intruders upon the public lands of the United States and "a set of unprincipled British spies, ever ready to communicate the measures of our govt. , and to defeat, as far as possible, its endeavors to maintain the relations of peace and friendly intercourse with the savages."

In this sort of atmosphere, clashes were inevitable. Determined to find someone to make an example of, Puthuff fixed on Elizabeth Mitchell, an Ottawa Indian, wife of Dr. David Mitchell, the surgeon of the British garrison. Mitchell was an Edinburgh Scot who had come to Canada before the War of Independence. He had married Elizabeth in 1776. They produced twelve children, all educated in Montreal or Europe. To flesh out his income as a frontier army doctor, Mitchell imported trade goods and outfitted winterers, including his own wife. Her customary wintering grounds were the Ottawa villages around Traverse Bay, Lake Michigan, especially the semiagricultural town of L'Arbre Croche, from which the island obtained much of the corn used by the voyageurs.

When McDouall withdrew the English garrison to Drummond Island, Dr. Mitchell of necessity went along. Mrs. Mitchell stayed behind to run their farm on Mackinac and to prepare for her winter's trade. At the time of Puthuff's arrival she was about fifty-five years old, tall, heavy, commanding. She dressed in black—a black beaver hat with a plume to one side, a black neckerchief, and voluminous black skirt with pockets in front into which she thrust her hands when she threw back her head and gave her orders. She spoke Indian and French, but no English.

The two-story Mitchell home was the largest in the village and was backed by a two-acre kitchen garden fenced with white pickets. Their farm outside the town, one of the very few on the island, grew rare hay, grain, potatoes. During the harvest season Mrs. Mitchell drove to her fields each day in a two-wheeled calash and strode about directing her indolent French Canadians, who evidently saw nothing untoward in being bossed by a squaw.

Her trouble with Puthuff started over her sending liquor to L'Arbre Croche with an assortment of trade goods. She defended herself by saying she had obtained the requisite permission from Captain Willoughby Morgan, commander of the American garrison. According to Puthuff, Morgan denied granting the clearance. The agent accordingly ordered Mrs. Mitchell arrested, then changed his mind and placed her on her own recognizance until he heard from Cass. After talking to Captain Morgan, Cass evidently wrote Puthuff to calm down; at least nothing more was heard of the charge.[2] It was remembered the next year, however, when Puthuff with incredible injudiciousness sent an Indian—a woman, too!—to L'Arbre Croche to barter liquor for some corn he needed for his own use.

Puthuff next got the notion that Mrs. Mitchell was promoting a secret council of Ottawas in Traverse Bay in order to stir up resistance to the Americans. On September 9, 1815, he therefore fastened to the door of the Mackinac church, where all important news was posted, an order forbidding her to hold any intercourse whatsoever with the Indians, though she was one herself. A son who had just returned from twelve years in the British army was also enjoined from "sauntering about through the village mixing with the savages." The mother defied the edict. On October 5 Puthuff charged her with "Illegal, Improper, Unjust, false, and Malicious practice." To escape arrest she fled at night in a small canoe to Drummond Island.

Her husband declared indignantly that "there is much more true Liberty at Algiers than at present at Michilimackinac." McDouall wrote his superiors that Puthuff "out Herods Herod, with his frantic violence, with an equal mixture of impudence and falsehood." To Lieutenant Colonel Talbot Chambers, who had just replaced Captain Morgan as commander of the American garrison, McDouall declared that Puthuff's charges against Mrs. Mitchell were "more puerile and absurd than perhaps ever before entered into the head of a man having pretensions of common sense."

The British colonel broadcast a few charges of his own. The Ottawas, he said, had given Mrs. Mitchell title to little Round Island at the entrance to Michilimackinac harbor. Colonel Chambers had unjustly taken it away from her. (Conceivably Chambers did not want so strategic an islet in unfriendly hands.) Mrs. Mitchell had been prevented from putting out her fishing nets; her garden and that of trader Jacob Franks had been broken into and pillaged. A British trader leaving the island in a canoe had been pelted with stones by American soldiers. Were not the Americans capable of maintaining order where British citizens were concerned?

Puthuff sent a special messenger to Cass denying everything. McDouall, he sniffed, was using the Mitchell affair to gain ascendancy over the Indians. He charged the British colonel with sending red wampum to the savages, and begged that Cass hurry back a clear statement of just what an agent's powers were in these emergencies.

The tempest was petty enough, but prophetic of the greater annoyances that came with spring. Puthuff decided that since most of the merchandise reaching Michilimackinac in 1815 had not paid its legal duties, the furs obtained with the goods were liable to seizure. McDouall protested: How could the traders have paid the excise when, at the time in question, Mackinac had been in the hands of the British? Waving the objection aside, Puthuff stationed informers along the different barge routes. In return for half the value of the furs to be impounded, these men spotted traders approaching with their winter harvest and raced ahead to alert the four boats from the military garrison which Talbot Chambers had placed in waiting.

The system worked. On June 5, 1816, Puthuff boasted to Cass that he already had impounded between $12,000 and $15,000 worth of furs. On the twentieth he promised that no one would elude him. He had collected the name of every trader operating out of Michilimackinac and data about where each had wintered and when he could be expected. Lieutenant Colonel Chambers' exertions in making the arrests were, he said, "unremitting."

The blockade was so efficient that when Pierre Rocheblave, the Montreal agent of the South West Company, reached Mackinac and estimated the situation, he hurried a letter to Green Bay, warning the traders not to try to run the gauntlet. It was wiser to submit and hope for justice at a court trial which he would try to schedule in Detroit in the fall. This threat of legal action made Puthuff a little less liberal in his promises of reward to his informers. He also agreed with Rocheblave to release the furs on the posting of bonds to their full value, the bonds to be forfeit if the suits went against the traders.

The gloom caused by the seizures deepened when word arrived that the new American law of April 29, 1816, would deny trading licenses to all foreigners unless the President of the United States himself granted exemptions. Naturally enough, the traders relayed the word to their customers, the Indians, who were flocking in to attend councils summoned by Puthuff on Mackinac and by McDouall on Drummond. (Reports of the meetings incline one to believe that the opportunistic savages made the most of the rivalry by nodding bland agreement with whoever was passing out presents at the moment.) This new cruelty of the Big Knives, the Canadians said, was intended to starve the Indians. In the presence of plenty, too, for as the red men could see, the usual boatloads of merchandise had just arrived from Montreal, yet could not be distributed.

A small ray of hope appeared when Jacob Franks received Astor's letter saying that he had applied to the President for blank licenses so that trade could go on. Triumphantly Franks waved the letter in Puthuff's face. Astounded, Puthuff wrote a long expostulation to Cass, outlining seizures made and councils held. He then burst out concerning Franks's letter:

I wish to god the President knew this man Astor as well as he is known here. Licenses would not be placed at his descretion to be distributed among British subjects, Agents, or Pensioners. I hope in god no such licenses will be granted . . . . that his [British friends] may be disappointed is my most sincere wish, should they succeed incalculable evil will assuredly grow out of the measure.[3]

Almost immediately he had a letter of his own to wave back at Franks and the Canadians. This one was the War Department's directive stating that the President had delegated his licensing powers to Governor Cass and the Indian agents—that is, to Puthuff himself. Confident now of his powers, he seized three additional cargos of fur and prepared to waylay more. The traders, he wrote Cass triumphantly on June 27, would no doubt do their best to circumvent him, but "they cannot hope to succeed. . . . I will firmly pursue that course which may, in my opinion best conform to my instructions and to the interest of the Country."

At this point Ramsay Crooks arrived, bearing the War Department's instructions that Puthuff should extend to Astor's agents "every facility and aid in the prosecution of their business, that may be compatible with your public duties." What these duties were Crooks crisply informed him. Just how were the Indians around Lake Superior, the upper Mississippi, the St. Peter's, and in central Wisconsin—Indians whom Puthuff was trying to impress by a mere show of pomp in a council house—just how were they to be supplied if every British citizen was excluded? No American trader had ever gone into those areas. None could go for years to come without the help of experienced Canadian interpreters and boatmen. Would Puthuff like to explain to the War Department how his Indians, to escape starvation, threw themselves into the arms of the British at Drummond Island?

These were "new and embarrassing principles," as Puthuff himself admitted in a letter to Cass. But the idea of the indiscriminate licensing which Crooks seemed to want stuck in his craw. He tried to compromise by saying that if a few persons of unimpeachable character who had committed no acts of aggression during the war were to appear before him in person, he would grant exceptions, provided the recipients agreed not to trade at any Indian village or hunting camp where an American also appeared. Since the great majority of the South West Company's traders had held various commissions from the British army during the war, Puthuff's proposal would have eliminated the best of Crooks's winterers. He rejected the suggestion. After fruitless debate they agreed that Crooks should go by sailing vessel to Detroit and obtain a ruling from Governor Cass.

Because Cass had recommended Puthuff for the agency job, the major may have counted on the governor to support him in this controversy. Instead Cass replied, ". . . that all the Agents and traders of [the South West Company] to whose personal character, and conduct there can be no objections should be furnished with licenses."

Puthuff did object. Several persons on Crooks's list had been connected with the British Indian Department during the war. But he could not produce evidence against their personal characters. With ill grace he issued the licenses. Then, nursing his pique, he began what he called a study of the "true state of the trade," hoping to prove "that there is not a necessity for the introduction of a *single foreigner* except perhaps on Lake Superior, to furnish an ample supply of goods for our Indians."

He never got around to citing on paper actual evidence in support of his contention. If he had, presumably it would have revolved around the handful of young American adventurers, like James Lockwood, who were inching into the area, and on an established and wealthy Detroit trader, David Stone, originally from New Hampshire, who had followed the American forces to the island, ready to harvest such plums as the peace treaty put within his reach. But although Stone, Lockwood, and the others might be American citizens, they too were obliged to rely on Canadians for conducting operations in the wilderness. Puthuff thus found his proof to be rather meager, after all.

For Crooks, David Stone posed a threat which perhaps Astor's ambitious young agent had not anticipated. The rival trader was able and experienced. He still maintained his voting residence at Walpole, New Hampshire, and through the state's complaisant senators and congressmen was able to exert political pressures not greatly inferior to Astor's. Younger than Astor, he was willing to visit the Indian country on his own errands, taking with him first-class merchandise he purchased in England on terms as favorable as any Astor could arrange.

On learning of the exclusion act of April 29 and foreseeing the demise of the South West Company, Stone hurried with his chief factotum, Oliver N. Bostwick (within a few years the firm would become Stone, Bostwick & Co.) to Mackinac, intent on filling whatever vacuum the Canadian concern left behind. They jumped quickly ahead of Crooks. Since the South West Company had at least one more year to run, after which its future was most unclear, Crooks could offer no immediate inducements to the unattached young Americans in the area. Stone and Bostwick could. They sold goods to young James Lockwood, for instance, and sent him off to the St. Peter's River, perhaps the first U.S. citizen ever to do any appreciable amount of business in that territory, though ever since the Louisiana Purchase it had belonged to the United States. They also dangled bait in front of the South West Company's Canadians, relying for licenses on exactly the same exemption privileges accorded to Astor. Some of the winterers listened, out of disgruntlement with the old company over unpaid debts or unsatisfactory merchandise, in the hope of better terms, or just through the normal human desire for change.

Grave uncertainties about the future hampered Crooks's efforts to meet this unexpected opposition. Although the provisional clause in Astor's new contract with the Montrealers said the South West Company should end in 1817 because of the exclusion law, many winterers fondly believed that some method of extension would be found. In that case they would like to continue with the familiar firm. If, however, the half-Canadian concern was replaced by the American Fur Company —well, who dared predict which would prove better, Stone or Astor?

Without being able to promise anything definite, Crooks proselytized as best he could. In at least one instance, his arrangements for the Fond du Lac district, he achieved notable success. The Fond du Lac post itself, luxurious with kitchen garden, cow barn, and horse stables, stood on a lovely, tree-spotted meadow a little above the mouth of the winding St. Louis River, on the outskirts of present Duluth. A dreadful portage on up the river's granite canyons brought traders into the Fond du Lac district, an almost unexplored sprawl of territory that embraced the entire northern part of today's Minnesota.

During the war winterers of the North West Company had occupied the scattered posts in the area. With the coming of peace they pulled back to their own side of the border. David Stone would have liked to move into Fond du Lac district behind them, for potentially it was one of the richest territories served through Michilimackinac. But the South West Company was allied to the North West Company through identical Montreal supply houses, and by playing on that connection, Crooks was able to employ the entire group of traders, clerks and voyageurs who had recently been working the district for the Nor'Westers. In charge of them he placed four tough, able veterans of the old struggles with the XY Company: James Grant, William Morrison, Eustache Roussain, Pierre Cotté. Obtaining licenses for them through Puthuff, he sent them off through Lake Superior with perhaps two dozen big barges loaded deep with goods, including seventy kegs of concentrated high wine.

He could hardly have made arrangements with such men for a single year and must have persuaded them that if the South West Company did die in 1817, their contracts would be shifted on advantageous terms to the American Fur Company. All told, it was a neat bit of personnel work and Crooks expected quick returns for the South West Company that winter as well as long-range benefits in the future. Actually, however, though he had no possible way of foreseeing it, he was sending the men into an eruption of violence that needs outlining here, even at the cost of moving a few months ahead of Crooks's own story.

The difficulty was an offshoot of the murderous conflict between the North West Company and the Earl of Selkirk. Shortly before the War of 1812 Thomas Douglas, Earl of Selkirk, had bought control of the Hudson's Bay Company, not because he was primarily interested in the fur trade but because he wished, out of pure benevolence, to obtain virgin land on which to locate colonies of poor farmers from Ireland

and Scotland. In May 1811 the Hudson's Bay Company deeded him out of its enormous holdings roughly 116,000 square miles of territory whose southern reaches extended deep across the border into today's western Minnesota and eastern North Dakota. The Red River of the North flowed through the heart of the area, and Selkirk established his principal settlements on the banks of the stream just north of the international border.

The North West Company took immediate alarm. Their half-breed hunters, the *métis*, made pemmican in the area; and pemmican was the essential, irreplaceable food of their western voyageurs. The company's canoe routes to Athabaska and the Rockies passed close enough to the colony lands to be vulnerable to all sorts of harassment. Harassment seemed certain. Competition between the two Canadian behemoths, the North West Company and the Hudson's Bay Company, was growing more and more intense. To prevent possible strangulation, the Nor'Westers decided to drive Selkirk's colonists out of the country. The long series of clashes that followed reached a gory climax on June 17, 1816, when *métis* led by North West winterers fell on a group of farmers and killed twenty-two of them, including their new governor, Robert Semple.

At the time of the massacre Selkirk was moving west through the lakes with a hundred ex-soldiers, recently demobilized, whom he had recruited as combination farmers and military police for his beleaguered settlement. Crooks knew of the movement and reached Mackinac from his conference with Cass at Detroit about the time that Selkirk rowed into Sault Ste Marie with his private army. At the Sault, Selkirk heard of the massacre. Vowing revenge, he coasted the north shore of Lake Superior to the North West Company's huge bastion at Fort William, captured it, and set about absorbing the trade of the surrounding area for the Hudson's Bay Company.

Without the least awareness of what was going on, Crooks's new traders rowed into Fond du Lac, assorted their outfits and started for their posts at the head of the Mississippi. Scouts sent out by Selkirk seized them at different points and took them as prisoners back to Fort William. The earl refused to heed their protestations about American territory—the boundaries had not yet been determined, he said loftily— and he considered their claim to be working for the South West Company, not the North West, as a distinction without a difference. (Grant, indeed, still had connections with the North West Company.) He confiscated goods worth $10,000, including the seventy kegs of high wine, and some furs. This left eight clerks and thirty or forty engagés with nothing to do for the winter but draw wages.

Grant's crime, in Selkirk's eyes, was that earlier in the year, while still in the employ of the North West Company, he had made public threats against the Red River colony. Morrison and Roussain were guilty, to the enraged earl, of *perhaps* intending to send supplies to the murderers of his farmers. It was flimsy enough, but Selkirk was in no mood to be reasonable. He ordered the trio taken to Montreal for trial. At Sault Ste Marie, Morrison and Roussain escaped. Securing a canoe and men, they made their way in bitter fall weather back to Fond du Lac arriving December 6. There and on the Mississippi they found Hudson's Bay men trading at their old stations, flooding the Indians with enough liquor (so Morrison reported the next summer to Puthuff, forgetting their own seventy kegs) to keep the savages "in a state of Intoxication all winter. . . . Every thing which malice could device or ingenuity invent was put in practise . . . to harrass annoy and drive from the country every person in the employ of the South west company." In spite of that, Morrison and Roussain set diligently about recouping and managed to make a fair trade—at the risk of their lives, Crooks later reported to Astor.

After talking to Grant in Montreal, William McGillivray wrote Astor of a plan to recapture Fort William and take Selkirk prisoner. He suggested that Astor aid the attack by a simultaneous descent on the Hudson's Bay people inside the United States. Astor, however, was too cautious to risk out-and-out freebooting. Seeking legal backing, he told President-elect Monroe that if the government would authorize a military force, the South West Company would furnish the guides, interpreters, and boatmen necessary for the soldiers to find their way to the enemy. The government declined, as perhaps Astor had anticipated when making the request to satisfy the Canadians. Meanwhile the Nor'Westers had second thoughts and called off their own ill-judged plans for physical violence. Recompense would have to come through legal action. Selkirk was dragged through the courts for the few remaining years of his life. (He died in 1820.) Among the many actions was James Grant's suit for $50,000 for false imprisonment and damages to his lost trade. The process was served on Selkirk at Detroit on September 6, 1818—a Sunday. Because of the timing, the case was thrown out of court by Judge A. B. Woodward, who adduced multitudinous authorities beginning with Christ's resurrection on the first Easter Sunday to show that the law could take no notice of actions begun so inauspiciously.

The outcome justified Crooks's own decision not to fall back on the law but to try to collect damages from Selkirk through direct conversations. In time he about broke even, save for the seventy kegs of high wine. As Astor already had sensed, Ramsay Crooks was an adroit negotiator.

Crooks was not immediately aware of the seizures. After dispatching the Lake Superior traders, he and Rocheblave prepared the outfits going to Indiana, Illinois, Michigan, Green Bay, Prairie du Chien and the

St. Peter's. It was a crowded, hectic period. He found time nevertheless to contract with a Chippewa girl a liaison about which almost nothing is known. Perhaps he married her in the fashion of the country, attesting to a contract before a magistrate. Perhaps it was a passing fancy. Whichever it was, he remained attached to the daughter born to him on Drummond's Island May 30, 1817. He gave the child his name, educated her, visited her, introduced her to his eventual white wife.

By the end of August, 1816, he had finished his season's chores at Michilimackinac. It was well he had worked rapidly. Puthuff, still brooding over the way in which his hands had been tied by the directive about licensing, had come up with another idea. Later the agent said the scheme was approved by such officials as Lieutenant Colonel Talbot Chambers at Mackinac and by John Bowyer, the Indian agent for Green Bay. Before the war, agents had charged a five-dollar clerk's fee for making out licenses. The postwar forms were much more onerous. Why not raise the fee for each license to fifty dollars? Would not the high price hold down the number of irresponsible applicants—meaning the British?

By the time the plan formed, Crooks had obtained most of the licenses he wished, and the bulk of the South West Company traders escaped the levy. But many independent winterers remained on the island. In return for the fifty-dollar payments, Puthuff scattered licenses with such exuberance among the very foreigners he had just been complaining about that the government factor, or trader, at Prairie du Chien asked indignantly how Major "Putoff" had received his unlimited freedom. "The blackest of characters were permitted, and are now trading with the Indians in every direction," many of them supplied by David Stone. (This extensive private trade of course hurt business at the factory, which added to the factor's pain.)

Seeing how profitable the device was, Puthuff next insisted that a different license be secured to cover every movement of goods away from a trading camp, even though in the normal usage of the trade the winter's entire operation was considered a single adventure. Crooks's old boss, James Aird, and Joseph Rolette were particular sufferers under this multiple charging. John Bowyer, it should be noted, also charged fifty dollars per license at Green Bay. Each protested later that his motives were pure; and each did give open receipts to those who paid. But neither made any accounting to the government and each put what he collected into his own pocket. Puthuff is said to have netted upward of $2000, a juicy addition to his salary of $1200 a year.[4]

This new bedevilment for the Canadian traders of the Northwest was just showing its teeth when Crooks started south to St. Louis, perhaps taking with him Montreal silverwork and capotes ordered by Astor's customers on the Missouri. As he visited the settlements along the way, he soon learned that Puthuff was not alone in rousing animosity among the old-time residents of the area. Green Bay seethed with protest against Lieutenant Colonel Talbot Chambers of the United States Army.

Chambers, it will be remembered, had commanded briefly at Fort Mackinac and while there had roused the ire of Mrs. Mitchell by depriving her (so her husband charged) of little Round Island just outside the harbor. A little later, Chambers was ordered to help in the building of Fort Howard at Green Bay. When his construction battalions sailed from Mackinac in the summer of 1816 to start the work, Chambers commandeered Stanislaus Chappu and Augustin Grignon to serve as pilots. They were furious. Both were busy preparing their assortments for the winter trade and were seriously inconvenienced at being forced to help a government which even then was trying to deprive them of the trading licenses which were the source of their livelihood.

Anticipating opposition from the Winnebago Indians, Chambers took with him to cover his landing at Green Bay several companies of infantry. The Indians never murmured, perhaps because of the show of force. But to the white inhabitants the sword rattling looked like an invasion by a conquering enemy. They resented it and grew hotter still when Chambers kept on acting as if he really were governing a defeated province and not a piece of United States territory. He scorned the French Canadians (but became friendly with the British residents). Since none of the Canadians possessed documents to prove that they had extinguished Indian title to the land they occupied, Chambers called them squatters. Arbitrarily he said they must abide by the laws forbidding liquor in Indian country; they could not import one drop for their own use, to say nothing of the Indian trade. Meantime they had to watch the erection of a government trading factory beside the new fort. This factory, supported by public funds, was openly intended to drive them out of business on the grounds that they excited the disloyalty of the savages. Naturally they were contentious, but their grumbling only strengthened Chambers' conviction of their untrustworthiness.

Prairie du Chien was equally unsettled. When Crooks arrived, troops who had ascended the Mississippi late in June were busy completing Fort Crawford, a log structure 340 feet to the side, situated at the edges of the village on low ground that later floods would inundate. During the bustle of construction several houses, including the South West Company warehouse, had been summarily appropriated for government use. Other houses had been dragged out of the way of the fort, and a cemetery had been disturbed. An influential trader, Michel Brisbois, who had accepted a lieutenant's commission in the Illinois militia in 1809 but who was suspected of helping the British in 1812, was arrested for treason and sent to St. Louis for trial. (Defended by

Thomas Hart Benton, Brisbois was acquitted and turned loose to make his way home as best he could, without compensation for time lost.) As at Green Bay, land titles were questioned and liquor was forbidden. A widely credited rumor said that General Thomas A. Smith, builder of Fort Crawford, advised its first commander, Captain Willoughby Morgan, to make life easier for the government by destroying the town and dispersing its inhabitants.

Crooks found that Willoughby Morgan was detaining several traders whom Puthuff had licensed. By law Puthuff should have apprised the neighboring agents and military commanders of his action. He had not. Lacking any evidence save the traders' own protestations that the licenses were legal, Morgan refused to let them proceed to their wintering grounds, a restriction which obviously could mean bankruptcy for them and heavy loss for their outfitters.

Crooks had anticipated trouble about the licenses. Authorities were not clear-cut. The War Department directive had placed the power to grant exemptions in the hands of Governor Cass of Michigan and the Indian agents at Mackinac, Green Bay, and Chicago—but not evidently, in the hands of old Nicholas Boilvin, agent at Prairie du Chien. Mackinac was in Michigan and Puthuff was clearly responsible to Cass. But Chicago, Green Bay, and Prairie du Chien lay under the jurisdiction of Illinois Territory and the Indian agents were responsible to Governor Edwards. The question thus might be raised whether or not Puthuff, or even Cass, could issue licenses good for the trade outside their direct jurisdiction.

Crooks insisted that they could. The center of the commerce, where outfits were prepared and furs returned, was Mackinac Island in Michigan. So long as licensing authority was available there, it would be unreasonable to make a man apply somewhere else, perhaps far out of his way, for the necessary permits. Cass backed the stand—obviously a convenient one if the agent at Mackinac happened to be more obliging than those at other stations.

Puthuff had started licensing all foreigners very grudgingly and Crooks anticipated that other government officials might be equally hostile. So he had come prepared to assert Puthuff's authority in the matter. Actually, Morgan was detaining the traders on slightly different grounds than those Crooks had anticipated, but the documents he brought with him proved adequate for answering the major's objections. The traders—in their number were some independents and some who had been equipped by David Stone—were told that they could go ahead.

By now Crooks was acquiring considerable prestige. Though he had visited Mackinac several times before, he had been just one more ambitious young trader, his name quite unknown to many of the hundreds who congregated there each summer. But in 1816 word sped with each

canoe into the Indian country that he had been a key figure in forcing
Puthuff to heed the directive about licensing foreigners and then in
persuading the army to honor those licenses. The triumphs were soon
followed by others. Many winterers knew that Crooks and Rocheblave
had protested Puthuff's seizure of South West Company furs early that
summer on the shaky ground that the 1815 merchandise had paid no
duties. A few men also knew that Crooks had questioned Puthuff's new
fifty-dollar license fees. When directives came from the War Department
declaring that both the seizures and the charges were out of line,[5]
Crooks received from the jubilant winterers more credit than he actually deserved. Nevertheless it added to the emerging image: here was
a new power to be reckoned with. It would have its effect on old
Astor as well: just as he had anticipated, this was a man who could
get things done.

His success continued in St. Louis. Stuart had disposed of their goods
to Cabanné & Company but had not been able to complete satisfactory
arrangements about future dealings between the Missouri merchants and
Astor. Crooks plunged into the job with the same energy he had shown
on the Lakes. Impressed, Charles Gratiot wrote Astor somewhat un-
grammatically, "The difficulties he meet with where [were] almost
unsurmountable, but his indefatigable activity conquered most every
difficulties." By the contracts John Jacob Astor & Co. became importing
agent and commission seller for Cabanné & Company and Berthold &
Chouteau. For the time being this took care of a substantial part of
the Missouri region. It also aroused jealousies that soon had serious
repercussions, as will appear.

The immediate tasks were finished; the next step was to transform
observations into policy. When the two young men arrived in New York
to report, Astor unquestionably listened with great care. He wanted the
fur trade of the entire United States neatly held within his own chubby
fists. The Lakes country, where an opening wedge had been shaped
by the South West Company, was the logical place to begin. But he
had long since given over acting from mere desire; never again, if he
could help it, would he be burned as he had been on the Pacific. This
new venture must be as certain as human calculation could make it.

Was Crooks absolutely sure?

Knowing his man, Crooks held nothing back. There would be trouble,
he admitted. Opposition would be immediate and strong, in part from
small, whisky-peddling independents but mostly from David Stone.
The government would harry them, both because of its determination
to drive the Canadians from the field and from its desire to replace
(or at least regulate) private enterprise with an extension of the factory
trading system. Even so, if Astor was willing to give free rein to his
own resources—capital enough for driving competitors from the field by

underselling them and political influence enough to hold back encroach-
ments by the government—then Crooks thought the job could be done.
And he, of course, helped by Robert Stuart, was the one to do it.

The South West Company offered no trouble. In 1815 the Montrealers
had wanted the firm to stay alive. But by the winter of 1816–17 they
were no longer willing to fight for what had been Montreal's private
domain since the beginning of the Indian trade. Gloomily Pierre Rocheblave wrote in French to their Green Bay traders—Jacques Porlier,
Augustin Grignon, John Lawe—that the firm simply could not continue
operations under "the endless restrictions that your insatiable Congress"
imposed.[6] "Your Congress": that must have twisted wry smiles in Green
Bay. So far as they could see, the government of the United States
wanted no part of them. But Rocheblave was too glum to heed his
own unconscious ironies. During the winter he went down to New
York to perform the last rites for the company and salvage what he
could out of a wartime defeat which, in the minds of every Canadian
trader, should have been a victory.

Exact terms have not survived. Presumably the Montrealers and Astor
would share equally in the returns of 1817 (furs brought back in payment for the goods Crooks had seen into the wilderness in 1816). For
their half of the assets in the Indian country—principally merchandise
stored at Detroit and Mackinac, plus also boats, real estate and buildings
at each center, and various miscellany—the Canadians asked approximately $100,000. Astor agreed, subject to inventories by his accountants.
The American Fur Company, originally chartered nine years before, had
at last come into active being.

Crooks was appointed principal agent for a term of three years, the
contract subject to renewal if Astor kept on with the trade after that
time—an unspoken warning, obviously, that Crooks had to succeed
within those three years or else lose the fruits of everything he did.
His compensation during this period was to be the profits that might
accrue from five shares of the hundred shares of stock in the company,
a salary of $2000 a year (at a time when good traders were paid $500
to $1000 annually) and expenses. Stuart became Crook's principal as-
sistant. His wage was $1500 a year and the income from a smaller
number of shares in the company. John Jacob Astor & Company was to
import at cost all goods used by the American Fur Company. In addition
to the income from ninety or more shares of the stock, Astor was to
receive interest on the capital he advanced and a 2½ per cent commission on the furs he sold through John Jacob Astor & Co. as exclusive
marketing agent for the American Fur Company.

The agreement was completed in March 1817. Crooks was thirty years
old, Stuart thirty-two, (and Astor fifty-four). Both had experienced
enough physical excitement to satisfy most lives. Crooks in particular

had received a thorough introduction to the kinds of competition that marked one of the roughest enterprises on the frontier. Now he and Stuart, both foreign-born, were delegated to turn, if possible, every fur caught between the Ohio and the upper Mississippi away from their former countrymen into the hands of an American merchant—a goal for which the frontier had long been shouting, not yet realizing how large a shadow John Jacob Astor could cast. If this thrust into the Lakes succeeded, the shadow would continue to grow: up the Missouri, into the Rockies, on to—what man in 1817 dared predict how far?

If the thrust succeeded, if the alien trade really could be Americanized . . . That was Ramsay Crooks's job, using whatever tools Astor provided for him. He began sanguinely. But before the year was out he was so battered that almost in spite of himself he had to turn ruthless in order to keep his infant company afloat.

CHAPTER 17

The Breath of Failure

His first frustrations came in Montreal. Promptly after signing his contract with Astor, he hurried there to reduce to specifics those generalities for closing the South West Company which Rocheblave and Astor had agreed on earlier in New York. The task bristled with annoyance. Forsyth, Richardon & Co. and McTavish, McGillivrays & Co. were displeased by some of Rocheblave's concessions and showed it by raising one picayune objection after another. Compounding the exasperations was Crooks's shortage of funds. Astor had not given his agent drafts enough to pay the Montrealers in full for the settlements Crooks reached with them or to buy all the supplies he needed for the American Fur Company's first rendezvous on Michilimackinac Island. In letter after letter, Crooks fired barbed remarks about money at Astor without visibly scratching the merchant's tough old hide. Astor may have been wiser than Crooks thought. It is just conceivable that a tight pocketbook was good training for an ambitious young manager dashing forth to restitch in a single summer the ancient, war-torn patterns of the Indian commerce of the Lakes.

During lulls in his protracted discussions with the Montrealers, Crooks wrote voluminous letters to the suppliers of foodstuffs that would be used by the voyageurs on their way to the wintering grounds—hundreds of sacks of hulled corn, half a ton of bacon in casks, twenty-five hundred pounds of "good common biscuit." He ordered from Kentucky thousands of pounds of trade tobacco in carrots and plugs, and from Pittsburgh a total of 2880 gallons of high wine (at $1.20 a gallon) and Monongahela whisky (at 70¢ a gallon). All this would have to be poled on barges up the Allegheny and French rivers to Erie, Pennsylvania, during the high water of spring. Knowing the likelihood of delay, Crooks underscored the need for maintaining schedules. The rendezvous at Michilimackinac lasted a short time only. If sales were lost through delays caused anywhere along the way, the lack could not be remedied until the next year, if ever.

He also had to oversee the "made-up work" that Montreal handicrafters prepared each winter—silver earbobs, hatbands and brooches; striped shirts; trousers and capotes sewn out of blue melton. He had run similar errands during his apprentice days as a clerk. Now, as Astor's chief executive, he was back at it, making dozens of personal calls at the little shops, not because he lacked help but because he wanted to win for his new company the good will of men who very recently had been at war with the United States. He grew to know them all: "William Edge paints the oilcloths and baskets. Baptisie Herichon of the Mountain will furnish the Portage Collars and Oxhide Shoes—Jean Baptiste Macon is the Trapmaker—and the Boatbuilder lives in the first street behind and nearly opposite the Citadel."[1]

He personally signed on the voyageurs. Although Rocheblave transferred to him the employment contracts held by the old South West Company, these alone were not sufficient. Crooks had to find replacements for men whose terms had expired, who had deserted, who were being released because of ill health or discharged for incompetence. He wanted additional men for the expanded activities he contemplated. Many workers were already at Detroit, Mackinac, or the Sault, but he needed sixty more from Montreal, to row the boats to the rendezvous and to take wintering jobs in the wilderness. Each of the sixty had to be approached individually, given an advance in clothing and cash against his wages, and exhorted to show up promptly after "warnings" about the brigade's departure time had been posted on church doors in the surrounding hamlets. Crooks did much of this time-consuming work himself. These men too had recently been at war and he wanted them to have whatever reassurance might stem from seeing their bourgeois face to face.

Under the restrictions imposed by the exclusion act of 1816, not one of these sixty men was entitled to cross the border into the United States without special permission from the government. Crooks was aware of that; he was also aware that when he applied for licenses, the government might ask why he did not use American workers instead.

He put his reasons in a long letter to Astor, although the merchant had been associated with the trade long enough to need no such instruction from his eager young agent. Americans, Crooks told him, were

too independent to submit quietly to a proper controul . . . Although
the body of a Yankee can resist as much hardship as any Man, tis
only in the Canadian we find the temper of mind to render him patient
docile and persevering in short they are a people harmless in themselves
whose habits of submission fit them peculiarly for our business and
if guided as it is my wish they should be, will never give just cause
of alarm to the government of the United States.[2]

The best traders in the area around the Great Lakes were likewise
British subjects and the licenses under which they had entered the wilderness the preceding winter would have to be renewed. Crooks wanted
to obviate a repetition of the difficulties caused in 1816 by Major
Puthuff. To that end Joseph Varnum, who had been on Mackinac with
Crooks the year before, had been collecting proof of the agent's illegal
fee charging. Crooks hoped the data could be used, he wrote Astor,
"to rid us of a man who unceasingly tries to annoy us in every way
and who scruples not to stake his official character to gratify his avarice
and ambition." But the wheels of government ground slowly; Puthuff
was not likely to be replaced by summer, and Crooks had to be sure
that his men reached the Indian country. At this point he could not
possibly list them all by name. Again he urged Astor to make one
more effort to obtain licenses in blank, so that they could be filled
in as necessity demanded. "For Gods sake go to Washington," he wrote
anxiously on April 19, "unless you are very sure of obtaining what we
want without making so disagreeable a journey."

The voyageurs and the made-up work were to travel from Montreal
up the St. Lawrence and through Lake Ontario in six big Mackinaw
barges. Farm wagons would portage the boats around the Canadian
side of Niagara Falls to Lake Erie. From York there was a choice of
ways—the long route via Detroit or the shortcut to Lake Simcoe and
Nottawasaga Bay. After considerable hesitation Crooks decided against
the latter. The North West Company had first call on the necessary
wagons and depots, and might enjoy shunting the new American company aside. The quicker route might well be the long one.

The man Crooks put in charge of the brigade was W. W. Matthews,
the former Astorian who since his return from the Columbia had been
buying and selling furs for Astor in Montreal and who the summer
before had gone with Crooks to Mackinac. Matthews was a responsible
manager; but like many an ambitious executive, Crooks could not bring
himself to delegate full responsibility to anyone. Although he needed
to go to New York to report to Astor about the Montreal arrangements,
he still wanted to keep in touch with the brigade during its long passage. Accordingly he purchased a light canoe and hired a famed guide,
François Xavier Dechanetorapé, to take it to Fort Erie, across from

Buffalo. Crooks would meet the canoe there and use it to check on the brigade's progress before dashing ahead to Mackinac.

Matthews had other causes for dissatisfaction. Believing himself fitted for the wilderness trade by his experiences on the Columbia, he had asked Crooks if he might not take charge of the rich Fond du Lac district between Lake Superior and the upper Mississippi. Unhappily for his request, John Johnston, the gentle Irishman of Sault Ste Marie, had asked that the same district be added to the Lake Superior outfits which he had managed for the South West Company and which he had agreed to continue for the American Fur Company.

In some ways Johnston's claims were better than Matthews'. No one knew the American shore of Lake Superior any better or commanded the loyalty of the Indians and voyageurs more fully. He was on good terms with the Nor'Westers, against whom the new American Fur Company was sure to clash along the border. It was even possible that he was too intimate with his territory, for he was able to run his Lake Superior outfits without leaving the Sault. He might not want to endure the rigors of Fond du Lac either. He was growing old and some of his zest had died after the destruction of his home by American raiders during the war.

Matthews, younger and more vigorous, would go into the Indian country in person, obviously an advantage. But he had scant notion of the Fond du Lac trade and might not be able to win the confidence of the voyageurs, to whom Johnston was a revered figure. What to do? The decision troubled the ambitious young manager, especially since each man was relying on personal friendship for help in carrying his case.

By nature Crooks was loyal. (Witness his staying at the risk of his own life with ailing John Day in the Snake River country of western Idaho.) Now, however, he was encountering, perhaps for the first time in his career, the aloofness which of necessity must stalk at the shoulder of responsibility. Instead of facing the choice squarely, he temporized. He asked Matthews to wait until they reached Mackinac and saw how things were shaping up.

The delay could hardly have seemed fair to Matthews. He knew that John Johnston was even then in Montreal and was planning to go with Crooks first to New York, where the Irishman could talk to Astor himself, and then on to Mackinac. From Fort Erie to the rendezvous Crooks and Johnston would ride in the same light canoe, share the same messes and the same tent. It would be incredible if they did not talk about Fond du Lac, a conversation Matthews would have no opportunity of matching. Yet what choice did he have but to comply?

They set May 1 for the brigade's departure. Twenty-three carts rattled off to Lachine with food and goods. The voyageurs began assembling for the regular blessing at St. Anne's chapel. Crooks went along in person to see this physical launching of the company. He may even have been congratulating himself; after all, this could be a tremendous moment for him. But if he did feel complacency, it was immediately jolted out of him. Of the sixty Canadian laborers he personally had signed on for sinewing the great project, only thirty-five showed up.

Some desertions were expected, but a forty per cent defection was abnormal. Its causes were rooted in a difficulty Crooks would meet in other forms throughout the summer: the company he now represented was no longer leavened by Canadian connections. It was American and therefore unpredictable. Among other things, exaggerated rumors were abroad about what the United States Government planned to do with foreigners it caught south of the border. Frightened by the talk, many of the engagés simply spent their advances and vanished.

Matthews took those who did appear up the river to a small island where further desertions would be difficult. There he camped while Crooks stormed back to Montreal and, as the law allowed, swore out warrants for the deserters. The police did not find many of the missing men. In hope of deterring recurrences in future years Crooks asked that the warrants be kept in force. Then he hired replacements, mostly second-rate men at that late date. Not until May 12 was Matthews able to go ahead. Edgy from the delays, Crooks hurried to New York City to report to Astor and to check on arrangements there.

During Crooks's stay in Montreal, the cloth, blankets, trade guns, flints, beads, and other imports from England had landed in New York City. Robert Stuart checked every bale, added the items obtained in the United States—kettles, knives, powder and so on—repacked them in something more than 900 bales and started them up the Hudson in river sloops. He was to overtake the merchandise at Albany (he left before Crooks came down from the north) and personally shepherd it along the rest of the slow trip to Mackinac. Traveling with him was an old friend of Astoria days, Russell Farnham of Massachusetts.

Few men have survived more rugged experiences than Farnham. He had sailed aboard the *Tonquin* with Stuart and had been one of those almost marooned on the Falkland Islands by Captain Thorn. He had lived through the lean days at Astoria, had been at the portage fight on the Columbia where John Reed was wounded, and had traded as far inland as Montana, the first white man to see sections of that country. He had arrived in New York only a few months before Stuart's departure, after a two-year walk across Siberia and northern Europe with dispatches for Astor. He was bound now for Michilimackinac, to be put in charge of whatever critical district Crooks decided might need a particularly stalwart and dependable manager.

About the time the freight caravan left New York, Stuart and Farnham heard with some wryness that the New York Legislature had just authorized the building of a canal between the Hudson near Albany and the eastern tip of Lake Erie at a terminus not yet determined. If ever the gigantic task were completed, and doing it probably would consume close to a decade, the costs and effort of the American Fur Company's annual shipping spasm would tumble significantly. In the meantime, however, the job was expensive and onerous. The company's consignment was, and for years would remain, the single biggest movement of merchandise into the West. No one forwarding company could handle it unaided. Various agents began working months ahead of time to line up suitable conveyances for various sections of the route.

Some of the bales went from Albany by water up the Mohawk, through Oneida Lake, and down Oswego Creek to Lake Ontario. Small schooners took the packs on to Lewiston, below Niagara Falls. They were portaged by wagon to Schlosser, above the falls, and put in bateaux for the rest of the journey to their embarkation point on Lake Erie. Merchandise not handled on the water route was freighted overland from Schenectady through Geneva in huge Pennsylvania freight wagons. These ponderous vehicles boasted iron tires a foot wide to keep them from sliding into ruts. Because the wheels acted like rollers and helped smooth the atrocious roads, the wagons were passed free of charge through the frequent turnpike gates. Whichever route was used, it was Stuart's job to check the bales at every transfer point and make sure nothing was misplaced, stolen or damaged. Small losses, particularly from petty thieving, were frequent in pre-canal days, and the source of a repetitious, irritable correspondence with the forwarding agents.[3]

While the clumsy serpentine of freight toiled toward Lake Erie, Crooks hurried from Montreal to spend a single day in New York discussing strategy with Astor. The most immediate problem was that of licenses. The merchant once again had failed to obtain blank forms, but he possessed the next best thing—a copy of a letter from George Graham, chief clerk of the War Department, dated May 4, 1817, and addressed to Lewis Cass, Governor of Michigan Territory. After obliquely censuring Puthuff for his fee charging, Graham finished:

Mr. Astor having represented to this department, that he had purchased the whole of the interest in what is termed the South West Company, you will afford to him and his agents, every facility in your power, consistent with the laws and regulations.

With that authority packed triumphantly in his traveling kit, Crooks started west with Johnston. After passing Stuart and Farnham en route, they reached Buffalo late in May. The last of the ice from an exceptionally long winter had only recently ceased bobbing down the Niagara River, and the small town (population less than 500) was just

emerging like an underfed bear from its harsh hibernation. The un-
healed sores of the war still showed—charred house timbers and can-
non-shattered tree stumps leaning forlornly along the muddy streets.
The inhabitants were bright with hope, however. Buffalo just might
become the terminus of the newly authorized Erie Canal. Buffalo Creek,
beside which the village sprawled, was big enough for lake vessels to
enter, if some means—a stone quay or breakwater—could be found to
keep sandbars from forming at the mouth of the stream. Then freight
would not have to be lightered inefficiently from the shore to vessels
waiting out in the lake.

The villagers in Black Rock, a hamlet of another five hundred persons
two miles north down the Niagara River, laughed raucously at Buffalo's
pretensions. *They* had the best harbor. Lake Erie is relatively shallow;
storms agitate it violently. Buffalo was exposed, but in the Niagara
River, just out from Black Rock, was a sheltering island behind which
ships took refuge. To be sure, the rapids at the entrance to the lake
were inconvenient; ships could not breast the swift water under sail
but had to be towed one at a time up the river by a dozen or more
yoke of oxen called "the horned breeze." A fat six-inch hawser more
than two hundred fathoms in length was run from each vessel's mast
to the shore and kept from sagging into the water by rowboats stationed
every fifty feet or so along the line. On reaching the lake, the ship
cast off the heavy hawser, which then had to be coiled in the different
rowboats and brought back. Awkward, yes. But a steamship was
scheduled to be built at Black Rock the next year (1818) and the
inhabitants were sure its power would easily overcome the rapids. Then
certainly the canal terminus would come to their town.

Crooks listened to the blandishments of forwarding agents at both
villages and decided to stick with Sill and Thompson at Black Rock.
He summoned the canoe waiting for him across the river near the remains of the Canadian Fort Erie and in it checked on Matthews' six
barges as they left the Niagara portage and struck into the lake, their
sails set. Then his singing voyageurs paddled him and Johnston to Erie,
Pennsylvania, so that Crooks could make sure the supplies ordered from
Pittsburgh would be ready when Robert Stuart appeared with the
schooners. He found tobacco and corn to be short. It was too late to
do anything about the tobacco, but by hurrying forty-five miles to Ashtabula, Ohio, and scouring the countryside in person, he was able to
make up the deficiencies in the grain. He had warned his agents
against just this sort of thing. Grimly he told them he had meant
what he said and that henceforth he would seek supplies through more
efficient sources.

On the canoe went, traveling each day from dawn until after dark.
On June 6 or 7 it reached Detroit. Crooks purchased additional goods

and supplies worth $2800 (including a yoke of oxen to be delivered to Johnston's farm at the Sault). He checked on the outfits being readied for the nearby fur country by the American Fur Company's Detroit agent, James Abbott. Once again he was exasperated by desertions when Matthews' brigade arrived and several more men vanished, including a master carpenter hired to supervise a contemplated building program at Mackinac. Perhaps the Lake Simcoe shortcut would have been better, after all. Swallowing his self-recriminations, he told Abbott to hire replacements, then he called on Governor Cass concerning licenses.

The two men—they had first met during the war—got along famously. Lewis Cass, whom the Indians called Big Belly, was a frontier politician through and through and was busy building a powerful personal political machine in his wilderness territory. He focused as automatically as a magnifying glass the diffuse, often unformulated, and frequently prejudiced energies of his constituents. Naturally most of them liked him.

In 1817 Michigan still lived in the shadow of fear. The Americans were intensely suspicious of the British. In times of peace why should the former enemy continue its annual summer distribution of Indian presents at Malden and Drummond Island, luring savages to the gatherings from hundreds of miles within the United States? Conversely, the humbler French Canadians around Detroit were just as suspicious of the new influx of American opportunists. What was going to happen to their lands, their businesses, their customs, their long-standing relations with the Indians?

The savages were equally unsettled. To whom did they turn now for guidance? The Americans issued directives, but the British were old friends. They went unhappily to Malden to receive gifts and listen to treacherous orations (so the American frontiersmen charged) about the wicked, land-grabbing propensities of the onrushing Yankees.

Cass's actions gave some ground to the Indians' fears. The governor subscribed fully, and without cynicism, to the frontier theory that the red men were a "provisional race," entitled to hold the land only until another group appeared who could make better use of God's blessings. President James Monroe, who was thoroughly briefed on the Old Northwest by Cass when visiting Detroit in the summer of 1817, stated this hypothesis to Congress in his first annual message on December 2. "The hunter state can exist only in the vast, uncultivated desert. It yields to the . . . greater force of civilized population and ought to yield, for the earth is given to mankind to support the greatest number of which it is capable, and no tribe or people have a right to withhold from the wants of others more than is necessary for their own support and comfort."

Convinced of Michigan's future greatness as a center of white civilization, Cass did everything in his power to attract the settlers who would realize God's blessings. An indefatigable boomer and optimist, he cried Michigan's charms from the housetops and at the same time assiduously negotiated treaties with the Indians which would remove them from the path of settlement. (When Crooks met him in 1817, Cass had just arrived in Detroit after negotiating with some of the Ohio tribes.)

Being a frontiersman, he often found himself at odds with the federal government over policies which he, as territorial governor, was supposed to execute. He vigorously opposed the factory trading system, of which more hereafter, and as a matter of honest political theory he wanted to see the Indian trade continue, under light federal regulation, in the hands of private enterprise. Like his American neighbors in Detroit, he was profoundly suspicious of the British; yet he was pragmatic enough to grasp the ironic truth that American companies could replace the long-established British firms only if they were allowed to draw on the experience and abilities of Canadian traders, clerks, boatmen and interpreters. It was that sort of thinking and not any particular complaisance before the awesome name of Astor that led him to listen attentively as Crooks requested bulwarks against the possible obstructions of Major Puthuff.

Cass obliged by writing to the agent a letter which Crooks himself carried to Michilimackinac for delivery. In this note the governor informed Puthuff:

> . . . it is the intention of the Government that Mr. Crooks as the agent of Mr. Astor should have the selection of such persons to enter the Indian Country and conduct the business as he may require. To such persons therefore as Mr. Crooks may designate you will please grant licenses, taking the security required by the law or the regulations of May 10, 1816.[4]

Exultantly Crooks wrote Astor a few days later that if Puthuff followed instructions, "he can serve our purpose almost as effectually as if foreigners had been excluded gene[r]ally and we had obtained the number of licenses in blank you at one time so confidentally expected." The rejoicing was premature. British subjects were not generally excluded; Cass ordered Puthuff to extend licenses admitting foreigners to all American trading companies in the Lakes area, notably David Stone & Co.[5]

On June 15 the speeding canoe landed Johnston and Crooks at Michilimackinac. The winterers were not yet assembled in any numbers. After only a brief pause to let key people know of the demise of the old South West Company and the ascendancy of the American Fur organization, Crooks continued to the Sault with Johnston. There he learned more details about the Earl of Selkirk's invasion of Fond du Lac and of the extraordinary exertions by which Morrison and Roussain had recovered part of their usurped trade. No doubt Johnston also reminded him again of his, Johnston's, efforts on behalf of the North West Company to return Fort William on Lake Superior peacefully to its owners. The explosive situation was not yet settled; the Fond du Lac manager, Crooks decided, should be familiar with the issues. Accordingly he told the Irishman to add the Fond du Lac outfits to the rest of his territory. Matthews would have to go somewhere else.

On the way from Sault Ste Marie back to Michilimackinac, Crooks paused on Drummond Island. While there he presumably visited one of the bark wigwams along the shore to see the daughter who had been born to him three weeks earlier. This is guesswork, however. His letters confine themselves to trade matters—swapping corn to the North West Company and pondering ways to bring into the United States furs accumulated at two posts on the northeast shore of Lake Huron, the only depots that the American Fur Company would ever maintain on foreign soil.

By the time he reached Mackinac, Stuart and Farnham had arrived with the New York importations and Matthews with the voyageurs. Traders were pouring in with their winter's take. As Crooks poked about among the smelly bales, reading the invoice labels attached to the deerhides which wrapped them, he was able to form a fair estimate of what the South West Company had achieved during the winter. Despite lingering unrest among the Indians, results in most places had been gratifying. Final audits would set Astor's share of the year's profit at $27,202.07.

The only soft spot was the Michigan Peninsula, and the trouble there had been partly due to Puthuff's negligence—or so Crooks wrote indignantly to Astor. The South West Company traders had obeyed the law by going into the area without a drop of liquor. Their rivals, however, had left Mackinac in broad daylight loaded with alcohol, yet Puthuff, the defender of law and order, had made no effort to stop them.

One of these debauchers of the savages, interestingly enough, was not a white man but an Indian woman, Madeline LaFramboise, of the Courtes Oreilles band of Ottawas. She was the widow of a French Canadian, Joseph LaFramboise, whose wintering grounds had stretched along the Grand River of western Michigan. Madeline and their children had been accustomed to going to the post with Joseph and his voyageurs. En route one evening in 1809, while the husband was kneeling at prayers in their tent, he was shot from behind by a drunken Indian to whom he had refused more liquor on credit. Madeline rallied her terrified children and the voyageurs, put the corpse in one of their Mackinaw barges, buried it near her home village at the mouth of Grand River, and then continued to the post, located a little above present-day Grand Rapids.

During the next dozen years she maintained the trade while raising her family, sending the boys to Montreal for their education. The girls received their polishing on Michilimackinac, where they stayed at the home of their mother's Ottawa sister, Therese Schindler, who was also a trader. (Another female Ottawa Indian trader, it will be remembered, was Elizabeth Mitchell, Puthuff's old foe, wife of Dr. David Mitchell of the British garrison.)

The most beautiful of the LaFramboise girls was Josette. During one of her stays on the island, Josette fell in love with Captain Benjamin Pierce of the American troops. They were married during the summer of 1817 in a resplendent ceremony in the Mitchell home. The military attended in their full regalia, as did the Indian members of the bride's family. Ramsay Crooks was on the island at the time but perhaps was not invited, for in 1817 the three Ottawa women were allied with rival concerns. Had Josette lived, all this might have titillated Washington gossips, for in 1852 her brother-in-law, Franklin Pierce, was elected President of the United States. Long before that, however, in 1821, both Josette and her infant son died on the island.[6]

Although trading liquor to Indians had caused her husband's death, Madeline LaFramboise was too imbued with its advantages to abandon its use. Crooks angrily gathered affidavits about her illegal activities and those of Jacob Smith of Detroit, who had employed alcohol to outdo the South West Company traders at Saginaw Bay, eastern Michigan. This evidence Crooks presented to Puthuff. The agent did nothing about it, perhaps because he felt he was not justified in acting after the fact on the basis of information supplied by a rival. Whatever the cause, the negligence did not inspire Crooks with high opinions about the impartiality of government officials. Bitterly he wrote Astor that he personally approved of total prohibition as being to the ultimate advantage of both the trade and the Indians. But the restriction had to be absolute: "to succeed in the trade when our opponents set the law at defiance . . . is wholly impossible." It was the beginning of a problem that was to plague the rest of his days in the fur trade.

As the rendezvous gathered headway and the winterers laid their plans, the new manager of the American Fur Company realized with dismay that competition from all sides was going to be more fierce than he had predicted to Astor. The government trading factories were actually taking the offensive in the struggle. The new Superintendent of Indian Trade, Thomas L. McKenney, was a grim humanitarian, outspoken in his hostility toward all private business with the Indians, American as well as British. He charged the new rush of Yankee traders with deliberate subversion of their country's laws. Did they not openly hire alien workers? Did they not corrupt the savages with intoxicating liquor? Did they not prey on the gullibility of their naïve customers in order to achieve inordinate profits? Well, he, Thomas L. McKenney, would end that. On May 2, 1817, he wrote John W. Johnson, the factor at Prairie du Chien, to do whatever he could to destroy profits and thus drive private traders from the field. "Every advantage over them that can be fairly taken . . . is within the limits of the duty we owe these unfortunate people [the Indians] whose want of knowledge of what constitutes their happiness alone prevents them from putting to flight these speculators on their toils."

The traders, vocally supported by Governor Cass, retorted that the trading factories cheapened the government of the United States in the eyes of the Indians: the British government grandly passed out gifts of merchandise as a true father should and did not basely dicker over handfuls of muskrat furs. They asserted that the Indians were not gullible, but recognized values to a fraction of a cent—recognized, too, with contempt, the inferiority of the government-contracted American goods sold at the factories. The savages wanted the superior English imports which only the private traders supplied. The whites further insisted that liquor was not a problem in the American wilderness but only on the Canadian frontier and near the settlements. But their sharpest pangs sprang from the price-cutting competition of these (in their minds) holier-than-thou government factors, who were supported by public funds and unrestrained by any need to show a gain on the capital invested.

The government investment was appreciable. John W. Johnson of Prairie du Chien alone had at his command a fund of $40,000. Furthermore the new government traders were more aggressive than those before the war. In the early days custom had decreed that Indians come to the factories to trade. In 1817 both Johnson at Prairie du Chien and Matthew Irwin at Green Bay altered this by equipping adventurers at cut rates to go into the field and compete directly with men backed by the private companies. And finally, adding a last rub to Crooks's personal grievances, Johnson conducted these hateful operations out of an American Fur Company building. The structure, originally a warehouse belonging to the South West Company, had been expropriated by General Thomas Smith during the building of Fort Crawford at Prairie du Chien. Afterward he turned it over to the government factory. Crooks demanded the building's return on the grounds that it had fallen to the American Fur Company on Astor's purchase of the South West Company's assets. General Smith denied this. He told Johnson the building belonged to the government and the factor could continue using it. The matter dragged through the Michigan courts for years before being settled in Astor's favor.

David Stone caused even more trouble than the factories. Determined to scramble with Crooks at full strength for the services of the winterers of the defunct South West Company, he went personally to England during the winter. There he drove such hard bargains with the manufacturers of blankets and guns that he knew he could meet any price offensive by Crooks without disaster to himself.[7] Returning to Montreal, he laid hold of Astor's long-time associate, Jacob Franks, and through him captured the entire body of Green Bay traders—John Lawe, Frederic Oliva, the numerous Grignons and Porliers. Among them they controlled the Wisconsin shore of Lake Michigan, the interior streams almost to Lake Superior, and much of the east bank of the Mississippi around Lake Pepin and its tributaries. Try as he might, Crooks could not break the front and had to reconcile himself to losing the Wisconsin trade at least for that year.

Stone intensified his attack on reaching Michilimackinac with what Crooks estimated to be 150 choice "pieces," that is, assortments of goods. The wilderness was drowned under merchandise. Part of the fault lay with Crooks himself. In his eagerness to overwhelm the trade, he had urged Astor to import more goods than the American Fur Company really needed in view of its commitment to absorb the quantities of South West Company cloth and hardware in storage at Detroit, Michilimackinac, and Prairie du Chien. Astor also had promised to receive whatever unsold bales the South West winterers brought back with them to the rendezvous of 1817. When Crooks added up the total it came to 100 pieces, on top of Stone's 150, the factories' outpourings, and the shiploads Stuart brought in. Still more was being smuggled across the border by French-Canadian coureurs de bois and by Indians as they returned from Malden or Drummond Island.

Glumly Crooks wrote Astor, "If all these goods go into the country, returns to pay for them can never be brought out." A vicious price war became inevitable. Stone began it by authorizing his Mackinac agent, Oliver N. Bostwick, to undercut by 25 per cent any figure offered by the American Fur Company.

There was no way to respond directly to that kind of attack, yet Crooks and Stuart had to devise some kind of answering lure. They came up with a canny one. They spread the word through the taverns and along the sandy white beach that this year the company would waive all interest charges on the merchandise it sold. Such fees were customary. The winterers did not pay on receipt of their goods but in furs delivered a year after the purchase. Since the risk was high that they would not harvest enough pelts to meet their obligations, carrying charges were also high and a continual source of irritation at the time of settlement. The thought of no interest payments to chop the heart out of a man's profits was dazzling, especially to those semiliterate traders who really did not understand cost accounting. In this way it was possible to let Stone quote figures lower than those shown on the American Fur Company price labels and still convince buyers that their real interest lay with Astor.

Naturally not everyone succumbed. Stone achieved one victory even more important than the winning of Jacob Franks. This was the semi-independent firm of Bertholet and Rolette, who formerly had bought their goods from the South West Company but had traded entirely on their own risk. The two French Canadians did some business on Drummond Island and along the north shore of Lake Huron, but their principal effort centered at Prairie du Chien. From there they dominated the west bank of the Mississippi to the vicinity of present Minneapolis, and the St. Peter's to its very head, where they set up a sphere-of-influence understanding with young James Lockwood, who was also supplied by Stone.

This was a princely district, drawing Sioux Indians to it from almost as far away as the Missouri. Unable to hold Bertholet and Rolette, Crooks then tried to find someone who would go into the area and compete with them even at a loss to be borne by the company. No one would take the risk; Rolette in particular was notorious for his rough tactics. Finally Crooks appealed to W. W. Matthews. At first blush, the opportunity looked as bright as the one Matthews had lost to John Johnston. But after listening to the talk around Mackinac and sizing up the combined strength of David Stone and Bertholet-Rolette, Matthews decided that if he accepted he might find himself wading out into an economic swamp from which he would never be able to escape. Pique over Fond du Lac may also have played a part in his decision. In any event he said he would rather stick to his eight-hundred-dollar-a-year job as Astor's agent in Montreal. And so the Mississippi above Prairie du Chien was also lost to Crooks, save for the headwaters served through Fond du Lac.

Even Fond du Lac, which Crooks thought he had secured the year before by his arrangement with Morrison, Cotté and Roussain (Grant dropped out), was invaded through a devious subterfuge that put him into a fury. The opening wedge was Charles Oakes Ermatinger, a British trader who lived on the Canadian side of the Sault, opposite the rebuilt home of John Johnston. Ermatinger knew in detail the border area as far west as Red River, and for some years had been acting as agent for the Earl of Selkirk in connection with supplies forwarded through the Sault to the beleaguered Red River colony.

In the spring of 1817 Ermatinger brought to the Sault a considerable quantity of Montreal trade goods. What his initial intention was cannot be said; for an English citizen to bring English goods into the United States was so totally illegal that he would have been rash indeed to contemplate using them south of the border. But suddenly Puthuff grew lax about granting licenses. Here indeed was irony. In the spring Ramsay Crooks had feared that the agent would be too strict. But under the bombardment of directives from Cass and the War Department about admitting whatever aliens were needed for the prosecution of the trade, Puthuff had caved in completely. Anyone, it seemed, could get a license.

Ermatinger applied to him for permission to trade along the south shore of Lake Superior and into Fond du Lac. Not the least guise of American connections accompanied the request. This was too much even for Puthuff, and he peremptorily denied the application.

Ermatinger next asked Crooks and Stuart to pretend to buy his merchandise and let him go across the lake as an agent of the American Fur Company. They declined. John Johnston of the Sault and William Morrison had just left Mackinac with twenty-eight loaded boats and nine clerks. This was ample to supply the areas named and the winterers would not relish competition from Ermatinger, no matter what cloak he traded under. Besides, Ermatinger was associated with Selkirk, "who," Crooks and Stuart wrote Astor, "so flagrantly abused and insulted the laws of the United States"—and who in the process had disrupted the trade of the South West Company by making prisoners of Grant, Roussain, and Morrison the year before. Crooks and Stuart even grew pious about the matter. They wouldn't dream of making a deal with an out-and-out Canadian, well knowing, they said, "your [Astor's] wish to give your utmost support to facilitate the full accomplishment of the intentions of the government, both in order to ameliorate the condition of the wretched natives, and as soon as advisable prevent all foreign communication with them."

Rebuffed by Crooks and Stuart, Ermatinger turned to Oliver Bostwick of David Stone & Co. Bostwick agreed to the Canadian's proposal. He made the dummy purchase and asked Puthuff to let Ermatinger, his new trader, visit the south shore of Superior and country beyond in Fond du Lac. Since Ermatinger now had American connections, Puthuff granted the license. This of course meant full-scale competition in what Crooks had considered a private preserve. He and Stuart rushed to the agency office to protest. Couldn't the major see that the whole thing was a fraud?

Puthuff, who just possibly was enjoying this, gave them a sour smile. He was merely obeying orders from Cass to issue licenses to whomever Bostwick recommended. What were they complaining about? They had been granted the same privilege. Or did they think they were something special? Well, he didn't. There was no reason why

Stone's men should not trade on equal terms with the American Fur Company in any district.

This was a wretched start. Astor wanted monopoly, yet nowhere had Crooks been able to achieve anything approaching that condition. He commanded the loyalty of only one experienced American trader who might have been able to fill some of the yawning gaps that had opened under his feet. That was Russell Farnham, the Astorian. But Farnham was unavailable for the north country. Crooks needed him even more acutely in an area where his American citizenship might prove crucial, in among the Sac and Fox Indians, who, with the Iowas, roamed both sides of the Mississippi below Prairie du Chien.

Neither Farnham nor his chief clerk, young Daniel Darling, another native-born American, knew the area or the Indians, but they were to be assisted by two redoubtable and, in the eyes of U.S. government officials, notorious French Canadians. One was Edward Lagoterie; the other, Joseph Laperche, *dit* St. Jean. Lagoterie had been Robert Dickson's deputy among the Sacs and Foxes during the war. Laperche was odious for having rowed into Prairie du Chien with three American scalps waving from his boat and using them to spark victory dances of Indians through the streets of the hamlet.

Jurisdictional quarrels between different departments of the government clouded operations in Farnham's district-to-be. Indian agents could grant licenses only in Indian country. In order to barter with the savages on land ceded to the United States, a trader had to obtain a permit from the governor of the territory claiming that land. On both the east and west banks of the Mississippi the border of the Indian country was in dispute. The United States insisted that the Sac and Fox chiefs had alienated that part of their land lying along the east bank of the river through a treaty signed in 1804 with William Henry Harrison. The tribe denied the contention, even though one term of their peace with the national government in 1816 was supposed to be a reaffirmation of the cession of 1804. The confusion was echoed west of the river, where Missouri Territory claimed more land in the area of the Des Moines River than the Indians were willing to grant.

Governor Ninian Edwards of Illinois (which then embraced Wisconsin) and Governor William Clark of Missouri wanted to control the trade in these disputed districts through their licensing powers on territorial lands. They were particularly hostile toward the British citizens who were crossing the hazy border on the strength of licenses obtained from the Indian agents at Michilimackinac, Green Bay, and, to a lesser extent, at Prairie du Chien. In Crooks's mind, Clark's and Edwards' animosity rose not so much from patriotism as from a desire to protect the traders of their districts, Cahokia and Kaskaskia in Illinois and St. Louis in Missouri.[8] Merchants from the three towns worked closely together on the Mississippi and up the Missouri, and Clark himself had fur-trade connections.

The Indians of course moved at will back and forth across the border, wherever it was; and the Great Lakes traders who through the years had grown accustomed to following them were outraged to discover after the war that they were barred, even though they possessed licenses. For instance, Jacques Porlier of Green Bay in 1816 held a license for the Indian country but could not obtain a territorial license to trade with the Sacs and Foxes along Rock River in land claimed by Illinois. As a result he had to rent a second-floor room in St. Charles, a village just north of St. Louis, and try to dispose of his goods to the white townspeople. That same year François Bouthillier of the South West Company finally obtained his territorial license through bribery, or so Porlier hinted.[9]

Edward Lagoterie, also of the South West Company, ran afoul of the same restriction but vanished among the Indians with their connivance and traded anyway. This annoyed the authorities, who sent out troops but could not find him. When Lagoterie came to St. Louis in the spring with forty-three bales of furs and some leftover merchandise and asked for permission to take the articles to the rendezvous at Mackinac, Clark refused him a passport, which as a British citizen he needed for passing through U. S. Indian country. Crossing the river, Lagoterie applied to Governor Edwards. Again he was refused. In the end he had to store furs and goods with a friend of Astor's, Joseph Philipson, and hire out as an interpreter to a trader bound up the Mississippi. To Crooks it was no coincidence that the employer was a friend of Clark's and hence able to obtain the passport which had been denied to Lagoterie personally.

After belatedly reaching Mackinac without his furs, Lagoterie was assigned, along with Laperche, to help Farnham and Darling learn the ways of the Sac, Fox, and Iowa Indians. Obtaining licenses to the Indian country from Puthuff proved easy. Crooks, however, was worried over possible harassment by zealous officials who, hoping to strike at Lagoterie and Laperche, might impound the outfits on the charge that the traders had strayed across the border. For additional protection Farnham would need territorial licenses as well. With both licenses in hand, the outfits could then operate wherever Farnham chose.

Timing complicated the problem. The Indians who annually congregated on Rock Island and along the Des Moines, waiting for the traders, would be eager to buy their necessities and be off on their fall hunt before Farnham could journey to St. Louis, obtain territorial licenses and return. Rival traders coming directly up the Mississippi from the Missouri capital would skim the cream well ahead of him. Crooks decided the thing for the outfits to do was stop inside the border of the Indian country and display their wares. While the Indians were buying on credit, Farnham should hurry to St. Louis for the territorial licenses and return to rescue the others in case they ran into trouble with the authorities. As soon as his clerks, Lagoterie and Laperche, were sure the licenses had been issued they could then move as business dictated onto Rock River, the Des Moines, or anywhere else in the disputed areas. Timewise they might walk a thin edge for a day or two; but otherwise everything seemed to Crooks perfectly legal, though he did recognize that the identity of the clerks might lift eyebrows here and there. Carefully he instructed Farnham:

> You must not listen to the thousand stories and perhaps threats you will hear against both Lagothry [sic] and St. Jean [Laperche], for such things will be attempted with the view of intimidating or checking your activity. . . . But actually to touch the persons or the goods belonging to these two outfits, is more than they dare.
> Be extremely cautious in giving vent to the hard things you may and will feel inclined to say to some people you may have to deal with . . . for be assured every word affecting these great men will be treasured up against you . . . . Should the Executive of either Territory dare to interrupt Lagothrie [sic] you will have to keep a watchful eye on the proceedings . . . and if he should (a thing that can hardly happen) be forced from his trading House to answer below to charges of a frivolous nature you must supply his place with some one who can speak the language.

The trouble Crooks anticipated shaped up well ahead of the trading houses at Rock Island and beside the Des Moines. Along the way, Farnham made a routine stop at Prairie du Chien to show his papers to Lieutenant Colonel Talbot Chambers, the commanding officer at Fort Crawford, and was thunderstruck to be told that Puthuff's licenses were not valid on the lower Mississippi.

As noted earlier, Chambers had gone from Michilimackinac to Fort Howard at Green Bay. After a short stay there he was transferred to Fort Crawford at the Prairie. At each place he treated the French Canadians under his jurisdiction as a species of creature not quite up to human level. Though he himself drank to excess, he insisted that since Green Bay and Prairie du Chien were in Indian country, the inhabitants could not have a drop of spirits. When Charles Menard was accused of selling liquor to the troops (Menard denied it), Chambers ordered him publicly flogged after an inadequate trial and paraded through the streets with a bottle tied around his neck, the military band playing the "Rogue's March" at his back. When another French Canadian interfered as Chambers was reeling down the street in pursuit of a young girl, that man too was ordered tied to a post and beaten—though in this case Chambers reconsidered and stopped the punishment after a lash or two had been delivered. For some alleged breach of morals, its nature not now recoverable, Joseph Rolette, the town's leading trader, was exiled for most of the winter to an island in the Mississippi and was allowed to return to his family only through the intervention of Governor Cass. Later, on the Missouri, Chambers beat a boatman so savagely that he received an official reprimand from the Secretary of War. In 1825 his drunkenness and improper conduct reached such depths that at last he was formally court-martialed and cashiered. Rolette summed up the opinion in Prairie du Chien about him by writing after his departure:

It is the first winter Since peace has taken place that we enjoy liberty and are dealt with as free men . . . It is a new World since that T. Chambers is no more here.

Crooks firmly believed that Chambers was motivated by an acute hostility toward the American Fur Company. The officer certainly showed favoritism toward its competitors. Although he railed to his superiors about foreign traders when discussing the French Canadians, he had formed, while at Fort Howard, strong friendships toward some of the British residents of Green Bay. After being transferred to Prairie du Chien, he wrote one of them, John Lawe, that he would help Lawe evade the restrictions against British traders: "The com^{dg} officer here has a great deal in his power, it shall be exerted to the utmost in your behalf, but keep every thing which I write you, *quiet*." The following September he passed boats belonging to Bertholet & Rolette and to Jacob Franks on the strength of licenses that had been obtained for them from Puthuff by David Stone. But when Farnham and Darling appeared with Lagoterie and Laperche a few days later, Chambers halted them.

He was abetted in the action by Benjamin O'Fallon, newly appointed Indian agent for Missouri, who had been at Prairie du Chien since spring. Crooks scented prejudice there too; O'Fallon was the nephew of William Clark, through whom he had obtained his appointment. And perhaps the nephew really did share his uncle's bias against the northern traders; shortly after reaching Prairie du Chien, O'Fallon wrote Clark that he was, as requested, "keeping a watchful eye over the feelings and the disposition and conduct of the *faithless Mackinac traders*."[10]

Chambers consulted O'Fallon about the legality of Farnham's license from Puthuff. The two men decided it did not apply on the Mississippi and that before Farnham, assisted by his notorious clerks, could open his assortments he would have to obtain a fresh license from Clark.

Because of the time involved in complying, the order amounted to handing over to competitors from St. Louis a large part of the fall trade among the Sacs and Foxes. Forgetting Crooks's instructions to guard his tongue, Farnham said violently in the hearing of several people that as soon as he reached Rock Island he was going to trade as planned, Chambers or no. The colonel thereupon handed Farnham written orders not even to converse with Indians on his way to St. Louis. In a message to Willoughby Morgan, in command at new Fort Armstrong on Rock Island, he characterized the American Fur Company men as "hardened Raschels" and directed Morgan to make sure the non-intercourse edict was enforced—"in order that the military might not be made the subject of derision by such named Raschels."

Farnham and Darling appeared at Rock Island on schedule with their clerks, went into camp near the Indian villages, and opened their bales. Morgan's soldiers arrested them. Morgan meanwhile debated with himself about the principles involved: could a military commander set aside on his own authority a license emanating from another government official, in this case an Indian agent? If not, would the civilians concerned be entitled to seek redress through the courts? If so, where did that put him, Willoughby Morgan, if he obeyed orders from his superior?

Being a good soldier, he obeyed and sent his prisoners to St. Louis under an escort of soldiers commanded by Lieutenant W. S. Blair. Clark's private opinions on the matter are not on record, but he evidently decided that Chambers had gone too far. He freed the prisoners and granted Farnham a license both to the public domain and to the Indian country for which Puthuff had earlier issued permits. He did observe grumpily that if agents could issue licenses for districts outside their assigned jurisdictions, as Puthuff was doing, confusions were bound to result.

To Crooks the discussion was academic. A harmful delay had occurred; a considerable amount of trade from still another promising fur area had to be subtracted from the total of his early anticipations. The extent of the trade lost throughout the area that initial year is suggested by the company ledgers. By dint of interest-waiving and through personal friendships formed the year before in helping traders reach their wintering grounds, Crooks managed to place goods worth $74,218.52. But he had to put into dead storage, there to eat up interest charges without profit, assortments invoiced at $51,794.[11] Astor was not going to be impressed.

Late in August, Stuart left Mackinac in charge of several hundred packs of furs brought to the rendezvous by the winterers of the defunct South West Company. Crooks stayed behind, unraveling accounts, devising ways to simplify procedures, and preparing importation orders for 1818. He hired Samuel Abbott to be the company's resident manager on the island, but in his anxiety he kept meddling with details as Abbott started carpenters to work building a dormitory for a hundred voyageurs and a cavernous warehouse for the better handling of furs. In October he heard of trouble at the Sault, its nature unrecorded, and hurried by canoe across the cold lake to see John Johnston, with whose business procedures he was growing dissatisfied. He returned in a snow-storm, wound up his affairs, and on November 3 caught a sailing ship, the *Tiger*, to Detroit on what proved to be a wildly stormy passage.

Boarding the *Tiger* with him was an influential friend, Adam D. Steuart (no relation to Robert Stuart), who was bound to Washington, where his uncle was mayor, in order to obtain confirmation of his interim appointment as collector of customs at Michilimackinac. The conjunction of this potent duo worried agent Puthuff. He knew that despite his liberality toward the American Fur Company, Crooks was furious at him for the favors granted Oliver Bostwick, especially in the case of Charles Ermatinger.

Thinking that a soft answer might turn away wrath, Puthuff concluded a letter to Cass defending his actions by saying,

Of Mr. Crooks as Agent for J. J. Astor I have good reason for believing that he had in his application for licenses, confined himself strictly to the Introduction of his own goods only, and indeed in all matters relating to his trade, I have never discerned a disposition . . . to violate the strict letter of his Country's laws.

Crooks voiced no such generosity in his own opinion of Puthuff. To Astor he wrote concerning the unhappy agent,

His shameful partiality makes it a matter of justice to ourselves to expose him, for he is totally unfit to fill the respectable office he now holds. For our success we want a man not to be cajoled or intimidated, one who will *on all occasions do his duty*.

Puthuff was Cass's friend. Knowing this, Crooks did not attack the agent directly in Detroit, but instead filled his time going over the accounts of the Detroit department with James Abbott (Samuel's brother) and drawing up detailed orders for foodstuffs. He added to the lists at Erie and Buffalo. In the latter town he was delayed by an icy dispute with a shipping firm over damage done in transit to several score packs of furs because of improper stowage.

On January 4, 1818, he at last reached New York to report on his first year's stewardship. By his own admission, the preliminary accounting he submitted to Astor bore "a reproving aspect." Although he projected a profit of $9475.02, the figure was achieved only by entering no interest against the goods put into storage at Detroit and Mackinac. Likewise, the forecast contained no immediate provisions for paying interest on the $146,348.48 which Astor had advanced to start the American Fur Company moving. And finally Crooks assumed, on the books, that all debts due from the winterers would be paid in full at the rendezvous of 1818. If traders defaulted to any substantial extent or if the furs on reaching market did not realize the values he anticipated, then, so he granted unhappily, "it will be a black business indeed."

A bad start after so much confidence. But at least he and Robert Stuart knew now what they were up against. Next year, instead of flailing blindly, they would take the offensive and hit first.

The place to begin, they decided, was the national capital. On January 24, 1818, they wrote a long joint letter to Astor, who was then in Washington. In this remarkable document they outlined the reasons for their poor showing and suggested cures which their employer could initiate through his friends in Congress and the War Department. First, the company must get rid of Puthuff. Next, they should make an example of Talbot Chambers, so that other military officers would be less inclined to interfere with duly licensed traders. And finally they should launch a determined drive to have the government trading factories abolished.

Those matters achieved in Washington, Crooks and Stuart would then be able to take care of whatever smaller problems might arise in the wilderness.

CHAPTER *18*

The Fist Closes

Results were immediate and striking. After failing in several attempts to meet with the new Secretary of War, John C. Calhoun, Astor on February 10, 1818, left a copy of the Crooks-Stuart letter in Calhoun's office. On March 2 the Secretary forwarded a copy to Cass in Detroit, asking for comment. Cass in turn relayed the charges against Puthuff to the agent at Michilimackinac and requested his observations. The rigamarole was pointless. Before Puthuff could reply, Calhoun fired the agent without a hearing.

Only surmise can explain the abrupt decision. Astor's influence was probably not as determining as that of Thomas L. McKenney, the strait-laced and ambitious Superintendent of Indian Trade. McKenney had been horrified earlier to learn not from Crooks or Stuart but from his own factory managers at Green Bay and Prairie du Chien of Puthuff's fee charging and of his wholesale licensing of foreign traders, whose competition cut painfully into the profits of the government posts. For these reasons he joined Astor in cries for the agent's scalp—strange bed-fellows indeed, in those days. Another telling witness may have been Adam D. Steuart, by then duly appointed as Collector of Customs at Michilimackinac and Crooks's traveling companion on the *Tiger*. After having had ample opportunity on shipboard to make his points to the presumptive Collector, Crooks then recommended Steuart to Calhoun as a "living witness" that the charges against Puthuff were true. Records are silent; but Steuart, who was in Washington at the time, quite possibly was consulted.

Notice of the dismissal troubled Lewis Cass. He protested to Calhoun that Puthuff had been a fine officer during the war and that since then had acted with a "Zeal, Capacity, and intelligence not surpassed in any agent within my knowledge." It was too late to revoke the order, however. Puthuff was granted a Hobson's choice only: he could stay on the island, drawing full salary and retaining full authority until his replacement arrived; or he could leave immediately for Washington to seek another government position, allowing Cass to designate a temporary substitute.

Cass suggested the latter course and promised to exert his influence toward helping Puthuff obtain a fresh position. The deposed agent elected to stay on Mackinac, however. He experienced one brief moment of hope. The man appointed in his place backed down, and Puthuff appealed for reinstatement.[1] The effort availed nothing. A second appointee accepted and in June 1819 Puthuff at last surrendered his agency. Thereafter he ran a store in Mackinac, functioned for a time as probate judge of the county court, and later was elected mayor of the village.

Meanwhile the attack against Talbot Chambers was grinding ahead more slowly but just as relentlessly. First, Astor made sure that the colonel was personally liable for damages—in other words, that the War Department had sent Chambers no orders that could be interpreted as authorizing such a seizure as that inflicted on Farnham and Darling. The man's hope for help from the government thus cut off, Astor hired a rising lawyer, politician and newspaper editor in St. Louis, Thomas Hart Benton, to institute suit for $10,000 for interruption to Farnham's trade.[2]

Crooks and Farnham would have to appear in St. Louis as early as possible to make the charges and swear to the necessary affidavits. This meant writing Cass for various papers, including corroboration of Puthuff's authority to issue licenses for the Indian country along the Mississippi. More strange bedfellows—for now Crooks was seeking to establish the strict licensing authority of the very man he was simultaneously challenging for abusing that authority. The unhappy agent simply could not win. Benjamin O'Fallon was concurrently writing letters to the St. Louis newspapers *defending* Chambers' actions and flaying Puthuff's laxness. The turmoil was symptomatic not only of the confused animosities of the postwar Indian trade, but also of the crippling ambiguities inherent in the government's effort to control a commerce it really did not understand.

Crooks insisted again and again that personal malice played no part in the actions against either Puthuff or Chambers. The American Fur Company was merely trying to clarify principles and establish its right to conduct lawful business unhampered by the whims of irresponsible government officials. Cass agreed, at least about Chambers. Any army officer who would usurp the law as Chambers had, so the Michigan governor wrote Crooks on May 7, 1818, "ought to be taught a practical lesson, no less wholesome to himself than to those disposed to approve his conduct and imitate his example."

And, indeed, a wholesome lesson may be all that Crooks and Astor intended. Still, a fist clenched under a man's nose tends to suggest malice to him and to look like a warning to his associates: see what happens when you interfere? Without question, Puthuff's discharge and Chambers' suit, however wholesome, acted as deterrents to other officers who, through similar zeal, might have been tempted to challenge the company.

The next attack of the spring, less personal in its focus, was aimed at the government trading factories. Opposition to them was not limited to Astor. His fur-trade rivals in St. Louis criticized the post at Fort Osage on the Missouri and the new "branch" of the Prairie du Chien factory near the mouth of the Des Moines River as intemperately as Crooks and Stuart belabored the establishments in their districts. Thomas Hart Benton, whose St. Louis paper, the *Enquirer,* was the public voice of the wilderness traders, formalized the objections in print. Factory goods were sneered at as inferior and factory policies stigmatized for alienating the Indians rather than winning them. Government traders were branded as lazy incompetents, squanderers of public funds at best and, at worst, sly profiteers who sold to their own gain the factory goods intrusted to them.

Heeding the outcries, the Senate early in 1818 ordered that appointments to factory positions could no longer remain the sole prerogative of the War Department, but would have to be referred to the Senate for confirmation. And on April 4, 1818, Secretary of War Calhoun, a proponent of the factory system, was put on the defensive by a resolution of the House of Representatives which directed him to study "a system providing for the abolition of the existing Indian trade establishments in the United States and providing for the opening of the trade with the Indians under suitable regulations." What part Astor played in the passage of these measures cannot be traced, but, in common with some of the St. Louis merchants who were also visiting Washington that winter, he surely dropped in at the offices of friendly congressmen.

The tug-of-war over the Indians was complicated by a sudden reversal of policies concerning licenses. As the new President, James Monroe, had promised to do, he reviewed the problem during a trip to the Northwest in the summer of 1817. No doubt the usefulness of foreigners in the trade was pointed out to him, perhaps by Cass. But other men also reached the President's ear. Military strategists warned of continued British councils with United States Indians at Malden and on Drummond Island. United States Indian agents, many of whom had served in the army during the war, questioned the advisability of letting a potential fifth column cross the border almost without restraint, merely on the specious claim that no one else, not even the government factories, could supply the tribes. Thomas McKenney, Superintendent of Indian Trade, blamed whisky-peddling aliens for corrupting the savages morally as well as politically, and for undermining the work of the government factories.

Monroe listened. The United States still feared British intrigue along the northern borders. Calhoun even then was working on plans to extend the country's frontier fortifications far up the Mississippi and the Missouri. Was it wise to license former enemies to dig in around the very sites of the proposed bastions? Deciding not, Monroe on November 26, 1817, revoked the exemptions granted by his predecessor and ordered that the total exclusion decreed by Congress in April 1816 be reinstated.

The rigors of this edict forcibly reminded Crooks and Astor of a necessity they had sensed before: sooner or later they were going to have to train young Americans to the Indian commerce. With this in mind they told Matthews in January 1818 to visit the border hamlets along Lake Champlain and hire, on five-year contracts at salaries of $140 to $240 a year, twelve or fourteen young clerks who knew Canadians and could speak French. In time the best of these young men could assume full charge of the outfits.

The critical word in the plan was *time*. No young man could learn Indian psychology and the involved, multitudinous, tedious details of the commerce during a single season. A long apprenticeship under an experienced winterer was necessary for turning a clerk into a trader. While that apprenticeship was being served, British veterans had to continue functioning at the heads of the outfits—and French-Canadian voyageurs as the workhorses. Otherwise the Indians would not be adequately served. Astor had made that point to government officials before. He was sure he could do it again, especially if this time he pleaded that he desired exemptions only until he had trained several young Americans, already hired, to do the very work their government wanted done.

Having initiated the scheme, Crooks and Astor did not want rivals to tumble to it. If the American Fur Company was the only firm offering young Americans as justification for exemptions, then perhaps the American Fur Company would be the only one to receive licenses. Crooks wrote Matthews to say nothing in Montreal about the clerks he had hired, "as it might open the eyes of our competitors."

It was a childish sort of secrecy. Other traders had reacted to Monroe's edict in exactly the same way. Jacob Franks, who had just ordered from David Stone "30 pieces Stroud . . . 300 Beavor Traps Baled up 250 half axes & 250 Caustettes [Tomahawks]" that he planned to transport in two barges to the Mississippi "with as many Winterers as I can procure," was confident of reaching his goal. To a Green Bay associate he explained, "Mr Stone who was here but a few days ago is of opinion that we can go on with our Trade . . . by imploying young Americans to take out the Goods."

Stone also suggested another device whereby some of the long-time residents of Detroit, Mackinac, Green Bay and Prairie du Chien could stay in business. Many of them had lived in those areas at the time of Jay's Treaty of 1794. They could have elected United States citizenship then. Perhaps they still could do so. Anyway, what was to prevent them from going to the agency offices and demanding licenses as American citizens under the terms of that old (and abrogated) treaty? By blustering enough, they could probably talk the agents out of at least temporary permits, good until some high official in Washington ruled on the matter. By then perhaps Astor and he could have worked out some legal way to relax Monroe's unfair edict—unfair at least in the eyes of the frontiersmen who were pinched by it.

Unaware of what the traders were up to, Thomas McKenney, Superintendent of Indian Trade, grew exultant. Now at last the government factories could establish their influence over the savages unimpeded. On March 6, 1818, he wrote one of the factors who had been most vocal about competition from private enterprise, Matthew Irwin of Green Bay, that he need worry no longer. "From the refusal on the part of the Govt. to let foreigners into a participation of our trade, I think you may calculate on success in the future."

But McKenney forgot the strength of Astor and Stone in Washington. Vigorously the two merchants reminded their friends in Congress and in the uneasy War Department that only foreigners were qualified to carry merchandise to Indians who lived far beyond range of the factories—Indians who, deprived of their livelihood, would listen more attentively than ever to British harangues at Malden and Drummond Island.

After "farther information and reflection" Monroe compromised.[3] On March 25 he decreed that trading firms might employ Canadian boatmen and interpreters if the engagés had not been notorious for cruelty during the war. A crippling barb accompanied the concession, however. No British fur *traders* were to be admitted to the United States. Only Americans could operate as heads of the outfits. To guarantee the observance of the order, the law required that each winterer furnish the nearest Indian agent with a descriptive list of his employees and post a $500 bond as surety that the men really were boatmen and interpreters, and not traders in disguise.[4]

The reservation caught Crooks and Astor by complete surprise. They indeed needed foreign voyageurs to man their boats and trading posts. But they also needed foreign *traders* to keep the commerce functioning while their young Americans were being trained. The crumbs in the President's compromise were, in their opinion, very little better than nothing. Except for this: it suggested to them, through its own requirements, an almost irresistible means of evading the law. Let the young traders Matthews had hired leave Mackinac that summer as ostensible heads of their outfits. Then, as soon as the trading posts were reached, far beyond the supervision of the Indian agents, the apprentices would retire to their normal positions as clerks, and the British traders, who had traveled along as interpreters, would take over. The descriptive lists required by the War Department to prevent exactly this sort of dodge would be no obstacle. Crooks need only stand in front of the appropriate Indian agent and solemnly swear that because of the government's restrictions the onetime chief traders really had been demoted in favor of these striplings.

One can almost imagine the palms-up gestures of protest with which Astor and Crooks excused the subterfuge. Their English importations were already landing in New York; the winterers were already baling furs to bring to Mackinac and gather in the goods which the Indians must have the following year. Should the men responsible for furnishing the supplies court bankruptcy for themselves and disaster for the savages in a mistaken highmindedness about meeting an unreasonable edict? They had meant to do what their government wanted, as their hiring of the young clerks amply proved. But now the government itself was making compliance next to impossible. Only for the time being, of course. As soon as the clerks were trained, the company would return to strict honesty. Or so Crooks and Astor may have assured themselves in order to salve their consciences, not reflecting perhaps that as a conscience becomes more and more calloused it requires less and less salve.

At the risk of getting ahead of the narrative, it might be well to indicate some of the specific law violations which Crooks authorized when he reached Mackinac in the summer of 1818. First, Fond du Lac. His initial step was to ease out John Johnston. As trader in charge of the southern shore of Lake Superior for the South West Company in the winter of 1816–17, Johnston had lost almost $6000 on a capital of $40,000, half provided by him and half by the company. Considering the postwar confusions, including the uproars caused by the Earl of Selkirk, the deficit was forgivable. But in the fall of 1817, it will be recalled, something had occurred at the Sault to make Crooks doubt Johnston's abilities. The suspicion was confirmed when Crooks reached

Mackinac in 1818 and learned that the Irishman probably would lose another $6000, although his district had been expanded at his own request to embrace Fond du Lac.

In Crooks's opinion, the district needed more vigorous management. Johnston's contract still had time to run, however. Under normal circumstances replacing him might have proved difficult, but the new law afforded an unexpected opportunity. Though prepared to violate the edict whenever violation proved convenient, Crooks now summoned it to his aid. Piously he wrote Johnston:

> The government of the United States having directed (under heavy penalties) that none but bona fide American citizens properly shall be admitted to the Indian country within its jurisdiction, you will at once perceive the impossibility of the connexion between yourself and the American Fur Company.[5]

On that same day Crooks wrote William Morrison, a foreigner who had been trading for the company during the winter in Fond du Lac under Johnston's general supervision:

> I hereby assure you that with regard to yourself or either of the gentlemen [Pierre Cotté and Eustache Roussain] in the employ of the American Fur Company in the Department of Fond du Lac, there does not exist any other regulations than those in force . . . last summer.

In short, the law did not apply where it was inconvenient.

Johnston out of the way, Crooks abandoned the old profit-sharing contracts under which the man had operated and dispatched the Fond du Lac outfits on straight salary arrangements. In charge of the different outfits (so far as Puthuff was concerned) were four of the youngsters whom Matthews had hired near Lake Champlain—William Farnsworth, John H. Fairbanks, Samuel Ashmun, and Goodrich Warner. Their salaries, as entered in the company ledgers, varied from $140 to $220 a year. Accompanying them as "interpreters" went the veterans William Morrison, salary $1000 a year, Eustache Roussain, salary $800, and Pierre Cotté, salary $400. Who were the bosses?

Johnston's Lake Superior territory was divided into four districts— Ance Quivinan (Keweenaw today), Lac Courte Orielles, Lac du Flambeau, and Follesavoines, the last named lying along the St. Croix River in northwestern Wisconsin. Employment terms were such a hodgepodge of salary and profit-sharing that parallel figures of remuneration are not so instructive as in Fond du Lac. But it is suggestive to note that an untrained eighteen-year-old youth, John Dyde, suddenly assumed command of Ance Quivinan and that the district's former head trader,

John Holiday, a hard-twisted onetime Nor'Wester, was put down on the books as Dyde's interpreter.[6]

The evidence seems clear enough. Yet against this lawbreaking, obviously long premeditated and carefully executed, should be set a letter of advice which Crooks wrote early in 1819 to another of those same young men hired near Lake Champlain, Edward Upham, who was learning the business in the Wabash country of Indiana under Alexis Réaume of Detroit, a British citizen. Crooks exhorted Upham:

> . . . the character of any man as a trader depends wholly on a reasonable and fair exercise of industry and perseverance; always bearing in mind that with Indians as in a civilized community *"Honesty is the best policy"* [Crooks's italics], for although the savage will seldom fail to cheat you of your credits when he can . . . he never tolerates similar actions in a white man—care must therefore be taken at all times to prevent his overreaching and outwitting you, but never consent to counteract his dishonesty at the expense of your own reputation for fairness and justice.

Was Crooks completely hypocritical and baldly expedient when he wrote of honesty, fairness and justice to a young man who had been employed at least in part for illegal purposes? Or was he half subconsciously remembering himself, aged eighteen at the threshold of a brave new career out at the edges of the Missouri wilderness, when almost certainly he would not have supposed aspiration and honor to be incompatible. (James Aird, his mentor, had resorted to subterfuge to avoid Wilkinson's 1805 edict against foreigners on the Missouri. Ramsay Crooks, not long over from Scotland, simultaneously had become an American from expediency. Where does dishonor take out its naturalization papers?) Foolish laws—the nub of course lies in who defines the foolishness—have often caused otherwise honest men to compromise, before and since. Unreasonableness in front, the tines of necessity sharp behind . . . then what?

Thus, as spring neared, the year's strategy had been set. Puthuff was all but out of office, Chambers and the factories were under attack, means had been devised to avoid inconvenient edicts about licenses. Only one major problem remained—to secure capable traders to invade the districts which had been without adequate representatives during the preceding winter. To that task Crooks now devoted himself with a concentration of energy that before the year was out would make inroads on his health.

Late in April 1818 he journeyed through Lake Champlain to Montreal, where Matthews was hiring six boatloads of new voyageurs for the American Fur Company and two boatloads for Cabanné & Co. in

St. Louis. (Matthews was also buying silver armbands, earbobs and brooches for the Missouri firm.) After approving the details, Crooks selected as a traveling companion one of the new young clerks, William Farnsworth, picked up a tailor, blacksmith and carpenter for the new company shops at Michilimackinac, and pushed in a special canoe up the spring-boisterous Ottawa River toward Lake Huron. A pause at Drummond Island (to see his Indian wife as well as the traders there?) delayed him so that he did not reach Michilimackinac until May 20.

The traders had not yet assembled. That accorded with Crooks's plan. He wanted to intercept the winterers on their way to the island and lure the best of them to his standards before Stone could counter with rival attractions. Most of this raiding he hoped to do at Green Bay and Prairie du Chien. Then he planned to continue down the Mississippi to St. Louis, picking up Russell Farnham en route, and with him initiate the suit against Chambers. That done, he would follow Marquette's and Jolliet's historic route up the Illinois River to Lake Michigan and reach Mackinac in time for the rendezvous. Physically it was an ambitious program, leaving little margin for delay, and he chafed irritably when high winds lashing across the lake forced him to postpone his departure day after day until June had arrived.

His frustrations continued with the Wisconsin traders he met at Green Bay and along the Fox River. Although they wavered under the radiant charm he turned on them, they finally decided to remain loyal to old Jacob Franks, who in turn was loyal to Stone. Without showing his vexation, Crooks distributed among them the mail he had brought them from Montreal (some from Franks himself) and continued to Prairie du Chien. There luck improved. He won over to his company the man who had taught him the fur business, James Aird. Grimly he told Aird to disregard cost and give the Green Bay people no rest the next year anywhere along the Wisconsin side of the Mississippi.

Aird was the man to harry them. Ever since the war his commercial raids on the Folles Avoines (Menominee) Indians claimed by the Green Bay men had so troubled them that Jacob Franks had exploded recently in writing, "I have never passed so wretched a winter as I have in Consequence of that Man's Conduct." Franks wanted certain papers from Aird so badly that he urged his partner and nephew, John Lawe, to stop at nothing, even "taking advantage when he is Drunk of serching his papers."[7] Aird was drunk all too often those days, as Crooks was well aware. But even drunk the old trader could circle the Green Bay crowd like a fox. He'd give them plenty to think about.

In Prairie du Chien, Crooks also signed up young James Lockwood to compete on the St. Peter's with Stone's most potent customers, the semi-independent firm of Bertholet & Rolette. Thus in one stop he succeeded in plugging two big holes in the American Fur Company's trading areas, western Wisconsin and southern Minnesota. In order to press the advantage home, he authorized unlimited price cutting. No matter what reductions Stone's people made, Aird and Lockwood were to match them. This was all-out war, and they soon would see who could hold out longest, Astor or the Yankee from New Hampshire.

Whatever pleasure he may have gained from his triumphs at Prairie du Chien evaporated when he met Farnham somewhere down the Mississippi near Rock Island. Because of the delay caused by Chambers, the former Astorian had lost $2721.09 and he said he wanted no more of so uncertain a business. Crooks would have to find someone else to run the Sac, Fox, and Iowa outfits. But who? Young Darling had proved incompetent and was fired. The clerks Lagoterie and Laperche were so odious in Missouri that Farnham warned Crooks not to try to have them licensed in any capacity; attempting to pass them off as interpreters would simply result in the confiscation of whatever goods they accompanied. They too should be let go and brand-new crews, untarnished by the past, brought in.

Unless, Crooks thought privately, he could somehow prevail on Farnham to change his mind. . . .

In a maneuver of extraordinary delicacy he prepared for either eventuality by making contact at Rock Island with wily old Maurice Blondeau, a French-Canadian half-breed who traded for Cabanné & Co. Blondeau had always been friendly with Americans. He had helped Zebulon Pike in 1805 and had been one of Nicholas Boilvin's most useful counterirritants to Robert Dickson during the war. Presumably he had become a citizen of the United States; at least he had experienced no trouble after the war in obtaining licenses—an important consideration to Crooks. The drawback of course lay in enticing him away from Cabanné & Company, a firm that Astor supplied and with whom the New Yorker had a gentleman's agreement about respecting each other's territories. Though nothing was written, this hands-off understanding about areas probably would be deemed to extend to men also.

Cautiously Crooks proposed to Blondeau that, if Cabanné agreed, Blondeau should continue trading in western Iowa for the Missouri company and at the same time supervise the territory farther east for the American Fur Company. Tentatively Blondeau agreed. Journeying on to St. Louis, where he arrived June 14, Crooks persuaded Cabanné to accede to Blondeau's serving of two masters. One assumes he managed the feat by saying he did not expect the dichotomy to develop, since he was sure he could change Farnham's mind. The unsuspecting Farnham, who with his own eyes watched these elaborate preparations, had no idea that it was all a show to gain time and that in actuality *he* was designed to be his own replacement.

In St. Louis, Crooks also showed William Clark a circular letter which

Governor Cass had sent to the Indian agents of Michigan Territory, directing them to follow the President's instructions about licensing foreign boatmen and interpreters, but not traders. Blandly Crooks said he assumed that the Missouri governor would follow the same instructions about admitting alien voyageurs to the Mississippi. With equal blandness Clark said he would take the matter under advisement.

Concurrent with these discussions Crooks and Benton launched the suit against Chambers. After settling a few business errands—among other things he hired another former boss, Wilson Price Hunt, to help fill the assortments of the American Fur Company's Illinois outfits—he then directed his eager men to turn the canoe up the Illinois River. At Chicago he arranged for trader John Kinzie to set up a portage adequate for handling the bulky packs of buffalo robes he expected Cabanné and Chouteau to send to Michilimackinac for marketing through the world-wide facilities of J. J. Astor & Son—no longer "& Co.," for recently young William Backhouse Astor had abandoned his studies in Germany to become general manager of his father's firm.

Just outside Chicago the driving pace caught up with Crooks. He fell desperately sick in the bobbing canoe of "fever," its exact nature no longer determinable. He stayed sick for several days after reaching Michilimackinac. Probably he should have remained in bed longer than he did. But the traders were assembling. He dragged himself out of bed to meet them, forced himself to bursts of hyperactivity, then collapsed again. Because he gave himself no real chance to recover, these intermittent collapses afflicted him for the next twelve months.

No doubt he would have said he could not afford to rest. Stuart had been delayed with his goods and did not arrive until July 16, his schooners loaded not only with finished merchandise but also with planks, hinges and door locks for an ambitious building program, with brick and tile for chimneys and hearths, bar iron and steel for making traps and tomahawks in the company's new blacksmith shops, buttons for the tailors, and enough sacked corn and ashes to make lye for hulling it to keep twenty-five voyageurs busy weeks preparing grits. Four days later Matthews appeared with his eight boatloads of men, having avoided Detroit, where desertions were likely, in favor of the laborious portage over the Toronto–Lake Simcoe "shortcut."

Little Michilimackinac's population of perhaps five hundred French Canadians, mixed bloods and soldiers (including twelve white women, wives of the garrison officers) exploded to more than ten times that figure. Upward of two thousand whites drank, fought, sang, yelled, and jockeyed fiercely with each other over every penny's advantage. They opened bales, beat the dust from the stinking pelts, graded them and repacked them, in 1818, into perhaps 1500 bundles.[8] Schooners arrived to pick up the furs and sailors joined the throngs. Axmen rowed in big barges to Bois Blanc Island to chop wood for hundreds of cook fires. Two or three thousand Indians padded about selling fish, game, wild rice, bark macocks full of maple sugar, blankets and silver the British had given them at Drummond Island, and sometimes the physical delights of their women. When the first outfits began leaving in gaily decorated barges and canoes for the more distant parts of the wilderness, the multitude streamed to the white-sand beach to wish them godspeed with waving scarves, howls, gunfire, and tears. Soon the watchers too would leave on separations that would last for at least a year.

Pale and miserable, Crooks drifted around among the houses and tents of the principal winterers, holding out his bait. He did his work well. On July 22 Robert Stuart (who was also sick much of that summer) wrote Astor, "Mr. Crooks has with much exertion, secured I may almost say every good Trader in the country." Even Madeline LaFramboise came into the fold. The air of excitement and accomplishment were too much for Russell Farnham. Just as Crooks had been sure he would—the wilderness never completely let go of its men—the former Astorian caught the fever and agreed to return to the Des Moines after all.

At first Crooks and Stuart worried about how Puthuff would treat their various requests, for they knew the agent had been informed of their charges against him. "I expect," Stuart wrote Astor, "nothing short of the Major's saluting us with the Butt end of a pistal." But the onetime martinet had been completely cowed. He passed every "interpreter" Crooks offered. In Missouri, however, William Clark proved less obliging. He refused to recognize Puthuff's authority and declined to let Farnham's foreign boatmen go into Iowa. Pinched much as Aird had been thirteen years before, Farnham discharged his crews and scoured St. Louis for acceptable men.

Clark's action put Crooks into a fury and he promised to take the matter to Secretary Calhoun himself. "We will try," he railed, "whether it is not possible to find means of convincing our enemies we are as good citizens as they . . . and *must* in all respects be allowed equal privileges." He won that point too. Never again would Farnham's outfits be challenged on the grounds of improper licenses.[9]

Farnham did not wait for the new papers. If his rivals thought he had been hopelessly delayed by his search for acceptable men, he soon disabused them. Instead of following his competitors back up the Mississippi, he decided to outflank them. He had his new crews row the barges up the Missouri River to the Grand in north-central Missouri Territory. He followed the Grand and its tributaries north to portages that let him reach the Des Moines. Thus he came on his rivals from behind, took them completely by surprise, and achieved so good a trade that Crooks became as sanguine about the Sac-Fox-Iowa outfits as he was about Fond du Lac. There was just one little trouble. Cabanné felt that the flanking movement violated his agreement with Astor and many long, soothing letters were needed to placate him. But Crooks managed that too.

Although Puthuff was willing to license such men as William Morrison as "interpreters" for the American Fur Company, he closed his ears to the plea of the Green Bay traders that they be recognized as United States citizens on the grounds that they had lived in United States territory since before Jay's Treaty. None of them received licenses. By various subterfuges they did slip a few men into the Indian country, but the restrictions were a staggering blow.

They filled the mails with lamentations. In a letter to Thomas Anderson of the British Indian Department on Drummond Island, John Lawe of Green Bay called the Americans "Hell Hounds," said the loss of a license was costing him £2000, and cried, "oh will their not come a Day of Resurrection, that we may rise once more. . . ." Jacques Porlier moaned to Forsyth, Richardson & Co., "I cannot make out what is going to become of us, abandoned as we are . . . In an obscure labyrinth, loaded incessantly with the most atrocious calumnies without means of unmasking them, what are we to do? . . . The word Liberty . . . does not mean the same thing as we commonly supposed."[10]

Redheaded Robert Dickson, who after the war had gone to work for the Earl of Selkirk, tried to take advantage of their discontent. Why, he asked, did not the Green Bay men migrate to the earl's Red River colony, bringing with them the Menominee Indians of Wisconsin, over whom they had great influence?[11] They could buy cattle for their new homes at Prairie du Chien, and he personally would see to it that the Sioux Indians let them, the cattle, and the Menominees pass unharmed. At Red River they could establish new trading houses undisturbed by American restrictions, and they and their Indians could develop farms as good as the ones they were leaving.

The Green Bay people were tempted enough that Porlier wrote his long-time friend Pierre Rocheblave for an opinion. This was a curious source, since Rocheblave, a Nor'Wester, was certain to feel only bitterness toward the earl. As Porlier might have expected, his answer was coldly sarcastic. Civilized men would be completely out of place in that barbaric colony, Rocheblave said. Starvation would stalk them. There were no markets for crops—and very few crops. Four harvests out of every six were lost to the frost. Even to keep a horse a man must

hold a Cord around his neck with one hand, and a Gun in the other, and thus pass the Summer Nights. There is more rest in winter, he need not watch any more, for the Snow indicates to him the direction the thieves have taken his Horse, he can follow their tracks as far as he pleases, but this will be in vain, if he does not take with him a Superior force, the Thieves will laugh at him, take his Gun and Capot, and boast of their moderation if they do not kill him.

The letter re-established the native inertia of the Green Bay men. Besides, they had appealed to the government of the United States for confirmation of their land titles at Green Bay. Until a decision was handed down, they were reluctant to abandon the work of decades in exchange for the uncertainties of Red River, as described by Rocheblave. So they ended up staying where they were, bemoaning their fate and hoping that somewhere out of the blue an angel of salvation might yet appear.

The refusal of licenses to them obviously benefited the American Fur Company, for it let Aird work among the Wisconsin Indians with no more opposition than Lawe and the others could provide by smuggling and by persuading a few Indians to come in from the distant forests to shop at their homes inside Green Bay. (Aird was not able to exploit the advantage for long, however. He fell mortally ill early in the winter and died just after the new year of 1819.) Indeed, the potential gain to Astor was so marked that one wonders whether Crooks could possibly have influenced Puthuff's decisions. It seems unlikely. The instant the Green Bay men were refused permits, Jacob Franks rushed from Mackinac to Detroit and appealed for consideration to William Woodbridge, secretary of Michigan Territory and acting governor during Cass's absence. Woodbridge declined to intervene, an abstention Crooks hardly suggested. But Crooks did write smugly to Astor on August 5, 1818, that at last Puthuff's ill nature was blowing some good their way.

New difficulties assail [our opponents] in the energy of Major Puthuff who refuses some indulgences he formerly accorded them, and pursues a line of conduct which had he exercised two years sooner would have saved us a few thousand [dollars] and relieved us from the disagreeable task of exposing to the government the unfairness of his administration.

But if the agent hoped to gain Crooks's friendship by his actions, he was wrong. The company managers made no move to help him recover the job they had deprived him of.

Having listed his successes to Astor, Crooks let slip a bit of pique. While he had been half sick and working like a horse to secure the best traders available, a letter had arrived from Astor complaining about extravagance. With elaborate bitterness Crooks wrote back:

Extravagance I assure you is not the order of the day, but we must adhere to the road before us or give to our opponents . . . the labor of years. We exert ourselves day and night for your interest, toil is forgotten in the hope of pleasing you: but if you do not think we merit your approbation we cannot consent to be blamed without cause.

That grievance off his chest, he saw the last of their outfits on the way to the Indian country. Then, still suffering from his mysterious ailment, he clambered on September 2 into one of a pair of barges carrying $1800 worth of goods to the company's two posts on the Canadian shore of Huron's Georgian Bay. There he settled with the Nor'Westers certain disagreements that had temporarily taken the stations from the control of the American Fur Company. That done, he returned to Mackinac and with Stuart boarded the new United States revenue cutter for an easy four-day trip to Detroit. There the two men called on Governor Cass to discuss the latest political developments.

Illinois had just been admitted to statehood. In the process she lost present Wisconsin and some of southern Minnesota to Michigan Territory. Cass was hard at work carving the new acquisition into three huge counties, a pleasant maneuver that added strength to the political machine he was building for himself. On October 26 he decreed that the lands draining into the south part of Lake Superior should be known as Michilimackinac County, its administrative seat at the island village of the same name. Brown County, its seat at Green Bay, embraced Wisconsin east of a north-south line through the Fox-Wisconsin portage. West of the line lay Crawford County, administered from Prairie du Chien. Local courts and law enforcement agencies had to be provided for each settlement. Trials for capital crimes and certain civil actions, however, still had to be heard at Detroit, hundreds of miles away, an obvious encumbrance on judicial machinery.

These unfamiliar procedures unsettled the tradition-loving French Canadians more than ever. In their confusion they turned for help to the only stability they knew, the fur companies. Crooks and Stuart obliged. They brought up the matter of licenses again and, though records are unclear, it seems that Cass promised to review matters with Woodbridge before the advent of next year's trading season. The development looked promising. Squeezed by Aird on one side and enticed by hopes of license relief from Crooks on the other, the Green Bay men quite possibly might forsake Stone at last. The irony of course was sharp, though Crooks may have refrained from pointing it out to the government men with whom he conferred. Without the fur companies, this unhappy minority group could not have been absorbed into the United States—and yet government agencies in the Northwest, particularly Thomas McKenney and his factors, continually railed at the American Fur Company for making common cause with "foreigners."

Cass's great increase in territory made him important to the fur company in still another way. The Indian agencies once attached to Illinois—

Green Bay, Prairie du Chien, and even Chicago—now fell under his jurisdiction. In conflicts along the Mississippi between the American Fur Company and the jealous traders of St. Louis, backed by William Clark, the friendly consideration of the Michigan governor in the matter of licenses and other exemptions might often make the difference between profit and loss.

To that extent, then, the new administrative setup was a gain to the company. But it also forecast trouble for the future. Settlement was pressing closer to the wilderness and Cass would exert himself to hurry the advance. Inexorably the Indians would be thrust out of their land, and the trade in furs in the border areas would shift from pelts taken by savages to those caught by white hunters. The American Fur Company would either adapt to the change or follow the Indians farther and farther west. The latter was the policy Crooks would urge on Astor for years; but the old merchant proved resistant to each new advance— strangely so, considering his bold leap to the Pacific less than a decade before. What course Crooks might have taken—and therefore, to an extent, what adaptations might have been imposed on western history— if Astor had given his agents their head cannot be guessed. What did develop was a careful consolidation of one district, a clenching of the fist hard upon it, before any move was made into a fresh area.

A noisy physical harbinger of the future appeared in Detroit at about the same time that Crooks and Stuart arrived in the fall of 1818. This was the steamship *Walk-in-the-Water*, first of her kind to ply the upper Lakes. She was 135 feet long, 32 feet wide, 8½ feet deep, and displaced 330 tons. The two paddlewheels affixed to her sides could drive her ahead in good weather at six or seven knots. Staterooms were crowded under her poop deck, gentlemen forward, ladies to the rear. A single tall smokestack rose between two masts rigged for supplemental sails. The ship's figurehead was a bust of Admiral Perry, an open reminder to the British of his spectacular victory on Lake Erie only five years before.

To the dismay of the civic boosters of Black Rock, where the *Walk-in-the-Water* was built, her engines were not stout enough to carry her up the Niagara rapids. Like the sailing ships, she had to be hauled into Lake Erie by a "horned breeze" of twenty oxen, and thereafter Buffalo was her home berth. She departed that city on her maiden trip August 23 and reached Detroit on the twenty-seventh. The popeyed Indians who swarmed to the riverbank to watch her were told that she was able to move without sails because white engineers had devised a method of harnessing huge sturgeons like draft horses. As the tale froze into folklore everyone became convinced that the savages really believed it.

The *Walk-in-the-Water* made another trip to Detroit in October. Crooks and Stuart boarded her on the twenty-second for the return to Buffalo. Speed and comfort were markedly improved over anything they had experienced before, but, as they instantly realized, the vessel's main significance lay in the swift handling of freight to Mackinac. Before the two men disembarked, Crooks had started preliminary talks that included a promise for the fur company to provide at a reasonable fee the firewood necessary for her boilers, if she would journey to Mackinac the next year. The steamship company agreed. With the signing of the contracts the strides of change insensibly quickened. Never again would life at the remote island outpost have quite the same feeling of lonesomeness and isolation, or quite the same indifference toward public opinion in the East.

CHAPTER *19*

Pressures

In March 1819 Crooks visited Washington to feed statistics to congressmen opposed to the factory system, to find documents Benton could use in pressing the lawsuit against Talbot Chambers, and to ask Secretary of War Calhoun that William Clark of Missouri be instructed to recognize the licensing authority of the Michigan Indian agents. Calhoun complied. During the course of their conversations, the secretary quite possibly mentioned to Crooks, an intensely interested citizen and potential opponent, something of his plans for protecting the northern frontier against that old bugaboo, the British traders and their Indian allies.

Calhoun's strategy called for reducing the forts at Osage on the Missouri, Rock Island and Prairie du Chien on the Mississippi, and Chicago, Green Bay, Mackinac and Gratiot around the Lakes to subsidiary posts intended mainly to impress the local Indians and to support the agents and factors in controlling the wilderness commerce. New advanced strongholds were to be rooted farther north, at Sault Ste Marie and at the confluence of the Mississippi and St. Peter's. Others were projected for the upper Missouri, one at the Mandan villages in the central part of today's North Dakota and a second at the mouth of the Yellowstone, almost astride the present North Dakota-Montana border. Military roads were planned for linking the Mississippi posts and those on the Missouri. Calhoun even talked of speeding traffic westward by means of a canal between the Fox and Wisconsin rivers, first recommended two decades earlier by Robert Dickson. So far as Crooks was concerned, the crucial point was not the forts themselves or roads for troops to march on, but the fact that Indian agencies and government trading factories would in all probability be established at each military post. His battle with the government, in short, was almost certain to spread.

Preliminary movements were already underway. In August 1818 Crooks's favorite enemy, Talbot Chambers, had gone up the Missouri to the vicinity of Fort Osage with 350 men, a vanguard of the contingent that the next year was supposed to reach the Mandan villages and perhaps the Yellowstone River. (The Missouri phase of the plan was dubbed the Yellowstone Expedition. It was the front that caught popular fancy —and was also the one that collapsed into almost ludicrous failure.) Shortly thereafter the Fifth Infantry began assembling at Detroit. As soon as the ice left the Lakes in the spring of 1819, those troops would sail by schooner to Green Bay, transfer to bateaux, and travel to Prairie du Chien, there to meet supplies and recruits toiling up the Mississippi from St. Louis. Under the general command of Colonel Henry Leavenworth, the combined force would then continue to the St. Peter's and build the first of the northern bastions.

A gold-braid trim to these thrusts into the wilderness was an official inspection trip of the Great Lakes by Major General Jacob Brown, commander of the Northern Department of the United States Army. Brown, his staff, and many of the men's wives planned to travel from Buffalo to Michilimackinac on the *Walk-in-the-Water*—the same sailing that would transport nearly a thousand packs of American Fur Company merchandise. And, at Erie, the steamboat would pick up Governor Cass and his entourage.

Also aboard the ship would be Puthuff's replacement as Indian agent, George Boyd. Boyd was a Virginian, courtly, handsome, debonair, and unfortunate. Through a misadventure in buying rifles which he hoped, mistakenly, to resell to the United States, he was deeply in debt. Because he was married and had children, his salary from his new position as agent was particularly critical.

Crooks probably did not know of the debt, and even if he had he may not have intended overt threats by strutting in front of the man whose predecessor Stuart and he had driven from office. But he did realize the virtues of a snug boat ride in the company of so many influential government men. As soon as another siege of illness let him return from Washington to New York, he ordered reservations on the *Walk-in-the-Water* for Robert Stuart, for Robert's hearty, home-loving, deeply religious Betsy, and for the Stuarts' two children, Mary, not quite five, and David, just three. Stuart was being moved to Michilimackinac as permanent resident manager. His place as transportation agent was to be filled by another Astorian, young Benjamin Clapp.

Crooks almost did not make the sailing. After a short pause in New York, he rushed on to Montreal, oversaw the routine purchasing and hiring there, and returned posthaste to Manhattan. John Jacob Astor was leaving in June for an extended stay in Europe. During his absence his twenty-six-year-old son, William Backhouse Astor, was to function as president pro tem of the American Fur Company. Most of the briefing necessary to familiarize him with the intricacies of the trade fell on Crooks. He managed to stay on his feet while doing it, but as he was on his way to Buffalo after the freight caravans, his health buckled again. He arrived so ill he had to stay in bed for a week and was barely able to haul himself aboard the *Walk-in-the-Water* when she weighed anchor at five o'clock Saturday afternoon June 12, 1819.

The trip was heady medicine. There was little to do but lounge under an awning spread above the deck, spin tales of adventure for the awed exclamations of the ladies, and drop casual remarks about the Indian trade to General Brown, Governor Cass, and agent Boyd. The ship reached Mackinac on the morning of June 19. The cannons of the fort above the village roared welcome; soldiers paraded smartly. A little later the *Walk-in-the-Water* took aboard a crowd of villagers and Indians for a short excursion. During the afternoon the pleasure-bent whites waltzed elegantly on one side of the deck. The Indians gyrated on the other, moving the party's diarist to pen:

> Ever and anon, a half-concealed, half naked, tawny thygh Was half un-
> covered, to white woman's lowering eye.

When the steamer started back to Detroit on June 21, she took the wives of the officers with her. Ready for business now, General Brown and his staff sailed on the government's revenue cutter (a sailing ship) for Sault Ste Marie to examine sites for a fort. As Crooks and Stuart waved good-by and then settled down for the hubbub of the rendezvous, they quite probably reflected that the trip had been as rewarding as any they were likely to take on the Lakes.

Several personnel problems awaited them. Some of the young clerks whom Matthews had hired the year before in the hope that they might grow into traders needed disciplining. One who had filled out his as-sortments by purchasing handkerchiefs, snuffboxes, earbobs, hawk bells and wampum from the government trading factory at Chicago was told icily that the company under no circumstances ever dealt with the or-ganizations the company was trying to have abolished. Another youth who persistently drank too much was reproved contemptuously—"You now stand before me," Crooks wrote him, "in all the depravity of an ill spent life"—and when scorn failed to sober him, he was fired.

A third who had ignored the instructions of his trader in the interior was warned, "You ought to recollect that to become a good Commander it is indispensable that you first learn to obey." By and large the object lessons worked. Considering the remote and violent circumstances of the trade, the company had relatively little trouble with its young men. Several of the neophytes not only developed into as good traders as Crooks hoped, but when civilization overtook them became useful citizens as well—Samuel Ashmun at the Sault, Gurdon Hubbard, the grand old man of Chicago, and, among a later group, Henry Hastings Sibley, first governor of Minnesota, to name only three.

A more serious breach of company standards revolved around an old-line trader named Alexis Réaume, who wintered in northern Indiana. In 1818 Crooks had assigned to Réaume, as clerk, William H. Wallace. Wallace had been hired in Montreal at the same time as the young Americans, but was no neophyte; he had been at Astoria. Hoping for an outfit of his own, he intended to show how good a dealer he was.

As soon as the party disembarked from their boats at the lower end of Lake Michigan, he realized that something was amiss. Réaume sulked, tried to shunt him off to areas where Wallace thought he should not be, and even encouraged the engagés to disobedience, telling them (so Wallace charged) that "if I should strike one . . . to prosecute me at Mackinac and they would recover too [sic] or three hundred dollars." Réaume also wrote such intemperate anti-Wallace letters to Crooks and Stuart in New York that they chided him, "Violence appears to have completely usurped the place of reason. . . . You must in the future write with at least common civility if you expect to be answered."

The reason for the strange antics soon emerged. Réaume was making life easy for himself by selling goods to and collecting furs from rival traders. This violated company policy. Opponents, public or private, were to be crushed, not kept afloat by profitable "understandings." Réaume feared that Wallace would interfere—and he did by reporting the *sub rosa* activities. When Réaume returned to Mackinac in 1819, Crooks and Stuart not only gave his outfit to Wallace but also clapped him into jail on charges of trover and conversion.[1] He was old and in poor health; even Stuart admitted he suffered in his cell. His plight excited sympathy and Captain Benjamin Pierce of the United States garrison undertook to help him by instituting suit against Crooks and Stuart—this in spite of the fact that Pierce's mother-in-law, Madeline LaFramboise, the female Ottawa trader of Grand River, had just transferred her allegiance to the Astor banners.

The meddling may not have been proper for a military officer on active duty, as Stuart charged, and certainly it brought Réaume no benefit. Pierce drank too much one night, swaggered with false confidence into Stuart's office to discuss the case, and ended up tipping his hand about the line of defense he proposed to follow. Thus alerted, Stuart, who acted as his own attorney, tangled Pierce in technicalities of pleading, and had the case thrown out of the Mackinac justice court.

Rather than appeal, Réaume agreed to arbitrate; each party submitted its financial charges against the other, and Réaume ended up being awarded $251, a thin victory for a winter's work and several days in jail. The company perhaps considered the sum a small price to pay for making a clear point to all its traders. Their loyalty must be absolute.

Opponents were warned also. During the winter of 1818–19, for instance, two rugged brothers, Paul and Basil Beaubien, set fire to the American Fur Company cabin at Lac du Flambeau, kicked holes into several canoes, and so frightened the trader, Roderick Lawrence, an American soldier whose enlistment had expired at Mackinac, that Crooks decided there was no point in sending the fellow back to the same area the following season.

Paul and Basil Beaubien were winterers for George Ermatinger, brother of the Charles Oakes Ermatinger of the Sault who had wormed into Fond du Lac in 1817 on a license from Puthuff. George had lived in Mackinac many years, claimed American citizenship, and was an expensive nuisance not only in northern Wisconsin but on the St. Peter's as well, where he worked in loose association with Bertholet and Rolette. Crooks had no intention of letting such a man get away with anything. He stormed over to the Indian agency office and asked permission for an American Fur Company trader, John Hogel, to drag the Beaubiens out of the Indian country. He also demanded that no traders associated with George Ermatinger be granted licenses until justice was done.

Boyd declined the last sweeping request. But he did authorize Hogel to take out a posse of voyageurs for dealing with the Beaubiens. If it occurred to the agent that there might be some impropriety in appointing an employee of the injured company to be its instrument of punishment, he perhaps excused the arrogation on the ground that no one else capable of doing the job was available. Off Hogel went. He apprehended Basil, but Paul escaped. Crooks accepted the half loaf as making the whole point: the company was not to be tampered with. As a reward for work well done, he appointed Hogel in place of the timorous Roderick Lawrence as head trader for Lac du Flambeau.

In still another case he persuaded Boyd to name a company employee as defender of the law. Liquor was becoming an acute problem along the border. Part of the difficulty stemmed from the ferocious competition between the Hudson's Bay Company and the North West Company. Mutual shock rising from the massacre of Selkirk's colonists at Red River in June 1816 had muted raw violence, but the seesaw struggle still went on, much of it refined by 1818–19 into a contest for the loyalties of the Indians. Robert Dickson's intrigues with the unhappy Green Bay traders, noted in the preceding chapter, were part of Selkirk's plan to lure great numbers of Indians and traders to the buffalo-rich prairies surrounding Red River. To hold the savages at home, the North West

Company spread blandishments of its own, including promises of alcohol.

Crooks took immediate alarm. The Nor'Westers might have their sights on the Hudson's Bay Company, but so big a scatter-gun was bound to wound the American Fur Company as well by luring Indians across the border with their furs. His initial reaction was the ancient one of fighting fire with fire: somehow he must get liquor out to the Indians as a counter-measure, legally if possible.

Adam D. Steuart, collector of the port of Michilimackinac, obligingly testified before Governor Cass that the North West Company had indeed laid dark plans to subvert the American Indians with ardent spirits. On the strength of Steuart's testimony Cass cautiously wrote Puthuff on July 4, 1818, that he would not object to temporary liquor permits for American traders (in general, not just Astor men). The final decision, however, he left up to Puthuff.

For reasons not now recoverable the company at the last minute decided not to put the matter to test and no liquor was sent into the border country for the winter of 1818–19. Results of the restraint were, in the eyes of some winterers, disastrous. Morrison and Roussain came out of Fond du Lac to the 1819 rendezvous hot with indignation, not so much against the Nor'Westers as against the Hudson's Bay Company. Three men from Selkirk's colony had brazenly called a council of United States Indians within sight of an American Fur Company post near Red River, south of the border, and had promised floods of "white man's milk" and cheap goods in 1820, if the savages came over to the Hudson's Bay Company. Duncan Graham, who had been one of Dickson's aides during the war—he was the one whom the St. Louis newspaper had reviled as Dickson's "deputy-scalping-master-general"—had sent messengers throughout southwestern Minnesota with similar promises. Aging Augustin Nolin of the Sault was among the Indians south of Lake Superior with ample whisky and soft urgings that they follow him to Selkirk's colony. These attacks, Morrison exploded, must be fought or the entire trade along the border would be lost to the unprincipled English.

Crooks hesitated, though he might have asked Boyd for permission to use liquor on the strength of Cass's earlier approval to Puthuff. He finally decided against it. He knew that one of McKenney's most telling arguments in favor of government factories against private traders was the use the latter made of liquor in their dealings with the Indians. As part of his attack on the factories during his visit to Washington the preceding March, Crooks had urged Calhoun to impose an absolute prohibition in the Indian country. He had written of what he was doing to Cass, to William Clark, to Russell Farnham, to many others. If he now resorted to what he had piously deplored only four months earlier, he would be putting a powerful weapon into McKenney's hands. Yet something had to be done.

His solution was to have Boyd grant to William Morrison on July 17, 1819, full authority to confiscate British goods south of the border, destroy any liquor he detected, and council the Indians against dealing with "improper persons"—i.e., Selkirk's siren-singing agents. A month later Boyd reinforced Morrison by appointing Adam D. Steuart, who at least was a government employee, as a sort of quasi-official marshal to pursue Duncan Graham to the head of the St. Peter's, seize his goods, and bring him back to Mackinac. One would have supposed that a detachment of the Fifth Infantry, even then ascending the Mississippi to build the fort at the mouth of the St. Peter's, would have been a more logical police force. But perhaps Boyd felt the troops would be too busy at their construction work to be able to serve. Or perhaps Crooks swayed him. Steuart, a proved friend of the company, was a known quantity; some eager young lieutenant out on patrol might do any number of unpredictable things.

Steuart came no closer to Graham than Prairie du Chien. There, instead of turning north, he went south to St. Louis and then to Washington, perhaps because of a last-minute message from Crooks, who had decided that the collector might be more useful at the capital, lobbying against the factories. From Washington, Steuart wrote Boyd that he would go in full strength to the St. Peter's the next summer. He didn't. Nor do records indicate that Morrison ever confiscated any whisky.[2] But the fact remains that they could have. Once again the company had showed its muscle in public, for competitors to take note.

Another problem which, paradoxically enough, reacted to the benefit of the company was the extreme restiveness of the Indians during 1819. As usual, the frontier blamed the British for the unsettled conditions. Even before summer came and before the savages made their usual trek to Malden and Drummond Island for English presents, old Nicholas Boilvin, the Indian agent at Prairie du Chien, was convinced he scented an uprising inspired by the former enemy. He hustled his family off to safety in St. Louis, then wrote Calhoun stoutly, "I shall await the demonstration of their barbarity to the end."

The commanding officer at Mackinac estimated, possibly with exaggeration, that the 6000 savages who had assembled on Drummond Island that year, half of them American Indians, received $95,000 worth of blankets, cloth, guns, gunpowder, knives, scissors, liquor and food. The Duke of Richmond, Governor General of Canada, himself attended the gathering at Malden, near Detroit, helped pass out the gifts, and joined Tecumseh's brother, the Prophet, in making speeches. Cass wrote Calhoun in agitation that as the Indians returned home from the Malden councils they "assault the Inhabitants, steal their horses, kill their

Cattle & Hogs, forcibly enter their houses . . . and thus keep this frontier in a continued state of alarm." At Chicago, traders John Kinzie and Jean Baptiste Chandonnai predicted Malden-inspired attacks at any moment.[3]

Though the frontier could hardly have realized it at the time, this American-eye view of the Indians' discontent had too narrow a focus. The British contributed to the restiveness, but a major cause was the unprecedented movement of United States troops throughout the Indian country. What did this invasion portend? Unhappy and angry, the savages crossed the border in greater numbers than ever to listen to the British.

The wild accusations by the frightened frontiersmen notwithstanding, they received no offers of direct help from their former allies, or probably there would have been an uprising. The attacks they made on the Michigan settlers were, rather, the fever sores of frustration. There were no battles and only a few feeble gestures of protest. As the vanguard of the Fifth Infantry started up the Fox River, the Winnebagos sent them word to go back; the door was locked. Colonel Leavenworth reputedly showed the messengers his rifle and declared, "I have the key." He passed through without trouble. A few weeks later, in August 1819, the savages did fire on a barge carrying Major Whistler and his children to Prairie du Chien, and a few balls did zing past the ears of George Ermatinger. Menominee Indians stabbed a soldier almost within sight of Fort Howard at Green Bay, and during the winter Winnebagos slew two troopers just outside Fort Armstrong on Rock Island. That was the extent of the predicted uprisings.

The occasional spurts of violence did, however, breed monstrous rumors, speculations, and alarms. In the face of such fears, timid traders might well have given up their work. Yet there is no indication that a single winterer abandoned his district because of dread of the Indians. Either the men did not believe each other's wild talk, or they were confident of their ability to control the savages among whom they lived. Or perhaps they were just plain desperate. Most of them had Indian families in the wilderness, and what other way was there to support them?

The traders were, in brief, ripe for whatever the supply companies offered them. It was another phase of a point that by now should be apparent: while it is true that the American Fur Company did indeed close a monopolistic fist upon the wilderness merchants, it is equally true that the United States Government through its unsettling policies helped drive those traders within the fist's accommodating reach.

Against this background Crooks spread his lures. John Crafts at Chicago and smaller winterers on the Michigan Peninsula capitulated that year. A far more satisfactory triumph (at the time; later it would be a source of infinite harassment) was the winning of the Green Bay men. The clincher was the matter of licenses. Jacques Porlier, contending he was an American citizen under Jay's Treaty, applied again for a permit, and perhaps through Crooks's representations to Cass it was granted to him, good until a final ruling could be received from the Attorney General of the United States. Heartened by the success, Lawe and the four Grignons—Augustin, Louis, Charles, and Pierre—also applied for licenses, claiming citizenship. Without waiting to hear the results of Porlier's test case, they then forsook David Stone and Jacob Franks, bought goods worth $8000 from the American Fur Company, and started for their trading grounds.

There were other satisfactions. Young James Lockwood, who had been put in charge of the entire upper Mississippi after Aird's death, began pressing Bertholet and Rolette so hard that soon Bertholet was ready to quit. In desperation Rolette began proposing "arrangements" with his rival. When Lockwood wrote Crooks for advice, the field manager replied loftily, "The American Fur Company does not depend for success on commercial coalitions with its opponents"—a statement Lockwood soon would recall with wryness.

Success in the market place did not match success in the field. A financial panic was shaking western Europe and the United States. Fur prices crumpled everywhere. After surveying the dismal auctions in London, Astor ordered Crooks to economize. The field manager had opened too many posts; he must cut back; indeed, Astor was contemplating giving up the whole business.

Crooks, who had just returned to New York, was dismayed. Every time he supposed he was showing progress, the old skinflint began crying economy. Crisply he replied that mere retrenchment would not suffice to offset the falling market. In his opinion this was the time to press ahead; for their opponents were also bedeviled by low prices. "Bertholet of Mackinac is quitting the trade, Ermatinger of St. Mary's is crippled, and David Stone & Company appear wavering." In another year, the American Fur Company could have things more nearly its own way. But, he added in mock humbleness, if Astor insisted, he of course would make arrangements to close down entirely.

Astor did not insist.

In that confident letter to Astor, Crooks did not mention an adverse ruling by the Attorney General on Porlier's license, which was a test case for all the Green Bay men. This official opinion declared that mere residence within United States territory at the time of Jay's Treaty did not automatically make a man a citizen. The resident had to give weight to his election by swearing an oath of allegiance. Since Porlier had not done this, he was not a citizen and his license must be revoked. Cass thereupon ruled that every permit issued to those claiming citizenship under the treaty be withdrawn.

The cancellation came after the men had purchased their outfits and had started for the Indian country. They vented their outrage in frantic charges. Michael Dousman, who was allied with David Stone, blamed the ruling on the machinations of Matthew Irwin, the factor at Green Bay. Bitterly he charged that Irwin's factory could show a profit only if it drove private competitors from the field, and that the government of the United States was stooping to unjust laws to gain its end.[4] The French Canadians of Green Bay told Stuart that shortly after they had received word of the revocations, Irwin and the Indian agent at the Bay unctuously offered to buy their land at ridiculous prices. The whole thing was a deliberate plot to deprive them of their property—an accusation that Stuart was halfway inclined to believe.

Louis Grignon declared violently that in spite of the law, "I shall trade all along my Route and take every Means proper or improper." He was restrained by John Lawe, who resorted to the old dodge of hiring Americans to act as fronts, while the actual owners went onto the rolls as interpreters.[5]

Results hardly justified the subterfuge. The restive Indians did not hunt energetically enough to pay back their credits, or else they went right by the Wisconsin posts to seek better prices from Rolette at Prairie du Chien. Porlier, who was ill much of the winter and grieved by the death of his youngest child, wrote in despair, "I am so put out with my Savages that I can scarcely see them without seizing them by the cravat [sic]." "I am at my wit's end," wrote Charles Grignon, and Louis Grignon mourned, "This Equipment is a total loss." By spring all of them could say amen to Robert Dickson when he wrote, trying once more to entice them to Red River, "The Indian trade in this Country is not in my opinion worth following, it is like walking in the Mud untill you get soussed over head & Ears." Yet how does one pull up the roots of a lifetime? The Green Bay men wrung their hands, drank more of their own cheap trade whisky than they should have, wrote doleful letters to each other—and stayed where they were.

Stuart protested on their behalf to Cass. The government's arbitrary ruling "will cause the total ruin of several honest and industrious men . . . [and] keep the Indians in continual discontent and ferment." He urged Crooks to go immediately to Washington: "For God's sake do not let us, if possible, be any longer pestered, I may say ruined by the inconsistency & wavering measures of Govt. Agents."

The situation was more alarming than Stuart realized. For months a special congressional committee appointed to investigate the Indian trade had been hearing testimony from Calhoun, McKenney, various agents, military men, and private merchants. Witnesses for the War and Indian departments poured opprobrium onto the private supply companies, accusing them of financing hordes of adventurers, mostly aliens, to ruin the business of the Green Bay and Chicago factories so that red-ink balance sheets would lead Congress to question the usefulness of the system. As long as such men could obtain licenses, the government's benevolent program for the Indians could not possibly meet the intentions of its founders. Had not the time come to strike for success by drafting a strong licensing law?

Crooks fought back furiously. The proposed law, he contended, was merely a device for squeezing private Indian trade into the hands of a few weak-kneed favorites who would play the government's game. Among their number, he predicted, "the American Fur Company would not [be] found: because we will not suffer ourselves to be trampled on with impunity, either by the military or any other power." Why, he cried, should private enterprise be strangled just so the inefficient factories could be made to look attractive to the voters?

In spite of his energetic lobbying, the bill passed the Senate. In desperation he turned to the House of Representatives, where his chief ally was William Woodbridge, territorial delegate from Michigan. He also enlisted the support of the Vice-President of the United States, "and through him I expect letters to . . . members who will essentially aid in defeating the outrageous system." William B. Astor wrote to key congressmen, and Oliver Bostwick of David Stone & Co. joined the counterattack. Strategies outlined, Crooks returned to New York to receive the year's importations from England, leaving Samuel Abbott in Washington to keep in touch with each day's developments.

As time for adjournment drew near, a House Committee appointed to determine what business should be considered during the rest of the session made no mention of the licensing bill. Exultantly Abbott reported to New York, ". . . those great pretended friends of the Indians have been frustrated at least on one of their plans."[6] Crooks, however, could not feel so airy. The company had won a delay, not a triumph. The battle, which each year grew more acrimonious, would have to continue until one side or the other was decisively bested.

At Detroit, on his way to Michilimackinac, Crooks had a stroke of luck in meeting the Reverend Jedidiah Morse, a man appointed by Calhoun to investigate the wilderness commerce. Morse was widely respected as a preacher, a writer of geography and history textbooks, and as an earnest supporter of Christian missionary work among the Indians. During the winter of 1819–20, missionary groups in both Scotland and the United States appealed to him to use his influence in obtaining from the government financial help for sending a qualified investigator among the distant Indian tribes "to acquire more accurate knowledge of their condition, and to devise the most suitable plan to advance their civilization and happiness."

Calhoun saw in Morse's assignment an opportunity to obtain a disinterested report on the operation of the factories. He prevailed on the reluctant minister to himself conduct the survey the missionary societies wished and promised at least $500 to help defray costs—more if Indian department appropriations allowed. He suggested that any valid survey of the tribes should also include a study of their economics. "The moral condition of the Indians," he told Morse, "will necessarily be dependent on the character of the trade with them. . . . You will report such facts, as may come within your knowledge, as will go to show the state of the trade . . . and the character of the traders."

Morse began his project in Detroit, where he spent twelve days interviewing military men, Indian agents, and private traders. He missed the man he wished most to see, however, Lewis Cass. The Michigan governor had left on May 24 with three canoeloads of scientists, frontiersmen, writers, soldiers, voyageurs, and Indians for a summer's exploration of his huge territory. During the trip he hoped to complete a project that had baffled both General Brown and Indian agent George Boyd— the purchasing from the Indians at Sault Ste Marie of enough land (sixteen square miles) to accommodate the military fort the War Department wanted to build at that strategic spot.

When Morse had finished his interviews at Detroit, he boarded the *Walk-in-the-Water* to continue to Mackinac. On the ship he met Ramsay Crooks together with members of an international commission that at last was launching an official survey of the boundary between the United States and Canada.[7] Both the preacher and the commissioners spent much of the trip pumping the trader for information.

Keenly aware of the influence Morse was likely to have on Calhoun, Crooks summoned up the full warmth of his sunny charm as he outlined his particular views of the Indian trade. But he could hardly have supposed that there would be no rebuttal by his opponents. Morse's headquarters during his sixteen days on the island were to be, by arrangement of the War Department, in the home of Captain Benjamin Pierce. Still smarting from his defeat by Robert Stuart during the Réaume affair, Pierce would welcome this opportunity of contradicting any favorable impressions Morse might have received. Both Crooks and the captain must have been in considerable suspense when Morse finally started back to Washington without revealing the conclusions he had reached.[8]

While Morse gleaned information on Mackinac, Crooks hurried by canoe to the Sault, hoping to overtake Cass's exploring party with mail he had picked up for them. (Additions at Mackinac had increased the governor's party to forty-two men in four big canoes.) Furthermore,

Crooks told Astor, he was worried about the governor's safety in the Indian country, though just what he proposed to do about the undefined dangers does not appear.

One ugly threat developed during Cass's conference with the Chippewas about buying the land at the Sault. At the conclusion of the first day's meeting, a principal chief kicked aside the pile of presents the governor had brought along as a good-will offering, strode to his lodge a short distance away, and raised a British flag—this on the American side of the border. Cass followed, tore down the banner, and stamped on it. The handful of soldiers behind him cocked their rifles. At that the Indians hesitated for a moment. This gave John Johnston's Chippewa wife a chance to intervene. By the next morning the savages had decided to sell the land. Bidding them a triumphant farewell, Cass moved on into Lake Superior. In his official report he declared that he found the rest of the border country in a state of "profound peace." He even prevailed on some of the western Chippewas to enter into a treaty with the Sioux of southern Minnesota. Like every other explorer from the first Frenchman on through Zebulon Pike, he congratulated himself on his success, only to learn that the two tribes returned to their fighting almost as soon as he was out of sight.

Crooks missed Cass at the Sault by only a few hours. Unable to continue the pursuit because of the duties waiting him at Mackinac, he entrusted the mail to a special express and made arrangements for an American Fur Company guide to overhaul the governor's party at Fond du Lac.

At the company's Fond du Lac post, Cass's group swapped their big lake canoes for smaller river craft and began the laborious portages toward the Mississippi—"swampy grounds—and rocky precipices—dark forest of hemlock and pine . . . a gloomy and dismal scene," wrote diarist Henry Schoolcraft. Where the river bends north the party split. Half waded southwest toward Sandy Lake. ("We seldom," wrote another journalist, James Doty, "found footing before we had sunk to our knees in mud, and frequently to our hips. . . . It is impossible to describe the fatigues.") Cass's group, seeking the sources of the Mississippi, pushed west to the lake that now bears his name. (It is not the river's true source, however; low water kept the governor from pressing on to the real beginning at Lake Itasca.)

The groups reunited at the American Fur Company's Sandy Lake post, where they were surprised to find in this "unknown" wasteland cows, horses, a vegetable garden, and comfortable living quarters equipped with a respectable library. Schoolcraft also noted a detached collection of huts where liquor could be passed out unobtrusively to the savages—or so he remarked in an account of the trip he published the next year. In the battle shaping up between McKenney and Crooks, the chance observation ballooned mightily—but more of that hereafter.

From Sandy Lake, the explorers continued down the Mississippi to the new fort being built on an imposing, three-hundred-foot bluff between the curling waters of the St. Peter's and the larger river. There Cass heard disturbing accounts of the misadventures that had befallen Calhoun's various expeditions into the northwest. The Mississippi part of the venture had been delayed by the slowness of the troops and supplies ascending the river from St. Louis. As a result there had been no time to build adequate winter barracks at what was optimistically called Cantonment New Hope, on the right bank of the St. Peter's, just above its mouth. Icy winds had ripped away some of the poorly constructed roofs. The cold was intense. Supplies failed, scurvy set in, forty men died. Blaming the site for the sickness, Colonel Leavenworth had moved as soon as spring allowed across the river to the top of the bluffs and began constructing a permanent post soon to be named Fort Snelling in honor of its first commander, Colonel Josiah Snelling.

The debacle on the Missouri had been even more tragic.[9] The steamboats intended to move troops to the Mandan villages and the Yellowstone had proved inadequate and the expedition crawled into winter quarters near present Omaha. There nearly a hundred men perished of scurvy. This and the financial scandals revolving around the steamboats led an angry Congress to cancel further appropriations for the so-called Yellowstone Expedition and to halt western military movements at Fort Atkinson, the cantonment just above the site of modern Omaha. Thus only Fort Snelling and yet-to-be-built Fort Brady at the Sault (Brady was finished in 1822) remained of Calhoun's ambitious plans for spreading the might of the United States along the northernmost frontier. For Ramsay Crooks, however, this was enough. Government forts—which in turn meant government Indian agents and perhaps government factories—were now rooted in the heart of some of the company's best country.

He learned of the progress at Fort Snelling from that part of Cass's group which returned through Mackinac. (The governor and the other part traveled back to Detroit through Chicago.) For the time being there was nothing he could do other than lay strategy for a renewed attack on the factories in Washington. Meanwhile his summer had been encouraging. He and Stuart had persuaded those of their British traders who had been in the area since 1794 to swear oaths of allegiance to the United States and thus become citizens, at least in name. This done, such men as William Morrison, Eustache Roussain, and most of the Green Bay traders were able to receive licenses not as a special favor but as their right.

More significant than this was a change in policy which Crooks finally brought himself to accept. Once he had vowed to end competition by crushing it. The goal proved impossible. Although he opened more posts than Astor approved of, the country was too big for his traders to blanket it completely. Growing numbers of frontiersmen, both Britons and Americans, threaded surreptitiously along its streams, financed by shoestring merchants in Detroit, Green Bay, Chicago and St. Louis. To undercut the bigger companies, all these wraiths used liquor without compunction, which was another reason Crooks kept urging total prohibition on the government.

The most effective of the wilderness supply houses was Bertholet & Rolette of Prairie du Chien. They bought their merchandise from David Stone, divided it into picayune lots, and sent it throughout the wilderness in charge of more unscrupulous operators than young James Lockwood, the American Fur Company trader at Prairie du Chien, could keep up with, though he too used liquor in the attempt. The intense competition that resulted hurt everyone. By the spring of 1820, Jean Baptiste Bertholet had grown so discouraged that he decided to leave United States territory and confine himself to Drummond Island, where he held a grant of land.

Joseph Rolette was made of stouter fiber. No matter what it cost, he was determined to stay in Prairie du Chien. He was the town's most noted citizen—not entirely for his virtues. He insisted that his traders did not take advantage of the Indians. The savages were too smart. "I have been trying to cheat them for years," he declared to one visitor, "and I have never once succeeded." On each trip to Mackinac he fell into terror whenever high waves broke across his boats—yet avarice kept him rowing on. Once when ice in the Mississippi threatened to crush his barge, he cried loudly that if the good Lord spared him, he would donate $1000 to start a Catholic church at Prairie du Chien. Landing safely, he reputedly said to the sky, "Collect if you can; I didn't sign any note." His second wife, Jane Fisher, the half-Indian daughter of the first American trader in the area, was less than thirteen years old when he married her in 1819—one account says she was ten. Though a teetotaler in his youth, Rolette later became a notorious drunkard and roué among the Sioux maidens.

He was forever on the go with new enterprises. He brought the first sheep to Prairie du Chien and had a share in the first sawmill. He established supply connections with Red River that enabled Selkirk's colonists to survive several disastrous winters. He bid successfully on several contracts to furnish beef, wheat, candles and other necessities to Fort Crawford at the Prairie and later to Fort Snelling. It behooved the army's purchasing agents to examine every clause of the agreements with a lawyer's microscope, but at least Rolette produced as if by magic what was needed, though other would-be merchants were throwing up their hands in despair. He exerted enormous influence on the Mis-

sissippi Sioux, who called him *Zica,* or Prairie Grouse, because of the
phenomenal speed with which he flew around the country from the
lead mines of northern Illinois to the headwaters of the St. Peter's.

Realizing at last that Rolette was not likely to give up, Crooks made
overtures about an association, though he had declared to James Lockwood only a year earlier that the company did not win battles by
entering into understandings with its competitors. Rolette held out for
an autonomous district extending north from Farnham's Iowa outfit to
Fond du Lac and embracing the entire St. Peter's. He promised to buy
his goods at a specified markup from the company, trade entirely on
his own risk, and sell his skins to the supplier, but within his own
territory he must remain supreme—King Rolette, his voyageurs would
soon be calling him.

Crooks must have seen the dangers in the proposal. Rolette had an
almost compulsive avarice that would lead him to crowd the other American Fur Company traders whose territories adjoined his. To judge from
past records, he was likely to be continually embroiled with government
officials. It was very well for him to insist on independence, but whenever trouble came, the company was certain to be involved in adjusting
his difficulties with the government and with his neighbors. Nevertheless Crooks thought that he and Stuart could manage the man. At
Rolette's insistence, they jettisoned Lockwood, who thereafter was an
intense though not very effective competitor, and, under the designation
of the Upper Mississippi Outfit, gave Rolette the territory he wanted.
The negotiations, which began in 1820, were not completed until 1821.
Almost immediately the company found it had caught a bear by the
tail—but that too comes later.

This and Crooks's other successes in coming to terms with opposition
traders completely discouraged David Stone about the trade out of
Mackinac. Furthermore, thanks to Astor's own caution, exciting new
prospects had opened for Stone in St. Louis. Manuel Lisa was once
again reforming his Missouri Fur Company, determined to reach the
headwaters of the muddy river from which the turmoils set off by the
war had driven him. In 1819 the Spaniard sounded out Crooks about
obtaining supplies through the American Fur Company and was turned
down; Astor was satisfied with the connections already established with
the Chouteaus. So then Lisa sought out Stone, ordered goods worth
$25,000 from him, and promised to market all his pelts through him.[10]

This opened a whole new area to the New Hampshireman and he
decided to leave Mackinac—at a profit if he could. Trying to hide his
eagerness to be away, he dangled various proposals in front of Crooks,
hoping to be well paid for leaving the American Fur Company a clear
field around the upper lakes. Crooks declined the bait. He would not
pay anyone for a mere opening. The most he would do, he said, was

buy Stone's stock of goods at Mackinac for a price that would allow some gain to the New Hampshireman and still allow Crooks to obtain at cut rates an excellent stock of merchandise without the headaches of transporting it. But he would add nothing for a clear field. That privilege must come with the goods. After half a year of sparring, Stone yielded late in 1820, selling his goods at Crooks's price and agreeing, for no extra consideration, to stay out of the Michilimackinac trade for at least five years.

Fortified by his full warehouses, Crooks next demanded lower freight rates on the *Walk-in-the-Water*. Since the ship was the sole steamer on the upper lakes, the shipping company thought it had a monopoly on quick transportation and refused to discuss the matter. Crooks thereupon canceled his contracts and made arrangements for the schooner *Michigan* to take the 1821 imports to Mackinac. Unaware that the amounts of freight involved would be far less than normal, thanks to Stone's goods, the steamer people took fright. After all, sailing ships until very recently had handled the entire Great Lakes freight and plenty of ships and experienced sailors were available for doing it again. Perhaps they had better reconsider. During the meetings Crooks hammered out the rate schedules he wanted, and in 1822 he returned the company shipments to the steamboat.[11]

Not everyone was happy with this spreading power. In mid-November 1820, after Crooks had left for New York, William Henry Puthuff and Captain Benjamin Pierce, both of them losers in earlier tiffs with the company, called a "mass meeting" of Mackinac residents to consider ways of combatting the octopus. Since most winterers were in the Indian country, the meeting was hardly representative. Furthermore, neither government official on the island, Indian agent George Boyd and collector Adam Steuart, was invited to attend, presumably because they might have supported the company. Robert Stuart, the company's representative, was also ignored.

This rump session appointed Puthuff to prepare a memorial severely criticizing the "American" Fur Company as being in reality almost one hundred per cent British. (It was a common charge that even Crooks and Stuart were aliens, and indeed their assumption of United States citizenship before the war had been expedient rather than deeply felt.) The memorial further declared that the company's traders followed a systematic plan in subverting the Indians. It added virulently that through its vast special privileges the company was turning itself into a monopoly against which small, true-American traders had no chance whatsoever.[12] The document was then mailed to the President of the United States aboard the last ship to leave the island before the annual freeze-up.

Word of the meeting soon leaked to Robert Stuart. He was convinced that the timing had been deliberately chosen so that months must pass before the fur company could send an answer after the charges. He did not even know what to answer. When he demanded that Puthuff let him see a copy of the memorial, the former Indian agent refused. George Boyd and Adam Steuart had no better luck with their requests. This left the trio with nothing better to do than write out generalized character references for each other. These they sent over the ice to Cass by a special Indian express which reached Detroit on January 20, 1821. In their letter to the governor, Boyd and Steuart declared:

> We have invariably found the principals as well as the subordinate agents of the American Fur Company, at this post, wholly disposed to meet our wishes, & the views of the Government in relation to the Indian trade, & the collection of the Revenue . . . . We feel also perfectly authorized to state as our opinion, that the dealings of the American Fur Company, with individuals & the public at large have been equally fair and honorable.

Cass in his turn wrote Calhoun, who had asked about the matter, that the memorialists had not been in possession of all the facts. During his explorations the previous summer he had found the company's traders to be fully cooperative and the Indians to be well disposed. As for being a monopoly, the company had been granted no special privileges; it simply had been more energetic than other traders in making the most of rights that were available to everyone. And with that letter the matter was dropped.

Crooks knew nothing of the episode until the summer of 1821. During the winter he went to Paris to discuss with Astor the renewal of his and Stuart's contracts, which were due to expire in March. Each man was rehired for five years at some advance in salary and profit sharing. With that assurance firmly in hand and anxious to increase the profits he shared, Crooks then suggested vigorous campaigns for the future. He wanted a steamship for plying the lakes, though he would settle for schooners. He argued that the time had come for some sort of definite policy concerning the Missouri River. For years the St. Louis firm of Berthold & Chouteau had been hinting at a truly colossal company: either they should absorb the American Fur Company or Astor should buy them out. But they had never really come down to cases about the matter, and because Astor imported some of their English goods and sold some of their furs for them he did not insist.[13] For the same reason Astor had told the American Fur Company traders in Illinois and Iowa not to crowd into territories claimed by the Missourians. But all that had been changed, so Crooks argued, by the entry of Stone, Bostwick & Company into St. Louis. The newcomers were seizing appreciable amounts of the Missouri business. (They were also colliding expensively with Farnham on the lower Mississippi.) If Astor waited too long to come to an understanding with the Chouteaus and Cabanné about moving west, Stone might grow too strong to be dislodged. The little profit Astor made as importer and selling agent no longer justified holding back. The time had come either to reach an agreement with the St. Louis Frenchmen, or to defy them and jump into the Missouri whirlpool.

Astor reacted typically. No, no—times were not right. The fur market had not recovered fully from the panic of 1819. The company could not afford to buy ships. A trade war along the Mississippi and up and down the Missouri would be disastrous, especially so long as Thomas L. McKenney and his government trading factories remained as a continual threat to private enterprise. In fact, it seemed wiser to him to retrench—close the Detroit department, for example, another place where Stone was giving them real trouble.

Crooks acquiesced—in Paris. When he reached New York on May 19, 1821, however, he wished he had been more insistent. During his absence the St. Louis fur traders, Oliver Bostwick, and the lobbyists of the American Fur Company had joined forces to put real pressure on Congress for the abolition of the trading factories. Thanks to the temper of the times, they had almost succeeded. A majority of congressmen, so Crooks was told, had pledged themselves to vote for ending the system, but by desperate maneuvers McKenney, Calhoun, and other supporters of the factories had kept the necessary bill off the floor until March 3, when Congress had had to adjourn for the inauguration of President Monroe at the beginning of his second term. Next session, under the leadership of Thomas Hart Benton, senator from the new state of Missouri, the battle would be rejoined and fought to the finish.

McKenney breathed confidence. He wrote a correspondent:

> . . . this contest of avarice with benevolence, of darkness with light, of confusion with order, of barrenness with fruitfulness and plenty, must be short.

The heads of the various supply houses were equally confident of defeating him. Their year had come at last. As Crooks reviewed the situation, his ambition boiled impatiently up again and he told himself he simply could not afford to rust at the Lakes while waiting on Astor's caution. The moment the factories were abolished, there would be a rush of traders into the more remote parts of the Indian country, where no one firm held dominance. It would be folly not to ease into St. Louis and at least start getting ready. He said as much to Astor in two or three letters from Mackinac that summer (he reached the island in mid-June on the schooner *Hannah*) and then toward fall decided to push ahead without Astor's authorization, in the hope that once the step had been taken the old skinflint would finally come around to his manager's way of thinking.

He sent Samuel Abbott to Prairie du Chien to check carefully on Rolette's Upper Mississippi Outfit, and then told him to continue down the river to St. Louis. There Abbott was to rent a store, draw up careful lists of the items most in demand for the western trade, estimate the financial responsibility of the Missouri River winterers, and "tamper" with some of them—the word is Crooks's. When first he wrote Astor about Abbott's errand, he soft-pedaled the touchy subject of expansion and justified the movement on the grounds of efficiency. Now that steamboats were plying the Mississippi from New Orleans and the National Road was speeding traffic across the Allegheny Mountains from the East, the company could operate its outfits in the lower Wabash country, in Illinois, and in Iowa more economically from St. Louis than from Mackinac. Therefore he had sent an agent to the Missouri to look things over—the Missouri River trade only as an incident in the other study.

All this while he was counting on a victory over the government trading factories to brighten Astor's outlook about the trade in general; indeed, such a triumph would cheer every wilderness merchant, himself included. Early in November, accordingly, he promised Astor to spend most of the winter in Washington, working "by every fair means" to effect the abolition of their most hated competitors. He let that statement soak for a month. Then, on November 30, he finally came out and stated flatly to Astor what he had only suggested before: the next spring he intended to move in on the Missouri trade. The next day he took his first step. He ordered Abbott to come directly to New York with the information he had gathered. More definitely, on December 22, he ordered Matthews in Montreal to hire boatmen for the Missouri as well as for the Lakes.

It was as far as he dared go without authorization from Astor. The next move had to be against the factories. Busily he began collecting statistics and witnesses. It was high time. Thomas L. McKenney, the United States Superintendent of Indian Trade, had already set about saving his government houses by launching in the public press a vitriolic offensive against the American Fur Company.

CHAPTER 20

Triumph

While looking for ammunition to fire at the private traders, Superintendent Thomas L. McKenney came across the affair of James Kinzie and pounced in glee. The young man, a winterer for the American Fur Company, had been caught red-handed taking liquor to the savages in the Milwaukee area and had been ordered from the Indian country. Here at last was not mere generalized rumor of the enemies' wicked ways, but proof. Picking up his pen, McKenney went to work. He knew nothing of James Kinzie's background, of course, and probably would not have been impressed even if the story had been brought to his attention. Yet the tale is not wholly irrelevant, for it suggests some of the wrenchings that shaped the frontier traders into what they were.

James Kinzie's mother was named, confusingly enough, McKenzie—Margaret McKenzie. Margaret's father, Moredock McKenzie, was a pioneer farmer of western Virginia (today's West Virginia). One May day in 1778 Moredock and his eldest son went into the woods to search for strayed horses, leaving three younger boys and two girls at home with their mother. Shawnee Indians raided, slew Mrs. McKenzie and the boys, and carried Margaret, aged ten, and her sister Elizabeth, aged eight, into captivity.

About ten years later two white traders from Detroit, John Kinzie and an associate named Clark, found the McKenzie girls in an Indian village beside the Maumee River in northeastern Indiana. They ransomed the pair—almost surely the sisters, one twenty and the other eighteen, were then the property of Shawnee braves. Although Kinzie and Clark went regularly to Detroit, they made no effort to legalize their acquisitions but simply lived with them.

It was a trying time. The American campaigns against the savages of the Ohio-Indiana area kept the frontier aflame; during the turmoil Clark's and Kinzie's posts were repeatedly burned and their credits lost. In between flights and alarms Elizabeth McKenzie bore Clark two children and Margaret bore John Kinzie three. James Kinzie was born in 1793.

All this while the girl's father, Moredock McKenzie of West Virginia, had been searching for some trace of his daughters. After Wayne's 1794 victory at Fallen Timbers had brought peace to the frontier, the old man wandered into Detroit. There he found the girls and prevailed on them to return home with him, bringing their children with them. There was no legal separation from their consorts. Since there had been no marriage, a divorce perhaps seemed superfluous.

Almost simultaneously John Kinzie, a native of Quebec, made another radical change. In order to keep on with his trade he elected United States citizenship under one of the clauses of Jay's Treaty. In 1798 he married, legally this time, the widow of a British soldier. No children were borne to the second union until 1803, when John H. Kinzie arrived, to be followed at rather widely spaced intervals by three more offspring. Meanwhile the father set up a trading company with one of his half-brothers, Thomas Forsyth, later agent for the Sac and Fox Indians. Forsyth established himself at Peoria, Illinois, John at Chicago. From those points they conducted extensive operations between southwestern Michigan and the Mississippi.

John Kinzie's friendship with the Potawatomi Indians saved his and his family's life when a band of those savages massacred the Fort Dearborn garrison at the outbreak of the War of 1812. He and his family were taken prisoners, however, and turned over to the British at Detroit. For a time they lived unmolested in the old Kinzie home there, but when Harrison launched his campaign against the city, John was suspected of sending information to the Americans. After being imprisoned for a time at Malden, he was started for England in irons to stand trial. Circumstances twice forced the ship he was on to turn back. Finally, without explanation, he was released.

In 1816 he and his family returned to Chicago with the troops that rebuilt Fort Dearborn. He was never able to rebuild his business, however. The war had scattered many of the Indians he knew best; other traders, including some of his own erstwhile clerks, had established themselves in his place. He eked out a living as best he could by operating the portage between the Chicago and Illinois rivers, by manufacturing silver trinkets, and by serving first as interpreter and then as subagent for the regular Indian officer in the area. In 1818, when Crooks and Matthews were searching for young American clerks, Kinzie apprenticed his son John H. to the company at Mackinac. This left only two young girls and an eight-year-old boy to help at home. Times were hard for the father, who at fifty-five was growing frail from a life of excessive hardship.

In this time of need two of his children by Margaret McKenzie appeared—James and Elizabeth. Possibly the father had written them; possibly they were dissatisfied at home, where their mother had remarried. It was not a youthful impulse, for both were over twenty when they arrived.[1] Delighted, the father made arrangements to set James up as a trader around Milwaukee for the American Fur Company.

Under the old man's guidance, the son did well. In fact, both John's boys at first gave him cause to rejoice. James was always willing to help at home and was a favorite with his young half-brother and sisters. On Mackinac, John H. was earning commendation from Robert Stuart, a notoriously stern taskmaster. The lad was at his chores at five o'clock every morning. In the evenings Mrs. Stuart took him into her parlor, and made him read aloud and explain to her the big words and hard sentences until he could scarcely hold up his head. How else was a youngster to get an education on Michilimackinac? On August 19, 1821, old John proudly wrote the boy, then eighteen years old:

> . . . a good name is better than wealth and we cannot be too circumspect in our line of conduct. Mr. Crooks speaks highly of you, and try to continue the favor of such worthy men . . . . James is here, and I am pleased that his returns are such as to satisfy the firm.

Fathers do not always see their sons clearly. Even as Old John wrote those lines, James was acting in such a way that rumors of his misbehavior reached as far as Mackinac. Exactly what he did does not appear; Crooks remarked only in one letter that his conduct was "disgusting and, some think, dishonest." The locale was a council of Indians which Governor Cass convened at Chicago in the summer of 1821. At the meeting, the savages ceded to the United States most of what is now southwestern Michigan. The treaty signed, the *government* passed out among the Indians, according to Isaac McCoy in his *History of Baptist Missions,* seven barrels of whisky; during the next twenty-four hours ten savages were killed in drunken brawls. McKenney, interestingly enough, did not mention those deaths when professing shock that 40 barrels of whisky had been traced to Green Bay alone and that the Sac and Fox Indians of Rock River had swapped two and a half tons of lead to a varicious *private* traders for nothing more than alcohol.

James Kinzie presumably had a tentful of trade cloth and hardware at the Chicago council. Unable to go to Mackinac himself, he sent in his orders by mail. The company returned the merchandise aboard a schooner that sailed from the island on September 13, 1821. The invoices, still surviving, show 151 blankets, 125 yards of various kinds of cloth, 400 pounds of gunpowder, 2400 earbobs, many knives, scissors, kettles, plug tobacco, a pair of cart wheels, and so on—including one gross jew's-harps, which should be remembered in connection with future developments. In this miscellany, which cost $5571.27, there was no whisky.[2]

Nevertheless James and the other traders around Chicago were regularly getting so much smuggled liquor from somewhere that protests had been lodged with Governor Cass when he passed through the area in August 1820, at the conclusion of his explorations of the upper Mississippi. Michael Dousman, Stone's trader at Milwaukee, was named specifically as a culprit. (Stone had not yet sold out to the American Fur Company.) Cass wrote agent Boyd at Mackinac to clamp down, and Boyd dutifully warned Dousman to watch his step.

Dousman was enraged. Did Boyd know what kind of place Milwaukee was? Save for a drunken blacksmith named Mirandeau, no white settlers lived in the area. The inhabitants were red renegades from every tribe in Wisconsin. The only restraint they acknowledged was that of the traders; even the Indian agent at Chicago, Alexander Wolcott, admitted the helpful influence of the winterers when writing Governor Cass in May 1821 to report the murder of a doctor who had been riding with the mail express between Green Bay and Chicago.[3] Without liquor, Dousman argued, no one could trade successfully at Milwaukee. Everyone used it: he knew James Kinzie was going to bring in barrels of the stuff for the winter of 1821–22. If Boyd persisted in his interdict, to hell with it. He, Dousman, would quit the unequal competition. And quit he did, transferring his activities to Prairie du Chien, where he soon found a kind of left-handed revenge by plunging another American Fur Company trader into trouble, as will appear.

Old John Kinzie seems to have known nothing of James's illegal doings, even though John was subagent at Chicago and responsible for enforcing the trade regulations. But someone alerted Wolcott, the head agent. He arrested James under circumstances that left no doubt of his guilt, revoked his license, and gave him sixty days to gather his personal property from his posts around Milwaukee and get out of the country.

News of the arrest came as a total surprise to Stuart and Crooks, the latter of whom was just preparing to leave Mackinac for the East to resume the fight against the factories. Stuart even jumped to the conclusion that the factor at Chicago was framing James in an effort to embarrass the company before Congress, and he began rumbling threats of legal action. Even agent Boyd entertained doubts enough about the arrest that Crooks prevailed on him to issue James a new license for replacing the one revoked by Wolcott.[4] But James's guilt became inescapable and the company had to back down.

The factor at Green Bay, Matthew Irwin, made the most of the opportunity. He gave an ancient of days, old Jacques Vieu, goods worth $2228.25 and hurried him south to the multiple rivers, the wild-rice swamps, and earthen bluffs of the Milwaukee region—so the Indians would not suffer from being without a trader, Irwin said. Louis Grignon wrote Crooks in a different vein: Irwin's government house had been operating in the red and now he was trying to redeem himself by making "a profit under the cover of care for the savages and of the Pretended benefits that they receive from the Factories." To Crooks, however, Irwin's opportunism was a minor consideration. What he feared was McKenney's reaction.

The blast came in the form of a letter to the editor signed "North West" and printed in the *Daily National Intelligencer* of Washington on December 17, 1821. McKenney's ostensible excuse for writing was an earlier letter to the same paper by Henry R. Schoolcraft, who had accompanied Cass through the Northwest in 1820. On his return East, Schoolcraft had issued a book about his travels. In the course of it he mentioned almost casually that a section of the American Fur Company post at Sandy Lake, far up the Mississippi, had looked as if it might be the scene of alcoholic presents to the Indians. The company protested and Schoolcraft wrote a vague sort of retraction to the *Daily National Intelligencer*, saying that he had not actually seen any Indians receive drink at Sandy Lake.

Crooks considered the explanation "highly honorable," but McKenney had struck hard at it, pointing out in his first letter to the editor that Schoolcraft's failure to see liquor did not mean that the Indians weren't "*drenched*" in it (McKenney's italics) when the officials were not looking. Now, triumphantly, he followed up his advantage with a second letter, chanting in print that thanks to Kinzie's arrest the world at last knew the identity of "these invisible nobodies . . . dealers in whisky, furs, and Indian blood . . . agent [s] of this same 'American Fur Company.'"

Crooks bristled. The use of quotation marks around the company name was by then a standard device to suggest to the public that the firm was really a British concern. Matthew Irwin of Green Bay even declared flatly, in testimony presented to the Senate, that Crooks was a British citizen—"the grossest perversion of truth," Crooks sputtered to Cass. In his outrage he momentarily contemplated suing Irwin for $5000, "to teach him," he told William Woodbridge, "to bridle his tongue in the future." Even more than these charges, however, he resented being held responsible for Kinzie's unauthorized lawbreaking. No one in the firm had given Kinzie whisky, and McKenney's implications to the contrary were inexcusable—or so he tried to act. Never, indeed, would Ramsay Crooks face fully up to the fact that the American Fur Company must accept censure for what its agents did, authorized or not. Like a baited bear he growled by letter to Stuart that "North West," as McKenney signed himself, "is not yet far enough *North* for us." He'd break the man's career yet.

Awesome forces marshaled against Thomas L. McKenney in Washington that winter. Some of the power plays were so indirect that deals can only be suspected, not proved. For instance: during that same winter of 1821–22, Michigan Territory was involved in extending its judicial system to the newly acquired counties in the west. Final plans had to be approved by Congress. The one that at length reached Washington proposed what amounted to a separate, almost autonomous west-end supreme court. In the opinion of one critic, the arrangement "is fraught with so many evils that no well wisher to the territory can ever want to see it adopted." Originator of the disturbing scheme was one of Governor Cass's retinue, James Duane Doty, twenty-two years old, who envisioned himself as chief judge of the sprawling new court—"a boy," another critic said in dismay, "who in any other place than this would be learning his profession."

As 1822 drew near, Doty was in Detroit, busily writing for the Detroit *Gazette* a eulogy of the American Fur Company. A message reached him that the court bill was foundering in Congress. He turned his eulogy over to the editor (it was printed under the pseudonym "Ottouwah" on January 25) and on horseback rode to Washington through one of the fiercest winters ever to afflict the Northwest. In the capital he stirred Crooks and Cass to energetic efforts on behalf of the court bill. Crooks's interest became so patent that the act was sneered at as "J. J. Astor's bill." It passed January 30, 1822. Three weeks later the boy Doty was appointed judge of the new court. Cass thus had another buttress for his political machine, and the American Fur Company had another influential friend in high places. Conceivably it is not just coincidence that Cass and Doty next enlisted their talents in support of Crooks's drive against the factories.

In formal testimony before the Senate Committee on Indian Affairs, Crooks contended that the goods sold by the factories were far inferior to the merchandise handled by the private traders. He insisted that through experience and willingness to go into the distant wilderness, private citizens served the savages far better than the factors could. He accused Irwin and other government traders of hiring aliens to carry goods among the savages, even though these employees had earlier been refused licenses for private commerce. He defended the credit system, which the factories eschewed, and questioned the ability of the factors to aid appreciably in the noble work of Christianizing the Indians. He produced figures designed to show that some of the factories, notably those at Green Bay, Chicago, and Prairie du Chien, had operated at so heavy a loss in spite of their favored positions that McKenney himself had proposed closing the first two of them and shifting their work to Fort Snelling. He accused them of selling goods designed for the Indians to soldiers and white residents of the nearby settlements, to the detriment of American storekeepers. Should the government, he demanded sarcastically, use public money—at a loss—to destroy its own citizens?

Powerful support was given him, in person and through the mails, by the government's own men. The Reverend Jedidiah Morse, whom Calhoun had sent to investigate the trade around the Lakes, said that the government houses were not fulfilling the hopes of their founders and should be abandoned. Captain John R. Bell, who had led part of the government's 1820 expedition to the Rocky Mountains, corroborated much of Crooks's testimony. Indian agents Benjamin O'Fallon from the Missouri River and John Biddle from Green Bay lent the strength of their voices to private enterprise.

McKenney struck back acidly, countering some of Crooks's statistics with figures of his own and casting doubt on the rest by pointing out the field manager's personal interest in seeing the public trade ended. Again and again he insisted that the factories were needed to keep a checkrein on the winterers, whose ruling passion was avarice. He used James Kinzie as an example, but agent John Biddle tut-tutted in reply that one case was not enough to support a sweeping generality. In his experience, Biddle said, the private traders were a decent group trying to get along in a hostile world, and were not nearly so bad as sensationalism pictured them.

One wonders what Crooks thought about as he mulled over those words of Biddle's. At the very time the Indian agent was defending the traders, Crooks began receiving private advice concerning the conduct of certain of his men above Prairie du Chien.

To understand the clashes we need to return to the company offices on Mackinac and a meeting held there in August 1821 between Stuart, Crooks, and the principal traders of Green Bay. Two years earlier the Green Bay winterers had forsaken David Stone for the American Fur Company, but the change had not proved successful and all of them were heavily in debt to the firm. Crooks told Stuart privately that he believed the fault lay in the men's own poor judgment and laxness. They regularly bought more than they could sell and then lounged wastefully around their posts rather than course the hunting grounds in an effort to keep the Indians at work. He doubted their ability ever to produce much profit for the company, but he certainly did not wish an opponent to slip into Green Bay, woo away its traders—an aggressive young American named Daniel Whitney was already making worrisome gestures in that direction—and then branch out toward more lucrative areas. If the Green Bay Frenchmen were able merely to keep the area neutralized, it was worth the company's while to hold them.

He did not say all that to the men themselves. He told them, rather, that he was hoping to bring order to their region. They were too ruggedly independent, he said. Each of them sent clerks into the same districts and fought each other to a standstill. What the five principal men of the town should do was establish a partnership—one share each for Jacques Porlier, John Lawe, Louis Grignon, Pierre Grignon, and Augustin Grignon.[5]

Cramped by their indebtedness to the American Fur Company, the resentful traders had to comply. Sullenly they watched Crooks write into their contracts almost schoolmasterish direction about how they should run their businesses: "Each of the partners . . . desirous of destroying old habits of extravagance . . . bind themselves to reduce every expense wherever practical . . . by going out themselves to winter in the Indian country . . . , by reducing the number of Boatmen, . . . and generally to practice the most rigid economy in every department." Nor was that the worst. When they began making up their assortments, Crooks refused to give them everything they wanted. Pierre Grignon grew especially virulent about his treatment. Weary of the tirades, Crooks at last wrote him bluntly that the Green Bay Company was in no position to complain. First they must offer the American Fur Company "adequate assurance that we will be regularly paid for our advances. Give us that security, and we will pledge ourselves to meet your wishes in all things."

They departed glumly. Competition was intense on all sides. The factories were sending traders deep into the wilderness. Daniel Whitney was dispatching bargeloads of supplies entirely across Wisconsin to the Mississippi. Lockwood, bitter at the company over being dumped overboard in favor of Rolette, was purchasing goods from Stone & Company in St. Louis and would push into Wisconsin from the west. In the face of these attacks, Crooks's stinginess seemed fatal. As Louis Grignon toiled up the Fox River, he wrote Lawe, "I leave As a man Entirely deprived of present and future Hope of Contentment. . . . I do not think that I am in Hell, but at the gate thereof."[6]

They did win one concession from Crooks. The Folles Avoines (Wild Rice or Menominee) Indians had stripped their hunting grounds, and Augustin Grignon wished to take the best hunters of the tribe to fresh country somewhere up the Mississippi, where they might have better luck. Crooks later insisted he thought Grignon meant to go above the Falls of St. Anthony, site of present Minneapolis. But that is not where Grignon landed. He settled with his Indians and his outfits beside the lower reaches of Lake Pepin, across the river, approximately, from modern Winona, Minnesota.

This was Rolette's country. Flying into a passion, the little Frenchman ordered one of his clerks, Jean Baptiste Mayrand, to get rid of the interlopers. Mayrand enlisted some of Wabasha's Sioux, priming them beforehand with two kettlefuls of alcohol. As soon as the Indians were deliciously drunk, they reeled into the clearing where Grignon had built his cabin, shot his two dogs in front of his eyes, and suggested they would like to do as much for him. He had no right, they said, to steal their wood and stone without permission.

The complaint was only an excuse, of course, and Grignon realized it. He produced his license to prove his permission. The Sioux spat on it. American paper!—their Father was British. They thereupon burned down his cabin, destroying considerable merchandise in the process. Thus beset, Grignon retreated downstream to the vicinity of present La Crosse and rebuilt. One of his brothers came to his rescue with a band of truculent Winnebago Indians, and although the Sioux continued their threats, the traders were able to maintain the new post throughout the rest of the winter.

The Green Bay men were reluctant to seek help from the government which so long had harried them as aliens. "We have no Rights since we are Foreigners," Louis Grignon moaned. Anyway a public airing of the affair might injure everyone. Therefore, Louis urged his brother, ". . . do not inform Against him [Rolette] as that will harm the [American Fur] Company rather than injure him."

Although the Green Bay men refrained from a public washing of the linen, they sent impassioned private protests to both Stuart and Crooks. The latter heard of the affair early in 1822, right while Thomas Mc-Kenney was lambasting the private fur traders and their entrepreneurs with every statistic he could produce. Obviously Crooks did not mention the Grignon-Rolette feud in any of the debates that followed. But the coincidence in timing must have troubled him and he probably was not writing only for the record when on March 22 he told Rolette in pained reproval:

> I trust you are innocent of the charges. Let me add I expect your con-
> duct will in all cases be so exemplary, as to put it out of the power
> of anyone to say you have done wrong in even a solitary instance, for
> it is not only necessary that you be free from reproach, but you must
> also be unsuspected.[7]

Rolette, however, was not conducting himself in a manner designed to leave him free from reproach. This time his troubles involved a public officer, Major Lawrence Taliaferro, pronounced Toliver, the hot-tempered, opinionated, stiff-necked Indian agent from Fort Snelling at the mouth of the St. Peter's.

Taliaferro's Italian ancestors had settled in Virginia in 1673. He had been born in the same state in 1794, had served as lieutenant during the War of 1812, and had remained in the army until 1818. He then resigned (so he says in his pompous "Auto-Biography") at the personal request of the President of the United States, a friend of his family's, who wanted him to take charge of the Indian agency at the new fort on the upper Mississippi.

During the winter of 1821–22, the agent at Prairie du Chien, old Nicholas Boilvin, was to be absent from his post, and Taliaferro was ordered from the St. Peter's to the Prairie to run both their agencies from that point. He went down the river during mid-October with the commander of the fort, Colonel Josiah Snelling, and a few other officers bound for St. Louis. Each time the travelers passed an Indian camp, Taliaferro ordered the boat to halt. Disembarking, he introduced himself to the savages as the representative of their Great Father, and to impress them passed out gifts of whisky—an official good-will offering by an official agent under the benign eye of an official military officer. All government agents and treaty makers gratified the Indians' inordinate love of alcohol, at least to an extent. But in private hands whisky was evil. Since an agent's personal profits were not involved, he was deemed likely to act with restraint. Still, it is not hard to see why the Indians were confused.

Taliaferro seems to have spent several weeks in Prairie du Chien without hearing of the Grignon affair, which occurred in mid-December. But in February, Michael Dousman (who had forsaken Milwaukee when ordered not to use whisky against the American Fur Company there) saw a chance to make trouble for the firm. He told Taliaferro that Rolette's clerk, Jean Baptiste Mayrand, had entrusted trade goods and liquor to an unlicensed alien named Bouchard, who lived at a primitive sawmill on the Black River, some seventy miles above Prairie du Chien and not far from Augustin Grignon's second establishment.

Thus alerted, "the agent [this is Taliaferro writing in his "Auto-Biography" fifty years later] moved steadily on in the performance of his arduous, responsible, and delicate duties." He deputized Dousman to help him, hired a horse, sleigh and driver, and started across the river ice to seize the contraband.

Getting wind of their errand, Rolette sent a very able half-breed Ottawa trader named Alexis Bailly up the river to warn the unauthorized traders. Taliaferro, who had had run-ins with Bailly on the St. Peter's, was suspicious. Encountering the messenger out on the winding river, he took him into custody. He then grew strangely lax. When the law officers paused at Augustin Grignon's new trading house, where at last Taliaferro learned of the Sioux attack, Bailly was able to slip away with his warning. Although Taliaferro did pounce on Mayrand and another Rolette hand the next morning as they were trying to remove several bales of merchandise from Bouchard's hut, he found no liquor —because of Bailly, he was sure. Or, just possibly, because none was there. Hearing that another unlicensed trader equipped by Mayrand (hence by Rolette) was over on the St. Croix River, he rushed Dousman over to arrest the fellow. The suspect turned out to be within his legal rights, however. He was duly bonded as an interpreter and was not trading, so far as appeared—merely watching over the goods during the absence of the licensed trader, he said righteously. In the end Taliaferro had to return to the owner everything he had impounded—eight packs of furs and merchandise worth $141.

None of the evidence against Rolette which Taliaferro unearthed during his sleigh rides over the icy Mississippi was very conclusive from a legal standpoint, whatever shape it may have taken in the agent's own nimble mind. But his journeys did bring to light the Grignon-Rolette clash, with all its suggestions about the ferocious rivalries of the trade. As soon as the participants realized the affair was in the open, each began writing long letters about his side of the story—some to Crooks, some to Calhoun, some to Cass. But this was February. Winter locked the land; late mail did not move. (Crooks, however, had learned of the feud through earlier dispatches.) Meanwhile, discussions before congressional committees about the best means of conducting the Indian trade were drawing to a close. And only Ramsay Crooks of all the people in Washington knew anything of the clash beside the distant Mississippi. He carefully said nothing.

After the committee hearings had ended, Senator Thomas H. Benton of Missouri carried the debate to the floor of Congress. He hammered home the charges made in committee by Jedidiah Morse, Ramsay Crooks, Benjamin O'Fallon, and the rest. Having thundered out against the economic and philosophic weaknesses in the system, he concentrated his sarcasm on McKenney's insistence that the factories would help civilize the Indians. The jew's-harps which he noted in the factory invoices were no doubt calculated to aid in this worthy end, he rumbled. After all, they were musical instruments and "it has been related of a musician of old, that he even tamed wild beasts, and bent down the tops of trees, and drew a woman out of hell by the potent charms of music." What might not an Indian accomplish with a jew's-harp?

McKenney had no chance to retort that some Indians liked to twang on jew's-harps and that the instruments were a standard item of trade. Nor had McKenney any chance to bring up the Roulette-Grignon-Taliaferro conflicts. He did not learn of them until late May. And by the sixth of the month both houses had passed and the President had signed into law a bill abolishing the government trading factories.

"Thank God for all his mercies!" Crooks wrote exultantly. To Benton he became downright fulsome. Because McKenney had made so much of the moral aspects of the factories—a picture which practice in the field hardly bore out—Crooks sneered at the system as a "pious monster." Unmasking so "gross and holy an imposition" was proof to the country of Benton's "talents, intelligence, and perseverance . . . You deserve the unqualified thanks of the community. . . . Without you . . . nothing could have been effected."[8]

The ending of government trade also ended Thomas McKenney's position as superintendent of that trade. Out of esteem for the man's work, Calhoun made an unauthorized spot for him in the War Department. Helped by two clerks and paid a pittance of $1600 a year, McKenney was to handle the department's voluminous correspondence on Indian matters. He accepted the onerous position on Calhoun's promise to push for the establishment of a semi-independent Bureau of Indian Affairs with McKenney at its head on a salary of $3000. In time, as we shall see, the hope of that shining job—the straining for it—would corrode the man's character to such an extent that he would bow even to his old enemies, the men of the American Fur Company.

One of the purposes behind the establishment of the factories had been to squeeze out of business those irresponsible traders who overcharged the Indians for goods, especially by bartering whisky. With the factory system eliminated, its defenders had asked again and again, what control remained? Congress answered with two new laws. One tightened the requirements for licenses; the other supposedly stiffened the old law of 1802 about the introduction of whisky into the Indian country.

That basic 1802 law concerning the Indian trade had sidestepped the prohibition problem by saying vaguely that the President of the United States could "take such measures . . . as to him may appear expedient to prevent or restrain the vending or distributing of spirituous liquors among all or any of the said Indian tribes." No uniform measures followed. The President's powers were delegated to the various territorial governors and Indian superintendents (often the responsibilities vested in the same person) and from time to time these men had issued edicts of varying severity, or had granted such exemptions as seemed useful.

The act's regulations were limited to the Indian country, and that restriction alone made it unworkable. The point is critical. Social custom sanctioned hard liquor as man's inalienable right—white man's, anyway—particularly on the frontier, where dirt-cheap whisky often was the only market for a pioneer farmer's corn or wheat crop. Nearly every trading center utilized by the American Fur Company and its rivals —Mackinac, Chicago, Sault Ste Marie, Green Bay, Prairie du Chien —was an enclave of American soil occupied by American citizens within the heart of the Indian country. Were residents there to be discriminated against by prohibition? For that matter, were citizens anywhere close to the border to be made the victims of unequal laws just because some savage might slip over the boundary for a nip?

The problem was complicated by forts at each of the centers named, plus other forts at Rock Island and the mouth of the St. Peter's. Enlisted men expected whisky as part of their rations after extra duty. They fleshed out their meager pay of $5.00 a month by working on nearby government construction jobs, such as building agency headquarters, at a standard wage of fifteen cents and a gill of whisky (one quarter of a pint) a day. The chief recreation of many of them when off duty was drunkenness, as surviving tales of army life on the frontier amply demonstrate.

All this took place inside Indian country and was watched by Indians who possessed thirsts as insatiable as that of the soldiers. So long as United States freedoms were deemed operative within these isolated enclaves, there simply was no way to keep spirits from leaking out to the savages.

White man's right to liquor extended to the hard-drinking voyageurs who manned the trading barges and wilderness posts. If the men did not receive their dram after a grueling day's work, they often refused to exert themselves the next day. On November 5, 1819, Roderick Lawrence reported from interior Wisconsin to Louis Devotion concerning the relative speed of two outfits, "Your boat would have got further but your boy will not give whiskey to drink & Rouse gives to each 5 glasses a day." Custom decreed therefore that each bourgeois was entitled to carry with him enough liquor to keep his engagés content. Obviously this opened a second loophole. Who was to determine what was "enough"? Loose custom again suggested a gill a day. Thus a ten-man crew setting out on a ten-month trip could load aboard close to one hundred gallons without causing an eyebrow to raise. If that much was waved through without trouble, why not add a little more? Few army officers, most of them heavy drinkers themselves, were likely to keep strict account. And after the boats had passed beyond sight of the forts, who was to say whether every gallon went to the engagés —or whether some of it occasionally reached Indians who chanced by with packs of furs?

The revisions of 1822 that accompanied the abolition of the factories were supposed to plug some of these loopholes. Under the new act Indian agents and military men were given the right to search on mere suspicion the effects of traders or anyone else passing through the Indian country. If liquor was found, the old penalties of 1802 were invoked: the trader's license was canceled; his goods were confiscated and sold. Informing was encouraged. If a tattler put the government onto a productive scent, he was to receive half of whatever was netted by the sale of the confiscated goods.

The first news about the law frightened some of the violators. One of their dodges had been to smuggle alcohol in casks passed off as containing pickled meat, tobacco, salt, and so on. In parts of Wisconsin "salt" became a private code word for liquor. When Louis Grignon learned of the new restrictions, he wrote in alarm to his brother Charles on July 23, 1822:

> You must Immediately get rid of the salt that you have as a Law has been passed that All Indian traders in whose possession is Found any Intoxicating Liquors shall have their merchandise confiscated by the informer, lose their Bond and honor . . . . Get rid of that which was passed up as provisions . . . . Go without Any Witness, without Any witness, without Any Witness.

Crooks's reaction was more law-abiding. He wrote Stuart that the new bill "deserves to be cordially approved of." He was quite sincere, for he knew that alcohol's troubles outdid its usefulness. As early as 1819 he had urged complete prohibition on Calhoun. He had not taken advantage of the special permit given him in 1818 to use liquor in competing with the North West Company along the border. He had repeatedly asked Cass to write William Clark about stricter supervision along the Mississippi. If this new law proved effective, then his company would no longer need anything more than its own superior resources for fighting its rivals.

Stuart too seemed to have glimpsed the light. On July 10, 1822, he wrote Governor Cass concerning James Kinzie:

> Rest assured Sir that whenever any person either employed by or having dealings of whatever nature with us, does not conform to the laws and regulations governing the Trade, . . . we will always be willing and happy to have him entirely excluded from the Indian country.

He did not mention Rolette in this protestation. Kinzie had been caught and hung up to public view, but news of Rolette's doings (which were not backed by official evidence) reached Washington after the debates were over and hence did not attract widespread attention. Besides, in 1822 Rolette's Upper Mississippi Outfit was the American Fur Company's best customer, save perhaps for Farnham's Lower Mississippi Outfit. It was not practical to be too rigid, now that victory had been won.

Other considerations intervened. As noted earlier, the traders at Green Bay, at Prairie du Chien, at Rock Island, at Chicago, at the mouth of the St. Peter's and at many other enclaves in the wilderness operated on United States ground. From their bark-covered huts they dispensed strong drink to United States citizens and soldiers—not to Indians on

Indian land. The American Fur Company had always ordered large stocks of whisky for these stores. The liquor was conveyed to them in the traders' boats, along with Indian merchandise. Surely the new law of 1822 was not meant to stop this legal business. Stuart appealed for an opinion to twenty-three-year-old Judge James Doty, who the preceding February had been appointed, with the support of the American Fur Company, to the bench of the supreme court for western Michigan. Doty replied that in his view any resident going to Green Bay or Prairie du Chien could take liquor with him if there was no intent to trade it to Indians. As the laden boats started from Mackinac for the Mississippi, Stuart covered them by sending along with each bourgeois a copy of Doty's opinion, addressed to the Indian agents and military commanders along the way. So obviously that loophole was going to stay gaping under the new legislation.

Other exemptions became advisable. In 1821 the British government had at last retaliated against American exclusion of British Indian traders by forbidding aliens to enter their fur trade. This forced the American Fur Company to close the posts it had operated on the shore of Georgian Bay. To replace them, Crooks and Stuart opened three new posts close to the Canadian border between Grand Portage on Superior's northwestern shores and Lake of the Woods.

The first winter proved to be a desperate one. Logistics were part of the problem. Traders east of the Great Plains seldom hunted on Indian lands even for their own subsistence, but used manufactured items for buying the provisions they needed. In starving times only liquor sufficed, and the winter of 1821–22 turned out to be unusually severe. The Indians could not find the normal amounts of game in the snowy woods. Anticipating trouble at the onrush of the first blizzards, Hudson's Bay Company traders ventured south of the border with sledloads of alcohol pulled by dogs. Before the American Fur Company winterers realized what was happening, the foreigners had stripped the Chippewa villages of meat, corn, maple sugar, and frozen fish. Perhaps they snatched some furs as well. But that became secondary. To escape starvation some of the Yankees had to make winter trips of more than five hundred miles to obtain what they needed.

They came into the Mackinac rendezvous furious over this illegal activity by the British. The old argument sprang alive: the only way to fight liquor was to use liquor. Unless they could obtain permission, the company might as well abandon the new posts.

Stuart passed their arguments on to George Boyd, the agent at Mackinac, assuring him in late July, 1822, that the American Fur Company "have on all occasions, most peremptorily ordered the people employed by them to avoid so degrading and illicit a practice." But now matters were desperate. If the company did not ask for an in-

dulgence—twelve barrels, or close to 400 gallons was the figure he suggested—"we might probably hereafter accuse ourselves of being the
means of sacrificing a number of fellow citizens" to death by starvation.
He cited as a precedent the exemption Cass had extended Crooks in
1818 for fighting the North West Company, then closed the request by
promising solemnly:

> I most religiously pledge myself that no improper use shall be made of
> your indulgence, nor one drop of liquor given but on the extreme frontier
> and where we are compelled so to do or sacrifice the wealth of that
> country entirely into the hands of strangers.

Boyd would rather have passed on the problem to higher authority,
but Cass was out of reach and the Lake Superior barges were ready to
leave. Rather uneasily he granted the permission for one year "only if
necessary to procure provisions." (Cass reaffirmed the permission in
June 1823.) Perhaps Stuart really meant for his traders to stay within
those bounds. He wrote Rolette that William Morrison at Fond du Lac
was using whisky only "if absolutely necessary to cope with the Hudson
Bay Co. in procuring provisions . . . but no where in the interior on
any consideration." He instructed Samuel Ashmun and a clerk named
Dingley, to whom he gave whisky, to "conform to the Laws and regulations governing the trade &c." But Fond du Lac was an enormous
area. Many of its posts were scores of miles from the border. Once
liquor was admitted, who was to say where it ended?[9]

The government's neglect of its own agents when they ran into trouble
was another reason the flood poured on undiminished. Consider, for
example, the clash between George Boyd and William Farnsworth.

Farnsworth was one of the young Americans whom Matthews had
hired as clerk-trainees in 1818. For unspecified reasons he was discharged before completing his five-year term. Like other disgruntled
employees, he continued in the trade on his own hook, a dedicated
enemy to his former employers. Boyd did not actually catch him using
liquor around the entrance to Green Bay in 1822, but the evidence was
sound enough in the agent's mind that in 1823 Boyd refused him a
license. Farnsworth thereupon went to the Sault and obtained a permit from the new agent there, Henry Schoolcraft. Returning to Mackinac, he triumphantly sued Boyd in the local justice court for his
travel expenses to the Sault—$80—and won. Boyd appealed to the county
court. In July 1824 a jury of Indian traders again held for Farnsworth
on the grounds that no agent could take it upon himself to withhold
a license on suspicion, however strong. Throughout this time the government said not a word on Boyd's behalf.

Using the permit obtained from Schoolcraft, Farnsworth meanwhile had traded during the winter of 1823–24 at the mouth of the Menominee River, near the entrance to Green Bay. There he obtained pelts by giving whisky not only to the savages but also to the singularly incompetent American Fur Company winterer who opposed him— then compounded the injury by seducing the befuddled fellow's Indian wife. Learning of all this, Robert Stuart prevailed on the commander at Fort Howard, Green Bay, to send out an officer and squad of soldiers to arrest Farnsworth. The winterer regaled them with brandy —private stock, not trade alcohol—and swore that the charges against him were the creations of the company's malice. The soldiers hiccoughed their sympathy, made only a perfunctory search, and returned to the fort saying they had found no illegal liquor. Baffled on that front, the company next dispatched Indians to harass Farnsworth—according to him. He scared them off by waving a lighted candle over a barrel of gunpowder.

When Farnsworth applied for a fresh license in 1824, Boyd again refused him. Schoolcraft, alerted this time by Boyd, also proved recalcitrant. Unlicensed, Farnsworth and two Indians started with a small cargo of merchandise toward the Menominee River. He said later he intended continuing to Green Bay and applying there for a permit. Boyd assumed, however, that he was off for the Indian country illegally and sent John Tanner with eight or nine Ottawa Indians to bring him back.[10]

Farnsworth was not jailed when he was landed on the island, but his goods were impounded at the agency and his two Indians were taken to the fort and given twelve lashes each at Boyd's order. The trader meanwhile obtained a writ of replevin for the recovery of his merchandise and a warrant for the arrest of Boyd for depriving him of liberty and property. The affair created enormous excitement. A mob of approving traders, clerks and voyageurs followed Farnsworth as he strode with the constable up the hill to the agency office. As the arrest was being made, the crowd roared threats against the agent and against the building itself, property of the United States Government.

In the end Boyd reached a settlement out of court with Farnsworth, whose illegal activities continued unchecked for years around Green Bay. Whatever the settlement cost, Boyd paid it himself, just as he paid his own attorney fees in the suit about the license. The government gave him no help.

This was not an isolated instance. Frontier sentiment was entirely behind the traders. Any winterer might secure the most outlandish of decisions against government men: one petty merchant caught redhanded without a license among the Creeks in Georgia in 1824 actually won a case of trespass against the agent who had had the effrontery to arrest him. Though the decision was a flagrant miscarriage of justice, the agent bore the costs unaided.

Military men fared no better. When Lieutenant Colonel Willoughby Morgan, who in 1822 was commanding at Fort Crawford, Prairie du Chien, received instructions about enforcing the new liquor laws in his district, he replied by outlining a long list of uncertainties regarding his powers. He approved of the law, he said, but he feared rendering himself liable to action by the traders. He did not add that he feared his government would not help him withstand suits, but almost surely the point was in his mind. The American Fur Company's continuing case against Talbot Chambers for interfering with Russell Farnham in 1817 was having exactly the effect Crooks wanted. "I anticipate a verdict that will have a salutary influence on the conduct of military men generally throughout the Indian Country," he had written Cass on April 5, 1820. And although the verdict was not yet in, Chambers' expenses and lack of support from the government in fighting the case were making army officers very careful about stepping a single inch out of line.

Within months traders everywhere knew that the "severe" new law of 1822 was not going to be any more effective than its predecessor. Meanwhile the factories and their small restraints were gone, thanks in large measure to Ramsay Crooks. Probably Crooks gave scant thought to the cost of his victory in terms of continued law violations out at the edges of the wilderness. He had approved the paper face of the prohibition, and in spite of his long experience with the roughest elements of the trade, he perhaps thought the restraints would work. In any event, he was in no mood now to strain at gnats. After years of fighting he had broken loose from the shackles of government competition.

His ambition surged. The monopoly Astor once had professed to want at last seemed within reach. Every area bordering the Lakes and upper Mississippi was in the hands of experienced winterers who, though they might quarrel among themselves, would strike back hard at opposition from the outside. With his flanks thus solidly protected from both the government and private rivals, he was free, he thought, to move onto the Missouri, where Samuel Abbott already was trying to come to some sort of agreement with the potent Chouteaus.

CHAPTER 21

Defeats

Crooks launched the western attack in person. He saw the year's goods start along the ninety-six miles of the Erie Canal so far open to traffic and then hurried ahead to Detroit, where James Abbott was revamping the Detroit department. After resolving certain problems, he rode horseback south through Fort Wayne and Fort Harrison (present-day Terre Haute, Indiana) to Vincennes, and there swung due west on the National Road across Illinois to St. Louis—six hundred spring-soggy, mosquito-plagued miles with only crude inns and Indian camps to furnish shelter for the night. By early June he was in the Missouri city, ready for battle. To his dismay he found more of it waiting than he had expected.

Driving energies were transfiguring Missouri. Statehood, achieved in 1820, had bred an optimism that looked far beyond geographic boundaries into the entire West. Although the so-called Yellowstone Expedition of 1818–20 had failed to guarantee the approach to the beaver-rich mountains, the private traders were confident enough of their growing strength that they started to exploit the area without government help.

The Missouri Fur Company was the first to jump. Although Manuel Lisa had died in 1820, his successors in the firm, Thomas Hempstead at St. Louis and Joshua Pilcher on the river, retained something of his old vigor. Supplied by Stone, Bostwick & Company, they built in 1821 Fort Recovery (sometimes called Cedar Fort) on an island near today's Chamberlain, South Dakota, then pressed on to the junction of the Bighorn and Yellowstone rivers in southeastern Montana. There, near the spot where Lisa had built his original Fort Raymond in 1807,

Pilcher erected a picket-surrounded wooden post that he named Fort Benton in honor of the senator who was so useful a friend of the fur men.

The sweeping ambitions of the Missouri Fur Company shook the Chouteau and Pratte families out of their snug routines. Until 1821 they had maintained a dominant position in the St. Louis trade by absorbing the bulk of the pelts produced in the wilder sections of the state and as far up the Missouri as the mouth of the Platte. But if the Missouri Fur Company succeeded in mastering the upper river, a monopoly could no longer be maintained by simply controlling the river's lower stretches. Rousing themselves—much too belatedly in Crooks's opinion—they asked Wilson Price Hunt to plant Berthold, Chouteau & Co. trading houses close to the ones Pilcher planned for the Sioux and the Mandans.

Hunt declined. Astor's Columbia adventure had given him as thorough a taste of wilderness-taming as he wanted. So in the end the job fell on Joseph Brazeau, Jr., of an ancient Illinois family, who was instructed to build Fort Lookout between the Missouri Company's Fort Recovery and the river's strange, north-looping Grand Detour. (Fort Lookout was more freqently called Fort Brazeau or Fort Kiowa.) As soon as Lookout was completed, Brazeau himself was to continue to the Mandans and build another post cheek-by-jowl with the one contemplated by the Missouri Company. Berthold, Chouteau & Co., in short, meant business. But they were not used to outfitting such massive spasms, and their river expeditions were still floundering among details when Crooks reached St. Louis. So, too, for that matter, were the 1822 outfits of their potent rivals.

Two other companies, both upstarts and both more intensely vigorous even than the Missouri Fur Company, were also invading the upper river that summer. One was led by William Ashley, lieutenant governor of the state, and his partner, Andrew Henry, prewar associate of Lisa's. Ashley and Henry possessed ample backing and had purchased quantities of first-class merchandise—six thousand dollars' worth of it from Oliver Bostwick in spite of his agreement with the Missouri Fur Company not to sell goods to rivals bound for the upper country. Ashley's and Henry's primary intention, however, was not to swap gimcracks to the savages for skins in the standard manner. Rather they were transporting to the mountains white trappers whom they had agreed to equip in return for half of whatever each man caught. They would also buy the other half of the pelts at rates to be determined at the posts each spring; the proceeds of these sales would be the trapper's profit for his years' work.

In the East, where the savages had learned the trade value of pelts, each Indian tribe considered itself the owner, in common for its members, of the game that roamed its homeland. In Indian minds a white man who hunted on Indian grounds was a thief. To prevent clashes, the United States Government had declared trapping by whites to be illegal. In the Far West, however, where the savages were unfamiliar with trade practices and unfamiliar with traps, the matter was less clear-cut. Lewis and Clark had recommended that whites be permitted to trap until the tribes learned the uses of commerce. The first parties on the upper river before the war had followed the suggestion, but had also endeavored to interest the Indians in barter.

As the reoccupation of the upper country got underway in the early 1820s, the Missouri Fur Company and, to a lesser extent the French Fur Company (Berthold, Chouteau & Co.) intended to use trappers again, but only as a supplement to trade. Ashley and Henry, on the other hand, meant to concentrate on trapping. Though trade would be accepted at the post they projected for the mouth of the Yellowstone, it was to be incidental, and with that shift in emphasis the Indian ceased to be a key figure in the commerce. Naturally the Indians could be expected to object. But Ashley's and Henry's hard-twisted crews were ready for that too.

Their dispatch matched their recklessness. Andrew Henry started upstream with one boat on April 3. The second, delayed by Bostwick's characteristic slowness in reaching St. Louis with merchandise, left May 8. On June 3 word reached St. Louis that this second craft had sunk. Ashley immediately scoured the neighborhood for fresh supplies and by June 21 was on his way, this time commanding the sailing in person. In spite of the setback, he was still ahead of his rivals.

Using his own early experiences on the Missouri and beyond as a yardstick, Ramsay Crooks must have tried to estimate the new company's chances of success. Perhaps memory made him pessimistic. At any event, he seems to have had no interest in trying to establish a commercial understanding with the untested firm. Perhaps, too, he felt that Astor would disapprove. Trappers used relatively few goods, yet much of the American Fur Company's profit depended on disposing of merchandise to, or through, wintering partners in the wilderness, who in turn bartered it to the Indians—not to trappers. What kind of sense did it make to further a development which in the long run might reduce the quantity of goods sold beyond the frontier?

During that same summer another of the West's startling developments took place under Crooks's nose. Two parties came in from Santa Fe with horse-packed bales of beaver and word that the Mexicans, recently independent of Spain, were clamoring for Yankee cloth, guns, and hardware.[1] From Hugh Glen, one of the leaders of the historic groups, and from some of Glen's men Crooks bought beaver to the amount of $4999.64. He and Bostwick together supplied another pioneer, James Baird, with goods to take back to Santa Fe. The two opponents even went out of their way to produce exactly the items Baird wanted, and Crooks instructed Abbott to charge as little as possible. So he was interested. But he made no effort to involve the American Fur Company permanently in the new trade. Mexico! For cautious old Astor?

The other new company he encountered in St. Louis was a direct threat to his established trade on the Mississippi, but at first he paid it little heed. This was Tilton & Company. Like Robert Dickson's prewar firm, Tilton & Co. was a tortured spin-off from the trade struggles in Canada. In 1821 the North West and Hudson's Bay companies had finally given up their violent feuding and amalgamated under the name of the Hudson's Bay Company.

The closing of some of the competing posts threw many men out of work. One of the displaced traders was Joseph Renville, a half-breed Sioux. Born about 1779 on the Mississippi below the mouth of the St. Peter's, Renville had been taken to Montreal as a youth and taught to read and write. Returning to the Mississippi before he was eighteen, he went to work first for Jacques Porlier and then for Robert Dickson. He served Pike as an interpreter in the winter of 1805–06, but that was his sole contact with the Americans until he fought them during the war. After the conflict he rejoined Dickson at Red River and traded out of the Hudson's Bay Company posts along that stream and its tributaries, some of them well within the borders of the United States.

At Red River he became friendly with two energetic young Scots who worked for Selkirk's colony—William Laidlaw and Daniel Lamont. Almost nothing is recoverable about their early days. Laidlaw was described by George Simpson, head of the newly amalgamated companies, as "thoughtless . . . dissipated and extravagant." But he was also warmhearted and daring. In 1820, when only nineteen, he rode several hundred miles through hostile Sioux country to Prairie du Chien to secure seed wheat and beef cattle for the starving colony, an adventure he shared with Rolette's half-breed clerk, Alexis Bailly. But he did not like farming and was ripe for a change. So too was Daniel Lamont, of whom we know nothing at all, save that he had been born about 1798 or 1799 in Greenock, Scotland, Ramsay Crooks's native town.

In 1821 a third Scot, twenty-five-year-old Kenneth Mackenzie, came tempestuously into the colony. Mackenzie had reached Canada shortly after the war and had bound himself to the North West Company with a five-year contract. On the amalgamation of the companies, he was transferred to Red River. But he had tasted the wilderness and did not like the farming community. When he came across Renville talking quietly to Laidlaw and Lamont about setting themselves up inside the United States in the country Renville knew best, the contiguous headwaters of the Red and St. Peter's rivers, Mackenzie instantly agreed to go along. There is inconclusive evidence that in doing it, he may have skipped out on the last few months of his contract with his employers. He seems also to have abandoned an Indian wife and children in the colony. But legalities never bothered Kenneth Mackenzie very much. Off he went with his new friends.

After rounding up an exceptionally able crew of foreign traders displaced by the amalgamation, the three Scots went to St. Louis and in 1822 declared their intentions of becoming Americans—Laidlaw and Mackenzie in February, Lamont in early July. This was a step only. Until full citizenship was achieved, they would need genuine Americans to front for them. The men they dug up—William P. Tilton and S. S. Dudley—are as obscure to frontier history as are the Scots themselves. Nevertheless, unknown though they were, they prevailed on Stone, Bostwick and Company to supply them with goods.[2] Officially their organization was known as Tilton & Company. Unofficially they called themselves the Columbia Fur Company, perhaps because the Columbia River was the ultimate goal of their ambitions. By the summer of 1822 it was clear that the group's driving force was neither Tilton, the nominal president, nor Renville, the founder. Rather it was Kenneth Mackenzie.

Renville's old stamping grounds at Lake Traverse between the St. Peter's and the Red became the hinge of their operations. They planned to swing east from there down the St. Peter's to the Mississippi, north up the Red, and west among the Sioux of South Dakota and the Mandans in North Dakota[3]—an old horseback route to the Missouri that had been tried after the Revolution by Robert Dickson and other Britons but which was largely ignored by American traders.

Crooks began to catch wind of the new company's plans while still in New York. He was not particularly concerned, even though Tilton & Company's eastern flank would overlap most of the territory he had assigned to Rolette's Upper Mississippi Outfit. Rolette, a scarred veteran of two decades of the ugliest sort of competition, would give them plenty to think about. Almost facetiously Crooks wrote the little Frenchman from New York that the Scots were preparing to ascend the river in a fine keelboat called *Clear the Way.* "I dare say," he finished, "you will keep the way clear enough." And after he reached St. Louis he wandered down to the docks to see what the upstarts had. The venture, he wrote Stuart later, seemed unlikely to succeed. Mackenzie's goods were second-rate; Crooks would not have taken them at three quarters of what the newcomers had paid. If Rolette's St. Peter's clerks, Hazen Mooers and Dennis Robinson, followed the invaders wherever they went, set up shop beside them, and undersold them each time they offered a bargain, they would not last long—he thought.

For his own initial connections on the Missouri he did not want newcomers, but tested men. He first tried to get them by raiding the Missouri Fur Company. He knew that the firm was heavily indebted to Stone, and with the arrogance of power he assumed that its key men would be delighted to leave their uneasy perch for a more substantial spot with him. He had written Pilcher from New York as early as March, suggesting an arrangement for the upper Missouri and perhaps even the Columbia. Replying from Fort Lisa, near Council Bluffs, on June 16, 1822, Pilcher politely but firmly turned him down. Crooks then sounded out Hempstead about breaking with Stone, Bostwick & Company and letting the American Fur Company supply trade goods for the Missouri group. Disgusted with Bostwick's inefficiencies, Hempstead yielded and asked for quotations—only to have Crooks suddenly back away.

The reason was Berthold and Chouteau. After Crooks had talked himself hoarse, that firm at last had agreed to let Astor import, on commission, more goods for their expanding ventures than they had ever bought from him before. But they demanded tight terms. Astor must not sell even a bead elsewhere on the Missouri. Yet they refused to grant Astor, in exchange, the exclusive marketing of their furs. They declined Crooks's vigorous proposals that they and the American Fur Company mutually own, under pelt-sharing arrangements, outfits to be sent into the distant Indian country. Whatever of the upper-river trade they were able to seize from their St. Louis rivals they intended to keep wholly to themselves. Certainly they were not going to let Astor, of all people, put his foot into the door.

These frustrations in St. Louis were Crooks's first considerable failures since becoming Astor's field manager. Yet times certainly were not out of joint. Benton's St. Louis *Enquirer* was even then rejoicing about the trade's vigor:

> Since the abolition of the United States factories, a great activity has prevailed in the operation of this trade. Those formerly engaged in it have increased their capital and extended their enterprises; new firms have engaged in it, and others are preparing to do so . . . . The Missouri Fur Company, which alone employs upwards of 300 men, has reached the mountains and will soon be on the Columbia river. Others have the same destination.

He who had been among the first to reach the Columbia, who more than any other individual had given the factories their *coup de grâce* —he could not join the forces he had released. The reason seemed clear enough. However much the St. Louis traders might fight each other, they were solidly combined to keep Astor away from the Missouri. And Crooks could find no way in which to breach that solid front.

Instead he was reduced to pettiness. He set up small outfits to trade in northern Missouri, especially along the Grand River. (One went to John Hogel, who had been shifted out of Lac du Flambeau because of a penchant developed there for wasting goods on young squaws.) He growled at Stone, Bostwick & Company for breaking its agreement about staying out of the Michilimackinac trade; they were equipping men like Lockwood (who could not buy material on the island) to take back up the Mississippi into Wisconsin. He wrote aggrieved letters to the government. The factories were not being closed in the orderly fashion he had expected; the men sent to shut them down were dumping the goods at bargain prices, with disastrous effects on everyone's business.

His greatest exasperation was the bickering between the company's own traders. Rolette and the Grignons wrote him violent letters about each other. Farnham complained that one of Rolette's men had invaded his territory at Rock Island to buy deer skins. (Rolette insisted that the fellow had not bought skins but tallow only, so that Rolette could make the candles he had agreed to supply to Fort Snelling.) Pensonneau, who ran most of Illinois save Chicago, charged Farnham with crowding him. And the Wabash outfits moaned that Pensonneau's clerks were selling blankets at cut rates inside their territory.

Such grubby intrafamily quarrels, Crooks exploded, were insanity. He grew sonorous about it in his letters: "Ambition in trade is in the abstract laudable: but it ought always to be under the Controul of justice." Justice, however, was also abstract; profits were concrete. So long as the heads and clerks of the different outfits depended on net proceeds for all or even part of their compensation, they were tempted to glean skins wherever they could. The problem was one for which Crooks never found a full solution.

The question of profits troubled his efforts to fight Stone, Bostwick & Company along the Iowa and Illinois banks of the Mississippi. Undercut them everywhere, he ordered Farnham. Farnham demurred; the effort would pinch his income too severely. To win his cooperation for a full-scale onslaught, Crooks had to put him on salary, $1000 a year. At that, Pensonneau in Illinois also asked for a salary. But Pensonneau, unlike Farnham, could not be counted on to exert himself if his income was guaranteed. So Crooks had to walk the tightrope between policies, keeping both men happy without hurting the company.

His only real success that summer was obtaining the services of George Davenport, an outstanding and surprisingly ethical trader in a cutthroat business. Born in Lincolnshire, England, in 1783, Davenport had started life as a common sailor. He broke his leg while rescuing a man who had fallen overboard and was put ashore at New York to mend. While on crutches, he lost interest in the sea. Ambulatory again, he enlisted in the United States Army, became a citizen, soldiered for ten years, and fought his former countrymen during the War of 1812. Discharged, he went as a sutler with the troops that built Fort Armstrong on Rock Island. He soon switched to trading with the Winnebago and Sac and Fox

Indians at their lead mines on either side of the Illinois-Wisconsin border. (They liked him partly because they considered him to be English.) In a small way he also followed Sac-Fox hunting parties into Iowa. There he came into conflict with Farnham.

Crooks tried to end the difficulties by setting up separate districts for the two men. The split was too artificial to endure; but rather than fight each other, as Rolette did with adjoining company men, they combined. Thereafter their names were inseparable. The settlement that grew up on the Iowa side of the Mississippi was named Davenport—and still is. Its twin city across the river in Illinois was called Farnhamsville until years after Farnham's death, when a newer group of citizens changed the name to Rock Island.

Davenport secured, Crooks gave up the St. Louis struggle and started for Michilimackinac. Earlier in the summer Stuart had sent him for the trip a thirty-foot birch canoe and a hand-picked crew of seven paddlers. The men had waited for him in a voyageur's tavern at St. Charles. Fever hit them there. One, Augustin Sonier, grew so ill that Crooks hired an oldster in town to nurse him, but after seventeen days Sonier died. When Crooks met the rest of the crew, and Sonier's replacement, at Portage des Sioux just below the mouth of the Illinois, they were all jaundiced and out of sorts.

For a day he fed them pills and exhortations. At dawn on August 2 they started up the winding Illinois. Their health grew worse. Before they reached Chicago three of them were so weak they had to be helped into and out of the canoe. Crooks himself picked up a paddle and took the foreman's place in the bow, a menial job no bourgeois performed except in times of acute emergency. He got them into Lake Michigan, and slowly the men recovered. But Crooks collapsed. He grew so violently ill that on occasion the alarmed men unloaded him on the beach and let him shake a day or two in his blankets until he was strong enough to wave them on again.

The canoe reached Mackinac August 23. Crooks was put to bed in a company house and the army surgeon summoned from the fort—William Beaumont, whom Crooks had first met aboard the *Walk-in-the-Water* in 1820. "He laid a heavy hand on me," the sick man wrote Samuel Abbott on September 2, apologizing for not being able to return to St. Louis for Abbott's wedding. Actually Beaumont was an uncommonly good doctor, already started toward a degree of fame that is closely enough associated with the American Fur Company to justify a digression here.

On June 6, eleven weeks before Crooks's arrival, a company voyageur, Alexis St. Martin, had been fooling around in the company store with a trade musket loaded with duck shot. Somehow it went off and tore a gaping hole in his stomach. According to Gurdon Hubbard, who was there, "The muzzle was not over three feet from him. . . . The wadding entered, as well as pieces of clothing; his shirt took fire; he fell, as we supposed, dead."

Stuart rushed in, pushed the crowd back, sent a messenger up the hill to the fort, and helped carry St. Martin to a cot. On Beaumont's arrival, Stuart assisted the doctor while he dug lead pellets and bits of cloth from the wound. Amazingly St. Martin lived. He stayed in the company store until he could be moved to the fort. There he recovered, but the wound, a hole 2½ inches in circumference, never closed. Whatever he ate could be held in his stomach only by dressings. The inconvenience also allowed the doctor to look inside his patient's anatomy at a time when no internal exploratory methods existed.

By April 1823 St. Martin had exhausted the welfare funds available to him from either the company or the town. Beaumont, who supported a wife and child on a salary of forty dollars a month and a small subsistence allowance, thereupon took St. Martin into his own home. His original motive was pure compassion, but as the voyageur moped around the house, all but helpless, the doctor conceived the idea of conducting experiments to determine the exact nature of the human digestive process. He began introducing various food tied to thread through the orifice and withdrawing them at timed intervals for study. When he was transferred in 1825 to Plattsburgh, beside Lake Champlain, he took St. Martin with him. By this time, however, St. Martin was tired of the performance and of the crude humor of his associates. Finding himself near Canada, he ran away.

His experiments still incomplete, Beaumont appealed to Crooks for help. Crooks instructed W. W. Matthews to keep an eye peeled as he went about the Montreal area hiring voyageurs for service in the West. In 1827 Matthews found St. Martin—and charged Beaumont fourteen dollars for expenses incurred during the search. Before Matthews received a reply from the doctor, St. Martin escaped again, this time into the Indian country with a Hudson's Bay Company brigade. Meanwhile Beaumont was transferred to Prairie du Chien. When St. Martin returned in abject poverty to the Montreal area, Matthews hired him as an American Fur Company voyageur for the 1829 season, gave his wife and two children free transportation in a company bateau and so returned the truant, his wound as wide open as ever, to the doctor. Beaumont kept him this time by paying him three hundred dollars a year to work around the house and yard. Experiments continued intermittently at various military stations until 1834, when St. Martin retreated permanently to Canada. By then Beaumont had published the results of three sets of experiments about human digestion. They constituted one of the first major contributions to medical knowledge by an American doctor and attracted world-wide attention.

In spite of Beaumont's treatments in 1822, Crooks did not mend appreciably. He declined even to see the Green Bay traders when they waited on him to pour out their grievances—and to stall on their debt payments. Fortunately, Stuart had a firm hand on the business. Of the forty-six traders licensed that year out of Michilimackinac, forty-one were connected with the American Fur Company. Of the five holdouts, Rix Robinson, future founder of Grand Rapids, Michigan, was ready to move into the fold in place of Madeline LaFramboise, who was retiring. With no major troubles in sight, Crooks decided to board the steamboat that was preparing to sail from the island and return by easy stages to New York, there to recuperate in anticipation of a visit from Astor, scheduled for late fall, 1822.

At New York he picked up a lone piece of good news. The long suit against Colonel Talbot Chambers over his interference with Russell Farnham's trade in 1817 had at last been decided in the company's favor, but the jury had scaled the damages requested from $10,000 down to $5000. Crooks was happy to settle for that. Henceforth military men would not be so likely to meddle with the company. Furthermore, he wrote Abbott, the decision "will also convince the impartial part of the community, how unjustly and shamefully the American Fur Co. has been slandered on the western frontier."[4]

It was his only good news. Astor arrived in New York finding fault with everything. Crooks had let expenses get out of hand. Too much money was tied up in credits to traders who too often defaulted. Too many non-productive posts were allowed to stay open. Even the engagés were extravagant. The company should retrench on all fronts. Under the circumstances the very thought of a trade war along the Mississippi with Stone, Bostwick & Company chilled him. Certainly he did not intend to move onto the Missouri. "Mr. Astor is so fervently opposed to *extension*," Crooks wrote Stuart on December 29, 1822, italicizing the word, "that he considered it wrong in me to make even the bargain I did last summer with Berthold & Company to import their goods for 1823."

Still, something had to be done about Stone. He was supporting the Columbia Fur Company on the St. Peter's, Lockwood in Wisconsin, and a host of small traders who were snapping at Farnham and Pensonneau out of St. Louis. Traders he outfitted in Detroit harried William Wallace and John Davis throughout the length of the Wabash River. What was to be the answer to all that?

Astor's retort was typical. Rather than endure an expensive fight, he would buy out his tormenters. In January 1823 he summoned Stone and perhaps Bostwick to New York and quickly came to terms with them. He bought up all their goods and contracts with various winterers. Then, to avoid having them move somewhere else and set up a new business to his hurt, as they had done after leaving Mackinac, he hired them. Bostwick was put in charge of St. Louis and Stone of the department he knew so well, Detroit. Stuart remained at Mackinac, and Crooks continued in general charge of all operations.

The agreement was to take effect April 1, 1823, and last until October 1, 1826. The peripheral arrangements were complex. They involved certain Boston merchants (Munson & Bernard) who had been associated with Stone in St. Louis and certain distributors of Kaskaskia (Menard and Vallé) who had ties with traders working throughout southern Missouri into Arkansas and what is now eastern Oklahoma. And although the American Fur Company agreed to meet all of Stone's commitments for the spring of 1823, it was obvious that to keep Rolette and the Green Bay Company content, the Columbia Fur Company and James Lockwood would thereafter have to be cut adrift. (Lockwood and the Columbia partners at once found new suppliers and stayed as troublesome to Crooks as ever.) Finally, there was the Missouri Fur Company, which had been buying heavily from Stone, Bostwick & Company. Was the American Fur Company to continue with Pilcher and Hempstead (the Missouri Fur Company)—or with Berthold, Chouteau & Pratte, soon to be called Bernard Pratte & Company?[5]

The Missouri Fur Company was the venturesome one; the St. Louis Frenchmen were solvent. Astor's preference was immediate—a choice that was a sore bruise to Crooks's ambitions, for a profit-sharing agreement with the Missouri Fur Company might have taken him back to the Rockies and a risky chance at dazzling profits. But the chance was too risky. Astor waved his arguments aside, and talks began with Bernard Pratte & Company about an exclusive contract for importing their European goods and selling their furs on a safe, uninspiring straight commission. Sensing their advantage, the St. Louis merchants grew demanding, and the conversations were postponed until Crooks came to St. Louis during the summer.

Astor then took fright at the size of the new commitments brought him by Stone, Bostwick & Company and redoubled his insistence on economy. He was so exercised that he almost went personally into the interior on an inspection, something he had never done since founding the company. In the end, however, he decided to return to Europe instead and contented himself with sending to all company traders on April 19, 1823, a stern directive about frugality.

The preamble stated that since the American Fur Company and Stone, Bostwick & Company were now one, the wastefulness that once had attended competition between them must also end. Unnecessary posts were to be closed. (Crooks and Stuart protested. How define unnecessary? Some posts, though profitless, were essential to keep rivals from sneaking in and obtaining a foothold. Others kept one band of

Indians from growing jealous of rivals that were nearer a trader.) The economy edict also cut at the small prerogatives of the employees. Wives and children could no longer live at the posts or travel with the brigades free of charge. Engagés could no longer run up bills against the company for supplies purchased while traveling to and from the wintering grounds. A man could not incur more than nominal debts at the company stores. Since few of them had spare cash available, this order amounted to depriving them of many of the small luxuries— tobacco, clay pipes, good knives, hats with small round brims and gay linings—that helped make the long monotonies of their lives endurable.[6]

Managers were ordered not to sell goods to winterers on credit. This was totally unreasonable. As Crooks and Stuart pointed out to Astor, there were not half a dozen traders in the entire Northwest who could stay in business a year if forced to put up some security other than the furs they anticipated each season. At least, they asked, let them have discretionary power in the matter so that they could continue dealing with men of proved dependability. While awaiting Astor's answer, they went ahead in the old way. Finally he consented on March 19, 1824 —very grudgingly: "Better that we do no business at all than Run Risks of Bade Debts."

With such cautions ringing in his ears, Crooks went to St. Louis in the summer of 1823 to settle matters with Bernard Pratte & Company. He succeeded but the terms were harsh: the St. Louis Frenchmen would not sign the contract unless the American Fur Company agreed to stay completely away from all save the lowest stretches of the Missouri River.[7] Conservatism entrenched—so far as Crooks could see, the American Fur Company was now grounded beside the Mississippi. This from the man who before the war had meant to sweep a continent into his grasp. It must have been a bitter change for Ramsay Crooks to accept.

He spent the rest of his time in St. Louis piddling with maple sugar and lead. Stuart had sent down two barrels and sixty-six kegs of the former; it was produced in such quantities by the Ottawa and Chippewa Indians of northern Wisconsin and Michigan that Stuart said he could supply up to ten tons of the stuff annually if it moved. George Davenport, meanwhile, was wondering how best to handle the lead he obtained at mines operated in northern Illinois by the Sac and Fox Indians and by illegal white squatters. He brought 46,000 pounds to St. Louis that summer and grew so optimistic about prospects that he ordered a fine new keelboat of twenty tons burden.

Crooks wrestled with those details and then toward the end of July disconsolately boarded another birchbark canoe Stuart had sent him along with the sugar and started his voyageurs up the Illinois. This time he stayed healthy. At Chicago he hailed a schooner, put his canoe and men aboard her, and reached Michilimackinac in comfort on August 18. There he learned to his dismay that his old mentor, Robert Dickson, had just died wildly insane on Drummond Island.

While he was downcast, he discovered that he must return to Chicago. The fault was David Stone's. The man had gone directly to Detroit from New Hampshire that summer. Disdaining James Abbott's advice to the contrary, he brought in gangs of his former traders, many of them once vicious rivals of the American Fur Company. With them he entered into a series of new contracts which, for technical reasons that need no detailing here, appalled Ramsay Crooks.

Among other things, Stone seemed bent on flooding the eastern department with more goods than the country could absorb, despite Astor's directions to the contrary. In particular he swept aside the old arrangements with the company's trader at Chicago, John Crafts. Then abruptly he left Detroit without letting James Abbott or anyone else know exactly what commitments he had incurred.

So many requisitions poured in on the startled Abbott that he had to send an express to Michilimackinac asking for help. Crafts too sent orders for far more material than Crooks felt the man needed—unless Stone had given him permission to extend his boundaries. If so, the delicate adjustments Crooks had worked out the year before were going by the boards and interfamily clashes were certain to develop. He wrote Stone a furious letter about it. (Stone replied with one so "crusty"— the word is Stuart's—that Stuart felt obliged to step in as peacemaker, decrying to both of them "the pernicious effects of any of us indulging in a spirit of rancour or hostility toward one another.") Then, on September 10, Crooks started wearily back down Lake Michigan in a Mackinac barge.

Stuart went with him as far as Green Bay. The subsidiary company there was in desperate shape. During the winter of 1822–23 its contentious partners had fought as usual with Rolette, had violated their contracts with the American Fur Company by dealing under the table with Lockwood and Whitney, and had ended the season deeper in debt than ever. So deplorable a showing would hardly lead Astor to soften his edicts against dealing with poor credit risks. Still, the Green Bay men were as useful a bulwark as ever against the peddlers infesting the area with their trinkets; and the American Fur Company already had invested so much in their trade that Crooks reluctantly decided, against Stuart's advice, to risk another outfit to them.

To secure the mounting debt, Stuart stopped off in Green Bay to insist that the winterers execute mortgages on their land in favor of the American Fur Company. He also proposed that they guarantee peace by entering into an arrangement with Rolette whereby each rival would contribute a certain portion of the merchandise used along the Mississippi and share the profits in the same ratio.

In spite of all this he was not very hopeful of success—nor were the men from Green Bay. In his usual semicoherent fashion, hard-drinking John Lawe moaned on September 5, 1823, to his uncle Jacob Franks about

> the Rabble opposition running about with a few bad goods & quantities of whiskey, it is as plentiful as water, that they trade out Slyly, & destroys the Indians . . . You never saw what a wretched place the Bay is, it is full of these dirty little Shantys, as they call them but the right name would be to give them is the dirty Grog shops where every crime is committed that you can think of, murder, Indians, squaws, Soldiers, all mixed together so that it is a complete nuisance, & every thing that is bad is there.

Whisky was bad. Everyone said so. But it lured furs. When the Green Bay men and Rolette drew up the contract Stuart had urged on them, they declared in one clause, just as though it were legal, "the liquors given to the savages this spring [1824] shall be mutually divided."

Since Stuart had initiated the contract, he presumably knew of the liquor arrangement. If so, he ignored it. Nor did the agreement change his mind about the inadvisability of keeping the men afloat. He wrote Crooks in November and again on January 22, 1824, that they should have closed out the Green Bay Company that fall: ". . . they are destitute of enterprize industry economy." His pessimism proved justified. Though their returns for 1823 showed a small profit, it was by no means enough to reduce their obligations or augur well for the future. Rolette was through with them too. Trying to get along with them, he wrote Samuel Abbott in St. Louis, had reduced his own income by $3000.

The Green Bay people accused Rolette and the American Fur Company of deliberately setting out to crush them. Lawe wrote Porlier on February 3, 1824:

> Our bourgeois at McKinac [Stuart] is to blame . . . . gives Secret Instructions to Rolette for to oppose & try to ruin us . . . . They have his money in their hands & they could make him pay well for . . . going contrary to Orders . . . but to the contrary they find he is just a proper person to serve as a tool for them to destroy us.

Destroyed they were. In the fall of 1824 the American Fur Company closed out the old concern. (The process brought their mortgages into Astor's hands and a dozen years later put him into Wisconsin real estate at no profit for himself.) After shaking loose the dead wood, Crooks and Stuart then set up a new Green Bay Company. One of its principal partners was Michael Dousman, erstwhile grim competitor of the American Fur Company. The other was John Lawe, the most vocal critic of Stuart and Crooks during the struggles of the original concern. His blistering and often incoherent attacks in his private correspondence during the years 1822–24 have been accepted by many commentators as proofs of the American Fur Company's unethical business practices; yet those same commentators for some reason ignore Crooks's and Stuart's efforts to keep the Green Bay winterers in operation. The American Fur Company most patently did not try to crush them. It needed them to control Lockwood, Whitney, and a host of small-time peddlers. To that extent it did make tools of them. But as one peruses the ledgers and letters, one can't help thinking that the real causes of failure were not Crooks and Stuart, but a shrinking of game coupled to the men's own inefficiencies, extravagances, and personal habits—Lawe, for instance, was so heavy a drinker that both Crooks and Stuart reprimanded him on several occasions. But once again we are ahead of the story.

After leaving Stuart at Green Bay, Crooks had his voyageurs row on to Chicago. Fort Dearborn had been abandoned and ships no longer called regularly at the hamlet. The diarist of Major Long's exploring party, bound that summer for the head of the St. Peter's, looked in distaste at the sterile land and at the traders' filthy little bark huts, then predicted that without a military establishment to support it Chicago would never amount to a hoot.[8] In one of those huts, Crooks found John Crafts. He straightened out the problems caused by Stone, and with great difficulty pushed on up the shallow, mud-bottomed, grass-grown Chicago River and over the portage to the Des Plaines.

He reached St. Louis about the first of October. Although at first he had resented having to return in that direction, he stayed until mid-November. Business led him to confer often with General Bernard Pratte, until the general left for Philadelphia, but business alone did not account for his lingering or for his frequent trips to the stately Pratte mansion on the bluff overlooking the riverside part of the city. The real attraction, gossips buzzed, was one of Pratte's daughters, teen-age Emilie. The interest was not new; young Judge Doty had remarked it the previous February in New York.[9] But it was growing, though in late 1823 Crooks's age doubled Emilie's—thirty-six to her eighteen.

During his courtship more business troubles under the Stone contract rose to plague him. Bartholomew Berthold complained heatedly that Bostwick had sent goods to Elly & Curtis on the Kansas River in violation of Pratte & Company's understanding with Astor. C. W. Munson of Munson & Bernard, Bostonians who had been drawn into the company's orbit through prior connections with Stone and Bostwick, bought up for private speculation certain furs Astor thought should have gone to him. All these irritations caused Crooks such obvious dissatisfaction that Berthold wondered in a letter of November 23, 1823, to Pratte in Philadelphia whether the association with Stone could last out the three and a half years called for in the contract of amalgamation.

Meanwhile one shocking news item after another was coming down the Missouri to the stunned city. The Indians had run wild. No company on the upper river in 1823 escaped a bloodletting. First, four deserters from a Missouri Fur Company party and an equal number from Andrew Henry's post at the mouth of the Yellowstone were murdered by Blackfeet. In May, more Blackfeet fell on Michael Immel and Robert Jones, the best mountain leaders of the Missouri Fur Company, killed them and five of their party, made off with horses, traps, and furs worth, at the company's official estimate, $13,445.

Two weeks later, Aricaras attacked William Ashley when he paused at their villages to trade for horses. In a twinkling they killed fifteen men, wounded nine or ten more, and destroyed every animal that Ashley had just acquired. He retreated to safety and sent expresses for help. Colonel Henry Leavenworth marched out of Fort Atkinson near Council Bluffs with a punitive expedition of soldiers heavily reinforced by trappers and Sioux auxiliaries under Joshua Pilcher of the Missouri Fur Company. The battle they fought was inconclusive. Pilcher was so disappointed by the results that he wrote Leavenworth a bitter open letter which Ramsay Crooks surely read in the *Missouri Republican* for October 15: "You come (to use your own language) to 'open and make good this great road'; instead of which, you have by the imbecility of your conduct and operations, created and left impassable barriers."

Bernard Pratte & Company (often called the French Fur Company along the river) had its turn next. When Joseph Brazeau, who ran Fort Lookout for the firm, arrived at his post from St. Louis about the first of October, he learned that the Aricaras had deserted their towns after Leavenworth's bombardment. No one knew where the Indians had gone. Perhaps Pilcher was wrong and the way was not impassable. Anyway, Brazeau decided to take a chance. Six trained men who knew the river might be able to slip north to the Mandan villages and cash in on the unusual lack of competition. The ones he sent ran into bad luck, however. The Aricaras had retreated to the Mandan villages themselves. They surprised the men from the French Fur Company and slew five.

The Columbia Fur Company shared in the disasters. During the fall of 1822 William Tilton left Lake Traverse with horses and wagons for the Missouri.[10] With him he took five men; one of them was James Kipp, a spectacularly able, thirty-four-year-old Canadian who had been trading out of Red River since shortly after the founding of the colony.

During the past four seasons Kipp had lived among the Mandans and knew their language well. On the way to the Missouri, Tilton's minuscule group managed to fight off a Sioux war party without casualties to themselves, but their limited strength made slow work of building a crude, picket-surrounded post a little below the largest Mandan town. They finished in November 1823 and named the place Fort Tilton.

The next month William Laidlaw brought six wagons creaking across the frozen prairies from Lake Traverse to resupply them. Aided by old Charbonneau, who with his wife Sacajawea had gone to the Pacific with Lewis and Clark, they did well for a time. But early in 1824, the Aricaras, blood-ugly still, stole several horses and killed one of their men at the very gates of the fort. Afterward tension mounted until the whites scarcely dared leave their post for food and water. Giving up finally, they retreated for protection inside the friendly Mandan village. In the spring Tilton and the voyageurs took their furs down river to St. Louis, leaving Kipp alone among the savages. To keep the Aricaras from burning Fort Tilton and claiming a victory, he dismantled it himself, giving the wood to the Mandans. That winter (1824–25) he was reinforced again from Lake Traverse, but the Aricaras kept the area in such uncertainty that his trade amounted to little.[11]

So continuous a tale of disaster must have made Crooks thank his lucky stars that he had not been able to send an American Fur Company brigade up the river in 1823—until electrifying news came from Ashley. Ashley's men, balked from going up the Missouri, had bought as many horses as friendly savages below the Aricara towns could scratch together, had borrowed more from the French Fur Company at Fort Lookout, and had headed west by land. It was one of the most famous expeditions of pioneering history, for during it a group of men under Jedediah Smith rediscovered South Pass, which Crooks and Stuart had traversed on their way back from the Columbia, and opened the West to the fabled stampede of the mountain men.

The first inklings of the riches waiting in the West reached St. Louis in September 1824. Instantly Ashley readied a supply outfit and left for the mountains in the teeth of winter. St. Louis buzzed with speculation as to what he was up to. Once again, perhaps a chance had come for the bold of heart to seize the Indian trade of the last wilderness.

What Crooks's thoughts may have been when the news reached him we can only guess. But he could hardly have been excited by what he had been reduced to during that period—fighting the government once again, sparring with Stone and William Astor about policy, trying to maintain shreds of integrity in a trade increasingly dishonest. If he hoped to keep following the wilds that had drawn him, while still a boy, to the Missouri, he must break away soon from the molds into which circumstances and Astor were steadily forcing him.

CHAPTER 22

Tensions

Like many Indian agents of the 1820s, Lawrence Taliaferro saw himself as an instrument of Utopia, appointed by destiny and the President of the United States to guide the Indians under his care from darkness into civilized awareness. He recognized a few prerequisites. He had to convince the sometimes dubious savages that the power of the United States really was sufficient to demand respect and assure happiness; he had to fend off the vices of civilization while illustrating its advantages; and he needed tranquility within his borders while he went about his work.

He did not travel very far through his enormous agency in pursuit of those ends. His headquarters were so strategically located at Fort Snelling, above the junction of two great river highways, that he found it more efficient to summon the Indians to meet with him. Bands that chanced by without a summons—there were many: canoe-borne groups delighted in long summer trips—were also gathered into his council chamber for harangues. At each meeting he asked the chiefs and influential warriors to surrender to him any British flags or medals they possessed; ten years after the war, skulduggery along the border was still suspected. He handed out American symbols in exchange and made a set speech: "It is true, your American Father was once like a small tree, but that day has passed and he has grown up like a large *Oak.*"

After each gathering he distributed presents. Since he had no help and his visitors were numerous, the activity became onerous. After one council in September 1821 he complained, with his usual erratic punctuation, to his journal:

I am compelled to cut the lead—open kegs of Powder—and—Tobacco—
wigh every article draw the whisky carry it to them, Count the flints,
needles, pins, awls, steeles, kettles, axes, hoes, traps. Blankets Calico—
in fact every article passes through my hands.

With unflagging zeal he inspected the licenses and cargoes of lawless white traders who might damage his work—in his mind "lawless"
and "American Fur Company" soon became synonyms: "These Mississippi demi-civilized Canadian mongrel English American citizens," he
once characterized the traders. He taught better farming practices to
his semiagricultural red villagers and introduced such Christian social
customs as marriage rites and Sunday rest, signaling the day's advent
by flying a flag from his agency house. When the Indians, who usually
placed their dead in trees, saw soldiers buried in coffins, they wished
that too. Taliaferro had to have the coffins made. He was also expected
to provide presents for burying with the deceased. For themselves the
mourners asked whisky; it helped them weep for their losses, they said.

His keenest interest was in establishing peace. The great sprawl of
his district—it embraced nearly all of present-day Minnesota and a
large slice of northwestern Wisconsin—was inhabited in the north and
northeast by Chippewas, in the southeast by Menominees, in the south
and southwest by Sioux. Hostility between the tribes, especially the
Sioux and Chippewas, was ancient enough to be a cultural pattern.[1]
Over the centuries three governments and many traders had tried without success to produce harmony. Undiscouraged by the record, Taliaferro convoked council after council, cajoled promises of truce from the
glowering opponents, and then saw the brief calms boil into violence
under the heat of some abrupt new quarrel.

A persistent source of trouble was one tribe's invasion of the other's
hunting grounds. Taliaferro believed that if firm boundaries could be
drawn between the several nations in the Upper Mississippi Valley, much
of the friction would end. Since the tribes in general refused to be
restricted by the acts of a few representatives, a lasting understanding
could be achieved only at a grand council attended by large delegations.
Such a council, Taliaferro further believed, needed selling to the Indians. His plan was to arrange a meeting in Washington between the
President of the United States and deputies from chosen bands. After
the President had impressed the importance of the coming council
onto the minds of the visitors, they would return home in a mood to
prepare their fellows.

In the spring of 1823 he persuaded bands of each nation to sit down
together while he explained the idea. At first matters moved amiably
enough. Then along came nineteen canoes carrying a hundred Chippewa

warriors led by Flat Mouth, who weighed 220 pounds and packed authority to match. Feeling his power, Flat Mouth refused to shake hands with the Sioux chiefs who stepped forward to greet him. The indignant Sioux held war dances that night; the Chippewas put their women and children in places of safety and joyfully made ready to fight back. In dismay Taliaferro rushed into Flat Mouth's camp and told the recalcitrant chief that four of his fellows had recently smoked a peace pipe with Sioux and Flat Mouth had better follow suit. If peace was broken now, Taliaferro threatened, he "would bring out a few pieces of artillery and drive off the whole party." At that Flat Mouth calmed down, delivered up his British medals and said he was ready to talk.

Trouble was not over. On August 2 a Sac-Fox war party killed nine Sioux, wounded five. The Sioux nation fell into such a turmoil that there was no longer any hope of taking a group of chiefs away that summer. But Taliaferro still hoped to go in 1824. To explain the change he brought Sioux and Chippewas together in September 1823 at still another conference. After the meeting three young Sioux bullyboys slipped into the Chippewa camp, smashed twelve canoes and stole five, leaving to their overworked agent the headache of keeping the Chippewas from going to war forthwith. That crisis was scarcely settled when Grignon's Folles Avoines (Menominee) Indians came up the Mississippi to hunt. Two years earlier Rolette had encouraged the Sioux to drive the Menominee away. This time, however, Rolette's brief partnership with the Green Bay winterers was operative and he told the Sioux to let the Menominees alone. The inexplicable shift outraged the Sioux, and Taliaferro found himself in the unhappy position of having to support his deadliest enemy by calming them down.

In spite of the continuing alarms he managed to start off in the spring with a mixed delegation of Sioux, Chippewas, and a few Menominees. While he was away he missed real trouble. A war party of Chippewas out hunting Sioux murdered four white traders instead. Since the Mississippi Indians for years had confined their killings to each other, this unexpected eruption terrified the local residents. Was their river to be visited by bloodlettings like those that had shaken the Missouri the year before? Heeding the ancient rule that white men could not be slain with impunity, a volunteer posse from Prairie du Chien joined the pursuit with soldiers from both Fort Snelling and Fort Crawford. Their determination softened when they lost the trail. Shamefaced, the amalgamated parties returned with no prisoners.

A lone American Fur Company trader, Jean Baptiste Corbin, solved the problem. The exultant Chippewas stopped near his post to dance over the fresh scalps. Corbin faced them down, recovered the trophies, and later gave the scalps to John Holiday, who was bound for Mackinac. Holiday delivered them in a small black coffin to agent Henry Schoolcraft at Sault Ste Marie; Schoolcraft in turn forwarded the scalps to Governor Cass. The exact purpose of this activity does not appear. Meanwhile Truman Warren and William Holiday went among the Chippewa villages, demanding the surrender of the murderers, who had scattered. They possessed influence enough to carry the point, and four braves, to match the number of slain whites, were handed over for trial at Mackinac. American Fur Company men delivered the accused to the sheriff. Cass was very impressed and wrote Thomas McKenney in Washington a glowing testimonial about the affair, finishing, "I consider the gentlemen composing this company highly honorable men and zealous and faithful citizens"—which is not quite the way Taliaferro was accustomed to describing them.[2] Later Robert Stuart would find the letter useful when answering certain charges emanating from the St. Peter's.

In Washington, meanwhile, Taliaferro was running into fine luck. On May 25, 1824, an act had been signed into law "to enable the President to hold treaties of trade and friendship with certain Indian tribes." The primary intent of the legislation was to pacify the tribes along the Missouri, a job entrusted during 1825 to General Henry Atkinson and agent Benjamin O'Fallon, supported by nearly five hundred soldiers and a fleet of eight keelboats.

To these Missouri plans Taliaferro at once added his ideas for a grand council of the tribes of the upper Mississippi—the Menominees, Winnebagos, Iowas, Sacs, Foxes, Sioux and Chippewas. Prairie du Chien was selected as the meeting place, August 1825 as the month. Governor Cass, William Clark, and lesser officials were ordered to attend. Henry Schoolcraft was to bring down a contingent of Lake Superior Chippewas. Taliaferro would bring the Sioux and as many Mississippi Chippewas as he could induce to travel with the enemy. Other agents would marshal the other tribes.

During the next year, preparations for the council engrossed Taliaferro's interest. He gave only scant attention to Section 4 of the same act, the so-called location law, which stated, "It shall be the duty of Indian agents to designate, from time to time, certain convenient and suitable places for carrying on trade with the different Indian tribes, and to require all traders to trade at the places thus designated, and at no other places."

The purpose of Section 4, as Taliaferro surely realized, was to help agents and the commanders of frontier military forts tighten their control over the Indian commerce. By confining traders to a few fixed spots, the authorities might have a better chance to check the traffic's sorest abuses—whisky peddling and the following of the savages to their hunting camps, there to steal credits, plant hostile ideas toward rival traders and the government, encourage excessive buying, and in general seduce the childlike emotions of the aborigines.

Years earlier, both the French and the British had decreed similar location laws. Their systems had never worked. But America's 1822 license and liquor laws were not working either. Proponents of the location law argued that the failure of earlier geographic restrictions had resulted from inadequate police forces in the wilderness; now that agencies and military forts had advanced close to the heart of the trading areas, the law could be made to function.

At some point after the passage of the act, a notion got abroad that Section 4 had been inserted into the bill through the political machinations of the American Fur Company. The firm supposedly hoped that if all traders were confined to a few spots, Astor's well-heeled winterers could easily undersell and crush the poor rivals. It seems unlikely, however, that the company wanted its own freedom of movement shackled by such an edict. When Calhoun had proposed a set of location laws some years earlier, Crooks, writing under the pen name of "Backwoodsman" in the *Washington Gazette* in March 1820 had protested the idea.[3] There is no reason to suppose he changed his mind later.

Possibly he approved of the act as a whole and so let Section 4 slip through unchallenged. Perhaps he did not even notice the minor clauses. His political activities that year were concentrated on an unsuccessful campaign to persuade Congress to increase the duty on furs imported to compete with American beaver and muskrat in the making of hats, while at the same time aiding *"the poor red children of the forest"* (actually the words, italics and cynicism are Robert Stuart's) by reducing the tariff on blankets, strouds, and trade guns brought into this country from England. But the speculation is bootless. All we know is that there was no outcry from the company for or against the law until suddenly it pinched one of the firm's prosperous traders, John Crafts of Chicago.

At the Mackinac rendezvous of 1824 Crafts spent $18,000 for goods to resell in the country that curved around the bottom of Lake Michigan. He hired twenty-six engagés and obtained the necessary licenses for them and for himself from George Boyd. Then, just as he was ready to leave the island for his winter's work, a form letter about locations arrived from Alexander Wolcott, the agent at Chicago. In this letter Crafts read that he was denied two areas he had used in preceding years and had counted on using again. His rivals, however, were being permitted to go to those locations.

Protests flew out to Cass, to the Indian office, and to various agents. Stuart persuaded Boyd to overrule Wolcott and issue Crafts licenses for the two disputed spots—a jurisdictional uncertainty the company had exploited before: how far did an agent's authority extend? Rolette also exploited it. When Thomas Forsyth, agent of the Sacs and Foxes, refused a location at the lead mines to one of Rolette's men, Rolette prevailed on Nicholas Boilvin at Prairie du Chien to issue the permission. But these were expedients only. Since a man could never be sure what ruling might strike him the next year, planning was difficult. Furthermore, none of the agents was authorizing as many locations as the traders were accustomed to visiting. The man at Green Bay, for instance, would allow no more than a single trader at a spot—no competitors side by side—and awarded the plum to whoever called on him first.

The Indians did not like the system. A delegation of Sacs called on Forsyth and said his locations were too far from the hunting grounds. Indians who ran out of gunpowder or clothing in the dead of winter would have to make trips as long as three hundred miles to replenish supplies at the authorized locations. They needed traders to come to them instead, so that they could keep on with their hunting.

Bernard Pratte & Company underscored the same point about the Missouri. Benjamin O'Fallon, they complained, had deprived many of the Sioux villages of their accustomed traders—and this after so severe a winter that the savages had lost many of their horses and had been forced to eat their "faithful dogs." Travel by horses and dog sled the next winter would be difficult. Yet if O'Fallon's edicts remained in force, many Sioux would have to journey from two to five days to buy what they needed—or else turn to the Hudson's Bay Company and "frustrate the hopes of the American traders." Amen to that, Stuart said and added that only rogues would benefit from the restrictions of the act. They would roam profitably through the wilderness with their shoddy gimcracks while law-abiding traders sat chained to arbitrarily assigned locations.

Into this simmer of dissatisfaction stalked agent Taliaferro with a belated circular letter dated April 10, 1825, announcing the locations each trader in his district could use during the ensuing year. The reaction was explosive. Indignant winterers called a meeting in Prairie du Chien to vote on a resolution censuring the assignments. It passed easily and copies were forwarded to William Clark, Governor Cass, and the Secretary of War. Angrily the document charged that Taliaferro had ignored suitable, familiar sites and had substituted new locations that were either impossibly remote from the best hunting ground or lacked such necessaries as wood for buildings and ground suited to gardens. The agent obviously did not know his geography, yet in preparing his list had been too high and mighty to consult the men who might have helped him most. The results were, in Stuart's words, a catalogue of "blundering absurdities."

So much for public complaints. Privately Stuart was more severe. In a letter to William B. Astor he charged that Taliaferro, backed by Colonel Snelling, was deliberately using the location law to favor the Columbia

Fur Company, hoping by such actions to end the American Fur Company's dominant position in the trade.[4]

William Astor forwarded a rather subdued summary of the public objections to James Barbour, who had replaced Calhoun as Secretary of War. The timing was ticklish. Among other things, the location law was designed to help check illicit whisky selling. Yet at that very moment the company was involved in still another controversy with the government over the confiscation of goods belonging to William H. Wallace, an American Fur Company trader in Indiana, on the charge that he had taken liquor among the savages. It was all very embarrassing.

At the 1824 rendezvous the only outfits to show a loss were the upper and lower Wabash groups run by Wallace and John Davis. Together they were in the red about $1200—not disastrous, but enough to draw exhortations from Stuart as the men started back to their posts in August. Davis was bound for the mouth of Tippecanoe Creek, Wallace for posts farther down the Wabash toward Fort Harrison. Each man carried thirty-five to forty gallons of spirits with him. Stuart knew this (which constitutes one small difference between the Wallace-Davis affair and James Kinzie's lawbreaking at Milwaukee), but he said later that he supposed the liquor was intended for the engagés.

In September an informer named Edward McCourtney hurried into the office of John Tipton, the new agent at Fort Wayne, and reported that Wallace and Davis were swapping liquor for horses over on the Wabash below Tippecanoe Creek.[5] This was a double illegality. Horse trading on Indian lands, a continual source of frontier friction, had been outlawed since 1802. Tipton recruited three deputies, hurried to the scene and placed fourteen men under arrest—a supineness on the traders' part that Stuart later described as "inconceivable," though one wonders if he really thought the suspects should have resisted.

The goods of both outfits were impounded, but somehow—the matter is not clear—the action came to focus on Wallace alone. Trial on his bond was set for January 24, 1825.

The company fought back instantly. This was standard policy: aggression helped keep government officials wary of interfering and also maintained before the public an image of corporate integrity. The usual spate of letters went to the governor of Michigan, the Secretary of War, and others in high office. In standard fashion both Stuart and William B. Astor accused company enemies of false informing and Tipton of deliberate malice. Young Astor characterized Wallace as honorable and respected, and asked for an investigation to "rescue the reputation of an injured man." Stuart clamored that the government had not a leg to stand on. Even if whisky was actually used, the trading occurred on lands ceded to the United States and hence the prohibitions of 1802 and 1822 did not apply. Furthermore, boatmen were entitled to their drams; any other construction of the law would be "more congenial to the meridian of Constantinople than that of the City of Washington." To show their confidence in Wallace (and to keep rivals from taking advantage of the opening) they rushed him a fresh assortment of goods from Detroit and Chicago.[6]

Attitudes changed after the trial. A jury took fifteen minutes to return a verdict of guilty. The company, to be sure, went through the routine of appealing, but when Wallace appeared at Mackinac the next summer, having done a poor trade with his fresh assortment, he was discharged—just as nearly every other winterer found guilty by law was summarily fired by the firm.[7] (Like other discharged employees, Wallace became a violent enemy. Somehow he obtained a license from Cass, the supposed tool of the American Fur Company, and really did flood the Wabash with liquor.) William Astor meanwhile took fright and told Stuart to clamp down on whisky as a trade item. In view of Stuart's earlier religious pledge about confining the use of spirits to the border regions, his reply makes interesting reading.

> . . . there are several parts of the country we had much better abandon than send without [liquor] . . . . If you think proper to leave this matter to my discretion I feel confident we shall not often get into difficulty . . . . Were it not for the bungling of such a sheep as Wallace, but little is ever to be feared.

William Astor's complaints about the location laws reached Barbour during the Wallace troubles. Without comment, Barbour referred the matter to Thomas McKenney, who was still angling to become head of the proposed new Indian department. Results were surprising. On hearing of James Kinzie's difficulties at Milwaukee a few years before, McKenney had rushed to the Washington newspapers with the story. This time, however, he made no public mention of Wallace's liquor, a wickedness the location law was supposed to help check. He purred instead to William Astor that "every disposition is felt to accommodate our enterprizing citizens who are engaged in the Indian trade." He then nudged William Clark about Taliaferro's assignments. Clark nudged Taliaferro. Rather ungraciously, Taliaferro added a few more locations. Astor's colossus was still able, evidently, to have its own way.

For a time during the initial stages of the Wallace affair Crooks thought he might have to go to Indiana to supervise the case personally. He did not want to. His courtship of Emilie Pratte had burgeoned into a "secret" engagement, and marriage was scheduled for March 10, 1825. Crooks planned to go west during the late fall with her father, General Bernard Pratte, and her cousin, Pierre Chouteau, Jr., who were in the East on business. Illness checked him. "Twelve leeches at my temples" did not relieve his fever enough for him to travel to St. Louis, or to Indiana either. As he recovered his strength after the New Year, he rambled around New York City house-hunting, settling on a two-story brick house "in the modern manner" on Garden Street, two doors from Broadway.

In February he at last started his final journey as a bachelor. With traders Menard and Vallé for company he rattled in an ice-cold public stage over the National Road to Wheeling, where he caught a steamboat to St. Louis.[8] By mid-April the newlyweds were back in New York, the bride homesick and exhausted by the rough trip. Her true honeymoon journey began in August. Proudly Crooks took her up the Hudson, through the nearly completed Erie Canal, past Niagara Falls, and aboard the busy little steamer that carried them to emerald Michilimackinac, dreaming in its crystal water.

Betsy Stuart, seven months pregnant with her fifth child, summoned the wives of principal traders and of the officers at the fort to greet the newcomers with appropriate gaiety. Even for a young girl from frontier St. Louis, related to the fabulous Chouteaus, the roaring rendezvous must have been a heady experience: those laden boats, flags fluttering, voyageurs singing, had made her husband's name a household word throughout the wilderness. But at times it must have been a bewildering experience too. Quite conceivably Crooks introduced her on this trip to her half-red stepdaughter, whom he had named Hester and who was about to enter the Presbyterian mission school recently opened on the island by the Reverend and Mrs. Ferry.

Honeymoon or no, Crooks's mood was not festive. Tensions were pulling at the fabric of the company. Too many of its officers were quarreling over procedures and policy. Both Crooks and John Jacob Astor were dissatisfied with the performances of Stone in Detroit and Bostwick in St. Louis. During the fall of 1824 Bostwick had been completely inefficient: he was late confirming Pratte & Company's importation order for 1825; he upset marketing procedures by his delays in dispatching furs to New York; he let competitors beat him to a choice batch of furs from New Mexico that created a sensation in the East. In spite of all this, however, William Astor seemed to like the pair. The year 1824 had been a good one. As though to give Stone and Bostwick much of the credit for it, in 1825 (and probably with Crooks's acquiescence) he suddenly extended the American Fur Company's contract with them for another year, to October 1, 1827.

David Stone had his dissatisfactions too. He particularly disliked Rolette. He questioned the honesty of the little Frenchman from Prairie du Chien, found continual fault with his operations, and felt he should be dumped overboard and the Columbia Fur Company be put in charge of the Upper Mississippi Outfit. Meanwhile Rolette had gone over Stuart's head to William Astor with certain complaints, inspiring Astor to snap so brusquely at the Mackinac manager's work in general that Stuart's fiery temper fumed up in another of its quick boils.

Indirectly Crooks placated his friend and chided young Astor by writing New York from Mackinac on July 29, 1825:

> Such dispatch I have never known before, and much credit is due Mr. Stuart for the excellent arrangement and good management of his department, for without a perfect knowledge of his complicated duties and constant application he could never have gotten through so much in so short a period.

More basic than any of these dissensions was Crooks's own growing resentment of John Astor's conservative policies and everlasting harping on economy. During the fall of 1824 Crooks had bluntly written him as much. Astor retorted from Europe, in the same letter in which he congratulated Crooks on his marriage:

> You think hard that I acquse you of being Sanguine—but you acknowledge that no one is perfect so are neyther you nor me. I am always ready to give you credit for your Industery your exertions & honrable Conduct —but at the same time I Do not hesitate to acknowladge that you are Sanguine & as your friend I recoment to you to remember that everything has two Sids which ought to be looked at.

In other words Crooks might as well give up any plans he had for expansion. The warning was underlined a little later in another letter in which old Astor—he was sixty-two in 1825—hinted that he might pull out of the trade when his contracts with Stone and Bostwick and also with Crooks and Stuart expired on October 1, 1826. William Astor's abrupt extension for another year of the Stone-Bostwick agreement muddied the picture completely. What should Crooks and Stuart do— pull out in 1826, or ride along for another year with the knowledge that the company might end then, or strive for reorganizations that might extend and expand the company's life?

The two friends must have talked endless hours on Mackinac about the decision. Records have not survived, but the matter grew acute enough that old Astor decided to return from Europe early the next winter for discussions. This time Stuart wanted not even his friend Ramsay Crooks to sign any papers for him by proxy. Instead he wrote William Astor asking permission to leave the island for New York to join the talks in person.

Betsy was excited. She had not been any appreciable distance from the island since their arrival and the prospect of a winter at her parents' home in Brooklyn overjoyed her. Unhappily her husband could not leave until the last winterer had departed for the trading grounds and accounts had been brought up to date—mid-September at the earliest. Betsy dared not wait that long. Her child was due the first part of October. So she left ahead of him, on August 13, with Ramsay and Emilie Crooks. Two of her children she put to board at the mission. With her on the steamboat she took three-year-old John and eleven-year-old Mary, the latter destined for her mother's former school, the Moravian seminary at Bethlehem, Pennsylvania.

As if the company did not already have enough trouble that summer, Lawrence Taliaferro and Colonel Josiah Snelling were preparing more. As soon as spring allowed, the agent had begun inviting Indians to attend the council he had initiated at Prairie du Chien. The Chippewas held back. Angrily Taliaferro blamed the traders of the American Fur Company for inspiring the reluctance. The company wanted familiar patterns to continue. Normally the Chippewas' fear of the Sioux kept their trading parties north in Fond du Lac, in the grip of William Morrison, John Holiday, Pierre Cotté, William Aitkin and other company stalwarts. If the Indians wished to visit an agent, they avoided the Sioux by traveling entirely across Lake Superior to Sault Ste Marie to see Henry Schoolcraft, whom Taliaferro disdained as an impractical literary figure and a mere blob of putty in the company's hands.

These advantages to the Fond du Lac traders would end if Taliaferro established peace and the Chippewas could move freely south to see him at Fort Snelling. So the Fond du Lac whites did what they could to poison the Chippewas against the council—at least Taliaferro charged them with it in his journal when he found he could enlist only twenty-six of the northern Indians to travel down the river with him and his Sioux. Even the Chippewas' own agent from the Lakes, that book-writing, soft-talking Henry Schoolcraft, could enlist only a hundred and sixty or so, practically none of them from Fond du Lac. Pure incompetence on Schoolcraft's part—or so Taliaferro still thought with sour satisfaction when he wrote his autobiography years later.

Aided by the Columbia Fur Company traders, he did much better, numerically at least, with the Sioux. He enlisted 359 of them.[9] He took these Indians and the twenty-six Chippewas to Prairie du Chien, boarded them, and brought them back, at a cost to the government of $812. Meanwhile Schoolcraft gave free rein about transportation and supplies to the American Fur Company traders who managed his group—Holiday, Cotté, Dingley, and Chapman—and they charged (Taliaferro recalled in his autobiography) $4700. That was why the cost of the council exceeded by $2500 the money appropriated for it.

It was a good show. Each band stopped outside town to deck itself in finery; then they lined their canoes in columns and paddled into

Prairie du Chien with guns firing and drums beating. Nearly two hundred Winnebagos and Menominees were waiting for the Sioux and Chippewas. The delegation of Sacs, Foxes, and Iowas arrived last. Everywhere horsehair decorations dangled from savage elbows; necklaces of grizzly-bear claws bobbed on the painted chests of the bravest warriors; a startling handprint of white clay adorned many a glistening, naked back. The American soldiers matched the display: high tar-bucket hats decorated with white pompons, tight blue jackets and crisscrossed white breast belts above snowy white trousers.

The chiefs and the government men—Cass, Clark, and the agents—met under a leafy bower erected near the fort's turreted blockhouse. Ordinary mortals sat around in ranks to watch and listen. For two weeks the interminable oratory went on, oiled by a minimum of liquor. When the thirsty savages mocked Clark's stinginess, he had soldiers fill the kettles as if for distribution; then, as the savages crowded eagerly up, he spilled the whisky onto the ground. Finish the work, he ordered. Sullenly they did, establishing between their hunting grounds boundary lines they would rarely observe. Then they celebrated.

On August 22 Taliaferro started his Indians home. The hot weather, unsanitary camps, strange diet, and excesses of government whisky had been hard on them, especially a group of ninety-six Sioux from the Lake Traverse area. Although the Columbia Fur Company had a main post at Lake Traverse, Taliaferro accepted Rolette's bid of $216 for taking this group home. Many fell ill. Near Lake Pepin on the Mississippi a chief died; terror and grief set his people rocking and wailing. Despite their feebleness, however, Taliaferro made them pick up fifteen sick Chippewas who had been inhumanly abandoned, Taliaferro charged, by the American Fur Company traders. Then Rolette's voyageurs caught the fever and had to abandon one of the convoying barges. The healthiest Indians walked the rest of the way.

At Fort Snelling two more Sioux died. Several were put into the hospital. Disgusted with the way Rolette's men were handling the transportation (Rolette himself had stayed at Prairie du Chien), Taliaferro made arrangements with William Laidlaw of the Columbia Fur Company to conduct the ambulatory part of the group on to Lake Traverse.

Before they reached their destination, fifteen Indians died. A wild rumor ran among the survivors that the white commissioners at the treaty had deliberately poisoned them. When Taliaferro heard the news he sent to the Columbia Fur Company a batch of merchandise and fifteen kegs of whisky (120 gallons) to distribute among the Indians as an antidote to their grief and an earnest of the government's good will. He may have felt the situation demanded exceptional remedies, but his choice of helpers was not politic. For by his act he placed the mantle of government favoritism on a particular private company, to the detriment of its rivals. The men of the Columbia Fur Company played the role to the hilt. Look, brothers! We are the ones the Father wants you to do business with.

Rolette's winterers along the St. Peter's were incensed. Out of pique over Taliaferro's favoring the Columbia men in awarding locations, they already had begun maneuvers to pry him out of office. Since the location law granted him discretionary powers about assignments, they had to attack him on some other score. So they claimed he was issuing licenses to foreigners—to Laidlaw at Traverse des Sioux, to Kenneth Mackenzie at Lake Traverse, to James Kipp and Honoré Picotte on farther west.

The foreign origins of the company's partners was an old charge. It had appeared in print in the St. Louis *Enquirer* on July 5, 1824, inspired, Mackenzie believed, by the American Fur Company. It was not wholly accurate. Laidlaw, Lamont, and Mackenzie had applied for citizenship in 1822 and had filled certain other requirements in 1824. The law about licenses made no provision for intent, however. Until a man was a full citizen he was not entitled to trade. Accordingly the Scots had entered themselves on their own descriptive lists as boatmen or interpreters—"too shallow and contemptible a farce to be played off anywhere," Stuart growled to Bostwick at one point, forgetting perhaps that Crooks and he had employed a similar dodge during their company's early days.

Seeking to prove the charges, Rolette had two young French Canadians spy on William Laidlaw at his post at Traverse des Sioux on the St. Peter's River. The pair swore out affidavits that Laidlaw was trading in violation of the law with Taliaferro's sanction. The agent's sending out liquor among the Sioux gave Rolette another lever—not an infallible one, for government men were entitled to use drink as a gift when necessary and Taliaferro would naturally insist that the unprecedented deaths of so many Indians had made the gesture unavoidable. Rolette nevertheless turned the episode to account. In four brief years, he wrote William Clark, Mackenzie's company had become established in the Indian country "as if by necromancy." Their magic? Illegal whisky and Taliaferro's favor, the latter exemplified by his choosing foreigners, of all people, to pass out the whisky, an act that gave the British in general and the Columbia Fur Company in particular great consequence in the eyes of the Indians. Were such an agent and such a company to be tolerated?

Taliaferro denied the charges about Laidlaw's trading. The Scot was practically a citizen. Anyway, he did not trade but was merely an ordinary hand employed by a duly licensed American. (Actually, of course, Laidlaw was a full partner in the company, and surely Taliaferro knew it.) The affidavits were beneath consideration: they had been sworn to by youths "so extremely simple" that their testimony was "very questionable." "As for Mr. Rolette, no statement coming from him deserves credit. . . . His character as a liar, drunkard and smugler [*sic*] of whiskey into the Indian country is too well established to be questioned."

(A parentheses from Taliaferro's Journal 3, December 31, 1825. On that snowy day the agent served as witness when Luther and Daniel Lamont, the latter surely the Daniel Lamont who was one of the partners of the Columbia Fur Company, purchased 1500 "Tamarac Trees" from the Indians for $180 in goods, to be paid in equal installments. The first payment consisted of lead, gunpowder, tobacco, knives, vermilion, and a large keg of whisky. When, in the agent's mind, did trade in whisky become illegal?)

Although he pretended the invulnerability of one whose cause is pure, he seems to have been worried. During the winter of 1825–26 (it was a severe one) he asked for a transfer to a southern station on the grounds of health. On the theory perhaps that the best defense is an offense, he decided meanwhile to show how really evil the American Fur Company was. During January 1826 he wrote several letters to William Clark, suggesting the advisability of sending Colonel Snelling with a military force through the countryside to scour the American Fur Company posts for liquor. Snelling agreed to the expedition, and Clark was informed that the raids would commence in February. A few places along the St. Peter's were visited that month, but weather postponed the search of Fond du Lac until spring.

Before learning the results of the search, Clark went to Washington on business connected with his Indian superintendency. While there he encountered Robert Stuart, who had come to the capital from the contract talks in New York in order to testify in favor of a bill abolishing the location law. During pauses in his lobbying Stuart pressed the company's complaints against Taliaferro on Clark, who was the agent's immediate superior and could recommend his discharge. In turn Clark showed Stuart the accusations about liquor which Taliaferro had entered against the company.

Once again the timing was inconvenient. The summer before, Colonel Snelling had taken a furlough from the fort that bore his name and had passed his vacation in Detroit. What he saw during his journey there had led him on August 23, 1825, to write Secretary of War James Barbour a blistering attack on the American Fur Company's use of whisky in the Indian trade. He railed that although he stopped liquor from passing the St. Peter's, traders to the north imported as much as they liked through Lake Superior under pretext of needing it to compete with the British along the frontier. Frontier indeed! The winterers were without morality; they promised anything, but used the whisky wherever they could get a fur. Without drawing distinction between Indian land and United States country he continued:

The neighbourhood of the trading houses where whisky is sold, presents a disgusting scene of drunkenness, debauchery, and misery . . . . In my route from St. Peters to this place, I passed Prairie des Chiens, Green bay, and Mackinac; no language can describe the scenes of vice . . . the most degraded picture of human nature I ever witnessed.

Where did this poison come from? "The present year there has been delivered to the Agent of the North [sic] American fur company at Mackinac (by contract) three thousand, three hundred gallons of whisky and two thousand five hundred of high wine." It was time, he finished, for an inquiry into the trade, especially as conducted "by the N. American fur company."

When Stuart appeared before the House Committee on Indian Affairs, unfriendly congressmen brought up both this letter and the Wallace affair. In the face of such charges, was it fitting for the American Fur Company to come before them and request the repeal of laws designed to control the wilderness commerce?

Stuart replied by pointing out the obvious fallacies in Snelling's letter. The company brought even more liquor to Mackinac, Sault Ste Marie, Green Bay, Chicago, and Prairie du Chien than the Colonel charged, but sold it to retailers in the settlements and to sutlers at the forts (including Fort Snelling), where its use by citizens and soldiers was perfectly legal. The scenes Snelling described were deplorable, but the places the colonel mentioned were not Indian country; the problem belonged to the local enforcement agencies and was not the responsibility of the American Fur Company, which had no direct dealings with Indians inside the towns. And he was sure, he said, that in spite of Colonel Snelling's imputations to the contrary, his brother officers at Fort Brady beside the Sault searched the trading barges that traveled through Lake Superior as diligently as the colonel's men searched those on the Mississippi. In other words, he implied, nothing leaked into Fond du Lac that was not authorized by Governor Cass.

He concluded his case by offering testimonials about the company's high principles from George Boyd, Adam Steuart, Governor Cass, and other government officials. The letter of Cass's which he used was the one of the preceding year in which the Michigan governor, commenting on the arrest of the Chippewa murders, had characterized the personnel of the American Fur Company as "zealous citizens." Stuart felt, all told, that he had done a good job. On April 4, 1826, he wrote Rolette that the location law would be repealed before Congress adjourned.

To his astonished chagrin, Congress voted instead to retain the law. From this distance it is not possible to say what influenced the decision. Almost surely, however, the turmoils about liquor—Wallace's arrest, Snelling's letter, and the raids proposed by Taliaferro on grounds the agent deemed sufficient—all had their effect.

Like Stuart and Crooks, old John Jacob Astor, who just recently had arrived in New York to determine the company's future, refused to admit openly that his unsupervised roughnecks in the far wilderness might be guilty as charged. He wrote Bostwick, "I trust however that on investigation it will be found that none of our pepal will have violated the law . . . I presume it not necessary to caution you against sending or permitting Liquir to go indirect or Direct with any outfits made by you." But he was also a careful old devil and those letters about raids which Taliaferro had written to William Clark worried him. Just suppose Snelling's troops did find whisky in Fond du Lac? They would undoubtedly confiscate the traders' property. In the spring the material would consist not of relatively durable hardware and cloth but of precious furs which might be destroyed by careless handling or by moths and worms during a long storage while bonds were in suit. To obviate this, he wrote on May 26, 1826, a remarkable letter to Secretary of War Barbour.

Snelling's search, he said, was ridiculous. The American Fur Company was duly licensed. It had put up bonds as guarantees of good behavior and had submitted its boats to search at the St. Peter's and the Sault. All had gone according to rule until a competitor, Tilton & Company (whose boats, he charged, were not searched with equal diligence) had stirred Taliaferro to this unfair action. If Snelling should seize furs on some mistaken grounds, Astor wanted them released on the posting of a bond equal to their value, in order to prevent loss during suit. Would Barbour issue a blanket order to the Indian agents to this effect? Plaintively Astor added that if irresponsible military men interfered with the company on no more basis than rumors originating in jealousy, "the trade will be too hazardous for us to pursue." And then he threatened: the verdict the company had won against Lieutenant Colonel Talbot Chambers showed what Snelling might expect if the property he seized was injured.

Barbour referred the letter to Thomas McKenney, who was still hoping that an Indian department might be formed with himself at its head. McKenney extended the authority Astor asked.[10] As a postscript it should be added that neither Snelling's searchers in Fond du Lac nor those whom Taliaferro accompanied a short winter's march up the St. Peter's found any liquor. Cynics of course remained unconvinced: secret expresses warned the traders in time. Or perhaps Snelling's troops arrived so late in the spring that the alcohol had already been translated into fur. None of this information reached Congress in time to have any effect, however. Though Stuart exulted over what he considered the company's vindication, the location law stayed firmly on the books.

During Stuart's ineffective struggle with the hostile House Committee on Indian Affairs, Crooks had been absent in St. Louis on weightier matters. J. J. Astor's summertime hints that he might abandon the trade had stiffened almost to a determination to do so. He postponed his scheduled return to the United States until March 1826 and ordered Crooks to hurry meanwhile to St. Louis and discuss the closure with Bernard Pratte & Company and with Oliver Bostwick.[11] Until a decision was reached, no new arrangements were to be made with winterers anywhere.

Although Crooks's first child, a daughter, had been born on February 8 and he might have used that as an excuse to delay the trip until a more pleasant season, he departed before the end of the month. By May he was back. No records of what he talked about or with whom have survived. He managed to change Astor's mind, however, and as soon as he returned Stuart and he began negotiating with Astor for new five-year contracts. Almost surely the extension was related at least in part to what Crooks had wrought in St. Louis.

This is one guess: he sounded out Bernard Pratte & Company (in which his father-in-law and his wife's cousin were two of the four principal partners) about the terms under which they would consent to a union with the Astor organization, so that the American Fur Company could at last obtain a foothold on the Missouri. They probably showed interest without making a definite commitment. Possibly they asked for assurance that Astor would act aggressively once he made his reluctant step across the Mississippi. For instance, what was to be done about the Columbia Fur Company, which was hurting the St. Louis Frenchmen on the Missouri as sorely as it was hurting the American Fur Company on the St. Peter's? Furthermore, if a union was consummated, Stone and Bostwick would have to be dropped.

These questions and conditions, or something like them, Crooks took back to New York. Astor indicated a willingness to talk farther and showed it by extending the contracts of his two chief agents. What persuaded him is uncertain. When he was actually faced by closing down, he perhaps discovered that he was strongly attached to this business on which he had laid the foundations of his enormous fortune—though other, later pursuits than fur, particularly New York real estate and the China trade, were what had fattened it to enormity. Perhaps Crooks warmed his imagination with tales of William Ashley's recent successes in the Rocky Mountains. At one time Astor had dreamed of capturing that trade for himself. Perhaps by joining Bernard Pratte & Company he could still reach for a share of it. The market for Rocky Mountain beaver was rising somewhat, and no doubt that influenced him. In any event, he suddenly decided to take a fresh new grip on the trade.

Stuart, who must hurry if he was to reach Mackinac with Betsy in time for the rendezvous, accepted his new contract on May 11, 1826. The terms were generous—a fifteen per cent interest in the company's profits and a salary of $2500 a year. Signing, he left at once for the Lakes, taking with him a new set of Astor's querulous orders about economy. Traders who smoked often sneaked free tobacco by pretending councils with Indians; the excuse was no longer acceptable; all men who used tobacco were to be automatically charged fifteen to twenty dollars a year. From that date on clerks were to pay for their own tents, traveling kits, liquor and the like. Single men were to be hired wherever possible in order to avoid the leakage that occurred where families were involved. And so on—though the shine of millions of dollars in the mountains was once again in the old man's fading eyes.

Crooks, who already held a twenty per cent interest in profits plus an indeterminate salary, was presumably offered an increase commensurate with Stuart's. For some reason he was dissatisfied. He and Astor argued with sharp tempers before reaching an agreement. As soon as it was signed, Crooks fell ill—as usual. But perhaps optimism brought him out of his bed quicker than otherwise might have been the case. By June 16 he was ready to travel again.

They decided to drop for the time being their efforts to remove Taliaferro from office. From Cass they had learned that the St. Peter's agent was seeking a new spot in the South. His and Snelling's search for liquor had turned into a fiasco. Why stir sleeping dogs? Pressing charges against Taliaferro would also involve the Columbia Fur Company. Since Crooks had made an appointment for Stuart, Rolette and himself to meet with Kenneth Mackenzie at Prairie du Chien and try to work out some sort of an understanding between their companies as a prelude to the more important compact with Bernard Pratte & Company, it was better to holster those affidavits against Taliaferro about the Columbia Fur Company's unlicensed trading, liquor distribution, and what not. The charges could be produced again quickly enough if Mackenzie proved recalcitrant.

He went west eagerly. After years of frustration he had at last broken through Astor's iron caution. Again the control of the future was partly his—if he could sweeten the acrimonies of his violent trade and impose cooperation on some of the frontier's most rugged individualists.

CHAPTER *23*

The Colossus

When Crooks reached St. Louis, he found Kenneth Mackenzie loading two keelboats for the St. Peter's with goods purchased from the supply firm of Collier and Powell. Times were changing. Since 1823 steamboats had been taking advantage of each spring's high water to snort up the Mississippi to Fort Snelling. In July they could not reach that far. But in this July, 1826, one hoped to make Prairie du Chien, and Mackenzie planned to avoid the crushing labor of cordelle and oar by having it tow his keelboats along that lower stretch of river. Crooks decided to ride with him.

This was the beginning of the three-way sparring between the gargantuas of the wilderness trade—Astor's American Fur Company, which dominated the Lakes and much of the Mississippi; Bernard Pratte & Company, whose tentacles reached up the Missouri into South Dakota and were groping southwestward into the new trapper center of Taos, New Mexico; and the Columbia Fur Company, which straddled the north country between the other two and was causing severe financial pain to both of them.

Rolette's Upper Mississippi Outfit, for instance, expended $60,000 to $70,000 a year without adequate return because of the Columbia Fur Company's competition throughout Minnesota and northern Iowa. Westward, Sioux Indians and even a few Cheyennes flocked to the Columbia Fur Company's Fort Tecumseh near the mouth of Bad River, in what is now central South Dakota. (No American trader, the War of 1812 still fresh in his memory, would have called a fort Tecumseh. Were Mackenzie's people, British by birth, using the name as subtle propaganda among the western Indians?) From Fort Tecumseh the Columbia men thrust south, leapfrogging Bernard Pratte & Company's Fort Lookout (or Kiowa) and building houses at the mouths of the rivers that flow into the Missouri from the north, the James, the Vermilion, and the Big Sioux—James Aird's old stamping ground. Throughout that entire distance they came into fierce conflict with the St. Louis Frenchmen. So Crooks and Chouteau, cousins by marriage, were both eager to push these young rivals from the north out of their way.

What the Columbia Fur Company was planning on its own part during these years is not known. Its papers have not survived, and incidental record keepers were fascinated not by them but by Ashley's men. After the bloodspillings of 1823 his trappers had left the river and had swung off by horseback to the western mountains. There they had upset traditional patterns; they supplanted Indian hunters with white trappers and supplied the latter at a summer rendezvous with goods transported on mule back. The spectacular success of this new system (and to a lesser extent, the returns gleaned by trappers working out of New Mexico) caught, and still catches, popular fancy. But the silence of the historians does not mean that the Missouri had been forgotten.

To traditionalists in the Indian trade, the surging river was still the logical approach to the Rockies. Despite the incredible labors involved in moving keelboats, water transport was cheaper than animal transport—for one thing, Indians were not inclined to steal boats, but they would snatch every unguarded horse they could lay hands on. Furthermore, the river Indians still needed the white man's cloth, knives, kettles, guns, and powder. A company eying the mountains could support itself on the way by slowly extending its trading posts up the river, and finally using the highest of the upper houses as jumping-off places for trapper brigades. If peace could be secured, they argued, then the river would prove to be a more economic highway west than the hazardous land routes.

The government helped by sending out the treaty-making Atkinson-O'Fallon expedition of 1825, which held peace councils with every river tribe as far into the northwest as the mouth of the Yellowstone River. The traders followed immediately. Bernard Pratte & Company sent a man named Bisonette among the Mandans. Tilton brought a keelboat to the same villages, to enable James Kipp (who had remained there throughout this time) to move still higher. In 1826 Kipp reached 140 miles upstream to the mouth of the White Earth River, where he collared the trade of the Assiniboins, whose friendship he had first gained while working out of Red River.

Beyond the Assiniboins the Blackfeet lived. Implacable enemies of the Americans, the Blackfeet obtained supplies by taking their furs to the

Hudson's Bay Company posts north of the border. (And almost certainly, the frontiersmen growled, Hudson's Bay traders slipped south to encourage the movement.) The Blackfeet had avoided Atkinson's treaty makers. No trader from the lower Missouri could expect anything but trouble from them. But the principal partners of the Columbia Fur Company had been working for the big Canadian firms only four years before and probably could count on passing themselves off as British. If that was accomplished, little chance would remain for anyone else to use the Missouri as an approach to the richest beaver country in the United States, the northern Rockies. So for that reason too something had to be done about Mackenzie's company.

Records for the dry plains west and south of the river are even more sparse. Beyond doubt, however, Columbia men were active there too. The ways were well known. From time immemorial, Cheyenne and Crow Indians had drifted east and north from Wyoming and eastern South Dakota to the Missouri to swap buffalo hides and, later, horses to the Mandans and Aricaras for dried vegetables. When white men appeared (first French and British out of Canada, then Spaniards and Americans from St. Louis), the same Indians began bartering for manufactured articles. Half-breeds and half-savage whites roamed off with them, carrying a few trinkets and bringing back a bale or two of beaver pelts.

There is no telling how far those peddlers went. The Vérendryes had reached at least to the Black Hills of South Dakota and perhaps to the Big Horn Mountains of Wyoming as long ago as 1742–43. François Laroque had gone to the Big Horns in 1805. Crooks himself, guided by that wild mulatto Edward Rose, had journeyed with the Astorians through northern South Dakota to the Rockies and beyond in 1811. Jedediah Smith had paralleled the route farther south in 1823. The Fort Tecumseh records that begin in 1828 show that by that year trips up the Missouri's western tributaries (the White, the Bad, the Cheyenne) were commonplace. So the Columbia Fur Company men were athwart the trails in that direction also—trails which, as every trader knew, led eventually to the mountains.[1]

Mackenzie had wanted to go to the Rockies ever since the founding of the company. But, as often happens, he had become so entangled in consolidating his first beachheads that he had never shaken free enough to effect his far-reaching plans. Though his firm might be causing Astor grievous hurt in Minnesota and Bernard Pratte & Company equal pain on the Missouri, they were clawing him just as severely. Neither the Columbia men nor their suppliers, Collier and Powell, could command nearly as much capital as their competitors could. Their greatest assets were intangibles: youth, energy, cohesion.[2] These had enabled them to hang on through three lean years. Finally, during the winter of

1825–26, they hit a $40,000 bonanza and paid off the most pressing of their obligations. If luck held, they might expand westward in spite of their two formidable opponents. But they were in no shape to begin with a rush. So they took a deep breath and sat down squarely in front of Astor and the Frenchmen. All three glared at each other like tomcats, growling prodigiously, but strengths were evenly enough matched that not one of them quite dared turn his back on the others and take that first step toward the West, lest the others be on his back in a trice.

Until the antipathies were resolved, no one could expand. As noted in the preceding chapter, Crooks's sudden spring trip to St. Louis to consult with Bernard Pratte & Company was a start. The next step was to sound out Mackenzie about the Columbia Fur Company's willingness to come to terms. It is inconceivable that Crooks passed through St. Louis in July, 1826, without discussing the problem again with his father-in-law and his wife's cousin. Yet it seems that no decisions concerning the Missouri were reached—at least no record survives—and Crooks was reduced to treating only about the Mississippi and the St. Peter's. This limitation of course gave Mackenzie a decided advantage. Every lead had to be made to him, for him to trump as he saw fit out of his strengths on the Missouri, where Crooks also yearned to go. No doubt he enjoyed the one-sided duel completely as the steamer dragged his keelboats up the river toward Prairie du Chien, where Daniel Lamont and Joseph Rolette were supposed to sit in with them on the final talks.

Low water halted the vessel at the Des Moines rapids. Somewhat disgruntled, the two bourgeois reverted to old ways and transferred to the keelboats. Crooks privately thought Mackenzie's voyageurs second-rate. Still, it was not an unpleasant trip. Cool weather discouraged mosquitoes; favoring winds let the boatmen spread their sails for long intervals. As the craft glided among the green islands, the two adversaries, lolling under the awning on the small deck, had ample opportunity to gauge each other. Respect was mutual; as fellow Scots, they may even have grown to like each other during those three weeks of close confinement. Certainly the tales they spun to pass the time must have been something to hear.

They reached Prairie du Chien on August 13. Lamont appeared on schedule. Rolette, who was buying and loading his goods at Mackinac, did not, which is strange, since the outcome of the discussions concerned him and his semiindependent Upper Mississippi Outfit more than anyone else. Eager to reach Lake Traverse as soon as possible, Mackenzie refused to wait and the talks began without Rolette.

Specifics have not survived. All we know is that Mackenzie demanded the American Fur Company's withdrawal from the St. Peter's save for a short stretch along its lower length. What Mackenzie offered in exchange, or how the Missouri may or may not have figured, remain a mystery. Anyway the concessions were not enough, and Crooks turned the proposal down.

Ten days of dickering did not break the deadlock. On August 23, ignoring the rumors of Winnebago hostility that filled the town, Mackenzie and Lamont left for the upper country. Crooks stayed in the frightened village (the scare at length blew over), waiting for Rolette and fretting about the collapse of the negotiations. He sent letters after Lamont and Mackenzie, suggesting a fresh meeting the following spring at either Fort Snelling or Prairie du Chien, "provided that you are inclined to be moderate in your expectations for I cannot consent to abandon the St. Peters from Travers des Sioux upwards."

He wrote Stuart asking for advice, though the letter took a month to reach Mackinac. In reply Stuart suggested buying the Columbia firm's merchandise at a reasonable profit to them and also paying them $5000 a year to stay completely out of the trade for a specified time, the costs to be borne jointly by the American Fur Company and Bernard Pratte & Company. The drawback was that new peddlers might rush into the vacuum. So perhaps setting the Columbia Fur Company up as a semiautonomous outfit, like Rolette's, would be preferable. If such an arrangement came about, Stuart wanted Mackenzie's people moved clear over to the Missouri—naturally, since that would remove their pressures from his Northern Department.

Rolette meanwhile had come into Prairie du Chien with his barges almost on the heels of Lamont's and Mackenzie's departure. Crooks told him to hit the Columbia people hard during the ensuing winter, probably granting the little Frenchman enough concessions that even a losing business on the St. Peter's would be worth his while.[3] Once again the hitting involved Lawrence Taliaferro, for the agent was still at Fort Snelling, his application for a southern post having been denied. Rolette should collect more evidence about Taliaferro's licensing of foreigners, distributing whisky through them, giving them the choice locations, and anything else that might embarrass Mackenzie. (But do not break the law yourself while getting after the Columbia men, Stuart warned Rolette from Mackinac after learning of the orders.)

Rolette had already begun a private attack on the Indian agent. The preceding April 2, Taliaferro had issued a circular letter stating that "no ardent spirits of any kind will be permitted to enter the limits of this Superintendency for any section of the country whatever, except for and on account of the United States." None for engagés? Rolette and Bailly decided to test the point, though possibly their hearts weren't bleeding so much for their men as for their trade. (Bailly, incidentally, had come back to Rolette's employ that spring; his sometime bourgeois, James Lockwood, had also reached an understanding with the little

Frenchman.) In pursuit of their plan, Bailly on June 30 obtained from agent Nicholas Boilvin at Prairie du Chien permission to take two barrels of whisky, about sixty-five gallons, to his post, provided that he report the liquor to the commanding officer at Fort Snelling.

He made the report on July 13. Taliaferro flew into a temper. Under authority emanating from the War Department to all Indian agents, he ordered the military to seize the offensive barrels. Colonel Snelling had the confiscation carried out the next day. Though glad enough to injure the company, Snelling nevertheless was worried by this old clash in jurisdiction between agents. Who had ultimate authority, Boilvin or Taliaferro? Remembering perhaps what had happened to Chambers, he tried to protect himself by writing Bailly for the record a stiffly formal note to the effect that the whisky was to be tried under the laws of the United States and condemned only if found illegal.

Taliaferro also began to have second thoughts. No ardent spirits whatsoever? On August 20 he authorized Alexander Faribault, one of Bailly's clerks, to take sixteen gallons to his trading post for the exclusive use of Faribault and his engagés. Unappeased, Bailly entered suit over the seizure against Taliaferro in the Prairie du Chien court.

Greatly agitated, the Indian agent offered lawyer John Turney of Galena, Illinois, $100 to undertake his defense, promising another $50 if Turney won. Quibbling, Taliaferro said he had not seized the liquor; Snelling had. But, he continued, he wanted the case to swing not on fine points but on principle. To William Clark he added, "Unless prompt and efficient measures be not taken in this case, it may prove needless to endeavor to restrain similar infractions of the law in the future." Despite his pleas, the government did not come to his help and Turney proved a poor lawyer. In the end, Bailly and Taliaferro settled out of court, with Taliaferro making an unrecorded payment of some sort to his opponent.[4]

Other difficulties for the agent were taking shape farther north. In company with Governor Cass, Thomas L. McKenney was making his first trip through the wilderness, the welfare of whose inhabitants had so long engrossed his attention. From Detroit to Sault Ste Marie, their party accompanied a military group headed by Inspector General George Croghan, who was examining the western forts. James Abbott of the American Fur Company traveled along with a bargeload of voyageurs to handle the provisions.

Near Drummond Island they saw a mob of Indians reeling through the night, howling like fiends and waving smoky torches of birch bark—"a scene of hell," McKenney wrote. The savages had just received their annual gifts of merchandise from the British and were swapping the blankets and kettles to uncontrolled traders for whisky—Canadian traders, not winterers of the American Fur Company, although conceivably some of the latter might have been jealous of the way their rivals across the border were raking in the business. It gave McKenney a notion of the border trade.

On St. Joseph Island they saw a few stark, white chimneys rising above grass-grown, almost indistinguishable debris. Only that remained of the settlement Croghan's men had burned during the War of 1812, while Ramsay Crooks watched. A few miles farther on they came to Fort Brady beside the Sault. There the parties split. Croghan and the military went south to inspect Fort Crawford at Prairie du Chien; McKenney and Cass picked up agent Henry Schoolcraft and sixty-six new military men, including four musicians. In three crowded barges and a bark canoe they rowed west through Lake Superior 553 miles (McKenney's calculation) to the American Fur Company's Fond du Lac establishment, a few miles up the lovely St. Louis River from the lake's farthest tip. More than seven hundred Chippewa Indians had assembled there to meet the whites and ratify the Prairie du Chien treaty that had been signed a year earlier without their presence.

The whites arrived in style, McKenney's bark canoe first and then Cass's barge, flanked on either side by welcoming Indians in a dozen swiftly moving vessels. The soldiers' Mackinaw boats brought up the rear, the musicians tootling mightily as the flotilla neared the company's establishments on the river's north shore, the heavily wooded mountains rising steeply behind it.

The post consisted of six or seven one-story log buildings, covered sides and top with bark. Pickets surrounded a garden of potatoes and wheat (the grain was used to feed the milk cows and not for making flour) and a graveyard, for whites and reds alike, that was beginning to take on sizable proportions. The clearing around the post and the small island out in the river were jammed with the bark wigwams of the Indians.

The military paraded to band music to impress the savages. The Chippewas painted, shook their rattles, and did their war dances to impress the soldiers. Business began with the firing of guns each morning. Though the treaty purported to be mainly about the boundary lines, the whites slipped in a clause that gave American citizens the right to exploit the great masses of copper on the Keweenaw Peninsula. The government paid the Chippewas a small annuity for this and then sat solemnly around conference tables in Washington, wondering how to draw up laws that would keep private merchants from cheating the ignorant savages.

Several traders had accompanied the Chippewas to the council from the interior sections of Fond du Lac. Catching McKenney's ear, they poured out their usual complaints about Taliaferro and then added one more. Using interpreter Scott Campbell as a blind, the Indian agent was engaging in the trade himself, a complete illegality. Could not something be done to relieve the commerce of such a monster?

McKenney said he would consider the matter.

The long trip home, moving sixteen hours a day, sun ablaze on the water, gave him time to think of many things. Those voyageurs! Every day they thrust their paddles into the lake 56,700 times. Perhaps they needed solace when evening came. Other calculations circled around the value of the furs taken in the area. By 1826 the amount had shrunk to $23,500, figured in highed-priced merchandise. This total allowed an income of three dollars a year to each Indian—man, woman, and child— in the district. The American Fur Company meanwhile sold those furs for $35,000—this profit on top of what the firm made from the goods. Yet smaller profits would not encourage men to accept the dreadful labors and risks involved—necessary risks, since the Indians had grown utterly dependent on the traders. Too, there was the problem of unpaid credits. The savages were improvident and wasteful. Many starved to death every winter. After hard times a high percentage of them defaulted on their debts. The only way a trader could protect himself was to increase his charges to those who were dependable. Unfair, perhaps, but what other solution was there?

And liquor. McKenney's trip made him believe that the more responsible traders understood the problem and did not use spirits where competition did not exist. But along the border and near the settlements restraint vanished, and then "no description can convey any adequate conception of the degraded and wretched condition in which the use of this article has involved this people." What was the answer?

Along the homeward route the canoes encountered John Holiday, bound toward his wintering grounds. He sent his men on with his barges, but turned back himself with the treaty makers. The year before, Taliaferro had described Holiday as a "drunken Scotchman." McKenney reached a different estimate: "This is a worthy man, and a meritorious trader." Less than a year later he would have occasion to recall those words.

On Michilimackinac, McKenney admired Betsy Stuart's work with the mission school and Robert Stuart's abilities as a wilderness entrepreneur. Sensing the drift, Stuart asked McKenney to make representations to the Secretary of War about the unwarranted hostility of Colonel Snelling and agent Taliaferro toward honest American businessmen. McKenney said he would. He also offered to make representations to the President himself about the Wallace seizure, which was still pending before the courts.

Amazed by this "revolution in his sentiments respecting us," Stuart hurried a letter ahead to Astor, still waiting in New York to learn the results of Crooks's western negotiations. In the note he suggested that the old merchant spread a little charm for their new friend on his return East. Astor thereupon entertained McKenney at dinner and reported, "I Do belive he is better inclined."

This new inclination (to jump ahead of the story) survived some remarkable onslaughts. In February 1827 the War Department, acting on Thomas McKenney's recommendations, took away from the various Indian Superintendents and territorial governors their right to grant exceptions to the prohibition act of 1822. Cass protested. He felt whisky necessary to counteract British influence along the border. He nevertheless obediently forwarded the directive to Henry Schoolcraft and ordered him to pass no more whisky through the Sault into Lake Superior.

Shortly after Schoolcraft received this order, that meritorious trader, John Holiday, sent an unlicensed employee with liquor to a jackknife post near the border to stop the flow of furs to a whisky-using British "shanty" on the other side of the line. Some squaws reported the matter to Schoolcraft. The agent seized the violator and began threatening full punishment—confiscation of Holiday's goods and furs, cancellation of his license, and so on.

At that juncture McKenney reappeared on his way to more treaty making, this time with the restive Winnebagos in Wisconsin. Stuart set about placating him. He arranged a meeting between McKenney and Holiday and then rushed warnings ahead urging the trader to prepare adequate excuses. Perhaps the unlicensed employee could be induced to say he had acted without his superior's knowledge; perhaps the squaws would say they had invented the liquor-selling yarn out of a desire to gain revenge for some wrong. In any event, the letter urged, "be careful not to admit anything that may condemn you. . . . All your ingenuity is necessary."

Whatever Holiday hit on, it satisfied McKenney. Smugly Stuart wrote Cass that after investigating the case, the War Department representative favored "a remission of sins—and I trust that Mr. Schoolcraft and yourself will cheerfully coincide." To Schoolcraft he added, "I therefore hope you will overlook whatever little indiscretion he or any of his people may be guilty of." Nor was that all. Though McKenney himself recently had ordered Cass to grant no further exceptions about liquor, he returned from the Sault so bemused that he personally wrote out permission for the company's winterers to take along in their outfits one gill per man per day.

Stuart, the real cynic of the company, sneered at McKenney as "slippery" and "feather-headed." The man was still angling to be put in charge of an independent bureau of Indian affairs and feared the company's opposition. Furthermore, Stuart went on to Astor, McKenney's trips through the lakes with Cass had brought him a "full knowledge . . . of the manner in which our business is conducted . . . and [he] takes every opportunity of lauding our humane and correct dealings with the Indians."[5]

During these trips through the lakes, McKenney decided to take the northern Chippewas away from Taliaferro's agency and assign them to Schoolcraft. To shorten the savages' trips to see their representative, he created a subagency at La Pointe on lovely Madeline Island. To run it he selected as subagent George Johnston, half-breed son of old John Johnston of the Sault, Schoolcraft's brother-in-law, and, until his appointment, a trader for the American Fur Company.

The loss of the northern Chippewas was a devastating blow to Taliaferro's vanity. He had always been jealous of Schoolcraft, that literary nincompoop. Now his wounded pride bled out through his pen into his journals in endless complaints. Did he deserve this? Had he not done his job well, "gaining the friendship & confidence of the Sioux & Chippewas to a degree almost without parallel in any age or Country[?]" To Clark he cried, "Every Chippeway on the Mississippi prefers me to any other man known to them . . . I am no *writer of books* nor do I expect to add to my fame or fortune in that way—but move on and do my country's service without such aid to give a more lovely and glowing colour to my humble operations."

George Johnston got his pummelings, too, in the journals. The Chippewas said they hated him; he struck them; he was always drunk; he would not listen to their problems. He even took some whisky from a few of them. *That* seizure, Taliaferro wrote in Journal 4, October 9, 1827, was an "unprovoked outrage." (Parenthetically it might be added that he was simultaneously receiving other humiliations. When assigning trading locations he had instructed the traders what names they should give the posts—he called them forts—and even told them how to build the establishments. The War Department crisply overruled him. Nonmilitary installations were not to be called forts; and it was not his place to dictate construction procedure to private citizens.)

When A. D. Dingley of the American Fur Company chanced by Fort Snelling, Taliaferro and his interpreter Scott Campbell put him on the carpet about his charge to McKenney that they were trading on the side. Dingley finally admitted (according to the journals) that he could not substantiate the canard but simply had been repeating Indian rumor. Nevertheless the lie had served its purpose, Taliaferro charged. Schoolcraft had used the tale to persuade McKenney to split the agency, give him the Chippewas, and thus "gratify certain favorites"—the American Fur Company.

The more the agent brooded, the angrier he became. On December 1, 1827, he boiled over. Seizing his pen, he wrote Schoolcraft a wild challenge to a duel. "My mind Sir is fixed, meet when and where we may."

There is no indication that Schoolcraft ever bothered to reply.

By this time the American Fur Company once again had dropped its charges against the agent, for he was no longer necessary to its plans. In September 1826 Crooks had returned to New York from his fruitless conference with Kenneth Mackenzie at Prairie du Chien. Pierre Chouteau followed him to the eastern city and began another series of exhausting talks about uniting their companies. They reached an agreement of sorts on December 15, broke it off sharply, got together again, and on the twentieth signed the contract. Beginning July 1, 1827, and continuing until the spring of 1831 (i.e., through the returns of the outfits of 1830), their firms would share equally in profits and losses of the trade on the Mississippi below Prairie du Chien and along the entire Missouri.

Management of this business fell to Bernard Pratte & Company, which became the Western Department of the American Fur Company. The department was completely independent, save that it agreed to buy all the merchandise used in the West through the American Fur Company, paying the organization a 5 per cent commission on materials imported from England (but nothing on goods bought in the United States) and 7 per cent interest on all money advanced by Astor. Each spring the American Fur Company would make the Western Department an offer for its pelts; if Bernard Pratte & Company declined, Astor would sell the furs for them at auction in New York or in Europe, charging the usual 2½ per cent commission for the service. Crooks remained general superintendent of affairs, but the Western Department was not necessarily bound to heed his directions if their judgment dictated otherwise. Actual ruler of the Missouri was Pierre Chouteau, Jr., who managed matters from St. Louis at a salary of $2000 a year, plus his share of the Western Department's profits. Berthold continued to run the company's posts in the Sioux country and Cabanné the big one at Council Bluffs, each at an annual salary of $1250, plus a share of profits. The American Fur Company even paid Bernard Pratte & Company $150 rent per year for its buildings in St. Louis and its cornfields at Council Bluffs. (A dollar, in short, had considerable purchasing power in 1827, a factor to bear in mind when evaluating Astor's statement, made in 1829, that his investment in the Indian trade amounted to a million a year.)

The union brought with it a tenuous connection with the Rockies. At the end of the mountain rendezvous of 1826, held in the broad, sage-filled valley of the Green River, William Ashley had sold his company to Jedediah Smith, David Jackson, and William Sublette. As part of the agreement Ashley promised to deliver them a fresh stock of merchandise at a rendezvous to be held during the summer of 1827 beside Bear Lake, astraddle today's Utah-Idaho border. The delivery, which would require forty men handling a pack train of more than 120 animals, would be risky. To minimize possible losses and to keep from tying up excessive amounts of his own capital, Ashley in October 1826 offered Bernard Pratte & Company a half interest in the enterprise.

The St. Louis Frenchmen held back, partly because of the pending negotiations with Astor and partly because Ashley wanted them to promise that their New Mexico trappers, headed by Bernard Pratte's son Sylvestre, would not interfere with the men Ashley might also put into the field during the winter of 1827–28, in competition with Smith, Jackson and Sublette. Ashley was in the East when the American Fur Company united with Bernard Pratte & Company, and when discussions about the Rocky Mountain adventure were resumed, Crooks almost certainly participated.

The result was a very limited agreement. The American Fur Company supplied half the goods Ashley took to Bear Lake and in return obtained half the 7400 pounds of beaver Smith, Jackson, and Sublette offered in payment. This completed the understanding. The Western Department refused to bind Sylvestre Pratte; he left Taos on schedule for the Green River in the fall of 1827 (but died en route and his outfit had to be continued with only moderate success by his clerk, Ceran St. Vrain). The St. Louis Frenchmen (and Crooks?) also declined to help outfit Ashley's proposed trapping parties (to which Sublette may likewise have objected when he reached St. Louis in March 1827) and they waved aside talk of further business in 1828. These limitations led Ashley to abandon his trapping plans and held the adventure to a matter of routine supply.[6]

So far as this account is concerned, the significance of the episode lies in what it shows about the thinking of the Western Department. A partnership with Ashley might have been an opportunity for them to outflank the Columbia Fur Company and reach the mountains at once. Neither Crooks nor Chouteau accepted it, however. They did not want to share their eventual invasion of the field with anyone else. More importantly, their planning (it is impossible to say whose voice dominated the discussions) still followed traditional lines. Bernard Pratte & Company owned several expensive posts beside the Missouri. Was it not logical to use these—and new ones to be built higher up the river—as bases for any expansion into the mountains? But to do it, they first must remove the Columbia Fur Company, not simply outflank it.

Alone, neither company had been able to handle Mackenzie. Together, however, they could exert grinding pressures. The job of applying them fell to Crooks. When he left New York in April 1827 he took Emilie with him. She was pregnant again. To avoid the arduous stage trip over the mountains, they traveled by ship to New Orleans and there transferred to a river boat. While Emilie stayed with her family in St. Louis, Crooks continued to the St. Peter's, still by steamboat, for the Mississippi was spring-high.

Taliaferro was aboard the same vessel. He had just learned through William Clark of the fur company's long list of charges against him, and he was bristle-stiff with indignation. Crooks let him stew without comment; the accusations, which also involved the Columbia Fur Company, could wait until after Mackenzie had made up his mind.

Stuart met the steamboat at Prairie du Chien. Still ignoring Taliaferro, the two friends continued to the Columbia Fur Company's Lands End Factory near Fort Snelling. Talks there with Mackenzie produced nothing. They talked again at Prairie du Chien, where Rolette joined them. Still nothing, though Crooks was sure that during the winter Rolette had badly hurt the Columbia company's Mississippi trade and that the rivals were alarmed over developments on the Missouri. But Mackenzie knew he had high nuisance value and he played it for high stakes.

To complete Crooks's frustration, fever felled him for a week at Prairie du Chien. He was still shaky and uncomfortable when the whole group of them, dickering and yarning, reached St. Louis. He could not rest. He still had to wind up the sticky business of ejecting Stone and Bostwick, whose contracts had several months yet to run. Meanwhile the usual competition for furs went on pell-mell in spite of the approaching amalgamations. Astor was anxious to secure western beaver in order to hold up prices in New York, and was enraged when Pratte ignored the union scheduled for July and sold his company's 1825–26 harvest to a rival. Next several hatters from the hustling young towns along the Ohio River paid such high prices for muskrat that both Mackenzie and Pierre Chouteau raised their sights on that article beyond reason. Disgusted, Crooks withdrew his own offers. Having filled their small requirements, the hatters left. Prices sagged back and Crooks bought every muskrat pelt in the West on his own terms. In New York the following September Astor disposed of 550,000 muskrat skins at an average price of thirty-six cents each. "So many," he wrote Crooks in satisfaction, "have never in the world been sold in a single day"—and he still had 200,000 left.

By the middle of June the squeeze on Mackenzie at last seemed to be taking effect. Crooks was so sure of him, in fact, that he told Clark the American Fur Company was going to drop its charges against Taliaferro.[7] At once Mackenzie grew shy again. On June 22 he postponed a final answer for three more days. When the period expired, he did not appear. Crooks went to his hotel and was told Mackenzie was too sick to talk. But the next day he was well enough to spring fresh demands on the astounded negotiator.

What he wanted now was an annual salary of $1500 for himself, liberal treatment for his partners and engagés, continued trade on the St. Peter's, and the exclusive privilege of sending hunting parties to the Rocky Mountains. Worst of all, he insisted that the American Fur Company take over at exorbitant markups (20 per cent to 25 per cent) the goods which Collier and Powell had imported for the 1827–28 season. "This would have cost us $10,000 more than we ever dreamed of," Crooks reported to Stuart, "and in a general consultation with B. Pratte & Co. it was unanimously decided that war was preferable to Peace on such conditions. . . . They must take the consequences."

Mackenzie had overplayed his hand. He realized it and two weeks later backed down. Collier and Powell reduced the markup on their goods by one half. In return for a payment of $2000 a year to the Western Department, a bill footed by Rolette and Bailly, the Columbia Fur Company quit the Mississippi and the St. Peter's entirely. Under title of the Upper Missouri Outfit and under general supervision of Chouteau's Western Department they assumed full control of the Missouri trade from the mouth of the Big Sioux to the mountains. Kipp, Laidlaw, and Lamont of the original company survived the transfer with Mackenzie, but Tilton, Dudley, the two original "front men," Honoré Picotte, and a few others were jettisoned. Renville, the originator of the company, was put on a pension of sorts: he was allowed to settle at Lac qui Parle on the upper St. Peter's and carry on a small, quasi-independent trade through Stuart's Northern Department. All in all, it was a signal victory for Ramsay Crooks—or so it seemed before he began to calculate the costs.

By this time hot weather lay heavily on St. Louis. Still shaky with ague, he was eager to escape with Emilie, whose confinement was drawing close. Just as they were about to leave, Pierre Chouteau fell ill. In some self-pity Crooks took over, writing Astor, "Desire must, as it always has done, give way to duty." He oversaw the preparation of the outfits bound up both rivers, switched the Western Department's accounting procedures to match those used at Mackinac and in New York, and arranged for the inventories of the property the Columbia Fur Company was turning over to the amalgamated concern.

Local worries plagued him. Warfare between the Sacs and Sioux upset Farnham's expectations. Winnebagos murdered some people near Prairie du Chien, attacked two keelboats below Fort Snelling (according to Taliaferro, the Indians were drunk on whisky furnished by Rolette), and stampeded the lead miners near Galena into shambling flight. Only quick action by Cass, traveling with McKenney to make a treaty with the Wisconsin Indians, forestalled a general uprising. During the excitement lightning struck the company warehouse at Chicago, damaging quantities of merchandise. All these things Crooks had to take into consideration as he prepared for fall.

On Mackinac a man named Currie, who was supposed to come to St. Louis to help him, juggled his books, forged some drafts, and vanished. Astor cried out with pain; it was the fault of Stuart's negligence, he charged, and grew suspicious of everyone, especially of Oliver Bostwick. So Crooks had to comb the books of that erstwhile agent for irregularities.

He found none. Then buying began again. Caravans came in from Santa Fe; Ashley's pack train returned from the mountains; free hunters arrived with small parcels. Crooks bid on every skin offered for sale. Most of them he obtained. What he missed went to Wilson Price Hunt at a higher price than Crooks felt the fur was worth.

During the latter part of August, Emilie returned to New York—just in time, for another daughter was born early in September. Crooks had to stay behind until November. Even his return trip to see his new child was dragged out with business. In Cincinnati he bought tobacco; in Wheeling, saddles; in Pittsburgh, bar iron, nails, axes, gunpowder, flour, and one hundred barrels of whisky. He also ordered two new keelboats built. One was to be towed by steamboat to St. Louis; the other, loaded with gunpowder, would have to be manned. And that meant lining up a captain who could hire the necessary crew in the spring.

Pierre Chouteau stayed so ill throughout the winter that he and his relatives talked seriously of his withdrawing from the business and turning management of the Western Department over to Crooks. For family reasons, both General Pratte and Emilie urged the change. But Benjamin Clapp, who was the work horse of the New York office, had left the firm to go into business for himself, and Crooks had to linger in New York most of the summer to keep procedures flowing. By the time he was free, Chouteau was up and about and had reconsidered his decision.

It might have been better for all the western wilderness if Ramsay Crooks had moved to St. Louis. The new firm was truly his creation. Though Astor had furnished the necessary capital and the European commercial connections, it was Crooks's work that had brought to life America's first great commercial colossus. Through the new connections he had established with Auguste Chouteau, with Bernard Pratte & Company, and with the Columbia Fur Company, American Fur now dominated the Indian trade from Arkansas Territory on the south to the Canadian border on the north; from the Wabash River westward to the edges of the mountains and the sleepy Spanish towns of New Mexico. Only the northern Rockies remained outside the fist's great reach, and Mackenzie was preparing to strike there too. But the monster's own size was its undoing. To get what he wanted, Crooks had surrendered control of local affairs to the distant outfit. Feeling their sudden new strength, they swept the initiative from him and leaped wildly ahead, beyond his power to check or even to guide them.

That was the price of what for a little while had seemed to be his greatest triumph.

CHAPTER 24

Strangling the Missouri

Mackenzie prepared for the mountains with the same thrust of naked energy that Rolette, bewildered by it, once had called "necromancy." His first step was to divest himself of routine chores. Immediately after signing the contract with Crooks and Chouteau, he went up the Mississippi with a bargeload of goods he had already ordered for the St. Peter's. On September 12, 1827, he arrived at the Columbia company's Lands End Factory under the frowning walls of Fort Snelling.[1]

There he met Alexis Bailly, whom Crooks had appointed as the American Fur Company's representative for the inventory of merchandise and property the Columbia people were turning over to the buyers. Presumably Bailly would be careful, for he was to accept for his own outfits, at prices he himself agreed to, two thirds of the merchandise to be transferred.

They pawed first through the shelves at Lands End, then moved up the river to the posts at Traverse des Sioux, Lac qui Parle, Lake Traverse. The usual conglomeration was inside each one: Tomahawks, knives, earbobs, gorgets, hawk bells, beads, buttons, hats, tobacco, beaver and muskrat traps, bridles, rope, guns, lead, handsaws, candle molds, cloth of many kinds, kettles, knives—even paper, ink, and women's hose. Outside there were boats, canoes, oars, mules, horses. And finally the buildings themselves, their furniture, tools, utensils.

During the counting Mackenzie was abrupt and overpowering with Bailly. He had to push on across the plains by horseback to the Missouri and repeat this tedium at Fort Tecumseh. No, he did not have the original invoices on the tools, animals, carts, and harnesses he had acquired from settlers leaving the Red River colony. But the value was such and such. Put it down and don't waste time. Bailly swallowed, wrote, added, and reached a total of $12,409.75.

From Lake Traverse, Mackenzie rode two hundred and fifty miles through the towering blue days of fall to Fort Tecumseh, which lay southwest across the river from today's Pierre, South Dakota. A man named Papin represented the American Fur Company during that inventory. The total came to $14,543—the usual goods plus six hogs, 4266 muskrat skins of varying quality, 1500 buffalo robes, 850 pounds of beaver, and buildings valued at $400.

When the figures reached Crooks he was astounded. What on earth, he demanded by letter, had led Bailly and Papin to accept such inflated valuations? Bailly answered plaintively that he had been imposed on. He had not expected Mackenzie to "barter his good name for a paltry sum." He, Bailly, would make good the losses to the company out of his own pockets; he practically was doing that anyhow, since he was taking some of the St. Peter's posts and the bulk of the merchandise for his own trade. Crooks declined to hold him responsible for the rest, but he did tell Chouteau to effect some sort of readjustment with Mackenzie— who, obviously, awed all of them more than a little.

Mackenzie passed the winter at Fort Tecumseh, trading, hunting buffalo for sport on his fleet ponies, as he loved to do, and dreaming of the Rockies. The mountains were beginning to look farther and farther away. An unusually severe winter had made horses hard to obtain; even Cabanné down at Council Bluffs could not obtain any for him. Mackenzie still hoped, though. As spring neared, he prepared his plans. Late in the summer James Kipp was to take a work crew from the Mandan villages to the mouth of the Yellowstone, locate a site near good grazing and water, and start erecting the first of the advanced posts the St. Louis partners wanted as bases for their mountain expeditions. As soon as the ice left the river, Mackenzie himself would head downstream to meet the keelboat bringing in supplies for his trapping adventure and see whether he could not speed the vessel along the way. If luck held, he would reach the Mandan towns before Kipp left and they could go to the Yellowstone together. But one never knew what accidents might delay voyageurs dragging a laden keelboat up fifteen hundred miles of spring-swollen river. Kipp was to leave the Mandans on schedule, whether Mackenzie appeared or not.

Extraordinary delays did occur. Mackenzie met the keelboat near the Little Platte, across from where the army had built Fort Leavenworth the year before. What he heard from the bourgeois aboard upset his plans completely. On he went to St. Louis. The mountain expedition was likely to be postponed.

During the enthusiasm that had followed the combining of the companies, Pierre Chouteau, Jr., had let himself be talked into something he really did not believe in. Crooks had been particularly eager to rush a brigade into the Rockies as soon as spring allowed. In January he had sent Mackenzie a hundred beaver traps; a little later he had written Chouteau that he felt it highly important that Mackenzie lead the expedition in person. As the time neared for starting, however, Chouteau had given way to second thinking.

He did not want the Missouri trade slighted for what might be a wild-goose chase. He preferred to get beaver by trading rather than by sending out trappers. Certainly he did not feel there was wisdom in the company's hurrying green hunters into country they knew nothing about in a reckless effort to beat the veterans Smith, Jackson, and Sublette at their own game.[2] Accordingly he returned to his insistence that the company depend primarily on a series of posts high up the Missouri. These would not only capture the trade of the river, but with their wares could also draw in from the Rockies both the mountain Indians and the increasing numbers of free trappers who were prowling the crystal streams. Secondarily, and only if competition demanded, the forts could serve as bases from which to dispatch hunting parties and supply caravans. Before rushing off to the mountains, Mackenzie should see that these strategic upper Missouri forts were well located and strongly established.

Mackenzie agreed. He even consented without fuss to the adjustments Chouteau suggested concerning the inventory prices. Then, accompanied probably by Laidlaw and Lamont, he began the long toil back up the river. They smashed the keel on their boat, and the vessel grew balky as a mule. September was at hand before they reached the company's post at Council Bluffs. Old Jean Pierre Cabanné wagged his head dubiously as he waved them on. They were not likely to beat the ice to the head of the river at that rate.

It is not known when they reached Fort Tecumseh, where Laidlaw and perhaps Lamont were to winter. But Mackenzie was writing letters from there on December 26, 1827, to send to St. Louis by the regular once-a-winter express he had established the year before to keep the forts in touch with each other and with civilization. Messages from above had already advised him that Kipp and a construction crew had left the Mandan towns aboard the keelboat *Otter* as instructed. They had reached the mouth of the Yellowstone without accident and work was underway.

Many men would have let it go at that. Not Mackenzie. Shortly after dispatching his reports to Chouteau, he set out to check Kipp's work in person. He probably traveled with the express that had brought down the mail from *le pays du haut*, the upper country. It was customary for the messengers from above and below to meet at Fort Tecumseh, exchange dispatches, and retrace their steps. Unless the winter was open, the upper party traveled by dog sled, and this is probably how Mackenzie went. They may have taken short cuts; but if they traveled by ice, the distance to the Yellowstone was six hundred bitter miles. Almost surely he paused at the Mandan villages and again at the post which Kipp had built three years earlier at the mouth of White Earth River. Trade with the Assiniboins was flourishing at the latter spot, but even the Indians agreed that the new location at the mouth of the Yellowstone, a few dozen miles farther up the Missouri, might prove better.[3]

On Mackenzie pressed into the teeth of the North Dakota wind. The ice-dull Missouri, erratically twisting, wound toward him from the west. Where it neared the Yellowstone it dipped southward in a broad V. The Yellowstone entered from the south through vast bottomlands broken by clumps of bare trees and small brush which only intensified the light-dazzled glare of immeasurable emptiness. Three miles farther up the Missouri from this tremendous joining the fort builders had picked their site on the north bank, where a treeless prairie rolled between the river and a line of bluffs two miles away. East and west of the prairie, tongues of cottonwood and ash licked toward the stream. These furnished fuel and wood for construction. The prairie itself grew ample grass for horses —in good years enough to cut for hay. Across the river were more trees. Behind them loomed a section of the stark-white cliffs that here and there bordered the valley for the next hundred miles or more.

The workers already had begun a quadrangular stockade 220 by 240 feet, twenty paces or so back from the river. They were cutting pickets twenty feet tall, snaking them in across the ice, hewing them square, and setting them upright in a deep trench lined with stone. Braces shaped like big X's supported the pickets on the insides. In time a promenade would be laid on these braces completely around the interior, five feet beneath the top of the pickets. Although the walkway was intended primarily for defense, it proved welcome during the years for amusement: taking a breath of air or shooting at the wolves and coyotes that at sundown began to skulk around the walls for refuse.

Plans called for a main house inside the enclosure a story and a half high and seventy-eight feet long by twenty-four wide, weather-boarded, painted white with green window shutters, and fronted by a deep porch. There would be tight warehouses for goods and hides, and a bunkhouse for men. Additional hutches for storage and living were built against the stockade, under the walkway. Two stone bastions twenty-four feet square and thirty feet tall, whitewashed eventually and covered with pyramidal roofs, stood guard at opposite corners of the quadrangle.

Mackenzie nodded approval. This may be the time when, with appropriate toasts, he christened the place Fort Floyd, after a Virginia congressman who supported measures deemed beneficial to the West. And then, one evening while pinpoints of ice seemed to dance in the moonlit air outside, he sat down by the fire to listen to bloodcurdling tales spun by old Hugh Glass, who had reached the fort from the Rockies with a group of shaggy mountaineers just as construction had been starting in the fall.

Old Glass was a breeder of folklore in his own lifetime. Everyone in the West knew his most famous adventure: how he had been clawed by a grizzly and abandoned to die of his wounds; how, broken and bleeding and starving, he had crawled scores of miles for help at Fort Kiowa; how, after searching for those who had deserted him, he had given up his revenge when it lay in the palm of his hand. After that yarn, further tales about his scrapes with Indians seemed pallid. Anyway Mackenzie was more interested right then in a firsthand report of conditions in the mountains.

Glass could give it. After his bear troubles and a hairbreadth escape from the Aricaras in 1824, he had wandered off to New Mexico. In 1828 he landed at the summer rendezvous beside Bear Lake. What he told of events there confirmed the opinions Chouteau had voiced in St. Louis about the dangers of mountain commerce. Each group that came into the Bear Lake gathering added to the toll of disaster. Blackfeet had hit the whites here, there, everywhere—at least ten men dead and many wounded; close to a hundred horses stolen; goods and furs worth thousands of dollars lost to the red devils. Crow Indians had made off with another hundred horses belonging to a hopeful new partnership that Joshua Pilcher had formed out of the ruins of the old Missouri Fur Company. On top of that, snow water leaking into a poorly built cache had ruined most of the goods which Pilcher and his partners—Charles Bent, Andrew Drips, Lucien Fontenelle, William Henry Vanderburgh—had hoped to sell at the rendezvous in competition with the supplies offered by Smith, Jackson, and Sublette. As a result Pilcher's company went broke and the others marked up their merchandise sky-high.

The free trappers decided they could not stand that pinch at another rendezvous. The obvious way of easing it was find other sources. Someone said the American Fur Company had combined with the St. Louis Frenchmen and with the Columbia people, and was planning a push up the Missouri. That looked like the answer. Off went Hugh Glass and a small party, east through South Pass, north to the Bighorn and down it and the Yellowstone to the Missouri. There they found the fort builders and, perhaps, entered into some kind of hunting-trading agreement with them in order to live out the winter. And there Kenneth Mackenzie listened to Glass's proposal about jumping into the mountains.

The company's new plans would not allow that. But, Mackenzie said, the upper Missouri was not a difficult summer trip from the mountains.

Times were slack in hot weather. Could not the trappers spend their leisure coming down the Yellowstone, as Glass had done, to Fort Floyd and use their beaver to buy what they needed? In fact, he planned to build another post two hundred miles or so higher up the river during the summer and call it Fort Union, since it was going to be the point of union between the river and mountain trades. Glass agreed. This compromise suggested and the plans for Union formulated, Mackenzie returned to Fort Tecumseh. He would meet the keelboats there and take them back up the river in person.

During that same fall and winter other men were trying to tug the company toward the mountains. In October 1828 three of Pilcher's bankrupt partners—Charles Bent, Lucien Fontenelle, William Vanderburgh—rode into Council Bluffs and hit Cabanné for jobs leading trapping parties back among the same high peaks that had broken them only months before.

Cabanné, who had been advocating mountain trapping since 1824, was sympathetic. But he also knew that it was not Astor's way, or Pierre Chouteau's either, to trust outfits to men who could not put up enough money of their own to guarantee diligence. Besides, Cabanné had just spent $3500 buying up the goods of Jean Baptiste Roi and Joseph Robidoux in order to get rid of their competition at the Black Snake Hills farther south. He had promised Robidoux a thousand dollars a year for two years and Roi eight hundred to work for the company. A little before this another ancient of days, trail-blazing Etienne Provost, had come in from Taos, and some sort of trapping deal had been cooked up with him. That was about as much involvement as Cabanné cared to risk for the time being.

Still, he did not want this able trio to fall into the arms of competitors. He put Vanderburgh on ice for the company, until his talents should be needed, by outfitting him to trade with the Poncas, up in what is now the northeastern corner of Nebraska. Fontenelle and Andrew Drips (the latter of whom had evidently lagged behind in the mountains) borrowed money enough, perhaps from Cabanné, to purchase Pilcher & Company's nearby post at Bellevue and worked it through some sort of agreement with the Western Department. Bent, staying more independent, drifted on and the next spring entered the Santa Fe trade.

A much more solvent man who talked to Cabanné about the mountains that same October 1828 was Pierre D. Papin, perhaps the same Papin who had helped take inventory at Fort Tecumseh a year earlier. Papin had three thousand dollars to invest. But he also had a growth on his neck that was giving him fits and he decided abruptly to go to St. Louis and have it treated. There he slipped through the net—briefly. He fell in with revengeful Honoré Picotte, who had been dumped overboard by Mackenzie when the Columbia Fur Company joined the Astor combine. In association with a few other St. Louis Frenchmen, Papin and Picotte bought goods invoiced at $16,000 and jumped into vigorous competition with the company from Council Bluffs up to Fort Tecumseh. They were troublesome enough that in the fall of 1830 Mackenzie went through the standard routine of quieting them. He bought their posts and goods for $21,266.21. (This cleared their debts and gave each partner a year's profit of $700.) He also hired several of their clerks and engagés and put the three principal partners, Picotte, Papin, and Gabriel Cerré, to work at top salaries of $1000 a year each.[4] It might have been cheaper just to have let Picotte come along with the company in the first place.

The purchasing of Papin's company ended all but nuisance opposition along the lower Missouri. But it did not end the internecine fights of one company outfit against another, a problem that had plagued Crooks since the beginning of these semiindependent "dealerships" through which Astor preferred to operate. Cabanné complained regularly of David Mitchell and Joshua Palen, who ran one of Farnham & Davenport's outfits from the Grand River of north-central Missouri and south-central Iowa west to the Black Snake Hills. Those villains, Cabanné cried, were interfering with the Indians he had just acquired from Robidoux. They even crossed the Missouri to undercut him with the Otos and Pawnees. Using whisky, too, the scoundrels! Cabanné always insisted he did not use spirits; during the fight with Robidoux in 1827 he wrote Chouteau, "I have abstained from giving whisky. Did I do right or wrong?"

The accused were just as righteous. They did not trade with Cabanné's savages; they most certainly avoided whisky: "We are two well aware of the Trouble and inconvenience attending this Illigal practice." Rather, the Indians themselves bought the whisky from peddlers in the settlements inching up the river in Missouri and took it with them across the boundary.

This veered Palen and Mitchell off into complaints about another perennial problem: the government took no action about bootlegging to the Indians in the settlements or at the military posts, but raised the devil with honest traders inside the line who simply wanted to protect themselves. In fact, the government was always in their hair. Look at Andrew Hughes, agent for the Iowas. He showered favors on a trader nephew. Worse, he refused Palen and Mitchell a location at Grand River, but illegally allowed his own interpreter, Vance Campbell (another disgruntled ex-employee of the company) to build a house there. Was this either honorable or fair?[5]

Northward, Farnham was having his usual run-ins with stormy Joseph Rolette. In August 1829 the little Frenchman threatened lawsuits because Farnham's invasion of the upper Des Moines had cost him $3000 —Rolette's estimate. Crooks and Chouteau calmed him down on that score, but they had more trouble solving his clash with William Dickson of Mackenzie's Upper Missouri Outfit.

William Dickson was a half-Sioux offspring of the British trader Robert Dickson. He knew every foot of the plains that his mother's people roamed between Lake Traverse and Rivère au Jacques, the James River of eastern South Dakota. The year the Columbia Fur Company was founded, Dickson went to work for it as a clerk, and he followed Mackenzie into the American Fur Company. It will be recalled that under terms of the amalgamation, Rolette had promised to pay the Western Department $2000 a year over a specified period; in exchange for this the Western Department would pull Mackenzie's people entirely away from the St. Peter's. Almost at once Rolette refused to make the payments. Dickson, he roared, was sending runners into his territory on the sly. Other Missouri traders were coming up the Vermilion from the south to seduce his Indians. If Chouteau had no better control than that over Mackenzie's people, Rolette would not yield a cent. While uttering these complaints, he tried with characteristic deviousness to bribe Dickson into leaving Mackenzie and coming to work for him!

A band of Rolette's Sioux complicated matters by emigrating to the neighborhood of Whitewood Lake in eastern South Dakota. Rolette obtained a license for the area from Jonathan Bean, subagent for the Missouri Sioux, and followed. He built posts not only at Whitewood Creek but beside the Rivière au Jacques. Dickson thereupon flew into a passion equal to Rolette's.

An apparent digression here: the Upper Missouri Outfit each year imported engagés from Montreal. The outfit used more than 250 voyageurs at its posts and replaced from thirty to forty of them each year. The new ones were hired by Gabriel Franchère, the Astorian, who recently had taken W. W. Matthews' place as the company's Canadian agent. In 1832 Franchère hired a total of 106 hands, 57 for the Missouri and 49 for Mackinac. Several deserted at Lachine, more at Detroit, for he traveled through the lakes rather than by the classic route up the Ottawa. By the time he reached Mackinac, so many had vanished that Stuart could spare only forty-one for the West. He sent these in charge of a sharp-eyed agent through Green Bay to Prairie du Chien. There they should have been met by William Laidlaw, who regularly escorted the weary "pork eaters" across the plains.

This year Laidlaw was late, for he and Dickson, who went along to help, did not leave the Missouri until July 1. They met the pork eaters a day's march above Fort Snelling, not far from Rolette's (i.e. Bailly's) post at Traverse des Sioux. Rolette was supposed to sell the cavalcade the supplies it needed at cost at each of his posts along their route. But he did not contemplate the sort of requisition Laidlaw made at Traverse des Sioux.

The river was low and the pork eaters were having a dreadful time moving their barges. Eventually the men would have to take to land travel anyway, so why not here? From the simple-minded voyageur who was alone at Rolette's post, Laidlaw coolly commandeered six horses, four carts, and four harnesses—the whole worth $1000, Rolette later estimated. He was sure the "theft" was done with deliberate intent to injure his trade. For when four of his bargemen came along later with goods destined for South Dakota, they found no carts. Unable to move the merchandise any farther by boat, they sat on their thumbs through the winter. That cost $3000 in lost wages and lost trade.

Meanwhile Laidlaw and Dickson herded their pork eaters on through the blistering heat of the plains. Two tried to desert but were returned by Indians. Yet somewhere between Mackinac and the Missouri five others succeeded in disappearing, for only thirty-six had to be ferried over the river to the fort. The job done, Dickson began moving merchandise for his winter trade back onto the plains. To his fury, he discovered that certain of Rolette's traders had come all the way to the Missouri and were trying to inveigle the Sioux to visit Rolette's posts on Whitewood Creek to trade. Utterly outraged, Dickson rushed with an armed group to the post, seized another three thousand dollars' worth of goods, and impounded the material in one of his own stockades.

Rolette erupted. "If robbing and pillaging make the law," he wrote Astor, "I think we can make them suffer more than we have." No such clash could be allowed, of course. But how stop it? Stuart, who was Rolette's superior, and Chouteau, who ran the Missouri, had been trying for years without success to bring peace between the outfits. They had no better luck this time. But Crooks did. He brought the contenders together in the fall of 1833, sifted through the records since 1827, and finally awarded Rolette $2817. Rivals from the outside were not so miserable to handle—but this has gotten us years ahead of our story.

Kenneth Mackenzie, it will be recalled, had made his first visit to Fort Floyd, under construction near the Yellowstone, during January 1829. After talking to Hugh Glass about the commerce of the Rockies, he decided to build Fort Union, for linking mountains and river, two hundred miles farther up the Missouri. He began the effort himself, traveling the next December (1829) as high, perhaps, as the mouth of Milk River near today's Fort Peck Dam, Montana. He started construction in January.[6] Then something went wrong. Possibly he was driven away by Blackfeet Indians, who hated all Americans and would not allow even their British suppliers from the Saskatchewan to send trapping parties onto their land. More probably, though, he was simply learning the lie of the western country and realized just in time that the site was poorly chosen for the union he had in mind.

The information must have come from his own men. By January 20, 1830, he was able to report on the fall hunt to Chouteau, so scouts must have ridden in to inform him. The company's traders and trappers had been scattered far and wide through the country south of him. Provost was along the Yellowstone, bartering with the Crows. William Gordon and a small party were trapping along the Powder near Wyoming's Big Horn Mountains. William Vanderburgh was off somewhere—perhaps up the Bighorn River—with a major party of fifty hunters. As they roamed, all of them were impressed with a key fact of western geography: the Yellowstone River has the logical highway from the upper Missouri to the Rocky Mountains. An inevitable corollary followed. The logical fort for uniting river and mountains already existed—Fort Floyd at the mouth of the Yellowstone. If the company wanted a base for mastering the Blackfeet, its site would have to be found much higher up the Missouri than the Milk.

Abandoning the unfinished post, Mackenzie dropped back to the mouth of the Yellowstone. He renamed the big post there Fort Union, then continued downriver to St. Louis to report and to urge on the company several new ideas.

The boldest was for a steamboat. Such vessels plied with fair regularity as high as the new town of Independence in western Missouri and even a little beyond to the army's Fort Leavenworth. They seldom went higher. Alarmists cried that the upper Missouri—twisting, tumultuous, full of sandbars and snags—was unnavigable. Mackenzie did not believe it. In his opinion a shallow-draft steamer could ride the spring floods nearly two thousand miles to Fort Union.

If so, steam offered many advantages. A single vessel could haul as much tonnage as several keelboats, at a tremendous saving in wages. Each keelboat had to be hauled upward foot by foot by thirty or forty men straining on the cordelle. These crews, hired each spring in St. Louis, demanded advances in cash, rather than in the marked-up goods which the company used for paying off its men in the Indian country. Keelboats were slow; occasionally winter froze them in before they reached their destinations. They capsized easily; one sank with all its cargo shortly before Mackenzie presented his arguments to Chouteau. A steamboat would be less vulnerable. The greatest danger would be breakage of machinery. This could be overcome by carrying along a blacksmith and plenty of spare parts. Even initial cost need not be frightening. Mackenzie thought a ship ample for their purposes could be built for $7000.

Chouteau was resistant at first, but finally agreed to talk to engineers at the shipbuilding yards in Louisville and Pittsburgh, and then sound out Crooks and Astor for their opinions.

Forced to be content with that, Mackenzie started back up the river, initiating more projects as he traveled. He wanted a better post at the Mandan villages than the rebuilt lodges that had been serving ever since the Aricaras had forced the abandonment of Fort Tilton in 1824. So he paused at the earthen towns to instruct Kipp to build a new stockade outside the largest of the villages. The site they picked was three hundred paces below the town on the south bank of the river, on a bluff well away from the highest flood line. It was to be named Fort Clark, in honor of William Clark.

The Aricaras were still around and still ugly. In August, shortly before Mackenzie arrived, they killed three hunters belonging to a rival firm and made off with four packloads of goods. They pounced on Mackenzie's group, too, after first entertaining them in one of their lodges, pillaged them and subjected them to unspecified indignities. But they stopped short of murder. And there is a postscript. That same winter (1830–31) the American Fur Company trader among the Crees obtained so many buffalo robes—more than 3000—that he had to send for extra boats to transport the pelts. Just the same, everyone, including the neighboring Indians, was relieved when the tribe announced they were tired of the Missouri and were going to move to the Platte to be near their relatives, the Pawnees.

Other forces had to enter Mackenzie's calculations as he moved up the river. (This was the month, October 1830, that he bought out Papin in a deal consummated at Fort Tecumseh.) To control the price of beaver in New York, the American Fur Company had to stop the leakage of pelts going to its competitors in St. Louis. One method was to strike for the sources in the mountains, both through trade and trapping. Under pressure from Astor and Crooks, Chouteau swallowed his reluctance about mountain hunting and in April 1830 the Western Department sent off its first brigade under Andrew Drips, Lucien Fontenelle, and Joe Robidoux for the central Rockies.

Mackenzie sent off Vanderburgh from farther north. In spite of his adventures the winter before in the Yellowstone Basin, Vanderburgh was still green and reckless. He figured he could avoid Blackfeet by going up the Yellowstone and crossing what is now called Bozeman Pass to the Madison River, in the rich Three Forks country. But the Blackfeet caught him, killed one man, wounded two, and destroyed so many horses that he had to reel back and winter on the Powder. The pressure was on the mountains, nevertheless. Sensing its approach, Smith, Jackson and Sublette had sold out in the summer of 1830 to the Rocky Mountain Fur Company—Jim Bridger, Thomas Fitzpatrick, Milton Sublette (William's brother), Henry Fraeb, and Jean Baptiste Gervais. They were a rough, knowledgeable quintet, hard-schooled. The only way the American Fur Company could learn the geography and methods the others long since had mastered was to follow them wherever they went, camp beside them wherever they sat down to trap. Grimly the company began. Mackenzie had fresh horses sent to Vanderburgh from Tecumseh so that he could return to the attack as soon as the snow let him move in the spring of 1831. The company had money; it could afford delays and accidents. The rival company, heavily indebted to its suppliers, couldn't.

Controlling the Blackfeet might be decisive in the approaching struggle. Trade was a way to start—and there was at Fort Union the very man who might be able to perform the magic. He was Jacob Berger. A former employee of the Hudson's Bay Company, Berger had been trading for twenty years with the Blackfeet who visited the Saskatchewan posts. Conceivably Mackenzie had written friends in Canada asking for just such a man. Or perhaps Berger had wandered down across the border in the footless way traders had. In any event he agreed to make the dangerous trip. In January, 1831, off he went, accompanied by four men.[7] They traveled on snowshoes and probably carried their goods by dog sled.

They walked a biblical forty days, according to one account, and then were surrounded by a war party of Piegans, one of the confederated tribes of Blackfeet. Fortunately a chief named Assapoke recognized Berger. Assapoke called off his glowering tribesmen, the whites handed around a few presents, and the Indians escorted the intruders to their main camp. There, for twenty days, Berger doled out more of his paltry gifts and enumerated the advantages of making peace with the Americans. No trappers—the Piegans insisted on that. But they would like a handier source of merchandise than the distant Saskatchewan. Yet to go to Fort Union, in the heart of the land of their ancient enemies, the Assiniboins and Crees . . .

The whites would protect them with big guns, Berger said, and added a few sneers about courage. At last, toward the end of March, he persuaded ninety-two Piegan braves and thirty-two squaws to march with him in the usual Indian pandemonium to the fort. Mackenzie was delighted. He regaled the visitors with gifts and liquor, promised security against the Assiniboins, and said that the next fall he would send up a party to build a trading post at the mouth of the Marias River, a little short of Great Falls and within easy striking distance of the mountains. The conferences ended, he hurried downriver by keelboat with a load of pelts to learn whether or not the steamboat would materialize.

On reaching Fort Tecumseh he learned to his dismay that the steamer, named *Yellowstone,* was trying to come up but had been balked by sandbars near the mouth of the Niobrara, two hundred and fifty winding river miles below. Pierre Chouteau himself was aboard. He had just sent messages to Fort Tecumseh asking for horses to extricate the gentlemen of the party, and for two keelboats to lighten the steamer so that perhaps she could crawl over the bars and resume her trip.

Mackenzie ordered out a small skiff. Accompanied only by John F. A. Sanford, protegé of William Clark and since 1826 subagent for the Mandans, he took after the rescuers. They got there just in time. Lightering by means of the keelboats had succeeded. The *Yellowstone* thrashed over the bars, Chouteau decided against horseback riding, Mackenzie climbed aboard, and they finished the trip without incident.

She was a beauty. She had been built at Louisville during the winter, was 130 feet long and 20 of beam. Her hold was a capacious six feet in depth. She sported triple decks; her cabin was seventeen feet wide and contained "four lengths of berths." Since she was designed to draw less than four feet of water empty and only five and a half when loaded to seventy-five tons, she seemed to rise out of the water to majestic heights. Two smokestacks towered forward. The paddlewheel, eighteen feet in diameter, was set on the side. But she had cost $9950, more then 40 per cent above Mackenzie's estimate.

On June 19 the *Yellowstone* pulled into the Fort Tecumseh docks to a rattle of musket fire from the voyageurs and awed stares from the Sioux. As Chouteau was being escorted in style into the main building, he banged his head painfully on the low door beam. In a sense, the accident was symbolic. The old ways cramped the company's new style and were being swept aside. Kipp had already replaced the earthlodge trading house at the Mandan villages with new Fort Clark and was slated to be the builder of the post Mackenzie had promised the Blackfeet. Chouteau promised that in the spring the *Yellowstone* would start earlier from St. Louis and try to reach Fort Union, ending the incredible labors with the keelboats. Even Fort Tecumseh, threatened by the steady chewing of the river, was doomed. Chouteau authorized a new establishment a mile or so farther upstream, still on the west bank but half a mile from the water's edge, where no flood could reach it. It was to be a powerful place, big enough to house the hundred men who would gather during busy seasons when furs and buffalo robes were being assembled from the outlying posts and packed into bales for shipment.

After filling her hold with buffalo robes and with several live buffalo calves to exhibit as curiosities at Chouteau's mansion in St. Louis, the *Yellowstone* started downstream. Mackenzie returned to Fort Union. He made plans for Sam Tulloch to build Fort Cass at the junction of the Bighorn and Yellowstone in the summer of 1832. He also outfitted Kipp for an immediate invasion of Blackfoot country along the Missouri. In the fall forty-four men (some accounts say twenty-five) started dragging his large keelboat up the surging river.

Immediately the Assiniboins objected. From the beginning of the

Indian trade, all tribes had fought to keep whites from going to enemy nations with guns, powder, knives, and the good things of life in general. The Assiniboins had not been able to prevent the Blackfeet from reaching the Saskatchewan, but the Missouri was something else. If they had power to prevent, Mackenzie was not going to use it as an easy highway to their deadliest foes. So they threatened. Given time, they might have worked themselves up to an attack, perhaps on Kipp as he returned with his winter harvest.

Mackenzie gave them no time. He gathered the principal chiefs into his council chamber, befuddled them with flattery, gifts, and liquor, and persuaded them to promise peace. It was November 30, 1831, St. Andrew's Day, dear to Scots. Perhaps he was a little befuddled himself. Anyway, he presented the Assiniboins with an extraordinary document to sign.

> We send greetings to all mankind! Be it known unto all nations that the most ancient, most illustrious, and most numerous tribes of redskins, lords of the soil from the banks of the great waters unto the tops of the mountains, upon which the heavens rest, have entered into a solemn league and covenant to make, preserve and cherish a firm and lasting peace . . . conforming to all ancient customs and ceremonies, and observing the due mystical signs enjoined by the great medicine lodges . . . hereafter to live as brethern of one large, united, and happy family; and may the Great Spirit who watcheth over us all approve our conduct and teach us to love one another.

No Blackfeet were named in the treaty, though the Assiniboin chiefs were, and no Blackfoot scratched down an X. Instead, Mackenzie signed for them, which leads to the presumption that none were about when Mackenzie went through the due mystical signs. Well, a man did as he must. And it might work. He wrote Chouteau on December 11 that he expected both nations to ratify the treaty. "If firm and durable it will be of great importance to this district."

When Kipp reached the Marias River where he was to build, waiting Piegans swarmed around him, a hundred lodges strong, before his men could unload the keelboat. His outnumbered party could not work with such a mob in the way. He persuaded the chiefs to leave for seventy-five days. Within that grace period, his voyageurs, working literally for their lives, erected a bunkhouse, storeroom and trading store surrounded by pickets twenty-five feet tall. They called the stockade Fort Piegan. Small cannon were in place: now let the Indians come.

They did, loaded with furs. By adding water, ginger, red pepper and black molasses to a barrel of high wine (thirty-two or -three gallons of almost pure alcohol), Kipp concocted two hundred gallons of what he called Blackfoot rum. (The Blackfeet liked the West Indies rum brought them by the Hudson's Bay Company.) In ten days he collected 2400 beaver skins. He had his troubles, though. The Bloods, another tribe of Blackfeet, did not like this commerce with Americans. Egged on perhaps by British traders, they arrived to put an end to it.[8] Kipp holed up inside the stockade. He did not want to start a war that would end all chances of wooing the Blackfoot nation. But after eleven days of siege he ran out of water. One tale says that he then used the rest of his alcohol to pacify the Bloods; another, that he loaded a cannon with an extra-heavy charge of grapeshot, blasted apart a nearby cotton-wood, and terrified the enemy into a change of heart. Be the truth as it may, the Bloods calmed down and by season's end Kipp had collected 6450 pounds of beaver.

Elsewhere liquor was hard to find. The unhappy Mandans and Yankton Sioux blamed Mackenzie for their thirsts. Actually, Mackenzie said, it was the fault of the Mandan's subagent, John Sanford. "I am neither able nor willing to bear the onus of debarring my old friends of their dearest comfort," he wrote David Mitchell, now trading among the Mandans; ". . . they should be made clearly to understand, that their magnanimous Father would drive me from the river, and I could no more have the satisfaction of trading with them, if I neglected to conform to his orders."[9]

Otherwise trade went on as usual. Small parties were sent from the company's half-dozen principal posts to whatever locales offered prospects, principally in buffalo robes and even buffalo tongues, which were smoked and shipped by the thousands to gourmets in cities along the Mississippi. (Because of transportation difficulties, the British traders on the Canadian plains did not want buffalo hides; the American Fur Company did and that is one reason they were able to pull the Blackfeet out of the British orbit.) White hunters could kill buffalo for hides not at all and for meat only with the Indians' permission; if it was denied, the posts had to buy their jerky from the savages. In mild weather game was hard to find. The Indians were generous with permissions then. But the white hunters had to roam three or four days from the posts, carrying wood for cook fires on their packhorses, since buffalo chips were hard to locate under the prairie snow. If they had poor luck (and at times every winter they did), there was a tightening of belts at the stockades and short diets of corn soup.

At "navy yards" where trees grew, boat builders whipsawed lumber into planks for constructing outsize Mackinaw barges that could carry fifteen tons of pelts each to St. Louis. Such craft never returned upstream; they were knocked apart in the city and the lumber sold. The consumption of wood along the river was fantastic. Even horses demanded it. Workers chopped cottonwoods into three-foot lengths, thawed the succulent bark so that the frozen edges would not cut the animals' mouths, stripped it from the logs with draw knives, and used the pieces to supplement the scanty hay harvested from the bottomlands during fall. The bared logs were then stacked beside the riverbank to fuel the insatiable steamboat. Seeing the havoc which the vessel's appetite caused to their groves, the Indians began exacting payment for wood too. And every chance they found, they stole horses belonging to the whites.

There were accidents. On January 19, 1832, after a good day's trade among the Oglala Sioux on the Cheyenne River, Thomas Sarpy's two engagés folded the fresh buffalo robes and passed them over the counter in the store to their bourgeois, who stacked them in the storeroom behind. Somehow the men knocked a lighted candle off the counter into a fifty-pound keg of gunpowder. The explosion killed Sarpy (Papin later wanted a lock of his hair for a souvenir but it was entirely burned off), destroyed three buildings, and scattered goods far and wide. Amazingly, the engagés lived. The Indian soldiers, as tribal policeman were called, kept looters away that night, collected the salvageable merchandise the next day, and turned it over to another company man who was trading with a village of Cheyenne Indians fifteen miles away.

Two weeks later at Fort Union, while everyone was asleep, embers fell from the fireplace between the floor cracks in clerk Chadron's room. Someone, waking choked and coughing in dense smoke, opened the door for air. A high wind was blowing. In came "a rush of air," Mackenzie wrote, "which fanned it to an almost immediate & unconquerable flame." Within minutes every building along the west wall of the stockade was ablaze. Mackenzie listed the damage:

> Trunks of wearing apparel, all the buffalo tongues of the year, near a thousand saw planks, the labour of two men for six months, stored to season in the lofts, rifles, pistols, white beaver skins . . . a cellar full of small kegs &c &c all fell sacrifice to the devouring element.

Fortunately the wind was from the east. The men chopped away communicating pickets and by dawn the fire had burned itself out. Hastily rooms were prepared for the homeless and the next day 170 trees were felled to start a new west wall. The half-starved horses took five days to haul the timbers in over the snow. Not until they were erected could the slow work of rebuilding inside go on in safety.

All in all, it was a spectacular beginning to the critical year of 1832, a year that no one in the Indian trade, Ramsay Crooks least of all, would ever forget.

CHAPTER 25

The Spasms of Change

Many things went wrong in the Western Department in 1832. Kipp's men at Fort Piegan were afraid to stay behind among the Blackfeet when their bourgeois started for Fort Union in the spring with three tons of beaver pelts and other furs. He let them come along and while they were absent, Indians burned the place down.

On learning of the destruction, Mackenzie ordered David Mitchell to replace the structure. Eight days upstream, Mitchell's keelboat hit a snag and sank with its cargo. One engagé and one Indian drowned. Mitchell made his way back to Fort Union. A packhorse party was hurried ahead with token goods to keep the waiting savages happy. Mitchell loaded a new boat and on June 19 started again. Foot by toilsome foot the engagés dragged the awkward craft between the crowding, fantastically eroded bluffs to what Mitchell thought was a better site six miles above the Marias. There he supervised the building of a post forty-seven paces square that he named Fort Mackenzie. The company was still in business with the Blackfeet.[1]

Southwest in the Rockies the company's caravans were late, as usual, in reaching the summer rendezvous. This was disastrous to business, which was already attracting several hungry new adventurers—Alexander Sinclair, Gantt and Blackwell, Wyeth, Bonneville. William Sublette, supplier for the Rocky Mountain Fur Company, reached the gathering first and skimmed the cream from both the Indians and the free trappers.

Afterward, competition forced the brigades to jockey for position with each other north into Blackfoot country. A party of those Indians under

Eagle Rib caught William Vanderburgh and a few men away from camp, scouting the land. One story says Eagle Rib was carrying dispatches from Fort Union to Vanderburgh and that some edgy white pulled his trigger without waiting to talk. Warren Ferris, Vanderburgh's clerk, says the Indians ambushed the group. Anyway, it was quick and costly. Vanderburgh and one trapper were killed, Ferris wounded. The Blackfeet stripped Vanderburgh's flesh from its skeleton and threw the bones into a river. At about the same time other Blackfeet took on another American Fur Company party under Andrew Drips, slew one man and wounded several. Those abrupt disasters canceled Mackenzie's half-formed plans to push on up the Missouri to Three Forks and build still another post there.

Matters were equally unsettled in the company's Mississippi Departments. Lead miners crowding into the Rock River country of northwestern Illinois for some years had been crying protest to their state government and to Washington over the continued presence of Sac and Fox Indians in the district. The Indians complained just as bitterly about the miners.

Justice lay on everybody's side. Certain Sac-Fox chiefs had sold the Illinois lands to William Henry Harrison in 1804, but Harrison's handling of the bargain was so tricky that the chiefs back home refused to acknowledge the treaty. After the War of 1812, however, the bulk of the tribe consented to a second treaty (1816) which confirmed the cession of 1804.

When whites attempted to move onto the twice-ceded lands, certain Indians repudiated the second document. They trotted out the two oldest Indian arguments in the book: they had not understood the 1816 treaty when signing it, which was quite likely; and besides it was morally wrong to sell land wherein lay the bones of their ancestors. Years of this sort of talk left the whites impatient. Twice ought to be enough for anyone's understanding. Furthermore, they said, Americans also were attached to their ancestral homes, but having sold the land at an agreed price, they had the grace to move. Not the Sacs. They clung stubbornly to their ancient village of Saukenuk and its fertile cornfields near the mouth of Rock River.

During the arguments game disappeared from northwestern Illinois. To secure skins for their own use and pelts to swap for necessary merchandise, the Sacs and Foxes had to cross the Mississippi and roam deep into Iowa. If they realized where the boundary ran that divided their lands from the Sioux, established at Prairie du Chien in 1825, they ignored it. Soon the tribes were at war. Thus a three-way row had shaped up—the Sacs and Foxes and allied Iowas and Winnebagos against the United States (the Winnebagos were under similar pressures to leave Wisconsin), and these same tribes against the Sioux and their allies, the Menominees. The unrest spread across the Missouri to set off Otos against Pawnees, and even Sioux and Mandans against Aricaras.

The troubles were further twisted by the Indians' habitual insistence on saving face. A man who felt injured or degraded soothed his vanity by hitting whoever was handy, not necessarily the one who had hurt him. This of course opened the way to endless retaliations. Early in 1828, for instance, a Fox half-blood chief named Morgan was prevailed on in St. Louis to sell to the United States the lead mines at Dubuque, Iowa, near the west bank of the Mississippi, several miles upstream from Rock River's mouth. When Morgan returned home, the tribe chided him angrily and refused to ratify the agreement. Feeling belittled, Morgan and his followers asserted their manhood by killing one Sioux woman and taking another prisoner. Sioux warriors pursued the Fox raiders, lost them, found some innocent Sacs instead, and satisfied themselves by killing a chief and his wife and stealing several horses.

Retaliations continued until the hunters of both tribes were afraid to leave their camps except in large bands that turned inevitably into war parties. The fur traders were distraught. Late in 1828 one of Farnham's winterers, David Mitchell (not yet transferred to the Upper Missouri Outfit) started several Sac hunters toward their beaver and muskrat grounds and went along to keep them at work. In spite of his vigilance some of the younger braves spotted an unguarded Sioux camp and seized a young woman. Fearing a Sioux counterattack, the rest of the Sac camp fell into panic and scurried for home "without," Mitchell reported in despair, "making one Skin."

Rolette's Sioux outfits suffered equally—$20,000 worth, the little Frenchman groaned to Chouteau. Unless the United States sent in soldiers to enforce peace, "I am afraid I will not be able to save myself." Noting how drastically the returns from all the Mississippi outfits were declining, J. J. Astor carried the matter on August 22, 1829, to Andrew Jackson's Secretary of War, John H. Eaton. "The welfare of the Indian nations so consistent with humanity and the character of our Government," he intoned, "will I have no doubt excite prompt and efficient measures." Stuart wrote Eaton to the same effect, and W. B. Astor urged Chouteau to hound William Clark in St. Louis until be acted: "'As our Mr. Crooks says 'give him no peace day or night.'"

After consulting Indian delegations in St. Louis, Clark called for a solemn meeting between Sac-Fox and Sioux representatives at Prairie du Chien in the early spring of 1830. The War Department then decided to swell the affair into a grand council of all the tribes in the area. Needing more time, the commissioners ordered the date postponed until July. No one notified the Foxes of the delay. Supposing that a precouncil truce prevailed, their delegations started toward Prairie du Chien according to the original timetable. Some opportunistic Sioux, arguing that the truce had been delayed along with the council, fell on an unprepared group of seventeen and killed all but one.

Clark mollified the outraged Foxes by "covering the dead" with a thousand dollars' worth of presents, and the July council convened under the watchful scrutiny of four companies of infantry. After long harangues the various tribes sold to the United States all their interests in a wide strip of land in Iowa running from the Mississippi to the Missouri. Part of this acquisition was to become a reservation for the Winnebagos, who in 1829 had alienated their eight-million-acre homeland east of the Mississippi and now needed somewhere to go. The rest of the Iowa cession was to become "neutral land." There each tribe could hunt without violating anyone else's territory. Wishful believing: by now animosities went beyond frictions over hunting. The next July (1831), for example, a band of Sacs came across a party of Sioux and Menominees—men, women, and children—sleeping off a drunk on an island near Prairie du Chien. They tiptoed in, knives drawn, killed twenty-five and wounded many more before the few survivors managed to scramble to their canoes.

Pressure from the whites mounted concurrently. Yielding to some of it, the Sacs offered, at the Prairie du Chien conference of 1830, to sell the Dubuque lead mines. The price was high—an annuity of $32,000 for fifty years and the payment of the tribe's debt to traders Farnham and Davenport of the American Fur Company.

Since 1824 the two partners had advanced credits to the Indians of $137,768.62 in marked-up merchandise. They had collected furs valued, by themselves, at $88,498. Their uncollected debts thus amounted to $49,270.62. By trade standards the figures were honest. Both men commanded good reputations even among Indian agents hostile to the company. The Indians acknowledged the debts. The savages had reason to be grateful. During the wars with the Sioux they seldom hunted and, in Farnham's words to Pierre Chouteau, ". . . if I had withdrawn the accustomed credits from them many must have perished with cold or Hunger."

There was nothing new about inserting provisions for debt payments into Indian treaties, although the techniques of fortifying claims had been highly refined by 1830. The Winnebago cession of 1829 had authorized $23,532.28 to Rolette, the Green Bay traders, and other eager creditors of the tribe. Clark thought the Farnham-Davenport claim might also be allowed, especially after the traders agreed to accept $40,000 in full settlement of their $50,000 claim. Amounts in general were so high, however (the annuities demanded by the Indians as well as the price set by the traders), that the government took no action.

Pressures from the whites meanwhile continued. Each winter while the Indians were hunting in Iowa, white squatters moved into Saukenuk, appropriated lodges, threw down fences, and usurped the cornfields, claiming full right to do so under the treaties of 1804 and 1816. For a time the government ejected the invaders (though it too claimed title to the area), but in 1830 lost patience with the Indians and declared the lower Rock River lands open for sale to qualified citizens. Traders Davenport and Farnham bought two thousand acres. The aging chief Black Hawk considered this an unfriendly gesture and was not mollified when they told him that he and his family could continue to live on the purchase.

The famous chief was then about sixty years old. Romanticists for the past century and a quarter have resolutely ignored mountains of evidence indicating that he was a vain, stubborn, quarrelsome old man, completely obtuse to the flow of history against his race. A younger chief, Keokuk, realizing the hopelessness of fighting, worked for compromises and ever since has been denigrated as an appeaser. Without question Black Hawk, by refusing Keokuk's advice, led his tribe into unnecessary misery. In his own memory he had defeated the Americans during the War of 1812 and he was convinced he could do it again. His belligerent supporters were called the British Band because of the frequent visits they made to the British at Malden for presents and advice, not all of it wholesome. A would-be prophet among the Winnebagos fueled the smoldering fires with ecstatic visions of victory.

The Winnebagos were proving recalcitrant about moving across the river to their new reserve.[2] Persuading himself that both they and the British would send him aid in the event of war, Black Hawk grew increasingly defiant. Although in 1831 he promised to stay away from Saukenuk, in April 1832, at the end of the winter hunt, he crossed stubbornly back into Illinois. Instantly General Atkinson marched out of Jefferson Barracks near St. Louis to drive him away. A thousand lead miners enlisted as militiamen under rambunctious Henry Dodge, and the Black Hawk "War" was on.

(Another parenthesis here. Black Hawk's "invasion" of Illinois terrified the frontier. Anything that might inflame the other tribes—whisky, for instance—was nervously rooted out. With singularly poor judgment, Rolette and Joseph Renville nevertheless started sixteen kegs of high wine toward the St. Peter's in two merchandise barges commanded by the veteran traders Hazen Mooers and Louis Provancelles. Informers sent warnings to Fort Snelling. Taliaferro was not about, but the commanding officer, Captain William R. Jouett, and Lieutenant Jefferson Vail rushed forth to intercept the liquor at Lake Pepin. There was a bit of a scuffle with the twelve engagés; afterward some of the merchandise, left uncovered, was damaged by weather. The American Fur Company and Renville promptly sued Jouett and Vail, contending mightily that the Mississippi was not Indian country but a public highway, and that Mooers and Provancelles had not intended to give the liquor to the Indians. This time, however, the Supreme Court of Michigan held in favor of the defendants, a legal upset against the company that constituted something of a milestone.[3])

The Black Hawk "War" actually amounted to little more than a skillful flight by the Indians and a bumbling pursuit by the Americans. Winnebago help did not materialize. Belatedly realizing that he had counted his resources too soon, Black Hawk drifted with his hundreds of men, women, and children through the thickets and swamps of Rock River Valley toward the Wisconsin line. Pursuit gathered. He was about ready to give up when, a little downstream from modern Rockford, he and forty warriors saw a chance to surprise a militia unit under Isaiah Stillman. Unable to resist temptation, they fell on the green whites, killed eleven, and terrified the others into abject flight. Heartened by the victory, the Indians chopped off the heads, limbs, and genitals of the fallen, dug out their hearts, drank blood, and changed their mind about surrendering. After this there was no hope for lenience, as they probably sensed.

The shock of the "massacre" brought volunteers pouring into the Illinois militia. In Washington Andrew Jackson ordered fresh troops under General Winfield Scott to sail through the Lakes to Chicago, march into the field, and end this foolishness. The numerical odds against Black Hawk were now utterly impossible and help account for the mists that have since dimmed sight of the bullheaded chief's share of responsibility for the inevitable end.

Cholera came briefly to the Indians' help. The disease, which devastated much of the Eastern United States during the summer of 1832 (1400 people died in New York in two weeks) caught up with Scott's command as it entered Lake Huron. He had to halt some of his ships near Detroit. The rest reached Chicago on July 11. There fifty-eight of two hundred cases died in seven days. But the thousands of other soldiers and militiamen already marching across Illinois were enough to handle the Indians.

Hoping desperately to regain the Iowa wilderness, Black Hawk fled through the beautiful Four Lakes country where Madison now stands, fought a delaying skirmish that enabled his women and children to cross the Wisconsin River with the men, and after a hungry, panicked fragmentation of his band in the timber, he reached the Mississippi near the mouth of the Bad Axe, above Prairie du Chien. An armed ship patrolled the river. Enemy Indians lined the banks. The debacle was brief, bloody, and complete.

General Scott moved his troops to Rock Island to dictate the peace. George Davenport was there to press his firm's claims. Russell Farnham was absent. Throughout the summer both men had worked grueling hours to keep the troops supplied; at the end of the fighting, Farnham had hurried far up the Des Moines River to restore his paralyzed trade. Before he could return or the Indians be assembled, cholera struck the troops once more. Cold rains sluiced the tight-packed tents. Men screamed and groaned. Davenport wrote his partner on September 2:

> our onse helthey Island is now a Buring Ground more than one sixt of the troops stationed here have died during the last 6 days the disease is yet Raging I am not verry well if I do not see you again God Bless you, my account you will find correct I now [know] you will do Justice.

A week later, writing Pierre Chouteau, he recommended as a "remede" two tablespoons of salt in a gill of vinegar to "stop the puking." General Scott felt temperance was a better preventative. Any soldier caught drunk was forced, on sobering, to dig a grave as a reminder—it was always used by someone. Stern sanitation and a shift of the tents to small groups on the Iowa bluffs probably helped more. The disease dwindled and negotiations began. The United States commissioners exacted from the Sacs and Foxes six million acres along the Mississippi border of Iowa, including the Dubuque mines, paying in return $22,000 a year for twenty years. They also agreed to add $40,000 to the first payment so that the Indians could meet their debt to Farnham and Davenport.

Joshua Pilcher, acting agent for the Indians, objected to the payment and threatened to go to Washington about it—"an evil Genious equell to the Cholra," Davenport growled. Street wrote Clark that this treaty and another with the Winnebagos "are well calculated to place the whole Indian frontier under the surveilance of the . . . A. Fur Company." In spite of the protests, however, the payments were allowed by the Senate.[4]

Farnham returned from the wilderness after negotiations had ended. He congratulated Davenport and continued to St. Louis to ready more goods and see his wife Susan, whom he had married three years before. On the morning of October 23, he was seized with violent cholera cramps. Two hours later he was dead. His partner, George Davenport, who had feared to die of the disease, lived until July 4, 1845, when he was murdered by robbers.

During the Sac-Fox troubles an uneasy Congress was reviewing the entire Indian trade. Beginning in 1828 and continuing through the fall of 1831, pages of data were assembled about wages, prices, expenses, profits, methods, quantities and kinds of merchandise used, the effects of the tariffs, and so on. Both Astor and his son testified, as did Lewis Cass, William Clark, Farnham and Davenport, other traders, and many

Indian agents.[5] The liquor problem was especially scrutinized. After nearly every agent had recommended total prohibition as the only solution, Congress decided to act. A clause banning liquor absolutely from the Indian country, even if carried by Indians, was inserted into a bill designed primarily to establish an office of Indian Affairs headed by a full-fledged commissioner of its own.

The company took alarm. As usual, it began crying out about the Hudson's Bay Company. A little earlier, in 1829, William Astor had been rebuffed when he proposed to the Canadian firm that both of them discontinue liquor along the border. The English refusal gave Robert Stuart a talking point that he used vociferously every time he wanted whisky for Fond du Lac. When the company decided to establish three new posts west of Red River, he appealed to Governor Porter of Michigan for permits to take two barrels annually to each post—the same amount authorized for each fort east of Red River.

> I make the present request but thro' sheer necessity—for the British Hudson Bay Company carry in large quantities all along our frontier: and unless our people have *a little* . . . we will not only lose the trade but all the influence we have hitherto managed to retain over the frontier tribes.

Liquor in amounts the Indians never before had dreamed of had been a major factor behind Mackenzie's instant success with the posts on the upper Missouri, and the company had no intention of letting the advantage go. While the proposed prohibition bill was under discussion, J. J. Astor wrote William Ashley, former fur trader and new congressman from Missouri:

> Our new posts on the Missouri river above the Mandans must yield to the superior attractions of our opponents, unless the government will permit us like them to use spiritous liquors; and the friendly relations we have at last succeeded in establishing with the Blackfeet (those inveterate enemies of the Americans) at so much expense and personal hazard, must inevitably be destroyed and the British be restored to the unlimited control they have heretofore exercised over these Indians.

Crooks alone seemed to feel reluctant to join the chorus. He preferred to ask the State Department to approach the British government in the hope that it too would issue an edict against alcohol and end the wretched problem entirely. Any such approach was likely to take a long time, however, and he reluctantly promised Chouteau to visit Washington and use what influence he had to wring permits from Ashley and Lewis Cass, the new Secretary of War following John Eaton's withdrawal during the Peggy O'Neill scandals. But he warned Chouteau not to be greedy (the italics are Crooks's): "Don't tell me how much *you would like to have,* but what will be required for *protection,* & for *that only."*

None of the maneuvers worked. As Crooks explained matters later, Ashley went along with the administration's measure because he was a dutiful Jackson man and Cass because he "is a temperance Society man in every sense of the word." On July 9, 1832, the bill became law.[6] Stricken by the upset, W. B. Astor moaned to Chouteau that the British would emerge triumphant, American prestige on the frontier would collapse. But, "if the executives will be blind to the real interests of the country I fear we cannot enlighten them."

Chouteau meanwhile was engaged in a more exciting adventure. On March 26, 1832, he boarded the *Yellowstone* in St. Louis for an epochal attempt to reach Fort Union by steamer.[7] Along with the dry goods in the ship's hold sloshed 1500 gallons of alcohol, duly authorized by William Clark as intended for the company employees. Another batch would come later. (The amounts were average. The year before, 1831, Clark had authorized 2766 gallons for keeping 217 men happy.) The military commander at Fort Leavenworth passed the ship without question and the *Yellowstone* belched and thundered on past Cabanné's post at Council Bluffs, on past the Niobrara—and stuck again in low water a little below the mouth of White River.

Some of the ship's passengers, mostly engagés and trappers, walked on up to the new post that had been built during the winter to replace Fort Tecumseh. Mackenzie and Kipp, who had reached the place on April 27 with nine Blackfeet Indians and 11,000 pounds of beaver and who had been waiting a month for the steamer, rushed down with a keelboat. The delay proved minor; the *Yellowstone* extricated herself and plowed on, reaching the new fort on May 31. Chouteau was given a noisy welcome; and with finer liquor than raw high wine the new establishment was christened Fort Pierre in his honor.

After four days of celebration, checking returns, and listening to local problems—Indians had just stolen every horse at the boat-building yards upstream; Frederick LaBoue had killed François Querrel by stabbing him seven times during an argument—he ordered the steamer on. Floods from melting snow in the Rockies gave a second lift to water levels and the vessel reached Fort Union without incident. It loaded aboard 700 packs of buffalo robes and beaver, squirmed around to point downstream, took on another 600 packs at Fort Pierre, and reached St. Louis early in July. The trip was so successful that the company ordered a second steamer, the *Assiniboine,* built along the same lines the next winter. Crooks wrote congratulations from New York. Astor added his from Europe, whither he had returned in June for a brief visit.

One theme was common to the many stories about the adventure: the Indians were so impressed by "the *Fire Boat* that walked on water"

(*New England Magazine*, September 1832) that the Hudson's Bay people would lose the border trade. Out in the wilderness, however, the winterers, both company men and opponents, still wanted alcohol.

A troublesome new opposition had arisen the year before, the firm of Valois and LeClerc. The more aggressive of the partners, P. N. LeClerc, had been an American Fur Company clerk at Fort Union during the post's early days. Why he left does not appear, but he was intent on damaging his ex-employers as severely as he could from Council Bluffs north into South Dakota. He had one advantage: the subagent for the Sioux, Jonathan Bean, whose headquarters were at Fort Lookout a score of miles above the White River, was his friend. Company traders grumbled among each other that Bean actually told the Sioux to deal with Valois and LeClerc rather than with the Upper Missouri Outfit. Like everyone else the new firm used liquor, presumably for its men. On July 12, 1832, Valois and LeClerc received a routine permit from William Clark for 262 gallons to care for thirty-two engagés for one year. To guarantee the legitimate use of the liquor they posted a bond of $3000.

On July 19 Pierre Chouteau applied for and received a second batch of permits. These authorized the company to take into the wilderness 1072 gallons for ninety-four men; bond, $10,000. The stuff was shipped in thirty-four barrels—twenty-eight aboard the *Yellowstone*, which was making a second trip as high as Council Bluffs, and six aboard a keelboat she was towing for Cabanné. Cabanné himself, now sixty years old, was aboard the *Yellowstone*. At some point well along the way the steamer cast off the keelboat, which proceeded by cordelle.

Though no one in Missouri yet knew it, the act of July 9, 1832, had made all this whisky toting illegal. Clark did not hear of the new law in St. Louis unofficially until August 16; officially, not until August 28. He did not send out formal notices to his agents until September 11. There is absolutely no evidence that word of the ruling had reached Fort Leavenworth on August 2, when the *Yellowstone* paused there for her routine check.

In May there had been no objection to the 1500 gallons of spirits carried by the steamboat. In August, Lieutenant J. Freeman, acting under orders of the commanding officer, searched the ship, found the twenty-eight barrels, and confiscated them. When the keelboat appeared on August 5, Freeman also confiscated her six barrels. Later he justified his action not by referring to the act of July 9, 1832, but to that of May 6, 1822, wherein army officers were given the right to search for liquor on mere suspicion. As for the permits, he snapped, without citing evidence, it was well known that the American Fur Company's exemptions were in general fraudulently obtained and grossly abused.

On August 6, 1832, *after* the seizures from the American Fur Company, along came P. N. LeClerc in the keelboat *Atlas,* carrying 262 gallons. Mixed with LeClerc's liquor and merchandise were annuity goods consigned to Jonathan Bean's Sioux agency at Fort Lookout. Lieutenant Freeman accepted LeClerc's permit from William Clark and waved the boat on without molestation.

A suspicion that someone was out to "get" the company becomes unavoidable. One name that suggests itself, quite without the support of evidence, is A. G. Morgan. Morgan was the sutler at Fort Leavenworth. He traded with the Indians in a small way on the side, and in 1832 furnished Valois and LeClerc with considerable financial backing. If LeClerc were able to carry alcohol into the wilderness and the American Fur Company were not, the advantages to the new opposition were obvious.[8]

His alcohol intact, LeClerc toiled triumphantly on toward John Dougherty's Indian agency at Bellevue, some two hundred and fifty river miles distant. Along the way he encountered four deserters from Cabanné's post rowing downstream in a small boat. He hired three of them. They were aboard his keelboat when he put in at Dougherty's agency on September 2.

Cabanné was there on business. When he saw the deserters, he ordered LeClerc to send them ashore. LeClerc gave certain suggestions to the choleric old trader (in his letters about the affair, LeClerc keeps referring to his opponent as "the old man") about where he could go. Cabanné thereupon rushed aboard with drawn pistol, took the men, and locked them in a shed—not very securely. They escaped and returned to LeClerc. The next morning Cabanné came after them. This time the old man pulled his pistol on LeClerc. Agent Dougherty separated them and got Cabanné ashore. One of the deserters went with him. The other two stayed defiantly with LeClerc.

Cabanné returned to his two-storied, deep-porched house a few miles upstream. When LeClerc followed about noon on September 5, traveling carefully along the river's opposite bank, Cabanné bawled at him across the water to send the two deserters over. You come get 'em, LeClerc bawled back, no doubt adding suitable epithets.

Cabanné came—roundabout. Arming a motley gang of French Canadians, a Negro, a mulatto, some half-breeds and Indians, he hurried by land ahead of the keelboat, shortcutting the river bends. Crossing to LeClerc's side of the stream, he set up a small cannon he had brought along, and waited. When his rival appeared, he pounced on the deserters and took them back to his post.

From them he learned that LeClerc's alcohol had been passed at Fort Leavenworth *after* his had been confiscated. While brooding about the unfairness, he learned, perhaps by express from St. Louis (it was now September 10 or so and word was spreading) of the total prohibition of July 9. Here was a solution! In hot triumph he ordered his clerk, J. B. Sarpy, to arm a posse and overhaul the lawbreaker.

By this time LcClerc was scores of miles ahead, too far for Cabanné's old bones. He did not go along. Sarpy was dependable, however. He overtook LeClerc 150 river miles away (but only seventy by land), at the site of the old Omaha villages where Ramsay Crooks had first met Robert McClellan. They stayed out of sight during the night. LeClerc's eighteen men bedded down aboard the boat and after the dreadful labors of the day slept like lead. At the first glimmer of dawn on September 17, Sarpy's gang cocked their guns and crept aboard.

There was no resistance. Sarpy told LeClerc of the prohibition and said he was looking for contraband under orders from Indian agent John Dougherty. Breaking open the bales and finding what he wanted, he declared the entire outfit condemned. He thereupon loaded his posse aboard and floated easily back to Council Bluffs, eating LeClerc's provisions en route. LeClerc's men had to walk, subsisting the while on starvation rations.

As soon as he could, LeClerc reported to Dougherty. The agent denied having given Sarpy any such orders. He stormed from the agency to Cabanné's post to check. LeClerc's liquor and some of Cabanné's was there. Reflecting that a total prohibition was now in effect, Dougherty sent the whole to St. Louis to await decision. Not knowing quite what to do with the legitimate merchandise, he locked it up in one of Cabanné's sheds.

A thunderous outcry followed. LeClerc hurried to St. Louis, poured out his wrongs to the press, and sued the company for trespass. Sutler A. G. Morgan, who had lost his hopes of profit to the seizure, wrote violent letters to Clark about this hypocritical monopoly that all at once had become so solicitous about enforcing the law. The American Fur Company he railed, was made up of outlaws, foreigners, and Canadian refugees. They thought they could get away with anything—". . . at this moment they have eight thousand gallons of whisky in the Upper Missouri . . . They have been known to sell it for fifty dollars per gallon at the mouth of the Yellow Stone."—and so on.

Agent Jonathan Bean at Fort Lookout dripped more venom with better chance of its taking effect. The seizure meant that the agency goods LeClerc had been hauling would not arrive in time for winter. (Actually Cabanné, realizing his folly, was belatedly hurrying them upstream.) "And thus," Bean cried:

> the poor Indian who is starving and shivering with cold is made to suffer even to death, merely that this overgrown monopoly may gratify a little spite against a more feeble opponent.

St. Louis was scandalized. So this was the end to which uncontrolled power could come! What would the government do now?

Clark moved cautiously. His permits for the spirits that had caused the uproar were dated after the prohibition law and he might easily become involved in whatever reckless charges started flying around. Very carefully, therefore, he collected full affidavits from everyone concerned before sending his dossier of the case to the new Commissioner of Indian Affairs in Washington, Judge Elbert Herring. The documents reached Herring in February 1833. Once again the timing was extraordinarily inopportune for the company.[9]

Kenneth Mackenzie was in the East during the winter of 1832-33. He carried with him additional schemes for increasing the company's prestige in the eyes of the Indians. The British passed out medals bearing the likeness of their king; American Indian agents occasionally had handed around bas-reliefs of presidential profiles. Why should not the company cast medals stamped with Astor's likeness and give them to important chiefs, to help convince the tribes as to who their Great Father really was? For his own prestige—he was already being called the King of the Missouri—he would like a coat of medieval mail. That ought to wow the savages.

William Astor agreed to write the company's representative in England about the armor. (Evidently it never materialized.[10]) Crooks, who was about to leave for Washington on routine business, agreed to ask whether medals in private hands were permissible. (They were, if called "ornaments"; evidently a few were actually struck off.)

By this time (November) Mackenzie of course knew of the prohibition law of July 9. He was dismayed. On learning of Crooks's errand to Washington, he urged him to talk to the highest government officers possible. Somehow—use any arguments that would work—somehow the Upper Missouri Outfit had to have liquor. He would depend on Crooks to get it. Then off Mackenzie went to visit friends in Montreal.

Crooks was reluctant about it, partly because of the Cabanné affair. He made no mention of the matter at all until he happened to run across Cass completely by accident in Washington. Then he probably wished he had kept his peace. Cass told him flatly there would be no exceptions.

The rebuff did not deject Crooks as much as it might have a few years earlier. His interest that fall lay not in liquor on the Missouri but in assembling a group of capitalists to buy from Astor the original American Fur Company—that is, everything except the Western Department. If his plans materialized, that department would revert to Bernard Pratte & Company, whose contract with the American Fur Company was due to expire in the summer of 1834. Little cash would be required for the St. Louis partners to resume independence, since in the main they would be retaining what they had brought to the company in 1827. The only major adjustment would concern the Iowa outfits, which had been transferred to the Western Department. If Chouteau wanted to keep Iowa he would have to pay Astor.

The cost to Crooks for the Great Lakes and the Upper Mississippi would be considerable, however. Not that there were many tangible assets to buy—buildings, boats, and so on. Most of the company's annual million-dollar investment went into merchandise that was fairly liquid. What Astor would put his price on would be the intangibles of a flourishing concern—good will, contacts, know-how, and the rest.

These assets had been created by Ramsay Crooks more than by anyone else. Still, the money and the patience had been Astor's. Between 1808 and 1823 he had poured hundreds of thousands of dollars into the venture (quite apart from his heavy losses at Astoria) with only the most meager returns. After 1823 profits had picked up. One thoughtful estimate concludes that he had netted well over a million dollars, although Astor himself never admitted to any such figure.[11] He was not going to let go of so lucrative a business (in spite of his other enormous profits from loans, real estate and some shipping) without exacting from the purchasers every cent he could make them agree to. In short, Crooks, the onetime cobbler's son, was faced with a major financial challenge.

Astor had flirted with the notion of retiring for some time, but Crooks had not taken him seriously until the winter of 1831–32. Then he had begun to think that the old merchant meant it. A flurry of letters went out to Chouteau about mutual arrangements. It was Crooks's hope that affairs could be settled—and that he, Ramsay Crooks, could step into Astor's fur-trading shoes—before his employer left for Europe on June 20, 1832. Details proved too numerous, however, and available capital too cautious. Astor left, promising to return in the fall, and negotiations continued desultorily by mail. Astor kept postponing his return, yet wrote only rarely. He was sixty-nine years old, unwell, and afflicted by the aches of a painful fall. Too, he hated to part irrevocably from this child of his creation.

An unshakable fur-trade myth says that Astor at last reached his decision shortly after arriving in Paris that summer and seeing a silk topper. According to the yarn, the horrid sight made him realize the beaver hat was doomed and led him to dump his holdings onto Crooks and associates. This of course is nonsense.

True, beaver prices were dropping. In August 1832 he wrote Chouteau from Paris, "I very much fear Beaver will not sell well very soon unless very fine, it appears they make hats of silk in place of Beaver." But he could equally well have blamed the decline on overproduction.

Stirred by William Ashley's spectacular success of 1824, a horde of trappers had stampeded into the Rockies from the Missouri. Alarmed by the onrush, the Hudson's Bay Company tried to reduce the allure of its Columbia River country stripping the intervening land bare of furs. A glut of beaver poured into the market. At first the fine quality of Rocky Mountain beaver sustained—even lifted—prices. But as always happens when a commodity is overpriced, substitutes began to catch hold—and not just silk, though silk eventually won the fashion war. William Astor wrote Chouteau from New York in October 1832, "An excellent good looking Hat, when napped with Nutria, can be sold for $4.50 and yield more profit to the manufacturer than one made of beaver at double the price."

Battered by these substitutes and overloaded with its own glut, the beaver market cracked. Of necessity the American Fur Company had to accept the beaver produced by its own mountain expeditions, but William Astor was no longer anxious to purchase more from outsiders. "We shall suffer sufficiently ourselves," he told Chouteau, "without taking on anyone else's returns."

Beaver was not the only fur in the trade, however. Fine raccoon (its price had jumped from twenty-five cents a skin to seventy cents in five years) abounded in southern Michigan, along the Wabash, and in some sections bordering the Mississippi. Muskrats, the favorite prey of the Indians because the animals were easy to trap, swarmed around the Lakes and throughout Minnesota. Deer roamed everywhere. Their prospects? In the same letter obliquely predicting beaver's fall Astor wrote, "There is a good demand for deer skins . . . Raccoon . . . are also expected to sell well. Muskrat skins have risen in London, but . . . I fear will fall again."

There were equally bright prospects in the West. The price of buffalo hides was rising, and if anything seemed limitless in 1832 it was the numbers of available buffalo. Consider a single comparison: in the spring of 1832 James Kipp brought 6450 pounds of beaver but very little buffalo down from the mouth of Marias River. Three years later, in 1835, when beaver were not so attractive, the trader at the Marias shipped to St. Louis about 1500 pounds of beaver—and 9000 buffalo robes, or *forty-five tons* (plus, oddly, 1500 prairie-dog skins). No, the pelt trade was not going to end just because one glamour fur weakened. In fact, the general market was strong and likely to stay so.

Astor knew the trends, of course. So did Crooks. And Crooks certainly was not stamped by the decline in beaver. Rather, he was eager to buy the company to which he had devoted most of his adult life as soon as he believed in Astor's willingness to sell. But no doubt the silk-hat myth will persist, perhaps because silk did help to ruin the mountain men of the Rockies. But it did not drive Astor from the trade. Age and illness did that.

Crooks raised $100,000 himself and found associates who would put up another $200,000.[12] In spite of the slowness of the transatlantic mails, bargaining with Astor had progressed far enough by the opening of 1833 that he thought he could complete the purchase in April—a logical month, since April 1833 marked the expiration of the American Fur Company's original charter from the New York State Legislature. He intended to use the old name for his new company, and hoped to stand in the same position toward Bernard Pratte & Company as had prevailed before 1827—namely, importer of goods and seller of furs for them on commission.

Chouteau, who admired Crooks, wanted a closer association. He offered him an interest in Pratte, Chouteau & Company, which was to be Bernard Pratte & Company's successor as heir to the Western Department. Crooks declined. "I am not sure," he wrote Chouteau on February 17, 1833, ". . . that my new associates would be willing for me to retain a separate interest from themselves in the same kind of trade." When Chouteau kept pressing him, he found a different excuse: if he did not take over the original company, Astor would sell to strangers who would push overland to the Missouri from the Mississippi, as the Columbia Fur Company once had done, and unleash a ruinous competition. It was better for Crooks to stay in a spot from which amiable trade agreements could be worked out to everyone's benefit.[13]

No doubt both these reasons entered his thinking. But as one reads the rest of his winter's correspondence another possibility keeps suggesting itself. The headstrong lawlessness of the Western Department, as typified by Cabanné and Mackenzie, was beginning to repel him. But more of that later.

Robert Stuart was also in the East that winter. The government was preparing a treaty to buy the last Indian lands in southwestern Michigan and northwestern Illinois, and then move the savages beyond the Mississippi. The document was to be presented to the Indians at a great council in Chicago late in the summer of 1833. At that time all claims held by traders against the savages were to be ruled on and paid if honored by the tribes. Dozens of wilderness merchants, Stuart among them, flocked to Washington to enter their names and those of their winterers on the various schedules. Stuart had dug out of the Mackinac records $20,000 in bad debts in the Chicago area and spent nearly a month in Washington with his books and other evidence persuading the commissioners to enter the defaulted credits for discussion.

During pauses in the work he learned that the American Fur Company was about to be sold to Ramsay Crooks and associates, and that he, Robert Stuart, was to have no place in the new organization. He was staggered. Why he was left out is unknown. Perhaps he was asked to buy a share of the Mackinac Department and lacked the necessary capital; he had seven children by then, three of them at boarding school in the East. Perhaps his harsh, peremptory ways had made him too many enemies. No one knows. Anyway, he was through. Gloomily he wrote his eldest daughter, Mary, on January 27, 1833:

It is more than probable that such arrangements will be made in our business between this & spring, as will cause *us* to leave Mackinac next fall . . . . The very thought of leaving that dear spot, where God's dear mercy & love have so long abounded to us all, is by no means pleasant to me, but if we are the Children of the most high; all will turn out for our best interest.[14]

Shortly after Stuart wrote that letter, Mackenzie returned from Montreal and insisted that Crooks travel with him to Washington to try once more to win permission to take liquor to the Upper Missouri—only for combatting the Hudson's Bay people, of course. The effort failed disastrously. While the men were in the capital, talking might and main, Clark's official dossier about Cabanné's seizure of LeClerc's boats and the government's Sioux annuities came in. Herring shook the papers under their noses. What did this mean?

Crooks, who had just been asking for exemptions to the prohibition law, was reduced to explaining that Cabanné, out of the purest motives, had simply been defending that same law by allowing *no* whisky to reach the Indians. That set Herring off on a somewhat illogical tack. Ignoring the government's own seizures of authorized liquor from the *Yellowstone*, he barked that LeClerc's spirits had been duly licensed by Clark and duly passed by Lieutenant Freeman. Just who did Cabanné and the American Fur Company think they were, to take the law in their own hands in such fashion?

The case, which already had created an ugly stir against the company in Missouri, now made headlines in Washington. Pressure grew for disciplinary action against the entire company. For a time it looked as if Herring might cancel the company's licenses (Cabanné had been operating under a license issued not to himself but to the American Fur Company) and put their extensive bonds in suit. Eventually, however, the commissioner was persuaded that Cabanné had acted entirely on his own responsibility. Besides, the Indians needed their traders. Relenting finally, Herring let the company's bonds and licenses stand, but ordered Cabanné and Sarpy out of the Indian country for a full year.

Under the circumstances, a quiet settlement of the suit LeClerc had instituted against the company seemed wise. Chouteau bought him off for $9200. To Chouteau's outrage the American Fur Company refused to contribute a cent. This was the Western Department's hot potato; let them handle it. (Chouteau got even, though. When the Sacs and Foxes paid their $40,000 debt to Davenport, the Western Department claimed every penny, though many of the credits antedated the amalgamation of 1827. William Astor rolled his eyes heavenward in hurt: Who would suppose old friends would advance their interest at the expense of ours? "Permit me to hope that on further consideration . . . you will accord what we are fairly entitled to.")

To calm Mackenzie, Crooks went to Cass with an idea about the liquor problem which he had been quietly working on for some months. Would not the American State Department make representations to the British government, so that the Hudson's Bay Company would also be forbidden to use spirits on the border? (This of course would help the new company's Fond du Lac affairs.) Cass agreed to mention the matter to the proper people. Meanwhile, in Europe, Astor came up with a more practical idea. He offered to pull his traders out of the upper Fond du Lac posts entirely and leave the country unchallenged to the Hudson's Bay Company if the firm would pay the American Fur Company £300 a year. They agreed, and thus liquor ceased to be a factor so far as the Canadians east of Red River were concerned. Crooks continued the arrangement for some years.

This was no help to Mackenzie. Without liquor, he said, he could not possibly fight the Hudson's Bay traders on the Missouri. Or local rivals either. Formidable opposition was mustering. Backed by William Ashley, Robert Campbell and William Sublette were preparing to enter both the Rocky Mountains and the Missouri River in strength. Though Ashley had supported the prohibition bill, Mackenzie was willing to wager that Campbell and Sublette would take liquor with them wherever they went. (They did.) Well, Mackenzie also intended to have it. If the shortsighted, unfair United States Government would not allow him to ship it in his boats, then he would set up a still at Fort Union and make what he needed out of Mandan corn.

The proposal disturbed Crooks. When dissuasion failed to budge Mackenzie, he wrote Chouteau on February 17 an unhappy twelve-page letter. The still was madness. These were times to be circumspect. "Every eye is upon us, and whoever can will annoy us with all his heart." He hoped that after the Cabanné uproar faded, the government might modigy the law "so as to afford us a fair chance with our Hudson Bay opponents." If not, he finished, "I would, hard as it is, rather abandon the trade than violate the statute."

Chouteau and Mackenzie refused to concede. Crooks then all but washed his hands of the West and concentrated on bringing the purchase from Astor to a conclusion. Delay after delay occurred. June 1833 arrived before the old merchant made the first official step, a formal notice to the Western Department that its contract would terminate in the summer of 1834. After that only time was needed to settle details of payment, inventories, trade boundaries, and so on. But since during the first part of the period, until Astor returned to America, letters had to pass between St. Louis, New York, and Geneva, these harassing matters dragged out for months.

During this period Kenneth Mackenzie created massive troubles for his department. According to formal charges made to Congressman William Ashley, Mackenzie deliberately incited Crow Indians to attack a brigade of the Rocky Mountain Fur Company and rob it of its horses and beaver pelts. Mackenzie denied everything, of course, but while the various letters were on their way, still another accusation rose like Frankenstein's monster: Rival traders reported his still to William Clark.

Mackenzie tried to bluster out of it. The informers, who he said had been disgustingly drunk all the way down the river, were bloated with spleen because he had refused to sell them some of the product of the still. Anyway, it was not his still. It belonged to a man named J. P. Bourke of Red River, who had hired Mackenzie to freight the apparatus up the Missouri on the *Yellowstone* and store it at Fort Union until Bourke could bring a wagon overland for it. It just happened that a man who knew wine making drifted by when the local wild fruits were ripening and was curious to know whether they would yield anything potable. Mackenzie let him experiment, and out of that innocent diversion the informers had made up their lies.

Chouteau was in the East, working on the details of the sale, when the stories arrived. He rushed to Washington and glibly persuaded Herring that there had been no intent to break the law. Furthermore, Herring continued in a resumé to Clark, Chouteau

> gives the assurance that if he can prevent it no just cause of complaint against the Company shall ever exist. Under these circumstances further action by the Department in this particular case seems to be inexpedient.

By an eyelash! Sardonically Crooks told Chouteau on February 23, 1834,

> Don't presume too much on your recent escape . . . The less of this sort of business the better . . . Your business so much resembles a monopoly that there will always exist strong jealousies against you.

Monopoly was a good word for it. In April 1834 Pratte, Chouteau and Company ignored Mackenzie's desire to crush the competition of Sublette and Campbell, who had built a post near Fort Union, and entered into an arrangement which left the St. Louis Frenchmen supreme on the Missouri.[15] They gave Mackenzie a sharp lesson as well. To prove to the government that their hearts were as pure as Chouteau had insisted to Herring, they abruptly ordered the rambunctious King of the Missouri out of the Indian country for a year. He did not suffer particularly from the enforced vacation. He went to Europe, visited Prince Maximilian zu Wied, studied—of all things—wine making, and returned to the Missouri in 1835. Within a few years, however, he left the river for good, though he did maintain business connections with Chouteau most of the rest of his life.

In April 1834, before the final papers were signed that would make him president of the American Fur Company, Crooks went with Emilie and their three children to lovely Mackinac, just turning a soft spring green above the crystal waters. His half-Indian daughter, Hester, was there, not quite seventeen. Later that summer she went to Yellow Lake in northwestern Wisconsin, to help teach the children of her mother's people at a new mission school. At Yellow Lake she met the Reverend William Boutwell. Another missionary married them at Fond du Lac (Duluth now) on September 10. Tea and doughnuts were her wedding supper. Her wedding trip was a forty-three-day canoe trip to wild Leech Lake, where her husband built a mission station of his own.

Back on Mackinac, her father made arrangements with Robert Stuart to take complete inventories after the rendezvous and then turn everything over to the company's new agent on the island, Samuel Abbott. That done, Stuart and his family moved to Detroit, where he built the city's first brick residence. He speculated in Michigan and Green Bay lands, later entered a bank, and remained a pillar of the church; but relations with Crooks were never quite friendly again, especially after he financed certain competitors on Mackinac Island itself. In 1840 he became State Treasurer of Michigan, and after that, for four years, he held Cass's former job as Superintendent of Michigan Indian Affairs. During a business trip to Chicago in 1848 he died in his hotel room. Betsy was with him.

Crooks returned to Mackinac in the summer of 1835 bursting with plans. The Erie Canal had reduced freight rates on merchandise incredibly. With careful management it was possible to trade the cheap goods for muskrat skins profitably even at their new rock-bottom prices. He reorganized the entire north, setting up two Superior outfits, one based under Franchère at Sault Ste Marie, the other at La Pointe on Madeline Island. La Pointe was headquarters for yet another pioneering enterprise. The Erie Canal had brought settlers to many points of the Lakes, and Crooks believed he could sell them Superior's famous trout and whitefish. He built schooners and established fisheries, but mismanagement by local people, untrained to the job, kept the business from meeting his expectations.

In the wilderness he was ruthless. No more of Astor's coming to terms with rivals. "Do not stop to count the cost of preventing Mr. Stitt by all fair means from making returns," he wrote William Aitkin in Fond du Lac. "Give him no rest." A little later he ordered Rolette, still in charge of the Mississippi, "There is to be no compromise & no buying out, but give them the benefit of your most persevering opposition."

His deadliest fight was with the totally unscrupulous Ewing brothers in the Wabash country. Raccoon caps had become a fad among the Jews of eastern Europe, and when the Russian army adopted raccoon head-gear for winter, demand became fantastic. German buyers from Leipzig entered the American market, made common cause with the company's enemies, and touched off a suicidal warfare.

Fur exports climbed steadily. During the later part of the 1830s more fur left the United States than ever before. During each of the closing years of the decade, Crooks's company exported nearly 600,000 small skins and sold another 170,000 abroad for Chouteau. But it was not the same. The Indians were hounded out of the East beyond the Missouri. In the Mississippi Valley farmers took over the trapping and small storekeepers began buying their product. As soon as trade ceased to be a controlling factor in the life of the Indians, it also ceased to be a molder of national, even international, policy. Instead it became just a business.

The Indian trade as a political force hung on longer on the plains. But the glamour was dying there too. Beaver prices at Philadelphia sagged from a high $6 a pound in 1831 to $2.62 in 1843. The mountain rendezvous flickered out and the western commerce shrank back to the buffalo of the short-grass country. There would be debaucheries of the natives still for the sake of those pelts, and wars would be fought again as the game disappeared and the ranges grew cramped. But no longer was that any part of Crooks's concern.

Thanks to continuing demands in Europe and improved techniques of cutting in on Indian treaties, the American Fur Company survived the depression of 1837–38. But the struggle with the Ewings exhausted both firms. They came so near mutual annihilation that G. W. Ewing wrote William Brewster, the company's agent in Detroit:

> The absurdity of such a course of policy as has been carried out by us and yourselves for the last two years is too glaring & manifest to require any comment. The whole country is jeering and laughing at both parties.

While they were staggering from the profitless fight, the European market broke. In desperation Crooks sold Rolette's Mississippi outfit to Pierre Chouteau. It wasn't enough. His last chance was to collect bad credits from the Sioux. That ended when the treaty was rejected on

September 9, 1842. The next day, September 10, the American Fur Company, lords once of the western wilderness, suspended payments. Its debts amounted to $300,000. In triumph one of the Ewings crowed:

The Great American Fur Company . . . has exploded. Disappeared, overwhelmed with the most miserable bankruptcy . . . They have met their just desert.

It was not quite so bad as that. By long, careful, adroit maneuvering Crooks paid off every cent. In 1845 he opened a small commission house in New York, dealing in pelts of all kinds. He lived very quietly. His principal pleasure was meeting friends from the wilderness and talking over old times.

Unhappily he never got around to writing any of it down, except once during the presidential campaign of 1856, when the new Republican party was trying to make political capital out of the pathfinding exploits of its candidate, John Charles Frémont. Some ill-advised publicist cried to the nation that Frémont had discovered South Pass, the gateway to Oregon, in 1842. Crooks snorted, reached for his pen, and prepared a long letter for the Detroit *Free Press*. Pathfinding, he said, did not necessarily qualify a man for the presidency. Besides, Frémont had not discovered the pass. Briefly he outlined Hunt's overland expedition of 1811–12, and then told of the first crossing of South Pass, west to east, "in the month of November, 1812," thirty years before Frémont saw it.

The seven persons forming the party were ROBERT McCLELLAND [*sic*], of Hagerstown, Maryland, who with the celebrated captain WELLS was chief of spies under General WAYNE in his famous Indian campaign, JOSEPH MILLER, of Baltimore, for several years an officer in the United States army, ROBERT STUART, a citizen of Detroit, BENJAMIN JONES, of Missouri, who acted as huntsman to the party, FRANÇOIS LE CLAIRE [*sic*], a half-breed, and ANDRE VALLEE, a Canadian voyageur, and RAMSAY CROOKS, who is the only survivor of this small band of adventurers.

The first man through—a continent in his hand when the world was young. It was something to remember as the days closed in. There were not many more. The last one came June 6, 1859. According to the New York *Herald*, "He seemed to die of no particular disease. He quietly passed from the world as one retired to sleep."[16] He was seventy-two years old.

A Note on the Bibliography

and

Acknowledgments

Among the many manuscript collections and volumes of printed letters listed in the bibliography which follows, half a dozen merit additional remarks. The first is a series of letters written by John Jacob Astor and Ramsay Crooks, 1813–43. I call these the Crooks–Astor letters in the bibliography. At one point in their career these letters were owned by a Mr. Hoguet of New York City, who allowed two reproductions of them. One is held by the Burton Historical Collection, Detroit Public Library. (The Missouri Historical Society has a typescript of the Burton reproduction.) The other reproduction of the Hoguet letters is two volumes of photostats at the New York Public Library. The latter are the ones I used.

The second source is three letter books, 1816–30 (actually there is almost nothing in them after 1827), containing copies of letters written by Ramsay Crooks and Robert Stuart. I call these the Crooks–Stuart letters. Of the originals, Volume I, 1816–20, is at the Missouri Historical Society; Volumes II and III, rather badly cared for, are in an iron safe on an upper floor of the Robert Stuart House on Mackinac Island. There are complete photostats of these three volumes at the State Historical Society of Wisconsin, an incomplete set of photostats and typescripts at the Chicago Historical Society, and complete microfilms at the Huntington Library, San Marino, California. In the course of checking and rechecking I managed to use all of these.

Both sets of letters should be supplemented by the American Fur Company ledgers and account books, 1817–35, preserved in the Public Archives of Canada at Ottawa and in the Burton Historical Collection, Detroit. Both the Huntington Library and the State Historical Society of Wisconsin have microfilms of these commercial papers. I used them from time to time at both places in order to shore up other readings.

The third essential source is the huge Chouteau collection of letters, diaries, bills, invoices, and what not at the Missouri Historical Society in St. Louis.

This collection has never been reproduced in full and hence must be used at the Society. So far as this study is concerned, it furnished most of the data about the Western Department of the American Fur Company, together with considerable material about affairs on the Missouri River prior to 1812.

Finally there is the overwhelming mass of material in Record Group 75, Records of the Office of Indian Affairs, National Archives, Washington. When it became obvious that I could not wade through this morass in the time I had available in Washington, the Huntington Library came to my rescue by providing for use nearer home microfilms of the correspondence of the Michigan and St. Louis Superintendencies, of the St. Peter's and Upper Missouri Agencies, and that great catchall, Miscellaneous Letters Received and Sent, which proved more valuable than the designation at first suggested.

Two indispensable printed supplements to the collections listed above are the miscellany of fur trade and Indian affairs letters printed in the *Wisconsin Historical Collections*, Volumes XIX and XX, and the documents scattered throughout Clarence Carter's superbly edited *Territorial Papers of the United States*, Volumes X (Michigan) and XIII, XIV, XV (Missouri).

Three bulky collections of letters and documents which here and there touch on the American Fur Company I did not examine in detail. One is the Astor Papers in the Baker Library of the Harvard University Graduate School of Business. These letters range over many of Astor's affairs other than the American Fur Company; and since a great many of those that do concern the Indian trade are on microfilm at the Missouri Historical Society, I contented myself with those selected reproductions. A second compromise had to do with the William Clark papers at the Kansas State Historical Society, Topeka, most of which pertain to the U. S. Superintendency of Indian Affairs, St. Louis. Copies of many of these letters are at Madison, St. Paul, and St. Louis, and are scattered through Record Group 75. Since these copies were available to me and time was not, I reluctantly did not visit Topeka. Finally there is the voluminous collection of American Fur Company papers in the New York Historical Society. Most of these were written after 1834. (Out of 18,181 letters, only 125 antedate 1835.) Since 1834 is this book's terminal date, I contented myself with skimming through the microfilms of this collection at the Huntington Library, using as my guide Grace Nute's *Calendar of the American Fur Company's Papers* (*Annual Report of the American Historical Association for 1944*, Washington, 1945).

All of the collections listed above have been combed several times for various purposes. Strangely, however, only one author of a published book has gone directly to them for a comprehensive account of the American Fur Company—Kenneth Wiggins Porter, whose two-volume study, *John Jacob Astor, Business Man,* was published by Harvard University Press in 1931. This was a pioneering work of such awesome thoroughness that later accounts have been satisfied to walk in Mr. Porter's footsteps, sometimes contributing nothing more than a slight rewriting, plus occasional infusions from Washington Irving's *Astoria,* Hiram Chittenden's 1902 study, *A History of the American Fur Trade of the Far West,* and oddments drawn from Paul C. Phillips, *The Fur Trade* (University of Oklahoma Press, 1961).

My own debt to Porter is profound. His untangling of Astor's intricate financial maneuvers is economic research of the most admirable sort. But Mr. Porter was writing of all Astor's affairs. The American Fur Company was only one, so that less than a third of *John Jacob Astor, Business Man* is concerned with the Indian trade. Furthermore, Mr. Porter was interested primarily in Astor as a businessman and only secondarily in the Indian trade as a historical force. These limitations, necessary and proper from the standpoint of what Mr. Porter was doing, narrowed his focus considerably. By the nature of things he could not relate the American Fur Company in detail to its broad context in the vanishing wilderness or to its historic and vigorous role as one of the determining voices in national and even international policies.

The Missouri trade in particular received only scanty attention from Mr. Porter. In covering that phase of the company's operations he relied mainly on Chittenden and, through one of the compromises we all must make sooner or later, did not examine the Chouteau papers. Chittenden's work, like Porter's, is monumental. It did depend on the Chouteau papers in its examination of the American Fur Company's Western activities. But Chittenden, like all of us, could be both careless and prejudiced. Moreover, he wrote in 1902. Quantities of material have come to light since then. It is quite impossible today to treat of the western phases of the American Fur Company only on the basis of Hiram Chittenden, without a fresh, direct examination of the Chouteau material in the light of these new investigations.

As stated in the Prologue, achieving a fresh view of this so-called first American monopoly involved shifting the focus away from Astor's often sensationalized glitter and onto Crooks and the field men of the American Fur Company. To do this I of necessity concentrated much of my research on a hunt for letters, journals, unpublished theses, and books of all kinds that might yield an understanding of the elusive tone of the wilderness society in which the company operated.

The chapter-by-chapter bibliography which follows indicates the manuscript collections I found most helpful. It lists at the proper place the books that furnished specific data. But many other books that revealed something of the texture of the times were involved, yet could not be conveniently listed because they did not tie in directly with the chapter under consideration. For example, there were many regional histories (among them R. C. Buley, *The Old Northwest, 1815–1840*, two volumes, Indiana University Press, 1950); state histories (William Folwell, *A History of Minnesota*, St. Paul, Minnesota Historical Society, 1956); local histories, (H. N. Ross, *La Pointe, Village Outpost*, St. Paul, 1960); political histories (Clarence Alvord, *The Mississippi Valley in British Politics*, two volumes, Cleveland, A. H. Clark, 1917); Indian histories (Emma Blair, *Indian Tribes of the Upper Mississippi Valley and the Region of the Great Lakes*, two volumes, Cleveland, A. H. Clark, 1911); social reminiscences (Timothy Flint, *Recollections of the Last Ten Years*, Boston, 1826); highly specialized accounts (John Parsons, "Gunmakers for the American Fur Company," New York Historical Society *Quarterly*, April 1952); and even novels (*Mark Logan the Bourgeois*, by Mrs. John H. Kinzie, who spent the early 1830s in Chicago and Wisconsin and on Mackinac as the wife of an American Fur

Company trader and Indian agent), and so on and so on—a list of whose reproduction in full here would probably serve no useful purpose.

Several unpublished theses submitted for degrees of master of arts and dissertations for degrees of doctor of philosophy also contributed help in various ways. They include:

Anson, Burt. "The Fur Traders in Northern Indiana, 1763–1850" (Ph.D.), U. of Indiana, 1953.

Bissell, Orpha L. "The Activities of the American Fur Company," (M.A.), U. of Minnesota, 1917.

Bridgwater, William R. "The American Fur Company," (Ph.D.), Yale University, 1938.

Jorstad, Erling. "The Life of Henry H. Sibley," (Ph.D.), U. of Wisconsin, 1957.

Keithann, Rollo. "The American Fur Company in the Upper Mississippi Valley," (M.A.), U. of Minnesota, 1929.

Lesley, L. B. "The Fur Trade of the Middle Northwest, 1796–1818," (M.A.), U. of California, 1923.

Nasatir, A. P. "The Chouteaus and the Indian trade of the West," (M.A.), U. of California, 1922.

Ratterman, Anne. "The Struggle for Monopoly of the Fur Trade," (M.A.), U. of Minnesota, 1917.

Webster, Archibald W. "Western Preliminaries of the War of 1812," (M.A.), Washington U., St. Louis, 1926.

Many persons guided and smoothed my long trail through this wilderness of words. Home base, so to speak, was the Henry E. Huntington Library, San Marino, California, where the director, Dr. John E. Pomfret, and several members of the library's most efficient staff—Constance Lodge, Anne Hyder, Mary Isabel Fry, Janet Hawkins—were always resourceful, cheerful, and prompt in helping me lay hands on whatever I needed. At the Minnesota Historical Society, St. Paul, I relied on Lucille Kane and her assistant, Kathryn A. Johnson; at the State Historical Society of Wisconsin, Madison, on Josephine Harper; at the Missouri Historical Society, St. Louis, on Mrs. Ernst A. Stadler and Mrs. John Dotzman in Archives, on Mrs. Fred Harrington and Mrs. Alice Johnson in the library; at the State Historical Society of Missouri, Columbia, on Kenneth Holmes, who helped me find my way through the society's collection of early Missouri newspapers. Knowledgeable guides through the National Archives were Mr. Wulgis and Dr. Ryan. In Chicago, Ray Billington, genial dean of Western historians, led me to Fred Hall at the Newberry Library, where the Ayer Collection yielded several original letters of interest, and to the Chicago Historical Society, where Archie Motley and the librarian, Mrs. Winslow Cope, answered questions and provided leads to useful documents.

Several persons gave generously of their time in providing materials and making helpful suggestions by mail: Don Rickey, Jr., of the Jefferson National Expansion Memorial, St. Louis; John Porter Bloom of the National Park Service offices in Washington; Ray H. Mattison and Merrill J. Mattes of the same service in Omaha; Richard Oglesby of Eastern Illinois College, Charleston; Dorothy Bridgwater of the Yale University Library; James M. Babcock, chief of the Burton Historical Collection, Detroit Public Library.

Mrs. Max Myer of St. Louis came to my rescue as a translator when I was stumped by the French written by Charles Gratiot, Joseph Rolette, Pierre Chouteau and others whose letters were essential to this account.

Bright point of the research was flying with John and Katie Batten in their plane from Racine, Wisconsin, over the gorgeous colors of October to Mackinac Island, eastward from there above Georgian Bay and westward around the south shore of Lake Superior, with a stop at Lake Owen and a visit to the museum at La Pointe on lovely Madeline Island, all of which added appreciably to an understanding of the controlling geography of the trade. On Mackinac, Mr. and Mrs. Hugh Rudolf, Mrs. John Bailly and Willard Lasley were helpful in introducing us to the historical and scenic highlights of that most sparkling of islands. Although the season was over and the fort closed, Director and Mrs. Carl Nordburg opened the doors to us, gave us a detailed and informative tour, and provided an armload of literature.

The financial strains of a protracted stay at the Huntington Library and of the zigzag automobile tour through the Indian trade country were eased by a grant from John Simon Guggenheim Memorial Foundation. Other major strains —the dreariness of living for long stretches in motels and the endless chore of typing and retyping—were evaporated by my wife's unfailing sunniness. In large measure this too is her book.

Abbreviations

I believe most of the abbreviations used in the bibliography and notes are self-evident. A few that may not be follow:

ASP ....*American State Papers* (generally the volumes concerned with Ind. Aff., or *Indian Affairs*).

Chout. Col. ....Chouteau Collection.

EWT ....Thwaites' editions of *Early Western Travels*.

Mich. P & H Col. .....*Michigan Pioneer and Historical Collections*.

MVHR ....*Mississippi Valley Historical Review*.

WHC ....*Collections of the State Historical Society of Wisconsin*.

Bibliography and Notes

CHAPTER 1
Michilimackinac: The Key and the Door

GENERAL BIBLIOGRAPHY

BACKGROUND MATERIAL ON THE FUR TRADE

Creighton, D. G. *The Commercial Empire of the St. Lawrence, 1760–1850.* New Haven: Yale University Press, 1937.

Davidson, Gordon C. *The North West Company.* Berkeley: University of California, 1918.

DeVoto, Bernard. *The Course of Empire.* Boston: Houghton Mifflin Company, 1952.

Innis, Harold A. *The Fur Trade in Canada.* 2d ed., Toronto: University of Toronto Press, 1956.

Johnson, Ida A. *The Michigan Fur Trade.* Lansing, 1919.

Kellogg, Louise P. *The French Régime in Wisconsin and the Northwest.* Madison, Wisconsin, 1925.

———. *The British Régime in Wisconsin and the Northwest.* Madison, Wisconsin, 1935.

EVENTS IN THE MICHILIMACKINAC AREA

Carver, Jonathan. *Three Years Travels Through the Interior Parts of North-America* . . . Philadelphia, 1789.

Cuneo, John. *Robert Rogers of the Rangers.* New York: Oxford University Press, 1959.

Henry, Alexander. *Travels and Adventures in Canada,* edited by James Bain. Toronto, 1901.

May, George, ed. *The Doctor's Secret Journal* (Journal of Daniel Morison). Mackinac Island, 1960.

Perrault, J. B. "Narrative of the Travels and Adventures of a Merchant Adventurer," edited by J. S. Fox. *Mich. P & H Col.,* XXXVIII.

Wood, E. O. *Historic Mackinac,* 2 vols. New York, 1918.

NOTES AND SPECIFIC REFERENCES

1. To forestall quibbling: When Ramsay Crooks was at the height of his influence in 1832–34, Texas, New Mexico, Arizona, California, Oregon, Washington, and Idaho were not part of the United States.

2. The 1790 figures are from Innis, *The Fur Trade in Canada*, p. 267.

3. In 1820 Ramsay Crooks told a seemingly tall tale about the Chicago portage to Colonel Wool of the commission that was surveying the boundary between the United States and Canada. While paddling a canoe over the portage during high water many years earlier, Crooks said, he and a companion each floated a feather from opposite ends of the craft. One feather started toward the Illinois River and the Gulf of Mexico; the other bobbed toward Lake Michigan and, conceivably, the North Atlantic. (Diary of Major Joseph Delafield, *The Unfortified Boundary*. New York, 1943.)

4. The invoice books of the American Fur Company clearly show that furs from the Iowa country were going up the Illinois River as late as 1819. (Charges of Louis Pensonneau and Russell Farnham, Account books of the American Fur Company, Public Archives of Canada, microfilm, Huntington Library.) No significant changes in the pattern occurred until the establishment of the company's Western Department in St. Louis in 1822 and the use of steamboats for shipping.

This supplying of St. Louis by way of Montreal and the Great Lakes at first glance seems illogically roundabout. But a route from New York or Philadelphia faced the expensive interruption of the Allegheny Mountains, while one from New Orleans had to use, in pre-steamboat days, human muscle and primitive sails to overcome the Mississippi's current. Nor did that current help a great deal in taking furs out of the interior. By the time the pelts had been gathered from the winter hunting camps and sorted in St. Louis, the humid heat of summer lay on the lower river. Worms and moths hatched expensive destruction. The cooler weather of the Great Lakes route helped compensate for its physical difficulties and the route was frequently used even after steamers had reached as high as present St. Paul.

5. Excerpts from several of these memorials of protest are given in Innis, op. cit., pp. 171–76.

6. The controlling of this jungle-style competition was one motive leading to associations of traders and eventually to monopoly; but a discussion of that phase of the commerce is apart from this chapter's purposes.

7. Compare Kay's antics with a solemn 1790 memorial of certain Montreal merchants protesting the Canadian government's attempts to control the liquor traffic. Outside regulations weren't necessary: "The Trader's personal interest and safety have been the best security against abuses. . . . For, tho' Rum might procure the hunt of a year, yet if obtained only by that means future Industry [in hunting] will cease. Murder might result and all its concomitant evils." (Innis, op. cit., p. 268.) The trouble with that pious reasoning was that many wilderness traders were as lacking in foresight as were the Indians; the North West Company finally had to institute rigorous penalties to quell drunkenness and licentiousness among its own partners and clerks.

The memorial of 1790 went on to admit giving (not selling) enough rum to the Indians "to prevent them from carrying their Furs to a distant or a Foreign market." John Astor's son, William B. Astor, forty years later offered the same sort of response to edicts by the United States Government that the American Fur Company keep liquor out of the Indian country. The American Fur Company, he said, would eschew spirits if the Hudson's Bay Company also did—i.e., he and Crooks and the company were patriotically keeping American furs from slipping away to foreign markets. (William B. Astor to Lewis Cass, May 27, 1833, Department of State, Territorial Papers, BIA, Miscellaneous. Also, W. B. Astor to Pierre Chouteau, Jr., Jan. 31, 1833; and Ramsay Crooks to Chouteau, Feb. 17, 1833; both in Chouteau Papers, Mo. Hist. Soc.)

In making these protestations the American Fur Company was not, as is sometimes charged, trying to booby-trap the Hudson's Bay Company into abandoning liquor so that it could then rush in a load to the thirsty savages and underhandedly seize the business. Rather, Astor and Crooks were mumbling one of the oldest liturgies of the trade: I'll be good if you will. Probably they would have—if. But the big companies were so suspicious of each other and so many unscrupulous outsiders were so eager to take advantage of them that no leading operator ever quite dared take that first radical step. It reminds one somewhat of proposals for international disarmament.

8. The French before 1763 and the Spanish at St. Louis before 1803 often sold licenses either to raise revenue for the government or to line the governor's pocket. But the main use of the permits was to establish a system of control.

CHAPTER 2

Robert Dickson and the Ways of the Trade

GENERAL BIBLIOGRAPHY

BACKGROUND ON THE FUR TRADE

As cited, same heading, Chapter 1, plus:

Innis, Harold. "Interrelations Between the Fur Trade of Canada and the United States," *MVHR*, XX (December 1933).

Stevens, Wayne. "The Organization of the British Fur Trade, 1760–1800," *MVHR*, III (September 1916).

Thwaites, R. G., ed. "The Fur Trade on the Upper Lakes" (a collection of letters). *WHC* XIX, pp. 234–375.

TRANSPORTATION, VOYAGEURS, LIVING IN GENERAL

Keating, William. *Narrative of an Expedition to the Source of the St. Peter's . . . 1823 . . .* 2 vols. London, 1825.

Lockwood, James H. "Early Times in Wisconsin," *WHC* II.

Long, John. *Voyages and Travels of an Indian Interpreter and Trader,* reprinted in Thwaites *EWT*, Vol. II. Cleveland, 1904.

McKenney, Thomas L. *Sketches of a Tour to the Lakes . . .* Baltimore, 1827.

Mackenzie, Alexander. *Voyages from Montreal . . .* Various editions.

Malhoit, François. "Journal, 1804–05," *WHC* XIX.

Nute, Grace L. *The Voyageur.* St. Paul: Minnesota Historical Society, 1955.

FOR ROBERT DICKSON

Cruikshank, Ernest A. "Robert Dickson, Indian Trader," *WHC* XII.
Tohill, Louis A. *Robert Dickson, British Fur Trader*, Ann Arbor, Michigan, 1927.
Documents relating to the trial of Ainse and Dease: *Mich. P & H Col.*, XI, 490–514; *ibid*, XXIII, 633–68. Some of the same are reprinted in *WHC*, XII.

THE INDIANS OF THE UPPER MISSISSIPPI

Robinson, Doane. *A History of the Dakota or Sioux Indians.* Facsimile edition, Minneapolis, 1956.
Warren, William W. (a half-breed Ojibway and trader). *History of the Ojibway Nation.* Facsimile edition, Minneapolis, 1957.

NOTES AND SPECIFIC REFERENCES

1. The quotations are from, in order, Phillips, *The Fur Trade*, op. cit., Vol. II, p. 16; and Innis, *The Fur Trade In Canada*, pp. 179–80. The Canadian fur men of the Great Lakes area could not be reconciled to the surrender of so much territory to the United States. As far as they were concerned, the War of 1812 was a war of conquest to regain by arms what their diplomats had lost.

2. Dickson's fish stories were noted on Michilimackinac by James Doty on July 4, 1822, and are with the Doty papers, State Historical Society of Wisconsin.

3. *Mich. P & H Col.*, XXXII, 340.

4. The kind of goods used in the trade are amply illustrated in the many invoices of the American Fur Company preserved in the Public Archives of Canada at Ottawa (microfilm, Huntington Library, San Marino, Calif.), the Burton Historical Collection, Detroit Public Library (microfilm, State Historical Society of Wisconsin), and records of the Western Department, Chouteau Collection, Missouri Historical Society, St. Louis. For specific details: "Indian Silver," *Wis. Mag of Hist.* XXXIV, 76 ff. David Thompson on clothing, pp. 421–22 of his *Narrative*, ed. by J. B. Tyrrell, Toronto, 1916. Cass on blankets, *WHC*, XX, 287–88. See also *ASP*, Ind. Aff. I, 425; Thomas L. McKenney, *Memoirs*, I, 309; Senate Document 106 (serial 298) 24th Congress, 2d session.

These sources indicate some variation in size, quality, etc. The surprising thing, however, is not variation but a remarkable uniformity over many decades. In buying, as in all other practices, the Indians were firm conservatives.

5. The name Chippewa, or Ojibway, means "to roast till puckered up," from the tribe's method of treating prisoners of war. Or perhaps, as some less violent etymologists suggest, it refers to the puckered seams of their moccasins. Tradition suggests that the Chippewas were driven westward up the St. Lawrence by the Iroquois. Some settled at Sault Ste Marie. Others drifted around both shores of Lake Superior and on toward the headwaters of the Mississippi. Possessing great numerical strength, they drove the Fox Indians out of northern Wisconsin to refuge among the Sauk, Sak, or Sac of northern Illinois and eastern Iowa. They chased the Sioux, more properly called Dakotas, away from the Lake Mille Lacs area. (The white man's name Sioux, incidentally, comes from a Chippewa word for "enemy"—roughly, Nadiousioux or its variants, there being at least 110 spellings of the word listed in Hodge's *Handbook of American Indians*, I, 379–80.) But when the triumphant Chippewas, a forest and lake people, reached the edge of the plains, the rear guard of

the Dakotas (the advance bands were edging to the Missouri River and beyond) turned and fought them to a standstill, thanks largely to horses, the use of which the Dakotas were beginning to master.

6. The Michilimackinac Company sprang from the so-called General Store of 1779, a combination to meet the threat of Clark's activities during the American Revolution. Beyond pooling resources, the company's main intent was to reduce competition by delineating spheres of influence. By 1783 its partners were operating in Wisconsin, southern Minnesota, the fringes of Iowa, and Illinois. Its store at Cahokia throve on smuggling goods into Spanish Louisiana, principally to Auguste Chouteau, who traded out of St. Louis among the Osage Indians. J. B. Perrault took goods from Michilimackinac to Cahokia in 1783–84—by way of the Fox-Wisconsin and Mississippi, not by the Illinois, which is one more bit of evidence about the routes of the trade. ("Narrative," op. cit., p. 508.) This early Michilimackinac Company endured after a fashion for an indeterminate number of years and Dickson evidently became a partner. But it withered completely before the turn of the century and should not be confused with the later Michilimackinac Company, which was formed on December 31, 1806, to meet the growing vigor of the Americans but which soon succumbed to Astor, as the text will show.

7. Robert Dickson's description of the Michilimackinac–Prairie du Chien route is in Elliott Coues, *The Expeditions of Zebulon M. Pike*, I, 294–303. Peter Pond's description of Prairie du Chien is in Charles Gates, ed., *Five Fur Traders of the Northwest*, pp. 27 ff. (Toronto, 1931).

8. Any account of Dickson's activities on the Ainse peace mission is guesswork. He was not yet important enough to be referred to often in the course of the trial, our principal source. But he did leave Prairie du Chien ahead of Ainse, so why not with Indians afraid to travel with the more numerous Sioux? He did retain the friendship of Aird, Cameron, Patterson and the other anti-Ainse traders of Prairie du Chien. And during Ainse's long trial for misappropriation of goods, no charges were leveled at Dickson. So evidently no one had reason to suppose that he had in any way shared in his superior's misdeeds.

CHAPTER 3

The Americans Stir

GENERAL BIBLIOGRAPHY

BACKGROUND ON THE FUR TRADE and on DICKSON

As cited, Chapters 1 and 2.

JAY'S TREATY

Bemis, Samuel. *Jay's Treaty*. New York, 1924.

THE SPANISH ON THE MISSOURI RIVER

Houck, Louis. *The Spanish Régime in Missouri*, 2 vols. Chicago, 1909. (Pages 183–92, Vol. II, contain portions of Mackay's diary.)

Nasatir, A. P. *Before Lewis and Clark,* 2 vols. St. Louis, 1952.
————. "Jacques D'Eglise on the Upper Missouri, 1791–95," *MVHR,* XIV (June 1927).
Quaife, M. M., ed. "Extracts from Captain Mackay's Journal," *Proceedings of the State Hist. Soc. of Wis., 1915* (Madison, 1916).

LEWIS AND CLARK

Abel, Annie H., ed. *Tabeau's Narrative . . . to the Upper Missouri.* Norman, Okla., 1939. Tabeau was on the Missouri just ahead of Lewis and Clark.
Bakeless, John. *Lewis and Clark.* New York: 1947.
DeVoto, Bernard, ed. *The Journals of Lewis and Clark.* Boston, 1953. DeVoto's introduction discusses the imperialistic aims of the expedition.
Lewis, Meriwether. *The Lewis and Clark Expedition,* 3 vols. Philadelphia and New York, 1961. A reprint of the Biddle-Allen edition of 1814.
Thwaites, Reuben Gold, ed. *The Original Journals of the Lewis and Clark Expedition,* 7 vols. New York, 1905.

FUR TRADE AND INDIAN AFFAIRS, MISSOURI TERRITORY, 1803–05.

Chouteau, Pierre, Senior. Ms "Letter Book, Oct. 1804–April, 1819," in the Chouteau Col., Mo. Hist. Soc. Especially for this chapter, letters of Nov. 19, 1804; March 11, May 11, May 19, 1805.
Carter, Clarence E., ed. *The Territorial Papers of the United States* Vol. XIII, *The Territory of Louisiana-Missouri, 1803–06.* Washington, 1948.

UNITED STATES INDIAN POLICY

Peake, Ora B. *A History of the United States Indian Factory System.* Denver, 1954.
Prucha, Francis Paul. *American Indian Policy in the Formative Years.* Cambridge, Mass., 1962.

NOTES AND SPECIFIC REFERENCES

1. By the time Dickson was established in western Minnesota, Alexander Mackenzie was insisting in his famous *Voyages from Montreal . . . to the Pacific* that the area belonged to Britain. His contentions were twofold. One, the Hudson's Bay Company's venerable charter granted it a trading monopoly over all streams flowing into Hudson Bay; the Red River, which drained parts of Minnesota and North Dakota did flow into the Bay. Second, the Treaty of Paris, 1783, stated that the international boundary should run *west* from Lake of the Woods to the head of the Mississippi. The Mississippi, however, heads south of Lake of the Woods. Mackenzie and other British fur men argued that therefore the boundary should go south to the forty-fifth parallel (near present St. Paul-Minneapolis), then veer west past the top of the Red, and continue to the Pacific. Such a line would give the British most of the rich fur area west of Lake Superior and, of more interest to Mackenzie, the Columbia River watershed in the Pacific Northwest.

The American diplomat, John Jay, blocked British attempts (but not British grumblings) to "rectify" the central border south from Lake of the Woods to the Mississippi. The Columbia dispute, however, hung in abeyance another fifty years. The

United States based her Oregon claims on the discovery of the Columbia's mouth by an American sea-otter trader, Robert Gray, in May 1792; on the Lewis and Clark expedition, 1804–06, and on John Jacob Astor's ill-fated Astorian expedition of 1811–13. Covered wagons following the paths of the fur traders were the irresistible force that finally carried the point.

2. Charles Mackenzie, "The Missouri Indians," in L. R. Masson, *Les Bourgeois de la Compagnie du Nord-Ouest* (Quebec, 1889–90) Vol. I, p. 332. The same Indian had other comments on the corrosion of the trade (p. 333). "In my young days there were no white men, and we knew no wants. . . . The white people came, they brought with them some good, but they brought the small pox, and they brought evil liquors; the Indians since diminish and they are no longer happy."

Reports vary as to how many beaver really inhabited the middle Missouri. Pierre-Antoine Tabeau, who tried to exploit the section just ahead of Lewis and Clark, insists there were not many. (Abel, ed., Tabeau's *Narrative*, pp. 83–87.) But members of the Lewis and Clark expedition on their way upstream seem to have trapped the animals everywhere without difficulty. Lewis specifically states that from central South Dakota northward, beaver abounded. (Lewis–Jefferson, Sept. 23, 1806, in Thwaites, *Original Journals*, VII, 334–37.)

3. The American advance down the Ohio toward the Mississippi was also recognized as a menace. To combat it the Spanish tried to weaken the United States by fostering frontier schemes designed to split the trans-Appalachian West from the Atlantic seaboard, and set up the former as a weak independent nation. George Rogers Clark's shabby treatment by his government after the Revolution led him to accept Spanish money for furthering the intrigues. James Wilkinson, who later became governor of Louisiana Territory, was another Spanish agent. Of Wilkinson, more hereafter.

4. Dickinson's figures are in Robert Hamilton's "Observations on the Trade of Upper Canada, 24 Sept. 1798," *Mich. P & H Col.*, XXV, 202–06.

5. Canadian memorials protesting American harassments are in William R. Manning, *Diplomatic Correspondence of the United States, Canadian Relations* (Washington 1940) pp. 571–79. See also *ASP, Foreign Relations*, III, 152–53, 164.

6. Figures from the memorial cited in Note 5 above.

7. So did Lewis and Clark. Acting, presumably, on government instructions, the explorers told the British traders whom they met at the Mandan villages during the winter of 1804–05 that aliens would not be restricted so long as they heeded the trading laws of the United States. To many of the British, the proclamation of August, 1805, denying them admission to Louisiana Territory, came as a total surprise.

8. Gurdon Hubbard, who like Ramsay Crooks entered the trade in his teens, gives a graphic example of Indian justice. He was at an Indian camp on Grand River, western Michigan, when a murderer who the previous year had drunkenly stabbed the son of a chief returned from his winter hunt without enough furs to satisfy the dead man's father. With his family at his heels, the guilty man marched up to the bereaved chief, thumping a drum and singing his death song. Stoically he presented himself to the old man, who handed a knife to another son and nodded. The son drove the blade hilt deep into the passive waiter. Not a sound stirred the camp until the body lay still; then the wife and children threw themselves onto the corpse with wails of grief. But there was a happy ending of sorts. Recognizing his responsibilities in the affair, the old chief adopted the widow and her family. (Henry E. Hamilton, ed., *Incidents and Events in the Life of Gurdon Saltonstall Hubbard*, Chicago, 1888, pp. 59–66.)

CHAPTER 4

Citizenship by Necessity

GENERAL BIBLIOGRAPHY

ROBERT DICKSON & COMPANY

Kellogg, Louise P. *The British Régime in Wisconsin and the Northwest*, pp. 225–60. Madison, 1935.
Tohill, Louis Arthur. "Robert Dickson, British Fur Trader," *North Dakota Historical Quarterly*, III (Oct. 1928), pp. 25–30.

EARLY ST. LOUIS, JAMES WILKINSON, AND THE INDIAN DELEGATION

Carter, Clarence E., ed. *The Territorial Papers of the United States*, XIII, op. cit., pp. 135–317 passim.
Scharf, J. Thomas. *History of St. Louis City and County*, Vol. I, Philadelphia, 1883.

ZEBULON PIKE

Coues, Elliott, ed. *The Expeditions of Zebulon M. Pike*, Vol. I, New York, 1895.

NOTES AND SPECIFIC REFERENCES

1. The North West Company post on St. Joseph Island was built in 1792. When the British garrison left Michilimackinac in 1796, it also established itself on St. Joseph in order to command the canoe route between Lake Superior and Lake Huron. Title was acquired from the Indians for £1200 in blankets, strouds, guns, fire, steel, silver medals for the chiefs, and fifty gallons of high wine diluted to one-third strength. The Indians got so drunk that the commissioners negotiating the sale fled in dismay.

Most of the island was covered with deciduous trees and was suitable for cultivation, but the site chosen for the new British fort was dismal—a round granite hump on a peninsula joined to the southwest side of the island by a marshy neck of land; this marsh was drained and turned into a vegetable garden of sorts. Trading houses and Indian camps grew up around the stockade, but the fort itself was never quite completed. (See John Johnston, "An Account of Lake Superior" in L. R. Masson, *Les Bourgeois de la Compagnie du Nord-Ouest* (Quebec, 1889–90) Vol. II, 172; also Joseph E. and Estelle L. Bayliss, *River of Destiny, the Saint Marys*. Detroit: Wayne University Press, 1955.

2. I have not endeavored to unravel Gillespie's connections with Crooks's first employers (Maitland, Garden and Auldjo) or with Dickson's chief backers, J. and A. McGill & Company. Gillespie was not a member of either firm; and so there is no apparent reason why Crooks would turn to him. (The different Montreal supply houses were as often linked as opposed, however.) For Gillespie, see index of W.

Stewart Wallace, *Documents Relating to the North West Company*, Toronto, 1943. Also frequent references in the Blackwood Letter Books, loc. cit. next chapter.

Tradition is firm that Gillespie hired Crooks. (Crooks's obituary in the New York *Journal of Commerce*, preserved in *Wisconsin Necrology*, I, 6, State Hist. Soc. of Wis. Also *WHC* IV, pp. 95–102.) Crooks himself wrote only, "I first went to Mackinaw in 1805, as a clerk to Robert Dickson & Co. . . . I was proud to call Robert Dickson my friend." (Crooks to H. M. Rice, Oct. 16, 1857, in E. D. Neill, *The History of Minnesota*, 5th ed. Minneapolis 1883, pp. 291–92n.)

3. A long time passed between ordering goods and realizing profits. Bales ordered from London in 1803 would be distributed to the traders at Michilimackinac in the summer of 1804. They would be traded for furs during the following winter. The furs would be assembled at Mackinac and shipped to Montreal in the late summer of 1805, and sold in London in the spring of 1806—at which time the debt for the original goods could be paid. Financing this long span of credit was one of the trade's severe burdens and a factor leading to repeated attempts at monopoly.

4. *Mich. P & H Col.*, XXXII, p. 339.

5. Henry Brevoort, one of Astor's early agents, left Montreal on May 16, 1811, with 14 paddlers and 4000 pounds of baggage. The party camped about nine each evening, started again at 3 A.M. On May 26 they were in Mackinac—eleven days to cover nine hundred miles. "These indefatigable Canadians," Brevoort wrote immediately afterwards, "surmount every obstruction by a sort of instinct unknown in any other animal." (George Hellman, ed., *Letters of Henry Brevoort to Washington Irving*, New York, 1918, pp. 20–25.) For routes, customs and the like, see Wayne Stevens, *The Northwest Fur Trade*, pp. 148–61; Gordon C. Davidson, *The North West Company*, pp. 212–26.

6. Manning, *Diplomatic Correspondence*, pp. 577–79.

7. Aird crossed the Chicago portage on May 21, 1805. (*Kinzie Account Book*, Chicago Historical Society.) This almost certainly means he came up the Illinois River that spring, which in turn strongly suggests that he was one of the British traders who had joined the rush to the Missouri River in the fall of 1804 and had wintered somewhere on that stream—presumably up toward the mouth of the James River, where he could meet Sioux Indians, whose language he knew. Quite possibly he was in St. Louis when Dickson brought down the Sioux delegation from Prairie du Chien early in May. If so, he perhaps shared some of the good will of agent Pierre Chouteau, Sr. This, as well as familiarity with the land, would be another reason for having Aird take charge of Robert Dickson & Company's operations on the Missouri.

No uncertainty whatsoever attends Aird's movements from the summer of 1805 on through the next winter; several official documents contain references to him. If Crooks was his clerk, then Crooks's movements also become clear. Reasons for assuming that Crooks was with him through the winter of 1805–06 are set forth in David Lavender, "Ramsay Crooks's First Ventures on the Missouri River," *Bulletin* of the Missouri Historical Society, Vol. XX (January, 1964), pp. 92–96.

8. Wilkinson was a notorious conspirator. During the Revolution he had risen to the rank of brigadier general but had been stripped of his honors for joining the Conway Cabal against Washington. Moving to the frontier as a trader, he became a highly paid Spanish agent on his promise to weaken the United States by working to split the trans-Appalachian West away from the Atlantic seaboard. During the Indian wars in Ohio he wormed back to high rank in the regular army and devoted his energies to trying to seize Wayne's command for himself. When France obtained Louisiana Territory, he was dropped from the Spanish payroll, but was reinstated when the Americans purchased the western lands. By that time many people dis-

trusted James Wilkinson. He was nevertheless able to knock at enough influential back doors to wangle an appointment as governor of Upper Louisiana.

While governor he became involved in Aaron Burr's fantastic conspiracy. (Later, when he saw the scheme fizzling, he betrayed Burr.) Zebulon Pike may have been, on both his Mississippi and Rocky Mountain adventures, a dupe of the two conspirators. A source of lead for shot would have been of interest to the schemers and may account for Wilkinson's desire to learn about Dubuque's mines. Or perhaps the new governor simply wanted to curry favor with Jefferson by fostering exploration, a pet hobby of the President's. In any event, Pike's expedition was put into motion somewhat extralegally by Wilkinson himself and not by the United States Government, as was the Lewis and Clark expedition. (W. Eugene Hollon, *The Lost Pathfinder, Zebulon Montgomery Pike*, Norman, Oklahoma: University of Oklahoma Press, 1949, pp. 18, 41–53.)

9. Crooks's father-in-law, Bernard Pratte, was married to a Chouteau. If my assumption that Crooks first reached St. Louis in 1805 is correct, his future wife, Emilie Pratte, was born within months of his arrival. For whatever little the romantic speculation is worth, he conceivably saw her in her cradle, or perhaps heard her crying somewhere out of sight if he was entertained at dinner.

10. Throughout the text the mileage figures given for distances on the Missouri, a very sinuous river, are those estimated by Lewis and Clark (Meriwether Lewis, *The Lewis and Clark Expedition*, Nicholas Biddle and Paul Allen, eds., introduction by Archibald Hanna, Philadelphia and New York: J. B. Lippincott Company, 1961. Vol. III, pp. 831–35). Land distances over today's highways are considerably shorter and so cloud the enormous effort expended by the early voyageurs.

11. Before fleeing their contaminated village, the survivors of the epidemic took Blackbird's corpse to the chief's favorite lookout on a hill commanding a long view of the twisting Missouri. There they buried him under a deep mound of earth and for many years carried food to his spirit. When Lewis and Clark visited the spot they found a staff eight feet tall set into the top of the mound. They too did obeisance of sorts to the old villain by fastening to the top of the staff "a white flag, bordered with red, blue, and white." Ramsay Crooks, who later spent many winter months in the vicinity, learned the legends clustered about the chief and the grave, and delighted in telling them to travelers. (John Bradbury, *Travels in the Interior of America*, in R. G. Thwaites, *Early Western Travels*, Vol. V, Cleveland, 1904.)

12. Aird to Jacob Franks, from St. Louis, June 7, 1806. *WHC*, XIX, pp. 316–17.

CHAPTER 5

The Meeting at La Charette

GENERAL BIBLIOGRAPHY

PIKE, as before.

ROBERT DICKSON & COMPANY, as before plus:

Blackwood, Thomas, ms "Letter Book, 1805–07," photostats at the state historical societies of Minnesota and Wisconsin.

LEWIS AND CLARK, as in Chapter 3.

ROBERT MCCLELLAN AND RAMSAY CROOKS

Finafrock, John. "Robert McClellan." Kittochtinny Historical Society. 1927? Chambersburg, Pa.

Kinzie Account Books. Chicago Historical Society. (This is a transcript of originals lost in the Chicago fire. The ledger is a tantalizingly incomplete record of persons who crossed the Chicago portage in the early 1800s.)

Lavender, David. "Ramsay Crooks's First Ventures on the Missouri River." *The Bulletin,* Missouri Historical Society, XX (January 1964).

Roosevelt, Theodore. *Winning the West,* part V, chapter 5. Various editions.

THE ARICARA CHIEF

Carter, op. cit., XIII, pp. 228, 235–36, 243–44, 247, 316–17, 355–59, 486–88.

NOTES AND SPECIFIC REFERENCES

1. This dichotomy persisted as long as the trade did. The Indians expected liquor to signalize important dealings with the whites. Even so ardent a prohibitionist as Lawrence Taliaferro, agent at St. Peter's in the 1820s, regularly gave alcohol to his Indians on important occasions. Yet selling it was forbidden. The distinction must have seemed subtle to primitive minds, especially since many traders obeyed the letter of the law by not "charging" for spirits yet often used "gifts" of alcohol to start bartering on its way.

2. It is unclear whether Murdock Cameron was a member of Robert Dickson & Company. He and Dickson had been associated on the St. Peter's before the forming of the organization, and later were together in the Michilimackinac Company. (P. L. Scanlan, *Prairie du Chien,* pp. 85–87. Menasha, Wisconsin, 1937.) Pike's journal, however, implies that Cameron was a rival of Dickson's during the winter of 1805–06—but Pike did not always assay accurately everything he saw.

Shortly after Pike had threatened Cameron with prosecution for selling liquor, he was approached by Cameron's clerk, wily Joseph Rolette, born in Quebec in 1781, educated by Jesuits, and destined to be Crooks's thorniest agent in the American Fur Company. Rolette offered Pike gifts of brandy, coffee, sugar. "I hesitated about receiving those articles from the partner of the man I intended to prosecute; their amount being trifling, however, I accepted of them, offering him pay. I assured him that the prosecution arose from a sense of duty, and not from any personal prejudice." Rolette would spend much of his stormy life in similiar light-footed maneuvers with government officials.

3. The packs that had come out of Michilimackinac in 1790 had been worth £20 each, on an average. (Innis, op. cit., p. 267.) Prices were lower in 1806. On July 18 of that year the factor in charge of the United States trading house at Fort Wayne wrote that the spring sales in London had been so bad that the fur traders in Indiana were bankrupt. (*ASP, Ind. Aff.* I, 370–71.) Affairs elsewhere must have been comparable.

4. Notice of suit, 1806, Lisa papers, Missouri Historical Society. Also Minute Book of the Missouri Supreme Court, 1805–08, Missouri Historical Society. These citations are by courtesy of Lisa's biographer, Richard Oglesby, whose book had not appeared when this was written.

5. Astor's purchases in Montreal are outlined by James McGill to Isaac Todd, Oct. 17, 1805, Blackwood Letter Book, 1805–07, loc. cit. The account of the draft on Astor to pay Dickson's duties is in Blackwood, on Mackinac, to J. and A. McGill & Co., July 1, 1806.

6. Blackwood to McGill & Co., June 28, 1807, ibid., says that Aird's 1806–07 outfit was worth 76,500 livres. A livre is an elusive quantity, say 16 to 20 cents.

7. Lewis, in St. Louis, to Jefferson, Sept. 23, 1806. In Thwaites, *Original Journals,* VII, pp. 334–37.

CHAPTER 6

Bold Hopes

GENERAL BIBLIOGRAPHY

INDIAN EARTH LODGES

Catlin, George. *North American Indians.* 2 vols. London, 1841. Letter 11.
Will, George F. "The Mandan Lodge at Bismarck," *North Dakota Historical Quarterly,* I (October 1925), pp. 38–48.

A TRADER'S LIFE

Hamilton, Henry E., ed., *Incidents and Events in the Life of Gurdon Saltonstall Hubbard,* Chicago, 1888.

TRADE PROBLEMS ON THE MISSOURI, 1807

Carter, Clarence E. *The Territorial Papers of the United States,* Vol. XIV, *The Territory of Louisiana-Missouri, 1806–1814.* Washington, 1952. pp. 108–09, 136–37, 153–54.
Chouteau, Pierre, Sr. *Letter Book,* and Chouteau, Auguste, *Papers.* Chouteau Collections. Mo. Hist. Soc.
Marshall, Thomas Maitland, ed. *The Life and Papers of Frederick Bates.* 2 vols. St. Louis, 1926.

TECUMSEH

Any general history of the Indians or even of the United States contains material. A useful summary is in Frederick W. Hodge, *Handbook of American Indians,* 2 vols. (reprint, Paterson, New Jersey: Pageant Books, 1959). II, pp. 714, 729.

NOTES AND SPECIFIC REFERENCES

1. This seems to contradict William Clark's statement in his journal that Reed and Mr. Aird's clerk were bound for the Osages (in western Missouri) and the Otos (near the mouth of the Platte). Aird, however, later testified that he met his boats near the Platte and ascended with them to his post among the Sioux, pausing en route at the Maha village, whose trade was lucrative enough to merit a clerk's attention. (Dep-

osition given Sept. 22, 1807, in St. Louis. Transcript of record in the General Court, April 6 and 10, 1810. Chouteau Papers. Missouri Historical Society.)

2. Annie H. Abel, *Tabeau's Narrative*, pp. 146–47.

3. Crooks and McClellan owned one wintering cabin near the Platte River that had three rooms. (Dr. Thomas' account of Lisa's 1809 adventure in the *Louisiana Gazette*, Nov. 30, 1809. State Hist. Soc. of Mo., Columbia, Mo.)

4. This account of Spanish custom on the river is from Meriwether Lewis' "Observations and Reflections on Upper Louisiana," Thwaites, *Original Journals*, VI, 369–88. Lewis, incidentally, was appointed governor of Missouri Territory in March 1807, but stayed in Washington for Burr's trial and did not reach St. Louis until March 8, 1808. His place was filled during the interim by Frederick Bates, Secretary of the Territory, who reached St. Louis April 1, 1807, and functioned as acting governor for almost a year. Clark was appointed Brigadier General of Louisiana Militia early in 1807 and was rushed to Missouri to organize the territory's armed forces against hypothetical Burr conspirators. Late in 1807 he returned East to be married, turned around and reached St. Louis again in June 1808.

5. Crooks and McClellan started up the river in August 1807 with eighty men. (Thomas Biddle to Henry Atkinson, from Camp Missouri, a little above present Omaha, October 29, 1819. *ASP, Ind. Aff.* II, 201–03. Biddle, writing twelve years after the episode, dated it 1808, a patent slip since related events clearly fix 1807 as the date.) Eighty men definitely means keelboats. At most a Mackinaw barge such as those Crooks and Aird had used in ascending the river in 1806 would carry only ten men, fewer if there were many goods.

6. McClellan and Aird were both at the Maha villages at least as late as May 11. (Court records, cited in Note 1 above.) Crooks was in St. Louis by May 1. (Thomas Blackwood to J. and A. McGill & Co., June 28, 1807. Blackwood Letter Book, loc. cit.) Robert McClellan and Company were given a trading license on May 1, 1807. (Thomas Maitland Marshall, ed., *The Life and Papers of Frederick Bates*, St. Louis, 1926, II, 31.) Since McClellan himself could not have taken out the license, Crooks probably did. Crooks may also have purchased boats, hired crews, and completed the other chores embraced in McClellan's remark of April 5 to Lewis: "I have arranged my business for to visit the upper parts of the Missouri as soon as I posably can after my arival at St. Louis." (This letter is in the Voorhis Memorial Collection, Missouri Historical Society.) Actually, no record exists to indicate where Crooks was between early May and mid-September, 1807. I assume he went to Mackinac as promptly as he could because Robert Dickson would have been anxious for his pelts (reports reaching Blackwood said Crooks had done well) and, furthermore, most goods used on the Missouri came from Michilimackinac. Certainly it was a logical place for Crooks to buy. But to do it he had to keep moving. We know that McClellan and he met Pryor near today's Omaha late in September or very early in October. They must have left St. Louis, therefore, about August 10–15. Crooks did not reach Michilimackinac until after June 28. (Blackwood on that date mentions rumors of him but not his presence.) A month from St. Louis to Mackinac by way of Chicago was good time; a return trip through Green Bay generally took less than a month. So if Crooks did go to the island, as I believe, he could not have sat around very long enjoying the rendezvous. All told, it was an extraordinary trust to be placed in one of his years.

7. Marked discrepancies exist concerning the number of men in the Chouteau-Pryor party. I use William Clark's in his letter to Secretary of War Dearborn, June 1, 1807, Carter, *Territorial Papers*, XIV, 126. (But see also Clark-Dearborn, May 18, 1807, ibid., 122, where different numbers are given.)

Most accounts have Pierre Chouteau, Jr., leading the traders, although Pierre was only eighteen in 1807. I follow the *Dictionary of American Biography* in ascribing leadership to his older brother, Auguste Pierre, who until January 1807 had served as an ensign under Wilkinson and thus fits various remarks about "young Chouteau" having been an officer.

8. William Clark to Secretary of War Dearborn, May 18, 1807 (Carter, *Territorial Papers*, XIV, 122), indicates that more parties than those named in the text were on their way up the river. McClellan's letter of April 5 to Lewis adds that "Mr. Corta a Kenedien who obtained Licenses to Traide with with [*sic*] the Sioux & Poncaws for the year 1806 Proceeds on a voige this spring up the Missouri Expecting To Reach the falls before he Stops." This suggests a possible explanation to two tantalizing mysteries—the authorship of the mysterious Jeremy Pinch letters ordering David Thompson of the North West Company out of the post he established in 1807 on the headwaters of the Columbia River; and the identity of the Mr. Courter who was killed on the upper Missouri in 1809.

If McClellan's Corta (whom Lewis and Clark met in 1806 near the Kansas River) did go to the falls and beyond, he probably preceded Lisa. If Corta heard from British traders at the Mandan villages of Thompson's intent to cross the Rockies that year and if he picked up western geographic names by running into Colter, who was trapping on the upper Missouri with Dixon and Hancock, he could very well be the man who tried to bluff Thompson out of the country by sending Indians to him with a letter purportedly written by a U.S. army officer. (For "Pinch," see Lavender, *Land of Giants*, p. 78, and *Western Vision*, pp. 129–32.)

David Thompson (*Narrative*, ed. by John Tyrrell, Toronto, 1916, p. 419) tells of rewarding Kullyspell Indians in Montana in 1809 for protecting the property and burying the corpse of a Mr. Courter who was killed on the headwaters of the Missouri because of his "imprudence . . . in going to the War Grounds with a small party to hunt the bison and set traps for the Beaver." Historians have speculated that Thompson meant John Colter, who in 1809 was working for Lisa on the headwaters of the Missouri, but who was *not* killed during his famous adventures with the Blackfeet. (For example, see Catherine White, ed., *Thompson's Journals . . .* Missoula, Montana, 1950, pp. 88–95.) McClellan's "Corta" is another possibility. The speculation is useful chiefly in suggesting that more men than history has recorded invaded the northern Rockies immediately on the heels of Lewis and Clark.

9. This identification of Labaddie and Auguste Chouteau as the backers of Crooks and McClellan rests on very shaky evidence, as presented in H. M. Chittenden, *A History of the American Fur Trade of the Far West*, p. 160, and Philip Ashton Rollins, *The Discovery of the Oregon Trial*, p. lxxxii, A discussion of it is in Lavender "Crooks's Early Ventures," op. cit. If the evidence does not hold up, then we do not know who the backers were.

10. Clark to Dearborn, July 17, 1807. Carter, *Territorial Papers*, XIV, pp. 136–37. See Note 1 above for citation of the trial.

11. Kinzie Account Books. Aird crossed the Chicago portage on July 12 with two boats and forty-six packs of furs. Forty-six packs are not half of what could be anticipated from the amount of trade articles he is known to have had. Some of his clerks (Crooks?) must have gone ahead of him with more furs. Kinzie did not note their passage; but his accounts are by no means complete.

12. The quotations concerning the Prophet and the suspicions of American officials concerning the British are, in order, John Askin Jr. to his father, Sept. 1, 1807, *WHC* XIX, 322. *ASP, Ind. Aff.* I, 798. Bates to Clark, July 25, 1807, and Bates to Dearborn, August 12, 1807, in Marshall, op. cit. I, pp. 166–68, 172. Dunning to Clark, Aug. 20, 1807, Carter, *Territorial Papers*, X (*Michigan Territory*), 127–28.

CHAPTER 7

Frustrations

GENERAL BIBLIOGRAPHY

TRADE PROBLEMS ON THE MISSOURI 1808–09

As in Chapter VI, especially correspondence between Secretary of War William Eustis and Meriwether Lewis, William Clark, Pierre Chouteau Sr. and Jr., Carter, pp. 285–353 passim.

ST. LOUIS MISSOURI FUR COMPANY

Douglas, Walter B. "Manuel Lisa," Missouri Historical Society *Collections,* III, No. 3, 1911.

James, Thomas. *Three Years Among the Indians and Mexicans,* Walter B. Douglas, ed., St. Louis, 1916. Chapter 1 and notes.

Oglesby, Richard. *Manuel Lisa and the Opening of the Missouri Fur Trade.* Norman, Okla.: University of Oklahoma Press, 1963.

ASTOR'S ENTRY INTO THE WESTERN FUR TRADE

Bridgwater, Dorothy, ed. "John Jacob Astor Relative to His Settlement on the Columbia River," The Yale University Library *Gazette,* XXIV, No. 2 (October 1949).

Creighton, op. cit. in Chapter 1, pp. 163–68.

Gratiot, Charles, ms *Letter Book.* Gratiot Papers, Missouri Historical Society.

Porter, Kenneth Wiggins. *John Jacob Astor, Business Man,* Cambridge, Mass.: Harvard University Press, 1931. I, 164 ff.

Stevens, Wayne. "Fur Trading Companies in the Northwest, 1760–1816." *Proceedings of the Mississippi Valley Historical Association,* 1916–17 (October 1918), pp. 288–90.

NOTES AND SPECIFIC REFERENCES

1. Pryor's report on the episode is in *Annals of Iowa,* third series, I, 616–19. Pierre Chouteau to President of the U.S., Nov. 14, 1807, re British influence, Letter Book, pp. 85–86. Mo. Hist. Soc. William Clark also suspected British instigation. (*Annals of Iowa,* op. cit., p. 620.)

2. Their occupying the vicinity in such force caused trouble for Aird. On Sept. 28, 1807, he secured a license to trade with the Otos and Omahas (Marshall, op. cit., I, 203), but when he found Crooks and McClellan dominating the area he dropped downstream to the Black Snake Hills, near today's St. Joseph, Missouri. There he competed vigorously with old Joseph Robidoux. This in turn annoyed Robidoux's backer, Auguste Chouteau, who thought he had obviated such difficulties through a deal with that far-ringing negotiator, George Gillespie.

American unfriendliness to alien traders had led the new Michilimackinac Company to send Gillespie to St. Louis in November 1807 to close the "store" (a store-house for its traders rather than a retail outlet) which the company had opened in the city a few months earlier. Gillespie disposed of the store's goods to Auguste Chouteau, promising as a part of the arrangement that traders of the Michilimackinac Company would not visit the Black Snake Hills. Then along came Aird. Chouteau demanded an explanation. Gillespie replied that Aird had gone up the river before the arrangement was completed and, anyway, Aird, although a member of the company, was actually trading on his own that winter. (Gillespie–Chouteau, August 18, 1808. Chouteau Collection, Mo. Hist. Soc.)

3. The memorial of the Canadian merchants protesting the seizure is reproduced in *Mich. P & H Col.*, XXV, pp. 250–58. Other correspondence over the seizure of the boats is in Manning, *Diplomatic Correspondence*, pp. 601–05, 800–01. The boats and goods were released by the United States after a year's detention, but no damages were paid.

4. Bates's letter to Dearborn and his aborted plans for the trading houses are in Marshall, op. cit. I, 176–77, 221 ff. For Dickson's license, Bates to Meriwether Lewis, Nov. 7, 1807.

5. For John Campbell's background, *Mich. P & H Col.*, XII, 38; for the duel, John Askin, Jr., on St. Joseph, to his father, August 17, 1808, *WHC*, XIX, 325.

6. Hoffman to Bates re Crooks, August 23, 1808, Marshall, II, 16–18. To Bates re Aird, Oct. 21, 1808. Bates mss., Missouri Historical Soc.

7. Indian Agent Pierre Chouteau, long-time friend of the Osages, always claimed that Clark's treaty was worthless and that he had had to go in afterward and repair matters. (Various letters in the transcript of the Pierre Chouteau Letter Book, Mo. Hist. Soc. Clark's negotiations are in his 1808 diary, *Westward With Dragoons,* Kate Gregg, ed., Fulton, Mo., 1937.)

8. When writing to James Madison on July 27, 1813, five years after the incorporation of the American Fur Company, Astor implied that he presented his plan not by letter but in person at a conference attended by Jefferson, Gallatin, Dearborn, and Madison, and that Jefferson, pleased by the idea of an American post on the Columbia, promised government help against North West Company threats "in the most Desided & explicit maner." Surviving records do not indicate such a personal interview. Astor sometimes remembered things the way he wanted them to be. Still, it is strange he would mention the conference to Madison, who supposedly was there, if in fact no such meeting took place. (Astor–Madison, July 27, 1813, in Dorothy Bridgwater, ed., "John Jacob Astor Relative to His Settlement on the Columbia River," op. cit.)

9. Davidson, *The North West Company*, Berkeley 1918, pp. 123–25. This appeal to the Board of Trade was not primarily directed at Astor, though Mackenzie did urge prompt action in granting the franchise so the company could forestall the Americans who might try to follow Lewis and Clark to the Pacific. Rather, the proposed charter was one more step in trying to solve the North West Company's difficult supply problems by developing Pacific ports. (At that time Mackenzie still thought that the Fraser and Columbia rivers were the same stream. Simon Fraser proved otherwise in 1808, but news did not reach Mackenzie until 1809.) This problem also involved establishing some sort of trade-sharing agreement with the Hudson's Bay Company. Everything the Nor'Westers did, including the bargaining with Astor, was undertaken with one eye on the Hudson's Bay Company. But *that* complexity is beyond the scope of this work, which is already involved enough.

10. Gratiot to Astor, April 29, 1800: "You are beyond question the greatest of the fur merchants," and so on. (Charles Gratiot ms "Letter Book," pp. 79–81, Missouri Historical Society.)

11. This is an imaginative reconstruction of how Hunt and Crooks became involved with Astor. Some sort of fresh evaluation is necessary; Washington Irving's offhand statement that it was all arranged by a letter or so is much too casual. An enterprise of such magnitude took a great deal of planning. But since none of Hunt's correspondence with either Astor or Crooks has survived, one must guess. Fortunately enough facts and dates have survived to lend reasonably solid support to the conjectures.

Preliminary plans for the overland expedition must have started far earlier than is generally stated. True, Hunt did not go to New York to settle the actual terms until November 1809, but the general notion had been in the air at least a year before. Gratiot touched on it in a December letter to Astor (Letter Book, 111–13). The firm of Hunt and Hankinson began liquidation early in June 1809. (*Missouri Gazette*, June 10, 1809.) Hunt hardly would have taken so radical a step without first having received fairly definite assurances from Astor. The initial assurances, probably motivated by the ending of the embargo, could have—and most likely did—reach St. Louis while Crooks was in from the Black Snake Hills in April. Hunt must have relayed the scheme to Crooks at the time. What else could have caused Crooks to cancel his plans for a dissolution of his partnership with McClellan and undertake instead a lightning trip to Michilimackinac for goods?

Hunt financed the trip to Mackinac. Gratiot (to Astor June 10, 1810, Letter Book, 121) says that Hunt equipped Crooks "last fall"—1809. As the text will show, Crooks was on the Missouri from July on. He could only have been equipped in the spring, when it is known he went to Mackinac. "Fall," as Gratiot used the word, means the time the expedition took to the field, not when preparations began.

Trader Thomas James of Lisa's party, writing of events in 1809, called Crooks Astor's agent. (Thomas James, *Three Years with the Indians and Mexicans*, reprint edition, Phila. and N.Y., 1962, p. 8.) James was reminiscing after Crooks became manager of the American Fur Co., and perhaps was using this later identification. On the other hand, he perhaps meant what he said; perhaps everyone in the St. Louis Missouri Fur Co. recognized Crooks *in 1809*, before the departure of the Astorians, as Astor's agent.

Astor and Hunt valued Crooks highly. When negotiations for the Pacific Fur Company were completed in 1810, he was awarded five shares of stock, the same amount that went to Hunt and the Canadian partners in the enterprise, though Crooks was only twenty-three years old. McClellan and Joseph Miller, much older hands in the trade, received only 2½ shares each. Was this extra recognition based on the enterprise and initiative Crooks showed in pushing up the river in 1809, hoping to found advance posts?

12. Crooks's journey from Michilimackinac aboard the *Selina* is indicated both by the Kinzie Account Book and by A. T. Andreas, *History of Chicago*, I, 240.

13. James says the party met Crooks. The surgeon of the group, Dr. Thomas, writing of the expedition for the *Louisiana Gazette*, Nov. 30, 1809, does not mention Crooks but was impressed by McClellan. "Brave, generous, and kind, he meets the untutored indian with a smile of complacence; or if the temerity of the savage should exceed the bounds of honesty or approach to menace: then M'Clelland discovers his exalted courage, surrounded with indians, with his rifle, pistols &c., sword, he bids defiance to whole nations; threatening or executing extermination on all who attempt to plunder him."

CHAPTER 8

Ripostes

GENERAL BIBLIOGRAPHY

ST. LOUIS MISSOURI FUR COMPANY

As in 7.

FORMATION OF THE PACIFIC FUR COMPANY

Bridgwater and Porter as in 7.
Irving, Washington, *Astoria,* various editions.
Perrault, Jean Baptiste, *Narrative,* as in 1.
Ross, Alexander, *Adventures of the First Settlers on the Oregon or Columbia River,* M. M. Quaife, ed., Chicago, 1923, pp. 7–14, 183–92.

ASTOR AND THE NORTH WEST COMPANY

Flandrau, Grace. *Astor and the Oregon Country,* St. Paul, n.d.
Morton, A. S. "The North West Company's Columbian Enterprise and David Thompson," including the appeals of the North West Company to the British government to forestall Astor. *Canadian Historical Review,* XVII (1936), pp. 267–310.
White, M. Catherine. *David Thompson's Journals Relating to Montana . . .* (cv– cxvi; 127–74, 247–55), Missoula, Montana, 1950.

NOTES AND SPECIFIC REFERENCES

1. Lydia Pomeroy reminiscing to Mrs. Atwater, March 6, 1866 (ms letter, Chicago Historical Society). Mrs. Pomeroy traveled from Buffalo to Chicago and back on the *Selina.* At Chicago she and the wife of the *Selina's* captain were housed with the Kinzies, "the first New England ladies that ever visited the post. There we met Mr. Crooks, who Embark^{d}. with us on our return [to Mackinac] to join his friends for the Rocky Mountains." Mrs. Pomeroy mistakenly remembers the incident as happening in 1809 and erroneously recalls Robert Stuart as being on the island when Crooks arrived.

2. The implementing of the contract demanded time-consuming conferences between Astor's agents and Russian officials in New York, St. Petersburg, and Sitka. (Porter, I, pp. 171–81, 192–98, 428–59 passim.) But although details were unsettled, the threat to the North West Company, with which this account is primarily concerned, remained firm.

3. The Winships actually started ahead of Astor and, like him, hoped to buttress themselves by dealing with the Russians. In May 1810 one of their ships, the *Albatross,* sailed thirty or forty miles up the Columbia and dropped off a party of fort builders headed by a man named Brown. Flood and Indians drove the party away. As Captain Ebbets of Astor's ship *Enterprise* heard the story in Sitka (Porter, 448–

53), Brown "expected to be join'd by others that were coming across the continent." No record remains of this overland group, which presumably should have left St. Louis in the summer of 1809 or very early in 1810. Perhaps Astor's sudden energy discouraged the Winships and they called off the plan. This could have put Brown in an uncomfortable position if he had stayed on the Columbia, depending on the arrival of reinforcements by land.

4. The letter is reproduced in the *Canadian Historical Review*, XVII, 304. The Montreal partners were following the standard British argument that Alexander Mackenzie's transcontinental crossing and Lt. Broughton's examination of the lower Columbia for Vancouver had given their country a better right to the Pacific Northwest than had accrued to the United States through Robert Gray's discovery of the river estuary and Lewis and Clark's explorations.

5. Chouteau papers, Missouri Historical Society.

6. The letter is in *Mich. P & H Col.*, XXV, 268.

7. Washington Irving mentions in *Astoria* the proposal that the North West Company absorb a third of the Astor's enterprise but gives no documentation and very few details about the maneuvering, which must be surmised from very few sources. Those I use include Alexander Henry in Montreal to John Askin in Detroit, Feb. 23, 1810 (*WHC* XIX, pp. 336–37): "I expect the Indian trade will fall into [the Americans'] hands, as Mr. Astore offered to purchas out the Mackenau Co. . . . I understand he is to be connected with the N.W. Company to make settlements on the North West coast of America, to communicate with the inland N.W. trade." Astor's provisional agreement of March 10, 1810 (Astor papers, Baker Library, Cambridge, Mass., reproduced in Grace Flandrau, op. cit.) shows very clearly that an arrangement with Michilimackinac Company was contemplated. Most revealing is the letter of the wintering partners of the North West Company to William McGillivray, reproduced in Dorothy Bridgwater, op. cit. What is generally left out of consideration in accounts dealing with the duels between Astor and the Canadians is the profound effect exerted by the unpredictable actions of the Congress of the United States.

8. David Thompson's abrupt turning back west from Rainy Lake coincides with the appeals of the North West Company to the British government to forestall Astor's settlement on the Columbia. The association led some historians (for example, Arthur S. Morton, *A History of the Canadian West to 1870;* Bernard DeVoto, *The Course of Empire*) to conclude that Thompson had been instructed to race the Astorians to the mouth of the river and set up a claim ahead of Astor. But Thompson did not race. Even when he reached the upper Columbia after his long delay in crossing the Rockies, he took his time going downstream. Morton contends that if Thompson had attended to business rather than dawdling along, Britain might now own most of what is now the American Northwest.

In rejecting Morton's contention, M. Catherine White says that Thompson was merely going about his normal business as a trader and had no interest in spreading imperialism, except incidentally. Both arguments overlook the fact that Thompson had been sent on a mission, but not a race. He went west supposing that his company owned a third of Astor's enterprise. There was no point in trying to fend Astor *away* from the lower river. Rather, he hoped to confine the Americans *to* the lower river and preserve for the North West Company the upper areas, where his posts were already established. Hence his famous claim stake, placed July 9, 1811, at the junction of the Snake and Columbia: "Know hereby that this country is claimed by Great Britain . . . and that the N. W. Company of Merchants from Canada . . . do hereby intend to erect a factory in this place . . ." This was the boundary: let Astor keep below it. To make that gesture Thompson did not have to hurry.

9. *WHC* XIX, pp. 337–38.

10. These interpretations, which are not the standard, hinge on a long letter which Astor wrote May 26, 1810, to Albert Gallatin, Madison's Secretary of the Treasury. (Gallatin papers, New York Historical Society, microfilm, St. Louis Historical Society.)

> In one of my letters I mentioned to you the contingency in the agreement with the Mackinac company say that if Mr. George Gillespie Did not arrive in the last month and agreed to becom interested in the purchas and act as agent it was not binding—that gentleman Did not arrive as was expected In consequence of which . . . I have this [day?] reluctantly been obliged to Declear off the Bargain—considering however the time which I have lost & the money spent . . . I could not abandon it altogether. I have therefor made arrangements to send a party of good men up the Missurie for the purpose of exploring the country and to assertain whether it afords furrs suficient to carry on an extensive trade & to learn the best and most proper situations for the establishing posts for trade.   this party it is intended are to cross the Rockey mountains to columbia's river where it is hoped they will meet with a party which will embark in a ship & go by watter which will leave here some time in July.
>
> Mr. Hunt a gentleman of considerable observation is to have charge of the party going by land they will set out next month . . .

At the end of the letter Astor added that if arrangements could be made to get bear and raccoon skins into Russia free of duty and if political considerations improved, he might yet purchase the Michilimackinac Company, "which I feel I can Do at anytime on near as good terms as now."

11. I assume the disagreement. The standard tale for so few men being hired in Montreal is the cold water thrown on the project by the North West Company, but it simply is not reasonable that Astor's Canadian partners, thoroughly conversant with all aspects of trade, could not have hired throughout May and June the thirty or so common workers (not prodigies) which were originally contemplated for the overland party. Hunt held the number down for some other reason. His arguments and McKenzie's are not of record, but those in the text fit the situation. They were heard again immediately after the War of 1812, when some frontiersmen wanted to rule every Briton of whatever cast out of the American wilderness, while others felt the peculiar virtues of the Canadian rivermen were needed to keep the trade functioning.

Ross says the antipathy between Hunt and McKenzie arose at the winter camp on the Missouri, when Astor removed McKenzie from the command he had been sharing with Hunt and made the American the supreme authority. I doubt any sharing. From the beginning Astor's letters specifically stated that Hunt was the leader of the party, inexperience nothwithstanding. The reason is clear. Missouri law excluded British traders. Obviously an American had to lead the group. But McKenzie did not have to like it and didn't, especially when Hunt went against McKenzie's judgment.

12. Irving is the source of the figure thirty and of the statement that it was Crooks who demanded more men. But Hunt was also familiar with the Missouri and one wonders why the thought had not occurred to him.

13. Aird, for example, traveled to the Missouri with the Astorians. He witnessed the delivery of the contracts to Crooks, Miller and McClellan. (Wilson Price Hunt ms notebook, Missouri Historical Society.) At the time Aird was trading for the Montreal-Michilimackinac Company, but the firm's difficulties with Astor did not bar his rendering this small service to old friends and a former employee.

14. The Kinzie account book names James Reed as crossing the Chicago portage with Crooks in 1806. If the transcription is correct, the Reeds are different men—but the difference, James to John, is too slight to be conclusive, and Kinzie's records were not always above reproach.

15. The dates for the trip, October 21 to November 16, are Irving's—twenty-six days to drag a keelboat over what Clark calculated as 450 miles. (Actually, it is close to 500.) If the dates are correct, the men were working desperately. Traveling the next spring with a single barge (against a swifter current), Hunt required thirty-one days to journey the same distance. Lisa, straining every muscle to overtake him, spent almost as long. Lewis and Clark took fifty-four days. The Falstaffian voyageurs at whom Irving and Ross sniff for the sake of humor could not have been so very bad, and Ross's statement that McKenzie could have taken the party on to the Columbia if given his head is absurd.

16. The letter, obviously edited, is quoted in Stella Drumm, "More About Astorians," *Oregon Historical Quarterly* XXIV (December 1923), p. 348. "Two hundred miles above" seems to locate the post near Council Bluffs. This was not within the normal range of the Sioux and it does not account for vague references that McClellan tried to make contacts with the Aricaras earlier in the year. (Chittenden, *The American Fur Trade*, p. 162.) Perhaps he started up the river and was turned back again by the Sioux, who then followed him and robbed him.

In May 1813, shortly after returning from the Pacific, McClellan was jailed for debt, but was released on taking bankruptcy. I do not know whether this was connected with the Sioux loss or, if so, how Crooks and Miller fared. Presumably they would also have been partly accountable.

Accounts of the Hunt party generally follow Irving in implying that McClellan knew nothing of the overland party until he met it and that Crooks prevailed on him to join. But I can't believe Hunt negotiated a contract for McClellan without McClellan's knowledge. If Crooks had to prevail on him, it was probably because of McClellan's resentment at being given only half as many shares as his junior.

CHAPTER 9

By Sea

GENERAL BIBLIOGRAPHY

Bridgewater, Irving (Chapters IV–XII), Porter (pp. 181–92), Ross (Chapters II–IX), op. cit., 7 and 8 above.

Franchère, Gabriel. *Narrative of a Voyage to the Northwest Coast of America,* in R. G. Thwaites, *Early Western Travels,* VI, 167 ff. Cleveland, 1904.

Thompson, David. *Narrative of His Explorations in Western America, 1784–1812,* ed. J. B. Tyrrell. Toronto, 1916. pp. 443–517.

Elliott, T. C., ed. Excerpts from Thompson's journals in *Oregon Historical Quarterly,* XV (Dec. 1914) and *Washington Historical Quarterly,* VI (Jan. 1915), VIII (Oct. 1917).

ROBERT STUART'S BACKGROUND

Marlott, Helen Stuart Mackay-Smith. *The Letters of Robert and Elizabeth Sullivan Stuart,* n.p., 1961. Vol. II, pp. 1021–33.

Rollins, Philip Ashton, ed. *The Discovery of the Oregon Trail, Robert Stuart's Narratives.* New York: Charles Scribner's Sons, 1935. (Biographical Note and Foreword.)

NOTES AND SPECIFIC REFERENCES

1. In May, Robert Stuart took a twelve-day trip to the Cascades of the Columbia, nearly 200 miles away, to investigate Indian rumors of a trading post of whites. They found a Spanish castaway and also made a side exploration up the Cowlitz River, of present-day Washington, but discovered no post.

2. Finan McDonald's letter suggests that John Stuart's Fort Estekatadene was built in late 1810 or was anticipated in early 1811. If so, I know nothing about it. In late 1812 John Stuart was at McLeod Lake well north of Prince George, British Columbia. (Stuart Lake in the same general area is named for him.) In 1813 he worked out what became the supply route for that remote wilderness. Boats would ascend the Columbia to the Okanogan River in northern Washington and go up that river to Lake Okanagan (the Canadian and American spellings differ). From Lake Okanagan packhorses moved the goods past Fort Kamloops on the Thompson River, through the Cariboo country (famous later for its gold deposits) and on to Prince George. This would have been a fantastic journey for the two Indian messengers, even if they had known where to go. But, as the text indicates, the letter may have been a ruse and not intended to reach any specific destination. (See Thompson's *Narrative*, 512–13.)

3. Ross says David Stuart's party had two Chinook canoes, each carrying 15–20 packs of merchandise—that is, a little less than a ton each. Irving, *Astoria*, 75, says three canoes. Thompson (*Narrative*, 510), whom I follow, says three heavy log canoes, or pirogues.

4. These critical letters (generally overlooked by historians, though printed in the *Yale Library Gazette*, XXIV, Oct. 1949, pp. 52–55) dispose of the charges by Irving, Ross, et al. that McDougall was being disloyal to Astor when he helped Thompson explore the Columbia's mouth, gave him supplies, and in general treated the explorer like a friend. For all McDougall knew, Thompson was not only a friend but a partner. Of course he was cordial.

5. Query: Could Thompson have been referring to the west side of the Cascade Mountains, not to the Rockies, as is generally supposed? The North West Company, to be sure, had no posts west of the Cascades to abandon; but Franchère, writing from memory, may have erred on that point. If the Cascades rather than the Rockies were to be the dividing line between the Pacific Fur Co. and the North West Co., then and only then do Thompson's activities east of the Cascades become logical.

Franchère says (p. 254) that Thompson produced a letter from McGillivray to support his, Thompson's, contentions about a dividing line at the Rockies. McGillivray's letter, however, was not about lines but about the proposal that the Nor'-Westers buy a third of Astor's Pacific enterprise. Franchère obviously did not remember details correctly—or perhaps never knew them. It is my own opinion that Thompson suggested using the Cascade line as part of his not very clever attempt to hold the Astorians to the coast.

CHAPTER 10

And by Land

GENERAL BIBLIOGRAPHY

Irving (Chaps. XIV–XXI), Porter (251–56, 454–69), Ross (Chap. X), as before.
Brackenridge, H. M. *A Journal of a Voyage up the River Missouri* . . . (in R. G. Thwaites, ed., *Early Western Travels*, VI, Cleveland, 1904).
Bradbury, John. *Travels in the Interior of America* . . . *1809–1811* . . . (in R. G. Thwaites, ed., *Early Western Travels*, V, Cleveland, 1904).

NOTES AND SPECIFIC REFERENCES

1. For an indication of the number of desertions, see K. W. Porter, "Roll of the Overland Astorians," *Oregon Historical Quarterly*, XXXIV (June 1933). The party's sporadic trading is indicated by the fact that Hunt sent at least twelve packs of buffalo robes through Auguste Chouteau to Astor in the summer of 1811. (Chouteau Papers, Missouri Historical Society.) Bradbury's entry for May 1, 1811, shows that Crooks traded as far from the Nodaway as the Platte. In spite of these desultory activities, the hired hands still had time to sit around, find fault, and worry about the future.

CHAPTER 11

The Harrowing

GENERAL BIBLIOGRAPHY

Irving (Chaps. XXII–L), Ross (XI–XII, XIV) as before, plus scattered bits in Franchère op. cit. and Ross Cox, *Adventures on the Columbia River* . . . New York, 1832.
Hunt's journal of the overland trip was redacted for *Nouvelles Annales des Voyages* . . . Vol. X, Paris 1821, and is translated in Rollins (op. cit.), pp. 281–308. The journal itself has not survived.
Robert Stuart's account of his return across the continent with Crooks, McClellan and their voyageurs is in Rollins, pp. 1–263.

THE SOUTH WEST COMPANY AND THE NON-INTERCOURSE ACT

Hellman, George S., ed. *Letters of Henry Brevoort to Washington Irving*, New York, 1918. pp. 20–38, 343–48.

NOTES AND SPECIFIC REFERENCES

1. Hunt notes (Rollins, 286) that all eight of the Indians left the party on Sept. 8 but later reports (p. 289) that "two Snake Indians who had followed us from the Absarokas [Crows] came to our camp" near the junction of the Snake and Hoback rivers. The pair move like shadows in and out of the narratives for the next year.

2. Shoshone Falls, 212 feet high, and Twin Falls, 182 feet high, were spectacular sights along the western part of this stretch. Hunt's diary curiously mentions "falls from ten to forty feet high." Mist and foreshortening may have distorted his view; perhaps he missed seeing the main falls when he retreated from the canyon rim to avoid obstructions along its brink; or perhaps, though he said he walked 35 miles, he overestimated the distance and did not quite reach the main cataracts.

3. Some historians with the wisdom of hindsight blame Hunt for having left the party's horses at Henry's Fort. Yet even after seeing the streams of the Rockies, what riverman from the Missouri or the Great Lakes could have anticipated the lava chasms of the Snake? In his efforts to hurry along the dangerously delayed party, Hunt chose as logically as his lack of geographical information allowed.

4. It is perhaps gratuitous to sit in a dry, warm study 150 years away from the event and find fault with the plan. But it does seem haphazard. Suppose none of the searchers found horses? Winter was at hand; there was little game in the vicinity. Under the circumstances, just how long was Hunt supposed to sit still with the bulk of his men, waiting on circumstances? Should not the whole group have marched west, dividing if they felt that small parties could travel more expeditiously, but not wasting precious time doing nothing?
Although neither Hunt's nor Irving's account suggests bickering, there may have been personality clashes behind the fragmentation. Also, did lassitude influence Hunt —the need just to be quiet for a while and regenerate? He was not a wilderness man, as the others were, and may have been overwhelmed by the enormity he faced. Let others move in their restlessness if they wished; he needed, subconsciously perhaps, time to learn to fight hopelessness.

5. The effort failed and McClellan rejoined McKenzie and Reed. Accounts of the wanderings are not clear. Even Irving, who tried diligently to follow them from first-hand sources and who consulted such wilderness figures as Captain Bonneville, came up with discrepancies. (*Astoria,* pp. 260, 284–86.)

6. This tortuous reasoning may be found in a letter of Thomas Jefferson to Astor, May 24, 1812. (Bridgwater, op. cit., pp. 55–56.)

7. Astor (to Jefferson, March 14, 1812, in Porter, op. cit., pp. 508–513) knew that sixty men had been sent west from Lake Superior in the summer of 1811. This party, led by John George McTavish, reached Spokan House and its subordinate posts in the fall. The next spring (1812) McTavish went east with David Thompson, picked up word of the war between Great Britain and the United States, and hurried back west to be ready for whatever developed. It was through him that the Astorians first learned, nearly seven months after the declaration of war, that hostilities had broken out.

8. Donald McKenzie, one of the overlanders, took charge of developing the trade in the Snake country. As Crooks perhaps anticipated, he found the effort unrewarding. The Indians would not trap energetically. Not until McKenzie went to work for the North West Company and instituted his famous fur brigades, based on Fort Nez Percé (at the junction of the Walla Walla and the Columbia) did the country begin

to pay—and then only because his men trapped it themselves. This, of course, was a total revolution in custom for the Canadians, who always before had relied on the Indians to take the furs.

9. The caches were robbed by the three men who had quit Hunt during the winter in eastern Oregon and had returned to the Snake to live with the Indians. After opening the caches they had journeyed with several Indians to the headwaters of the Missouri to hunt. Blackfeet drubbed them soundly and they fled back to the Boise River in western Idaho. There they picked up Dubreuil, the voyageur who had starved with Crooks and Day. There too they were joined by three of the four trappers who had been detached from Hunt's party at the mouth of the Hoback River in western Wyoming. This quartet also had been robbed by Indians and one of its members slain. The reunited seven were rescued by John Reed when he came to retrieve the caches. The following summer (1813) Hoback, Reznor, and Robinson joined Reed. They, Reed, Dorion, and several others were massacred in January 1814. Only Dorion's wife and children escaped the bloodletting.

10. This probably was the first traverse of the gateway through the Continental Divide that became famous during the later migrations to Oregon and California. The War of 1812 slowed expansion to the West, and South Pass was all but forgotten. Not until after its "rediscovery" in March, 1824, by a chilled, hungry party of mountain men under Thomas Fitzpatrick, did it become the standard thoroughfare to the Pacific.

11. The *Missouri Gazette,* May 15, 1813, reporting the party's return from the West, says they learned at the Oto village that Tecumseh's brother, the Shawnee Prophet, had sent wampum to the Otos, inviting them to join a general Indian war against the Americans. The Otos refused, saying that they could make more money trapping beaver.

CHAPTER 12

The Pawns of War

GENERAL BIBLIOGRAPHY

THE WAR OF 1812

Considerable material—much of it in disagreement—exists on the causes of the conflict and on the frontier campaigns. I relied chiefly on

Abel, Annie H. "A History of Events Resulting in Indian Consolidation West of the Mississippi," American Historical Association, *Annual Report for 1906,* I (Washington, 1908).

Bernie, Francis. *The War of 1812.* New York, 1949.

Caruso, John Anthony. *The Great Lakes Frontier.* Indianapolis: Bobbs-Merrill Co., 1961. Chaps. 7–8.

Gilpin, Alec R. *The War of 1812 in the Old Northwest.* East Lansing, Mich.: Michigan State University Press, 1958.

Pratt, Julius. *Expansionists of 1812.* Gloucester, Mass.: Peter Smith, 1949.

Wood, William, ed., *Select British Documents of the Canadian War of 1812,* 3 vols. Toronto, 1920. Vol. I, pp. 24, 432–52.

Hacker, Louis M. "Western Land Hunger and the War of 1812," MVHR, X, (March, 1924).

Pratt, Julius. "Western Aims in the War of 1812," MVHR, XII, (June, 1925).

SPECIAL LOCALITIES AND CAMPAIGNS

Boilvin Letters, typescripts at State Historical Society of Wisconsin.

Robert Dickson Papers, 1790–1822. Copies at the Minnesota Historical Society of originals in the Public Archives at Canada, Ottawa, and in the State Historical Society of Wisconsin. Also, some Dickson correspondence, *WHC*, X, pp. 96–7, XI, 271–303 passim.

Files of *Missouri Gazette* under its various names at the State Historical Society of Missouri, Columbia, Mo.

Cruikshank's and Tohill's studies of Robert Dickson, as cited in Chapter 2 above.

Hagan, William T. *The Sac and Fox Indians*. Norman, Okla.: University of Oklahoma Press, 1958, Chaps. 3–7.

Kellogg, Louise P. *The British Régime in Wisconsin and the Northwest*. Madison, 1935.

Landon, Fred. *Lake Huron*. Indianapolis: Bobbs-Merrill Co., 1944, pp. 72–92.

Luttig, John C. (Stella Drumm, ed.) *A Fur Trading Expedition on the Upper Missouri, 1812–13*. St. Louis, 1920.

Oglesby, Richard. *Manuel Lisa*. Norman, Okla.: University of Oklahoma Press, 1963, pp. 126–57.

Quaife, Milo M. *Chicago and the Old Northwest*. Chicago, 1913. pp. 196–242.

Horsman, Reginald. "Wisconsin and the War of 1812," *Wisconsin Magazine of History*, XLVI (Autumn, 1962).

Irwin, Matthew (who was captured on Michilimackinac) to John Mason, Oct. 16, 1812. Carter, op. cit., X, pp. 411–15.

Kellogg, Louise P. "The Capture of Mackinac," Wis. Hist. Soc. *Proceedings*, II (1912).

Van Der Zee, Jacob. "Forts in the Iowa Country," *The Iowa Journal of History and Politics*, XII (April 1914).

NOTES AND SPECIFIC REFERENCES

1. If Elliott actually made so inflammatory a promise, it was contrary to policy emanating from London. The relaxing of the United States embargoes in 1809 had belatedly led the government of Great Britain to frown on efforts to incite the frontier savages. London instructed Quebec and Quebec instructed Elliott to restrain the Indians from fighting—in order, some cynical Americans believed, to preserve the savages as an effective force when the English were ready to use them. The slow-moving orders may not have reached Elliott until after Tecumseh's visit. (The delicately shifting policies of the English in connection with the Indians of the United States is discussed by Reginald Horsman in "British Indian Policy in the Northwest, 1807–17," *MVHR*, XLV, June 1958.)

2. There seems to have been an altercation along the way. The *Louisiana Gazette* (St. Louis) reported on Oct. 12, 1812, and again on June 6, 1813, that an officer of the customs collector at Mackinac was knocked down when trying to seize goods being smuggled past the island. The June 6 story names Dickson as the one who did the pummeling. Dickson's own recital (a memorandum of Dec. 3, 1812, claiming compensation for services, photostat in the Dickson papers, Minnesota Historical Society) says only ". . . notwithstanding the impediments thrown in my way by the American government, I was fortunate enough to reach the country where I usually carried on my trade."

3. As typical examples, *c'est l'avril* came out *cel avrille; j'espère* as *jais pairre,* and so on. English proper names floored him. "Pittsburgh" he rendered "Piteschebuewrgue." It is unlikely that anyone in the War Department ever read very many of the almost indecipherable letters and reports Boilvin wrote between 1811 and 1823. They were translated in the early 1940s, with prodigious effort and ingenuity, by Marian Scanlan, who deposited typescripts of them in the State Historical Society of Wisconsin.

4. Astor may have been foolish in writing so many letters about the war to so many Canadians; however, his intent was not treason but the protection of his property. He probably assumed (if he thought anything at all about the possibility of revealing secrets) that both the American and British government were already rushing the news to their military commanders. His private commercial channels were swifter than those of either government, however, and he unwittingly may have been the source of the leak. (For Astor's responsibility, see Porter, op. cit., 258–63, and for Abbott, Carter, op. cit., X, *Michigan Territory,* pp. 442–48, 493.

5. By chance the United States factor from Chicago was on the island at the time of the attack, looking for an interpreter to take the place of one recently killed by trader John Kinzie during a quarrel. Dickson and Crawford told Irwin triumphantly that the first thing they were going to do on overrunning the border strong points was destroy the United States government trading houses. (Carter, op. cit., X, 411–15.) This would seem to show that the houses were more effective than their opponents liked to admit. It would also indicate that Astor and Crooks did not invent the animosity toward the government houses out of their own selfishness, as some critics charge, when they lashed out at them a few years later.

6. When Dickson learned of Chandonnai's perfidy, he ordered the young man's uncle to apprehend him. Chandonnai killed the older man. Later Dickson captured Chandonnai and his associate, Chicago trader John Kinzie, a half-brother of Thomas Forsyth, and started with them for Canada. Chandonnai escaped, but Kinzie was in prison in Quebec for some time. Though he returned to Chicago in 1816, he never regained his former affluence.

CHAPTER 13

Small Fights for Large Stakes

GENERAL BIBLIOGRAPHY

As in 12, plus:
Astor-Crooks Letters, Vol. I (1813–19), photostats, New York Public Library.

NOTES AND SPECIFIC REFERENCES

1. It is possible that the *Forester,* intended for Astoria's salvation, and the *Isaac Todd,* bent on the post's destruction, sailed in the same convoy. (Porter, op. cit., 217–18.)

2. The quotation is from a letter to Secretary Jones, July 27, 1813, printed in Bridgwater, op. cit. Additional data concerning Astor's efforts to protect the Columbia River post are in Porter, op. cit., 523–26, 533–39, 541–43.

3. Astor to Pliny Moore, *Moorsfield Antiquarian*, Vol. I, (Nov. 1937), p. 192. Other letters dealing with the Lake Champlain fur exit are ibid., February 1938, and microfilms, held at the Missouri Historical Society, of select letters from the Astor papers at the Baker Library, Harvard University School of Business.

4. Information about the affair is sketchy. There is a summary in Sister Marietta Jennings, *A Pioneer Merchant of St. Louis . . . Christian Wilt* (New York: Columbia University Press, 1939, pp. 144–46). Porter mentions it (p. 275) and there are allusions in Carter's *Territorial Papers*, XIV, 637, 593–94. In reconstructing details I have assumed a great deal. For instance, Pothier's involvement: Why else would Cabanné and Chenié have transported Astor's furs? And the shortage of transport on the Lakes: Why else should the furs go by way of St. Louis?

Accounts generally state that Cabanné and Chenié had two boats, but transporting 602 packs of furs, plus merchandise, would take more than two of the relatively small barges usable on the Fox-Wisconsin route. It is conceivable that the traders exchanged barges for keelboats at Prairie du Chien, but why? Besides, Governor Howard (Carter, XIV, 593) says he seized "several" boats from Mackinac. The smuggled merchandise, incidentally, seems to have been forgotten in the louder hue and cry about the furs, whose importation was legal.

5. I assume this. During the winter of 1813–14 Crooks kept suggesting that he go to St. Louis, as the text will later show; and his first move when peace was declared was to buy goods for entering the Missouri trade with Stuart.

6. Crooks was away from New York City between early October 1813 and early May 1815, and could hardly have met Betsy Sullivan Stuart during his absence. Yet a letter from Stuart to Crooks dated March 21, 1815, (*WHC*, XIX, 369–72) indicates that Crooks had already won a warm place in the affections of Betsy, her brother, and their mother. This acquaintanceship must have ripened during August and September, 1813, after Stuart's marriage of July 21, as dated in the family Bible. (Rollins, op. cit., liv, lv, notes 12, 23.)

In spite of this, Astor remarked to Crooks, Feb. 14, 1814 (Astor–Crooks letters, loc. cit.), as though it were fresh news, that Stuart had married Miss Sullivan. Even more curiously, Crooks replied, March 3, 1814, that the marriage would explain why he had not heard from his friend.

This raises a query: Were Robert Stuart and Elizabeth Sullivan married secretly? There is a persistent legend that they were, but the marriage is said to have occurred before Stuart sailed on the *Tonquin* in 1810. (*Mich. P & H Col.*, III, 54, 58.) The Bible entries seem to preclude that theory. But perhaps they were married secretly *after* Stuart's return from the Pacific. Unless the mother still objected (yet she apparently welcomed both Stuart and Crooks to her home), I have no useful theory for explaining the deception. But at least it accounts for the tradition and also for Astor's delay in learning of the wedding. Surely Astor would have been invited to a normal ceremony.

It is harder to account for Crooks's ignorance, for he evidently was a favored friend of the bride and her family. Possibly he was not ignorant, but was playing along with Stuart's desire for secrecy when he pretended in his letter of March 3 to Astor that the marriage was news to him also.

The revelation of the marriage in February 1814 may have been necessitated by Betsy's pregnancy. The Stuarts' first child, Mary, was born June 27.

7. Lt. Col. Robert McDouall–General Drummond, July 16, 1814, (*WHC*, XI, 260–63). There is no confirmation of this in any other source, though it is the sort of story which, if true, would have been remembered and repeated afterward. Some of

Clark's and Perkins' correspondence about the move against Prairie du Chien is reprinted in Carter, op. cit., XIV, 738–86, passim.

8. The letter is in *Mich. P & H Col.*, XV, 629–30.

CHAPTER 14

Sweet Fruits of Defeat

GENERAL BIBLIOGRAPHY

As in 12–13, plus:

THE FIGHTING AT PRAIRIE DU CHIEN AND MICHILIMACKINAC

"The Bulger Papers," and related documents, *WHC*, XIII, 1–162. Photostats of these and other of Andrew Bulger's papers, including his "Autobiographical Sketch," are in the Minnesota Historical Society.

Anderson, Thomas G. "Journal, 1814." *WHC*, IX, 207–61.

Grignon, Augustin. "Seventy-Two Years Recollections . . ." *WHC*, III, 271–79.

"Prairie du Chien Documents, 1814–15." *WHC*, IX, 263–81.

Sinclair, Arthur. Various reports in *Niles Weekly Register*, supplement to Vol. VII, 129–31.

Dickson's troubles with Rolette: *Mich. P & H Col.*, XVI, 1–32.

ASTORIA AND THE NORTH WEST COMPANY FUR BRIGADE

Ross Cox, Washington Irving, and Kenneth Porter as cited earlier, with more specific details from:

Franchère, Gabriel, *Narrative . . .* , in Thwaites, *EWT*, VI, 336–97.

McDonald, John, of Garth. "Autobiographical Notes, 1791–1816," in L. R. Masson, *Les Bourgeois de la Compagnie du Nord-Ouest*. (Quebec, 1890) II, 43–55.

NOTES AND SPECIFIC REFERENCES

1. If any of Astor's furs were stored in the warehouses, neither Crooks nor Sinclair mentions them. They may already have been transferred to Mackinac. In any event Crooks could not have removed them in naval vessels bound for war. (Reports of the campaign include Crooks–Astor, Aug. 21, 1814. Letters, loc. cit. and *WHC*, XIX, 361–64; Arthur Sinclair to Secretary of Navy William Jones, July 22, 1814, in *Niles Weekly Register*, VII, supplement, p. 129.)

2. Indian agent Henry R. Schoolcraft, Johnston's son-in-law and a prolific writer on Indian affairs, left a tribute in "Memoir of John Johnston," *Mich. P & H Col.*, XXXVI.

3. Legend says that sailors corked Holmes's corpse in a hollow log and towed it through Huron's sparkling waters, in order to keep it cool during the return to Detroit.

4. The estimate is Gabriel Franchère's and quite likely is high.

5. In his "Autobiographical Notes" (loc. cit.), McDonald does not mention the notorious Jane, who later demoralized the post. He fixed his disgust on the ship:

"She proved to be a miserable sailor, with a miserable commander, a rascally crew . . . I left the *Todd* without regret." (pp. 44, 47) But he was a strait-laced man and could hardly have approved of Jane or of her violently autocratic paramour. For a start on the literature about Miss Barnes, see the latter part of the journals of Alexander Henry the Younger, ed. by Elliott Coues, in *New Light on the Early History of the Greater Northwest*, (New York, 1897) or, for a more recent summary, Walter O'Meara, *The Savage Country* (Boston: Houghton Mifflin Co., 1960).

6. The memorandum is in G. C. Davidson, *The North West Company* (Berkeley, Calif., 1918) p. 296.

7. This may be as good a place as any to note that most pelts were sought not for decorative wearing but for their woolly underfur. This underfur was the raw material of the felt that went into military cocked hats and tall, fashionable civilian hats with various crowns and brim curls. Hatters first shaved the greasy pelts, collected the underfur, and then felted and shaped it under warmth, moisture, and pressure. After the moist hat was shellacked for hardness, a coating of fine fur was worked into the surface to give the effect of growing there. Finally the hat was dyed, brushed, ironed and polished.

Muskrat was used for cheap hats—about two dollars each. Beaver made a better felt because the tiny barbs on each soft hair provided density and cohesion. Nutria from South America, cony, hare and other wools were used as substitutes or adulterants.

Raccoon was in demand for caps. And of course mink, martin, and fine furs in general were used for trimming fashionable garments. Deer skins (while we are on the subject of the economic ends of the fur trade) were tanned by tens of thousands into leather. By the end of the War of 1812, the tanning industry was doing $12,000,000 worth of business. The great bulk of the hides it absorbed was provided by the Indians.

CHAPTER 15

Bright New Vistas, American Style

NOTES AND SPECIFIC REFERENCES

1. Both this letter and Stuart's are in "Astor–Crooks Letters," I, 146–50.

2. Astor, writing Charles Gratiot May 26, 1816, (Bogy Collection, photostat in Mo. Hist. Soc.) speaks of "Mr. Robert Stuart, with whom I believe you are allready acquainted." Gratiot and Stuart may have met in St. Louis on Stuart's return from Astoria in the spring of 1813, but the tenor of the sparse surviving correspondence of the period suggests to me (quite unprovably) a more recent acquaintanceship formed probably in the summer of 1815. There is very little more evidence about Crooks's activities. The statement that he actually went to Mackinac rests on James Lockwood's reminiscences, "Early Times and Events in Wisconsin," (*WHC*, II), written forty years after the event.

3. *Mich P & H Col.*, XVI, 67–69.

4. In 1818 the commissioners ruled that Astoria had been seized and therefore must be restored to American ownership. Otherwise there was no agreement on terri-

torial claims to the Oregon country. As a compromise the negotiators signed a convention of joint occupation, which gave citizens of Great Britain and the United States equal rights of trade and settlement in the Pacific Northwest. By then, however, the North West Company was too deeply entrenched to buck. Astor made no attempt to reoccupy Astoria, but confined his operations to the undisputed territories of the United States, from which British Indian traders were excluded and where he had only local rivals to worry about.

5. Astor to Charles Gratiot, St. Louis, May 21, 1816. (Bogy Collection, photostat, Mo. Hist. Soc.)

6. Astor–Monroe, May 27, 1816, reproduced in Porter, op. cit., II, 1145–46. Various writers have followed Porter in citing the request as an example of Astor's "cool" presumption with government people. "It seems, however, that President Madison did not accede to this cool request." (Porter, II, 695.) There was no reason for the President to accede. Other channels had been established by the War Department seventeen days earlier. Astor followed them as soon as he learned of them. Porter also calls the request for blank licenses an effort by Astor to secure an advantage over his American rivals. Those rivals, however, could obtain and did obtain permits exactly as Astor did. No special grants were made on Astor's behalf. He requested only what the law said any United States citizen might ask for.

For Monroe's debt to Astor, see Porter, II, 725–27.

7. William W. Matthews, a native of New York, had gone to Astoria aboard the *Tonquin* and had stayed on the Columbia until 1815, at which time he returned overland through Canada with his Clatsop Indian wife. For many years thereafter he served as Astor's agent in Montreal; his name will reappear often in this account.

Joseph B. Varnum was one of two Indian-trading sons of a United States senator from Massachusetts (1811–16). His father's position and his own experience should have made him a logical agent for Astor. He did not work out well, however. After the 1816 season (and the defeat of his father for re-election), he abandoned the wilderness trade for merchandising in New York City.

CHAPTER 16

Taste of Power

GENERAL BIBLIOGRAPHY

CONDITIONS AROUND THE LAKES IN GENERAL

Record Group 75, National Archives, Washington: letters scattered throughout Microcopy 1, roll 2 of Michigan Superintendency of Indian Affairs, Letters Received and Sent, 1814–17. Also Microcopy 271, roll 1, Letters Received by the Office of the Secretary of War Relating to Indian Affairs, pp. 346–440, passim. Also, same office, the original letters in Letter Books C, D, E. To an extent these sources duplicate. A few of the letters have been printed in the historical collections cited below.

INDIAN AFFAIRS AROUND THE LAKES

The British side: Letters by Robert McDouall in the Dickson papers, loc. cit., Chap. 12 above, and *Mich. P & H Col.*, XVI, 193–302 passim.
The American view: *WHC*, XIX, 375–487, passim.

PUTHUFF AND MRS. MITCHELL

Mich. P & H Col., XVI, 252–381, passim.
Baird, Elizabeth. "Reminiscences of Early . . . Mackinac," WHC XIV, 35–37.

PUTHUFF AND THE TRADERS

WHC XIX, 415–32. Ibid., XX, 19–20.
Mich. P & H Col., 463–65.

THE SELKIRK TROUBLES

Morrison to Puthuff, July 19, 1817, Mich. P & H Col., XXXVI, 340–43.
Porter, Kenneth W. "John Jacob Astor and Lord Selkirk," North Dakota Historical
    Quarterly, V (Oct. 1930), 5–13.
"Summary of Evidence in the Controversy Between the Hudson's Bay Company
    and the Northwest Company," Collections of the State Historical Society of
    North Dakota, IV, 449–643.

AFFAIRS IN ST. LOUIS

Astor–Gratiot correspondence in Mo. Hist. Soc.: (1) Gratiot Letter Book, 175–95;
    (2) photostats of select letters from the Astor papers at the Baker Library, Har-
    vard; (3) photostats of Astor letters in the Bernard P. Bogy collection.

NOTES AND SPECIFIC REFERENCES

1. W. W. Blume, ed., Transactions of the Supreme Court of Michigan, 1814–24,
Ann Arbor, 1938, III, 504–12; IV, 233–34. The decision was not necessarily fair. One
historian says of the Michigan court during this period (Silas Farmer, The History
of Detroit and Michigan, Detroit, 1884, pp. 179–80), "Many cases were decided as
whim or convenience dictated; favoritism was often grossly manifest; and court rules
were made for the benefit of particular and special cases." I find no evidence of
overt prejudice in the Puthuff case, save that the frontier was in general biased
against government officials, particularly army officers.

2. Prohibition caused trouble in Green Bay also. After Governor Edwards of Illinois, which then included Wisconsin, reminded his agents and justices of the peace
to keep spirits out of the Indian country, three of Green Bay's principal traders wrote
in agitation to their justice that the order would place their men in jeopardy.
". . . they cannot resist a number of Savages resolved to go to extremes. . . . Liquor,
having once been allowed among the savages it is not possible to restrain them from
it." (Porlier, Grignon, Lawe to Charles Réaume, WHC, XIX, 400.)

3. This letter is sometimes quoted out of context as indicative of Astor's evil reputation in the fur country. All Puthuff meant was that everyone in the fur country knew
that the New Yorker worked hand in glove with Canadians, in Puthuff's eyes a
major crime. The President of course was perfectly aware of Astor's Canadian connections; Astor had written Monroe of them when asking for exceptions. (Puthuff's
letter of protest is reproduced in WHC, XIX, 417 ff.)

4. Thomas McKenney, new Superintendent of Indian Trade, heard that Puthuff
had collected as much as $4000. (WHC, XIX, 481–82.) George Graham of the War
Department (to Cass, May 4, 1817, Letter Book D, p. 35, Sec. of War Letters Sent,

Indian Affairs, Record Group 75, National Archives) says $3000. Crooks says the
agent collected $2000. (Crooks and Stuart to Astor, Jan. 24, 1818.) Puthuff's defense
to Cass, Oct. 15, 1818, is ibid., 88–90. I can find no really solid evidence about how
much he did collect, but I believe it was no more than $2000 and perhaps less.

5. Secretary Crawford to the agents, Letter Book C, Secretary of War, Letters
Sent, Indian Affairs, pp. 344–47, 439–40.

6. Rocheblave–Porlier, Grignon, Lawe; Porlier Papers, Wis. Hist. Soc.

CHAPTER 17

The Breath of Failure

GENERAL BIBLIOGRAPHY

Details for the launching of the American Fur Company in the Great Lakes area
are drawn from the Crooks–Stuart Letter Books (photostats at the State Historical Society of Wisconsin), the Astor–Crooks letters (photostats, New York
Public Library), the ledgers of the American Fur Company in the Public Archives of Canada (microfilm at the Huntington Library, San Marino, California);
Records of the Michigan Superintendency of Indian Affairs, Letters Received
and Sent, Vol. 2, April 24, 1817–June 3, 1818, Record Group 75, National Archives; (microcopy 1, roll 3. A copy is at the Huntington Library)—all this
fortified by the miscellany of letters printed in *WHC*, XIX, 445–88; XX, 1–62.
The famous Crooks–Stuart letter to Astor of Jan. 24, 1818, opening their campaign against certain government officials appears in full in the Michigan records, supra; lenghty excerpts are in *WHC*, XX, 17–31.
For Farnham's seizure: Carter, *Territorial Papers*, XV, 312–19; 520; 532–33; *WHC*,
XIX, 477–84; plus Crooks letters in Crooks–Stuart Letter Books.

NOTES AND SPECIFIC REFERENCES

1. Crooks and Stuart to Matthews, Jan. 10, 1818 (Crooks–Stuart Letter Book I),
giving directions for 1818. Though Matthews had been in Montreal with Crooks in
1817, he obviously had not visited the workers as Crooks had. It is interesting to note
how meticulous Crooks was, during these early days, to have Stuart sign important
letters with him; he carefully treated his long-time friend and onetime superior as
a business equal, although from the beginning authority rested with Crooks.

2. The next sentence in this letter adds that Astor should try to further monopoly
by keeping out of the United States all foreign boatmen save those licensed to the
American Fur Company. (Crooks–Stuart Letter Book, I, 12. The date is missing but
is probably April 5, 1817.) Porter, op. cit., II, 702–03, uses this sentence as one more
bit of evidence to support a charge that in his drive to monopolize the American
fur trade, Astor exerted undue influence on government officials in order to gain
special favors. But Astor was not quite so naïve as to follow Crooks's naïve suggestion
that they rule out all boatmen except their own. All he did was ask the War Department for licenses for his own men. There was nothing special about such requests. Other traders, notably David Stone, asked for and received the same consideration.

3. I could not find detailed records for the shipments of 1817; the routes described in the text were those used in 1820, but the pattern probably had been established earlier. (Crooks–Stuart Letter Books, I, various letters between March 30, 1820, and June 10, 1820.) For general data on Erie shipping, see Thomas Symons and John Quinter, "The History of Buffalo Harbor," Publications of the Buffalo Historical Society, V, 239–85.

4. Immediately following the instructions quoted in the text, Cass added this paragraph: "On mature reflection on the subject I would recommend that as few licenses as may be consistent with those regulations be granted, rather than exceeding the number." (Cass to Puthuff, June 8, 1817, WHC, XIX, 460–61.) Porter, op. cit., II, 702, who consistently (and in my opinion unjustly) belabors Cass as a spineless tool in the hands of the American Fur Company, construes the sentence to mean that Puthuff was supposed to limit other traders' licenses while giving Crooks whatever he wanted. But the sentence can be interpreted just as easily to mean that the number of all licenses to all traders should be limited. Certainly neither Cass nor Puthuff tried to exclude men working for other American concerns, as see note 5 below.

This may be the place to dispense with the story that Astor bribed Cass for his favors. According to certain 1909 newspaper reports describing American Fur Company account books then being displayed for sale in a New York City gallery, a mysterious ledger entry suggested that on either May 3 or May 13, 1817, Cass was in Montreal and received $35,000 to take to Michilimackinac. Gustavus Myers, History of the Great American Fortunes, I, p. 130, interprets the payment as a bribe and adds darkly that Cass, as Secretary of War, was worth bribing since he had jurisdiction over the Indian trade. Cass, however, did not become Secretary until 1831, fourteen years after the reputed payment, which is giving Astor credit for remarkable foresight.

No one since 1909 has been able to find these reputed entries. Curiously, an American Fur Company account book in the Detroit Public Library does have a page missing after the entry for May 12, 1817. Even so, after analyzing the "evidence," Porter (op. cit., II, 723–25), no admirer of Cass, concludes against bribery on the ground that such crudity was foreign to the natures of both men. John Upton Terrell (Furs by Astor, New York 1963, p. 251) repeats Porter's data and then states flatly that Cass was in Astor's pay. Neither man seems to have wondered whether Cass actually was in Montreal in May, 1817, to receive the $35,000 as charged. Apparently he wasn't. At least the government thought he was in Ohio, conferring with the Indians about land cessions. (W. L. G. Smith, The Life and Times of Lewis Cass, N.Y., 1856, p. 110; see also a letter Cass wrote from Zanesville, Ohio, April 12, 1817—Burton Historical Collections, Detroit Public Library.) Physically, it was barely possible for Cass to have sneaked off from these government duties long enough to journey through the Lakes and down the St. Lawrence to receive his "bribes" in Montreal, but wouldn't it have been infinitely easier (to say nothing of more logical) just to have met Astor in New York or Washington, which cities Cass visited annually? But I doubt even this. As Porter contends, bribery was not in character for either man.

5. "The goods I have imported from Michil^a Were purchased from the House of David Stone & Co Who have obtained the Same privilege as the American Fur Comp^y" F. Oliva of Green Bay to U. S. Indian Agent John Bowyer, also at Green Bay, Sept. 16, 1817, WHC, XIX, 476–77.

6. For Madame LaFramboise, see Elizabeth Baird, "Reminiscences of Early Days on Mackinac Island," WHC, XIV, 38–43. Also Mich. P & H Col., XVII, 326.

7. It may be well at this point to review at length the methods of selling goods. The policies of the American Fur Company emerge quite clearly through ledgers

still preserved in the public archives of Canada at Ottawa. (The Huntington Library has microfilms of these. See also the testimony of H. R. Schoolcraft, Sen. Doc. 90, 22nd Congress, 1st Sess., and Porter, op. cit., II, 820–29.) The details of Stone's operations are not so well preserved, but presumably they were similar.

Charges were made this way. The company added during the 1820s an average markup of 81¼% to goods imported for its account from England by J. J. Astor & Son. This markup covered transportation, insurance, excise duties, etc. Goods sent to Mackinac from New York City were marked up 13% to 15% to cover insurance, transportation, and the like. I cannot determine whether these markups represented fair charges or contained hidden profits. Crooks himself testified to the Senate (Sen. Doc. 60, 17th Congress, 1st Sess.) that the 10% markup charged for transportation by the government factories was exorbitant. As Porter notes (II, 847–48) this suggests that the Fur Company's markup was still more exorbitant. It is not clear, however, what insurance the government charged against the goods or what provision it took against a certain amount of inevitable loss not covered by insurance. The government, not having to show a profit, could absorb more of these costs than private capital could; and therefore what might be overcharging by the factories might not be for the traders.

John Jacob Astor & Co. provided goods at cost for the American Fur Company. The Fur Company added a 5% commission (on top of the markups noted above) for handling these goods. In some cases, where traders were not reliable or where they were associated with competitors also, this commission might soar to over 30%. But the average was 5%, which was not unreasonable—or would not have been if the traders had bought the goods for cash. But they made their returns in fur (and also paid a year's interest on the debt they owed the company). The company agents on Mackinac, generally Robert Stuart for the American Fur Co., accepted these furs at the lowest price they thought they could get away with in view of market quotations in New York and London (sent them by special courier) and the amount of competition from outside buyers. Obviously the company hoped to turn a profit on the furs it resold in New York, London, Leipzig, or Canton. One reason Astor hoped to obtain a monopoly on the furs produced inside the United States was so that he could control or at least influence prices on the world market. He never quite succeeded, but in general he was able to withhold furs or shift them about advantageously enough to realize the profits he was after. From 1823 to 1834 the net for the American Fur Company seems to have averaged about 10% per year on the investment involved. On top of this Astor collected, through J. J. Astor & Co., interest on money advanced the fur company and a 2½% commission on furs which he sold for the fur concern.

The American Fur Company moved the goods into the wilderness under three different schemes. In the early days, when competition from Stone was keen, very few traders (save for John Johnston of the Sault) were willing to risk investing their own capital. Therefore the company had to send out traders on salary, absorbing all the gains and losses. Astor and Crooks disliked this method. It cut out the 5% handling commission and the possibilities of manipulation when receiving the furs. Furthermore, salaried men did not exert themselves as diligently as did those who had a chance of sharing in the profits. As soon as competition was reduced, Crooks and Stuart tried to employ traders on a profit-sharing basis. Generally speaking, a trader working under this arrangement paid half the cost of the goods, including markup and handling commission, and furnished half the cost of boats, voyageurs and food supplies for the winter. At the end of the trading season the winterer turned in all his furs to the company—there were always fierce arguments over price—and shared profits or losses on a scale matching his original investment.

A few semiindependent firms bought goods outright from the company and traded the merchandise entirely on their own risk. Often they resold part of the merchandise at stiff markups to small traders who maintained posts among the tribes they knew best, generally through marriage. These small traders returned their furs to the so-called independents, who then took them to Mackinac for settling their accounts with the American Fur Company.

For the traders, the main virtue in aligning themselves with the company was its help in fighting interference by government officials and the factories, and in eliminating some of the cutthroat competition which from the beginning had made the Indian commerce as hazardous, economically and even physically, as any on the continent. The company tried to establish boundaries between its outfits, but those who had an interest in the profits they made, as opposed to salaries, frequently encroached on one another; and settling such quarrels was, as the text will indicate, a continual headache.

Where the competition arose not within the family but from an outsider, an attempt was sometimes made to control it by letting the trader concerned buy his merchandise in equal proportions from the American Fur Company and from the rival, turning furs back in the same proportion. Some of the Fond du Lac outfits were handled this way: William Aitkin bought half from the American Fur Company and half from a Canadian, Charles Oakes Ermatinger, and in theory worked with equal diligence for both suppliers.

The American Fur Company often sold directly to its own rivals. In 1817 Crooks sold the Prairie du Chien firm of Bertholet and Rolette goods charged at $4000 so that they could fill out certain assortments obtained in the main through David Stone & Co. That same year Crooks also sold to Stone odds and ends amounting to $3000. The different traders then took these goods into the wilderness and used them to commit mercantile mayhem on each other. It is something like today's filling stations buying gasoline from each other's distributors during a price war.

8. Crooks to Farnham, Feb. 5, 1818, (Crooks–Stuart Letter Books) after Farnham's troubles about licenses says that events "tell us too plainly how shamefully the Illinois confederatcy leagued to harass, persecute, & finally ruin you." On August 9, 1818 (ibid.) he wrote Nicholas Boilvin, Indian agent at Prairie du Chien, "A species of civil war has already been too long waged by the St. Louis interests against those of the Lakes. Our rights to the Indian trade are precisely the same, and surely the men of Mackinac are entitled to equal protection and advantage with those from the Illinois country."

9. "Mr. Bouteiller, that Sheep of the Good God, after so many hardships, having been taxed with being at the head of the savages during the war . . . has succeeded in dissipating the prejudice against him with the aid of his purse." (Porlier to Pierre Rocheblave, undated, 1817, *WHC*, XIX, 445–47.)

10. The italics are O'Fallon's (to Clark, May 10, 1817, *ASP Ind. Aff.* II, 358). For Chambers' characteristics: James H. Lockwood, "Early Times and Events in Wisconsin," *WHC*, II; Col. John Shaw, "Personal Narrative," ibid.; plus letters in *WHC*, XIX, 458–59; 483–84; and XX, 23–24, 29–30, 59–62, 150–51, and 389–90, in the last of which O'Fallon testified that in the controversy with Farnham "no officer in the place filled by Col. Chambers could have acted with more moderation and integrity." Secondary mentions of the situation at the Prairie are in Peter L. Scanlan, *Prairie du Chien* (Menasha, Wis., 1937), pp. 100, 125–26; Bruce Mahan, *Old Fort Crawford and the Frontier* (Iowa City, 1926), pp. 72–74, 80–81.

11. The accounting is summarized in Crooks to Astor, Feb. 1, 1818. (Crooks–Astor Letters I, 174–75.)

CHAPTER 18

The Fist Closes

GENERAL BIBLIOGRAPHY

Crooks–Stuart and Crooks–Astor letters and American Fur Company ledgers as cited in XVII.
Michigan Superintendency of Indian Affairs, Letters Received and Sent, vols. 2 and 3, microcopy 1, rolls 3 & 4, loc. cit.
Wisconsin Historical Collections, XIX, XX, as cited.

THE YOUNG CLERKS

Hamilton, Henry E. *Incidents and Events in the Life of Gurdon Saltonstall Hubbard*, Chicago, 1888, pp. 1–27.
Letters by John Fairbanks and Samuel Ashmun in *Moorsfield Antiquarian*, Vol. II, May 1938.

NOTES AND SPECIFIC REFERENCES

1. On first learning of Puthuff's dismissal, Cass dropped his investigation of Crooks's charges. On receiving Puthuff's appeal for reinstatement, Calhoun ordered the hearings continued. Puthuff offered his defense to Cass during a belated visit to Detroit in October 1818. The bulk of it was oral and consisted in the main of uncorroborated denials of the allegations. Cass tended to believe the agent, though admitting that neither Crooks nor Stuart had been on hand to defend their own contentions. Cass also admitted that Puthuff's anti-British zeal had led him into rash decisions—but nothing dishonest or disloyal. As for Crooks and Stuart, Cass added, he knew both to be "correct and highminded." Their zeal to develop trade matched Puthuff's zeal against the British. It was all an unhappy conflict in interpretations, and so on. (Cass to Calhoun, Oct, 20 and 24, 1818, Mich. Sup., Letters Received and Sent, Vol. 3, pp. 44–51.) Once again the investigation was strangely unnecessary. Calhoun appointed George Boyd as Puthuff's successor before hearing the results of the defense he himself had ordered.

2. Willoughby Morgan, the commander at Rock Island who had done the arresting, and W. S. Blair, the lieutenant who had escorted the prisoners to St. Louis, were also named as defendants; but since they had been acting under orders, their inclusion was a formality and the action centered on Chambers.

3. Monroe's $5000 debt to Astor may have made him listen to the merchant's protests about licenses but Porter at least (op. cit., II, 725–27) thinks it did not lead the President to act against his conscience. Besides, it was difficult to favor Astor without also favoring his American competitors, who were not without resources of their own. David Stone, for instance, told Jacob Franks in Montreal that he could obtain "*as much* from the Interests of his friends who are Members of Congress" as could Astor. (Franks to John Lawe, March 11, 1818, *WHC*, XX, 34–36). Michael Dousman of Mackinac, one of Stone's traders, wrote Lawe on May 10, 1818 (ibid. 55–56) with the naïve faith which most winterers placed in their suppliers,

". . . there is a report that British Subjects are totaly Excluded but I presume there will be Some other aranjment. . . . J. J. Astor & D. Stone will have Interest Suficient to mack Sum Satisfactory arangment." Monroe did not owe Stone anything, but Stone obviously obtained as much from him as Astor did.

4. The lists became so routine that the American Fur Company had the forms printed wholesale in nine columns, affording space for the man's name, his job, height, color of eyes, hair, complexion, "make" (i.e., stout or slender) and place of birth. Strangely, there was no column for age. The lists furnish interesting anthropological data. For instance, one list of 24 men for 1824, chosen at random from the holdings of the Minnesota Historical Society, shows that eighteen of the voyageurs described were stout, six slender. The smallest was 5 feet 3 inches tall (and stout). Two were 5 feet 10 inches (one stout, one slender). The average height of 5 feet 7 inches compares favorably with average of native-born Americans of the period, although the voyageurs are generally described as exceptionally short and bandy-legged. Grace Nute (*The Voyageur*, p. 13) presumably on the basis of more than 24 measurements, gives 5 feet 6 inches as the voyageurs' average height.

5. Eventually Johnston's losses for 1816–17 and 1817–18 were compromised at $11,000. (A resumé is in a letter of Robert Stuart's, August 14, 1838, Warren papers, State Hist. Soc. of Wis.) In spite of the poor showing, some of it caused by Ermatinger's competition, Johnston felt throughout the rest of his life that he had been ill used by the company.

6. American Fur Company ledgers, loc. cit. Also William Bridgwater's unpublished doctoral dissertation (Yale, 1938) "The American Fur Company." (Microfilm courtesy Yale University Library.)

The evidence against David Stone is not quite so direct, but evidently he was equally guilty, though on a smaller scale. Franks wrote Lawe May 1, 1818, "I re^d a letter a few days ago from Mr Stone saying he intended to take up 4 or 5 Young Men to Mackinac this spring which will serve to take out the goods as Americans." (*WHC*, XX, 52.)

7. Franks, in Montreal, April 23 and May 1, 1818, to John Lawe, Green Bay. Morgan L. Martin papers, Box 1, State Hist. Soc. of Wisconsin.

8. The figures are partly guesswork. But the ships did haul out that summer 63 packs belonging to the South West Company and 866 packs belonging to the American Fur Company. Records of Stone's harvest and that of various small buyers flitting around the edges of the camps are not available, but it seems reasonable to assume they added 600 packs to the total.

9. Crooks made a personal protest to Calhoun in Washington on March 2, 1819. Since Clark clearly had violated the terms of Monroe's directive about exemptions, Calhoun informed the Missouri governor and all other civil and military authorities on the frontier that thereafter they must honor properly issued licenses and not throw the wilderness into turmoil by conflicting rules.

While in Washington, Crooks also saw Clark's nephew, Indian agent Benjamin O'Fallon, who had been at Prairie du Chien at the time of Farnham's trouble with Chambers. Crooks convinced O'Fallon "of the falcity of these monstrous reports" about the American Fur Company. O'Fallon even "promised to undeceive the officers. . . . On the whole we may have reason to believe the reign of persecution is . . . near its close." (Crooks to Farnham, March 17, 1819, Crooks–Stuart Letter Books, I, 172–74.)

So far as the government was concerned, Crooks added, Farnham could go anywhere in the United States he wished with his Mackinac men, so long as he did not violate Astor's understandings with a few St. Louis merchants. Interestingly enough,

Farnham wanted to go completely outside the country and open a commerce with Santa Fe—this in 1819, while the pioneers who had tried to break into New Mexico in 1812 were still in jail and long before the men who finally did open the Santa Fe Trail in 1821–22 had set about forming their parties. One wonders what might have happened if he had been allowed to go ahead. But Crooks refused permission, saying he should venture no farther than Arkansas Territory. This did not appeal to Farnham and he stayed along the middle Mississippi and in Iowa.

10. The two letters are quoted in full, Porlier's in translation, in *WHC*, XX, 90–95.

11. Dickson also tried to persuade certain bands of Sioux and other Indians of the United States to migrate to Red River. Not many heeded him. Nevertheless his activities created profound distrust among frontier army officers. What did Dickson really plan to do in Canada with this potential striking force? Talbot Chambers in particular was outraged when Dickson visited Prairie du Chien in the spring of 1818, on the strength of a passport issued him by Puthuff. Chambers denied the validity of the document, arrested the trader, and sent him to St. Louis for trial on vague charges of alien sedition. The courts released Dickson even more promptly than Clark had released Farnham and Darling.

(Some correspondence about the proposed move of the Green Bay men to Red River is printed in *WHC*, XX, 102–03, 105–07, 109–14.)

CHAPTER 19

Pressures

GENERAL BIBLIOGRAPHY

As cited earlier: Crooks–Stuart and Crooks–Astor Letter Books; George Boyd papers; Michigan Superintendency Letters, Letters Received and Sent, Vol. III; Letter Received, 1820 through 1821, Vols II, III, IV. Also *WHC*, XX, Miscellaneous letters, pp. 64–215, especially those relating to Green Bay, licensing, and the factories.

TROOP MOVEMENTS, 1818–19

American State Papers, Military Affairs, I, 324–25, 669, 779; II, 32–34. (Washington, 1832–34.)

Carter, Clarence E. *Territorial Papers*, XV, passim. (Washington, 1952.)

Goodwin, Cardinal. "A Larger View of the Yellowstone Expedition, 1819–20," *MVHR*, IV (Dec., 1917), 299–313.

Forsyth, Thomas. "Journal . . . to the Falls of St. Anthony," *WHC*, VI, 188–219.

Hansen, Marcus. *Old Fort Snelling*, 18–30 (Minneapolis, 1958).

Jameson, J. Franklin. "The Correspondence of John C. Calhoun," *Annual Rep. of the Am. Hist. Ass'n*, II (1899), pp. 134–36, 150–70.

Jones, Roger. "Memoranda of General Brown's Inspection to the Lakes in 1819," Buffalo Hist. Soc. Pub., XXIV (1920), 295–323.

Schoolcraft, Henry R. *Narrative Journal of Travels . . . in the Year 1820* (Mentor Williams, ed.) East Lansing, 1953.

INDIAN POLICY, LICENSING, FACTORIES

Coman, Katherine. "Government Factories; An Attempt to Control Competition in the Fur Trade," *Bulletin of the American Economic Association*, I, No. 2, 4th Series (April, 1911), pp. 368–88.

Peake, Ora B. *A History of the United States Indian Factory System, 1795–1822.* Denver: Sage Books, Inc., 1954.

Prucha, Francis Paul. *American Indian Policy in the Formative Years*, esp. Chap. V. Cambridge, Mass.: Harvard University Press, 1962.

Way, Royal B. "The United States Factory System . . . ," *MVHR*, VI, No. 2 (Sept. 1919).

JOSEPH ROLETTE

Anecdotes in Elizabeth Baird, "Reminiscences . . ." *WHC*, XIV, 55–63; B. W. Brisbois, "Recollections of Prairie du Chien," *WHC*, IX, 293–94; Mrs. John H. Kinzie, *Wau-Bun* (Chicago, 1932), pp. 31–33, 46–47, 120; Col. John Shaw, "Personal Narrative," *WHC*, II, 226.

NOTES AND SPECIFIC REFERENCES

1. Another of Réaume's clerks was Edward Upham, the same young American who bought the gimcracks from the Chicago factory. Upham supported Réaume in the controversy with Wallace. This may be why Upham left the company, though Crooks says the young man requested his release in order to develop some land he has bought in Indiana. On his way back to the Hoosier state, Upham caught "bilious fever" and died very suddenly. (Crooks to Upham's sister, Maria Hastings, April 29, 1820; Crooks–Stuart Letter Books, I. For the Réaume affair, ibid., Crooks to Wallace or Réaume, Jan. 8, 9; March 17, July 9, Oct. 18, 21, 25, Dec. 17, 1819. Also Wallace to Crooks, Dec. 7, 1818, original in the Chicago Historical Society.)

2. The company began using whisky on the border in 1820, perhaps deciding that loss of furs was worse than loss of reputation to McKenney. The American Fur Company ledger for that year (page 167) shows that the Fond du Lac outfit was provided with 127½ gallons of high wine, 99¼ gallons of whisky. Ance Quivinan, on the south shore of Superior, had 83 gallons of high wine, 37 of whisky. Lac du Flambeau received 26 gallons of high wine, 11 of whisky. Theoretically this liquor was for the use of the boatmen, who indeed had enormous capacities. But no doubt enough remained for a brisk trade in furs when the Indians came in from the hunting grounds. In any event, it would hardly do to have Steuart and Morrison smashing the kegs of their rivals while those belonging to the company remained untouched. This may be one reason why there was no follow-up to Boyd's authorization. However, as the text indicates, the point about the company's strength had been made.

3. For the restiveness, Boilvin to Calhoun, Dec. 1, 1818; March 1 and June 11, 1819—letters 46, 53, 55, State Hist. Soc. of Wis. Cass's correspondence on the subject is in Carter, *Territorial Papers*, X, 864–70; 885–87. The reports reaching him from the agencies are in *Letters Recieved and Sent by the Mich. Superintendency*, Vol. 3, microcopy 1, roll 4, 127–36.

4. The Green Bay men had some reason for feeling that way. On learning of the Attorney General's ruling, McKenney on Sept. 10, 1819 (*WHC*, XX, 123) wrote

triumphantly to Irwin, "This will rid you, I hope of a number of the greatest enemies of your factory and enable you to carry on an advantageous trade with the Indians." (For Dousman's charges, see *Mich. P & H Col.*, XXXVI, 417–19.)

5. The men Lawe used as fronts were John Gunn and Roderick Lawrence, the latter the American Fur Company trader who had been frightened away from Lac du Flambeau by the Beaubiens. (*WHC*, XX, 130–31, and passim.)

6. Abbott to Crooks, May 12, 1820, original among Astor papers at Minnesota Historical Society, St. Paul.

7. Anecdotal accounts of the survey are in John J. Bigsby, *The Shoe and Canoe,* London, 1850; and Major Joseph Delafield's *The Unfortified Boundary, A Diary of the First Survey of the Canadian Boundary Line,* New York, 1943.

8. Morse's penetration of the Indian country extended no farther than Green Bay. For additional information he depended on the voluminous letters written him, at his request, by members of Cass's exploration party, and by military men, traders, and agents in Prairie du Chien, Rock Island, Chicago, and so on. (See Jedidiah Morse, *A Report to the Secretary of War of the United States on Indian Affairs.* New Haven, 1822.)

Morse himself believed that the ultimate solution of the Indian problem must depend on assimilating the red men into white communities. Again and again he urged the savages he met to give up their hunting, settle on farms, learn English, "dress and live like white people . . . and be prepared in due time, to sit and deliberate with them in the councils of the nation." They were to be helped through the transition by missionaries, whom Morse dubbed Education Families in order to avoid certain unfavorable connotations released by the word *mission.* The chief weapon of the Education Families was to be religion. As Morse explained it to the Indians, "We will bring you the best, and only *effectual,* means of making you truly happy—we will bring you our BIBLE, the best of all books. . . . This book causes the wide difference which exists . . . between the white man and the Indian." Unhappily, this long-range program did not meet the immediate problem of what to do about the factories. He pondered the matter a full year before finally making his recommendations.

9. Information about the winter disasters on the Missouri was brought to the St. Peter's just ahead of Cass's arrival by a military party exploring for a wagon road through Iowa to link the Mississippi and Missouri forts. Stephen Watts Kerny's account of the survey is in *Mo. Hist. Coll.* III, 8–29, 99–131.

10. For Stone and Lisa, see Richard Oglesby, *Manuel Lisa* op. cit., pp. 171–75.

11. The shipments by sail in 1821 were considerable, nevertheless—786 barrel bulk (a unit of measurement) on the Michigan, 146 on the *Erie* and *Hannah* (Crooks–Stuart Letter Books, II, 78, 81).

The *Walk-in-the-Water* was wrecked in a gale in the fall of 1821 and the fur company's freight was hauled by her successor, the *Superior.*

12. I have not been able to locate the original memorial but deduce its charges from Crooks and Stuart to Cass. Sept. 1, 1821, Letter Books, II, 34–36; George Boyd's letters, 106, 107, 109, 110, 114, Boyd Papers, I, loc. cit.; Cass to Calhoun, Oct. 26, 121, Mich. Super. of Indian Affairs, Letters Received and Sent, III. The matter was complicated by a simultaneous clash between Boyd and the military over the running of the Indian agency.

13. I have not attempted to follow the shifting alignments of the Missouri River traders between 1815–22, nor Astor's dealings as importer and commission seller for certain of their combinations, following the contracts Crooks and Stuart established in 1817. In general it may be said, however, that his chief customers

during that period were Berthold & Chouteau, founded 1813 by Bartholomew Berthold and young (twenty-four in 1813) Pierre Chouteau, Jr., and Cabanné & Co. The latter firm dissolved in 1819. Cabanné in early 1823 joined the expanding company of Berthold, Pratte & Chouteau, commonly called the French Fur Company. On Cabanné's admission the firm name became Bernard Pratte & Company; late in 1826 the group joined the American Fur Company as its Western Department.

CHAPTER 20

Triumph

GENERAL BIBLIOGRAPHY

THE KINZIE FAMILY

Andreas, A. T. *History of Chicago*, I, 72–75 (Chicago, 1884).
Quaife, Milo. Introduction to Lakeside edition of Mrs. John H. Kinzie's *Wau-bun*. (Chicago, 1932.) Also pp. 208–96.

THE UNITED STATES GOVERNMENT TRADING FACTORIES

As in Chapter 19, "Indian Policy," plus:
American State Papers, Indian Affairs, II, 326–64.
Benton, Thomas H. *Abridgement of the Debates of Congress*, VII, 180–88. (New York, 1858.)
"The Fur Trade and Factory System at Green Bay, 1816–21." (This contains many letters by Matthew Irwin, the Green Bay factor.) *WHC*, VII, 269–382.
McKenney, Thomas L. *Memoirs, Official and Personal*, I, 285–92. (New York, 1846.)
Smith, Alice E. *James Duane Doty, Frontier Promoter*, Chapter 2. (Madison, 1954.)

THE GREEN BAY COMPANY, ROLETTE, AND TALIAFERRO

Crooks–Stuart Letter Books, II, 119–290 passim. (This section also contains, along with routine business affairs, considerable material on the factories and the company's commercial invasion of St. Louis.)
WHC, XX, 196–247, passim.
Taliaferro, Lawrence. "Auto-Biography," *Min. Hist. Col.*, VI, 189–255.
Taliaferro Papers, Minnesota Historical Society. A hodgepodge of letters, letter books, and journals. Taliaferro sometimes wrote from the back of a journal forward, from front to back, crossed out, overwrote, hopped from date to date, and in general confused matters thoroughly for future researchers.
Babcock, Willoughby M., Jr. "Major Lawrence Taliaferro, Indian Agent." *MVHR*, XL (Dec. 1924), 358–75.

FARNSWORTH–BOYD

Baird, Henry S. "Early History . . . Wisconsin," *WHC*, II, 84–86.
Boyd to Cass Aug. 23, 1824, *WHC*, XX, 345–49.
Childs, Ebenezer. "Recollections . . ." *WHC*, IV, 156–59.
Morgan, L. M. "Sketch of William Farnsworth," *WHC*, IX, 397–400.

NOTES AND SPECIFIC REFERENCES

1. Either with them or following them came one of trader Clark's sons by Elizabeth. A John Kinzie Clark, described as old John's nephew, was at Milwaukee in 1822. (*WHC*, XX, 270–71.) The pilgrimage of these adult cousins back to the father (and uncle) whom they could not have remembered is an extraordinary search for identity, not paralleled so far as I know anywhere else in frontier history.

2. There is no reason to suppose incriminating figures were excised from the ledgers, for invoices of whisky remain clearly visible for other years, and for other outfits in 1821. Actually the trading season of 1821–22 was relatively dry, perhaps because the company once again wanted to keep its hands clean during the coming battle with McKenney. Two Lake Superior outfits received from Mackinac a total of 167 gallons; four received none. No spirits went to Indiana; Illinois received 175 gallons. A mere 41 gallons went into western Michigan, an amount that could easily have been consumed during the long winter by the engagés of the two outfits involved. The only large quantities went to outfits operating out of settlements where troops were stationed—1331 gallons of both whisky and high wine to Joseph Rolette at Prairie du Chien (at a cost of $545 out of his total order of $24,-147) and 2051 gallons, whisky and high wine both, to Green Bay ($1020 of a total order of $14,946.80). Conceivably soldiers and settlers at both spots consumed far more than the Indians did, though some of course reached the savages, as the text will indicate.

3. Alexander Wolcott to Cass, May 20, 1821, *Mich. Sup., Letters Received,* II, microcopy 1, roll 7.

One more Kinzie connection with Milwaukee might be noted: In 1812, shortly before the outbreak of the war, Old John and a man named LaLime engaged in a private fight with pistols and knives in John's front yard at Chicago. LaLime was killed. Kinzie was severely wounded. His friends spirited him away to Milwaukee, as a suitable hideout where LaLime's revengeful friends would not venture. Recovering from his wound, John returned to Chicago just in time for the massacre.

4. Stuart's suspicions about the factor are in Crooks–Stuart Letter Books, II, 277, 288. Crooks sent the new license to James on Oct. 2, 1821 (ibid., II, 153. The American Fur Co., incidentally, was paying part of the tuition for Boyd's son Joshua, who was being educated in the East, so Boyd was perhaps inclined to be amenable to suggestion). In mailing the license, Crooks warned that from now on James's conduct must be so exemplary "as not to furnish even malice with the means of raising a surmise. . . . You must not only be pure but you must also be unsuspected." In the end, however, they had to withdraw their support from James. He returned defiantly with whisky to Milwaukee the next summer, but a marshal was sent after him (*WHC*, XX, 275–76) and thereafter he lived pretty much hand-to-mouth around Chicago. For a brief time in 1825 the company's Chicago trader, John Crafts, did employ James against Stuart's wishes ("I cannot easily alter my opinion of him," Stuart wrote Crafts March 2, 1825, Crooks–Stuart Letter Books, "but as you think it of consequence to have him employed, I leave the whole affair to your good judgment."). When settlers began entering the area, James helped in the development of Chicago—he was the first sheriff of Cook County! Later he moved to Iowa County, Wisconsin, where he died an honored and influential citizen.

5. Others of the interlocking families became clerks, especially those who were reluctant to become citizens of the United States; they of course had to pretend

to be interpreters or boatmen. A sixth important trader of the area, Louis Rouse, although a native of the United States and hence useful, was so nearly insolvent that he had to be left out of the first partnership. Crooks wanted him in, helped him find relief under the bankruptcy laws, and sustained him on an individual basis so that he could join later. After Pierre Grignon died in the winter of 1822–23, Rouse took Pierre's place. It was no real help to him, however; like the other Green Bay men, he stayed perpetually indebted to the American Fur Company.

6. L. Grignon to John Lawe, Oct. 25, 1821 (*WHC*, XX, 223–24). Ten days or so after this, Robert Stuart passed through Green Bay on his way to Prairie du Chien, traveling with Michael Dousman, no friend of the American Fur Company. (Ibid., 225, 234.) It was a dreadful trip—blinding snow, ice-clogged rivers. Why Stuart undertook such a journey at the onset of winter is, so far as records go, a mystery. Presumably it had to do with telling Rolette in person of the arrangements with the Green Bay Company. If Stuart meant to insure peace in the countryside, his effort was wasted, as the text will show. After six days in Prairie du Chien, he made his way back through ice and storm to Mackinac. He must have been discouraged when reports of Rolette's antics reached him only two or three weeks later.

7. The last of the quoted clauses is an almost exact echo of what Crooks had written James Kinzie nearly five months earlier. See note 4 above.

8. Writers on the factory system persistently edit Crooks's words to "pious [*sic*] monster," as if the word somehow wasn't likely, and to "[un] holy imposition." But Crooks meant what he said. In his eyes McKenney had used the benevolent aspects of the system as an unfair screen against more pertinent attacks. For example, Crooks wrote Astor, April 23, 1822, (Crooks–Stuart Letter Books, II, 265), "Missionaries throughout the Union have bewailed the downfall of the factories as destroying the Means of Propogating the gospel among the Heathen . . . but the pious imposition has been stripped of its Cloak, and exposed in all its deformity."

9. The more pertinent of the many letters related to the liquor laws of 1822 and their aftermath include the following from *WHC*, XX: L. Grignon–C. Grignon, July 23, 1822, p. 269; Willoughby Morgan–General Gaines, Nov. 15, 1822, pp. 291–97; Cass to Schoolcraft, June 10, 1823, pp. 306–07. From the Crooks–Stuart Letter Books, II and III: Stuart–Cass, July 10, 1822; to the agent at Green Bay, Aug. 11, 1822; to Boyd, July n.d. 1822. (Original is in Boyd papers II, 117, as is Boyd's answer); to Ashmun, Aug. 2, 1822; to Stone, May 19, 1823; to Rolette, May 17, 1824.

10. John Tanner had been captured when aged nine by Shawnee Indians in Kentucky in 1789. They traded him to Ojibways (Chippewas), who brought him up as an Indian. About 1820 Tanner returned to his own people, was unhappy, came back to the Northwest, and tried to make a place for himself in the half-red, half-white world of the wilderness trade. For a time he worked in Fond du Lac for the American Fur Company, a more arduous experience than anything else he had ever encountered. When he tried to bring his Indian wife and daughters to Mackinac in 1823, the reluctant woman hired another Indian to shoot him. After a dreadful ordeal, the wounded man reached the Sault, where he dictated his extraordinary *Narrative* to Dr. Edwin James of the U. S. Army. Afterward he found employment with Boyd as an interpreter. Later he drifted back to the Sault. The story is sketchy until it picks up again in 1846 when Tanner was falsely accused of murdering James Schoolcraft. For a recent account of his career, see Walter O'Meara, *The Last Portage* (Boston: Houghton Mifflin Co., 1962).

CHAPTER 21

Defeats

GENERAL BIBLIOGRAPHY

MISSOURI RIVER COMMERCE IN THE EARLY 1820S

Oglesby, Richard. *Manual Lisa*. Norman, Okla.: University of Oklahoma Press, 1963, 179–96.
Chittenden, Hiram M. *The American Fur Trade of the Far West*. (Stanford, Calif., 1954). I, 149–55, 247–61, 309–20.
Morgan, Dale L. *Jedediah Smith and the Opening of the West*. (Indianapolis and New York: Bobbs-Merrill Co., 1953), 1–114 passim.
Letters showing the relationships between the American Fur Company, Stone, Bostwick & Co. and Bernard Pratte & Co. are in Crooks–Stuart Letter Books, II, page 305–end; III, 1–34; Crooks–Astor Letter Books, II, 202–18; and the Chouteau Collection, Mo. Hist. Soc., filed by year.

THE GREEN BAY COMPANY

Crooks–Stuart Letter Books, II, 321–94 passim; III, 21–52 passim. *WHC*, XX, 309–34 passim.

THE COLUMBIA FUR COMPANY

Abel, Annie H., ed. *Chardon's Journal at Fort Clark, 1834–39*, (Pierre, So. Dak., 1932). Miss Abel's notes contain a great deal of scattered information about the company and its founders. See esp., pp. 216–20; 331–37.
Neill, E. D. "A Sketch of Joseph Renville," *Minn. Hist. Col.* I, 350–56.

WILLIAM BEAUMONT

Hamilton, H. E., ed. *Incidents . . . in the Life of Gurdon Saltonstall Hubbard*, (Chicago 1888), 117–18.
Selleck, Henry B. *Beaumont and the Mackinac Island Miracle*, (East Lansing, Mich., 1961).

DAVENPORT AND FARNHAM

Wilkie, F. B. *Davenport, Past and Present*. (Davenport, Iowa, 1858), 145 ff.
Brandt, Frank Erwin, "Russell Farnham, Astorian," *Transactions of the Illinois State Hist. Soc.*, 1930.
Van Der Zee, Jacob. "Fur Trade Operations in Iowa, 1800–33," *Iowa Journal of History and Politics*, XII, No. 4 (Oct. 1914).

NOTES AND SPECIFIC REFERENCES

1. Actually three parties reached Missouri from Santa Fe in 1822. The first to arrive, William Becknell's, halted at Franklin. The other two, returning together some months later, continued to St. Louis. Though by no means the first Americans to penetrate New Mexico, these three groups did initiate the flow of commerce that became known as the Santa Fe trade—a venture, it will be recalled from Note 9, Chapter 18, that Russell Farnham had wanted to try in 1819.

2. The trading license William Clark issued the company in 1822 indicates a capital expenditure for goods of $9907.78. Boats, wages, provisions, and so on surely increased the investment by another 50%. A large part of this $15,000 was no doubt in the form of credit, to be repaid in fur.

3. Local histories generally say that the Columbia Fur Company operated as far east as Green Bay. I find no conclusive evidence of this. Even at Prairie du Chien their interest was confined mostly to facilities for storage, transport, and supply. Though they maintained a few posts along the Mississippi above Prairie du Chien and on the St. Croix River, their concentration was the St. Peter's, the James, and the Missouri. Their principal post on the Missouri was Fort Tecumseh, built in 1822 or 1823 on the west bank of the river a little below present-day Pierre, South Dakota.

4. Gratification was all the company received. Three St. Louis attorneys without charge to Chambers carried the case through the Missouri Supreme Court into the Federal District Court. (Geyer, Struther, Magnis to Sec. of War, Nov. 1825; Indian Office Records, microcopy 271, roll 4. See also Chambers–Calhoun, Sept. 19, 1823, Letters Received by Office of Ind. Aff., microcopy 234, roll 429.) Crooks felt the trio were paid by the St. Louis merchants as part of the anti-Astor campaign, but Chambers said they simply wanted to see justice done. At this point there seems no way of determining the truth.

In the end the company's award was reduced to $200, so small a sum that Chambers' attorneys counseled against spending the time and money necessary to carry the matter on to the Supreme Court of the United States. Or so they said. But possibly they were tired of Col. Chambers. At that point he had begun the misbehaviors that led to his dishonorable discharge from the army. He later went to Mexico, hired out to the Mexican army and fought his former countrymen during the Mexican war. If he ever paid the American Fur Co. the $200 the court awarded, records are silent.

5. Sometime toward the end of 1822, as nearly as I can determine, old General Bernard Pratte, an accomplished merchant, linked his mercantile firm with that of Berthold & Chouteau. (Young Chouteau was related to Pratte by marriage.) On May 26, 1823, J. P. Cabanné joined the organization, which thereafter was known as Bernard Pratte & Company. It consisted of four partners: Bartholomew Berthold, Pierre Chouteau, Jr., Bernard Pratte, and J. P. Cabanné.

6. A common censure of the American Fur Company's policy toward its employees runs like this: the workers were encouraged to buy clothes, tobacco, etc., at exorbitant rates through the company store so that when their terms of service ended they would be heavily in debt and would have to sign up for another hitch at ruinous wage. Foundation for the belief seems to be Lockwood's "Early Days and Events in Wisconsin," *WHC*, II, 110–11. The charge does not accord with the facts. Astor's economy order of April 19, 1823, flatly outlawed any such practice.

Crooks and Stuart both frowned on the custom. (For example, Crooks–James Kinzie, Sept. 13, 1821, Crooks–Stuart Letter Books, II, 143; Stuart–S. Abbott, Aug. 10, 1823, ibid., III, 8–9.) The reasons are obvious: the voyageurs were not rooted to the land as tenant farmers of another era were and, as Crooks put the matter to Kinzie, "always have it in their power to Cheat us, by leaving the country clandestinely."

7. Bernard Pratte & Company watched the American Fur Company like hawks, lest the agreement be violated. In 1824, a year after the signing of the contract, Crooks told Rolette to have his men follow the Columbia Fur Company traders wherever they went, even to the Missouri. Since the Columbia Fur Company cut heavily into the business done by Bernard Pratte & Co. along the central Missouri, conceivably they might have welcomed Rolette's help against the common enemy. Not so. Just hearing that he wanted Pawnee and Mandan interpreters was enough to frighten them concerning his destination and they roared protests. Stuart had to calm them with long letters of apology: it was all a mistake, Rolette hadn't understood his geography, and so on. (Crooks–Stuart Letter Books, III, 100, 109, 117–19. Also Rolette–Bostwick, June 13, 1824, Chout. Col.)

Some history books say that with the establishment of a Western Department at St. Louis under Oliver Bostwick, the Astor juggernaut had at last crossed the Mississippi and was started up the Missouri toward the mountains. Actually Astor in 1823 had deliberately precluded any such possibility; the moment one of his traders made the least move in that direction the man was peremptorily pulled back.

8. Keating, William H., *Narrative of an Expedition to the Source of the St. Peter's River* . . . (London, 1825), p. 164.

9. Smith, *James Duane Doty*, p. 34.

10. Or perhaps another member of the company made the first trip that fall in a cart pulled by dogs, and Tilton followed with the horses and wagons (and James Kipp) in the spring of 1823. The episode is not clear. See Keating, op. cit., 434 and Abel, op. cit., 333.

11. What little is known of Kipp's adventures comes from what Prince Maximilian heard from him in 1833. (Maximilian, Alexander, Prince of Wied, *Travels in the Interior of North America*, EWT., XXIII, 223–28.)

CHAPTER 22

Tensions

GENERAL BIBLIOGRAPHY

Sources for this chapter are primarily manuscript letters: Crooks–Stuart Letter Books, III, 100–323; Crooks–Astor Letter Books, II, 218–56; Taliaferro papers, principally Letter Book A and Journal 3; letters received by O. N. Bostwick, mostly from W. B. Astor, in the Chouteau Collection for the years 1824–26. Also letters in the National Archives, Washington, Records Group 75: Office of Indian Affairs, Letters Received, Miscellaneous, 1824–26, Vols. 2 and 3; microfilm rolls 429, 434. Records of the St. Peter's Agency, 1824–36, microfilm roll 757.
Also a few miscellaneous letters printed in *WHC*, XX, 353–87.

Other printed material utilized for the chapter:

American State Papers, Indian Affairs, II, 657 ff.

Benton, Thomas Hart, *Abridgements of the Debates of Congress,* loc. cit., VII, 543–56.

Blackburn, Glen; Nellie Robertson, Dorothy Ricker (eds.) *The John Tipton Papers,* (Indianapolis, 1942), I, 373–74, 401–12.

Hansen, Marcus. *Old Fort Snelling,* loc. cit., 103–45.

Mahan, Bruce E. *Old Fort Crawford and the Frontier* (Iowa City, 1926), 89–99.

NOTES AND SPECIFIC REFERENCES

1. All districts were similarly troubled. The Sioux fought the Sacs and Foxes as eagerly as they fought the Chippewas. This hurt both Rolette's business and Farnham's, for scalping parties were not interested in animal pelts. The two traders repeatedly urged the agents concerned—Forsyth, Boilvin, Taliaferro—to do something about the wars. When the efforts of the agents failed, Stuart and Crooks asked the winterers themselves to take steps. This, however, would cost an appreciable sum in gifts. Rolette and Farnham could not agree on how much each should contribute, and the project fizzled out in recriminations.

2. The accused Indians cut their way out of the log jail and returned to their villages. Though one term of an 1826 treaty with the Lake Superior Chippewas demanded their return, they stayed at large. For the affair in general, see W. W. Warren, *History of the Ojibway Nation* (Minneapolis: Ross & Haines, Inc., 1957), 389–93, 467. A copy of Cass's letter is enclosed with a memorial of Robert Stuart's, February 24, 1826, *Letters Received by the Office of Indian Affairs,* Misc., 1824–26, microcopy 234, roll 439.

3. Ebenezer Childs ("Recollections of Wisconsin Since 1820," *WHC,* IV, 156–57) seems to have initiated this oft-repeated charge against the company. A month after the act's passage, W. B. Astor, who never visited the Indian country and did not understand field operations, wrote Bostwick (June 22, 1824, Chout. Col.) that he approved of the law. But that does not necessarily mean he lobbied for its passage. I find only one case where the company deliberately bent the location law to its own advantage. When would-be rivals whom Robert Stuart suspected of smuggling started in 1825 with their goods for the south shore of Superior, he tried to push them within the company's grasp by sending to the acting Indian agent at the Sault a list of the locations designated earlier by Schoolcraft. He then told trader William Morrison to sit close to the opponents and give them "a touch of *Old Times.*" (Stuart to N. S. Clarke, and Stuart to William Morrison, Crooks–Stuart Letter Books, III, 162, 228.)

4. Not every objection to Taliaferro's assignments came from the American Fur Company. One particularly outspoken protest (undated, Office of Indian Affairs, Letters Received, Miscellaneous, 1824–26, microfilm roll 439, frames 218–19) was signed by Rolette, his clerks Robinson, Roc, Pizanne—and by James Lockwood, a bitter enemy of the company, and by Alexis Bailly, who that year was working for Lockwood.

Stuart's charges that Taliaferro favored the Columbia Fur Company are in a letter of June 4, 1825, to W. B. Astor. (Crooks–Stuart Letter Books, III, 178.) Taliaferro's own journals bear out the charge; for example, this entry for March 27, 1827 (Journal 3): "The Agents & others—a majority of them, of the Am Fur Cpy on the Mississippi and west of it—are men of *mean* principles and low origin—jealous, evil disposed &

great vagabonds. . . . Not so with the Col Fur Cpy. . . . A large majority of them being Gentlemen—I suppose is the real cause of this great difference."

5. John Tipton was an exceptional agent. He had fought under Harrison at Tippecanoe, had served in the militia during the War of 1812. Politically ambitious, he had functioned as a county sheriff from 1816–20 and thereafter was elected to a seat in Indiana's House of Representatives. In 1823 he accepted the job of Indian agent to stay solvent. Eventually he became one of Indiana's United States Senators.

6. Since Wallace's license was in abeyance pending suit, he must have planned to use the goods along the border of the Indian country, not inside it. It is worth while noting, perhaps, that in 1819 Crooks had specifically ordered Wallace, who had requested liquor to use at Fort Harrison, "Whiskey you must not trade in the *Indian Country* [Crooks's italics] for it is not only in violation of the law, but a conviction would forfeit the bond given for your licenses. Neither must any go to our outfits, more than may be necessary for private use." (Wallace's request, Dec. 7, 1818, is in Chicago Hist. Soc. Crooks's answer, Jan. 8, 1819, is in Crooks–Stuart Letter Book, I.)

7. The company carried the Wallace case into the Supreme Court of the United States and in 1829 won a reversal of the conviction on the ground that the alleged violation had really occurred outside Indian country. This "vindication" did not do Wallace's career any good, however.

8. From Wheeling, Crooks wrote George Boyd (Feb. 24, 1825, Boyd papers, loc. cit., II, 78): "Perhaps the only good objection there is to the match, is, that my Emilie is only about 20, while I am—(let me see—but it is no great matter now that the die is cast—) very considerably older. [He was thirty-eight.] My intended is not a beauty neither is she rich except in goodness, of which I hope and believe she possesses a large share."

9. William Clark's journal of the council (Kansas Historical Collections, copy at Wis. His. Soc.) gives slightly different figures. Clark says Taliaferro brought 354 Sioux; Schoolcraft, 132 Chippewas and 70 related Ottawas.

10. This victory achieved, Astor next brought pressure on Barbour to release the goods of Wallace's which had been impounded at Fort Wayne and were "in a state of destruction." This time Albert Gallatin, former Secretary of Treasury and newly appointed ambassador to England, served as character witness. In so large a company, Gallatin wrote Barbour on June 30, 1826 (Office of Indian Affairs, Letters Received, 1824–26, microfilm roll 429), some unsupervised traders possibly did evade the law, but their derelictions should not be held against the firm as a whole. Astor was a man of "great merit." America's claim to the Oregon country rested primarily on the Astorian adventure, which had cost the merchant $1,000,000. "I think therefore he is at least entitled to a liberal treatment, so far as is consistent with the law." Barbour agreed and on July 5, 1826, ordered the release of Wallace's goods on the posting of a bond for their full value, the bond to be forfeit if the appeal in the case went against the company. It did not. As noted earlier, the Supreme Court decided for the company.

11. W. B. Astor wrote of the projected dissolution and of Crooks's errands in connection with it to O. N. Bostwick on February 25, 1826. (Chout. Col.) By this time Bostwick's sloppy methods had exasperated even young Astor. For example, he snapped on January 20 (ibid.), "I have reasoned matters with you too long already. . . . I shall convince you by my future acts that you must conform to such instructions as are sent you from this office."

CHAPTER 23

The Colossus

GENERAL BIBLIOGRAPHY

Crooks–Stuart Letters, III, page 323 to the end of the volume; Crooks–Astor Letters, II, 283–359, passim; Taliaferro's Letter Book A and Journal 4; the Chouteau Collections for the years treated in this chapter, and, as additional printed matter:

MCKENNEY, THOMAS L.

———. *Sketches of a Tour to the Lakes.* (Baltimore, 1827.)

NOTES AND SPECIFIC REFERENCES

1. In 1824, James Clyman and Thomas Fitzpatrick of the Smith party found the Platte River–Sweetwater Creek route to the central Rockies. This became the main highway to the West but by no means eliminated land routes from Fort Tecumseh (later Fort Pierre) into Wyoming; or farther north, along the Bighorn and Yellowstone rivers. A considerable traffic in buffalo hides and furs followed both these northern ways even after the Oregon Trail was firmly established.

2. On this point Crooks once remarked to Chouteau (Feb. 29, 1828, Chout. Col.), "I am satisfied that our Upper Mississippi folks were uniformly actuated toward each other like cats and dogs, while McKenzie's people acted as one man for the general good."

3. As usual, Rolette did not confine his hitting to the company's competitors. He sent Lockwood with merchandise to the lead mines and drew angry threats of a lawsuit from George Davenport. "The shuffling and unprincable procedings of Mr. Rolette must be put a stop to." (Davenport–Bostwick, Oct. 17, 1826. See also Davenport–Crooks, Nov. 3, 1826; both in Chout. Col.)

4. This 1826 seizure of Bailly's liquor is generally offered by local historians as one more example of Taliaferro's unbending integrity—and, as a corollary, as an example of the company's lawbreaking. Whisky for a trader's employees was legal, however, and Taliaferro had arrogated indefensible powers to himself with his sweeping prohibition of April 2, 1826. Having led with his chin, he could expect it to be rapped. In this connection it is worth noting a letter he wrote Captain John Garland at Fort Crawford on March 12, 1829 (Letter Book A), stating that he and Bailly had settled their difficulties and adding, "What the Am. Fur Company has done to affect my standing has *long since been forgiven* [italics Taliaferro's] and their traders have not fared the worst for it." He went on to say he would like to see even more traders in the Indian country. His experience evidently had chastened him, at least temporarily.

For Bailly's side of the affair, see the Bailly papers, Box 1, Correspondence 1826–29, Minn. Hist. Soc.

5. For McKenney's conversion (and it is hard to believe it was based only on hypocrisy) see Crooks–Stuart Letter Books, III, 400–70, passim. Corroborative data

on the 1827 "tightening" of the liquor laws is in Prucha, *American Indian Policy in the Formative Years*, 114. Concerning Schoolcraft, a recent biographer estimated him thus: "A deeply religious man, he actively supported the temperance movement and as Indian agent vigorously enforced the federal laws prohibiting the sale of liquor to Indians." (Philip Mason (ed.) *Schoolcraft's Expedition to Lake Itasca*, East Lansing, Mich., 1958, xi.)

6. The incomplete file of letters in the Chouteau collection about the Ashley agreement does not fully clarify the details. For the wrestling which recent historians have done with the problem see Dale Morgan, *Jedediah Smith*, op. cit., 220–25; John Sunder, *Bill Sublette, Mountain Man*, 72–73; Don Berry, *A Majority of Scoundrels*, 125–40.

7. Taliaferro naturally enough took the dropping of the charges as a vindication of his own conduct. Historians in general have been inclined to take him at his own estimate. For example, Porter, op. cit., II, 757: "Stuart and Crooks seem soon to have recognized the insubstantial character of the accusations leveled against Taliaferro. . . . They therefore withdrew their charges and William Clark was able to write, 'No evidence has been produced by the company in support of their charges or Statements, and it is believed they do not wish to go into further investigation.'"

Of course they did not wish to—but not because of the flimsy nature of the charges. With McKenney backing them in the War Department, the case was far from insubstantial. Besides, the company had clung grimly to other cases no stronger, carrying them into the highest federal courts in pursuit of a point. Far more relevant, it seems, is the timing. The charges, which involved the Columbia Fur Company, were dropped *in the same week* that Crooks supposed he had reached a preliminary understanding with Kenneth Mackenzie.

CHAPTER 24

Strangling the Missouri

GENERAL BIBLIOGRAPHY

The Chouteau Collection, esp. *Upper Missouri Outfit, Letter Book A*. Also at the Missouri Historical Society is a useful selection of microfilmed letters from the National Archives relative to this period along the Missouri.

Printed matter concerning the river, in addition to Abel, *Chadron's Journal* and Chittenden, *American Fur Trade*, I, 325–41, both cited Chapter 21, *ante*, includes:

Catlin, George. *Letters and Notes on . . . the North American Indians*, 2 vols., (London, 1841).

Chittenden, Hiram M. *History of Early Steamboat Navigation on the Missouri River* (New York 1903), I.

Larpenteur, Charles. *Forty Years a Fur Trader on the Upper Missouri*. Elliott Coues, ed., (New York, 1898), I.

Wied-Neuwied, Maximilian. *Travels in the Interior of North America*. ETW, XXII–XXIV (Cleveland, 1906), esp. XXIII.

DeLand, Charles, and Doane Robinson, eds. "The Fort Tecumseh and Fort Pierre Journal and Letter Book," So. Dak. Hist. Soc. *Collections*, IX (1918), 69–240.

The glamour of the Rocky Mountain fur trade has resulted in several studies which shed light on Missouri River activities. In addition to Morgan, *Jedediah Smith*, cited 21, the following are useful:

Alter, J. Cecil. *Jim Bridger* (rev. ed., Norman, Okla.: University of Oklahoma Press, 1962).

Berry, Don. *A Majority of Scoundrels* (New York: Harper & Row, 1961).

DeVoto, Bernard. *Across the Wide Missouri* (Boston: Houghton Mifflin Co., 1947).

Ferris, Warren A. *Life in the Rocky Mountains* (Denver: Old West Publishing Co., 1940).

Sunder, John E. *Bill Sublette, Mountain Man* (Norman, Okla.: University of Oklahoma Press, 1959).

Two useful Indian studies:

Denig, Edwin T. *Five Indian Tribes of the Upper Missouri* (John C. Ewers, ed., Norman, Okla.: University of Oklahoma Press, 1961).

Ewers, John C. *The Blackfeet* (Norman, Okla.: University of Oklahoma Press, 1958).

NOTES AND SPECIFIC REFERENCES

1. Taliaferro, Journal 4. At this point the agent learned that the gentlemen of the Columbia Fur Company, as he once had called them, had joined his mortal enemies. He was staggered. It went to show, he wrote William Clark on Oct. 1, 1827, (Letter Book A) how little dependence could be placed on any fur trader.

2. Chouteau to Mackenzie, April 25, 1828 (quoted in Chittenden, I, 329n):

For three years these enterprises [mountain trapping] have succeeded well with General Ashley, but with him alone. Many others, and even he before this time, have met with great disasters. . . . One of the principal dangers is loss of horses at the hands of the Indians. It is necessary to be prudent, firm, and especially to exact obedience from the engagés, who are generally very insubordinate.

A short trial with trapping parties did nothing to change his mind. On May 4, 1833, he wrote Astor (ibid., I, 366):

I am convinced that these expeditions have been an annual loss. . . . If [they] had confined themselves entirely to the trade [at the regular posts] returns would have been greater and expenses much less.

3. This account of Mackenzie's movements in conjectural. Chittenden (I, 328), citing Mackenzie's December 26 letter from Ft. Tecumseh, suggests the trader was at the Mandan villages in September, when Kipp left—Kipp by tradition rather than by specific evidence. But letters from Cabanné at Council Bluffs to Pierre Chouteau definitely put Mackenzie on the lower river at that time. (Sept. 23 and Oct. 14, 1827, Chout. Col. Cabanné wrote his French in such a tiny hand that although Lamont's name is decipherable, with Mackenzie's, I am not sure about Laidlaw.) Unhappily Mackenzie's own letters of Dec. 26, 1827, and March 15, 1828, on which Chittenden drew in 1902 and which he quotes in part only, seem to have vanished from the files, along with any additional clues they might have contained.

My remark about the pause at White Earth River is based on Larpenteur, *Forty Years a Fur Trader*, I, 108–09.

4. *Articles of Agreement*, Oct. 14, 1830; Theodore Papin–P. M. Papin, Feb. 24, 1831; the company's list of "Persons Employed for the Upper Missouri Outfit . . . 1830," all in Chout. Col. Also Abel, op. cit., 202–03, 227–28.

5. Palen & Mitchell's defense against Cabanné's charges are in their letter to him of Nov. 29, 1829 (Chout. Col.). Many letters (1830–31) by Palen, Joe Robidoux, C. McLeod and others (ibid.) fulminate against agent Hughes, his nephew, and his interpreter. Without question the Indian agents had trouble with the company's traders. But, and this point is generally overlooked by writers eager to pummel the "monopoly," the traders also had trouble with some government agents—many of them, like Hughes, displaced army officers who had neither the knowledge nor the temperament for their new jobs.

David Dawson Mitchell, incidentally, was transferred to Mackenzie's Upper Missouri Outfit in 1830. During the next decade he became famous as a trader and, later, as Superintendent of Indian Affairs at St. Louis.

6. Data about the first Fort Union depends on a letter cited by Chittenden (II, 959) no longer in the Chouteau Collections. On April 19, 1830 Pierre Chouteau, Jr., wrote Astor: ". . . j'ai trouvé des lettre de M. McKenzie du 28 Décembre, 1829, et de 2 et 20 Janvier, 200 milles au dessus de la Roche Juane." In the same letter he specifies, "les trois posts d'en haut, chez les Mandans, à l'embouchure de la Roche Juane, et Fort Union 200 milles audessus." Two hundred miles—by boat, by horse?— is too vague for pinpointing the first Fort Union's location, but assuming river miles and the tendency to spot trading forts near river junctions, I guess at the mouth of the Milk in east-central Montana.

7. Some accounts say Berger left in October, 1830. Since Mackenzie could not have reached Fort Union in October (he was at Fort Tecumseh on October 14 and was later delayed by his troubles with the Aricaras), this seems unlikely. I chose January 1831 by deductions from the journal of Father Point, who had the story from James Kipp in 1847 (Abel, op. cit., 401–04). Another account about Berger and the Blackfoot forts that derives in part from Kipp's personal reminiscences is in those sections of "The Bradley Manuscript" printed in Montana Historical *Contributions* III, 200 ff., VIII, 244–50. Larpenteur, who also heard the stories firsthand, gives his version in *Forty Years a Fur Trader*, I, 108–16. Prince Maximilian added to the lore during his trip of 1833–34 (*EWT*, XXIII, passim). Indian traders Edwin Denig and Alexander Culbertson supplied additional data to John James Audubon in 1843. (Maria Audubon, *Audubon and His Journals*, II, 180–95.) A recent summary of much of the above is John C. Ewers, *The Blackfeet*, Norman, Okla., 1958, 55–60.

8. According to J. F. A. Sanford to William Clark, July 17, 1832, the Indians themselves blamed the Hudson's Bay Company for inciting the attack.

9. Mackenzie from Fort Union to Mitchell at Fort Clark, Feb. 14, 1832. Later that same year, on Nov. 22, 1832, Sanford married one of Pierre Chouteau's daughters. He continued as subagent to the Mandans until 1834, when he entered his father-in-law's service. It is said that when he was an Indian agent he was totally subservient to the American Fur Company (Abel, op. cit., xxxix, 252–55). Mackenzie's letter above does not bear this out; and on Dec. 26, 1832, a month *after* the marriage, Cabanné complained to Chouteau that Sanford was "ill-disposed" toward Mackenzie and Laidlaw. Like most generalities, this one about Sanford's toadying to the monopoly seems a little sweeping.

Sanford, incidentally, owned a slave named Dred Scott, who achieved a more lasting fame than did his master.

CHAPTER 25

The Spasms of Change

GENERAL BIBLIOGRAPHY

As in 24, plus Upper Missouri Outfit, Letter Book B (1832–35); Fort Union Letter Book, pp. 1–56, both in Chout. Col.

The National Archives, Records Group 75, Office of Indian Affairs, Letters Sent, Misc., Vols. 9, 10, 11 contain many letters, mostly by D. Kuntz and Elbert Herring, that touch on affairs both along the Mississippi and Missouri. Also relevant, ibid., Letters Received, Misc., microfilm roll 434.

INDIAN TROUBLES ALONG THE MISSISSIPPI

Street, Joseph M., Manuscript items, Numbers 1–31; State Hist. Soc. of Wis.

Hagan, William T. *The Sac and Fox Indians,* (Norman, Okla., 1958), 92–204.

Mahan, Bruce E. *Old Fort Crawford and the Frontier* (Iowa City, 1926).

Quaife, Milo M. *Chicago and the Old Northwest* (Chicago, 1913), 328–66.

Gallaher, Ruth. "Indians Agents In Iowa," *Iowa Journal of History and Politics,* XIV (July, 1916), 360–85.

Van Der Zee, Jacob. "Early History of Lead Mining in the Iowa Country," ibid., XII (Jan. 1915), 39–52.

———. "The Neutral Ground," ibid., XIII (July 1915), 311–48.

THE LAST DAYS

A few selected letters from the American Fur Company papers in the New York Historical Society. Microfilms at the Huntington Library.

NOTES AND SPECIFIC REFERENCES

1. Mackenzie's St. Andrew's Day peace between Assiniboins and Blackfeet was short-lived. On August 28, 1833, six hundred allied Assiniboins and Crees jumped a small camp of Piegans immediately outside the walls. The victims whistled up reinforcements and a day-long battle swirled off from the fort toward the mouth of the Marias. Artist Carl Bodmer, visiting Fort Mackenzie with Prince Maximilian zu Wied, watched the uproar from the stockade and afterward made it the subject of one of the most famous paintings of the early West.

The Crows resented the fort's trade with the Blackfeet just as much as the Assiniboins did. In June 1834 a great mob of them laid siege to the post. After two weeks, Mackenzie reported, the defenders were living on boiled rawhide ropes. Contradictions pile up; trader Culbertson says the attack lasted only two days; trader Denig says it lasted a month. Whatever the siege's length, it was ended by Blackfeet coming in to trade. See Denig, op. cit., 172–82, and editor Ewers' notes.

2. The Winnebagos' long-time agent at Prairie du Chien, Nicholas Boilvin, drowned late in 1827. He was replaced by Joseph M. Street. Street had to borrow $200

from Pierre Chouteau in order to bring his family to his new station. He never repaid the loan; his obsequious letters stalling Chouteau make painful reading. But he did not become obsequious to the company. He opposed Rolette actively and in 1830 blamed the little Frenchman for urging the Winnebagos to stay east of the river, lest he lose trade if they moved. A typical Street outburst (to Commissioner Elbert Herring, June 29, 1833,): "The American fur company's agents, and their overwhelming moneyed influence with the whites, and whiskey influence with the Indians in that quarter, have heretofor been too powerful" to fight. (See Sen. Doc. 512, 1st Sess. 23rd Congress, Vol. X, 61–63, 87, 178–79, 475–85, etc.)

3. For the circumstances and the case: *American State Papers, Military Affairs,* V, 506–11; *Transactions of the Supreme Court of Michigan,* op. cit., V, 563–69. Two interesting comments by observers. First, Alexis Bailly to agent Street (Street papers, ⅜28) ". . . consternation among those [Indians] who have not yet joined the temperance Societies. . . . They cannot be made to comprehend it is all for their benefit." And the Reverend William Boutwell (Philip Mason, ed., *Schoolcraft's Expedition to Lake Itasca,* East Lansing, Mich., 1958, p. 340), praising Jouett in his journal entry of July 25 as a friend the frontier needed: "The fur traders in this vicinity have been in that habit of bringing in whiskey with the permission of the Indian Agent, Mr. Taliaferro."

4. Enemies of the company suggested darkly, and some historians have followed along, that Farnham and Davenport deliberately pushed Black Hawk into war so that a treaty would be forced on the tribe and under it their claims might be recognized. (Van Der Zee, "Fur Trade Operations . . ." *Iowa Journal of History and Politics,* XII, 562.) But Black Hawk took no pushing. And at the behest of Keokuk, leader of the "peace party" among the Sacs and Foxes, Davenport carried the problem to Washington in February 1832, hoping to work out a solution that would appease Black Hawk and avert war. He even tried, without success, to gain an interview with that notorious opponent of the Indians, President Jackson. Also, the unsettled conditions of the war cost Farnham and Davenport $5050.03 in trade in 1832 (W. B. Astor–Chouteau, Aug. 17, 1833, Chout. Col.), but Davenport made no effort to add the sum to the $40,000 the partners had agreed to settle for.

5. Much of the material was published by the government: 20th Cong., 2nd Sess., Sen. Doc. 67 (serial 181); 21st Cong., 2nd Sess., Sen. Doc. 39 (serial 203); 22nd Cong., 1st Sess., Sen. Exec. Doc. 90, (serial 213). There is considerable carry-over in the massive, ten-volume, 23rd Cong., 1st Sess., Sen. Doc. 512 (serials 244–48).

6. This was the bill that Thomas L. McKenney had long hoped would make him head of a semiautonomous Indian Department—the bill for which he had all but sold himself to the American Fur Company. He lost. Judge Elbert Herring became commissioner.

7. A company's guest on the trip was artist George Catlin, on his way to find material for his famous paintings of North American Indians. The Upper Missouri posts frequently entertained distinguished visitors. Prince Paul of Württemberg stopped by in 1830–31; Prince Maximilian zu Wied and his artist Carl Bodmer in 1833. Their reminiscences furnish valuable source material.

8. This not the orthodox version of the case. Historians of the episode invariably follow Chittenden (I, 347–49). Chittenden, however, overlooks dates and ignores, or was unfamiliar with, LeClerc's own reports, Clark's long letters to Cass about the matter, and Lieutenant Freeman's testimony in St. Louis. (Much of it is now on microfilm at the Missouri Historical Society.) The result is an interpretation of the case that is far more unfavorable to the company than seems to me justifiable.

9. Unofficially the War Department knew about the affair by the end of October.

10. Correspondence about the coat of mail continued at rare intervals through the summer of 1833; thereafter no more is heard. If it had been delivered, some reminiscence surely would have mentioned it. The cancellation may have resulted from Mackenzie's abrupt removal from the Indian country in 1834.

In 1837 William Drummond Stewart, Scottish sportsman and boon companion of the mountain men, brought a suit of armor west. Jim Bridger pranced around in it at the summer rendezvous. Whether or not there is any connection with Mackenzie's coat of mail I do not know.

11. Porter, op. cit., II, 815–23. On January 29, 1829, Astor told the Senate of the United States that in spite of an annual investment of one million dollars the company had never paid a dividend, whereas the Hudson's Bay Company, thanks to better support from its government, averaged 10% per annum on its capital stock. His statement is true only in the narrowest sense. The American Fur Company paid no dividends until 1830—but they were then retroactive to 1823. By 1834 dividends alone amounted to more than $1,000,000 and Astor of course held the bulk of the stock. He also profited personally from loans he made the company and commissions earned through J. J. Astor & Son for merchandise imported and furs sold for the fur company.

William Astor's remark to the Senate in 1831 that the company's returns averaged half a million a year refers of course to the gross value of the furs traded for—not, as some wide-eyed commentators have supposed, to the year's net.

12. Among the other investors, some of them corporate, were John C. Halsey & Co., $60,000; W. and F. Brewster, Detroit traders, $50,000; John Catlin, $20,000; John B. Whetten, a relative of Astor's wife, $20,000; Samuel Abbott, Gabriel Franchère, Joseph Rolette, and several "others," including possibly some English supply firms, $50,000.

13. Crooks–Chouteau, April 10, May 31, 1834 (Chout. Col.).

14. (Marlott, Helen Stuart, Stuart Letters . . . n.p., 1961, pp. 17–18.) After joining the Reverend William Ferry's Mackinac church on April 12, 1829, Stuart became oppressively religious. It was said he would no longer unload fur barges on Sundays even when weather threatened (but he kept on requesting exemptions from the liquor laws). Excerpts from another letter to Mary will illustrate:

> Be sure to get no gaudy, foolish dress . . . As I hope you call yourself a follower of the meek & lowly Jesus; I pray you . . . let nothing draw you from the consistent Christian walk [even though] you may be laughed at. . . . I fear you have a very fiery spirit—this is not the spirit of Christ.

15. Westerners continued to call Pratte, Chouteau & Company and its successor (Pierre Chouteau, Jr., & Co.) by the old name, the American Fur Company. Actually, however, that designation belonged exclusively to Crooks's company around the Lakes and on the Mississippi.

16. Both newspaper quotations are lifted from Philip Ashton Rollins, The Discovery of the Oregon Trail, cxxxvi and xci.

Index

Abbott, James, 185, 262, 275, 344, 372
Abbott, Samuel, 275, 304, 313, 331, 335, 339, 341, 345, 417
Act of 1802, 43, 45, 48
Ainse, Joseph L., 27–32, 59, 429
Aird, George, 179–80
Aird, James, 47, 58–62 ff, 65–67 ff, 71–78 *passim*, 82, 83, 88, 90 ff, 102, 148, 154, 191, 220, 284, 439–40, 444; Ainse dispute, 32; Crooks hires, 285, 286, 290; death, 290; and Jay Treaty, 104; and license charges, 249; meets Dickson, 31; returns to St. Louis, 91, 92; and smuggling, 179–80
Aitkin, William, 359, 418, 460
Alaska, 120–21, 172, 217
Albany, N.Y., 4, 20, 21, 58, 109
Albatross (ship), 216, 442
Alcohol, 10, 11–13, 43, 46, 250, 265–66, 298–300, 306, 308, 314 ff, 323, 325–31, 345, 355–56, 361–64, 371–72 ff, 402, 405, 406, 407–10, 414–17 (*See also* specific companies, traders using alcohol); "Blackfoot rum," 395–96; packing of rum, 42–43; Pike and, 69, 70, 71
Allegheny Mountains, 313
Allegheny River, 58
American Fur Company, 5, 10, 14, 33, 54, 63, 85, 148, 184, 234, 253–419 (*See also* specific posts, rival companies, traders, etc.); becomes active, 253–54; first failures, 255 ff; formation of, 109–10 ff; later defeats, difficulties, 332 ff, 349 ff; memorial against, 310–11; Missouri monopoly, 382 ff; power achieved, pressures used, triumphs, 277 ff, 294 ff, 314 ff; South West Company shifted to, 246; 3-way sparring with Pratte & Co., Columbia Fur Co., 367 ff; times change, Crooks takes over, final days, 398–419; Western Department of (*See* Western Department)
Ames, Daniel, 238–39
Amherstburg, 101, 179, 183
Ance Quivinan (Keweenaw), 283, 373, 464
Anderson, Thomas, 180–81, 208, 209, 211, 227, 230, 289
Ange, Augustin, 191
Arapaho Indians, 175, 176
Arkansas, 7, 342
Aricara Indians, 35, 36, 45, 73, 76–77, 88, 118, 155, 157–58, 369, 400; attacks on whites, 97–98, 117, 347, 348, 392; chief in St. Louis, 50–51, 64; chief in Washington, death of, 72, 77; lodge described, 83

Ashley, William, 333, 334, 348, 368, 377–78, 381, 405, 406, 415, 416
Ashmun, Samuel, 283, 297, 329
Ashtabula, Ohio, 261
Askin, John, Jr., 94, 185, 186, 187, 205
Assapoke, Chief, 393
Assiniboin Indians, 368, 385, 393, 394–95, 478
Assiniboine (steamer), 406
Assiniboine River, 37
Astor, George, 202–3, 204, 213, 214, 219, 220, 221
Astor, John Jacob, 4–5, 15, 79, 92, 119–32 *passim*, 135, 146–47 ff, 171 ff, 216–17 ff, 227–36 *passim*, 243–49 *passim*, 252–54, 255–60 *passim*, 263–71 *passim*, 274–82 *passim*, 286–92 *passim*, 296, 306–13 *passim*, 334, 337, 341–48 *passim*, 357, 358, 364 ff, 387–92 *passim*, 400, 404, 405, 410 ff (*See also* American Fur Co.; specific employees, projects, etc.); at Beaver Club dinner, 104; considers giving up business, sells out, 302, 365, 411–13, 415, 416; and 1812 war, 184 ff, 194 ff, 223; and formation of American Fur Co., 108–13 ff; and North West Co.'s purchase of Astoria, 216–17
Astor, John Jacob, & Son, 54, 252, 253, 287, 459
Astor, William B., 287, 296, 304, 354–58 *passim*, 400, 404 ff, 410, 412, 415, 426–27, 472
Astoria and Astorians, 137–39 ff, 144–45, 164, 169 ff, 192–93 ff, 214 ff, 231. *See also* specific Astorians
Astoria (Irving), 130
Athabaska country, 27, 56
Athabaska Pass, 125, 140
Atkinson, Henry, 352, 368, 369, 402
Atlas (keelboat), 408

Bad Axe River, 403
Bad River, 367, 369
Bailly, Alexis, 323, 335, 371–72, 380, 382–83, 474
Baird, James, 334–35
Baranoff, Alexander, 121, 174, 215, 216
Barbour, James, 355, 356, 362, 364, 473
Barges, described, 56
Barnes, Jane, 217
Bates, Frederick, 90, 91, 94, 95, 102, 103, 437, 440
Bathurst, Earl of, 204
Bean, Jonathan, 389, 407–9
Bear Lake, 377, 378, 386
Beaubien, Paul and Basil, 298
Beaumont, William, 339–41